P9-BZP-940

Microsoft®

Exploring

Office XP

Volume II

Robert T. Grauer

University of Miami

Maryann Barber

University of Miami

Prentice
Hall

PRENTICE HALL   *Upper Saddle River, New Jersey 07458*

Senior Acquisitions Editor: David Alexander
VP/Publisher: Natalie Anderson
Managing Editor: Melissa Whitaker
Marketing Managers: Sharon Torkovich & Emily Knight
Assistant Editor: Kerri Limpert
Editorial Assistant: Maryann Broadnax
Technical Editor: Cecil Yarbrough
Media Project Manager: Cathleen Profitko
Marketing Assistant: Jason Smith
Production Manager: Gail Steier de Acevedo
Project Manager: Lynne Breitfeller
Production Editor: Greg Hubit
Associate Director, Manufacturing: Vincent Scelta
Manufacturing Buyer: Lynne Breitfeller
Design Manager: Pat Smythe
Interior Design: Jill Yutkowitz
Cover Design: Blair Brown
Cover Illustration: Marjorie Dressler
Composition: GTS
Printer/Binder: Banta Menasha

Microsoft and the Microsoft Office User Specialist logo are trademarks or registered
trademarks of Microsoft Corporation in the United States and/or other countries.
Prentice Hall is independent from Microsoft Corporation, and not affiliated with
Microsoft in any manner. This publication may be used in assisting students to prepare
for a Microsoft Office User Specialist Exam. Neither Microsoft Corporation, its designated review company, nor Prentice Hall warrants that use of this publication will
ensure passing the relevant Exam.

Use of the Microsoft Office User Specialist Approved Courseware Logo on this product signifies that it has been independently reviewed and approved in complying with
the following standards:

Acceptable coverage of all content related to the core level Microsoft Office Exam
entitled "Access 2002" and the expert level of Microsoft Office Exams entitled, "Excel
2002" and "Word 2002" and sufficient performance-based exercises that relate closely
to all required content, and based on sampling of text, in conjunction with Volume 1.

Copyright © 2002 by Pearson Education, Inc., Upper Saddle River, New Jersey, 07458.
All rights reserved. Printed in the United States of America. This publication is protected by copyright and permission should be obtained from the publisher prior to any
prohibited reproduction, storage in a retrieval system, or transmission in any form or
by any means, electronic, mechanical, photocopying, recording, or likewise. For information regarding permission(s), write to: Rights and Permissions Department.

10 9 8 7 6 5 4 3 2 1
ISBN 0-13-034260-2

To Marion —
my wife, my lover, and my best friend

Robert Grauer

To Frank —
for giving me the encouragement, love, and the space

Maryann Barber

APPROVED COURSEWARE

What does this logo mean?

It means this courseware has been approved by the Microsoft® Office User Specialist Program to be among the finest available for learning **Excel 2002**, **Word 2002**, and **Access 2002**. It also means that upon completion of this courseware, you may be prepared to become a Microsoft Office User Specialist.

What is a Microsoft Office User Specialist?

A Microsoft Office User Specialist is an individual who has certified his or her skills in one or more of the Microsoft Office desktop applications of Microsoft Word, Microsoft Excel, Microsoft PowerPoint®, Microsoft Outlook® or Microsoft Access, or in Microsoft Project. The Microsoft Office User Specialist Program typically offers certification exams at the "Core" and "Expert" skill levels.[*] The Microsoft Office User Specialist Program is the only Microsoft approved program in the world for certifying proficiency in Microsoft Office desktop applications and Microsoft Project. This certification can be a valuable asset in any job search or career advancement.

More Information:

To learn more about becoming a Microsoft Office User Specialist, visit www.mous.net

To purchase a Microsoft Office User Specialist certification exam, visit www.DesktopIQ.com

To learn about other Microsoft Office User Specialist approved courseware from Prentice Hall, visit http://www.prenhall.com/phit/mous_frame.html

---

[*]The availability of Microsoft Office User Specialist certification exams varies by application, application version and language. Visit www.mous.net for exam availability.

Microsoft, the Microsoft Office User Specialist Logo, PowerPoint and Outlook are either registered trademarks or trademarks of Microsoft Corporation in the United States and/or other countries.

CONTENTS

MICROSOFT® WORD 2002

APPENDIX A: TOOLBARS 355

MICROSOFT® EXCEL 2002

5

CONSOLIDATING DATA 3-D WORKBOOKS AND LINKING 217

6

A FINANCIAL FORECAST: WORKGROUPS, AUDITING, AND TEMPLATES 261

7

LIST AND DATA MANAGEMENT: CONVERTING DATA TO INFORMATION 307

MICROSOFT® ACCESS 2002

7

BUILDING APPLICATIONS: MACROS AND A MULTILEVEL SWITCHBOARD 313

8

CREATING MORE POWERFUL APPLICATIONS: INTRODUCTION TO VBA 367

A VBA Primer: Extending Microsoft® Office XP

GLOSSARY

INDEX

PREFACE

Continuing a tradition of excellence, Prentice Hall is proud to announce the latest update in Microsoft Office texts: the new Exploring Microsoft Office XP series by Robert T. Grauer and Maryann Barber.

The hands-on approach and conceptual framework of this comprehensive series helps students master all aspects of the Microsoft Office XP software, while providing the background necessary to transfer and use these skills in their personal and professional lives.

WHAT'S NEW IN THE EXPLORING OFFICE SERIES FOR XP

The entire Exploring Office series has been revised to include the new features found in the Office XP Suite, which contains Word 2002, Excel 2002, Access 2002, PowerPoint 2002, Publisher 2000, FrontPage 2002, and Outlook 2002.

In addition, this revision includes fully revised end-of-chapter material that provides an extensive review of concepts and techniques discussed in the chapter. Many of these exercises feature the World Wide Web and application integration.

Building on the success of the Web site provided for previous editions of this series, Exploring Office XP will introduce the MyPHLIP Companion Web site, a site customized for each instructor that includes on-line, interactive study guides, data file downloads, current news feeds, additional case studies and exercises, and other helpful information. Start out at www.prenhall.com/grauer to explore these resources!

Organization of the Exploring Office Series for XP

The new Exploring Microsoft Office XP series includes four combined Office XP texts from which to choose:

■ ***Volume I*** is MOUS certified in each of the major applications in the Office suite (Word, Excel, Access, and PowerPoint). Three additional modules (Essential Computer Concepts, Essentials of Windows, and Essentials of the Internet) are also included.

■ ***Volume II*** picks up where Volume I left off, covering the advanced topics for the individual applications. A VBA primer has been added.

■ The ***Brief Microsoft Office XP*** edition provides less coverage of the individual applications than Volume I (a total of 8 chapters as opposed to 14). The supplementary modules (Windows, Internet, and Concepts) are not included.

■ A new volume, ***Getting Started with Office XP***, contains the first chapter from each application (Word, Excel, Access, and PowerPoint), plus three additional modules: Essentials of Windows, Essentials of the Internet, and Essential Computer Concepts.

Individual texts for Word 2002, Excel 2002, Access 2002, and PowerPoint 2002 provide complete coverage of the application and are MOUS certified. For shorter courses, we have created brief versions of the Exploring texts that give students a four-chapter introduction to each application. Each of these volumes is MOUS certified at the Core level.

To complete the full coverage of this series, custom modules on Microsoft Outlook 2002, Microsoft FrontPage 2002, Microsoft Publisher 2002, and a generic introduction to Microsoft Windows are also available.

This series has been approved by Microsoft to be used in preparation for Microsoft Office User Specialist exams.

APPROVED COURSEWARE

The Microsoft Office User Specialist (MOUS) program is globally recognized as the standard for demonstrating desktop skills with the Microsoft Office suite of business productivity applications (Microsoft Word, Microsoft Excel, Microsoft PowerPoint, Microsoft Access, and Microsoft Outlook). With a MOUS certification, thousands of people have demonstrated increased productivity and have proved their ability to utilize the advanced functionality of these Microsoft applications.

By encouraging individuals to develop advanced skills with Microsoft's leading business desktop software, the MOUS program helps fill the demand for qualified, knowledgeable people in the modern workplace. At the same time, MOUS helps satisfy an organization's need for a qualitative assessment of employee skills.

Customize the Exploring Office Series with Prentice Hall's Right PHit Binding Program

The Exploring Office XP series is part of the Right PHit Custom Binding Program, enabling instructors to create their own texts by selecting modules from Office XP Volume I, Volume II, Outlook, FrontPage, and Publisher to suit the needs of a specific course. An instructor could, for example, create a custom text consisting of the core modules in Word and Excel, coupled with the brief modules for Access and PowerPoint, and a brief introduction to computer concepts.

Instructors can also take advantage of Prentice Hall's Value Pack program to shrinkwrap multiple texts together at substantial savings to the student. A value pack is ideal in courses that require complete coverage of multiple applications.

The **Instructor's CD** that accompanies the Exploring Office series contains:

- Student data disks
- Solutions to all exercises and problems
- PowerPoint lectures
- Instructor's manuals in Word format enable the instructor to annotate portions of the instructor manual for distribution to the class
- A Windows-based test manager and the associated test bank in Word format

Prentice Hall's New MyPHLIP Companion Web site at www.prenhall.com/grauer offers current events, exercises, and downloadable supplements. This site also includes an on-line study guide containing true/false, multiple-choice, and essay questions.

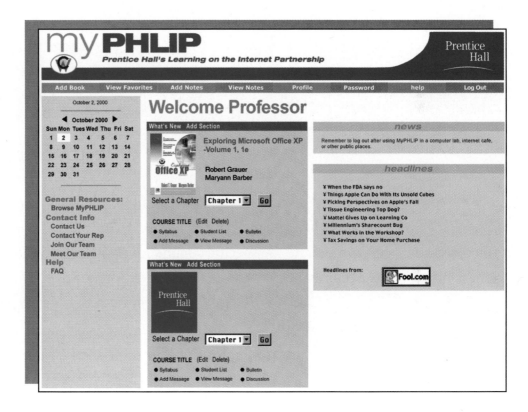

WebCT www.prenhall.com/webct

GOLD LEVEL CUSTOMER SUPPORT available exclusively to adopters of Prentice Hall courses is provided free-of-charge upon adoption and provides you with priority assistance, training discounts, and dedicated technical support.

Blackboard www.prenhall.com/blackboard

Prentice Hall's abundant on-line content, combined with Blackboard's popular tools and interface, result in robust Web-based courses that are easy to implement, manage, and use—taking your courses to new heights in student interaction and learning.

CourseCompass www.coursecompass.com

CourseCompass is a dynamic, interactive on-line course management tool powered by Blackboard. This exciting product allows you to teach with marketing-leading Pearson Education content in an easy-to-use customizable format.

Exploring Microsoft Office XP assumes no prior knowledge of the operating system. A 64-page section introduces the reader to the Essentials of Windows and provides an overview of the operating system. Students are shown the necessary file-management operations to use Microsoft Office successfully.

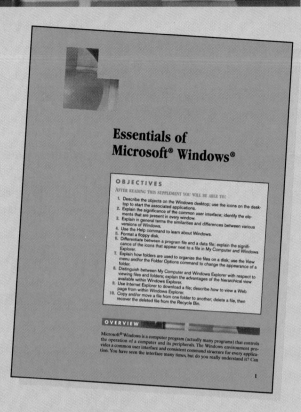

In-depth tutorials throughout all the Office XP applications enhance the conceptual introduction to each task and guide the student at the computer. Every step in every exercise has a full-color screen shot to illustrate the specific commands. Boxed tips provide alternative techniques and shortcuts and/or anticipate errors that students may make.

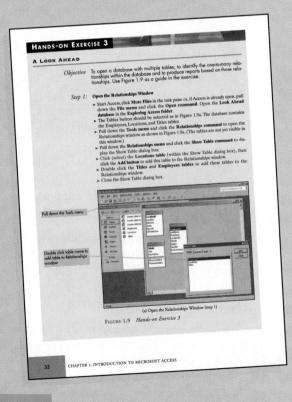

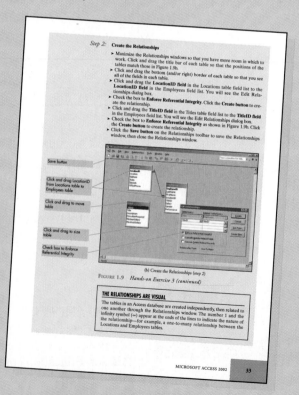

The authors have created an entirely new set of end-of-chapter exercises for every chapter in all of the applications. These new exercises have been written to provide the utmost in flexibility, variety, and difficulty.

Web-based Practice Exercises and On Your Own Exercises are marked by an icon in the margin and allow further exploration and practice via the World Wide Web.

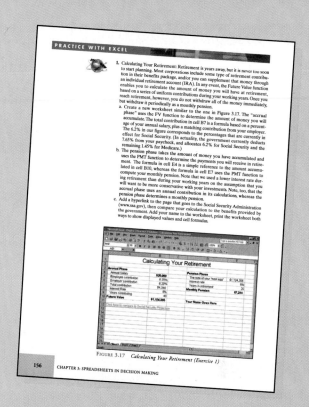

FIGURE 3.17   *Calculating Your Retirement (Exercise 1)*

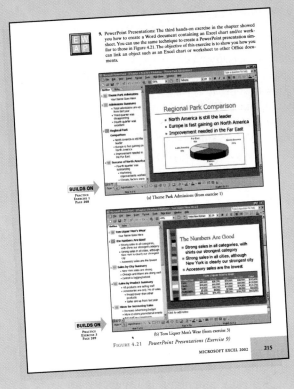

FIGURE 4.21   *PowerPoint Presentations (Exercise 9)*

Integration Exercises are marked by an icon in the margin. These exercises take advantage of the Microsoft Office Suite's power to use multiple applications in one document, spreadsheet, or presentation.

BUILDS ON   ➤   ***Builds On Exercises*** require students to use selected application files as the starting point in later exercises, thereby introducing new information to students only as needed.

The end-of-chapter material includes multiple-choice questions for self-evaluation plus additional "on your own" exercises to encourage the reader to further explore the application.

ACKNOWLEDGMENTS

We want to thank the many individuals who have helped to bring this project to fruition. David Alexander, senior editor at Prentice Hall, has provided new leadership in extending the series to Office XP. Cathi Profitko did an absolutely incredible job on our Web site. Melissa Whitaker coordinated the myriad details of production and the certification process. Greg Christofferson was instrumental in the acquisition of supporting software. Lynne Breitfeller was the project manager and manufacturing buyer. Greg Hubit has been masterful as the external production editor for every book in the series. Cecil Yarbrough did an outstanding job in checking the manuscript for technical accuracy. Chuck Cox did his usual fine work as copyeditor. Kerri Limpert was the supplements editor. Cindy Stevens, Tom McKenzie, and Michael Olmstead wrote the instructor manuals. Patricia Smythe developed the innovative and attractive design. We also want to acknowledge our reviewers who, through their comments and constructive criticism, greatly improved the series.

Lynne Band, Middlesex Community College
Don Belle, Central Piedmont Community College
Stuart P. Brian, Holy Family College
Carl M. Briggs, Indiana University School of Business
Kimberly Chambers, Scottsdale Community College
Alok Charturvedi, Purdue University
Jerry Chin, Southwest Missouri State University
Dean Combellick, Scottsdale Community College
Cody Copeland, Johnson County Community College
Larry S. Corman, Fort Lewis College
Janis Cox, Tri-County Technical College
Martin Crossland, Southwest Missouri State University
Paul E. Daurelle, Western Piedmont Community College
Carolyn DiLeo, Westchester Community College
Judy Dolan, Palomar College
David Douglas, University of Arkansas
Carlotta Eaton, Radford University
Judith M. Fitspatrick, Gulf Coast Community College
James Franck, College of St. Scholastica
Raymond Frost, Central Connecticut State University
Midge Gerber, Southwestern Oklahoma State University
James Gips, Boston College
Vernon Griffin, Austin Community College
Ranette Halverson, Midwestern State University
Michael Hassett, Fort Hays State University
Mike Hearn, Community College of Philadelphia
Wanda D. Heller, Seminole Community College
Bonnie Homan, San Francisco State University
Ernie Ivey, Polk Community College
Mike Kelly, Community College of Rhode Island
Jane King, Everett Community College

Rose M. Laird, Northern Virginia Community College
John Lesson, University of Central Florida
David B. Meinert, Southwest Missouri State University
Alan Moltz, Naugatuck Valley Technical Community College
Kim Montney, Kellogg Community College
Bill Morse, DeVry Institute of Technology
Kevin Pauli, University of Nebraska
Mary McKenry Percival, University of Miami
Delores Pusins, Hillsborough Community College
Gale E. Rand, College Misericordia
Judith Rice, Santa Fe Community College
David Rinehard, Lansing Community College
Marilyn Salas, Scottsdale Community College
John Shepherd, Duquesne University
Barbara Sherman, Buffalo State College
Robert Spear, Prince George's Community College
Michael Stewardson, San Jacinto College—North
Helen Stoloff, Hudson Valley Community College
Margaret Thomas, Ohio University
Mike Thomas, Indiana University School of Business
Suzanne Tomlinson, Iowa State University
Karen Tracey, Central Connecticut State University
Antonio Vargas, El Paso Community College
Sally Visci, Lorain County Community College
David Weiner, University of San Francisco
Connie Wells, Georgia State University
Wallace John Whistance-Smith, Ryerson Polytechnic University
Jack Zeller, Kirkwood Community College

A final word of thanks to the unnamed students at the University of Miami, who make it all worthwhile. Most of all, thanks to you, our readers, for choosing this book. Please feel free to contact us with any comments and suggestions.

Robert T. Grauer
rgrauer@miami.edu
www.bus.miami.edu/~rgrauer
www.prenhall.com/grauer

Maryann Barber
mbarber@miami.edu
www.bus.miami.edu/~mbarber

CHAPTER 5

Desktop Publishing: Creating a Newsletter and Other Documents

OBJECTIVES

AFTER READING THIS CHAPTER YOU WILL BE ABLE TO:

1. Design and implement a multicolumn newsletter; explain how sections are used to vary the number of columns in a document.
2. Define a pull quote and a reverse; explain how to implement these features using Microsoft Word.
3. Define typography; explain how styles can be used to implement changes in typography throughout a document.
4. Use the Insert Picture command to insert clip art into a document; explain how the Format Picture command is used to move and size a graphic.
5. Discuss the importance of a grid in the design of a document; describe the use of white space as a design element.
6. Use the Drawing toolbar to add objects to a Word document; describe the function of at least four different drawing tools.
7. Use object linking to create a Word document that contains an Excel worksheet and an Excel chart.

OVERVIEW

Desktop publishing evolved through a combination of technologies, including faster computers, laser printers, and sophisticated page composition software to manipulate text and graphics. Desktop publishing was initially considered a separate application, but today's generation of word processors has matured to such a degree that it is difficult to tell where word processing ends and desktop publishing begins. Microsoft Word is, for all practical purposes, a desktop publishing program that can be used to create all types of documents.

217

The essence of ***desktop publishing*** is the merger of text with graphics to produce a professional-looking document without reliance on external services. Desktop publishing will save you time and money because you are doing the work yourself rather than sending it out as you did in traditional publishing. That is the good news. The bad news is that desktop publishing is not as easy as it sounds, precisely because you are doing work that was done previously by skilled professionals. Nevertheless, with a little practice, and a basic knowledge of graphic design, you will be able to create effective and attractive documents.

Our chapter begins with the development of a simple newsletter in which we create a multicolumn document, import clip art and other objects, and position those objects within a document. The newsletter also reviews material from earlier chapters on bullets and lists, borders and shading, and section formatting. The second half of the chapter presents additional tools that you can use to enhance your documents. We describe the Drawing toolbar and explain how it is used to add objects to a Word document. We also describe how to create a Word document that contains an Excel worksheet and an Excel chart. The document is created in such a way that any changes to the underlying Excel workbook are automatically reflected in the Word document.

THE NEWSLETTER

The newsletter in Figure 5.1 demonstrates the basics of desktop publishing and provides an overview of the chapter. The material is presented conceptually, after which you implement the design in two hands-on exercises. We provide the text and you do the formatting. The first exercise creates a simple newsletter from copy that we provide. The second exercise uses more sophisticated formatting as described by the various techniques mentioned within the newsletter. Many of the terms are new, and we define them briefly in the next few paragraphs.

A ***reverse*** (light text on a dark background) is a favorite technique of desktop publishers to emphasize a specific element. It is used in the ***masthead*** (the identifying information) at the top of the newsletter and provides a distinctive look to the publication. The number of the newsletter and the date of publication also appear in the masthead in smaller letters.

A ***pull quote*** is a phrase or sentence taken from an article to emphasize a key point. It is typically set in larger type, often in a different typeface and/or italics, and may be offset with parallel lines at the top and bottom.

A ***dropped-capital letter*** is a large capital letter at the beginning of a paragraph. It, too, catches the reader's eye and calls attention to the associated text.

Clip art, used in moderation, will catch the reader's eye and enhance almost any newsletter. It is available from a variety of sources including the Microsoft Media Gallery, which is included in Office XP. Clip art can also be downloaded from the Web, but be sure you are allowed to reprint the image. The banner at the bottom of the newsletter is not a clip art image per se, but was created using various tools on the ***Drawing toolbar***.

Borders and shading are effective individually, or in combination with one another, to emphasize important stories within the newsletter. Simple vertical and/or horizontal lines are also effective. The techniques are especially useful in the absence of clip art or other graphics and are a favorite of desktop publishers.

Lists, whether bulleted or numbered, help to organize information by emphasizing important topics. A ***bulleted list*** emphasizes (and separates) the items. A ***numbered list*** sequences (and prioritizes) the items and is automatically updated to accommodate additions or deletions.

All of these techniques can be implemented with commands you already know, as you will see in the hands-on exercise, which follows shortly.

Creating a Newsletter

Volume I, Number 2   Spring 2001

Desktop publishing is easy, but there are several points to remember. This chapter will take you through the steps in creating a newsletter. The first hands-on exercise creates a simple newsletter with a masthead and three-column design. The second exercise creates a more attractive document by exploring different ways to emphasize the text.

Clip Art and Other Objects
Clip art is available from a variety of sources. You can also use other types of objects such as maps, charts, or organization charts, which are created by other applications, then brought into a document through the Insert Object command. A single dominant graphic is usually more appealing than multiple smaller graphics.

Techniques to Consider
Our finished newsletter contains one or more examples of each of the following desktop publishing techniques. Can you find where each technique is used, and further, explain, how to implement that technique in Microsoft Word?
1. Pull Quotes
2. Reverse
3. Drop Caps
4. Tables
5. Styles
6. Bullets and Numbering
7. Borders and Shading
8. The Drawing Toolbar

Newspaper-Style Columns
The essence of a newsletter is the implementation of columns in which text flows continuously from the bottom of one column to the top of the next. You specify the number of columns, and optionally, the space between columns. Microsoft Word does the rest. It will compute the width of each column based on the number of columns and the margins.

Beginners often specify margins that are too large and implement too much space between the columns. Another way to achieve a more sophisticated look is to avoid the standard two-column design. You can implement columns of varying width and/or insert vertical lines between the columns.

The number of columns will vary in different parts of a document. The masthead is typically a single column, but the body of the newsletter will have two or three. Remember, too, that columns are implemented at the section level and hence, section breaks are required throughout a document.

Typography
Typography is the process of selecting typefaces, type styles, and type sizes, and is a critical element in the success of any document. Type should reinforce the message and should be consistent with the information you want to convey. More is not better, especially in the case of too many typefaces and styles, which produce cluttered documents that impress no one. Try to limit yourself to a maximum of two typefaces per document, but choose multiple sizes and/or styles within those typefaces. Use boldface or italics for emphasis, but do so in moderation, because if you use too many different elements, the effect is lost.

A pull quote adds interest to a document while simultaneously emphasizing a key point. It is implemented by increasing the point size, changing to italics, centering the text, and displaying a top and bottom border on the paragraph.

Use Styles as Appropriate
Styles were covered in the previous chapter, but that does not mean you cannot use them in conjunction with a newsletter. A style stores character and/or paragraph formatting and can be applied to multiple occurrences of the same element within a document. Change the style and you automatically change all text defined by that style. You can also use styles from one edition of your newsletter to the next to insure consistency.

Borders and Shading
Borders and shading are effective individually or in combination with one another. Use a thin rule (one point or less) and light shading (five or ten percent) for best results. The techniques are especially useful in the absence of clip art or other graphics and are a favorite of desktop publishers.

All the News That Fits

FIGURE 5.1   *The Newsletter*

Typography

Typography is the process of selecting typefaces, type styles, and type sizes. It is a critical, often subtle, element in the success of a document, and its importance cannot be overstated. You would not, for example, use the same design to announce a year-end bonus and a plant closing. Indeed, good typography goes almost unnoticed, whereas poor typography calls attention to itself and detracts from a document. Our discussion reviews basic concepts and terminology.

A *typeface* (or *font*) is a complete set of characters (upper- and lowercase letters, numbers, punctuation marks, and special symbols). Typefaces are divided into two general categories, serif and sans serif. A *serif typeface* has tiny cross lines at the ends of the characters to help the eye connect one letter with the next. A *sans serif typeface* (sans from the French for *without*) does not have these lines. A commonly accepted practice is to use serif typefaces with large amounts of text and sans serif typefaces for smaller amounts. The newsletter in Figure 5.1, for example, uses *Times New Roman* (a serif typeface) for the text and *Arial* (a sans serif typeface) for the headings.

A second characteristic of a typeface is whether it is monospaced or proportional. A *monospaced typeface* (e.g., Courier New) uses the same amount of space for every character regardless of its width. A *proportional typeface* (e.g., Times New Roman or Arial) allocates space according to the width of the character. Monospaced fonts are used in tables and financial projections where items must be precisely lined up, one beneath the other. Proportional typefaces create a more professional appearance and are appropriate for most documents.

Any typeface can be set in different styles (such as bold or italic) to create *Times New Roman Italic*, **Arial bold**, or `Courier New Bold Italic`. Other effects are also possible, such as small caps, shadow, and outline, but these should be used with moderation.

Type size is a vertical measurement and is specified in points. One *point* is equal to $1/72$ of an inch. The text in most documents is set in 10- or 12-point type. (The book you are reading is set in 10 point.) Different elements in the same document are often set in different type sizes to provide suitable emphasis. A variation of at least two points, however, is necessary for the difference to be noticeable. The headings in the newsletter, for example, were set in 12-point type, whereas the text of the articles is in 10-point type. The introduction of columns into a document poses another concern in that the type size should be consistent with the width of a column. Nine-point type, for example, is appropriate in columns that are two inches wide, but much too small in a single-column term paper. In other words, longer lines or wider columns require larger type sizes.

There are no hard and fast rules for the selection of type, only guidelines and common sense. Your objective should be to create a document that is easy to read and visually appealing. You will find that the design that worked so well in one document may not work at all in a different document. Good typography is often the result of trial and error, and we encourage you to experiment freely.

USE MODERATION AND RESTRAINT

More is not better, especially in the case of too many typefaces and styles, which produce cluttered documents that impress no one. Try to limit yourself to a maximum of two typefaces per document, but choose multiple sizes and/or styles within those typefaces. Use boldface or italics for emphasis, but do so in moderation, because if you emphasize too many elements, the effect is lost.

The Columns Command

The columnar formatting in a newsletter is implemented through the ***Columns command*** as shown in Figure 5.2. Start by selecting one of the preset designs, and Microsoft Word takes care of everything else. It calculates the width of each column based on the number of columns, the left and right margins on the page, and the specified (default) space between columns.

Consider, for example, the dialog box in Figure 5.2, in which a design of three equal columns is selected with a spacing of ¼ inch between each column. The 2-inch width of each column is computed automatically based on left and right margins of 1 inch each and the ¼-inch spacing between columns. The width of each column is computed by subtracting the sum of the margins and the space between the columns (a total of 2½ inches in this example) from the page width of 8½ inches. The result of the subtraction is 6 inches, which is divided by 3, resulting in a column width of 2 inches.

You can change any of the settings in the Columns dialog box, and Word will automatically make the necessary adjustments. The newsletter in Figure 5.1, for example, uses a two-column layout with wide and narrow columns. We prefer this design to columns of uniform width, as we think it adds interest to our document. Note, too, that once columns have been defined, text will flow continuously from the bottom of one column to the top of the next

Return for a minute to the newsletter in Figure 5.1, and notice that the number of columns varies from one part of the newsletter to another. The masthead is displayed over a single column at the top of the page, whereas the remainder of the newsletter is formatted in two columns of different widths. The number of columns is specified at the section level, and thus a ***section break*** is required whenever the column specification changes. A section break is also required at the end of the last column to balance the text within the columns.

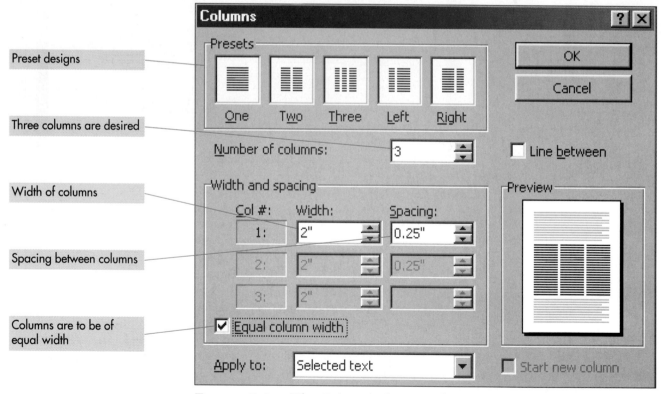

FIGURE 5.2 *The Columns Command*

NEWSPAPER COLUMNS

Objective To create a basic newsletter through the Format Columns command; to use section breaks to change the number of columns. Use Figure 5.3.

Step 1: **The Page Setup Command**

➤ Start Word. Open the **Text for Newsletter document** in the Exploring Word folder. Save the document as **Modified Newsletter**.

➤ Pull down the **File menu**. Click **Page Setup** to display the Page Setup dialog box in Figure 5.3a. Change the top, bottom, left, and right margins to .75.

➤ Click **OK** to accept these settings and close the Page Setup dialog box. If necessary, click the **Print Layout View button** above the status bar. Set the magnification (zoom) to **Page Width**.

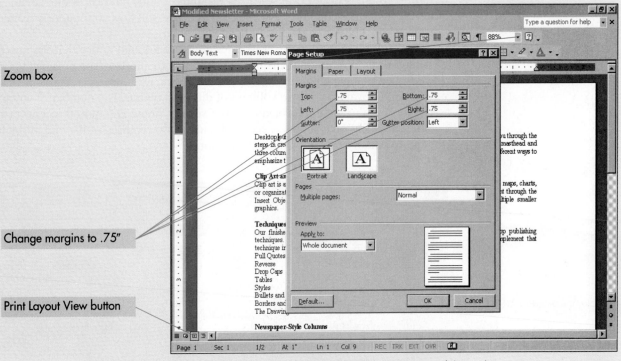

Zoom box

Change margins to .75″

Print Layout View button

(a) The Page Setup Command (step 1)

FIGURE 5.3 *Hands-on Exercise 1*

CHANGE THE MARGINS

The default margins of 1 inch at the top and bottom of a page, and 1¼ inches on the sides, are fine for a typical document. A multicolumn newsletter, however, looks better with smaller margins, which in turn enables you to create wider columns. Margins are defined at the section level, and hence it's easiest to change the margins at the very beginning, when a document consists of only a single section.

Step 2:   **Check the Document**

> ➤ Pull down the **Tools menu**, click **Options**, and click the **Spelling and Grammar tab**. Click the **drop-down arrow** on the Writing style list box and select **Grammar & Style**. Click **OK** to close the Options dialog box.
> ➤ Click the **Spelling and Grammar button** on the Standard toolbar to check the document for errors.
> ➤ The first error detected by the spelling and grammar check is the omitted hyphen between the words *three* and *column* as shown in Figure 5.3b. (This is a subtle mistake and emphasizes the need to check a document using the tools provided by Word.) Click **Change** to accept the indicated suggestion.
> ➤ Continue checking the document, accepting (or rejecting) the suggested corrections as you see fit.
> ➤ Save the document.

Spelling and Grammar button

Flagged error

Suggested change

Click change

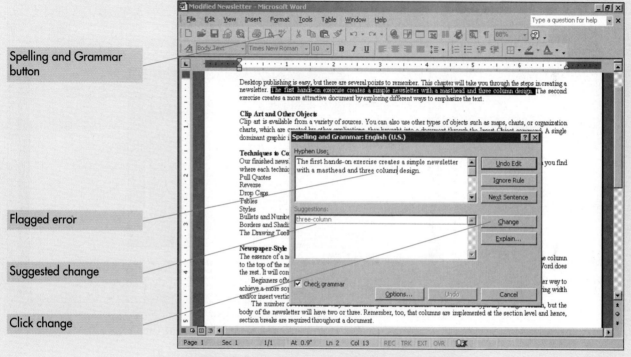

(b) Check the Document (step 2)

FIGURE 5.3   *Hands-on Exercise 1 (continued)*

USE THE SPELLING AND GRAMMAR CHECK

Our eyes are less discriminating than we would like to believe, allowing misspellings and simple typos to go unnoticed. To prove the point, count the number of times the letter f appears in this sentence, *"Finished files are the result of years of scientific study combined with the experience of years."* The correct answer is six, but most people find only four or five. Checking your document takes only a few minutes. Do it!

Step 3: **Implement Column Formatting**

➤ Pull down the **Format menu**. Click **Columns** to display the dialog box in Figure 5.3c. Click the **Presets icon** for **Two**. The column width for each column and the spacing between columns will be determined automatically from the existing margins.

➤ If necessary, clear the **Line between box**. Click **OK** to accept the settings and close the Columns dialog box.

➤ The text of the newsletter should be displayed in two columns. If you do not see the columns, it is probably because you are in the wrong view. Click the **Print Layout View button** above the status bar to change to this view.

➤ Save the document.

Click preset design for Two columns

Clear check box for Line between columns

Preview of column design

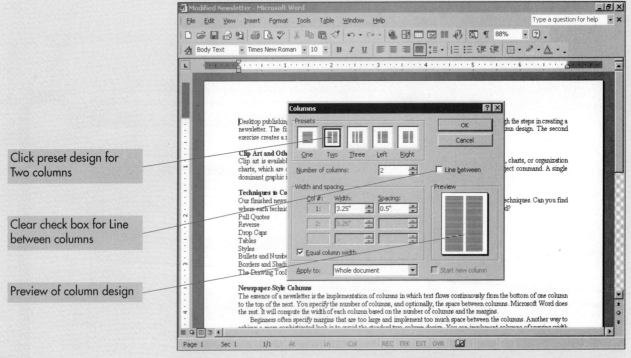

(c) Implement Column Formatting (step 3)

FIGURE 5.3   *Hands-on Exercise 1 (continued)*

PAGE BREAKS, COLUMN BREAKS, AND LINE BREAKS

Force Word to begin the next entry on a new page or column by inserting the proper type of break. Pull down the Insert menu, click the Break command to display the Break dialog box, then choose the option button for a page break or column break, respectively. It's easier, however, to use the appropriate shortcut, Ctrl+Enter or Shift+Ctrl+Enter, for a page or column break, respectively. You can also use Shift+Enter to force a line break, where the next word begins on a new line within the same paragraph. Click the Show/Hide button to display the hidden codes to see how the breaks are implemented.

Step 4: **Balance the Columns**

➤ Use the **Zoom box** on the Standard toolbar to zoom to **Whole Page** to see the entire newsletter as shown in Figure 5.3d. Do not be concerned if the columns are of different lengths.

➤ Press **Ctrl+End** to move the insertion point to the end of the document. Pull down the **Insert menu**. Click **Break** to display the Break dialog box in Figure 5.3d. Select the **Continuous option button** under Section breaks.

➤ Click **OK** to accept the settings and close the dialog box. The columns should be balanced, although one column may be one line longer than the other.

➤ Save the document.

Zoom box

Press Ctrl+End to move to end of document

Click Continuous

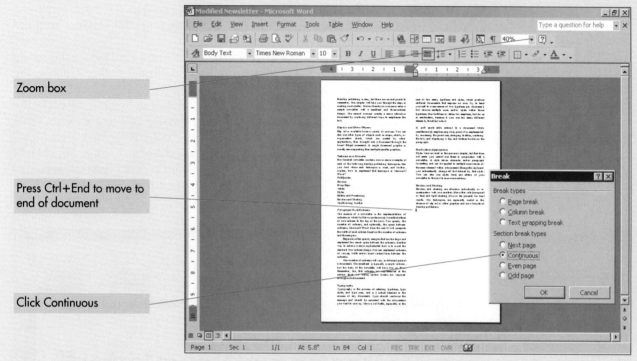

(d) Balance the Columns (step 4)

FIGURE 5.3 *Hands-on Exercise 1 (continued)*

USE THE RULER TO CHANGE COLUMN WIDTH

Click anywhere within the column whose width you want to change, then point to the ruler and click and drag the right column margin (the mouse pointer changes to a double arrow) to change the column width. Changing the width of one column in a document with equal-sized columns changes the width of all other columns so that they remain equal. Changing the width in a document with unequal columns changes only that column. You can also double click the ruler to display the Page Setup dialog box, then click the Margins tab to change the left and right margins, which in turn will change the column width.

Step 5: **Create the Masthead**

➤ Use the **Zoom box** on the Standard toolbar to change to **Page Width**. Click the **Show/Hide ¶ button** to display the paragraph and section marks.

➤ Press **Ctrl+Home** to move the insertion point to the beginning of the document. Pull down the **Insert menu**, click **Break**, select the **Continuous option button**, and click **OK**. You should see a double dotted line indicating a section break as shown in Figure 5.3e.

➤ Click immediately to the left of the dotted line, which will place the insertion point to the left of the line. Check the status bar to be sure you are in section one.

➤ Change the format for this section to a single column by clicking the **Columns button** on the Standard toolbar and selecting one column. (Alternatively, you can pull down the **Format menu**, click **Columns**, and choose **One** from the Presets column formats.)

➤ Type **Creating a Newsletter** and press the **enter key** twice. Select the newly entered text, click the **Center button** on the Formatting toolbar. Change the font to **48-point Arial Bold**.

➤ Click underneath the masthead (to the left of the section break). Pull down the **Table menu**, click **Insert** to display a submenu, then click **Table**. Insert a table with one row and two columns as shown in Figure 5.3e.

➤ Click in the left cell of the table. Type **Volume I, Number 1**. Click in the right cell (or press the **Tab key** to move to this cell and type the current semester (for example, **Spring 2001**). Click the **Align Right button**.

➤ Save the document.

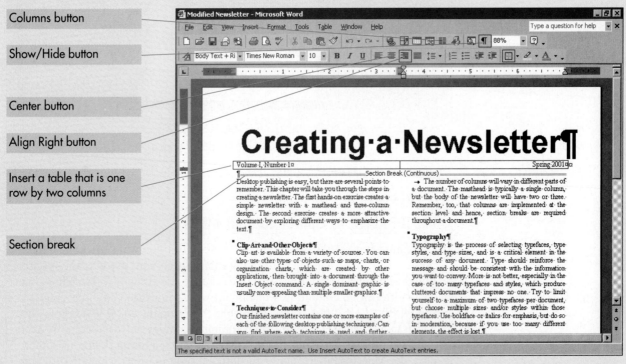

(e) Create the Masthead (step 5)

FIGURE 5.3 *Hands-on Exercise 1 (continued)*

Step 6:   **Create a Reverse**

➤ Press **Ctrl+Home** to move the insertion point to the beginning of the newsletter. Click anywhere within the title of the newsletter.

➤ Pull down the **Format menu**, click **Borders and Shading** to display the Borders and Shading dialog box, then click the **Shading tab** in Figure 5.3f.

➤ Click the **drop-down arrow** in the Style list box (in the Patterns area) and select **Solid (100%)** shading. Click **OK** to accept the setting and close the dialog box. Click elsewhere in the document to see the results.

➤ The final step is to remove the default border that appears around the table. Click in the selection area to the left of the table to select the entire table.

➤ Pull down the **Format menu**, click **Borders and Shading**, and if necessary click the **Borders tab**. Click the **None icon** in the Presets area. Click **OK**. Click elsewhere in the document to see the result.

Shading tab

Click drop-down arrow on
Style list box

Click Solid (100%)

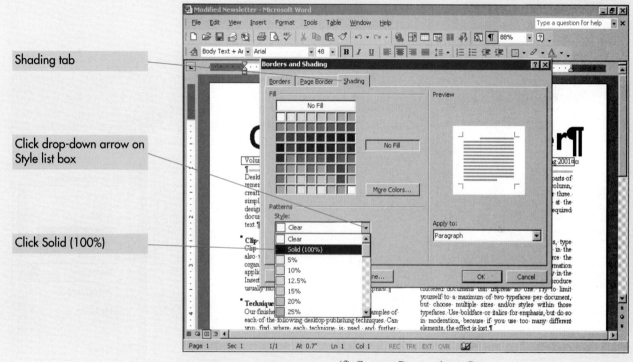

(f) Create a Reverse (step 6)

FIGURE 5.3   *Hands-on Exercise 1 (continued)*

LEFT ALIGNED	CENTERED	RIGHT ALIGNED

Many documents call for left-, centered, and/or right-aligned text on the same line, an effect that is achieved through setting tabs, or more easily through a table. To achieve the effect shown at the top of this box, create a 1 × 3 table (one row and three columns), type the text in the cells, then use the buttons on the Formatting toolbar to left-align, center, and right-align the cells. Select the table, pull down the Format menu, click Borders and Shading, then specify None as the Border setting.

Step 7: **Modify the Heading Style**

➤ Two styles have been implemented for you in the newsletter. Click in any text paragraph, and you see the Body Text style name displayed in the Style box on the Formatting toolbar. Click in any heading, and you see the Heading 1 style.

➤ Pull down the **View menu** and click the **Task Pane command** to open the task pane. Click the **down arrow** within the task pane and choose **Style and Formatting**.

➤ Point to the **Heading 1** style to display a down arrow, then click the **Modify command** to display the **Modify Style** dialog box shown in Figure 5.3g.

➤ Change the font to **Arial** and the font size to **12**. Click **OK** to accept the settings and close the dialog box. All of the headings in the document are changed automatically to reflect the changes in the Heading 1 style.

➤ Experiment with other styles as you see fit. (You can remove the formatting of existing text by clicking within a paragraph, then clicking **Clear Formatting** within the task pane.)

➤ Save the newsletter. Close the task pane.

Click drop-down arrow and select Styles and Formatting

Style box

Click Clear Formatting to remove formatting from selected text

Click drop-down arrow to select font size

Point to Heading 1 style

Click drop-down arrow when it appears

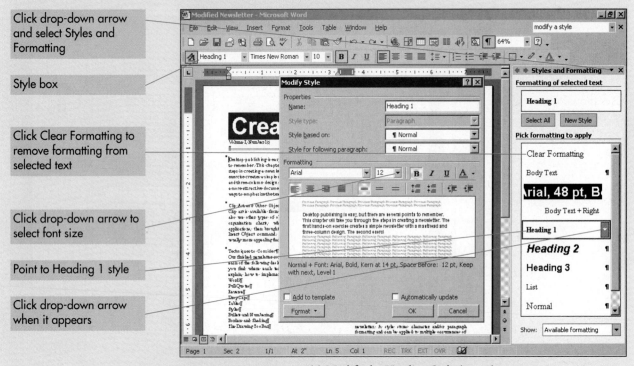

(g) Modify the Heading Style (step 7)

FIGURE 5.3 *Hands-on Exercise 1 (continued)*

USE STYLES AS APPROPRIATE

Styles were covered in the previous chapter, but that does not mean you cannot use them in conjunction with a newsletter. A style stores character and/or paragraph formatting and can be applied to multiple occurrences of the same element within a document. Change the style and you automatically change all text defined by that style. Use the same styles from one edition of your newsletter to the next to ensure consistency. Use styles for any document to promote uniformity and increase flexibility.

Step 8: **The Print Preview Command**

➤ Pull down the **File menu** and click **Print Preview** (or click the **Print Preview button** on the Standard toolbar) to view the newsletter as in Figure 5.3h. This is a basic two-column newsletter with the masthead appearing as a reverse and stretching over a single column.

➤ Click the **Print button** to print the newsletter at this stage so that you can compare this version with the finished newsletter at the end of the next exercise.

➤ Click the **Close button** on the Print Preview toolbar to close the Preview view and return to the Page Layout view.

➤ Exit Word if you do not want to continue with the next exercise at this time.

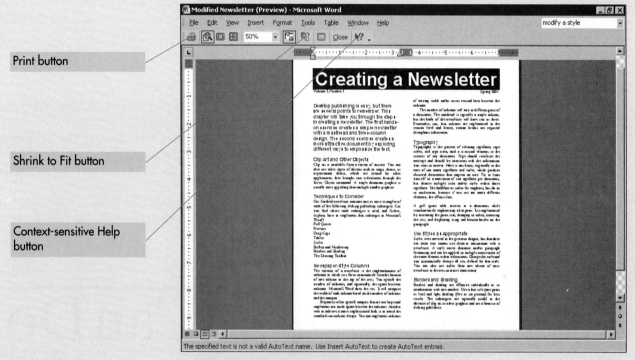

Print button

Shrink to Fit button

Context-sensitive Help button

(h) The Print Preview Command (step 8)

FIGURE 5.3 *Hands-on Exercise 1 (continued)*

THE PRINT PREVIEW TOOLBAR

The Print Preview toolbar appears automatically when you switch to this view, and it contains several tools that are helpful prior to printing a document. The Shrink to Fit button is especially useful if a small portion of a document spills over to a second page—click this button, and it uniformly reduces the fonts throughout a document to eliminate the extra page. The context-sensitive Help button, on the extreme right of the toolbar, explains the function of the other buttons. Click the button (the mouse pointer changes to an arrow and a question mark), then click any other button for an explanation of its function. We suggest that you avoid the Full Screen button and that you close the full screen immediately if you wind up in this view.

We trust you have completed the first hands-on exercise without difficulty and that you were able to duplicate the initial version of the newsletter. That, however, is the easy part of desktop publishing. The more difficult aspect is to develop the design in the first place because the mere availability of a desktop publishing program does not guarantee an effective document, any more than a word processor will turn its author into another Shakespeare. Other skills are necessary, and so we continue with a brief introduction to graphic design.

Much of what we say is subjective, and what works in one situation will not necessarily work in another. Your eye is the best judge of all, and you should follow your own instincts. Experiment freely and realize that successful design is the result of trial and error. Seek inspiration from others by collecting samples of real documents that you find attractive, then use those documents as the basis for your own designs.

The Grid

The design of a document is developed on a **grid**, an underlying, but *invisible,* set of horizontal and vertical lines that determine the placement of the major elements. A grid establishes the overall structure of a document by indicating the number of columns, the space between columns, the size of the margins, the placement of headlines, art, and so on. The grid does *not* appear in the printed document or on the screen.

Figure 5.4 shows the "same" document in three different designs. The left half of each design displays the underlying grid, whereas the right half displays the completed document.

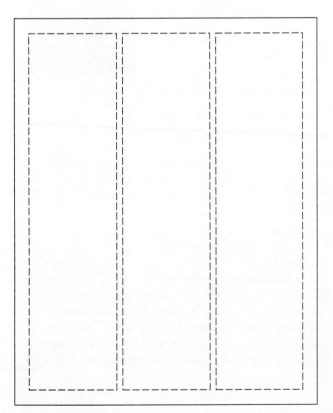

(a) Three-column Grid

FIGURE 5.4   *The Grid System of Design*

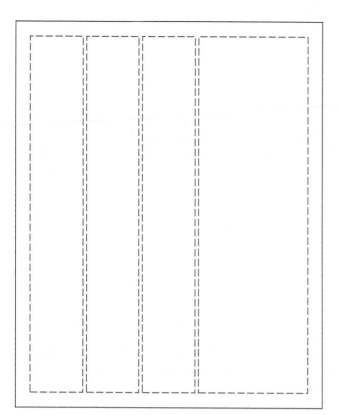

No Can Do

He felt more and more pressure to play the game of not playing. Maybe that's why he stepped in front of that truck.

People wonder why people do things like this, but all you have to do is look around and see all the stress and insanity each person in responsibility is required to put up with. There is no help or end in sight. It seems that managers are managing less and shoveling the workloads on to their underlings. This seems to be the overall response to the absence of raises or benefit packages they feel are their entitlement. Something must be done now!

People wonder why people do things like this, but all you have to do is look around and

see all the stress and insanity each person in responsibility is required to put up with. There is no help or end in sight. It seems that managers are managing less and shoveling the workloads on to their underlings. This seems to be the overall response to the absence of raises or benefit packages they feel are their entitlement. Something must be done now!

People wonder why people do things like this, but all you have to do is look around and see all the stress and insanity each person in responsibility is

required to put up with. There is no help or end in sight. It seems that managers are managing less and shoveling the workloads on to their underlings. This seems to be the overall response to the absence of raises or benefit packages they feel are their entitlement.

People wonder why people do things like this, but all you have to do is look around and see all the stress and insanity each person in responsibility is required to put up with. There is no help or end in sight. It seems that managers are

managing less and shoveling the workloads on to their underlings. This seems to be the overall response to the absence of raises or benefit packages they feel are their entitlement. Some-thing must be done now!

People wonder why people do things like this, but all you have to do is look around and see all the stress and insanity each person in responsibility is required to put up with. There is no help or end in sight. It seems that managers are managing less. Something must be done now!

People wonder why people do things like this, but all you have to do is look around and see all the stress and insanity each person in responsibility is required to put up with. There is no help or end in sight. It seems that managers are managing less and shoveling the workloads on to their underlings. This seems to be the overall response to the ▼

(b) Four-column Grid

People wonder why people do things like this, but all you have to do is look around and see all the stress and insanity each person in responsibility is required to put up with. There is no help or end in sight. It seems that managers are managing less and shoveling the workloads on to their underlings. This seems to be the overall response to the absence of raises or benefit packages they feel are their entitlement. Something must be done!

People wonder why people do things like this, but all you have to do is look around and see all the stress and insanity each person in responsibility is required to put up with. There is no help or end in sight. It seems that managers are managing less and shoveling the workloads on to their underlings. This seems to be the overall response to the absence of raises or benefit packages they feel are their entitlement. Something must be done now!

People wonder

why people do things like this, but all you have to do is look around and see all the stress and insanity each person in responsibility is required to put up with. There is no help or end in sight. It seems that managers are managing less and shoveling the workloads on to their underlings. This seems to be the overall response to the absence of rais-es or benefit packages they feel are their entitle-ment. Something must be done now!

People wonder why people do things like this, but all you have to do

is look around and see all the stress and insanity each person in responsi-bility is required to put up with. There is no help or end in sight. It seems that managers are man-aging less and shoveling the

He felt more and more pressure to play the game of not playing. Maybe that's why he stepped in front of that truck.

workloads on to their underlings. This seems to be the overall re-sponse to the ab-sence of raises or benefit packages they feel are their

entitlement. Some-thing must be done now!

People wonder why people do things like this, but all you have to do is look around and see all the stress and insanity each person in responsi-bility is required to put up with. There is no help or end in sight. It seems that managers are managing less and shoveling the workloads on to their underlings. This seems to be the overall re-sponse to the absence of raises or benefit packages they feel are their entitle-ment. Some-thing

must be done!

People wonder why people do things like this, but all you have to do is look around and see all the stress and insanity each person in responsibility is required to put up with. There is no help or end in sight. It seems that man-agers are managing less and shoveling the workloads on to their underlings. This seems to be the overall response to the absence of rais-es or benefit pack-ages they feel are their entitlement. Something must be done!

People wonder why people do things like this, but all you have to do is look around and see all the stress and insanity each person in responsibility is required to put up with. There is no help or end in sight. It seems that man-agers are managing less and shoveling the workloads on to their underlings. Something must be done now!

People wonder why people do things like this, but all you have to do ▼

(c) Five-column Grid

FIGURE 5.4 *The Grid System of Design (continued)*

A grid may be simple or complex, but it is always distinguished by the number of columns it contains. The three-column grid of Figure 5.4a is one of the most common and utilitarian designs. Figure 5.4b shows a four-column design for the same document, with unequal column widths to provide interest. Figure 5.4c illustrates a five-column grid that is often used with large amounts of text. Many other designs are possible as well. A one-column grid is used for term papers and letters. A two-column, wide-and-narrow format is appropriate for textbooks and manuals. Two- and three-column formats are used for newsletters and magazines.

The simple concept of a grid should make the underlying design of any document obvious, which in turn gives you an immediate understanding of page composition. Moreover, the conscious use of a grid will help you organize your material and result in a more polished and professional-looking publication. It will also help you to achieve consistency from page to page within a document (or from issue to issue of a newsletter). Indeed, much of what goes wrong in desktop publishing stems from failing to follow or use the underlying grid.

Emphasis

Good design makes it easy for the reader to determine what is important. As indicated earlier, *emphasis* can be achieved in several ways, the easiest being variations in type size and/or type style. Headings should be set in type sizes (at least two points) larger than body copy. The use of **boldface** is effective as are *italics,* but both should be done in moderation. (UPPERCASE LETTERS and underlining are alternative techniques that we believe are less effective.)

Boxes and/or shading call attention to selected articles. Horizontal lines are effective to separate one topic from another or to call attention to a pull quote. A reverse can be striking for a small amount of text. Clip art, used in moderation, will catch the reader's eye and enhance almost any newsletter.

Clip Art

Clip art is available from a variety of sources including the Microsoft Media Gallery and Microsoft Web site. The Media Gallery can be accessed in a variety of ways, most easily through the *Insert Picture command*. Once clip art has been inserted into a document, it can be moved and sized just like any other Windows object, as will be illustrated in our next hands-on exercise.

The *Format Picture command* provides additional flexibility in the placement of clip art. The Text Wrapping tab, in the Advanced Layout dialog box, determines the way text is positioned around a picture. The Top and Bottom option (no wrapping) is selected in Figure 5.5a, and the resulting document is shown in Figure 5.5b. The sizing handles around the clip art indicate that it is currently selected, enabling you to move and/or resize the clip art using the mouse. (You can also use the Size and Position tabs in the Format Picture dialog box for more precision with either setting.) Changing the size or position of the object, however, does not affect the way in which text wraps around the clip art.

The document in Figure 5.5c illustrates a different wrapping selection in which text is wrapped on both sides. Figure 5.5c also uses an option on the Colors and Lines tab to draw a blue border around the clip art. The document in Figure 5.5d eliminates the border and chooses the tight wrapping style so that the text is positioned as closely as possible to the figure in a free-form design. Choosing among the various documents in Figure 5.5 is one of personal preference. Our point is simply that Word provides multiple options, and it is up to you, the desktop publisher, to choose the design that best suits your requirements.

Top and bottom wrapping style

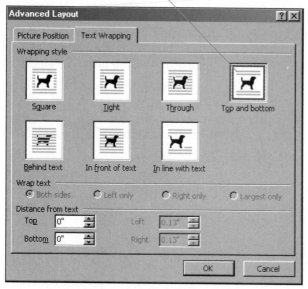

(a) Advanced Layout Dialog Box

(b) Top and Bottom Wrapping

(c) Square Wrapping (both sides)

(d) Tight Wrapping (both sides)

FIGURE 5.5   *The Format Picture Command*

Did you ever stop to think how the images in the Media Gallery were developed? Undoubtedly they were drawn by someone with artistic ability who used basic shapes, such as lines and curves in various combinations, to create the images. The Drawing toolbar in Figure 5.6a contains all of the tools necessary to create original clip art. Select the Line tool for example, then click and drag to create the line. Once the line has been created, you can select it, then change its properties (such as thickness, style, or color) by using other tools on the Drawing toolbar. Draw a second line, or a curve—then, depending on your ability, you have a piece of original clip art.

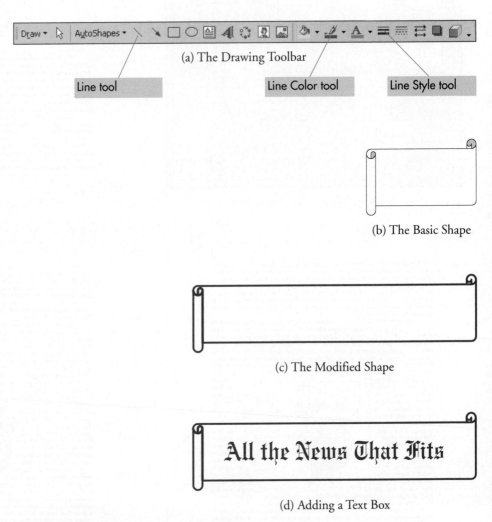

(a) The Drawing Toolbar

Line tool   Line Color tool   Line Style tool

(b) The Basic Shape

(c) The Modified Shape

All the News That Fits

(d) Adding a Text Box

FIGURE 5.6   *The Drawing Toolbar*

We don't expect you to create clip art comparable to the images within the Media Gallery. You can, however, use the tools on the Drawing toolbar to modify an existing image and/or create simple shapes of your own that can enhance any document. One tool that is especially useful is the AutoShapes button that displays a series of predesigned shapes. Choose a shape (the banner in Figure 5.6b), change its size and color (Figure 5.6c), then use the Textbox tool to add an appropriate message.

The Drawing toolbar is displayed through the Toolbars command in the View menu. The following exercise has you use the toolbar to create the banner and text in Figure 5.6d. It's fun, it's easy; just be flexible and willing to experiment. We think you will be pleased at what you will be able to do.

COMPLETE THE NEWSLETTER

Objective   To insert clip art into a newsletter; to format a newsletter using styles, borders and shading, pull quotes, and lists. Use Figure 5.7a as a guide in the exercise.

Step 1:   **Change the Column Layout**

➤ Open the **Modified Newsletter** from the previous exercise. Click in the masthead and change the number of this edition from 1 to **2**.

➤ Click anywhere in the body of the newsletter. The status bar should indicate that you are in the second section. Pull down the **Format menu**. Click **Columns** to display the dialog box in Figure 5.7a. Click the **Left Preset icon**.

➤ Change the width of the first column to **2.25** and the space between columns to **.25**. Check (click) the **Line Between box**. Click **OK**.

➤ Save the newsletter.

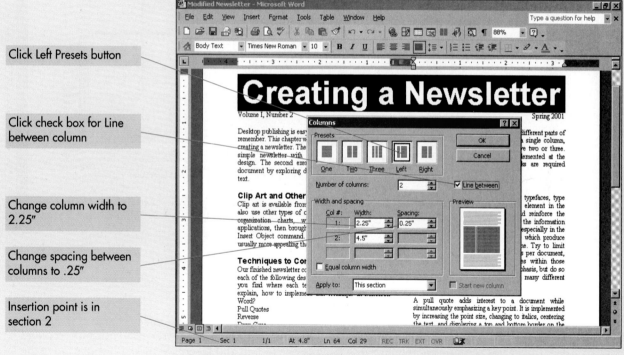

Click Left Presets button

Click check box for Line between column

Change column width to 2.25"

Change spacing between columns to .25"

Insertion point is in section 2

(a) Change the Column Layout (step 1)

FIGURE 5.7   *Hands-on Exercise 2*

EXPERIMENT WITH THE DESIGN

The number, width, and spacing of the columns in a newsletter is the single most important element in its design. Experiment freely. Good design is often the result of trial and error. Use the Undo command as necessary to restore the document.

Step 2: Bullets and Numbering

➤ Scroll in the document until you come to the list within the **Techniques to Consider** paragraph. Select the entire list as shown in Figure 5.7b.

➤ Pull down the **Format menu** and click **Bullets and Numbering** to display the Bullets and Numbering dialog box.

➤ If necessary, click the **Numbered tab** and choose the numbering style with Arabic numbers followed by periods. Click **OK** to accept these settings and close the Bullets and Numbering dialog box.

➤ Click anywhere in the newsletter to deselect the text.

➤ Save the newsletter.

Numbered tab

Click the numbering style

Select the list of items

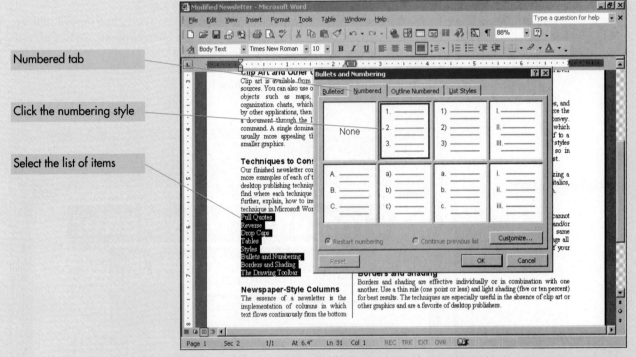

(b) Bullets and Numbering (step 2)

FIGURE 5.7 *Hands-on Exercise 2 (continued)*

LISTS AND THE FORMATTING TOOLBAR

The Formatting toolbar contains four buttons for use with bulleted and numbered lists. The Increase Indent and Decrease Indent buttons move the selected items one tab stop to the right and left, respectively. The Bullets button creates a bulleted list from unnumbered items or converts a numbered list to a bulleted list. The Numbering button creates a numbered list or converts a bulleted list to numbers. The Bullets and Numbering buttons also function as toggle switches; for example, clicking the Bullets button when a bulleted list is already in effect will remove the bullets.

Step 3:   **Insert the Clip Art**

➤ Click immediately to the left of the article beginning **Clip Art and Other Objects**. Pull down the **Insert menu**, click **Picture**, then click **Clip Art** to display the Insert Clip Art task pane.

➤ Click in the **Search text box** and type **goals** to search for all pictures that have been catalogued to describe this attribute. Click the **Search button**. The search begins and the various pictures appear individually within the task pane.

➤ Point to the image you want in your newsletter, click the **down arrow** that appears, then click **Insert** to insert the clip art.

➤ The picture should appear in the document, where it can be moved and sized as described in the next several steps. Click the **Close button** on the task pane.

➤ Save the document.

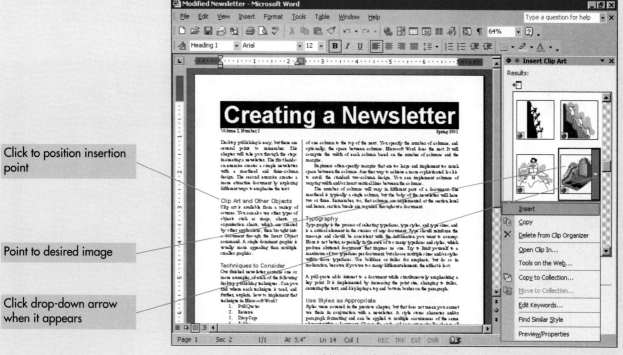

Click to position insertion point

Point to desired image

Click drop-down arrow when it appears

(c) Insert the Clip Art (step 3)

FIGURE 5.7   *Hands-on Exercise 2 (continued)*

CLIPS ONLINE

Why settle for the same old clip art when you can get new images from the Microsoft Web site? Pull down the Insert menu, click the Picture command, then choose Clip Art to open the task pane. Click the Clips Online button to connect to the Microsoft site, where you have your choice of clip art, photographs, sounds, and motion clips in a variety of categories. Click any image to see a preview, then click the preview box to download the image to your PC. Click the image after it has been downloaded to display a shortcut menu from where you insert the image into your document.

Step 4: **Move and Size the Clip Art**

➤ Click the **drop-down arrow** on the Zoom list box and select **Whole Page**.
➤ Point to the picture, click the **right mouse button** to display a context-sensitive menu, then click the **Format Picture command** to display the Format Picture dialog box as shown in Figure 5.7d.
➤ Click the **Layout tab**, choose the **Square layout**, then click the option button for left or right alignment. Click **OK** to close the dialog box. You can now move and size the clip art just like any other Windows object.
➤ To size the clip art, click anywhere within the clip art to select it and display the sizing handles. Drag a corner handle (the mouse pointer changes to a double arrow) to change the length and width of the picture simultaneously and keep the object in proportion.
➤ To move the clip art, click the object to select it and display the sizing handles. Point to any part of the object except a sizing handle (the mouse pointer changes to a four-sided arrow), then click and drag to move the clip art.
➤ Save the document.

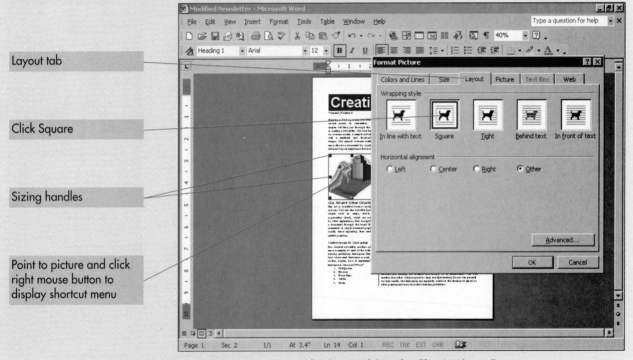

Layout tab

Click Square

Sizing handles

Point to picture and click right mouse button to display shortcut menu

(d) Move and Size the Clip Art (step 4)

FIGURE 5.7 *Hands-on Exercise 2 (continued)*

CROPPING A PICTURE

Select a picture, and Word automatically displays the Picture toolbar, which enables you to modify the picture in subtle ways. The Crop tool enables you to eliminate (crop) part of a picture. Select the picture to display the Picture toolbar and display the sizing handles. Click the Crop tool (the ScreenTip will display the name of the tool), then click and drag a sizing handle to crop the part of the picture you want to eliminate.

Step 5: **Borders and Shading**

➤ Change to **Page Width** and click the **Show/Hide ¶ button** to display the paragraph marks. Press **Ctrl+End** to move to the end of the document, then select the heading and associated paragraph for Borders and Shading. (Do not select the ending paragraph mark.)

➤ Pull down the **Format menu**. Click **Borders and Shading**. If necessary, click the **Borders tab** to display the dialog box in Figure 5.4e. Click the **Box icon** in the Setting area. Click the **drop-down arrow** in the Width list box and select the **1 pt** line style.

➤ Click the **Shading tab**. Click the **drop-down arrow** in the Style list box (in the Patterns area) and select 5% shading. Click **OK** to accept the setting.

➤ Click elsewhere in the document to see the results. The heading and paragraph should be enclosed in a border with light shading.

➤ Save the document.

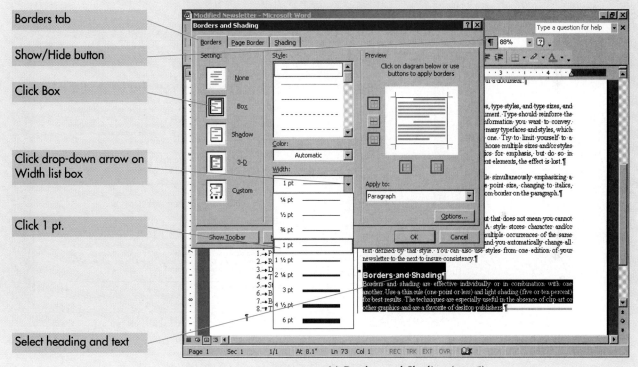

(e) Borders and Shading (step 5)

FIGURE 5.7 *Hands-on Exercise 2 (continued)*

USE THE TOOLBAR

The Outside Border button on the Formatting toolbar changes the style of the border for the selected text. That tool is also accessible from the Tables and Borders toolbar, which contains additional tools to insert or merge cells and/or to change the line style, thickness, or shading within a table. If the toolbar is not visible, point to any visible toolbar, click the right mouse button to show the list of toolbars, then click the Tables and Borders toolbar to display it on your screen.

Step 6: **Create a Pull Quote**

➤ Scroll to the bottom of the document until you find the paragraph describing a pull quote. Select the entire paragraph and change the text to **14-point Arial italic**.

➤ Click in the paragraph to deselect the text, then click the **Center button** to center the paragraph.

➤ Click the **drop-down arrow** on the **Border button** to display the different border styles as shown in Figure 5.7f.

➤ Click the **Top Border button** to add a top border to the paragraph.

➤ Click the **Bottom border button** to create a bottom border and complete the pull quote.

➤ Save the document.

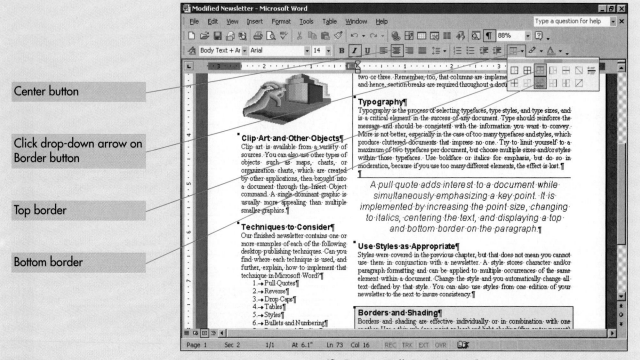

Center button

Click drop-down arrow on Border button

Top border

Bottom border

(f) Create a Pull Quote (step 6)

FIGURE 5.7   *Hands-on Exercise 2 (continued)*

EMPHASIZE WHAT'S IMPORTANT

Good design makes it easy for the reader to determine what is important. A pull quote (a phrase or sentence taken from an article) adds interest to a document while simultaneously emphasizing a key point. Boxes and shading are also effective in catching the reader's attention. A simple change in typography, such as increasing the point size, changing the typeface, and/or the use of boldface or italics, calls attention to a heading and visually separates it from the associated text.

Step 7:   **Create a Drop Cap**

➤ Scroll to the beginning of the newsletter. Click immediately before the D in *Desktop publishing.*

➤ Pull down the **Format menu**. Click the **Drop Cap command** to display the dialog box in Figure 5.7g.

➤ Click the **Position icon** for **Dropped** as shown in the figure. We used the default settings, but you can change the font, size (lines to drop), or distance from the text by clicking the arrow on the appropriate list box.

➤ Click **OK** to create the Drop Cap dialog box. Click outside the frame around the drop cap.

➤ Save the newsletter.

Position Insertion Point to left of D

Click Dropped

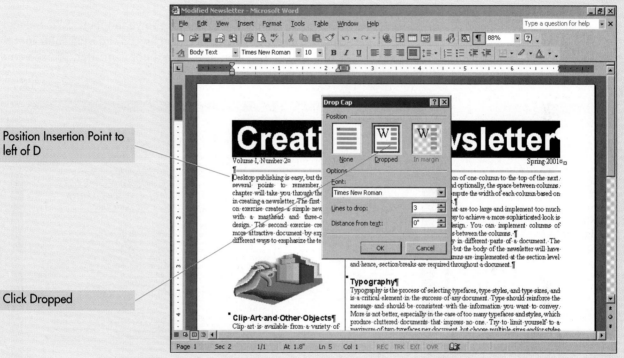

(g) Create a Drop Cap (step 7)

FIGURE 5.7   *Hands-on Exercise 2 (continued)*

MODIFYING A DROP CAP

Select (click) a dropped-capital letter to display a thatched border known as a frame, then click the border or frame to display its sizing handles. You can move and size a frame just as you can any other Windows object; for example, click and drag a corner sizing handle to change the size of the frame (and the drop cap it contains). Experiment with different fonts to increase the effectiveness of the dropped-capital letter, regardless of its size. To delete the frame (and remove the drop cap), press the delete key.

Step 8: **Create the AutoShape**

➤ Click the **Show/Hide button** to hide the nonprinting characters. Pull down the **View menu**, click (or point to) the **Toolbars command** to display the list of available toolbars, then click the **Drawing toolbar** to display this toolbar.

➤ Press **Ctrl+End** to move to the end of the document. Click the **down arrow** on the AutoShapes button to display the AutoShapes menu. Click the **Stars and Banners submenu** and select (click) the **Horizontal scroll**.

➤ Press **Esc** to remove the drawing canvas. The mouse pointer changes to a tiny crosshair. Click and drag the mouse at the bottom of the newsletter to create the scroll as shown in Figure 5.7h.

➤ Release the mouse. The scroll is still selected as can be seen by the sizing handles. (You can click and drag the yellow diamond to change the thickness of the scroll.)

➤ Click the **Line Style tool** to display this menu as shown in Figure 5.7h. Select a thicker line (we chose **3 points**). Click the **down arrow** on the **Line color tool** to display the list of colors (if you have access to a color printer. We selected **blue**).

Show/Hide button

Line Style button

Line Color tool

Click yellow diamond to change width of AutoShape

Sizing handles

AutoShapes button

Drawing toolbar

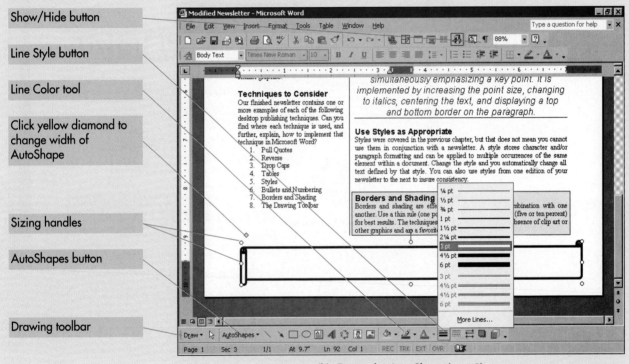

(h) Create the AutoShape (step 8)

FIGURE 5.7   *Hands-on Exercise 2 (continued)*

DISPLAY THE AUTOSHAPE TOOLBARS

Click the down arrow on the AutoShapes button on the Drawing toolbar to display a cascaded menu listing the various types of AutoShapes, then click and drag the menu's title bar to display the menu as a floating toolbar. Click any tool on the AutoShapes toolbar (such as Stars and Banners), then click and drag its title bar to display the various stars and banners in their own floating toolbar.

Step 9: **Create the Text Box**

➤ Click the **Text Box tool**, then click and drag within the banner to create a text box as shown in Figure 5.7i. Type **All the News that Fits** as the text of the banner. Click the **Center button** on the Formatting toolbar.

➤ Click and drag to select the text, click the **down arrow** on the **Font Size list box**, and select a larger point size (22 or 24 points). If necessary, click and drag the bottom border of the text box, and/or the bottom border of the AutoShape, in order to see all of the text. Click the **down arrow** on the **Font list box** and choose a different font.

➤ Right click the text box to display a context-sensitive menu, then click the **Format Text Box command** to display the **Format Text Box dialog** box as shown in Figure 5.7i. Click the **Colors and Lines tab** (if necessary), click the **down arrow** next to Color in the Line section, click **No Line**, then click **OK** to accept the settings and close the dialog box.

➤ Click anywhere in the document to deselect the text box. Save the document.

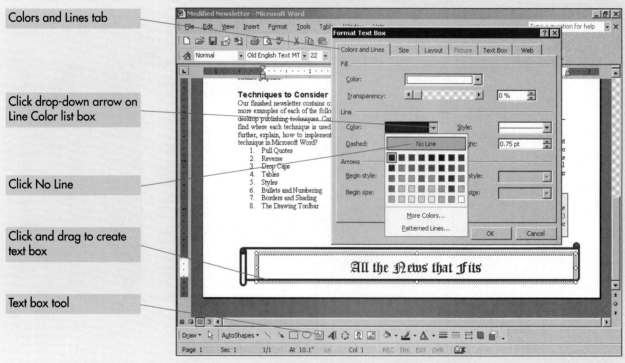

Colors and Lines tab

Click drop-down arrow on Line Color list box

Click No Line

Click and drag to create text box

Text box tool

(i) Create the Text Box (step 9)

FIGURE 5.7 *Hands-on Exercise 2 (continued)*

DON'T FORGET WORDART

Microsoft WordArt is another way to create decorative text to add interest to a document. Pull down the Insert menu, click Picture, click WordArt, choose the WordArt style, and click OK. Enter the desired text, then click OK to create the WordArt object. You can click and drag the sizing handles to change the size or proportion of the text. Use any tool on the WordArt toolbar to further change the appearance of the object.

Step 10: **The Completed Newsletter**

➤ Zoom to **Whole Page** to view the completed newsletter as shown in Figure 5.7j. The newsletter should fit on a single page, but if not, there are several techniques that you can use:

- Pull down the **File menu**, click the **Page Setup command**, click the **Margins tab**, then reduce the top and/or bottom margins to .5 inch. Be sure to apply this change to the **Whole document** within the Page Setup dialog box.
- Change the **Heading 1 style** to reduce the point size to **10 points** and/or the space before the heading to **6 points**.
- Click the **Print Preview button** on the Standard toolbar, then click the **Shrink to Fit button** on the Print Preview toolbar.
- Save the document a final time. Print the completed newsletter and submit it to your instructor as proof you did this exercise. Congratulations on a job well done.

Print Preview button

Zoom box

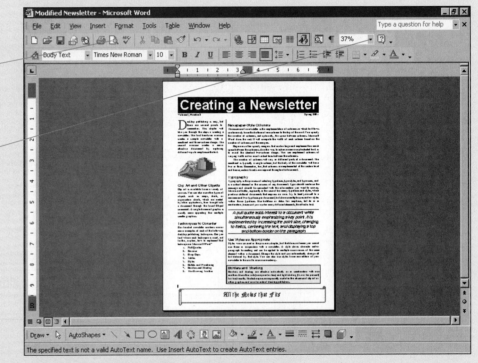

(j) The Completed Newsletter (step 10)

FIGURE 5.7 *Hands-on Exercise 2 (continued)*

A FINAL WORD OF ADVICE

Desktop publishing is not a carefree operation. It is time-consuming to implement, and you will be amazed at the effort required for even a simple document. Computers are supposed to save time, not waste it, and while desktop publishing is clearly justified for some documents, the extensive formatting is not necessary for most documents. And finally, remember that the content of a document is its most important element.

Microsoft Office enables you to create documents that contain data (objects) from multiple applications. The document in Figure 5.8a, for example, was created in Microsoft Word, but it contains objects (a worksheet and a chart) that were developed in **Microsoft Excel**. **Object Linking and Embedding** (**OLE**, pronounced "oh-lay") is the means by which you create the document.

Every Excel chart is based on numerical data that is stored in a worksheet. Figures 5.8b and 5.8c enlarge the worksheet and chart that appear in the document of Figure 5.8a. The worksheet shows the quarterly sales for each of three regions, East, West, and North. There are 12 **data points** (four quarterly values for each of three regions). The data points are grouped into **data series** that appear as rows or columns in the worksheet. (The chart was created through the Chart Wizard that prompts you for information about the source data and the type of chart you want. Any chart can be subsequently modified by choosing appropriate commands from the Chart menu.)

The data in the chart is plotted by rows or by columns, depending on the message you want to convey. Our data is plotted by rows to emphasize the amount of sales in each quarter, as opposed to the sales in each region. Note that when the data is plotted by rows, the first row in the worksheet will appear on the X axis of the chart, and the first column will appear as the legend. Conversely, if you plot the data by columns, the first column appears on the X axis, and the first row appears as a legend.

Look closely at Figures 5.8b and 5.8c to see the correspondence between the worksheet and the chart. The data is plotted by rows. Thus there are three rows of data (three data series), corresponding to the values in the Eastern, Western, and Northern regions, respectively. The entries in the first row appear on the X axis. The entries in the first column appear as a legend to identify the value of each column in the chart. The chart is a **side-by-side column chart** that shows the value of each data point separately. You could also create a **stacked column chart** for each quarter that would put the columns one on top of another. And, as with the stacked-column chart, you have your choice of plotting the data in rows or columns.

After the chart has been created, it is brought into the Word document through Object Linking and Embedding. The essential difference between linking and embedding depends on where the object is stored. An embedded object is physically within the Word document. A **linked object**, however, is stored in its own file, which may in turn be tied to many documents. The same Excel chart, for example, can be linked to a Word document and a PowerPoint presentation or to multiple Word documents and/or to multiple presentations. Any changes to a linked object (the Excel chart) are automatically reflected in all of the documents to which it is linked. An **embedded object**, however, is stored within the Word document and it is no longer tied to its source. Thus, any changes made in the original object or in the embedded object are not reflected in one another.

EMPHASIZE YOUR MESSAGE

A graph exists to deliver a message, and you want that message to be as clear as possible. One way to help put your point across is to choose a title that leads the audience. A neutral title such as *Sales Data* does nothing and requires the audience to reach its own conclusion. A better title might be *Eastern Region Has Record 3rd Quarter* to emphasize the results in the individual sales offices. Conversely, *Western Region Has a Poor Year* conveys an entirely different message. This technique is so simple that we wonder why it isn't used more frequently.

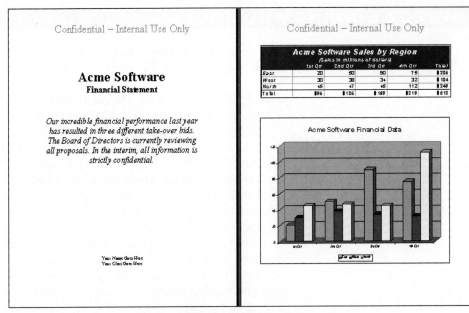

(a) The Word Document

Excel formatting is copied into the Word document

	1st Qtr	2nd Qtr	3rd Qtr	4th Qtr	Total
Acme Software Sales by Region					
(Sales in millions of dollars)					
East	20	50	90	75	$235
West	30	38	34	32	$134
North	45	47	45	112	$249
Total	$95	$135	$169	$219	$618

(b) The Excel Worksheet

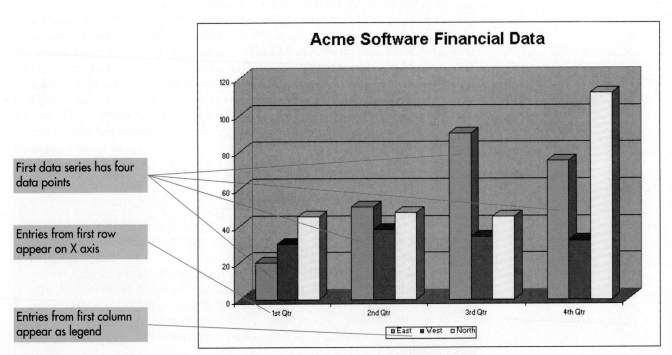

First data series has four data points

Entries from first row appear on X axis

Entries from first column appear as legend

(c) Alternate Chart

FIGURE 5.8   *Object Linking and Embedding*

OBJECT LINKING AND EMBEDDING

Objective   Use object linking to create a Word document that contains an Excel worksheet and an Excel chart. Use Figure 5.9 as a guide in the exercise.

Step 1:   **Create the Title Page**

> ➤ Start Word. Click the **New button** on the Standard toolbar to open a new document. Press the **enter key** several times, then enter the title of the document, **Acme Software Financial Statement**, **your name**, and the **course number** with appropriate formatting. Save the document as **Confidential Memo**.
> ➤ Click the **Print Layout View button** above the status bar, then click the **down arrow** on the Zoom list box and select **Two Pages**. Your document takes only a single page, however, as shown in Figure 5.9a.
> ➤ Pull down the **View menu** and click the **Header and Footer command** to display the Header and Footer toolbar. The text in the document (its title, your name, and class) is dim since you are working in the header and footer area of the document.
> ➤ Click the **down arrow** on the Font Size box and change to **28 points**. Click inside the header and enter **Confidential - Internal Use Only**. Center the text.
> ➤ Click the **Close button** on the Header and Footer toolbar to close the toolbar. The header you just created is visible, but dim.

New button

Zoom box

Enter header text in header area

Enter title

Close button

Enter name and course number

Print Layout View button

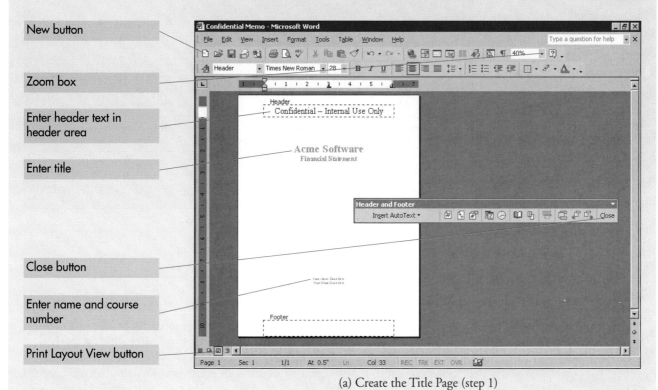

(a) Create the Title Page (step 1)

FIGURE 5.9   *Hands-on Exercise 3*

Step 2: **Copy the Worksheet**

➤ Click the **Start button**, click **Programs,** then click **Microsoft Excel** to start Excel. The taskbar now contains buttons for both Word and Excel. Click either button to move back and forth between the open applications. End in Excel.

➤ Pull down the **File menu** and click the **Open command** (or click the **Open button** on the Standard toolbar) to display the Open dialog box.

➤ Click the **down arrow** on the Look in list box to select the Exploring Word folder that you have used throughout the text. Open the **Acme Software workbook**.

➤ Click the **Sales Data** worksheet tab. Click and drag to select **cells A1 through F7** as shown in Figure 5.9b.

➤ Pull down the **Edit menu** and click the **Copy command** (or click the **Copy button** on the Standard toolbar). A moving border appears around the entire worksheet, indicating that it has been copied to the clipboard.

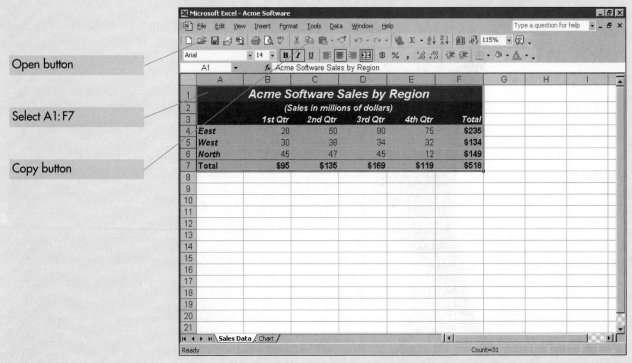

(b) Copy the Worksheet (step 2)

FIGURE 5.9 *Hands-on Exercise 3 (continued)*

THE COMMON USER INTERFACE

The common user interface provides a sense of familiarity from one Office application to the next. Even if you have never used Microsoft Excel, you will recognize many of the elements that are present in Word. The applications share a common menu structure with consistent ways to execute commands from those menus. The Standard and Formatting toolbars are present in both applications. Many keyboard shortcuts are also common; for example: Ctrl+X, Ctrl+C, and Ctrl+V to cut, copy, and paste, respectively.

Step 3: **Create the Link**

> Click the **Word button** on the taskbar to return to the document as shown in Figure 5.9c. Press **Ctrl+End** to move to the end of the document, which is where you will insert the Excel worksheet.

> Press **Ctrl+Enter** to create a page break, which adds a second page to the document. This page is blank except for the header, which appears automatically.

> Pull down the **Edit menu** and click **Paste Special** to display the dialog box in Figure 5.9c. Select **Microsoft Excel Worksheet Object**. Click the **Paste Link** option button. Click **OK** to insert the worksheet into the document.

> Do not be concerned about the size or position of the worksheet at this time. Press the **enter key** twice to create a blank line between the worksheet and the chart, which will be added later.

> Save the document.

Header appears automatically on new page

Click Microsoft Excel Worksheet Object

Click Paste Link

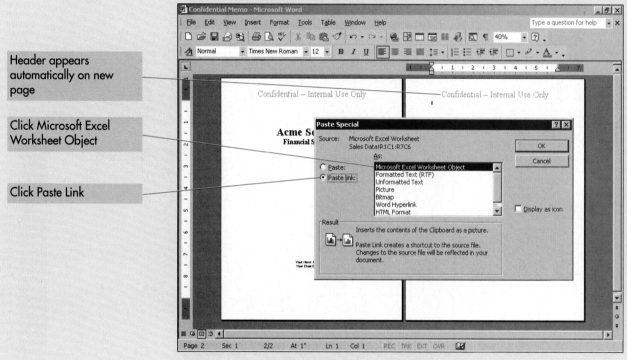

(c) Create the Link (step 3)

FIGURE 5.9 *Hands-on Exercise 3 (continued)*

THE WINDOWS TASKBAR

Multitasking, the ability to run multiple applications at the same time, is one of the primary advantages of the Windows environment. Each button on the taskbar appears automatically when its application or folder is opened and disappears upon closing. (The buttons are resized automatically according to the number of open windows.) You can customize the taskbar by right clicking an empty area to display a shortcut menu, then clicking the Properties command. You can resize the taskbar by pointing to the inside edge and then dragging when you see the double-headed arrow. You can also move the taskbar to the left or right edge, or to the top of the desktop, by dragging a blank area of the taskbar to the desired position.

Step 4: **Format the Object**

➤ Point to the newly inserted worksheet, click the **right mouse button** to display a context-sensitive menu, then click the **Format Object command** to display the dialog box in Figure 5.9d.

➤ Click the **Layout tab** and choose **Square**. Click the option button to **Center** the object. You can now move and size the object.

➤ Select (click on) the worksheet to display its sizing handles. Click and drag a corner sizing handle to enlarge the worksheet, keeping it in its original proportions.

➤ Click and drag any element except a sizing handle to move the worksheet within the document.

➤ Right click the worksheet a second time and click the **Format Object command** to display the associated dialog box. Click the **Colors and lines tab**, click the **drop-down arrow** next to color in the line area and choose **black**. Click the **Spin button** next to weight and choose **.25.**

➤ Click **OK** to accept these settings and close the dialog box. Save the document.

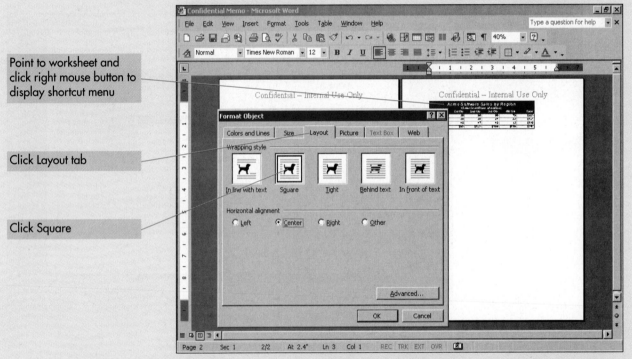

Point to worksheet and click right mouse button to display shortcut menu

Click Layout tab

Click Square

(d) Format the Object (step 4)

FIGURE 5.9 *Hands-on Exercise 3 (continued)*

TO CLICK OR DOUBLE CLICK

An Excel chart that is linked or embedded into a Word document retains its connection to Microsoft Excel for easy editing. Click the chart to select it within the Word document, then move and size the chart just as any other object. (You can also press the Del key to delete the graph from a document.) Click outside the chart to deselect it, then double click the chart to restart Microsoft Excel (the chart is bordered by a hashed line), at which point you can edit the chart using the tools of the original application.

Step 5: **Copy the Chart**

➤ Click the **Excel button** on the taskbar to return to the worksheet. Click outside the selected area (cells A1 through F7) to deselect the cells.

➤ Click the **Chart tab** to select the chart sheet. Point just inside the border of the chart, then click the left mouse button to select the chart. Be sure you have selected the entire chart as shown in Figure 5.9e.

➤ Pull down the **Edit menu** and click **Copy** (or click the **Copy button** on the Standard toolbar). Once again you see the moving border, indicating that the selected object (the chart in this example) has been copied to the clipboard.

➤ Click the **Word button** on the taskbar to return to the document.

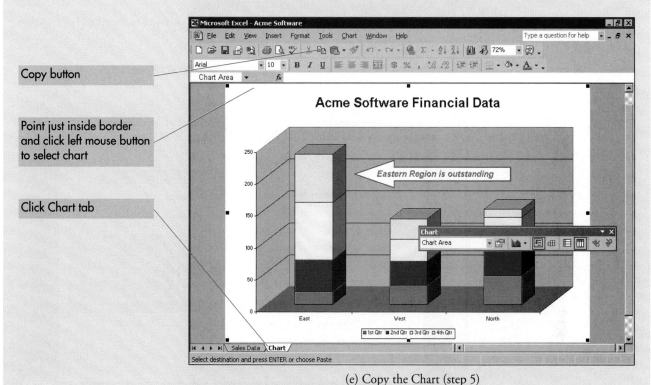

Copy button

Point just inside border and click left mouse button to select chart

Click Chart tab

(e) Copy the Chart (step 5)

FIGURE 5.9 *Hands-on Exercise 3 (continued)*

KEEP IT SIMPLE

Microsoft Excel provides unlimited flexibility with respect to the charts it creates. You can, for example, right click any data series within a graph and click the Format Data Series command to change the color, fill pattern, or shape of a data series. There are other options, such as the 3-D View command that lets you fine-tune the graph by controlling the rotation, elevation, and other parameters. It's fun to experiment, but the best advice is to keep it simple and set a time limit, at which point the project is finished. Use the Undo command at any time to cancel your last action(s).

Step 6:   **Complete the Word Document**

➤ You should be back in the Word document, where you may need to insert a few blank lines, so that the insertion point is beneath the spreadsheet. Press **Ctrl+End** to move to the end of the document, where you will insert the chart.

➤ Pull down the **Edit menu**, click the **Paste Special command**, and click the **Paste Link** option button. If necessary, click **Microsoft Excel Chart Object**.

➤ Click **OK** to insert the chart into the document. (Do not be concerned if you do not see the entire chart.)

➤ Select the chart, pull down the **Format menu**, and click the **Object command**.

➤ Select the **Layout tab** and change the layout to **Square**. **Center** the chart. Select the **Color and Lines tab**, and add a **.25″ black line**.

➤ Move and size the chart as shown in Figure 5.9f. Save the document. Print this version of the document for your instructor.

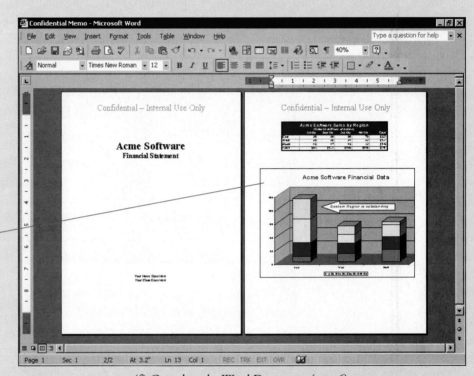

Move and size chart as shown

(f) Complete the Word Document (step 6)

FIGURE 5.9   *Hands-on Exercise 3 (continued)*

LINKING VERSUS EMBEDDING

The Paste Special command will link or embed an object, depending on whether the Paste Link or Paste Option button is checked. Linking stores a pointer to the file containing the object together with a reference to the server application, and changes to the object are automatically reflected in all documents that are linked to the object. Embedding stores a copy of the object with a reference to the server application, but changes to the object are not reflected in the document that contains the embedded (rather than linked) object.

Step 7: **Modify the Chart**

➤ Click the **Excel button** on the taskbar to return to Excel. Click the **Sales Data tab** to return to the worksheet.

➤ Click in **cell E6**, the cell containing the sales data for the Northern region in the fourth quarter. Type **112**, then press **enter**. The sales totals for the region and quarter change to 249 and 219, respectively.

➤ Click the tab for the chart sheet. The chart has changed automatically to reflect the change in the underlying data. The bars for the Eastern and Northern regions are approximately the same size.

➤ Pull down the **Chart menu** and click the **Chart Type command** to display the Chart Type dialog box. Click the **Standard Types tab**. Select the **Clustered Column Chart with 3D Visual Effect** (the first chart in the second row).

➤ Click **OK** to accept this chart type and close the dialog box. The chart type changes to side-by-side columns as shown in Figure 5.9g.

➤ Select the arrow on the chart. Press the **Del key** since the text is no longer applicable. Save the workbook.

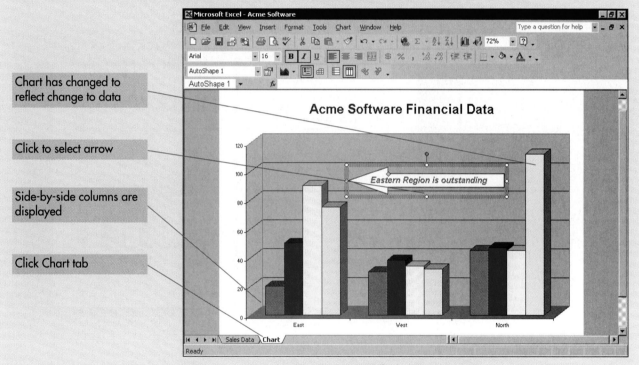

Chart has changed to reflect change to data

Click to select arrow

Side-by-side columns are displayed

Click Chart tab

(g) Modify the Chart (step 7)

FIGURE 5.9 *Hands-on Exercise 3 (continued)*

THE DRAWING TOOLBAR

The Drawing toolbar is common to all applications in Microsoft Office. Click the down arrow next to the AutoShapes button to display the various shapes, then click Block Arrows to display the arrows that are available. Select an arrow. The mouse pointer changes to a tiny crosshair that you click and drag to create the arrow within the document. Right click the arrow, then click the Add Text command to enter text within the arrow. Use the other buttons to change the color or other properties.

Step 8: **The Modified Document**

➤ Click the **Word button** on the taskbar to return to the Word document, which should automatically reflect the new chart. (If this is not the case, right click the chart and click the **Update Link command**.)

➤ Move and/or resize the chart and spreadsheet as necessary. Save the document.

➤ Complete the document by adding text as appropriate as shown in Figure 5.9h. You can use the text in our document that describes a confidential takeover, or make up your own.

➤ Place a border around the chart. Click the chart to select it, pull down the **Format menu**, click the **Object command**, and click the **Colors and Lines tab**.

➤ Click the **down arrow** on the Color text box (in the Line section of the dialog box) and select a line color. Click **OK**. Click elsewhere in the document to deselect the graph.

➤ Save the document a final time. Click the **Print button** on the Standard toolbar to print the document for your instructor.

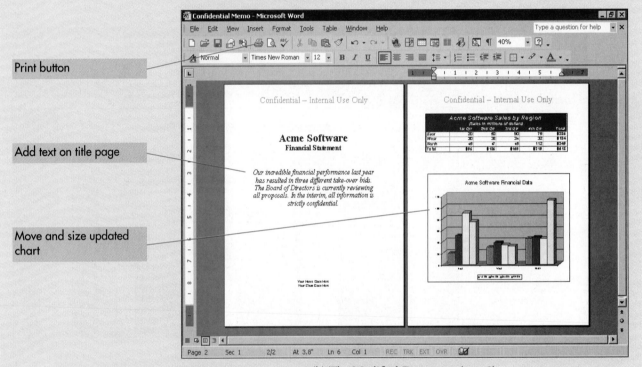

(h) The Modified Document (step 8)

FIGURE 5.9   *Hands-on Exercise 3 (continued)*

ALT+TAB STILL WORKS

Alt+Tab was a treasured shortcut in Windows 3.1 that enabled users to switch back and forth between open applications. The shortcut also works in all subsequent versions of Windows. Press and hold the Alt key while you press and release the Tab key repeatedly to cycle through the open applications, whose icons are displayed in a small rectangular window in the middle of the screen. Release the Alt key when you have selected the icon for the application you want.

The essence of desktop publishing is the merger of text with graphics to produce a professional-looking document. Proficiency in desktop publishing requires knowledge of the associated commands in Microsoft Word, as well as familiarity with the basics of graphic design.

Typography is the process of selecting typefaces, type styles, and type sizes. A typeface (or font) is a complete set of characters (upper- and lowercase letters, numbers, punctuation marks, and special symbols). Type size is a vertical measurement and is specified in points. One point is equal to $\frac{1}{72}$ of an inch.

The design of a document is developed on a grid, an underlying but invisible set of horizontal and vertical lines that determine the placement of the major elements. A newsletter can be divided into any number of newspaper-style columns in which text flows from the bottom of one column to the top of the next. Columns are implemented by clicking the Columns button on the Standard toolbar or by selecting the Columns command from the Format menu. Sections are required if different column arrangements are present in the same document. The Page Layout view is required to see the columns displayed side by side.

Emphasis can be achieved in several ways, the easiest being variations in type size and/or type style. Boxes and/or shading call attention to selected articles in a document. Horizontal lines are effective in separating one topic from another or calling attention to a pull quote (a phrase or sentence taken from an article to emphasize a key point). A reverse (light text on a solid background) is striking for a small amount of text.

Clip art is available from a variety of sources, including the Microsoft Media Gallery, which is accessed most easily through the Insert Picture command. Once clip art has been inserted into a document, it can be moved and sized just like any other Windows object. The Format Picture command provides additional flexibility and precision in the placement of an object. The Drawing toolbar contains various tools that are used to insert and/or modify objects into a Word document.

Graphic design does not have hard and fast rules, only guidelines and common sense. Creating an effective document is an iterative process and reflects the result of trial and error. We encourage you to experiment freely with different designs.

Object linking and embedding enables the creation of a document containing data (objects) from multiple applications. The essential difference between linking and embedding is whether the object is stored within the document (embedding) or stored within its own file (linking). The advantage of linking is that any changes to the linked object are automatically reflected in every document that is linked to that object.

Arial (p. 220)
AutoShape (p. 242)
AutoShapes toolbar (p. 242)
Borders and Shading (p. 218)
Bulleted list (p. 218)
Clip art (p. 218)
Columns command (p. 221)
Common User Interface (p. 248)
Data points (p. 245)
Data series (p. 245)
Desktop publishing (p. 218)
Drawing toolbar (p. 218)
Dropped-capital letter (p. 218)
Embedded object (p. 245)

Emphasis (p. 232)
Font (p. 220)
Format Picture command (p. 232)
Grid (p. 230)
Insert Picture command (p. 232)
Linked object (p. 245)
Masthead (p. 218)
Microsoft Excel (p. 245)
Monospaced typeface (p. 220)
Numbered list (p. 218)
Object linking and embedding (OLE) (p. 245)
Paste Special command (p. 249)

Proportional typeface (p. 220)
Pull quote (p. 218)
Reverse (p. 218)
Sans serif typeface (p. 220)
Section break (p. 221)
Serif typeface (p. 220)
Side-by-side column chart (p. 245)
Stacked column chart (p. 245)
Text box (p. 243)
Times New Roman (p. 220)
Type size (p. 220)
Typeface (p. 220)
Typography (p. 220)

1. Which of the following is a commonly accepted guideline in typography?
   (a) Use a serif typeface for headings and a sans serif typeface for text
   (b) Use a sans serif typeface for headings and a serif typeface for text
   (c) Use a sans serif typeface for both headings and text
   (d) Use a serif typeface for both headings and text

2. Which of the following best enables you to see a multicolumn document as it will appear on the printed page?
   (a) Normal view at 100% magnification
   (b) Normal view at whole page magnification
   (c) Print Layout view at 100% magnification
   (d) Print Layout view at whole page magnification

3. What is the width of each column in a document with two uniform columns, given 1¼-inch margins and ½-inch spacing between the columns?
   (a) 2½ inches
   (b) 2¾ inches
   (c) 3 inches
   (d) Impossible to determine

4. What is the minimum number of sections in a three-column newsletter whose masthead extends across all three columns, with text balanced in all three columns?
   (a) One
   (b) Two
   (c) Three
   (d) Four

5. Which of the following describes the Arial and Times New Roman fonts?
   (a) Arial is a sans serif font, Times New Roman is a serif font
   (b) Arial is a serif font, Times New Roman is a sans serif font
   (c) Both are serif fonts
   (d) Both are sans serif fonts

6. How do you balance the columns in a newsletter so that each column contains the same amount of text?
   (a) Check the Balance Columns box in the Format Columns command
   (b) Visually determine where the break should go, then insert a column break at the appropriate place
   (c) Insert a continuous section break at the end of the last column
   (d) All of the above

7. What is the effect of dragging one of the four corner handles on a selected object?
   (a) The length of the object is changed but the width remains constant
   (b) The width of the object is changed but the length remains constant
   (c) The length and width of the object are changed in proportion to one another
   (d) Neither the length nor width of the object is changed

8. Which type size is the most reasonable for columns of text, such as those appearing in the newsletter created in the chapter?
   (a) 6 point
   (b) 10 point
   (c) 14 point
   (d) 18 point

9. A grid is applicable to the design of:
   (a) Documents with one, two, or three columns and moderate clip art
   (b) Documents with four or more columns and no clip art
   (c) Both (a) and (b)
   (d) Neither (a) nor (b)

10. Which of the following can be used to add emphasis to a document?
    (a) Borders and shading
    (b) Pull quotes and reverses
    (c) Both (a) and (b)
    (d) Neither (a) nor (b)

11. Which of the following is a recommended guideline in the design of a typical newsletter?
    (a) Use at least three different clip art images in every newsletter
    (b) Use at least three different typefaces in a document to maintain interest
    (c) Use the same type size for the heading and text of an article
    (d) None of the above

12. Which of the following is implemented at the section level?
    (a) Columns
    (b) Margins
    (c) Both (a) and (b)
    (d) Neither (a) nor (b)

13. How do you size an object so that it maintains the original proportion between height and width?
    (a) Drag a sizing handle on the left or right side of the object to change its width, then drag a sizing handle on the top or bottom edge to change the height
    (b) Drag a sizing handle on any of the corners
    (c) Both (a) and (b)
    (d) Neither (a) nor (b)

14. A reverse is implemented:
    (a) By selecting 100% shading in the Borders and Shading command
    (b) By changing the Font color to black
    (c) Both (a) and (b)
    (d) Neither (a) nor (b)

15. The Format Picture command enables you to:
    (a) Change the way in which text is wrapped around a figure
    (b) Change the size of a figure
    (c) Place a border around a figure
    (d) All of the above

ANSWERS

1. b	**6.** c	**11.** d
2. d	**7.** c	**12.** c
3. b	**8.** b	**13.** b
4. c	**9.** c	**14.** a
5. a	**10.** c	**15.** d

1. **Study Tips:** Create a simple newsletter similar to the document in Figure 5.10. There is no requirement to write meaningful text, but the headings in the newsletter should follow the theme of the graphic. The intent of this problem is to provide practice in graphic design.

   a. Develop an overall design away from the computer—that is, with pencil and paper. Use a grid to indicate the placement of the articles, headings, clip art, and masthead. You may be surprised to find that it is easier to master commands in Word than it is to design the newsletter; do not, however, underestimate the importance of graphic design in the ultimate success of every document you create.

   b. Use meaningful headings to give the document a sense of realism. The text under each heading can be a single sentence that repeats indefinitely to take up the allotted space. Your eye is the best judge of all, and you may need to decrease the default space between columns and/or change the type size to create an appealing document.

   c. Insert clip art to add interest to your document, then write one or two sentences in support of the clip art. Use the clip art within Microsoft Office or any other clip art you have available. You can also download pictures from the Web, but be sure to credit the source. The image you choose should be related to studying in some way.

   d. More is not better; that is, do not use too many fonts, styles, sizes, and clip art just because they are available. Don't crowd the page, and remember white space is a very effective design element. There are no substitutes for simplicity and good taste.

   e. Submit the completed newsletter to your instructor for inclusion in a class contest. Your instructor might want to select the five best designs as semifinalists and let the class vote on the overall winner.

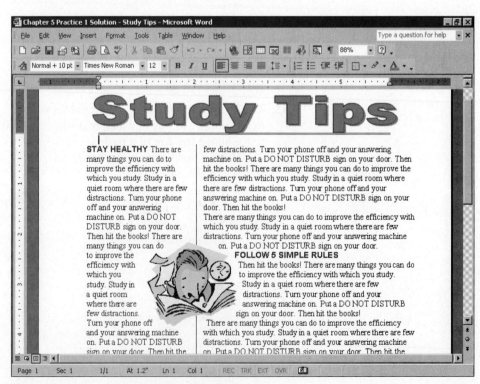

FIGURE 5.10 *Study Tips (Exercise 1)*

BUILDS ON

HANDS-ON
EXERCISE 2
PAGES 235–244

2. Alternate Design: The document in Figure 5.11 contains the same text as the newsletter that was developed in the chapter, but it is formatted differently. Start with the original text of the newsletter and implement a new design. You can match our formatting, or better yet, develop your own design. The completed newsletter must fit on a single page. Clip art is optional. Submit the completed newsletter to your instructor for inclusion in a class contest to pick the best design.

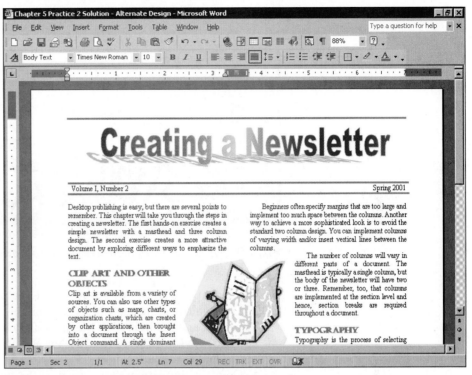

FIGURE 5.11 *Alternate Design (Exercise 2)*

3. A Guide for Smart Shopping: This problem is more challenging than the previous exercises in that you are asked to consider content as well as design. The objective is to develop a one- or two-page document with helpful tips to the novice on buying a computer as shown in Figure 5.12. We have, however, written the copy for you and put the file on the data disk.

   a. Open and print the *Chapter 5 Practice 3 document* on the data disk, which takes approximately a page and a half as presently formatted. Read our text and determine the tips you want to retain and those you want to delete. Add other tips as you see fit.

   b. Examine the available clip art through the Insert Picture command or through the Microsoft Media Gallery. There is no requirement, however, to include a graphic; that is, use clip art only if you think it will enhance the effectiveness of your document.

   c. Use an imaginary grid to develop a rough sketch of the completed document showing the masthead and the placement of the text and clip art. Do this away from the computer.

   d. Implement your design in Microsoft Word. Try to create a balanced publication, which completely fills the space allotted; that is, your document should take exactly one or two pages (rather than the page and a half in the original document on the data disk).

   e. Submit the completed newsletter to your instructor for inclusion in a class contest. Your instructor might want to select the five best designs as semifinalists and let the class vote on the overall winner.

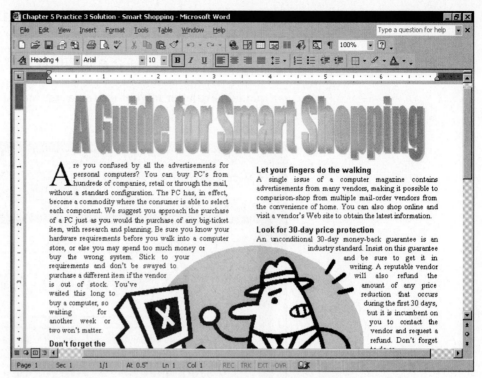

FIGURE 5.12 *A Guide for Smart Shopping (Exercise 3)*

4. The Equation Editor: Microsoft Office includes several shared applications, each of which creates an object that can be inserted into a Word document. (WordArt and the Microsoft Media Gallery are both shared applications.) The newsletter in Figure 5.13 illustrates the Equation Editor, a shared application of particular use to math majors.

   a. Create a simple newsletter such as the two-column design in Figure 5.13. There is no requirement to write meaningful text, as the intent of this exercise is to illustrate the Equation Editor. Thus, all you need to do is write a sentence or two, then copy that sentence so that it fills the newsletter.

   b. To create the equation, pull down the Insert menu, click the Object command, click the Create New tab, then select Microsoft Equation to start the Equation Editor. This is a new application, and we do not provide instruction in its use. It does, however, follow the conventions of other Office applications, and with trial and error, and reference to the Help menu, you should be able to duplicate our equation.

   c. Once the equation (object) has been created, you can move and size it within the document. Clicking an object selects the object and displays the sizing handles to move, size, or delete the object. Double clicking an object loads the application that created it, and enables you to modify the object using the tools of the original application.

5. The Flyer: Any document can be enhanced through Microsoft WordArt, an application included in Microsoft Office to create decorative text. Pull down the Insert menu, click Picture, click WordArt, choose the desired style, then click OK. Enter the desired text, then click OK to insert the WordArt object into your document. Use the Format Object command to change to a square layout, then move and size the WordArt within the document.

   Create at least two flyers, consisting of text, clip art, and WordArt, similar to the flyers in Figure 5.14. You can duplicate the flyers in our figure, or better yet, create your own. The flyers can describe a real or hypothetical event. Submit your work to your instructor.

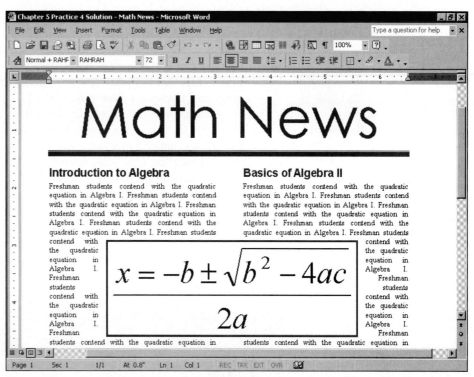

FIGURE 5.13 *The Equation Editor (Exercise 4)*

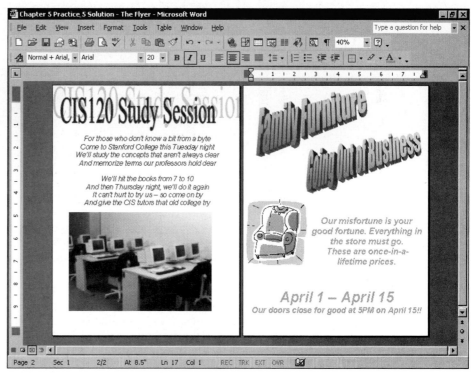

FIGURE 5.14 *The Flyer (Exercise 5)*

6. My Favorite Car: The document in Figure 5.15 consists of descriptive text, a photograph, and a worksheet to compute a car payment. We have created the spreadsheet, but you will have to obtain the other information via the Web.
   a. Choose any vehicle you like, then go to the Web to locate a picture of your vehicle together with descriptive material. *Be sure to credit your source in the completed document.* Start a new Word document. Enter a title for the document, then insert the photograph and descriptive information. Do not worry about the precise formatting at this time.
   b. Open the *Chapter 5 Practice 6 workbook* that is found in the Exploring Word folder. Enter the necessary information for your vehicle. The monthly payment will be computed automatically, based on the amount you are borrowing, the interest rate, and the term of your loan. Save the workbook.
   c. Click and drag to select the appropriate cells within the worksheet, return to Word, and use object linking and embedding to include this information in the document.
   d. Move and size the various objects to complete the document. Add your name and submit the completed document to your instructor.

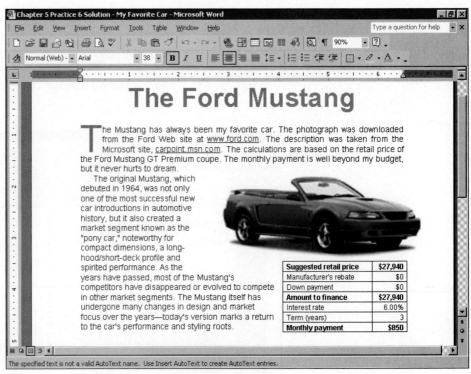

FIGURE 5.15 *My Favorite Car (Exercise 6)*

BUILDS ON

HANDS-ON
EXERCISE 3
PAGES 247–254

7. PowerPoint Presentation: The third hands-on exercise described how to create a Word document that contains an Excel worksheet and associated chart. Object linking and embedding can also be used to create a PowerPoint presentation similar to the examples in Figure 5.16. Moreover, the same object can be linked to both the PowerPoint presentation and the Word document, so that any changes to the worksheet are automatically reflected in both documents.
   a. Create a PowerPoint presentation similar to Figure 5.16a that is based on the worksheet from the third hands-on exercise. Add text and clip art as appropriate. You can duplicate our presentation or you can create your own.
   b. Create a second presentation similar to Figure 5.16b that is based on the Ford Mustang example in practice exercise 6.

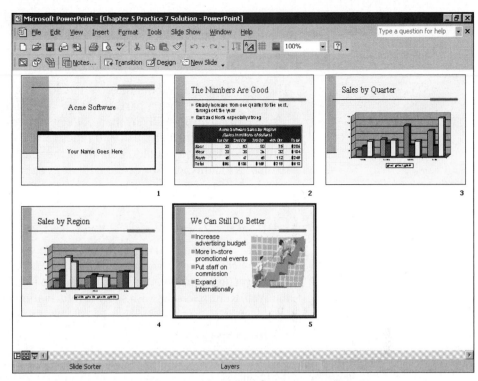

(a) Acme Software

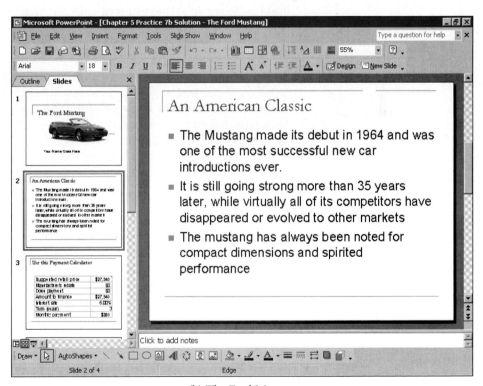

(b) The Ford Mustang

FIGURE 5.16 *PowerPoint Presentations (Exercise 7)*

Before and After

The best way to learn about the do's and don'ts of desktop publishing is to study the work of others. Choose a particular type of document—for example, a newsletter, résumé, or advertising flyer, then collect samples of that document. Choose one sample that is particularly bad and redesign the document. You need not enter the actual text, but you should keep all of the major headings so that the document retains its identity. Add or delete clip art as appropriate. Bring the before and after samples to class for your professor.

Clip Art

Clip art—you see it all the time, but where do you get it, and how much does it cost? Scan the computer magazines and find at least two sources for additional clip art. Better yet, use your favorite search engine to locate additional sources of clip art on the Web. Return to class with specific information on prices and types of the clip art.

Color Separations

It's difficult to tell where word processing stops and desktop publishing begins. One distinguishing characteristic of a desktop publishing program, however, is the ability to create color separations, which in turn enable you to print a document in full color. Use your favorite search engine to learn more about the process of color separations. Summarize the results of your research in a short paper to your instructor.

Photographs versus Clip Art

The right clip art can enhance any document, but there are times when clip art just won't do. It may be too juvenile or simply inappropriate. Photographs offer an alternative and are inserted into a presentation through the Insert Picture command. Once inserted into a presentation, photographs can be moved or sized just like any other Windows object. Use your favorite search engine to locate a photograph, then incorporate that photograph into the newsletter that was developed in this chapter.

Subscribe to a Newsletter

Literally thousands of regularly published newsletters are distributed in printed and/or electronic form. Some charge a subscription fee, but many are available just for the asking. Use your favorite search engine to locate a free newsletter in an area of interest to you. Download an issue, then summarize the results of your research in a brief note to your instructor.

CHAPTER 6

Introduction to HTML: Creating a Home Page and a Web Site

OBJECTIVES

AFTER READING THIS CHAPTER YOU WILL BE ABLE TO:

1. Define HTML and its role on the World Wide Web; describe HTML codes and explain how they control the appearance of a Web document.
2. Use the Insert Hyperlink command to include hyperlinks, bookmarks, and/or an e-mail address in a Word document.
3. Use the Save As Web page command to convert a Word document to HTML.
4. Use the Format Theme command to enhance the appearance of a Web document.
5. Use an FTP program to upload a document to a Web server; add a Web page to the catalog of a search engine.
6. Explain how to view HTML codes from within Internet Explorer; describe the use of the Telnet program that is built into Windows.
7. Use the Web Page Wizard to create a Web site with multiple pages.
8. Explain how the use of frames and/or bookmarks facilitates navigation between multiple documents.

OVERVIEW

Sooner or later anyone who cruises the World Wide Web wants to create a home page and/or a Web site of their own. That, in turn, requires an appreciation for *HyperText Markup Language (HTML)*, the language in which all Web pages are written. A Web page (HTML document) consists of text and graphics, together with a set of codes (or tags) that describe how the document is to appear when viewed in a Web browser such as Internet Explorer.

In the early days of the Web, anyone creating a Web document (home page) had to learn each of these codes and enter it explicitly. Today, however, it's much easier as you can create a Web document within any application in Microsoft Office XP. In essence, you enter the text of a document, apply basic formatting such as boldface or italics, then simply save the file as a Web document. Office XP also provides an FTP (File Transfer Protocol) capability that lets you upload your documents directly on to a Web server.

There are, of course, other commands that you will need to learn, but all commands are executed from within Word, through pull-down menus, toolbars, or keyboard shortcuts. You can create a single document (called a home page) or you can create multiple documents to build a simple Web site. Either way, the document(s) can be viewed locally within a Web browser such as Internet Explorer, and/or they can be placed on a Web server where they can be accessed by anyone with an Internet connection.

As always, the hands-on exercises are essential to our learn-by-doing philosophy since they enable you to apply the conceptual material at the computer. The exercises are structured in such a way that you can view the Web pages you create, even if you do not have access to the Internet. The last exercise introduces the Web Page Wizard to create a Web site that contains multiple Web pages.

LEARN MORE ABOUT HTML

Use your favorite Web search engine to search for additional information about HTML. One excellent place to begin is the resource page on HTML that is maintained by the Library of Congress at http://lcweb.loc.gov/global/html.html. This site contains links to several HTML tutorials and also provides you with information about the latest HTML standard.

INTRODUCTION TO HTML

Figure 6.1 displays a simple Web page that is similar to the one you will create in the hands-on exercise that follows shortly. Our page has the look and feel of Web pages you see when you access the World Wide Web. It includes different types of formatting, a bulleted list, underlined links, and a heading displayed in a larger font. All of these elements are associated with specific HTML codes that identify the appearance and characteristics of the item. Figure 6.1a displays the document as it would appear when viewed in Internet Explorer. Figure 6.1b shows the underlying HTML codes (*tags*) that are necessary to format the page.

Fortunately, however, it is not necessary to memorize the HTML tags since you can usually determine their meaning from the codes themselves. Nor is it even necessary for you to enter the tags, as Word will create the HTML tags for you based on the formatting in the document. Nevertheless, we think it worthwhile for you to gain an appreciation for HTML by comparing the two views of the document.

HTML codes become less intimidating when you realize that they are enclosed in angle brackets and are used consistently from document to document. Most tags occur in pairs, at the beginning and end of the text to be formatted, with the ending code preceded by a slash, such as <p and </p> to indicate the beginning and end of a paragraph. Links to other pages (which are known as hyperlinks) are enclosed within a pair of anchor tags <A and </A> in which you specify the URL address of the document through the HREF parameter.

Heading is in a larger font

Bulleted list

Underlined links

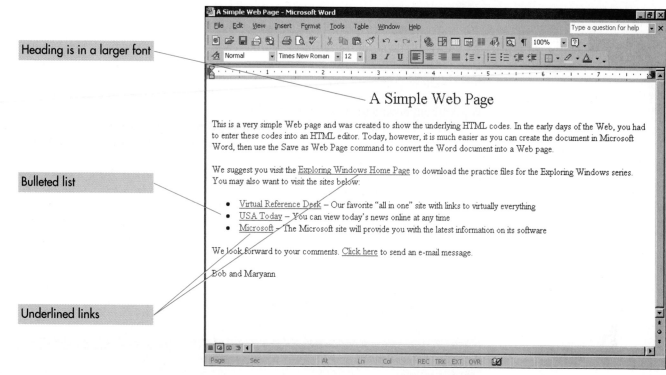

(a) Internet Explorer

Paragraph tags

Anchor tags enclose URL address

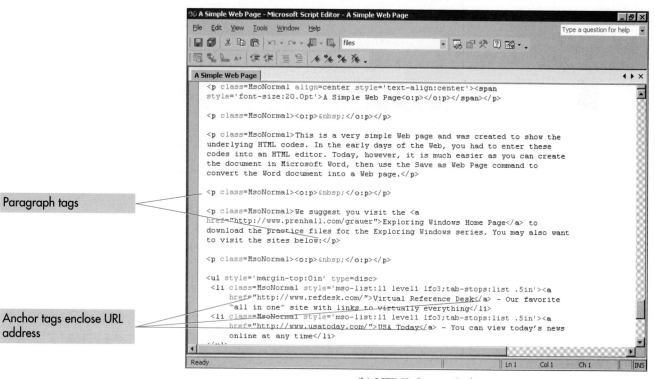

(b) HTML Source Code

FIGURE 6.1   *Introduction to HTML*

Microsoft Word

As indicated, there are different ways to create an HTML document. The original (and more difficult) method was to enter the codes explicitly in a text editor such as the Notepad accessory that is built into Windows. An easier way (and the only method you need to consider) is to use Microsoft Word to create the document for you, without having to enter or reference the HTML codes at all.

Figure 6.2 displays David Guest's *home page* in Microsoft Word. You can create a similar page by entering the text and formatting just as you would enter the text of an ordinary document. The only difference is that instead of saving the document in the default format (as a Word document), you use the ***Save As Web Page command*** to specify the HTML format. Microsoft Word does the rest, generating the HTML codes needed to create the document.

Hyperlinks are added through the Insert Hyperlink button on the Standard toolbar or through the corresponding ***Insert Hyperlink command*** in the Insert menu. You can format the elements of the document (the heading, bullets, text, and so on) individually, or you can select a *theme* from those provided by Microsoft Word. A theme (or template) is a set of unified design elements and color schemes that will save you time, while making your document more attractive.

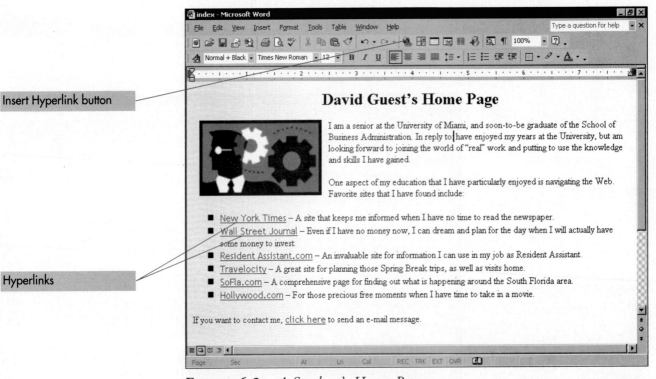

FIGURE 6.2 *A Student's Home Page*

ROUND-TRIP HTML

Each application in Microsoft Office XP lets you open an HTML document in both Internet Explorer and the application that created the Web page initially. In other words, you can start with a Word document and use the Save As Web Page command to convert the document to a Web page, then view that page in a Web browser. You can then reopen the Web page in Word (the original Office application) with full access to all Word commands, should you want to modify the document.

INTRODUCTION TO HTML

Objective To use Microsoft Word to create a simple home page with clip art and multiple hyperlinks; to format a Web page by selecting a theme. Use Figure 6.3 as a guide in the exercise.

Step 1: **Enter the Text**

➤ Start Microsoft Word. Pull down the **View menu** and click the **Web Layout command**. Enter the text of your home page as shown in Figure 6.3a. Use any text you like and choose an appropriate font and type size. Center and enlarge the title for your page.

➤ Enter the text for our links (e.g., *New York Times* and the *Wall Street Journal* sites), or choose your own. You do not enter the URL addresses at this time.

➤ Click and drag to select all of your links, then click the **Bullets button** on the Formatting toolbar to precede each link with a bullet.

➤ The Bullets button functions as a toggle switch; that is, click it a second time and the bullets disappear. Click anywhere to deselect the text.

➤ Click the **Spelling and Grammar button** to check the document for spelling. (There is absolutely no excuse for not checking the spelling and grammar in a document, be it a printed document or a Web page.)

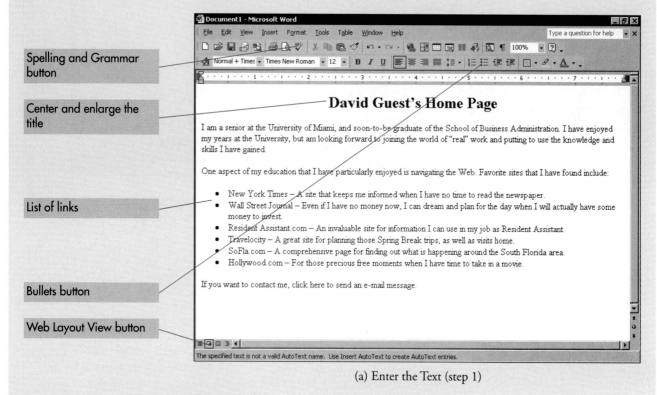

(a) Enter the Text (step 1)

FIGURE 6.3 *Hands-on Exercise 1*

Step 2: **Save the Document**

➤ Pull down the **File menu** and click the **Save As Web Page** command to display the Save As dialog box in Figure 6.3b.

➤ Click the **drop-down arrow** in the Save In list box to select the appropriate drive—drive C or drive A. Click to open the **Exploring Word folder** that contains the documents you have used throughout the text.

➤ Change the name of the Web page to **index**. (Use index as the name of the document to be consistent with the convention used by a Web browser—that is, to automatically display the index document, if it exists.)

➤ Click the **Change Title button** if you want to change the title of the Web page as it will appear in the Title bar of the Web browser. (The default title is the opening text in your document.)

➤ Click the **Save button**. The title bar reflects the name of the Web page (index), but the screen does not change in any other way.

Click to select drive and folder

Change Title button

Enter index as name for Web page

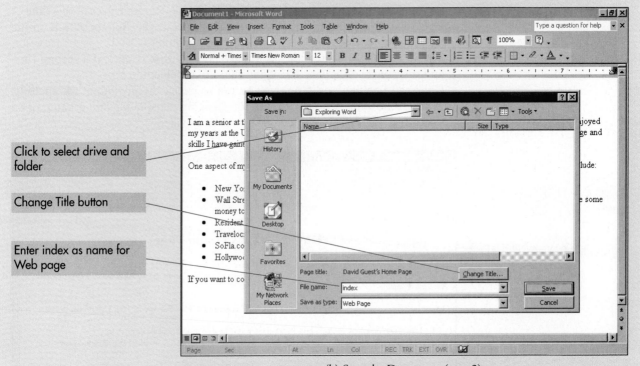

(b) Save the Document (step 2)

FIGURE 6.3   *Hands-on Exercise 1 (continued)*

THE FILE TYPES ARE DIFFERENT

Click the Start button, click (or point to) the Programs command, then start Windows Explorer. Select the drive and folder where you saved the index document. If necessary, pull down the View menu and change to the Details view. Look for the index document you just created, and note that it is displayed with the icon of a Web browser (Internet Explorer or Netscape Navigator) to indicate that it is an HTML document, rather than a Word document.

Step 3:   **Insert the Clip Art**

➤ Pull down the **Insert menu**, click (or point to) **Picture**, then click **Clip Art** to display the Insert Clip Art task pane in Figure 6.3c.

➤ Click in the Search text box and type **man** to search for all pictures that have been catalogued to describe this attribute. Click the **Search button**. The search begins and the various pictures appear individually within the task pane.

➤ Point to the image you want in your newsletter, click the **down arrow** that appears, then click **Insert** to insert the clip art.

➤ The picture should appear in the document. Close the task pane.

➤ Point to the picture and click the **right mouse button** to display the context-sensitive menu. Click the **Format Picture command** to display the Format Picture dialog box.

➤ Click the **Layout tab**, choose the **Square layout**, then click the option button for Left or Right alignment. Click **OK** to close the dialog box. Click and drag the sizing handles on the picture as appropriate. Save the document.

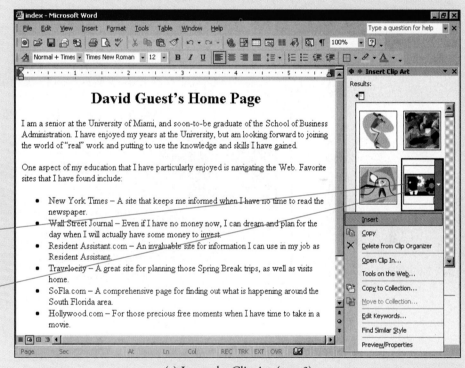

Point to image

Click the drop-down arrow when it appears

(c) Insert the Clip Art (step 3)

FIGURE 6.3   *Hands-on Exercise 1 (continued)*

SEARCH BY COLLECTION

The Media Gallery organizes its contents by collections and provides another way to select clip art. Pull down the Insert menu, click (or point to) the Picture command, then click Clip Art to open the task pane, where you can enter a key word to search for clip art. Instead of searching, however, click the link to Media Gallery at the bottom of the task pane to display the Media Gallery dialog box. Close the My Collections folder if it is open, then open the Office Collections folder, where you can explore the available images by collection.

Step 4:   **Add the Hyperlinks**

➤ Select **New York Times** (the text for the first hyperlink). Pull down the **Insert menu** and click **Hyperlink** (or click the **Insert Hyperlink button**) to display the Insert Hyperlink dialog box in Figure 6.3d.

➤ The text to display (New York Times) is already entered because the text was selected prior to executing the Insert Hyperlink command. If necessary, click the icon for **Existing File or Web Page**, then click **Browsed Pages**.

➤ Click in the second text box and enter the address **www.nytimes.com** (the http is assumed). Click **OK**.

➤ Add the additional links in similar fashion. The addresses we used in our document are: **www.wsj.com**, **www.residentassistant.com**, **www.travelocity.com**, **www.sofla.com**, and **www.hollywood.com**.

➤ Click and drag to select the words, **click here**, then click the **Insert Hyperlink button** to display the Insert Hyperlink dialog box.

➤ Click the **E-mail Address icon**, then click in the E-mail Address text box and enter your e-mail address. Click **OK**.

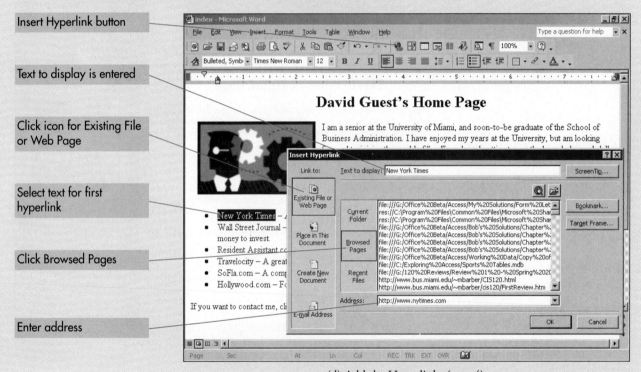

Insert Hyperlink button

Text to display is entered

Click icon for Existing File or Web Page

Select text for first hyperlink

Click Browsed Pages

Enter address

(d) Add the Hyperlinks (step 4)

FIGURE 6.3   *Hands-on Exercise 1 (continued)*

CLICK TO EDIT, CTRL+CLICK TO FOLLOW

Point to a hyperlink within a Word document, and you see a ToolTip that says to press and hold the Ctrl key (Ctrl+click) to follow the link. This is different from what you usually do, because you normally just click a link to follow it. What if, however, you wanted to edit the link? Word modifies the convention so that clicking a link enables you to edit the link. Alternatively, you can right click the hyperlink to display a context-sensitive menu from where you can make the appropriate choice.

Step 5: **Apply a Theme**

➤ You should see underlined hyperlinks in your document. Pull down the **Format menu** and click the **Theme command** to display the Theme dialog box in Figure 6.3e.

➤ Select (click) a theme from the list box on the left, and a sample of the design appears in the right. Only a limited number of the listed themes are installed by default, however, and thus you may be prompted for the Microsoft Office XP CD depending on your selection. Click **OK**.

➤ You can go from one theme to the next by clicking the new theme. There are approximately 65 themes to choose from, and they are all visually appealing. Every theme offers a professionally designed set of formatting specifications for the various headings, horizontal lines, bullets, and links.

➤ Make your decision as to which theme you will use. Save the document.

Preview of theme

Select a theme

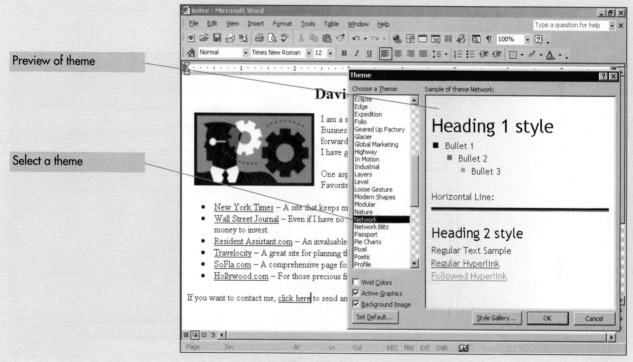

(e) Apply a Theme (step 5)

FIGURE 6.3   *Hands-on Exercise 1 (continued)*

KEEP IT SIMPLE

Too many would-be designers clutter a page unnecessarily by importing a complex background, which tends to obscure the text. The best design is a simple design—either no background or a very simple pattern. We also prefer light backgrounds with dark text (e.g., black or dark blue text on a white background), as opposed to the other way around. Design, however, is subjective, and there is no consensus as to what makes an attractive page. Variety is indeed the spice of life.

Step 6: **View the Web Page**

➤ Start your Web browser. Pull down the **File menu** and click the **Open command** to display the Open dialog box in Figure 6.3f. Click the **Browse button**, then select the drive folder (e.g., Exploring Word on drive C) where you saved the Web page.

➤ Select (click) the **index document**, click **Open**, then click **OK** to open the document. You should see the Web page that was just created except that you are viewing it in your browser rather than Microsoft Word.

➤ The Address bar shows the local address (C:\Exploring Word\index.htm) of the document. (You can also open the document from the Address bar, by clicking in the Address bar, then typing the address of the document—for example, c:\Exploring word\index.htm.)

➤ Click the **Print button** on the Internet Explorer toolbar to print this page for your instructor.

➤ Exit Word and Internet Explorer if you do not want to continue with the next exercise at this time.

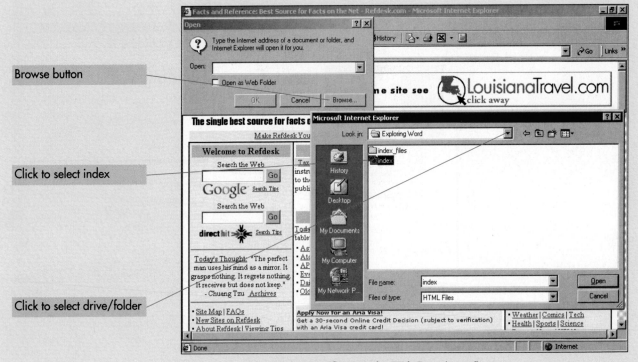

Browse button

Click to select index

Click to select drive/folder

(f) View the Web Page (step 6)

FIGURE 6.3   *Hands-on Exercise 1 (continued)*

AN EXTRA FOLDER

Look carefully at the contents of the Exploring Word folder within the Open dialog box. You see the HTML document you just created as well as a folder that was created automatically by the Save As Web Page command. The latter folder contains the various objects that are referenced by the Web page. Be sure to copy the contents of this folder to the Web server in addition to your Web page if you decide to post the page.

The previous exercise described how to create a Web document and view it through a browser such as *Internet Explorer*. The document was stored locally and thus you are the only one who can view it. It's more fun, however, to place the document on a Web *server*, where it becomes part of the World Wide Web and is therefore accessible by anyone with an Internet connection. The next several pages tell you how.

To place your page on the Web you will need Internet access, and further, you will need permission to store your document on a computer connected to the Internet. Thus, you will need the address of the server, a username, and a password. You will also need the name of the folder where you are to store your document (typically the public_html folder) as well as the path to that folder. Your instructor will provide this information for you if, in fact, your school is able to offer you this service. If not, you can still do the exercise if you have a computer at home and your Internet Service Provider enables you to store documents on its server. (Most ISPs provide several megabytes of online storage in conjunction with their service.)

The procedure to place your document on the Web is straightforward. First you create the document as you did in the previous exercise. However, in addition to (and/or instead of) storing the document locally, you have to upload it to your Web server. This is accomplished through *FTP* (*File Transfer Protocol*), which transmits files between a PC and a server. (There is an FTP capability built into Office XP, but we find it easier to use an independent program.) There are many sites on the Web where you can download a shareware version. Once the file has been saved on the Web server, it may be viewed by anyone with Internet access. (FTP can also be used to upload duplicate copies of important files to a remote site to provide backup for these files.)

The following exercise takes you through the procedure in detail as we upload David Guest's home page to the Web server at the University of Miami. The username (or User ID) is specific to David, and the address of the server is that of the university. The combination of the two, homer.bus.miami.edu/~fze79cav, is the address of David's home page. (The university uses the ~ symbol in front of the username to indicate that the complete path to the folder need not be specified.) You will have to obtain similar information from your instructor or local Internet Service Provider.

You can upload and maintain a Web page entirely through a combination of Microsoft Word and FTP. Occasionally, however, it is advantageous to connect directly to the Web server and execute commands as though you were attached directly to that computer. This is known as a *terminal session* and it is established through a program called *Telnet*. (A terminal, unlike a PC, is a device without memory or disk storage that communicates with a computer via a keyboard and display.) Telnet is illustrated in the last step of the hands-on exercise.

THE INTRANET

The ability to create links to local documents and to view those pages through a Web browser has created an entirely new way to disseminate information. Indeed, many organizations are taking advantage of this capability to develop an *Intranet*, in which Web pages are placed on a local area network for use within the organization. The documents on an Intranet are available only to individuals with access to the LAN on which the documents are stored. This is in contrast to loading the pages onto a Web server where they can be viewed by anyone with access to the Web.

PUBLISHING YOUR HOME PAGE

Objective To use FTP to upload an HTML document onto a Web server; to demonstrate Telnet. Use Figure 6.4 as a guide in the exercise.

Step 1: **Start FTP**

> ➤ This exercise requires that you have an account on a Web server in order to store your Web page, and further that you have access to an FTP program to upload the files from your PC to the server. (You can use your favorite search engine if you are working at home to locate a shareware site where you can download the software.)
> ➤ Click the **Start button** to start the FTP program. The left side of the FTP window displays the contents of a folder on your computer. The right side of the window shows the content of the FTP site, which is currently empty.
> ➤ Click the **Connect button** to display the Session Properties dialog box in Figure 6.4a. The entries in the dialog box are specific to one student at the University of Miami. In any event, you will need to enter:
>   • The address of the Web server (homer.bus.miami.edu in our example).
>   • The User ID (or username, f2e79cav in our example).
>   • Your Password (not visible in Figure 6.4a).
> ➤ Click the **OK button** to connect to the Web site. The Session Properties dialog box will close, and you should be connected to your server.
> ➤ You are ready to upload files from your PC to the Web server.

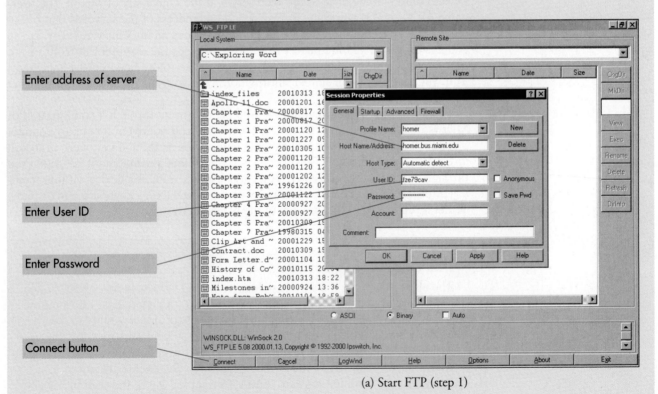

(a) Start FTP (step 1)

FIGURE 6.4 *Hands-on Exercise 2*

Step 2: **Upload the Files**

➤ Change to the folder on your computer that contains the home page you created earlier. We are using the Exploring Word folder on drive C, but your files may be in a different location.

➤ Change to the **public_html** (or similar) **folder** on the Web server. Typically, all you have to do is double click the public_html folder that appears when you first log into the site.

➤ You *must* be in the public_html folder or its equivalent on your system. Check the address bar in the right pane to see that it ends with the name of the folder as shown in Figure 6.4b.

➤ Select (click) the **index_files folder** that appears in the left pane. Press and hold the **Ctrl key** to select the **index.htm file** as well. Both files must be selected!

➤ Click the → button to upload the files. Click **Yes** if asked whether you want to transfer the selected folders and their contents.

➤ The file transfer should take a few seconds, after which the index.htm file and the associated file should appear in the right pane, indicating that the files have been transferred to the server. Close the FTP window.

Folder on your PC

Click index_files folder

Address should end with public_html

Click → button

Press Ctrl as you click index.htm

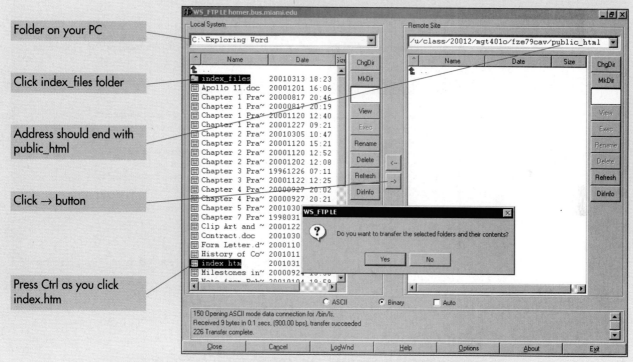

(b) Upload the Files (step 2)

FIGURE 6.4 *Hands-on Exercise 2 (continued)*

IT'S EASY TO MAKE A MISTAKE

It's easy to create a Web page. The hard part, if there is a hard part, is uploading the page and its associated folder to a Web server. Be sure that you select both the index.htm (home page) as well as the index_files folder (the supporting files) for the file transfer. One common mistake is to forget the folder, in which case you will not see the graphic elements when you view the page. In addition, be sure that you change to the public_html folder on the server prior to uploading the files.

Step 3:   **View Your Home Page**

➤ Start your Internet browser. Click in the **Address bar** and enter the name of your server followed by your username (preceded by the ~ character); for example, homer.bus.miami.edu/~pze79cav. Your server may follow a different convention.

➤ You should see your home page as shown in Figure 6.4c. You do not have to specify the document name because the browser will automatically display a document called index.html if that document is present in the public_html folder.

➤ Click the hyperlinks on your page to be sure that they work as intended. (You should have tested the hyperlinks in the first exercise, but we suggest that you try one or two at this time anyway.)

Click in Address bar and enter address of your Web page

Hyperlinks

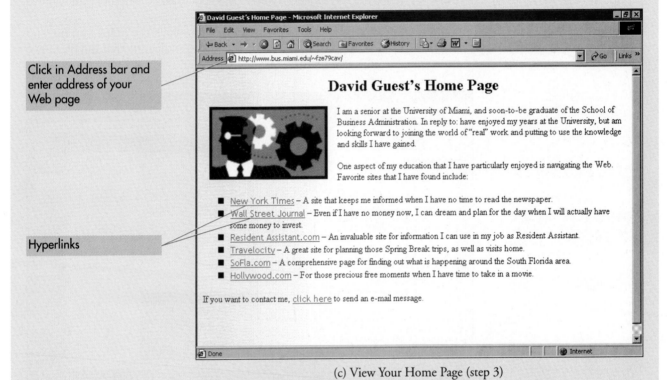

(c) View Your Home Page (step 3)

FIGURE 6.4   *Hands-on Exercise 2 (continued)*

HYPERLINKS BEFORE AND AFTER (INTERNET EXPLORER)

Hyperlinks are displayed in different colors, depending on whether (or not) the associated page has been displayed. You can change the default colors, however, to suit your personal preference. Pull down the Tools menu, click the Internet Options command to display the Internet Options dialog box, and click the General tab. Click the Colors button, then click the color box next to the visited or unvisited links to display a color palette. Select (click) the desired color, click OK to close the palette, click OK to close the Colors dialog box, then click OK to close the Internet Options dialog box.

Step 4: **Add Your Home Page to a Search Engine Database**

➤ Click in the **address bar**, enter **www.lycos.com/addasite.html**, then press the **enter key**. Scroll down the page until you see the section to add your site as shown in Figure 6.4d.

➤ Enter your URL (the address of your home page) and your e-mail address. Click the button to **Add Site to Lycos**, then read the additional information that is displayed on the screen.

➤ Wait a week or two, then see if your Web page has been entered into the Lycos database. Start Internet Explorer, then type **www.lycos.com** to access the Lycos search engine. (You can also access the Lycos search engine by clicking the **Search button** on the Internet Explorer toolbar.)

➤ Enter your name in the Search for text box at the top of the page, then click the **Search button**, to see if your page is recognized by the Lycos search engine. Try a different search engine and compare the results.

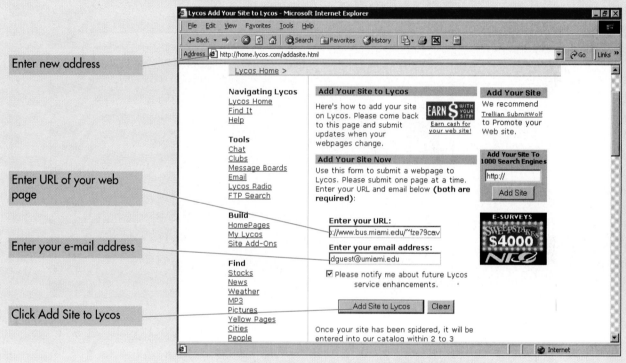

(d) Add Your Home Page to a Search Engine Database (step 4)

FIGURE 6.4 *Hands-on Exercise 2 (continued)*

ADD YOUR E-MAIL ADDRESS TO A DIRECTORY

Add your personal information to various directories on the Internet. Click the Address bar, type www.whowhere.com, press the enter key to display the form for one such directory, then enter your name and other information as appropriate. Click the Search button to see whether you are listed. If not, scroll down the page until you can click Adding Your Listing to add your e-mail address to the directory. As with all directories, there are advantages/disadvantages to an unlisted address.

Step 5:   **Print the Web Document**

➤ Right click the **Back button**, then click the address of your home page. Pull down the **File menu**, click the **File menu**, and click the **Print command** to display the dialog box in Figure 6.4e.

➤ Click the **Options tab**. Check the box to **Print table of links**, then click **OK** to print your home page.

➤ Look closely at the printed document. You will see the text of your home page (as you did in the previous exercise). You will also see a list of the hyperlinks in your document together with the associated URLs (Web addresses).

➤ Look at the header and/or footer of the printed page. You should see the address of your Web page as well as today's date. If not, you can modify this information through the Page Setup command.

➤ Submit the printed document to your instructor.

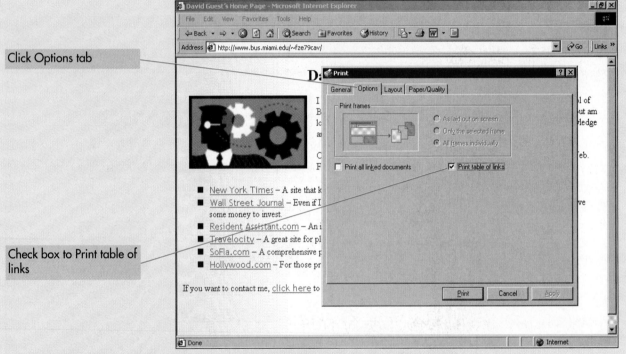

Click Options tab

Check box to Print table of links

(e) Print the Web Document (step 5)

FIGURE 6.4   *Hands-on Exercise 2 (continued)*

THE PAGE SETUP COMMAND

Pull down the File menu and click the Page Setup command to display the Page Setup dialog box that controls the appearance of the printed page. The contents of the header and footer text boxes are especially interesting as they contain information such as the URL of the page and/or the date the page was printed. The precise information that is printed is a function of the code that is entered in the text box—for example, &u and &d for the URL and date, respectively. Click the Help button (the question mark at the right of the title bar), then point to the Header or Footer text boxes to see the meanings of the various codes, then modify the codes as necessary.

Step 6: **Telnet to Your Account**

➤ Click the **Start button** on the Windows taskbar, click the **Run command** to display the Run dialog box. Type **Telnet**, then click **OK**.

➤ Pull down the **Connect menu**, click the **Remote Server command**, then enter the address of your Web server (homer.bus.miami.edu in our example) in the Host Name text box. Click **Connect**.

➤ Enter your username and password (the same entries you supplied earlier). The system will then display an opening message (e.g., University of Miami on our system), followed by a prompt (homer> on our system). Our Web server uses the Unix operating system as shown in Figure 6.4f.

➤ Type the command **ls −l** to display the files and folders that are stored in your account. You should see the public_html folder (the folder you specified when you uploaded your Web page).

➤ Type the command **cd public_html** to change to this directory, then type the command **pwd** to print the name of the working directory. You should see an address corresponding to the path you specified when you saved your Web page.

➤ Type the command **ls −l** to see the contents of the public_html directory. You should see index.htm (the name of your home page) and index files (the folder that contains the graphic elements on that page).

➤ Type **exit** to log out; you will then see a dialog box indicating that the connection to the host is lost. Click **OK**.

➤ Close the Telnet window. Close Internet Explorer. Close Microsoft Word if you do not want to do the next exercise at this time.

Home page

Enter ls −1

Enter cd public_html

Enter pwd

Enter ls −1

Enter exit

Path to your home page

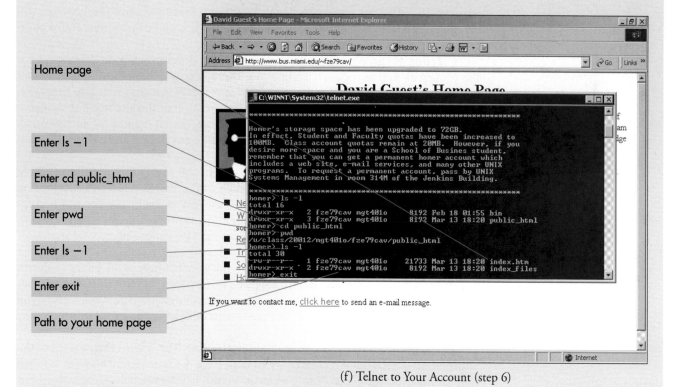

(f) Telnet to Your Account (step 6)

FIGURE 6.4   *Hands-on Exercise 2 (continued)*

Thus far, you have created a home page and have placed it on a Web server. The next logical task is to extend your home page to reference additional pages that are stored on the server. In other words, you want to create a **Web site**, as opposed to a single home page.

Figure 6.5 displays a Web site for a hypothetical travel agency. The Address bar in both Figures 6.5a and 6.5b shows that the document (named default.htm) is stored in the World Wide Travel folder on drive C. (The document would be subsequently renamed to index.htm prior to uploading it onto the Web.) The reference to drive C indicates that the site is being developed on a local machine and has not yet been uploaded to a Web server.

The default.htm document is divided into two vertical **frames**, each of which displays a different document. The left frame is the same in both Figure 6.5a and 6.5b, and it contains a series of hyperlinks that are associated with other pages at the site. Click the About the Agency link in the left pane of Figure 6.5a, for example, and you display information about the agency in the right pane. Click the New York Weekend in Figure 6.5b, however, and you display a page describing a trip to New York City. Note, too, that each frame has its own vertical scroll bar. The scroll bars function independently of one another. Thus, you can click the vertical scroll bar in the left pane to view additional links, or you can click the scroll bar in the right pane to see additional information about the agency itself.

The document in the right pane of Figure 6.5a also illustrates the use of a **bookmark** or link to a location within the same document. A bookmark is a useful navigation aid in long documents, as it lets you jump from one place to another (within the same document) without having to manually scroll through the document. Thus, you can click the link that says, "click here for travel tips", and the browser will scroll automatically to the paragraph about travel tips and display that entire paragraph on the screen.

Creation of the Web site will require that you develop separate documents for the agency, as well as for each destination. There is no shortcut because the content of every site is unique and must be created specifically for that site. You can, however, use the **Web Page Wizard** to simplify the creation of the site itself as shown in Figure 6.6. The wizard asks you a series of questions, then it creates the site based on the answers you supply. The wizard takes care of the navigation and design. The content is up to you.

The wizard begins by asking for the name of the site and its location (Figure 6.6a). It's easiest to specify a local folder, such as the World Wide Travel folder on drive C, and then upload the entire folder to the Web server once the site is complete. Next you choose the means of navigation through the site (Figure 6.6b). Vertical frames are the most common, but you can also choose horizontal frames or a separate window for each document.

The essence of the wizard, however, is in the specification of the pages as shown in Figures 6.6c and 6.6d. The wizard suggests three pages initially (Figure 6.6c), but you can add additional pages or remove the suggested pages. The wizard gives you the opportunity to rename any of the pages and/or change the order in which they will appear in Figure 6.6d.

You choose the theme for your site in Figure 6.6e. The wizard then has all of the information it needs, and it creates the default page in Figure 6.6f. This page is much simpler than the completed site we saw in Figure 6.5. Nevertheless, the wizard has proved invaluable because it has created the site and established the navigation. It's now your task to complete and/or enhance the individual pages. The ease with which you create the documents in Figure 6.6 depends on your proficiency in Microsoft Word. Even if you have only limited experience with Microsoft Word, however, our instructions are sufficiently detailed that you should be able to complete our next exercise with little difficulty.

Document is on local drive

Right frame displays page when associated hyperlink is clicked

Left frame displays hyperlinks

Bookmark: click link and you jump to bookmark within document

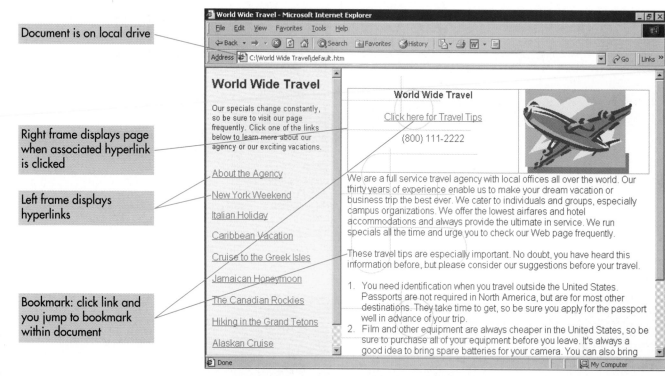

(a) About the Agency Page

Click link

Associated page is displayed in right frame

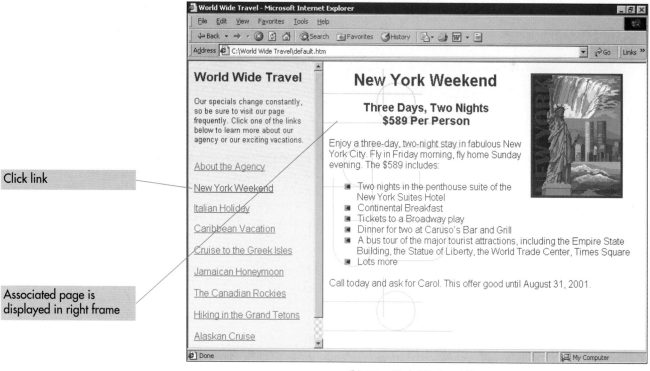

(b) New York Weekend Page

FIGURE 6.5 *A Web Site*

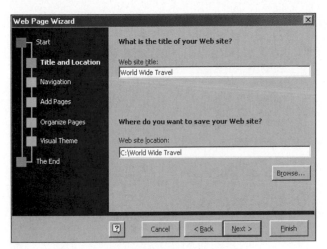

(a) Create the Site

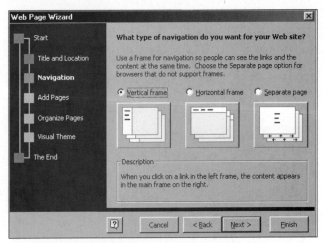

(b) Choose the Navigation

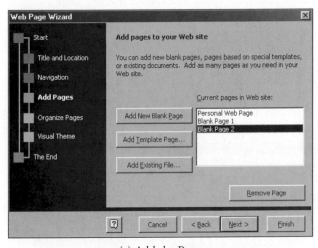

(c) Add the Pages

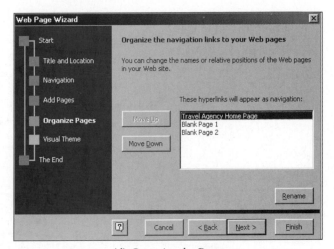

(d) Organize the Pages

(e) Choose the Theme

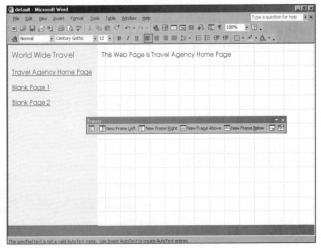

(f) The Initial Site

FIGURE 6.6   *The Web Page Wizard*

CREATING A WEB SITE

Objective To use the Web Page Wizard to create a Web site; to facilitate navigation within a document by creating a bookmark. Use Figure 6.7.

Step 1: **Start the Web Page Wizard**

> Start Word. Pull down the **File menu** and click the **New command** to display the task pane. (If a new document is already open, pull down the **View menu** and click the **Task Pane command**.)
> Click the link to **General templates** to open the Templates dialog box. Click the **Web pages** tab, then double click the **Web Page Wizard** icon to start the wizard. Click **Next**.
> Enter **World Wide Travel** as the title of the Web site. Choose a separate folder to hold all of the documents for the site. We suggest **C:\World Wide Travel** as shown in Figure 6.7a. Click **Next**.
> The option button for **Vertical frame** as the means of navigation is already selected. Click **Next**.

Enter World Wide Travel

Enter name of folder for Web site

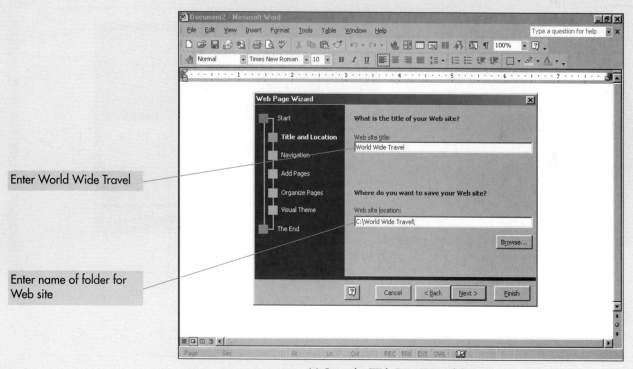

(a) Start the Web Page Wizard (step 1)

FIGURE 6.7 *Hands-on Exercise 3*

WIZARDS AND TEMPLATES

Office XP includes wizards and templates for a variety of documents. A template is a partially completed document that contains formatting, text, and/or graphics. A wizard introduces additional flexibility by first asking you a series of questions, then creating a template based on your answers.

Step 2: **Specify the Pages**

> ➤ The Web Page Wizard creates a site with three pages: Personal Web Page, Blank Page 1, and Blank Page 2. You can, however, add, remove, and/or rename these pages as appropriate for your site.
> ➤ Select (click) **Personal Web page** and click the **Remove Page button**. Click the **Add New Blank Page button** to add Blank Page 3. Click **Next** to display the screen in Figure 6.7b.
> ➤ Select **Blank Page 1** and click the **Rename button** (or simply double click **Blank Page 1**) to display the Rename Hyperlink dialog box. Enter **About the Agency** and click **OK**. Rename Blank Page 2 and Blank Page 3 to **New York Weekend** and **Italian Holiday**, respectively.
> ➤ Check that the order of pages is what you intend (About the Agency, New York Weekend, and Italian Holiday). Click **Next**.
> ➤ Click the **Browse Themes button** and choose a suitable theme. We chose **Capsules**. Click **OK**. Click **Next**. Click **Finish**.

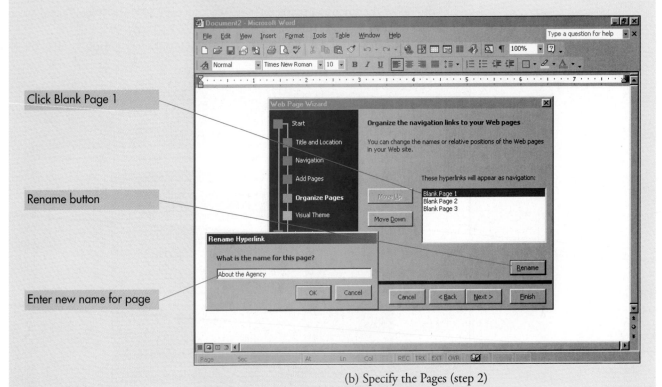

Click Blank Page 1

Rename button

Enter new name for page

(b) Specify the Pages (step 2)

FIGURE 6.7   *Hands-on Exercise 3 (continued)*

CHANGING THE WEB SITE

The Web Page Wizard is intended to get you up and running as quickly as possible. It takes you through all of the steps to create a Web site, and it builds the appropriate links to all of the pages on that site. You will, however, need to modify the site after it has been created by adding text, adding new links, and/or deleting or modifying existing links.

Step 3: **Modify the Default Page**

➤ You should see the default page for the World Wide Travel site as shown in Figure 6.7c. Our figure, however, already reflects the changes that you will make to the default page. Close the Frames toolbar.

➤ Click and drag to select **World Wide Travel**. Click the **Bold button**. Click to the right of the text to deselect it. Press the **enter key** twice. Enter the text shown in Figure 6.7c.

➤ Click the **Save button** to save the changes to the default page. Pull down the **File menu** and click the **Close command** to close the default page but remain in Microsoft Word.

➤ We will reopen the default page in Internet Explorer later in the exercise to view the page as it will appear to others.

Save button

Bold button

Enter text

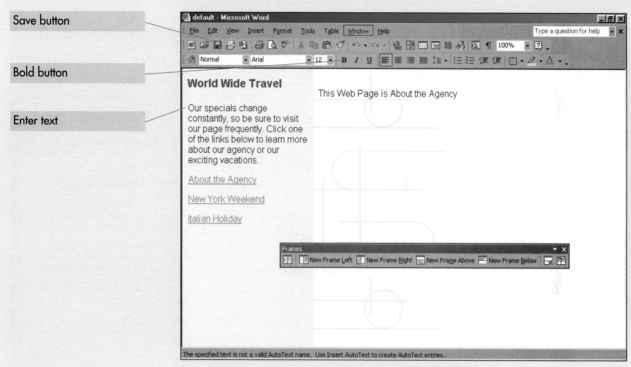

(c) Modify the Default Page (step 3)

FIGURE 6.7   *Hands-on Exercise 3 (continued)*

OBTAINING A PASSPORT

You can't obtain a passport online, but you can get all of the information you need. Go to travel.state.gov, the home page of the Bureau of Consular Affairs in the U.S. Department of State, then scroll down the page until you can click the link to Passport Information. You will be able to download an actual passport application with detailed instructions including a list of the documents you need to supply. You can also access a nationwide list of where to apply. See practice exercise 3 at the end of the chapter.

Step 4:   **Modify the Agency Page**

➤ You should still be in Microsoft Word. Click the **Open button** on the Standard toolbar to display the Open dialog box. Click the **down arrow** on the Look in text box, then double click the **World Wide Travel folder** on drive C (the location you specified when you created the Web site).

➤ Double click the **About the Agency document** that currently consists of a single line of text. Click at the end of this sentence and press the **enter key**.

➤ Pull down the **Insert menu** and click the **File command** to display the Insert File dialog box. Change to the **Exploring Word folder** and insert the **Text for Travel document**.

➤ Your document should match the document in Figure 6.7d. Click and drag to select the original sentence as shown in the figure. Press the **Del key** to delete this sentence. Delete the blank line as well. Save the document.

Select original sentence and press Del key

Insert text for Travel document

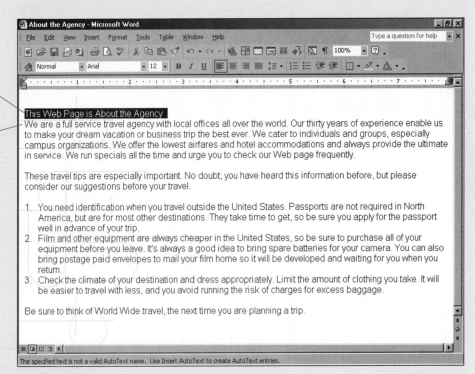

(d) Modify the Agency Page (step 4)

FIGURE 6.7   *Hands-on Exercise 3 (continued)*

THE WORLD WIDE TRAVEL FOLDER

A Web site consists of multiple Web pages, each of which is saved as a separate document. Each document in turn may contain graphical elements that are also saved separately. Thus the World Wide Travel folder contains an About the Agency document that in turn references graphic elements in its own folder. The other pages (e.g., Italian Holiday and New York Weekend) have their own folders. The World Wide Travel folder also contains additional documents such as a default page and a TOC (table of contents) frame that is displayed in the left pane.

Step 5:   **Test the Navigation**

> ➤ Start your Web browser. Pull down the **File menu** and click the **Open command** to display the Open dialog box. Click the **Browse button**, then select the drive (e.g., drive C) and folder (e.g., World Wide Travel).
> ➤ Select (click) the **default** document, click the **Open command button**, then click **OK** to display the document in Figure 6.7e. You should see the Web page that was created earlier, except that you are viewing it in your browser rather than Microsoft Word. The Address bar reflects the local address of the document (C:\World Wide Travel\default.htm).
> ➤ Click the link to **New York Weekend** to display this page in the right pane. The page is not yet complete, but the link works properly. Click the link to **Italian Holiday** to display this page. Again, the page is not complete, but the link works properly.
> ➤ Click the link to **About the Agency** to access this page.

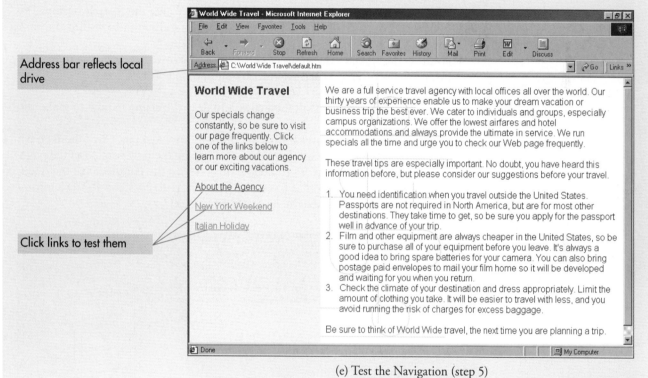

Address bar reflects local drive

Click links to test them

(e) Test the Navigation (step 5)

FIGURE 6.7   *Hands-on Exercise 3 (continued)*

UNDER CONSTRUCTION

Use prototyping to let the end user experience the "look and feel" of a site before the site has been completed. The user sees the opening document, and is provided with a set of links to partially completed documents. This provides a sense of the eventual site even though the latter is far from finished. Prototyping also provides valuable feedback to the developer, who is able to make the necessary adjustments before any extensive work has been done. See practice exercise 4 at the end of the chapter.

Step 6:   **Insert the Clip Art**

➤ Click the **Word button** on the Windows taskbar. The About the Agency document should still be open. Press **Ctrl+Home** to move to the beginning of the document. Press the **enter key** to add a blank line.

➤ Click the **Insert Table button** on the Standard toolbar, then click and drag to select a one-by-two grid. Release the mouse. Click in the **left cell**. Type **World Wide Travel**.

➤ Press the **enter key** twice. Type the sentence **Click here for Travel Tips** (we will create the link later), press the **enter key** twice, and enter the agency's phone number, **(800) 111-2222**.

➤ Select all three lines and click the **Center button**. Choose a suitable point size. We suggest 18 point for the first line and 12 point for the other text.

➤ Click in the **right pane**. Pull down the **Insert menu**, click **Picture**, then click **Clip Art** to display the Insert Clip Art task pane in Figure 6.7f.

➤ Click in the **Search text box** and type **airplane** to search for all pictures that have been catalogued to describe this attribute. Click the **Search button**. The search begins and the various pictures appear individually within the task pane.

➤ Point to the image you want, click the **down arrow** that appears, then click **Insert** to insert the clip art. The picture should appear in the document. Close the task pane.

➤ Click the picture to select it, then click and drag the sizing handle to make the picture smaller.

➤ Click the **Internet Explorer button** on the Windows taskbar. Click the **Refresh button** on the Internet Explorer toolbar to display the new version of the page.

➤ If necessary, return to the Word document to resize the picture. Save the document, then return to Internet Explorer. Remember to click the **Refresh button** in Internet Explorer to see the most recent version.

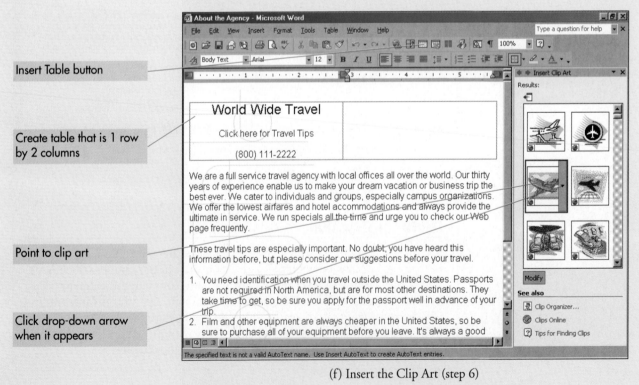

Insert Table button

Create table that is 1 row by 2 columns

Point to clip art

Click drop-down arrow when it appears

(f) Insert the Clip Art (step 6)

FIGURE 6.7   *Hands-on Exercise 3 (continued)*

Step 7: **Insert a Bookmark**

➤ Return to the Agency page in Microsoft Word to create a bookmark.
➤ To create the bookmark:
  - Click at the beginning of the second paragraph. Pull down the **Insert menu** and click **Bookmark** to display the Bookmark dialog box.
  - Enter **TravelTips** (spaces are not allowed) as the name of the bookmark, then click the **Add button** to add the bookmark and close the dialog box.
➤ To create the link to the bookmark:
  - Click and drag the text **Click here for Travel Tips** as shown in Figure 6.7g, then click the **Insert Hyperlink button** to display the dialog box.
  - Click the icon for **Place in This Document**, click the **plus sign** next to Bookmarks, then click **TravelTips**. Click **OK**.
➤ The sentence, Click here for Travel Tips, should appear as underlined text to indicate that it is now a hyperlink. Save the document.

Insert Hyperlink button

Click and drag to select text

Click Place in This Document

Click TravelTips

Click here and create TravelTips bookmark

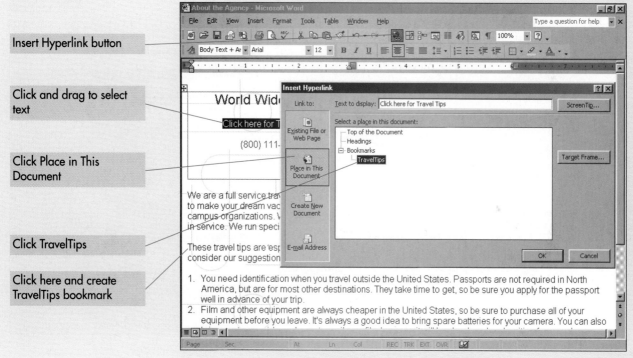

(g) Insert a Bookmark (step 7)

FIGURE 6.7 *Hands-on Exercise 3 (continued)*

THE TOP OF DOCUMENT BOOKMARK

Simplify the navigation within a long page with a link to the top of the document. Press Ctrl+End to move to the bottom of the document (one of several places where you can insert this link), then click the Insert Hyperlink button to display the Insert Hyperlink dialog box. Click the icon for Place in This Document, click Top of the Document from the list of bookmarks (Word creates this bookmark automatically), then click OK. You will see the underlined text, Top of Document, as a hyperlink.

Step 8: **View the Completed Page**

> ➤ Click the **Internet Explorer button** on the Windows taskbar. Click the **Refresh button** to view the completed document as shown in Figure 6.7h.
> ➤ If necessary, click the link to **About the Agency** to display the completed Agency page. There is a scroll bar in the right frame, because you cannot see the entire agency page at one time. Note, however, that you do not see a scroll bar in the left frame because this page can be seen in its entirety.
> ➤ Click in the **right pane**. Pull down the **File menu** and click the **Print command** to display the Print dialog box in Figure 6.7h. Click the option button to print **Only the selected frame** but check the box to **Print all linked documents** (which effectively prints every document in the site).
> ➤ Click **OK**, then submit the printed pages to your instructor as proof that you did this exercise.

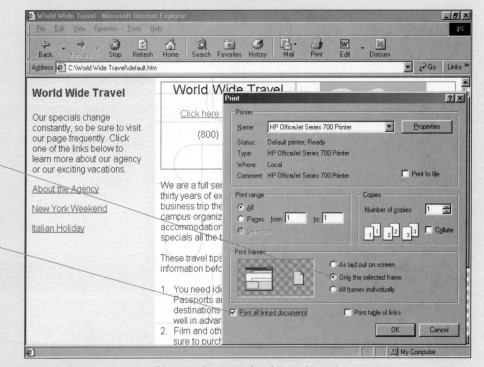

Click Only the selected frame

Check box to Print all linked documents

(h) View the Completed Page (step 8)

FIGURE 6.7 *Hands-on Exercise 3 (continued)*

CHANGE THE FONT SIZE

Internet Explorer enables you to view and/or print a page in one of five font settings (smallest, small, medium, large, and largest). Pull down the View menu, click the Text Size command, then choose the desired font size. The setting pertains to both the displayed page as well as the printed page.

All Web documents are written in HyperText Markup Language (HTML), a language that consists of codes (or tags) that format a document for display on the World Wide Web. The easiest way to create an HTML document is through Microsoft Word. You start Word in the usual fashion and enter the text of the document with basic formatting. Then you pull down the File menu and click the Save As Web Page command.

Microsoft Word does the rest, generating the HTML tags that are needed to create the document. The resulting document can be modified with respect to its content and/or appearance just like an ordinary Word document. The Insert Hyperlink command is used to link a document to other pages. Graphics may come from a variety of sources and are inserted into a document through the Insert Picture command. The Format Theme command applies a professional design to the document. The Web page may be subsequently opened in Microsoft Word for additional editing and/or it can be opened in Internet Explorer for viewing.

After a Web document has been created, it can be placed on a server or local area network so that other people will be able to access it. This, in turn, requires you to check with your professor or system administrator to obtain the necessary username and password. Once you have this information, you use the FTP protocol to upload your page to the Web server. (FTP can also be used to upload duplicate copies of important files to a remote site to provide backup for these files.) There is an FTP capability within Office XP, but it is easier to use a standalone program. (Many sites on the Web provide a shareware version of FTP.) Even if your page is not placed on the Web, you can still view it locally on your PC through a Web browser.

The Web Page Wizard simplifies the creation of a multipage site. The wizard asks you a series of questions, then it creates the site based on the answers you supply. The opening page is divided into horizontal or vertical frames that provide links to subsidiary pages. Every page has a consistent format according to the theme that you selected. Additional pages can be added at any time. Existing pages can be modified or deleted. In short, the wizard takes care of the navigation and design. The content is up to you.

Prototyping can be used during the development process to provide the look and feel of the finished site. The navigation is complete, but the individual pages are still "under construction."

KEY TERMS

Bookmark (p. 282)
File Transfer Protocol (FTP) (p. 275)
Frame (p. 282)
Home page (p. 268)
Hyperlink (p. 268)
Hypertext Markup Language (HTML) (p. 265)

Insert Hyperlink command (p. 268)
Internet Explorer (p. 275)
Intranet (p. 275)
Prototyping (p. 289)
Save As Web Page command (p. 268)
Server (p. 275)
Tag (p. 266)

Telnet (p. 275)
Terminal session (p. 275)
Theme (p. 268)
Web Page Wizard (p. 282)
Web site (p. 282)

1. Which of the following requires you to enter HTML tags explicitly in order to create a Web document?
   (a) A text editor such as the Notepad accessory
   (b) Microsoft Word
   (c) Both (a) and (b)
   (d) Neither (a) nor (b)

2. What is the easiest way to switch back and forth between Word and Internet Explorer, given that both are open?
   (a) Click the appropriate button on the Windows taskbar
   (b) Click the Start button, click Programs, then choose the appropriate program
   (c) Minimize all applications to display the Windows desktop, then double click the icon for the appropriate application
   (d) All of the above are equally convenient

3. When should you click the Refresh button on the Internet Explorer toolbar?
   (a) Whenever you visit a new Web site
   (b) Whenever you return to a Web site within a session
   (c) Whenever you view a document on a corporate Intranet
   (d) Whenever you return to a document that has changed during the session

4. How do you view the HTML tags for a Web document from Internet Explorer?
   (a) Pull down the View menu and select the Source command
   (b) Pull down the File menu, click the Save As command, and specify HTML as the file type
   (c) Click the Web Page Preview button on the Standard toolbar
   (d) All of the above

5. Internet Explorer can display an HTML page that is stored on:
   (a) A local area network
   (b) A Web server
   (c) Drive A or drive C of a standalone PC
   (d) All of the above

6. How do you save a Word document as a Web page?
   (a) Pull down the Tools menu and click the Convert to Web Page command
   (b) Pull down the File menu and click the Save As Web Page command
   (c) Both (a) and (b)
   (d) Neither (a) nor (b)

7. Which program transfers files between a PC and a remote computer?
   (a) Telnet
   (b) FTP
   (c) Homer
   (d) PTF

8. Which of the following requires an Internet connection?
   (a) Using Internet Explorer to view a document that is stored locally
   (b) Using Internet Explorer to view the Microsoft home page
   (c) Both (a) and (b)
   (d) Neither (a) nor (b)

9. Which of the following requires an Internet connection?
   (a) Telnet
   (b) FTP
   (c) Both (a) and (b)
   (d) Neither (a) nor (b)

10. Assume that you have an account on the server, www.myserver.edu, under the username, jdoe. What is the most likely Web address to view your home page?
    (a) www.myserver.edu
    (b) www.jdoe.edu
    (c) www.myserver.edu/~jdoe
    (d) www.myserver.edu.jdoe.html

11. The Insert Hyperlink command can reference:
    (a) An e-mail address
    (b) A bookmark
    (c) A Web page
    (d) All of the above

12. The Format Theme command:
    (a) Is required in order to save a Word document as a Web page
    (b) Applies a uniform design to the links and other elements within a document
    (c) Both (a) and (b)
    (d) Neither (a) nor (b)

13. The Web Page Wizard creates a default Web site and enables you to specify:
    (a) The means of navigation such as vertical or horizontal frames
    (b) The number of pages (links) that are found on the default page
    (c) The theme (design) of the Web site
    (d) All of the above

14. The Web Page Wizard creates a site with a Personal Web page, Blank Page 1, and Blank Page 2, but you can
    (a) Delete any of these pages
    (b) Add new pages to those it creates for you
    (c) Rename any pages it supplies
    (d) All of the above

15. Assume that the Web Page Wizard was used to create a site called Personal Computer Store, and further, that the site contains links to four separate pages, each of which contains one or more graphics. Which of the following is true?
    (a) You can expect to see a Personal Computer Store folder on your system
    (b) The Personal Computer Store folder will contain a separate document for each of the four pages
    (c) The Personal Computer Store folder will contain a separate folder for each of the four pages
    (d) All of the above

ANSWERS

1. a	6. b	11. d
2. a	7. b	12. b
3. d	8. b	13. d
4. a	9. c	14. d
5. d	10. c	15. d

1. **Web Page Review:** The document in *Chapter 6 Practice 1* provides a quick review of the process to create a Web page and upload to a server. Your assignment is to open the document shown in Figure 6.8 and fill in the blanks. Use boldface and italics to highlight your answers, then print the completed document for your instructor. This is a valuable exercise to review the material from the chapter.

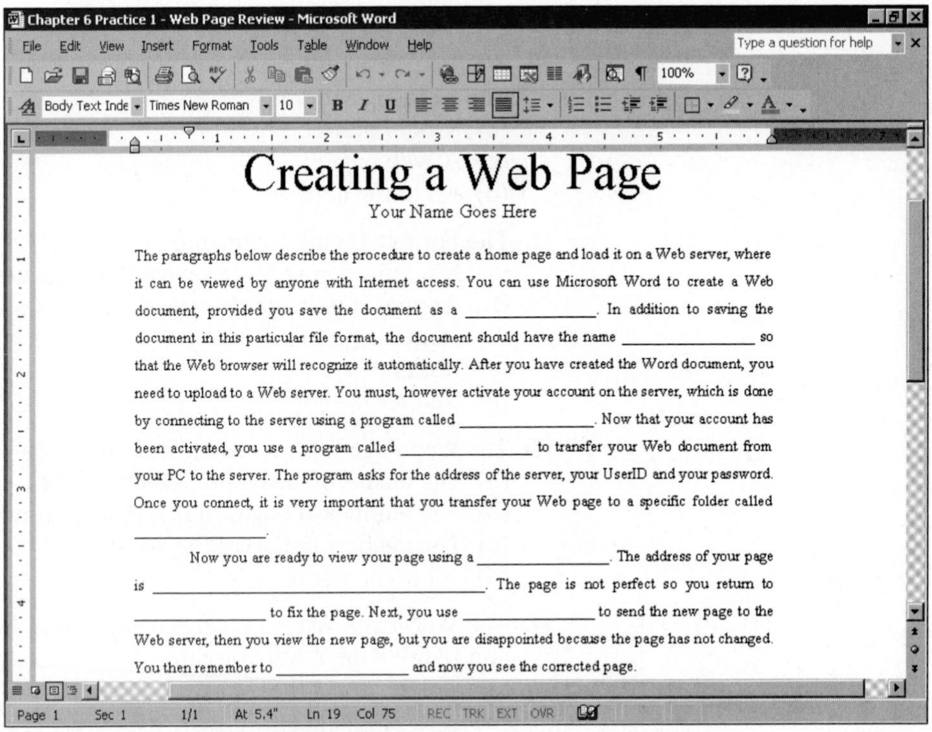

FIGURE 6.8 *Web Page Review (Exercise 1)*

2. **New York Weekend:** Create the World Wide Travel Web site as described in the third hands-on exercise. Test the site to be sure that the navigation works. The About the Agency page is complete, but the New York Weekend and Italian Holiday documents exist only as one-sentence documents. Open either document and complete the page. Our suggestion for the New York weekend is shown in Figure 6.9, but you need not use our design. Print the additional page(s) and submit them to your instructor as proof you did this exercise.

    Use FTP to upload the Travel Web site to a Web server, provided you have this capability. Be sure to transfer the complete contents of the World Wide Travel folder from your local machine to the public_html folder on the server. What is the Web address of your site?

3. **Adding an External Link:** Open the default.htm document in the World Wide Travel folder, then add the link to Passport information to display the State Department page (travel.state.gov) shown in Figure 6.10. This site contains a wealth of information for the would-be traveler, including information on how to obtain a passport. Print the revised page for your instructor.

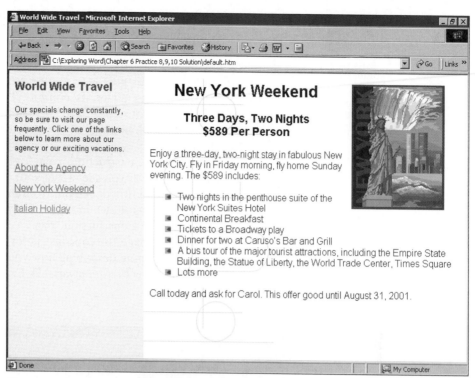

FIGURE 6.9 *New York Weekend (Exercise 2)*

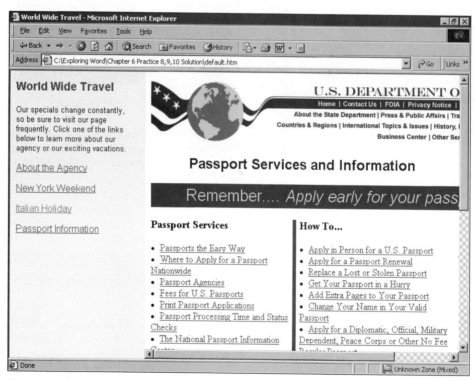

FIGURE 6.10 *Adding an External Link (Exercise 3)*

BUILDS ON

PRACTICE
EXERCISE 2
PAGE 296

4. Under Construction: The creation of a Web site is an interactive process between the client who is paying for the site and the developer. It's important for the client to get the "look and feel" of the site during the early stages of development, so that any errors can be corrected as soon as possible. One way to accomplish this goal is to implement the navigation for the complete site, prior to creating all of its content. This is done through an "Under Construction" (or prototype) page such as the document in Figure 6.11. The client obtains the look and feel of the eventual site and can communicate any changes immediately.

a. Create an "Under Construction" page for the World Wide Travel agency. You can use our design or you can create your own.

b. Expand the default.htm document from the previous exercise to include the additional vacations shown in Figure 6.11. Each of the additional links is to display the "Under Construction" page.

c. Print the revised page for your instructor as shown in Figure 6.11. In addition, write a short note describing how you will add content to the site as the additional vacations become available. Explain how to remove a link if it is no longer available.

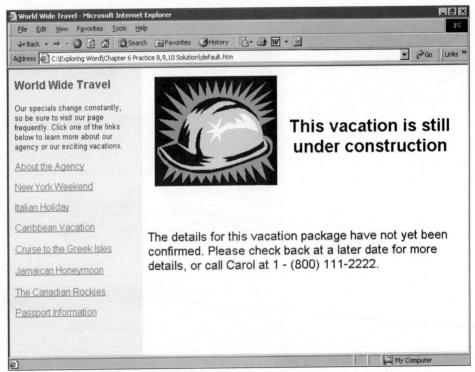

FIGURE 6.11   *Under Construction (Exercise 4)*

5. Frequently Asked Questions: Pull down the File menu, click the New command, and click the Web Pages tab to display a dialog box containing several templates for use as Web pages. Open the Frequently Asked Questions template, and use it to create a document with questions and answers about any subject that interests you. You could, for example, create a document with questions about travel, then add a link to this document to your World Wide Travel site. Print the completed document for your instructor as proof you did this exercise. Be sure to explore the bookmarks that are created automatically within the template. Include a short note explaining how to add new bookmarks and/or to remove existing bookmarks that are no longer relevant.

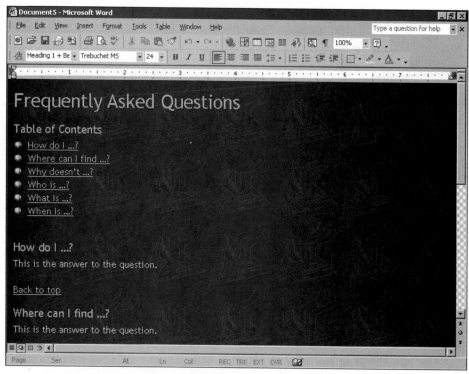

FIGURE 6.12 *Frequently Asked Questions (Exercise 5)*

6. Personal Web Page: Use the Personal Web Page template in Office XP to develop a page about yourself. The template in Figure 6.13 is intended to give you a quick start, but you are not obligated to use all of the headings. Choose an appropriate theme, then print the completed page for your instructor. Add a short note that compares the personal Web page in this exercise with the home page that you developed in the first hands-on exercise in the chapter.

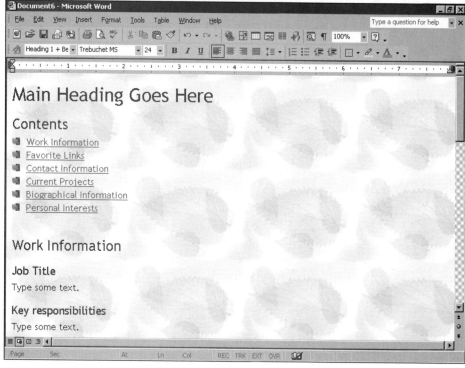

FIGURE 6.13 *Personal Web Page (Exercise 6)*

7. A Commercial Web Site: Use the Web Page Wizard to create a Web site for a hypothetical Computer Super Store as shown in Figure 6.14. Use the Web Page Wizard to create a site with horizontal or vertical frames. Choose any theme you like. Use the text in our document, *Chapter 6 Practice 7* for the home page. The subsidiary pages do not have to be completely developed; that is, the pages can be "under construction." The navigation, however, has to work. Print the completed home page and at least one subordinate page for your instructor.

There is no requirement to upload the page to the Web, but it is worth doing if you have the capability. You will need additional information from your instructor about how to obtain an account on a Web server (if that is available), and further how to upload the Web page from your PC to the server.

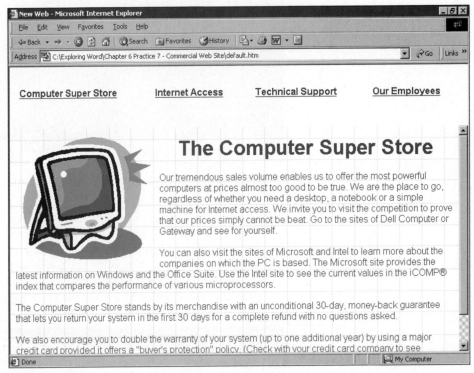

FIGURE 6.14 *A Commercial Web Site (Exercise 7)*

8. Milestones in Communications: The use of hyperlinks enables the creation of interactive documents such as the document in Figure 6.15. Open the unformatted document in *Chapter 6 Practice 8* in the Exploring Word folder. Pull down the Format menu, click the AutoFormat command to display the AutoFormat dialog box, verify that the AutoFormat option is selected, and click OK.

Modify the Body Text style and/or the Heading 1 style after the document has been formatted in any way that makes sense to you. The most important task, however, is to create the hyperlinks at the beginning of the document that let you branch to the various headings within the document. To create a hyperlink, pull down the Insert menu, click the Hyperlink command, then click the Place in this Document button to select from the bookmarks that are contained within the document. (Each heading in the document appears as a bookmark.)

You also need to insert a hyperlink after each article to return to the top of the document. Follow the same procedure as before, but select the Top of the Document bookmark. The result is an interactive document that lets the user browse through the document in any sequence you choose. Complete the formatting, save the document as a Web page, then view it in a Web browser. Print the completed document for your instructor.

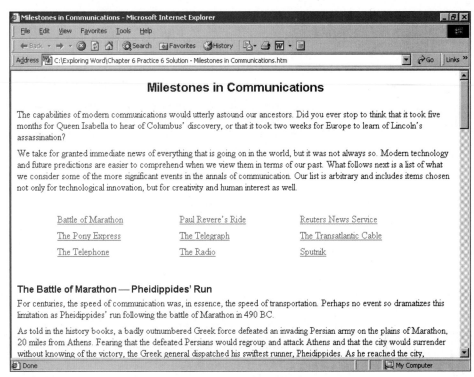

FIGURE 6.15 *Milestones in Communication (Exercise 8)*

9. Meet Bob and Maryann: Bob Grauer and Maryann Barber are full-time faculty at the University of Miami. The authors welcome you to visit their Web sites (www.bus.miami.edu/~rgrauer and www.bus.miami.edu/~mbarber) to view this semester's assignments. Maryann's site is shown in Figure 6.16 and should have a familiar look—it is based on the Web Page Wizard. Choose either author, look around, and summarize your findings in a brief note to your instructor.

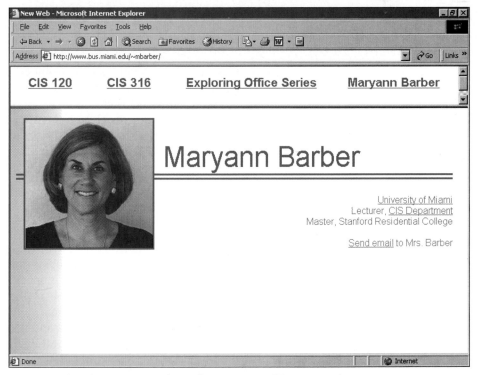

FIGURE 6.16 *Meet Bob and Maryann (Exercise 9)*

Designer Home Pages

Everyone has a personal list of favorite Web sites, but have you ever thought seriously about what makes an attractive Web page? Is an attractive page the same as a useful page? Try to develop a set of guidelines for a designer to follow as he or she creates a Web site, then incorporate these guidelines into a brief report for your instructor. Support your suggestions by referring to specific Web pages that you think qualify for your personal "Best (Worst) of the Web" award.

Register a Domain Name

InterNIC is the government agency responsible for assigning and maintaining domain names on the Web. A domain name is a mnemonic (easy-to-remember) name such as www.microsoft.com that corresponds to a numeric Internet Protocol (IP) address that represents the true location of the site. Use your favorite search engine to locate the InterNIC site, then search on the name for a hypothetical business and report your success to your instructor. Is the name of your potential business taken? If so, who owns the name and when was it registered? Remain at the site until you can find a name suitable for your business that is not yet taken. How much does it cost to register the name? Summarize your findings in a short note to your instructor.

Employment Opportunities

The Internet abounds with employment opportunities, help-wanted listings, and places to post your résumé. Your home page reflects your skills and experience to the entire world, and represents an incredible opportunity never before available to college students. You can encourage prospective employers to visit your home page, and make contact with hundreds more companies than would otherwise be possible. Update your home page to include a link to your résumé, and then surf the Net to find places to register it.

Front Page

Microsoft Word is an excellent way to begin creating Web documents. It is only a beginning, however, and there are many specialty programs with significantly more capability. One such product is Front Page, a product aimed at creating a Web site as opposed to isolated documents. Search the Microsoft Web site for information on Front Page, then summarize your findings in a short note to your instructor. Be sure to include information on capabilities that are included in Front Page that are not found in Word.

UNIX Permissions

As a developer, you need to be able to log on to your account, to add or modify documents. You also want others to be able to go to your URL to view the page, but you want to prevent the world at large from being able to modify the documents. This is controlled on the Web server through the operating system by setting appropriate permissions for each document. Return to the second hands-on exercise that described how to Telnet to a Web server and view the associated documents on that server. Look to the left of the listed files and note the various letters that indicate different levels of permission for different users.

CHAPTER 7

The Expert User: Workgroups, Forms, Master Documents, and Macros

OBJECTIVES

AFTER READING THIS CHAPTER YOU WILL BE ABLE TO:

1. Describe how to highlight editing changes in a document, and how to review, accept, or reject those changes.
2. Save multiple versions of a document and/or save a document with password protection.
3. Create and modify a form containing text fields, check boxes, and a drop-down list.
4. Create and modify a table; perform calculations within a table.
5. Sort the rows in a table in ascending or descending sequence according to the value of a specific column in the table.
6. Create a master document; add and/or modify subdocuments.
7. Explain how macros facilitate the execution of repetitive tasks; record and run a macro; view and edit the statements in a simple macro.
8. Use the Copy and Paste commands to duplicate an existing macro; modify the copied macro to create an entirely new macro.

OVERVIEW

This chapter introduces several capabilities that will make you a true expert in Microsoft Word. The features go beyond the needs of the typical student and extend to capabilities that you will appreciate in the workplace, as you work with others on a collaborative project. We begin with a discussion of workgroup editing, whereby

303

suggested revisions from one or more individuals can be stored electronically within a document. This enables the original author to review each suggestion individually before it is incorporated into the document, and further, allows multiple people to work on a document in collaboration with one another.

The forms feature is covered as a means to facilitate data entry. Forms are ideal for documents that are used repetitively, where much of the text is constant but where there is variation in specific places (fields) within the document. The chapter also extends the earlier discussion on tables to include both sorting and calculations within a table, giving a Word document the power of a simple spreadsheet. We also describe the creation of a master document, a special type of structure that references one or more subdocuments, each of which is saved under a different name. A master document is useful when many individuals work on a common project, with each person assigned to a different task within the project.

The chapter ends with a discussion of macros, a technique that lets you automate the execution of any type of repetitive task. We create a simple macro to insert your name into a document, then we expand that macro to create a title page for any document. As always, the hands-on exercises enable you to implement the conceptual material at the computer.

WORKGROUPS

As a student, you have the final say in the content of your documents. In the workplace, however, it's common for several people to work on the same document. You may create the initial draft, then submit your work to a supervisor who suggests various changes and revisions. Word facilitates this process by enabling the revisions to be stored electronically within the document. The revisions can come from a single individual or from several persons working together on a project team or *workgroup*.

Consider, for example, Figure 7.1, which displays two different versions of a document. Figure 7.1a contains the original document with suggested revisions, whereas Figure 7.1b shows the finished document after the changes have been made. The persons who entered the revisions could have made the changes directly in the document, but decided instead to give the original author the opportunity to accept or reject each change individually. The suggestions are entered into the Word document and appear on screen and/or the printed page, just as they might appear if they had been marked with pencil and paper.

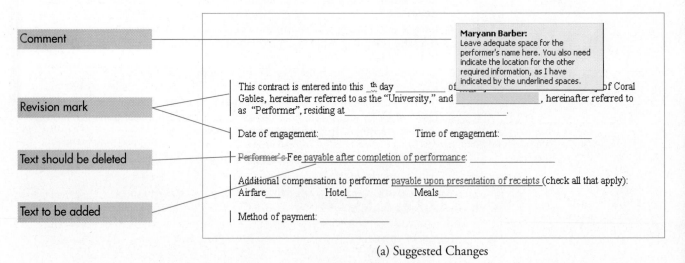

(a) Suggested Changes

FIGURE 7.1   *Workgroup Editing*

This contract is entered into this ___th day _____ of 20__, by and between the University of Coral Gables, hereinafter referred to as the "University," and _____, hereinafter referred to as "Performer", residing at _____.

Date of engagement: _____   Time of engagement: _____

Fee payable after completion of performance: _____

Additional compensation to performer payable upon presentation of receipts (check all that apply):
Airfare ___   Hotel ___   Meals ___

Method of payment: _____

(b) Revised Document

FIGURE 7.1   *Workgroup Editing (continued)*

The notation is simple and intuitive. A ***revision mark*** (a vertical line outside the left margin) signifies a change (an addition or deletion) has been made at that point in the document. A line through existing text indicates that the text should be deleted, whereas text that is underlined is to be added. The suggestions of multiple reviewers appear in different colors, with each reviewer assigned a different color. Yellow highlighting denotes a comment indicating that the reviewer has added a descriptive note without making a specific change. The comment appears on the screen when the cursor is moved over the highlighted text. (Comments can be printed at the end of a document.)

The review process is straightforward. The initial document is sent for review to one or more individuals, who enter their changes through tools on the ***Reviewing toolbar*** or through the ***Track Changes command*** in the Tools menu. The author of the original document receives the corrected document, then uses the ***Accept and Review Changes command*** to review the document and implement the suggested changes.

Versions

The Save command is one of the most basic in Microsoft Office. Each time you execute the command, the contents in memory are saved to disk under the designated filename, and the previous contents of the file are erased. What if, however, you wanted to retain the previous version of the file in addition to the current version that was just saved? You could use the Save As command to create a second file. It's easier to use the ***Versions command*** in the File menu because it lets you save multiple versions of a document in a single file.

The existence of multiple versions is transparent in that the latest version is opened automatically when you open the file at the start of a session. You can, however, review previous versions to see the changes that were made. Word displays the date and time each version was saved as well as the name of the person who saved each version.

Word provides two different levels of ***password protection*** in conjunction with saving a document. You can establish one password to open the document and a different password to modify it. A password can contain any combination of letters, numbers, and symbols, and can be 15 characters long. Passwords are case-sensitive.

Forms are ubiquitous in the workplace and our society. You complete a form, for example, when you apply for a job or open any type of account. The form may be electronic and completed online, or it may exist as a printed document. All forms, however, are designed for some type of data entry. Microsoft Word lets you create a special type of document called a *form*, which allows the user to enter data in specific places, but precludes editing the document in any other way. The process requires you to create the form and save it to disk, where it serves as a template for future documents. Then, when you need to enter data for a specific document, you open the original form, enter the data, and save the completed form as a new document.

Figure 7.2 displays a "forms" version of the document shown earlier in Figure 7.1. The form does not contain specific data, but it does contain the text of a document (a contract in this example) that is to be completed by the user. It also contains shaded entries, or *fields*, that represent the locations where the user enters the data. To complete the form, the user presses the Tab key to go from one field to the next and enters data as appropriate. Then, when all fields have been entered, the form is printed to produce the finished document (a contract for a specific event). The data that was entered into the various fields appears as regular text.

The form is created as a regular document with the various fields added through tools on the *Forms toolbar*. Word enables you to create three types of fields—text boxes, check boxes, and drop-down list boxes. A *text field* is the most common and is used to enter any type of text. The length of a text field can be set exactly; for example, to two positions for the day in the first line of the document. The length can also be left unspecified, in which case the field will expand to the exact number of positions that are required as the data is entered. A *check box*, as the name implies, consists of a box, which is checked or not. A *drop-down list box* enables the user to choose from one of several existing entries.

After the form is created, it is protected to prevent further modification other than data entry. Our next exercise has you open an existing document, review changes to that document as suggested by members of a workgroup, accept the changes as appropriate, then convert the revised document into a form for data entry.

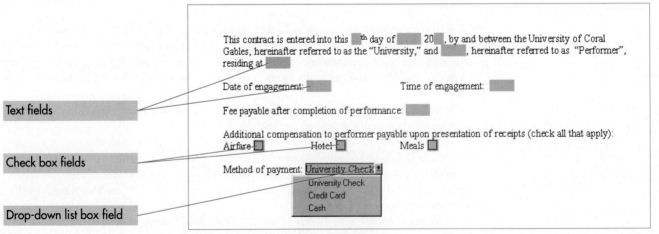

FIGURE 7.2   *A Blank Form*

WORKGROUPS AND FORMS

Objective To review the editing comments within a document; to create a form containing text fields, check boxes, and a drop-down list.

Step 1: **Display the Forms and Reviewing Toolbars**

> ➤ Start Word. If Word is already open, pull down the **File menu** and click the **Close command** to close any open documents.
> ➤ Point to any visible toolbar, click the **right mouse button**, then click the **Customize command** to display the Customize dialog box as shown in Figure 7.3a.
> ➤ If necessary, click the **Toolbars tab** in the Customize dialog box. The boxes for the Standard and Formatting toolbars should be checked.
> ➤ Check the boxes to display the **Forms** and **Reviewing toolbars** as shown in Figure 7.3a. Click the **Close button** to close the Customize dialog box.

Toolbars tab

Click Forms toolbar

Click Reviewing toolbar

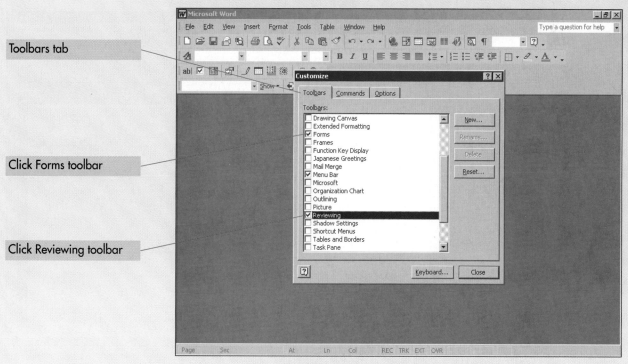

(a) Display the Forms and Reviewing Toolbars (step 1)

FIGURE 7.3 *Hands-on Exercise 1*

DOCKED VERSUS FLOATING TOOLBARS

A toolbar is either docked along an edge of a window or floating within the window. To move a docked toolbar, click and drag the move handle (the vertical line that appears at the left of the toolbar) to a new position. To move a floating toolbar, click and drag its title bar—if you drag a floating toolbar to the edge of the window, it becomes a docked toolbar and vice versa. You can also change the shape of a floating toolbar by dragging any border in the direction you want to go.

Step 2:   **Highlight the Changes**

➤ Open the document called **Contract** in the **Exploring Word folder** as shown in Figure 7.3b. Save the document as **Modified Contract**.

➤ Pull down the **Tools menu**, click (or point to) the **Track Changes command**.

➤ The Track Changes command functions as a toggle switch; that is, execute the command, and the tracking is in effect. Execute the command a second time, and the tracking is off. You can track changes in one of three ways:
  • Pull down the **Tools menu** and click the **Track Changes command**.
  • Double click the **TRK indicator** on the status bar.
  • Click the **Track Changes button** on the Reviewing toolbar.

➤ Tracking is in effect if you see the TRK indicator on the status bar.

➤ Press **Ctrl+Home** to move to the beginning of the document. Press the **Del key** four times to delete the word "The" and the blank space that follows. You will see an indication in the right margin that the text was deleted.

➤ Move to the end of the address (immediately after the zip code). Press the **space bar** three or four times, then enter the phone number, **(305) 111-2222**. The new text is underlined.

Deleted: The appears as a screen note

Entered text is green and underlined to indicate an addition

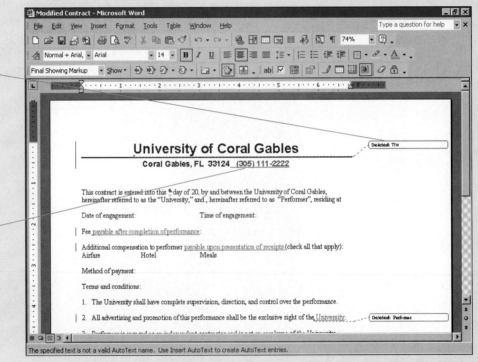

(b) Highlight the Changes (step 2)

FIGURE 7.3   *Hands-on Exercise 1 (continued)*

CHANGE THE EDITING MARKS

Red is the default color used to indicate changes to a document. Text that is added to a document is underlined in red, whereas text that is deleted is shown with a line through the deleted portion. You can, however, change either the color or the editing marks. Pull down the Tools menu, click the Track Changes command, click Highlight Changes to display the Highlight Changes dialog box, then click the Options buttons to display the Track Changes dialog box. Enter your editing preferences and click OK.

Step 3: **Accept or Reject Changes**

> ➤ Press **Ctrl+Home** to move to the beginning of the document, then click the **Next button** on the Reviewing toolbar to move to the first change, which is your deletion of the word "the".
> ➤ Click the **Accept Change button** to accept the change. Click the **Next button** to move to the next change, where you will review the next change.
> ➤ You can continue to review changes individually, or you can accept all of the changes as written. Click the **down arrow** on the Accept Change button and click **Accept All Changes in Document** as shown in Figure 7.3c.
> ➤ Save the document.

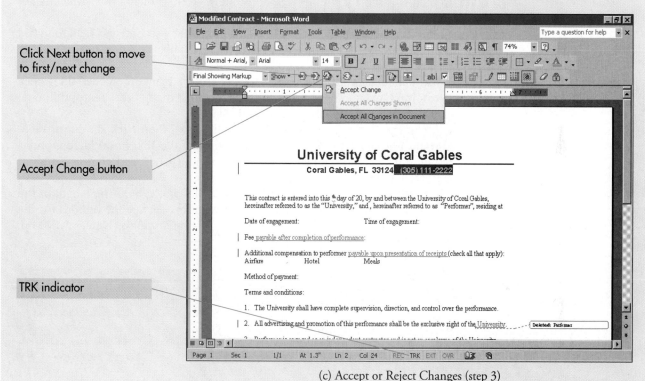

Click Next button to move to first/next change

Accept Change button

TRK indicator

(c) Accept or Reject Changes (step 3)

FIGURE 7.3   *Hands-on Exercise 1 (continued)*

INSERT COMMENTS INTO A DOCUMENT

Add comments to a document to remind yourself (or a reviewer) of action that needs to be taken. Click in the document where you want the comment to appear, then pull down the Insert menu and click the Comment command to open the Comments window. Enter the text of the comment, then close the Comments window. The word containing the insertion point is highlighted in yellow to indicate that a comment has been added. Point to the highlighted entry, and the text of the comment is displayed in a ScreenTip. Edit or delete existing comments by right clicking the comment, then choosing the Edit Comment or Delete Comment command.

Step 4: **Create the Text and Check Box Fields**

➤ Click the **Track Changes button** on the Reviewing toolbar to stop tracking changes, which removes the TRK indicator from the status bar. Click the button a second time and tracking is again in effect. (You can also double click the **TRK indicator** on the status bar to toggle tracking on or off.)

➤ Move to the first line of text in the contract, then click to the right of the space following the second occurrence of the word "this".

➤ Click the **Text Form Field button** on the Forms toolbar to create a text field as shown in Figure 7.3d. The field should appear in the document as a shaded entry (see boxed tip). Do not worry, however, about the length of this field as we adjust it shortly via the Text Form Field Options dialog box (which is not yet visible).

➤ Click after the word **of** on the same line and insert a second text field followed by a blank space. Insert the six additional text fields as shown in Figure 7.3d. Add blank spaces as needed before each field.

➤ Click immediately after the word **Airfare**. Add a blank, then click the **Check Box Form Field** to create a check box as shown in the figure. Create additional check boxes after the words **Hotel** and **Meals**.

➤ Click in the first text field (after the word *this*), then click the **Form Field Options button** on the Forms toolbar to display the Text Form Field Options dialog box. Click the **down arrow** in the Type list box and choose **Number**. Enter **2** in the Maximum Length box.

➤ Click **OK** to accept these settings and close the dialog box. The length of the form field changes automatically to two positions. Change the options for the Year (Number, 2 positions) and Date of Engagement fields (Date, MMMM d, yyyy format) in similar fashion. Save the document.

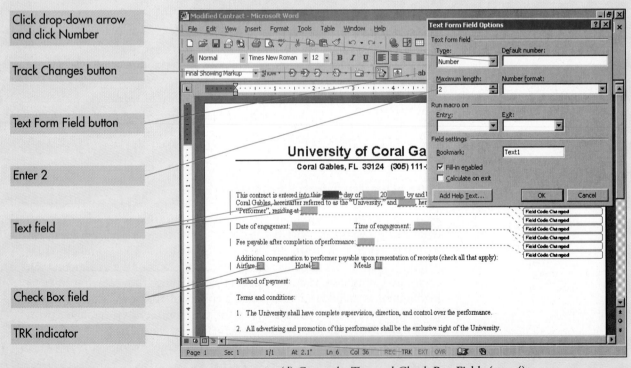

(d) Create the Text and Check Box Fields (step 4)

FIGURE 7.3 *Hands-on Exercise 1 (continued)*

Step 5:   **Add the Drop-Down List Box**

➤ Double click the **TRK indicator** on the status bar to stop tracking changes. (The indicator should be dim after double clicking.)

➤ Click the **down arrow** on the Accept Changes button on the Reviewing toolbar. Click **Accept All Changes in Document**.

➤ Click in the document after the words **Method of Payment**, then click the **Drop-down Form Field button** to create a drop-down list box. **Double click** the newly created field to display the dialog box in Figure 7.3e.

➤ Click in the Drop-down Item text box, type **University Check**, and click the **Add button** to move this entry to the Items in drop-down list box. Type **Credit Card** and click the **Add button**. Type **Cash**, then click the **Add button** to complete the entries for the drop-down list box.

➤ Click **OK** to accept the settings and close the dialog box. Save the document.

Click down arrow on Accept Changes button and click Accept All Changes in Document

Click Drop-down Form Field button

Enter items for drop-down list

Double click TRK indicator

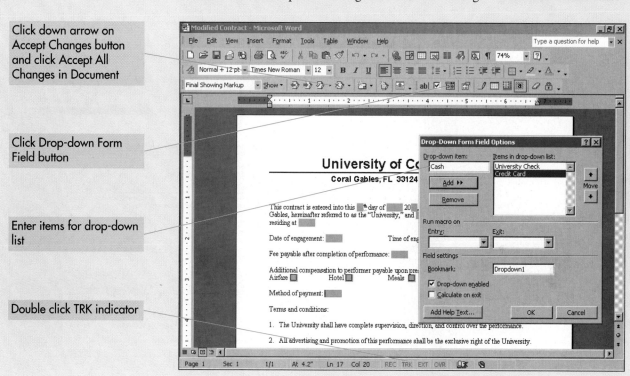

(e) Add the Drop-down List Box (step 5)

FIGURE 7.3   *Hands-on Exercise 1 (continued)*

FIELD CODES VERSUS FIELD RESULTS

All fields are displayed in a document in one of two formats, as a field code or as a field result. A field code appears in braces and indicates instructions to insert variable data when the document is printed; a field result displays the information as it will appear in the printed document. (The field results of a form field are blank until the data is entered into a form.) You can toggle the display between the field code and field result by selecting the field and pressing Shift+F9 during editing.

Step 6: **Save a New Version**

➤ Proofread the document to be sure that it is correct. Once you are satisfied with the finished document, click the **Protect Form button** on the Forms toolbar to prevent further changes to the form. (You can still enter data into the fields on the form, as we will do in the next step.)

➤ Pull down the **File menu** and click the **Versions command** to display the Versions dialog box for this document. There is currently one previous version, the one created by Robert Grauer on August 28, 1998.

➤ Click the **Save Now button** to display the Save Version dialog box in Figure 7.3f. Enter the text of a comment you want to associate with this version. The author's name will be different on your screen and will reflect the person who registered the version of Microsoft Word you are using.

➤ Click **OK** to save the version and close the dialog box.

Click Save Now button

Protect Form button

One existing version is listed

Enter comment on version

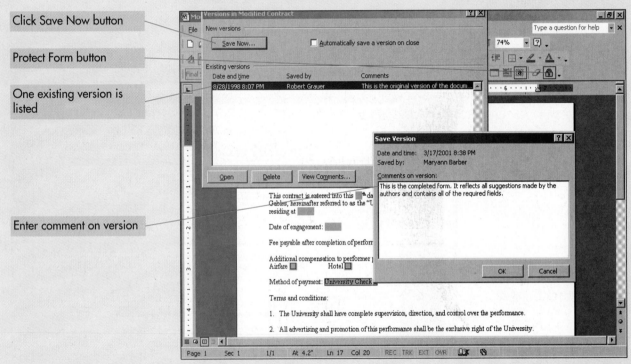

(f) Save a New Version (step 6)

FIGURE 7.3   *Hands-on Exercise 1 (continued)*

CREATE A BACKUP COPY

Microsoft Word enables you to automatically create a backup copy of a document in conjunction with the Save command. Pull down the Tools menu, click the Options button, click the Save tab, then check the box to Always create backup copy. The next time you save the file, the previously saved version is renamed "Backup of document", after which the document in memory is saved as the current version. In other words, the disk will contain the two most recent versions of the document.

Step 7: **Fill In the Form**

➤ Be sure that the form is protected; that is, that all buttons are dim on the Forms toolbar except for the Protect Form and Form Field Shading buttons. Press **Ctrl+Home** to move to the first field.

➤ Enter today's date, press the **Tab key** (to move to the next field), enter today's month, press the **Tab key**, and enter the year.

➤ Continue to press the **Tab key** to complete the form. Enter your name as the performer. Press the **space bar** on the keyboard to check or clear the various check boxes. Check the boxes for airfare, hotel, and meals, and enter a fee of $1,000. Click the **down arrow** on the Method of Payment list box and choose **University Check**.

➤ Your completed form should be similar to our form as shown in Figure 7.3g. You can make changes to the text of the contract by unprotecting the form. Do not, however, click the Protect Form button after data has been entered or you will lose the data.

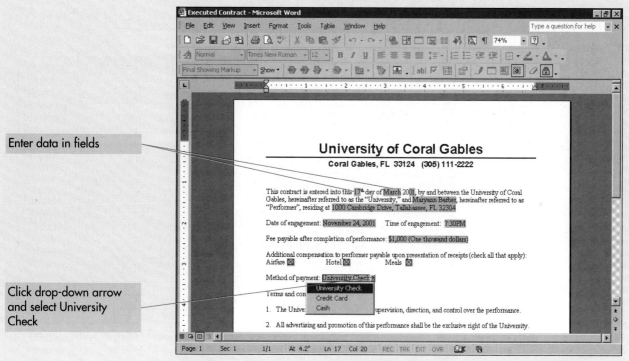

Enter data in fields

Click drop-down arrow and select University Check

(g) Fill In the Form (step 7)

FIGURE 7.3 *Hands-on Exercise 1 (continued)*

PROTECTING AND UNPROTECTING A FORM

The Protect Form button toggles protection on and off. Click the button once, and the form is protected; data can be entered into the various fields, but the form itself cannot be modified. Click the button a second time, and the form is unprotected and can be fully modified. Be careful, however, about unprotecting a form once data has been entered. That action will not create a problem in and of itself, but protecting a form a second time (after the data was previously entered) will reset all of its fields.

Step 8: **Password Protect the Executed Contract**

➤ Pull down the **File menu**, click the **Save As command** to display the Save As dialog box, then type **Executed Contract** as the filename.

➤ Click the **drop-down arrow** next to the Tools button and click the **General Options command** to display the Save dialog box in Figure 7.3h. Click in the **Password to open** text box and enter **password** (the password is case-sensitive) as the password. Click **OK**.

➤ A Confirm Password dialog box will open, asking you to reenter the password and warning you not to forget the password; once a document is protected by a password, it cannot be opened without that password. Reenter the password and click **OK** to establish the password.

➤ Click **Save** to save the document and close the Save As dialog box. Exit Word if you do not want to continue with the next exercise at this time.

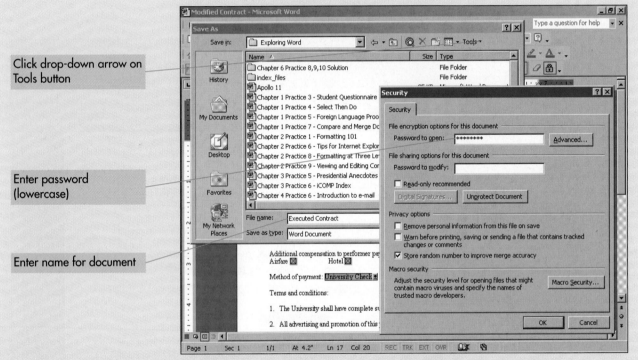

Click drop-down arrow on Tools button

Enter password (lowercase)

Enter name for document

(h) Password Protect the Executed Contract (step 8)

FIGURE 7.3 *Hands-on Exercise 1 (continued)*

AUTHENTICATE YOUR DOCUMENTS

What if you sent a contract or other important document to a third party and the document was intercepted and altered en route? Or more likely, what if someone sent a forged document to a third party in your name? You can avoid both situations by using a digital signature to authenticate your correspondence. A digital signature is an electronic stamp of authenticity that confirms the origin and status of an e-mail attachment. You can obtain a digital signature from a variety of sources, then use Word to apply that signature to any document. See exercise 6 at the end of the chapter.

Tables were introduced in an earlier chapter and provide an easy way to arrange text, numbers, and/or graphics within a document. This section extends that discussion to include calculations within a table, giving a Word document the power of a simple spreadsheet. We also describe how to *sort* the rows within a table in a different sequence, according to the entries in a specific column of the table.

We begin by reviewing a few basic concepts. The rows and columns in a table intersect to form *cells*, each of which can contain text, numbers, and/or graphics. Text is entered into each cell individually, enabling you to add, delete, or format text in one cell without affecting the text in other cells. The rows within a table can be different heights, and each row may contain a different number of columns.

The commands in the *Tables menu* or the *Tables and Borders toolbar* operate on one or more cells. The Insert and Delete commands add new rows or columns, or delete existing rows or columns, respectively. Other commands shade and/or border selected cells or the entire table. You can also select multiple cells and merge them into a single cell. All of this was presented earlier, and should be familiar.

Figure 7.4 displays a table of expenses that is associated with the performer's contract. The table also illustrates two additional capabilities that are associated with a table. First, you can sort the rows in a table to display the data in different sequences as shown in Figures 7.4a and 7.4b. Both figures display the same 6×4 table (six rows and four columns). The first row in each figure is a header row and contains the field names for each column. The next four rows contain data for a specific expense, while the last row displays the total for all expenses

Figure 7.4a lists the expenses in alphabetical order—airfare, hotel, meals, and performance fee. Figure 7.4b, however, lists the expenses in *descending* (high to low) *sequence* according to the amount. Thus the performance fee (the largest expense) is listed first, and the meals (the smallest expense) appear last. Note, too, that the sort has been done in such a way as to affect only the four middle rows; that is, the header and total rows have not moved. This is accomplished according to the select-then-do methodology that is used for many operations in Microsoft Word. You select the rows that are to be sorted, then you execute the command (the Sort command in the Tables menu in this example).

Figure 7.4c displays the same table as in Figure 7.4b, albeit in a different format that displays the field codes rather than the field results. The entries consist of formulas that were entered into the table to perform a calculation. The entries are similar to those in a spreadsheet. Thus, the rows in the table are numbered from one to six while the columns are labeled from A to D. The row and column labels do not appear in the table per se, but are used to enter the formulas.

The intersection of a row and column forms a cell. Cell D4, for example, contains the entry to compute the total hotel expense by multiplying the number of days (in cell B4) by the per diem amount (in cell C4). In similar fashion, the entry in cell D5 computes the total expense for meals by multiplying the values in cells B5 and C5, respectively. The formula is not entered (typed) into the cell explicitly, but is created through the Formula command in the Tables menu.

Figure 7.4d is a slight variation of Figure 7.4c in which the field codes for the hotel and meals have been toggled off to display the calculated values as opposed to the field codes. The cells are shaded, however, to emphasize that these cells contain formulas (fields), as opposed to numerical values. (The shading is controlled by the Options command in the Tools menu. The *field codes* are toggled on and off by selecting the formula and pressing the Shift+F9 key or by right clicking the entry and selecting the Toggle Field Codes command.)

The formula in cell D6 has a different syntax and sums the value of all cells directly above it. You do not need to know the syntax since Word provides a dialog box which supplies the entry for you. It's easy, as you shall see in our next hands-on exercise.

Header row

Expenses are in alphabetical order

Totals are displayed

Expense	Number of Days	Per Diem Amount	Amount
Airfare			$349.00
Hotel	2	$129.99	$259.98
Meals	2	$75.00	$150.00
Performance Fee			$1000.00
Total			**$1758.98**

(a) Expenses (Alphabetical Order by Expense)

Descending order by amount

Expense	Number of Days	Per Diem Amount	Amount
Performance Fee			$1000.00
Airfare			$349.00
Hotel	2	$129.99	$259.98
Meals	2	$75.00	$150.00
Total			**$1758.98**

(b) Expenses (Descending Order by Amount)

Column labels

Row labels

Field codes

	A	B	C	D
1	Expense	Number of Days	Per Diem Amount	Amount
2	Performance Fee			$1000.00
3	Airfare			$349.00
4	Hotel	2	$129.99	{=b4*c4}
5	Meals	2	$75.00	{=b5*c5}
6	Total			{=SUM(ABOVE)}

(c) Field codes

Shading indicates a cell formula

	A	B	C	D
1	Expense	Number of Days	Per Diem Amount	Amount
2	Performance Fee			$1000.00
3	Airfare			$349.00
4	Hotel	2	$129.99	$259.98
5	Meals	2	$75.00	$150.00
6	Total			$1758.98

(d) Field Codes (Toggles and Shading)

FIGURE 7.4 *Sorting and Table Math*

TABLE MATH

Objective   To open a password-protected document and remove the password protection; to create a table containing various cell formulas. Use Figure 7.5.

Step 1:   **Open the Document**

> Open the **Executed Contract** in the **Exploring Word folder** from the first exercise. You will be prompted for a password as shown in Figure 7.5a.
> Type **password** (in lowercase) since this was the password that was specified when you saved the document originally.
> Pull down the **File menu** and click the **Save As command** to display the Save As dialog box. Click the **Tools button**. Click **Security Options**.
> Click and drag to select the existing password (which appears as a string of eight asterisks). Press the **Del key** to remove the password. Click **OK** to close the Save dialog box. Click the **Save command button** to close the Save As dialog box. The document is no longer password protected.

Enter password (lowercase)

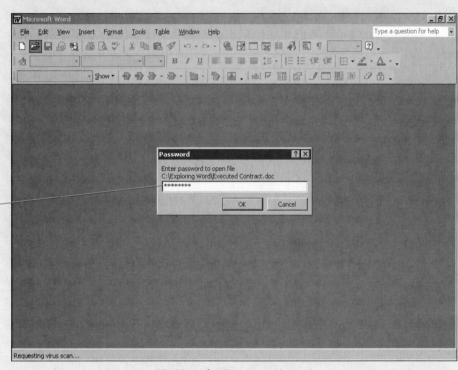

(a) Open the Document (step 1)

FIGURE 7.5   *Hands-on Exercise 2*

CHANGE THE DEFAULT FOLDER

The default folder is the folder where Word saves and retrieves documents unless it is otherwise instructed. To change the default folder, pull down the Tools menu, click Options, click the File Locations tab, click Documents, and click the Modify command button. Enter the name of the new folder (for example, C:\Exploring Word), click OK, then click the Close button.

Step 2: **Review the Contract**

➤ You should see the executed contract from the previous exercise. Click the **Protect Form button** on the Forms toolbar to unprotect the document so that its context can be modified.

➤ Do *not* click the Protect Form button a second time or else the data will disappear. (You can quit the document without saving the changes, as described in the boxed tip below.)

➤ Point to any toolbar, and click the **right mouse button** to display the list of toolbars shown in Figure 7.5b. Click the **Forms toolbar** to toggle the toolbar off (the check will disappear). Right click any toolbar a second time, and toggle the Reviewing toolbar off as well.

Right click an existing toolbar to display shortcut menu

Protect Form button

Click Forms toolbar to toggle it off

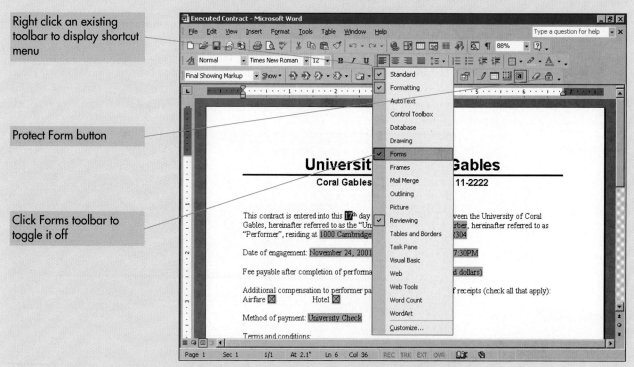

(b) Review the Contract (step 2)

FIGURE 7.5   *Hands-on Exercise 2 (continued)*

QUIT WITHOUT SAVING

There will be times when you do not want to save the changes to a document—for example, when you have edited it beyond recognition and wish you had never started. Pull down the File menu and click the Close command, then click No in response to the message asking whether you want to save the changes to the document. Pull down the File menu and reopen the file (it should be the first file in the list of most recently edited documents), then start over from the beginning.

Step 3:   **Create the Table**

➤ Press **Ctrl+End** to move to the end of the contract, then press **Ctrl+Enter** to create a page break. You should be at the top of page two of the document.
➤ Press the **enter key** three times and then enter **Summary of Expenses** in **24-point Arial bold** as shown in Figure 7.5c. Center the text. Press **enter** twice to add a blank line under the heading.
➤ Change to **12-point Times New Roman**. Click the **Insert Table button** on the Standard toolbar to display a grid, then drag the mouse across and down the grid to create a 6 × 4 table (six rows and four columns). Release the mouse to create the table.
➤ Enter data into the table as shown in Figure 7.5c. You can format the column headings by selecting multiple cells, then clicking the **Center button** on the Standard toolbar. In similar fashion, you can right justify the numerical data by selecting the cells and clicking the **Align Right button**.
➤ Save the document.

Insert Table button

Center button

Align Right button

Enter title and format as 24-point Arial bold, centered

Create a 6-row by 4-column table and enter data as shown

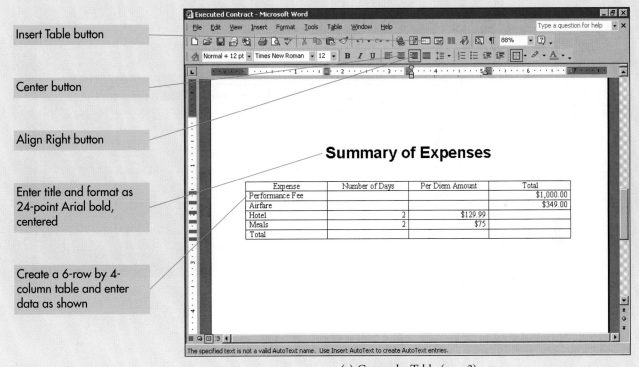

Summary of Expenses

Expense	Number of Days	Per Diem Amount	Total
Performance Fee			$1,000.00
Airfare			$349.00
Hotel	2	$129.99	
Meals	2	$75	
Total			

(c) Create the Table (step 3)

FIGURE 7.5   *Hands-on Exercise 2 (continued)*

TABS AND TABLES

The Tab key functions differently in a table than in a regular document. Press the Tab key to move to the next cell in the current row (or to the first cell in the next row if you are at the end of a row). Press Tab when you are in the last cell of a table to add a new blank row to the bottom of the table. Press Shift+Tab to move to the previous cell in the current row (or to the last cell in the previous row). You must press Ctrl+Tab to insert a regular tab character within a cell.

Step 4: **Sort the Table**

➤ Click and drag to select the entire table except for the last row. Pull down the **Table menu** and click the **Sort command** to display the Sort dialog box in Figure 7.5d.
➤ Click the **drop-down arrow** in the Sort by list box and select **Expense** (the column heading for the first column). The **Ascending option button** is selected by default.
➤ Verify that the option button to include a Header row is selected. Click **OK**. The entries in the table are rearranged alphabetically according to the entry in the Expenses column. The Total row remains at the bottom of the table since it was not included in the selected rows for the Sort command.
➤ Save the document.

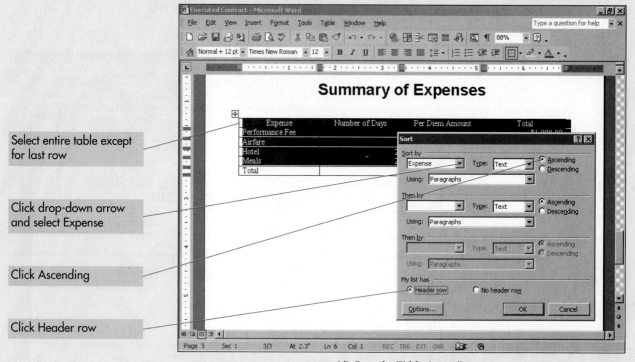

Select entire table except for last row

Click drop-down arrow and select Expense

Click Ascending

Click Header row

(d) Sort the Table (step 4)

FIGURE 7.5   *Hands-on Exercise 2 (continued)*

THE HEADER ROW

The first row in a table is known as the header row and contains the column names (headings) that describe the value in each column of the table. The header row is typically included in the range selected for the sort so that the Sort by list box displays the column names. The header row must remain at the top of the table, however, and thus it is important that the option button that indicates a header row be selected. In similar fashion, the last row typically contains the totals and should remain as the bottom row of the table. Hence it (the total row) is not included in the rows that are selected for sorting.

Step 5: **Enter the Formulas for Row Totals**

➤ Click in **cell D3** (the cell in the fourth column and third row). Pull down the **Table menu** and click the **Formula command** to display the Formula dialog box.

➤ Click and drag to select the =SUM(ABOVE) function, which is entered by default. Type **=b3*c3** as shown in Figure 7.5e to compute the total hotel expense. The total is computed by multiplying the number of days (in cell B3) by the per diem amount (in cell C3). Click **OK**. You should see $259.98 in cell D3.

➤ Click in **cell D4** and repeat the procedure to enter the formula **=b4*c4** to compute the total expense for meals. You should see $150.00 (two days at $75.00 per day). Save the document.

Click in D3

Enter formula =b3*c3

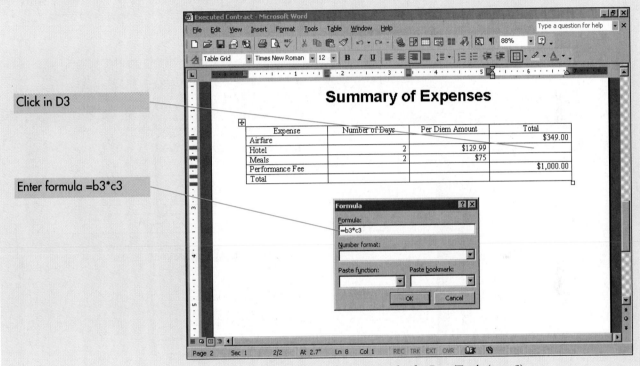

(e) Enter the Formulas for Row Totals (step 5)

FIGURE 7.5   *Hands-on Exercise 2 (continued)*

IT'S NOT EXCEL

Your opinion of table math within Microsoft Word depends on what you know about a spreadsheet. If you have never used Excel, then you will find table math to be very useful, especially when simple calculations are necessary within a Word document. If, on the other hand, you know Excel, you will find table math to be rather limited; for example, you cannot copy a formula from one cell to another, but must enter it explicitly in every cell. Nevertheless, the feature enables simple calculations to be performed entirely within Word, without having to link an Excel worksheet to a Word document.

➤ Click in **cell D6** (the cell in row 6, column 4), which is to contain the total of all expenses. Pull down the **Table menu** and click the **Formula command** to display the Formula dialog box in Figure 7.5f.

➤ The =SUM(ABOVE) function is entered by default. Click **OK** to accept the formula and close the dialog box. You should see $1,758.98 (the sum of the cells in the last column) displayed in the selected cell.

➤ Select the formula and press **Shift+F9** to display the code {=SUM (ABOVE)}. Press **Shift+F9** a second time to display the field value ($1,758.98).

➤ Click in **cell D2** (the cell containing the airfare). Replace $349 with **$549.00** and press the **Tab key** to move out of the cell. The total expenses are *not* yet updated in cell D6.

➤ Point to **cell D6**, click the **right mouse button** to display a context-sensitive menu, and click the **Update Field command**. Cell D6 displays $1,958.98, the correct total for all expenses.

Click in D6

=SUM(ABOVE) is entered by default

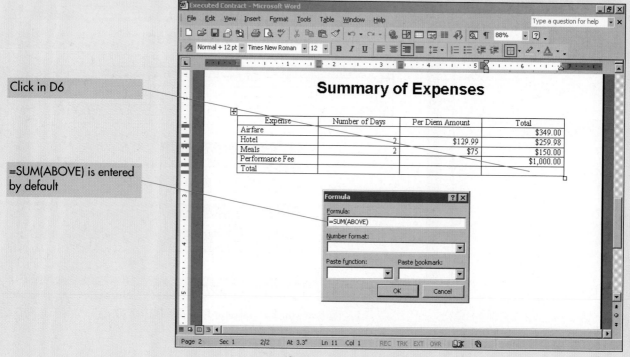

(f) Enter the SUM(ABOVE) Formula (step 6)

FIGURE 7.5 *Hands-on Exercise 2 (continued)*

FORMATTING A CALCULATED VALUE

Word does its best to format a calculation according to the way you want it. You can, however, change the default format by clicking the down arrow on the Number format list box and choosing a different format. You can also enter a format directly in the Number format text box. To display a dollar sign and comma without a decimal point, enter $#,##0 into the text box. You can use trial and error to experiment with other formats.

Step 7: **Print the Completed Contract**

➤ Zoom to two pages to preview the completed document. The first page contains the text of the executed contract that was completed in the previous exercise. The second page contains the table of expenses from this contract.

➤ Pull down the **File menu** and click the **Print command** to display the Print dialog box in Figure 7.5g. Click the **Options command button** to display the second Print dialog box.

➤ Check the box to include **Field codes** with the document. Click **OK** to close that dialog box, then click **OK** to print the document.

➤ Repeat the process to print the document a second time, but this time with field values, rather than field codes. Thus, pull down the **File menu**, click the **Print command** to display the Print dialog box, and click the **Options command button** to display a second Print dialog box.

➤ Clear the box to include **Field codes** with the document. Click **OK** to close that dialog box, then click **OK** to print the document.

➤ Exit Word if you do not want to continue with the next exercise at this time. Click **Yes** if asked to save the changes.

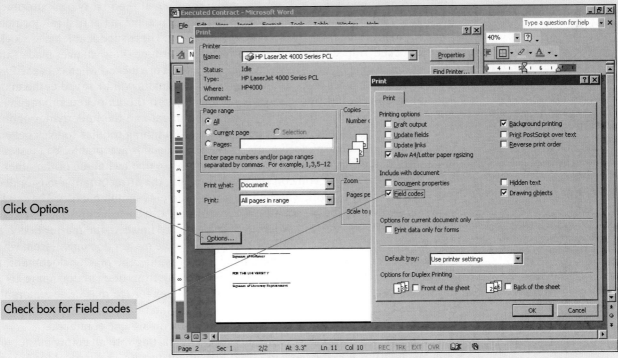

Click Options

Check box for Field codes

(g) Print the Completed Contract (step 7)

FIGURE 7.5 *Hands-on Exercise 2 (continued)*

DOCUMENT PROPERTIES

Prove to your instructor how hard you've worked by printing various statistics about your document, including the number of revisions and the total editing time. Pull down the File menu, click the Print command to display the Print dialog box, click the drop-down arrow in the Print What list box, select Document properties, then click OK.

A *master document* is composed of multiple *subdocuments*, each of which is stored as a separate file. The advantage of the master document is that you can work with several smaller documents, as opposed to a single large document. Thus, you edit the subdocuments individually and more efficiently than if they were all part of the same document. You can create a master document to hold the chapters of a book, where each chapter is stored as a subdocument. You can also use a master document to hold multiple documents created by others, such as a group project, where each member of the group is responsible for a section of the document.

Figure 7.6 displays a master document with five subdocuments. The subdocuments are collapsed in Figure 7.6a and expanded in Figure 7.6b. (The *Outlining toolbar* contains the Collapse and Expand Subdocument buttons, as well as other tools associated with master documents.) The collapsed structure in Figure 7.6a enables you to see at a glance the subdocuments that comprise the master document. You can insert additional subdocuments and/or remove existing subdocuments from the master document. Deleting a subdocument from within a master document does *not* delete the subdocument from disk.

The expanded structure in Figure 7.6b enables you to view and/or edit the contents of the subdocuments. Look carefully, however, at the first two subdocuments in Figure 7.6b. A padlock appears to the left of the first line in the first subdocument, whereas it is absent from the second subdocument. These subdocuments are locked and unlocked, respectively, and the distinction determines how changes made within the master document are saved. (All subdocuments are locked when collapsed as in Figure 7.6a.) Changes made to the locked subdocument will be saved in the master document, but not in the subdocument. Changes to the unlocked subdocument, however, will be saved in both the master document and the underlying subdocument. (The Lock Subdocuments button on the Outlining toolbar toggles between locked and unlocked subdocuments.) Either approach is acceptable. You just need to understand the difference, as you may want to use one technique or the other.

Regardless of how you edit the subdocuments, the attraction of a master document is the ability to work with multiple subdocuments simultaneously. The subdocuments are created independently of one another, with each subdocument stored in its own file. Then, when all of the subdocuments are finished, the master document is created and the subdocuments are inserted into the master document, from where they are easily accessed. Inserting page numbers into the master document, for example, causes the numbers to run consecutively from one subdocument to the next. You can also create a table of contents or index for the master document that will reflect the entries in all of the subdocuments. And finally you can print all of the subdocuments from within the master document with a single command.

Alternatively, you can reverse the process by starting with an empty master document and using it as the basis to create the subdocuments. This is ideal for organizing a group project in school or at work, the chapters in a book, or the sections in a report. Start with a new document, enter the topics assigned to each group member as headings within the master document, then use the *Create Subdocument command* to create subdocuments based on those headings. Saving the master document will automatically save each subdocument in its own file. This is the approach that we will follow in our next hands-on exercise.

The exercise also illustrates the *Create New Folder command* that lets you create a new folder on your hard drive (or floppy disk) from within Microsoft Word, as opposed to using Windows Explorer. The new folder can then be used to store the master document and all of its subdocuments in a single location apart from any other documents.

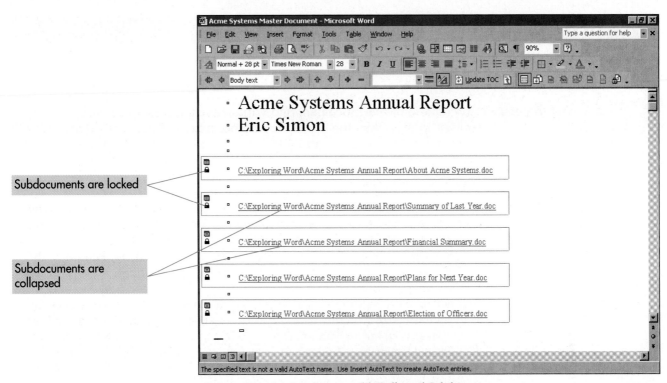

(a) Collapsed Subdocuments

Subdocuments are locked

Subdocuments are collapsed

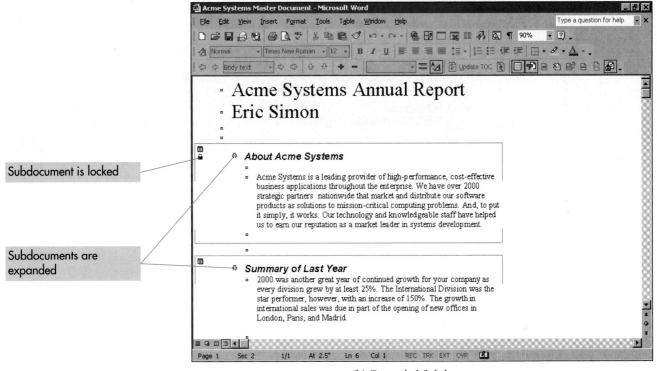

(b) Expanded Subdocuments

Subdocument is locked

Subdocuments are expanded

FIGURE 7.6 *A Master Document*

MASTER DOCUMENTS

Objective To create a master document and various subdocuments; to create a new folder from within the Save As dialog box in Microsoft Word. Use Figure 7.7 as a guide in the exercise.

Step 1: **Create a New Folder**

➤ Start Word. If necessary, click the **New button** on the Standard toolbar to begin a new document. Enter the text of the document in Figure 7.7a in **12-point Times New Roman**.

➤ Press **Ctrl+Home** to move to the beginning of the document. Pull down the **Style list box** on the Formatting toolbar, then select **Heading 2** as the style for the document title.

➤ Click the **Save button** to display the Save As dialog box. If necessary, click the **drop-down arrow** on the Save in list box to select the **Exploring Word folder** you have used throughout the text.

➤ Click the **Create New Folder button** to display the New Folder dialog box. Type **Acme Systems Annual Report** as the name of the new folder. Click **OK** to create the folder and close the New Folder dialog box.

➤ The Save in list box indicates that the Acme Systems Annual Report folder is the current folder. The name of the document, **About Acme Systems**, is entered by default (since this text appears at the beginning of the document).

➤ Click the **Save button** to save the document and close the Save As dialog box.

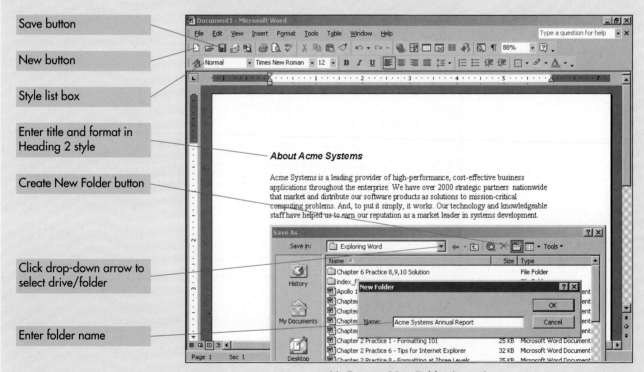

(a) Create a New Folder (step 1)

FIGURE 7.7 *Hands-on Exercise 3*

Step 2: **Create the Master Document**

➤ Click the **New button** on the Standard toolbar. Enter **Acme Systems Annual Report** as the first line of the document. Enter your name under the title.
➤ Press the **enter key** twice to leave a blank line or two after your name before the first subdocument. Type **Summary of Last Year** in the default typeface and size. Press **enter**. Enter the remaining topics, **Financial Summary**, **Plans for Next Year**, and **Election of Officers**.
➤ Change the format of the title and your name to **28-pt Times New Roman**.
➤ Pull down the **View menu** and click **Outline** to change to the Outline view. Click and drag to select the four headings as shown in Figure 7.7b. Click the **drop-down arrow** on the Style list box and select **Heading 2**.
➤ Be sure that all four headings are still selected. Press **Create Subdocument button**. Each heading expands automatically into a subdocument.

New button

Click drop-down arrow
and select Heading 2

Enter title and name

Click and drag to select
four headings

Create Subdocument
button

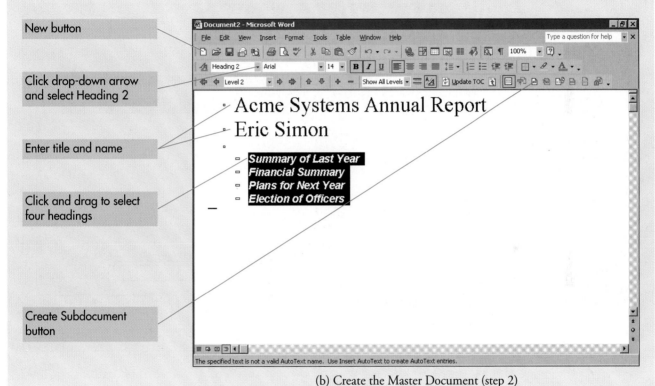

(b) Create the Master Document (step 2)

FIGURE 7.7 *Hands-on Exercise 3 (continued)*

THE CREATE SUBDOCUMENT BUTTON

You can enter subdocuments into a master document in one of two ways, through the Insert Subdocuments button if the subdocuments already exist, or through the Create Subdocument button to create the subdocuments from within the master document. Start a new document, enter the title of each subdocument on a line by itself that is formatted in a heading style, then click the Create Subdocument button to create the subdocuments. Save the master document. The subdocuments are saved automatically as individual files in the same folder.

Step 3: **Save the Documents**

➤ Click the **Save button** to display the Save As dialog box in Figure 7.7c. If necessary, click the **drop-down arrow** on the Save In list box to select the **Acme Systems Annual Report folder** that was created in step 1. You should see the About Acme Systems document in this folder.

➤ Enter **Acme Systems Master Document** in the File name list box, then click the **Save button** within the Save As dialog box to save the master document (which automatically saves the subdocuments in the same folder).

➤ Press the **Collapse Subdocuments button** to collapse the subdocuments. You will see the name of each subdocument as it appears on disk, with the drive and folder information. Press the **Expand Subdocuments button**, and the subdocuments are reopened within the master document.

Collapse Subdocuments button

Click drop-down arrow to select folder

Enter File name

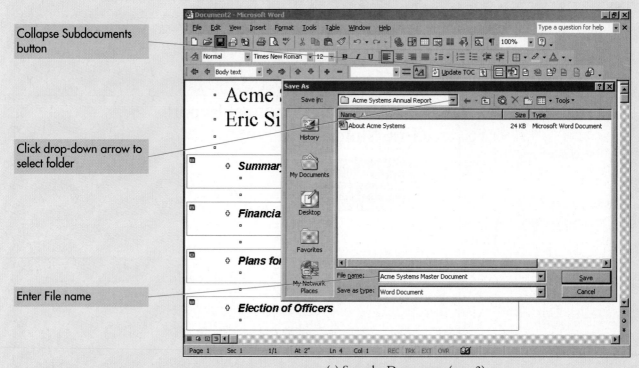

(c) Save the Documents (step 3)

FIGURE 7.7   *Hands-on Exercise 3 (continued)*

HELP WITH TOOLBAR BUTTONS

The Outlining toolbar is displayed automatically in the Outline view and suppressed otherwise. As with every toolbar you can point to any button to see a ToolTip with the name of the button. You can also press Shift+F1 to change the mouse pointer to a large arrow next to a question mark, then click any button to learn more about its function. The Outlining toolbar contains buttons that pertain specifically to master documents such as buttons to expand and collapse subdocuments, or insert and remove subdocuments. The Outlining toolbar also contains buttons to promote and demote items, to display or suppress formatting, and/or to collapse and expand the outline.

Step 4: **Insert a Subdocument**

➤ Click below your name, but above the first subdocument. Click the **Insert Subdocument button** to display the Insert Subdocument dialog box in Figure 7.7d. If necessary, click the **drop-down arrow** on the Look in list box to change to the Acme Systems Annual Report folder.

➤ There are six documents, which include the About Acme Systems document from step 1, the Acme Systems Master document that you just saved, and the four subdocuments that were created automatically in conjunction with the master document.

➤ Select the **About Acme Systems** document, then click the **Open button** to insert this document into the master document. Save the master document.

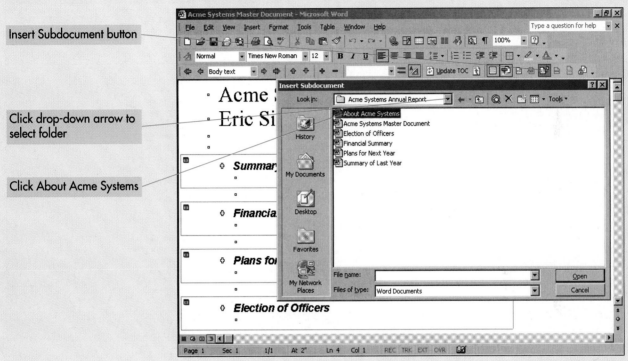

Insert Subdocument button

Click drop-down arrow to select folder

Click About Acme Systems

(d) Insert a Subdocument (step 4)

FIGURE 7.7 *Hands-on Exercise 3 (continued)*

CHANGE THE VIEW

The Outline view is used to create and/or modify a master document through insertion, repositioning, or deletion of its subdocuments. You can also modify the text of a subdocument within the Outline view and/or implement formatting changes at the character level such as a change in font, type size, or style. More sophisticated formatting, however, such as changes in alignment, indentation, or line spacing has to be implemented in the Normal or Print Layout views.

Step 5: **Modify a Subdocument**

➤ Click within the second subdocument, which will summarize the activities of last year. (The text of the document has not yet been entered.)

➤ Click the **Lock Document button** on the Outlining toolbar to display the padlock for this document. Click the **Lock Document button** a second time, which unlocks the document.

➤ Enter the text of the document as shown in Figure 7.7e, then click the **Save button** to save the changes to the master document. Be sure the subdocument is unlocked so that the changes you have made will be reflected in the subdocument file as well.

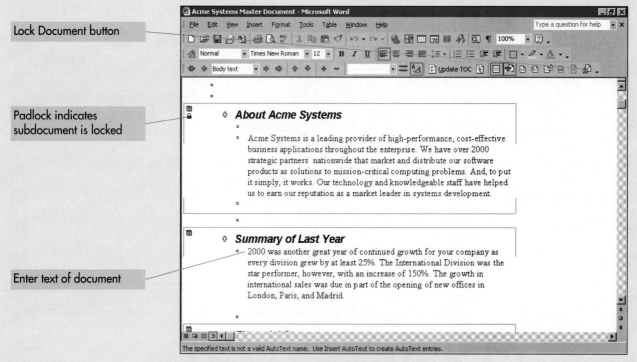

(e) Modify a Subdocument (step 5)

FIGURE 7.7 *Hands-on Exercise 3 (continued)*

OPEN THE SUBDOCUMENT

You can edit the text of a subdocument from within a master document, but it is often more convenient to open the subdocument when the editing is extensive. You can open a subdocument in one of two ways, by double clicking the document icon in the Outline view when the master document is expanded, or by clicking the hyperlink to the document when the Master Document is collapsed. Either way, the subdocument opens in its own window. Enter the changes into the subdocument, then save the subdocument and close its window to return to the master document, which now reflects the modified subdocument.

Step 6: **Print the Completed Document**

➤ Click the **Collapse Subdocuments button** to collapse the subdocuments as shown in Figure 7.7f. Click **OK** if asked to save the changes in the master document.

➤ Click the **Print button** on the Standard toolbar to print the document. Click **No** when asked whether to open the subdocuments before printing. The entire document appears on a single page. The text of the subdocuments is not printed, only the address of the documents.

➤ Click the **Print button** a second time, but click **Yes** when asked whether to open the subdocuments before printing.

➤ Submit both versions of the printed document to your instructor as proof that you did this exercise. Exit Word if you do not want to continue with the next exercise at this time.

Print button

Collapse/Expand Subdocuments button

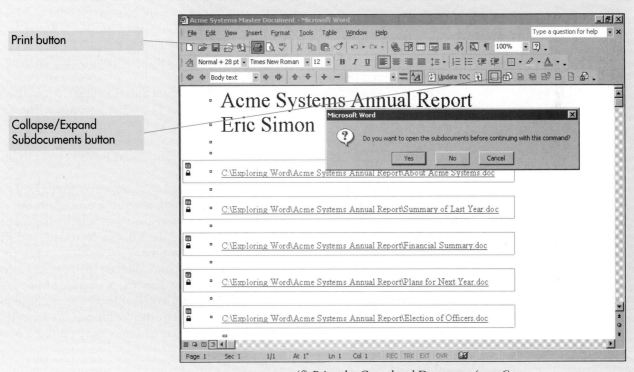

(f) Print the Completed Document (step 6)

FIGURE 7.7 *Hands-on Exercise 3 (continued)*

THE DOCUMENT MAP

The Document Map is one of our favorite features when working with large documents. Be sure that the master document is expanded to display the text of the subdocuments, then click the Document Map button on the Standard toolbar to divide the screen into two panes. The headings in a document are displayed in the left pane, and the text of the document is visible in the right pane. To go to a specific point in a document, click its heading in the left pane, and the insertion point is moved automatically to that point in the document, which is visible in the right pane. Click the Document Map button a second time to turn the feature off.

Have you ever pulled down the same menus and clicked the same sequence of commands over and over? Easy as the commands may be to execute, it is still burdensome to continually repeat the same mouse clicks or keystrokes. If you can think of any task that you do repeatedly, whether in one document or in a series of documents, you are a perfect candidate to use macros.

A *macro* is a set of instructions (that is, a program) that executes a specific task. It is written in *Visual Basic for Applications (VBA)*, a programming language that is built into Microsoft Office. Fortunately, however, you don't have to be a programmer to use VBA. Instead, you use the *macro recorder* within Word to record your actions, which are then translated automatically into VBA. You get results that are immediately usable, and you can learn a good deal about VBA through observation.

Figure 7.8 illustrates a simple macro to enter your name, date, and class into a Word document. We don't expect you to be able to write the VBA code by yourself, but, as indicated, you don't have to. You just invoke the macro recorder and let it create the VBA statements for you. It is important, however, for you to understand the individual statements so that you can modify them as necessary. Do not be concerned with the precise syntax of every statement, but try instead to get an overall appreciation of what the statements do.

Every macro begins and ends with a Sub and End Sub statement, respectively. These statements identify the macro and convert it to a VBA *procedure*. The *Sub statement* contains the name of the macro, such as NameAndCourse in Figure 7.8. (Spaces are not allowed in a macro name.) The *End Sub statement* is always the last statement in a VBA procedure. Sub and End Sub are Visual Basic key words and appear in blue.

The next several statements begin with an apostrophe, appear in green, and are known as *comments*. Comments provide information about the procedure, but do not affect its execution. The comments are inserted automatically by the macro recorder and include the name of the macro, the date it was recorded, and the author. Additional comments can be inserted at any time.

Every other statement in the procedure corresponds directly to a command that was executed in Microsoft Word. It doesn't matter how the commands were executed—whether from a pull-down menu, toolbar, or keyboard shortcut, because the end results, the VBA statements that are generated by the commands, are the same. In this example, the user began by changing the font and font size, and these com-

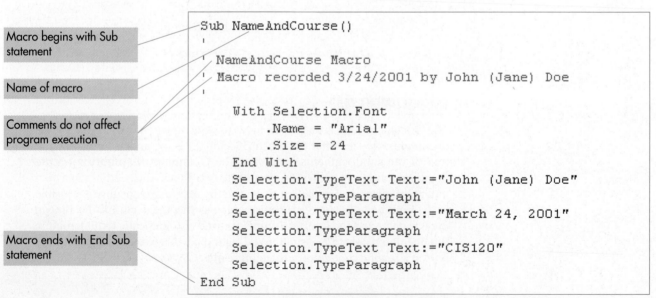

Macro begins with Sub statement

Name of macro

Comments do not affect program execution

Macro ends with End Sub statement

```
Sub NameAndCourse()
'
' NameAndCourse Macro
' Macro recorded 3/24/2001 by John (Jane) Doe
'
    With Selection.Font
        .Name = "Arial"
        .Size = 24
    End With
    Selection.TypeText Text:="John (Jane) Doe"
    Selection.TypeParagraph
    Selection.TypeText Text:="March 24, 2001"
    Selection.TypeParagraph
    Selection.TypeText Text:="CIS120"
    Selection.TypeParagraph
End Sub
```

FIGURE 7.8   *The NameAndCourse Macro*

mands were converted by the macro recorder to the VBA statements that specify Arial and 24-point, respectively. Next, the user entered his name and pressed the enter key to begin a new paragraph. Again, the macro recorder converts these actions to the equivalent VBA statements. The user entered the date, pressed the enter key, entered the class, and pressed the enter key. Each of these actions resulted in an additional VBA statement.

You do not have to write VBA statements from scratch, but you should understand their function once they have been recorded. You can also edit the statements after they have been recorded, to change the selected text and/or its appearance. It's easy, for example, to change the procedure to include your name instead of John Doe. All changes to a macro are done through the Visual Basic Editor.

The Visual Basic Editor

Figure 7.9a displays the NameAndCourse macro as it appears within the ***Visual Basic Editor (VBE)***. The Visual Basic Editor is a separate application (as can be determined from its button on the taskbar in Figure 7.9), and it is accessible from any application in Office XP. The left side of the VBE window displays the ***Project Explorer***, which is similar in concept and appearance to the Windows Explorer. Macros are stored by default in the Normal template, which is available to all Word documents. The VBA code is stored in the NewMacros module. (A ***module*** contains one or more procedures.)

The macros for the selected module (NewMacros in Figure 7.9) appear in the ***Code window*** in the right pane. (Additional macros, if any, are separated from one another by a horizontal line.) The VBA statements are identical to what we described earlier. The difference between Figure 7.8 and 7.9a is that the latter shows the macro within the Visual Basic Editor.

Figure 7.9b displays the TitlePage macro, which is built from the Name-AndCourse macro. The new macro (a VBA procedure) is more complicated than its predecessor. "Complicated" is an intimidating word, however, and we prefer to use "powerful" instead. In essence, the TitlePage procedure moves the insertion point to the beginning of a Word document, inserts three blank lines at the beginning of the document, then enters three additional lines that center the student's name, date, and course in 24-point Arial. The last statement creates a page break within the document so that the title appears on a page by itself. The macro recorder created these statements for us, as we executed the corresponding actions from within Word.

Note, too, that the TitlePage macro changed the way in which the date is entered to make the macro more general. The NameAndCourse macro in Figure 7.9a specified a date (March 24, 2001). The TitlePage macro, however, uses the VBA InsertDateTime command to insert the current date. We did not know the syntax of this statement, but we didn't have to. Instead we pulled down the Insert menu from within Word, and chose the Date and Time command. The macro recorder kept track of our actions and created the appropriate VBA statement for us. In similar fashion, the macro recorder kept track of our actions when we moved to the beginning of the document and when we inserted a page break.

A SENSE OF FAMILIARITY

Visual Basic for Applications has the basic capabilities found in any other programming language. If you have programmed before, whether in Pascal, C, or even COBOL, you will find all of the logic structures you are used to. These include the Do While and Do Until statements, the If-Then-Else statement for decision making, nested If statements, a Case statement, and calls to subprograms.

Project Explorer window

Selected module

Macro in selected module

Specific date

Specific course

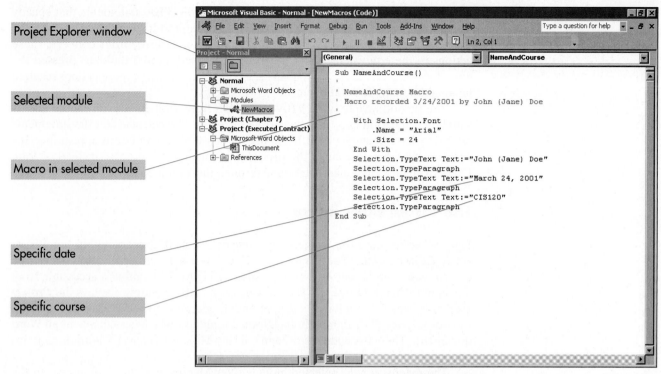

(a) NameAndCourse Macro

Command to Insert Date

User will specify course
during macro execution

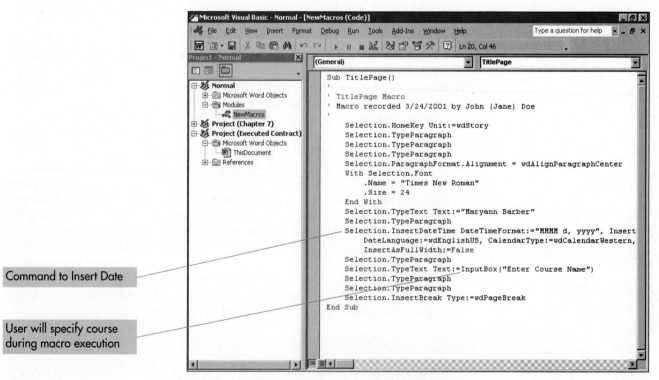

(b) TitlePage Macro

FIGURE 7.9   *The Visual Basic Editor*

INTRODUCTION TO MACROS

Objective To record, run, view, and edit simple macros; to run a macro from an existing Word document via a keyboard shortcut. Use Figure 7.10.

Step 1: **Create a Macro**

> ➤ Start Word. Open a new document if one is not already open.
> ➤ Pull down the **Tools menu**, click (or point to) the **Macro command**, then click **Record New Macro** to display the Record Macro dialog box in Figure 7.10a.
> ➤ Enter **NameAndCourse** as the name of the macro. (Do not leave any spaces.) If necessary, change the description to include your name.
> ➤ Click **Yes** if asked whether you want to replace the existing macro. (The existing macro may have been created by another student or if you previously attempted the exercise. Either way, you want to replace the existing macro.)
> ➤ Click **OK** to begin recording the macro. The mouse pointer changes to include a recording icon, and the Stop Recording toolbar is displayed.

Enter macro name

Change description to include your name

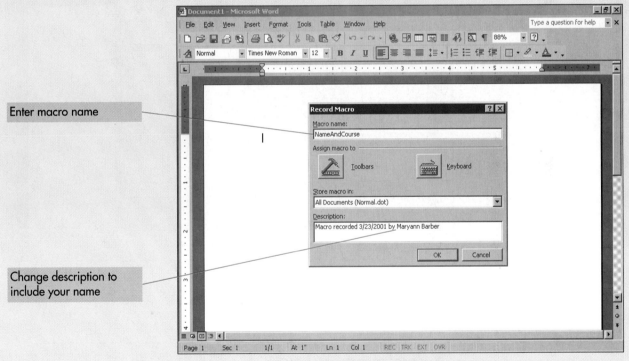

(a) Create a Macro (step 1)

FIGURE 7.10 *Hands-on Exercise 4*

MACRO NAMES

Macro names are not allowed to contain spaces or punctuation except for the underscore character. To create a macro name containing more than one word, capitalize the first letter of each word and/or use the underscore character; for example, NameAndCourse or Name_And_Course.

Step 2:   **Record the Macro**

➤ The first task is to change the font. Normally we would change the font by using the Font list box on the Formatting toolbar, but there appears to be a bug in the macro recorder in that the font change is not recorded from the list box. Thus, we changed the font via the Font list box.

➤ Pull down the **Format menu** and click the **Font command** to display the Font dialog box in Figure 7.10b. Select **14-point Arial**. Click **OK** to accept the setting and close the dialog box.

➤ Pull down the **Insert menu** and click the **Date and Time command** to display the Date and Time dialog box in Figure 7.10b. Choose the format of the date that you prefer. Check the box to **Update Automatically**, then click **OK** to accept the settings and close the dialog box. Press the **enter key**.

➤ Enter the course you are taking this semester. Press the **enter key** a final time. Click the **Stop Recording button** to end the macro.

Stop Recording toolbar

Stop Recording button

Click Arial

Click 14

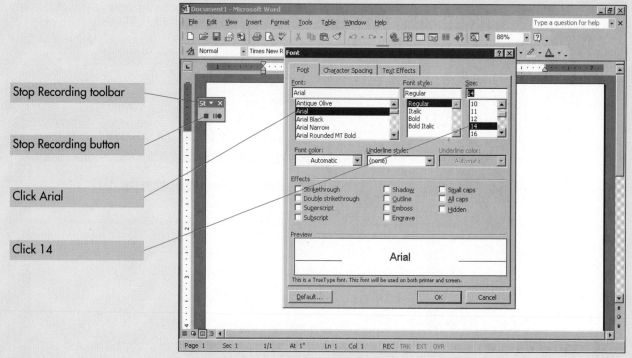

(b) Record the Macro (step 2)

FIGURE 7.10   *Hands-on Exercise 4 (continued)*

THE INSERT DATE COMMAND

A date is inserted into a document in one of two ways—as a field that is updated automatically to reflect the current date or as a specific value (the date and time on which the command is executed). The determination of which way the date is entered depends on whether the Update Automatically check box is checked or cleared, respectively. Be sure to choose the option that reflects your requirements.

Step 3:   **Test the Macro**

> ➤ Click and drag to select your name, date, and class, then press the **Del key** to erase this information from the document.
> ➤ Pull down the **Tools menu**. Click **Macro**, then click the **Macros . . . command** to display the Macros dialog box in Figure 7.10c. Select **NameAndCourse** (the macro you just recorded) and click **Run**.
> ➤ Your name and class information should appear in the document. The typeface is 14-point Arial, which corresponds to your selection when you recorded the macro initially. Do not be dismayed if the macro did not work properly as we show you how to correct it in the next several steps.
> ➤ Press the **enter key** a few times. Press **Alt+F8** (a keyboard shortcut) to display the Macros dialog box.
> ➤ Double click the **NameAndCourse** macro to execute the macro. Your name and class information is entered a second time.

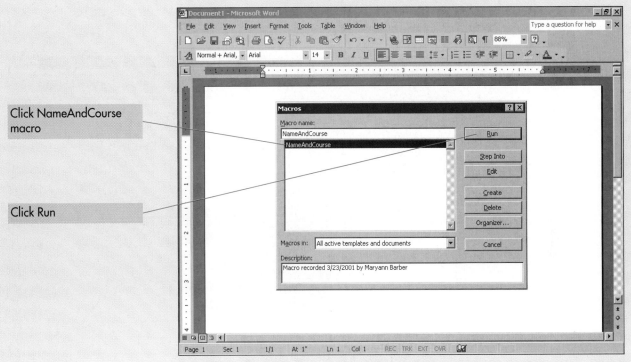

Click NameAndCourse
macro

Click Run

(c) Test the Macro (step 3)

FIGURE 7.10   *Hands-on Exercise 4 (continued)*

KEYBOARD SHORTCUTS

Take advantage of built-in shortcuts to facilitate the creation and testing of a macro. Press Alt+F11 to toggle between the VBA editor and the Word document. Use the Alt+F8 shortcut to display the Macros dialog box, then double click a macro to run it. You can also assign your own keyboard shortcut to a macro, as will be shown later in the exercise.

Step 4: **View the Macro**

➤ Pull down the **Tools menu**, click the **Macro command**, then click **Visual Basic Editor** (or press **Alt+F11**) to open the Visual Basic Editor. Maximize the VBE window. If necessary, pull down the **View menu** and click **Project Explorer** to open the Project window in the left pane. Close the Properties window if it is open.

➤ There is currently one project open, Document1, corresponding to the Word document on which you are working. Click the **plus sign** next to the Normal folder to expand that folder. Click the **plus sign** next to the **Modules folder** (within the Normal folder), then click **NewMacros**.

➤ Pull down the **View menu**, and click **Code** to open the Code window in the right pane. If necessary, click the **Maximize Button** in the Code window.

➤ Your screen should be similar to the one in Figure 7.10d except that it will reflect your name within the macro. The name in the comment statement may be different, however (especially if you are doing the exercise at school), as it corresponds to the person in whose name the program is registered.

➤ Delete the superfluous statements.

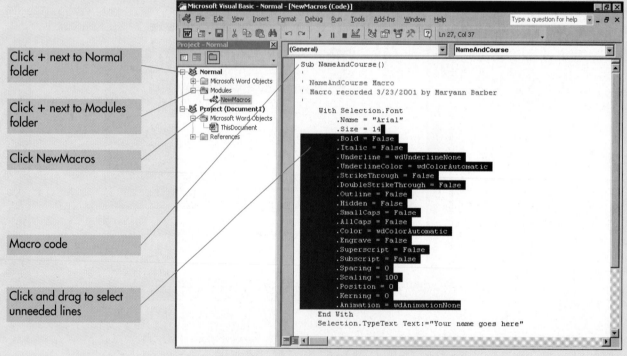

(d) View the Macro (step 4)

FIGURE 7.10 *Hands-on Exercise 4 (continued)*

RED, GREEN, AND BLUE

Visual Basic automatically assigns different colors to different types of statements (or a portion of those statements). Comments appear in green and are nonexecutable (i.e., they do not affect the outcome of a macro). Any statement containing a syntax error appears in red. Key words such as Sub and End Sub, With and End With, and True and False, appear in blue.

Step 5: **Edit the Macro**

➤ If necessary, change the name in the comment statement to reflect your name. The macro will run identically regardless of the changes in the comments. Changes to the statements within the macro, however, affect its execution.

➤ Click and drag to select the existing font name, **Arial**, then enter **Times New Roman** as shown in Figure 7.10e. Be sure that the **Times New Roman** appears within quotation marks. Change the font size to **24**.

➤ Click and drag to select the name of the course, which is "CIS120" in our example. Type **InputBox("Enter Course Name")** to replace the selected text.

➤ Note that as you enter the Visual Basic key word, InputBox, a prompt (containing the correct syntax) is displayed on the screen as shown in Figure 7.10e.

➤ Ignore the prompt and keep typing to complete the entry. Be sure you enter a closing parenthesis. Click the **Save button**.

Enter your name in comments

Enter Times New Roman

Enter 24

Enter InputBox statement

Prompt is displayed

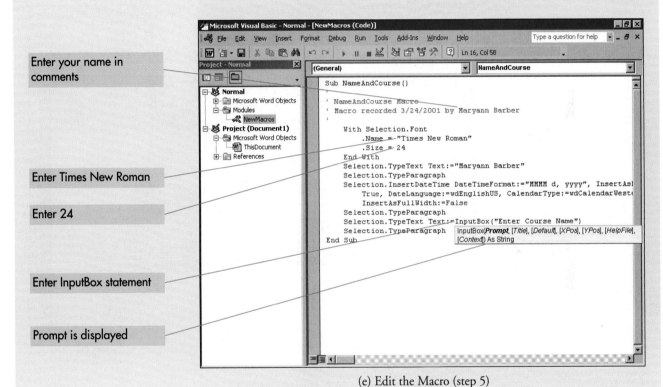

(e) Edit the Macro (step 5)

FIGURE 7.10   *Hands-on Exercise 4 (continued)*

COPY, RENAME, AND DELETE MACRO

You can copy a macro, rename it, then use the duplicate macro as the basis of a new macro. Click and drag to select the entire macro, click the Copy button, click after the End Sub statement, and click the Paste button to copy the macro. Click and drag to select the macro name in the Sub statement, type a new name, and you have a new (duplicate) macro. To delete a macro, click and drag to select the entire macro and press the Del key.

Step 6: **Test the Revised Macro**

➤ Press **Alt+F11** to toggle back to the Word document (or click the **Word button** on the taskbar). **Delete any text that is in the document**. If necessary, press **Ctrl+Home** to move to the beginning of the Word document.

➤ Press the **Alt+F8 key** to display the Macros dialog box, then double click the **NameAndCourse macro**. The macro enters your name and date, then displays the input dialog box shown in Figure 7.10f.

➤ Enter any appropriate course and click **OK** (or press the **enter key**). You should see your name, today's date, and the course you entered in 24-point Times New Roman type.

➤ Press **Alt+F11** to return to the Visual Basic Editor if the macro does not work as intended. Correct your macro so that its statements match those in step 5.

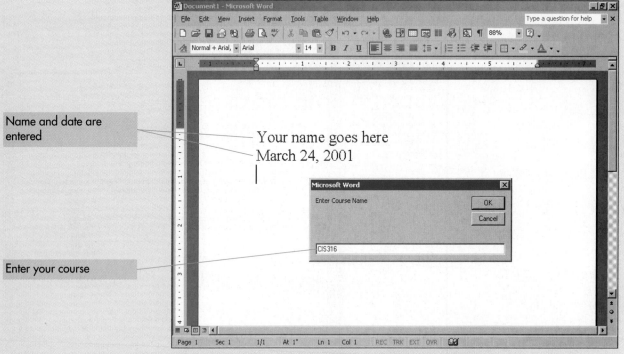

(f) Test the Revised Macro (step 6)

FIGURE 7.10 *Hands-on Exercise 4 (continued)*

HELP FOR VISUAL BASIC

Click within any Visual Basic key word, then press the F1 key for context-sensitive help. You will see a help screen containing a description of the statement, its syntax, key elements, and several examples. You can print the help screen by clicking the Options command button and selecting Print. (If you do not see the help screens, ask your instructor to install Visual Basic Help.)

Step 7: **Record the TitlePage Macro**

➤ If necessary, return to Word and delete the existing text in the document. Pull down the **Tools menu**. Click the **Macro command**, then click **Record New Macro** from the cascaded menu. You will see the Record Macro dialog box as described earlier.

➤ Enter **TitlePage** as the name of the macro. Do not leave any spaces in the macro name. Click the **Keyboard button** in the Record Macro dialog box to display the Customize Keyboard dialog box in Figure 7.10g. The insertion point is positioned in the Press New Shortcut Key text box.

➤ Press **Ctrl+T** to enter this keystroke combination as the new shortcut; note, however, that this shortcut is currently assigned to the Hanging Indent command:

  • Click the **Assign button** if you do not use the Hanging Indent shortcut,

  • *Or,* choose a different shortcut for the macro (or omit the shortcut altogether) if you are already using Ctrl+T for the Hanging Indent command.

➤ Close the Customize Keyboard dialog box.

➤ You are back in your document and can begin recording your macro:

  • Press **Ctrl+Home** to move to the beginning of the document.

  • Press the **enter key** three times to insert three blank lines.

  • Click the **Center button** to center the text that will be subsequently typed.

  • Press the **enter key** to create an additional blank line.

  • Press **Ctrl+Enter** to create a page break.

➤ Click the **Stop Recording button** to end the macro.

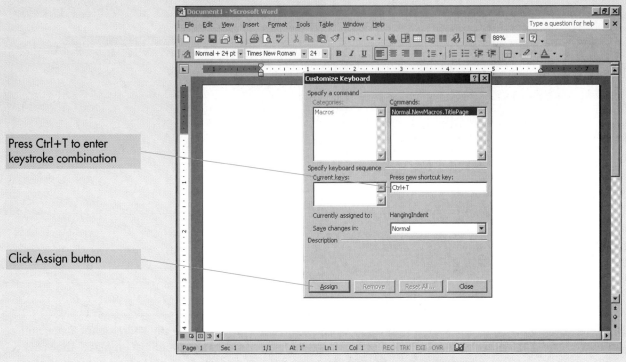

Press Ctrl+T to enter keystroke combination

Click Assign button

(g) Record the TitlePage Macro (step 7)

FIGURE 7.10 *Hands-on Exercise 4 (continued)*

Step 8: **Complete the TitlePage Macro**

➤ Press **Alt+F11** to return to the Visual Basic Editor. You should see two macros, NameAndCourse and TitlePage. Click and drag to select the statements in the **NameAndCourse macro** as shown in Figure 7.10h. Do not select the End Sub statement.

➤ Click the **Copy button** on the Standard toolbar (or use the **Ctrl+C** shortcut) to copy these statements to the clipboard.

➤ Move to the TitlePage macro and click after the VBA statement to center a paragraph. Press **enter** to start a new line. Click the **Paste button** on the Standard toolbar (or use the **Ctrl+V** shortcut) to paste the statements from the NameAndCourse macro into the TitlePage macro.

➤ You can see the completed macro by looking at Figure 7.10j, the screen in step 10. Click the **Save button** to save your macros.

➤ Press **Alt+F11** to return to Word. Pull down the File menu and click the **Close command** to close the document you were using to create the macros in this exercise. There is no need to save that document.

Copy button

Paste button

Click and drag to select macro statements

TitlePage macro

Click and press Enter to add a blank line

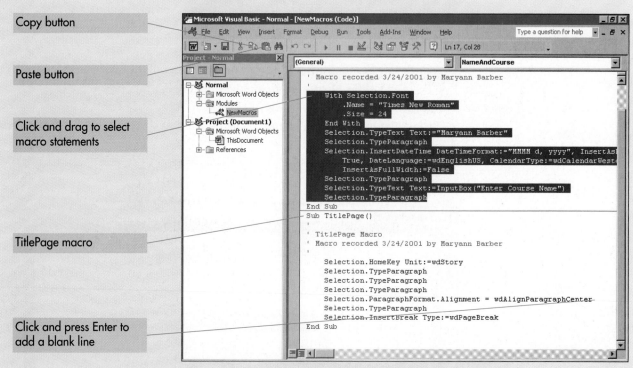

(h) Complete the TitlePage Macro (step 8)

FIGURE 7.10 *Hands-on Exercise 4 (continued)*

THE PAGE BORDER COMMAND

Add interest to a title page with a border. Click anywhere on the page, pull down the Format menu, click the Borders and Shading command, then click the Page Border tab in the Borders and Shading dialog box. You can choose a box, shadow, or 3-D style in similar fashion to placing a border around a paragraph. You can also click the drop-down arrow on the Art list box to create a border consisting of a repeating clip art image.

Step 9: **Test the TitlePage Macro**

➤ Open the completed Word document (Executed Contract) from the second hands-on exercise.
➤ Pull down the **Tools menu** and click the **Unprotect command**. Click anywhere in the document, then press **Ctrl+T** to execute the TitlePage macro.
➤ Your name and date should appear, after which you will be prompted for your course. Enter the course you are taking, and the macro will complete the title page.
➤ Pull down the **View menu** and change to the **Print Layout view**. Pull down the **View menu** a second time, click the **Zoom command**, click the option button for **Many Pages**, then click and drag the monitor to display three pages.
➤ You should see the executed contract with a title page as shown in Figure 7.10i. Print this document for your instructor. Save the document.

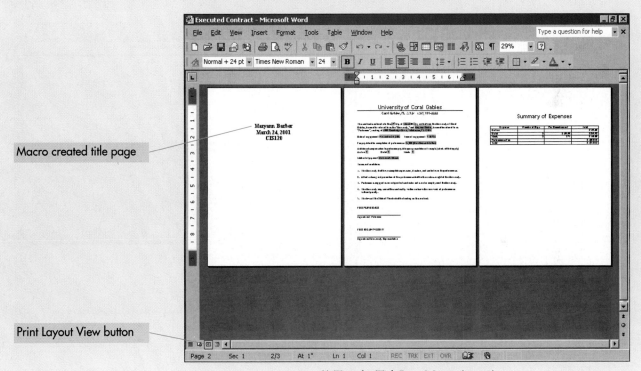

Macro created title page

Print Layout View button

(i) Test the TitlePage Macro (step 9)

FIGURE 7.10   *Hands-on Exercise 4 (continued)*

TROUBLESHOOTING

If the shortcut keys do not work, it is probably because they were not defined properly. Pull down the View menu, click Toolbars, click Customize, then click the Keyboard command button to display the Customize Keyboard dialog box. Drag the scroll box in the Categories list box until you can select the Macros category. Select (click) the macro that is to receive the shortcut and click in the Press New Shortcut Key text box. Enter the desired shortcut, click the Assign button to assign the shortcut, then click the Close button to close the dialog box.

Step 10: **Print the Module**

➤ Press **Alt+F11** to return to the Visual Basic Editor. Delete the second **Selection.TypeParagraph** line, as it is unnecessary.

➤ Pull down the **File menu**. Click **Print** to display the Print dialog box in Figure 7.10j. Click the option button to print the current module. Click **OK**. Submit the listing of the current module, which contains the procedures for both macros, to your instructor as proof you did this exercise.

➤ Delete all of the macros you have created in this exercise if you are not working on your own machine. Pull down the **File menu**. Click the **Close and Return to Word command**.

➤ Exit Word. The Title Page macro will be waiting for you the next time you use Microsoft Word provided you did the exercise on your own computer.

Click Current Module

Click OK

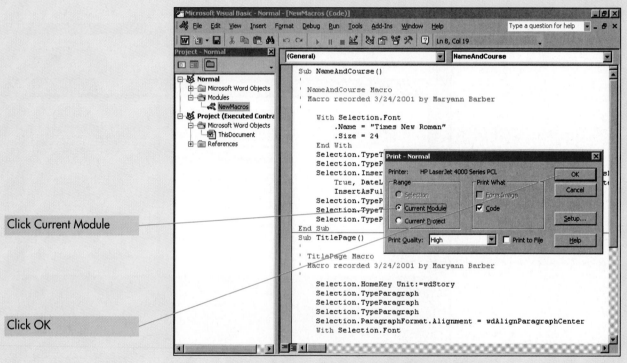

(j) Print the Module (step 10)

FIGURE 7.10 *Hands-on Exercise 4 (continued)*

INVEST IN MACROS

Creating a macro takes time, but that time can be viewed as an investment, because a well-designed macro will simplify the creation of subsequent documents. A macro is recorded once, tested and corrected as necessary, then run (executed) many times. It is stored by default in the Normal template, where it is available to every Word document. Yes, it takes time to create a meaningful macro, but once that's done, it is only a keystroke away.

Multiple persons within a workgroup can review a document and have their revisions stored electronically within that document. The changes are entered via various tools on the Reviewing toolbar. A red line through existing text indicates that the text should be deleted, whereas text that is underlined is to be added. Yellow highlighting indicates a comment where the reviewer has added a descriptive note without making a specific change.

A form facilitates data entry when the document is made available to multiple individuals via a network. It is created as a regular document with the various fields added through tools on the Forms toolbar. Word enables you to create three types of fields—text boxes, check boxes, and drop-down list boxes. After the form is created, it is protected to prevent further modification other than data entry.

The rows in a table can be sorted to display the data in ascending or descending sequence, according to the values in one or more columns in the table. Sorting is accomplished by selecting the rows within the table that are to be sorted, then executing the Sort command in the Tables menu. Calculations can be performed within a table using the Formula command in the Tables menu.

A master document consists of multiple subdocuments, each of which is stored as a separate file. It is especially useful for very large documents such as a book or dissertation, which can be divided into smaller, more manageable documents. The attraction of a master document is that you can work with multiple subdocuments simultaneously.

A macro is a set of instructions that automates a repetitive task. It is in essence a program, and its instructions are written in Visual Basic for Applications (VBA), a programming language. A macro is created initially through the macro recorder in Microsoft Word, which records your commands and generates the corresponding VBA statements. Once a macro has been created, it can be edited manually by inserting, deleting, or changing its statements. A macro is run (executed) by the Run command in the Tools menu or more easily through a keyboard shortcut.

KEY TERMS

Accept and Review Changes command (p. 305)
Cells (p. 315)
Check box (p. 306)
Code window (p. 333)
Comment (p. 332)
Create New Folder command (p. 324)
Create Subdocument command (p. 324)
Descending sequence (p. 315)
Drop-down list box (p. 306)
End Sub statement (p. 332)
Field (p. 306)
Field codes (p. 315)

Form (p. 306)
Forms toolbar (p. 306)
Header row (p. 320)
InputBox function (p. 339)
Insert Date command (p. 336)
Keyboard shortcut (p. 337)
Macro (p. 332)
Macro recorder (p. 332)
Master document (p. 324)
Module (p. 333)
Outlining toolbar (p. 324)
Password protection (p. 305)
Procedure (p. 332)
Project Explorer (p. 333)
Reviewing toolbar (p. 305)

Revision mark (p. 305)
Shortcut key (p. 337)
Sort (p. 315)
Sub statement (p. 332)
Subdocument (p. 324)
Tables menu (p. 315)
Tables and Borders toolbar (p. 315)
Text field (p. 306)
Track Changes command (p. 305)
Versions command (p. 305)
Visual Basic for Applications (VBA) (p. 332)
Visual Basic Editor (VBE) (p. 333)
Workgroup (p. 304)

1. Which of the following is a true statement regarding password protection?
   (a) All documents are automatically saved with a default password
   (b) The password is case-sensitive
   (c) A password cannot be changed once it has been implemented
   (d) All of the above

2. Which statement describes the way revisions are marked in a document?
   (a) A red line appears through text that is to be deleted
   (b) A red underline appears beneath text that is to be added
   (c) Yellow highlighting indicates a comment, where the user has made a suggestion, but has not indicated the actual revision in the document
   (d) All of the above

3. Which of the following types of fields *cannot* be inserted into a form?
   (a) Check boxes
   (b) Text fields
   (c) A drop-down list
   (d) Radio buttons

4. Which of the following is true about a protected form?
   (a) Data can be entered into the form
   (b) The text of the form cannot be modified
   (c) Both (a) and (b)
   (d) Neither (a) nor (b)

5. Which of the following describes the function of the Form Field Shading button on the Forms toolbar?
   (a) Clicking the button shades every field in the form
   (b) Clicking the button shades every field in the form and also prevents further modification to the form
   (c) Clicking the button removes the shading from every field
   (d) Clicking the button toggles the shading on or off

6. You have created a table containing numerical values and have entered the SUM(ABOVE) function at the bottom of a column. You then delete one of the rows included in the sum. Which of the following is true?
   (a) The row cannot be deleted because it contains a cell that is included in the sum function
   (b) The sum is updated automatically
   (c) The sum cannot be updated unless the Form Protect button is toggled off
   (d) The sum will be updated provided you right click the cell and select the Update field command

7. Which of the following is suitable for use as a master document?
   (a) An in-depth proposal that contains component documents
   (b) A lengthy newsletter with stories submitted by several people
   (c) A book
   (d) All of the above

8. Which of the following is true regarding changes made to a subdocument from within a master document?
   (a) The changes will be saved in the master document only
   (b) The changes will be saved in both the master document and the subdocument provided the subdocument is unlocked
   (c) The changes will be saved in both the master document and the subdocument provided the subdocument is locked
   (d) Changes cannot be made to a subdocument from within a master document

9. What happens if you click inside a subdocument, then click the Lock button on the Outlining toolbar?
   (a) The subdocument is locked
   (b) The subdocument is unlocked
   (c) The subdocument is locked or unlocked depending on its status prior to clicking the button
   (d) All editing to the subdocument is disabled

10. Which of the following describes the storage of a master document and the associated subdocuments?
    (a) Each document is saved under its own name as a separate file
    (b) All of the subdocuments must be stored in the same folder
    (c) Both (a) and (b)
    (d) Neither (a) nor (b)

11. Which of the following best describes the recording and execution of a macro?
    (a) A macro is recorded once and executed once
    (b) A macro is recorded once and executed many times
    (c) A macro is recorded many times and executed once
    (d) A macro is recorded many times and executed many times

12. Which of the following is true regarding comments in Visual Basic?
    (a) A comment is not executable; that is, its inclusion or omission does not affect the outcome of a macro
    (b) A comment begins with an apostrophe
    (c) Both (a) and (b)
    (d) Neither (a) nor (b)

13. Which commands are used to copy an existing macro so that it can become the basis of a new macro?
    (a) Copy command
    (b) Paste command
    (c) Both (a) and (b)
    (d) Neither (a) nor (b)

14. What is the default location for a macro created in Microsoft Word?
    (a) In the Normal template where it is available to every Word document
    (b) In the document in which it was created where it is available only to that document
    (c) In the Macros folder on your hard drive
    (d) In the Office folder on your hard drive

15. Which of the following correctly matches the shortcut to the associated task?
    (a) Alt+F11 toggles between Word and the Visual Basic Editor
    (b) Alt+F8 displays the Macros dialog box
    (c) Both (a) and (b)
    (d) Neither (a) nor (b)

ANSWERS

1. b	**6.** d	**11.** b
2. d	**7.** d	**12.** c
3. d	**8.** b	**13.** c
4. c	**9.** c	**14.** a
5. d	**10.** a	**15.** c

1. Reviewing a Document: Open the *Chapter 7 Practice 1* document shown in Figure 7.11, then revise that document by incorporating all of the suggested revisions. Delete the existing comment, which appears as a ScreenTip in Figure 7.11, then insert your own comment indicating that you have completed the necessary revisions. Click the Show button on the Reviewing toolbar to display the Reviewing Pane as shown in the figure. Note that the document contains revisions from multiple reviewers. Look closely and you will see that the comments for each reviewer appear in a different color. (You can also click the Show button, then click the Reviewers command to toggle the comments from individual reviewers on or off.)

   Save the revised document as its own version within the Chapter 7 Practice 1 document. Print both versions of the document, the original and the one you created, and include the associated comments and properties for each version. These elements can be included with the printed document by clicking the Options button within the Print command.

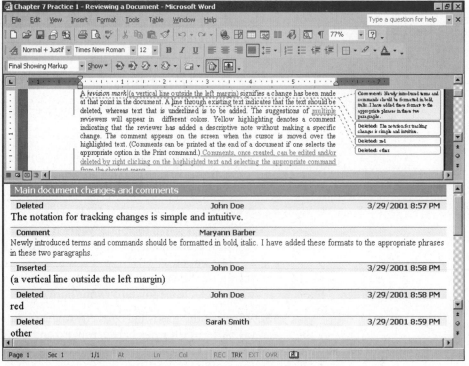

FIGURE 7.11   *Reviewing a Document (Exercise 1)*

2. Route a Document for Review: Do the first two hands-on exercises as described in the text, then send a copy of the executed contract to your instructor as shown in Figure 7.12. You can use the Send To Mail Recipient button on the Reviewing toolbar to start your e-mail program, which in turn attaches the document automatically. Alternatively, you can start your e-mail program independently, then use the Insert Attachment command to select the appropriate document.

   Either way, you will be sending an attached file to an e-mail recipient. You can include multiple attachments in the same message and/or send attachments of any file type. It's faster and cheaper than sending an overnight package.

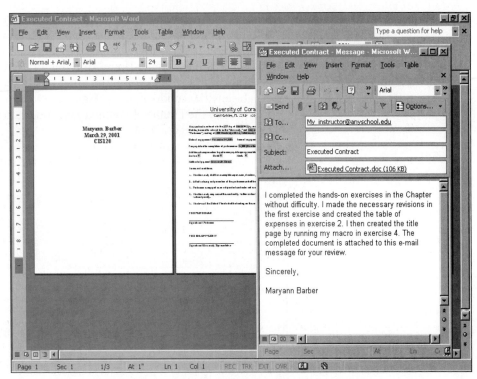

FIGURE 7.12 *Route a Document for Review (Exercise 2)*

3. Table Math: Figure 7.13 displays two versions of a table. Figure 7.13a shows the original table prior to any modification, whereas Figure 7.13b displays the table at the end of the exercise.
   a. Open the *Chapter 7 Practice 3* file in the Exploring Windows folder.
   b. Click in the cell containing "Enter your name" and enter your last name. (White was the person added in our exercise.)
   c. Sort the table so that the names appear in alphabetical order. (By coincidence the names in our example are in the same sequence after sorting.)
   d. Enter the appropriate formula for each person to compute the gain in sales.
   e. Enter the appropriate formulas in the total row to complete the totals as shown in Figure 7.13b.
   f. Add a short memo to your instructor indicating that you have completed the table. Print the memo twice, once with displayed values as shown in Figure 7.13b, then a second time to show the cell formulas.

Sales Person	Last Year	This Year	Gain
Brown	200	225	
Jones	200	300	
Smith	125	140	
Your Name Goes Here	100	450	
Total			

(a) Original Table (as it exists on disk)

Sales Person	Last Year	This Year	Gain
Brown	200	225	**25**
Jones	200	300	**100**
Smith	125	140	**15**
White	100	450	**350**
Total	**625**	**1115**	**490**

(b) Completed Table

FIGURE 7.13 *Table Math (Exercise 3)*

4. The Master Document: Do the third hands-on exercise as described in the chapter, then modify the master document as follows:

   a. Complete the subdocument, "Election of Officers" in which you propose nominations for the Board of Directors. Nominate yourself as the CEO and various classmates to fill the other positions.

   b. Delete the subdocument, "Plans for Next Year".

   c. Modify the Financial Summary document to include the table of fiscal results shown in Figure 7.14.

   d. Print the completed master document for your instructor. Print the document twice, in both the expanded and the collapsed format.

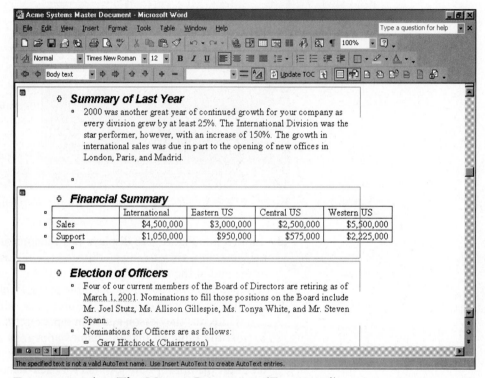

FIGURE 7.14 *The Master Document (Exercise 4)*

5. Customizing Toolbars and Menus: The chapter illustrated different ways to execute a macro—from the Tools menu in Word, by pressing Alt+F8 to display the Macros dialog box, and via a keyboard shortcut. You can also add a customized button to a toolbar (or a command to a menu) as shown in Figure 7.15. Do the following:

   a. Pull down the View menu, click Toolbars, then click Customize to display the Customize dialog box in Figure 7.15. Click the Commands tab, click the down arrow in the Categories list box until you see the Macros category, then click and drag the TitlePage macro from the Commands area in the Customize dialog box (it is not visible in Figure 7.15) to an existing toolbar. (You can add the macro to a menu by dragging the macro to the menu and placing it wherever you like within the commands in that menu.)

   b. Click the Modify Selection command button, click the Change Button Image command, then click the image you want for the toolbar button. Click the Modify Selection command button a second time, then click the Default style option to display just the image on the button as opposed to the image and the text. Click the Close button to accept the settings.

   c. Open an existing Word document, then click the button to test it. Experiment with other options in the Customize dialog box, then summarize your findings in a brief note to your instructor.

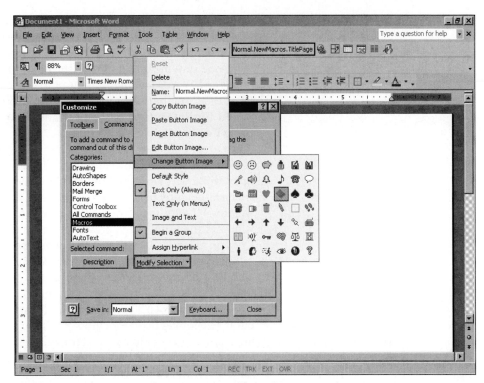

FIGURE 7.15 *Customizing a Toolbar (Exercise 5)*

6. Authenticating a Document: Open any document, pull down the Tools menu, click the Options command, then click the Security tab to display the dialog box in Figure 7.16. Click the Digital Signatures command button to display the associated dialog box, then click the Add button to authenticate the open document. Note, however, that you can add a signature only if you have applied for a digital certificate. Summarize your thoughts on authentication for your instructor.

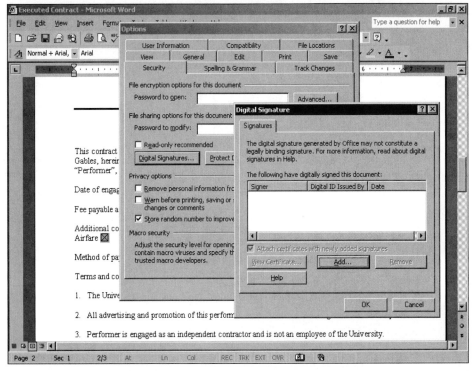

FIGURE 7.16 *Authenticating a Document (Exercise 6)*

7. Debugging a Macro: A "bug" is a mistake in a computer program; hence, "debugging" refers to the process of correcting a programming error. One useful tool for debugging a macro is the STEP Into command, in which you execute a macro one statement at a time as shown in Figure 7.17:

   a. Open any Word document, then press Alt+F11 to open the VBE window. Click the Close button in the left pane to close the Project window within the Visual Basic Editor. The Code window expands to take the entire Visual Basic Editor window.

   b. Point to an empty area on the Windows taskbar, then click the right mouse button to display a shortcut menu. Click Tile Windows Vertically to tile the open windows (Word and the Visual Basic Editor). Your desktop should be similar to Figure 7.16. It doesn't matter if the document is in the left or right window. (If additional windows are open on the desktop, minimize the other windows, then repeat the previous step to tile the open windows.)

   c. Click in the Visual Basic Editor window, then click anywhere within the TitlePage macro. Pull down the Debug menu and click the STEP Into command (or press the F8 key) to enter the macro. The Sub statement is highlighted. Press the F8 key a second time to move to the first executable statement (the comments are skipped). The statement is selected (highlighted), but it has not yet been executed. Press the F8 key again to execute this statement and move to the next statement.

   d. Continue to press the F8 key to execute the statements in the macro one at a time. You can see the effect of each statement as it is executed in the Word window.

   e. Do you think this procedure is useful in finding any bugs that might exist? Summarize the steps in debugging a macro in a short note to your instructor.

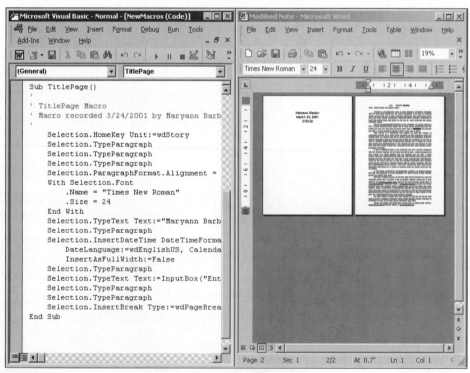

FIGURE 7.17   *Debugging a Macro (Exercise 7)*

Customize the Toolbar

The Create Envelope button is a perfect addition to the Standard toolbar if you print envelopes frequently. Pull down the Tools menu, click Customize, then click the Toolbars tab in the dialog box. If necessary, click the arrow in the Categories list box, select Tools, then drag the Create Envelope button to the Standard toolbar. Close the Customize dialog box. The Create Envelope button appears on the Standard toolbar and can be used the next time you need to create an envelope or label.

¿Cómo Está Usted?

The Insert Symbol command can be used to insert foreign characters into a document, but this technique is too slow if you use these characters with any frequency. Alternatively, you can use the predefined shortcut keys; for example, Ctrl+' followed by the letter "a" will insert á into a document. It's cumbersome, however, to remember the apostrophe, and we find it easier to create a macro and assign the shortcut Ctrl+A. Parallel macros can be developed for the other vowels or special characters, such as Ctrl+q for ¿. Try creating the appropriate macros, then summarize the utility of this technique in a short note to your instructor. Be sure to address the issue of using shortcuts that are already assigned to other macros; Ctrl+A, for example, is assigned to the Select All command by default.

Object Linking and Embedding

Table math is fine for simple calculations, but it is exceedingly limited when compared to Microsoft Excel. Thus, if you know Excel, you would be wise to explore the ability to link or embed an Excel workbook into a Word document. What is the difference between linking and embedding? Can the same workbook be associated with multiple Word documents? Does Object Linking and Embedding (OLE) pertain to applications other than Word and Excel? Use Chapter 5 as a starting point to learn about OLE, then summarize your findings in a short note to your instructor.

File Management in Microsoft Office

Most newcomers to Microsoft Office take the Open and Save As dialog boxes for granted. Look closely, however, and you will discover that these dialog boxes provide access to virtually all of the file management capabilities in Windows. You can create a folder, as was done in the chapter. You can also search for specific documents or create entries in the Favorites list. Write a short note to your instructor that summarizes the file management capabilities within the Open and Save dialog boxes. What additional capabilities are available through Windows Explorer that are not found within these dialog boxes?

Macros in Microsoft Excel

Do you use Microsoft Excel on a regular basis? Are there certain tasks that you do repeatedly, whether in the same document or in a series of different documents? If so, you would do well to explore the macro capabilities within Microsoft Excel. Does Excel have a macro recorder? Does it convert its macros to VBA? Can you modify an Excel macro after it has been created? Summarize the creation and execution of macros in Excel as compared to Word in a short note to your instructor.

APPENDIX A

Toolbars

OVERVIEW

Microsoft Word has multiple toolbars that provide access to commonly used commands. The toolbars are displayed in Figure A.1 and are listed here for convenience. They are: the Standard, Formatting, 3-D Settings, AutoText, Control Toolbox, Database, Diagram, Drawing, Drawing Canvas, Equation Editor, Extended Formatting, Forms, Frames, Function Key Display, Header/Footer, Japanese Greeting, Mail Merge, Microsoft, Organization Chart, Outlining, Picture, Reviewing, Shadow Settings, Shortcut Menus, Tables and Borders, Visual Basic, Web, Web Tools, Word Count, and WordArt. The Standard and Formatting toolbars are displayed by default and appear on the same row immediately below the menu bar. The other predefined toolbars are displayed (hidden) at the discretion of the user.

The buttons on the toolbars are intended to indicate their functions. Clicking the Printer button (the sixth button from the left on the Standard toolbar), for example, executes the Print command. If you are unsure of the purpose of any toolbar button, point to it, and a ScreenTip will appear that displays its name.

- To separate the Standard and Formatting toolbars and simultaneously display all of the buttons for each toolbar, pull down the Tools menu, click the Customize command, click the Options tab, then clear the check box that has the toolbars share one row. Alternatively, the toolbars appear on the same row so that only a limited number of buttons are visible on each toolbar and hence you may need to click the double arrow (More Buttons) tool at the end of the toolbar to view additional buttons. Additional buttons will be added to either toolbar as you use the associated feature, and conversely, buttons will be removed from the toolbar if the feature is not used.
- To display or hide a toolbar, pull down the View menu and click the Toolbars command. Select (deselect) the toolbar(s) that you want to display (hide). The selected toolbar(s) will be displayed in the same position as when last displayed. You may also point to any toolbar and click with the right mouse button to bring up a shortcut menu, after which you can select the toolbar to be displayed (hidden).

- To change the size of the buttons, suppress the display of the ScreenTips, or display the associated shortcut key (if available), pull down the View menu, click Toolbars, and click Customize to display the Customize dialog box. If necessary, click the Options tab, then select (deselect) the appropriate check box. Alternatively, you can right click on any toolbar, click the Customize command from the context-sensitive menu, then select (deselect) the appropriate check box from within the Options tab in the Customize dialog box.

- Toolbars are either docked (along the edge of the window) or floating (in their own window). A toolbar moved to the edge of the window will dock along that edge. A toolbar moved anywhere else in the window will float in its own window. Docked toolbars are one tool wide (high), whereas floating toolbars can be resized by clicking and dragging a border or corner as you would with any window.
  - To move a docked toolbar, click anywhere in the gray background area and drag the toolbar to its new location. You can also click and drag the move handle (the vertical line) at the left of the toolbar
  - To move a floating toolbar, drag its title bar to its new location.

- To customize one or more toolbars, display the toolbar(s) on the screen. Then pull down the View menu, click Toolbars, and click Customize to display the Customize dialog box. Alternatively, you can click on any toolbar with the right mouse button and select Customize from the shortcut menu.
  - To move a button, drag the button to its new location on that toolbar or any other displayed toolbar.
  - To copy a button, press the Ctrl key as you drag the button to its new location on that toolbar or any other displayed toolbar.
  - To delete a button, drag the button off the toolbar and release the mouse button.
  - To add a button, click the Commands tab in the Customize dialog box, select the category from the Categories list box that contains the button you want to add, then drag the button to the desired location on the toolbar. (To see a description of a tool's function prior to adding it to a toolbar, select the tool, then click the Description command button.)
  - To restore a predefined toolbar to its default appearance, click the Toolbars tab, select the desired toolbar, and click the Reset command button.

- Buttons can also be moved, copied, or deleted without displaying the Customize dialog box.
  - To move a button, press the Alt key as you drag the button.
  - To copy a button, press the Alt and Ctrl keys as you drag the button.
  - To delete a button, press the Alt key as you drag the button off the toolbar.

- To create your own toolbar, pull down the View menu, click Toolbars, click Customize, click the Toolbars tab, then click the New command button. Alternatively, you can click on any toolbar with the right mouse button, select Customize from the shortcut menu, click the Toolbars tab, and then click the New command button.
  - Enter a name for the toolbar in the dialog box that follows. The name can be any length and can contain spaces. Click OK.
  - The new toolbar will appear on the screen. Initially it will be big enough to hold only one button, but you can add, move, and delete buttons following the same procedures as for an existing toolbar. The toolbar will automatically size itself as new buttons are added and deleted.
  - To delete a custom toolbar, pull down the View menu, click Toolbars, click Customize, and click the Toolbars tab. *Verify that the custom toolbar to be deleted is the only one selected (highlighted).* Click the Delete command button. Click OK to confirm the deletion.

MICROSOFT WORD 2002 TOOLBARS

Standard Toolbar

New Blank Document · Save · Print Preview · Cut · Paste · Undo · Insert Hyperlink · Insert Table · Columns · Document Map · Zoom

Open · E-mail · Search · Print · Spelling and Grammar · Copy · Format Painter · Redo · Tables and Borders · Insert MS Excel Worksheet · Drawing · Show/Hide · Microsoft Word Help

Formatting Toolbar

Styles and Formatting · Font · Bold · Underline · Center · Justify · Numbering · Decrease Indent · Borders · Font Color

Style · Font Size · Italic · Align Left · Align Right · Line Spacing · Bullets · Increase Indent · Highlight

Normal | Times New Roman | 12

3-D Settings Toolbar

3-D On/Off · Tilt Up · Tilt Right · Direction · Surface

Tilt Down · Tilt Left · Depth · Lighting · 3-D Color

AutoText Toolbar

AutoText · Create AutoText

All Entries · New...

All Entries

Control Toolbox

Design Mode · View Code · Text Box · Option Button · Combo Box · Spin Button · Label · More Controls

Properties · Check Box · Command Button · List Box · Toggle Button · Scroll Bar · Image

Database Toolbar

Data Form · Add New Record · Sort Ascending · Insert Database · Find Record

Manage Fields · Delete Record · Sort Descending · Update Field · Mail Merge Main Document

Diagram Toolbar

Insert Shape · Move Shape Forward · Layout Menu · Change to Menu

Insert Shape | Layout ▾ | Change to ▾

Move Shape Backward · Reverse Diagram · AutoFormat · Text Wrapping

Drawing Toolbar

Draw Menu · AutoShapes Menu · Arrow · Oval · Insert WordArt · Insert Diagram or Organization Chart · Fill Color · Font Color · Dash Style · Shadow Style

Draw ▾ | AutoShapes ▾

Select Objects · Line · Rectangle · Text Box · Insert ClipArt · Insert Picture · Line Color · Line Style · Arrow Style · 3-D Style

FIGURE A.1   *Toolbars*

Drawing Canvas Toolbar

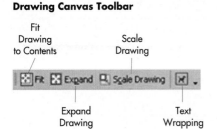

Fit Drawing to Contents

Scale Drawing

Expand Drawing

Text Wrapping

Extended Formatting Toolbar

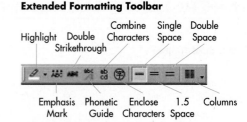

Highlight

Double Strikethrough

Combine Characters

Single Space

Double Space

Emphasis Mark

Phonetic Guide

Enclose Characters

1.5 Space

Columns

Equation Editor Toolbar

Relational Symbols

Spaces and Ellipses

Embellishments

Operator Symbols

Arrow Symbols

Logical Symbols

Set Theory Symbols

Miscellaneous Symbols

Greek Characters (lowercase)

Greek Characters (uppercase)

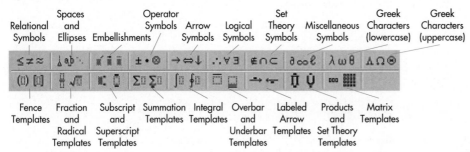

Fence Templates

Fraction and Radical Templates

Subscript and Superscript Templates

Summation Templates

Integral Templates

Overbar and Underbar Templates

Labeled Arrow Templates

Products and Set Theory Templates

Matrix Templates

Forms Toolbar

Text Form Field

Drop-down Form Field

Draw Table

Insert Frame

Reset Form Fields

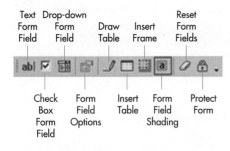

Check Box Form Field

Form Field Options

Insert Table

Form Field Shading

Protect Form

Function Key Display Toolbar

Frames Toolbar

Table of Contents in Frame

New Frame Right

New Frame Below

Frame Properties

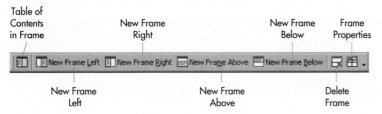

New Frame Left

New Frame Above

Delete Frame

Header/Footer Toolbar

Insert AutoText Menu

Insert Number of Pages

Insert Date

Page Setup

Same as Previous

Show Previous

Close Header and Footer

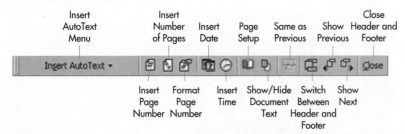

Insert Page Number

Format Page Number

Insert Time

Show/Hide Document Text

Switch Between Header and Footer

Show Next

FIGURE A.1   *Toolbars (continued)*

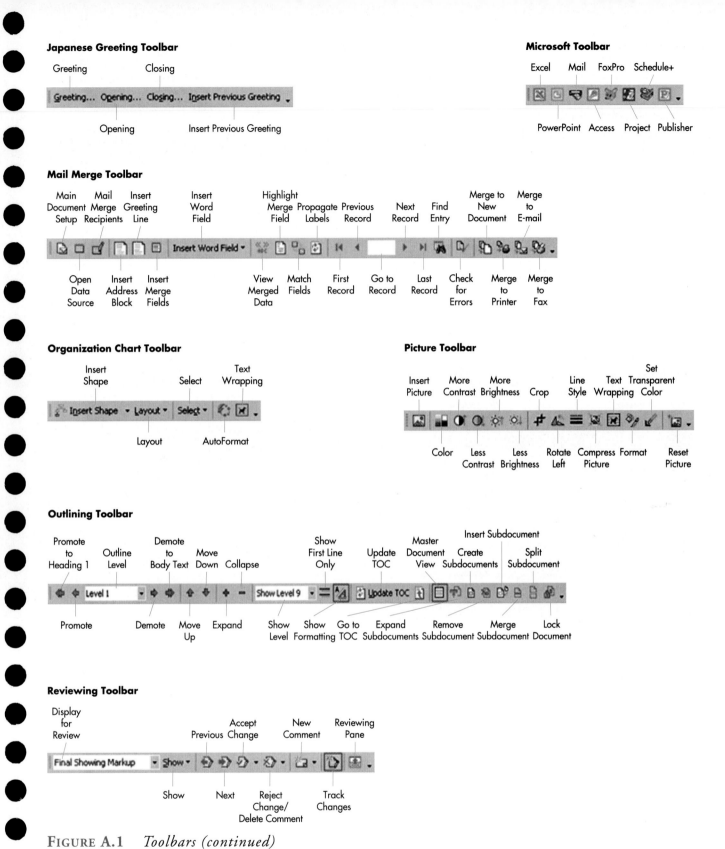

FIGURE A.1   *Toolbars (continued)*

Shadow Settings Toolbar

Shortcut Menus Toolbar

Text   Draw

Text ▾ Table ▾ Draw ▾

Table

Visual Basic Toolbar

Run
Macro   Security   Control   Microsoft
                          Toolbox   Script Editor

Record   Visual   Design
Macro   Basic   Mode
                 Editor

Tables and Borders Toolbar

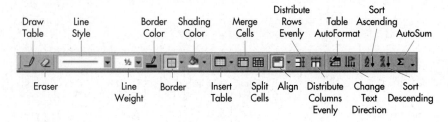

Web Toolbar

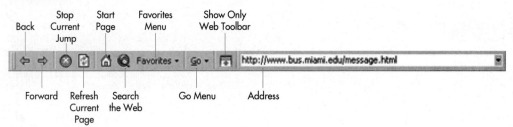

Web Tools Toolbar

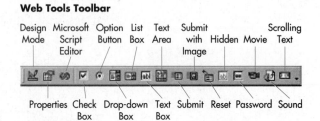

Word Count Toolbar

Word Count Statistics

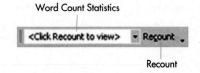

Recount

WordArt Toolbar

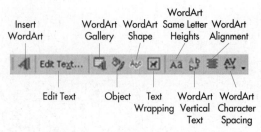

FIGURE **A.1**   *Toolbars (continued)*

CHAPTER 5

Consolidating Data: 3-D Workbooks and File Linking

OBJECTIVES

AFTER READING THIS CHAPTER YOU WILL BE ABLE TO:

1. Distinguish between a cell reference, a worksheet reference, and a 3-D reference; use appropriate references to consolidate data from multiple worksheets within a workbook.
2. Select and group multiple worksheets to enter common formulas and/or formats.
3. Use the AutoFormat command to format a worksheet.
4. Explain the advantage of using a function rather than a formula when consolidating data from multiple worksheets.
5. Explain the importance of properly organizing and documenting a workbook.
6. Use the Copy and Paste commands to copy selected data to a second workbook; copy an entire worksheet by dragging its tab from one workbook to another.
7. Distinguish between a source workbook and a dependent workbook; create external references to link workbooks.

OVERVIEW

This chapter considers the problem of combining data from different sources into a summary report. Assume, for example, that you are the marketing manager for a national corporation with offices in several cities. Each branch manager reports to you on a quarterly basis, providing information about each product sold in his or her office. Your job is to consolidate the data into a single report.

The situation is depicted graphically in Figure 5.1. Figures 5.1a, 5.1b, and 5.1c show reports for the Atlanta, Boston, and Chicago offices, respectively. Figure 5.1d shows the summary report for the corporation.

217

Atlanta Office

	Qtr 1	Qtr 2	Qtr 3	Qtr 4
Product 1	$10	$20	$30	$40
Product 2	$1,100	$1,200	$1,300	$1,400
Product 3	$200	$200	$300	$400

(a)

Boston Office

	Qtr 1	Qtr 2	Qtr 3	Qtr 4
Product 1	$55	$25	$35	$45
Product 2	$150	$250	$350	$450
Product 3	$1,150	$1,250	$1,350	$1,400

(b)

Chicago Office

	Qtr 1	Qtr 2	Qtr 3	Qtr 4
Product 1	$850	$950	$1,050	$1,150
Product 2	$100	$0	$300	$400
Product 3	$75	$150	$100	$200

(c)

Corporate Totals

	Qtr 1	Qtr 2	Qtr 3	Qtr 4
Product 1	$915	$995	$1,115	$1,235
Product 2	$1,350	$1,450	$1,950	$2,250
Product 3	$1,425	$1,600	$1,750	$2,000

(d)

FIGURE 5.1   *Consolidating Data*

You should be able to reconcile the corporate totals for each product in each quarter with the detail amounts in the individual offices. Consider, for example, the sales of Product 1 in the first quarter. The Atlanta office has sold $10, the Boston office $55, and the Chicago office $850; thus, the corporation as a whole has sold $915 ($10+$55+$850). In similar fashion, the Atlanta, Boston, and Chicago offices have sold $1,100, $150, and $100, respectively, of Product 2 in the first quarter, for a corporate total of $1,350.

The chapter presents two approaches to computing the corporate totals in Figure 5.1. One approach is to use the three-dimensional capability within Excel, in which one workbook contains multiple worksheets. The workbook contains a separate worksheet for each of the three branch offices, and a fourth worksheet to hold the corporate data. An alternate technique is to keep the data for each branch office in its own workbook, then create a summary workbook that uses file linking to reference cells in the other workbooks.

There are advantages and disadvantages to each technique, as will be discussed in the chapter. As always, the hands-on exercises are essential to mastering the conceptual material.

THE THREE-DIMENSIONAL WORKBOOK

An Excel workbook is the electronic equivalent of the three-ring binder. It contains one or more worksheets, each of which is identified by a tab at the bottom of the document window. The workbook in Figure 5.2, for example, contains four worksheets. The title bar displays the name of the workbook (Corporate Sales). The tabs at the bottom of the workbook window display the names of the individual worksheets (Summary, Atlanta, Boston, and Chicago). The highlighted tab indicates the name of the active worksheet (Summary). To display a different worksheet, click on a different tab; for example, click the Atlanta tab to display the Atlanta worksheet.

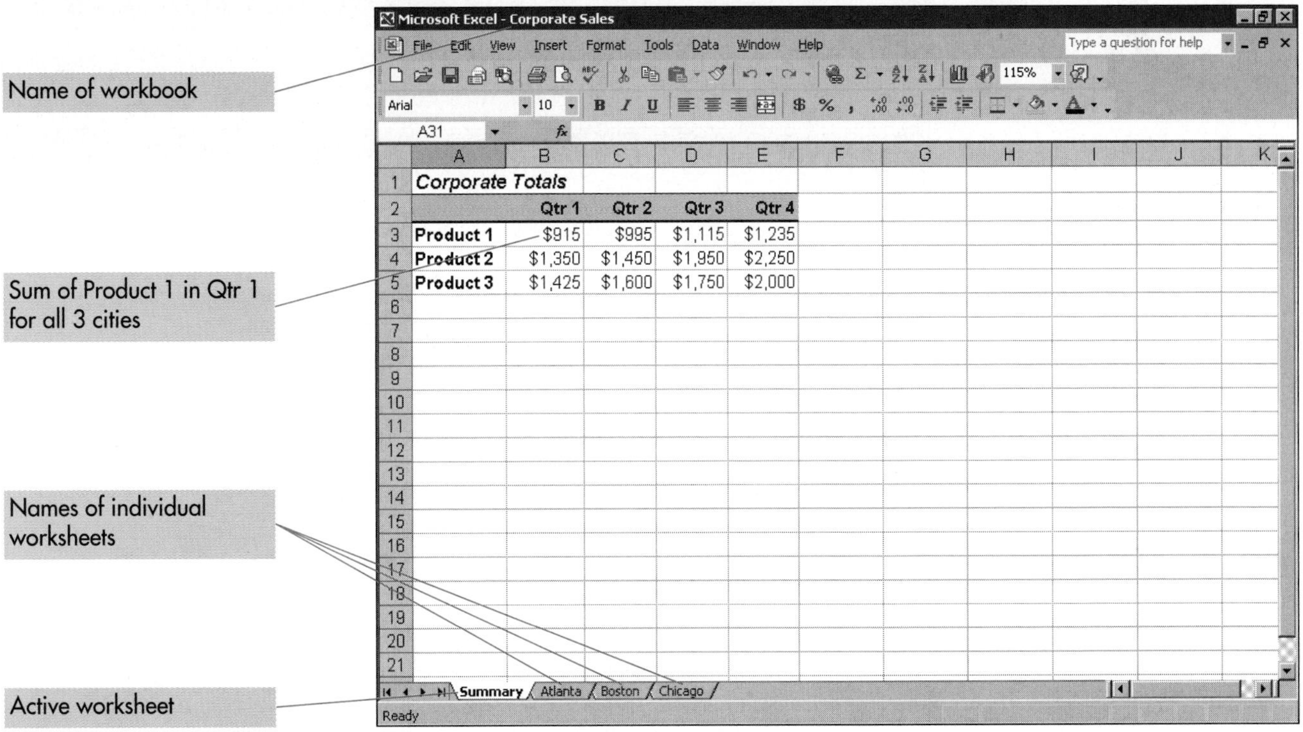

FIGURE 5.2 *A Three-dimensional Workbook*

The Summary worksheet shows the total amount for each product in each quarter. The data in the worksheet reflects the amounts shown earlier in Figure 5.1; that is, each entry in the Summary worksheet represents the sum of the corresponding entries in the worksheets for the individual cities. The amounts in the individual cities, however, are not visible in Figure 5.2. It is convenient, therefore, to open multiple windows in order to view the individual city worksheets at the same time you view the summary sheet.

Figure 5.3 displays the four worksheets in the Corporate Sales workbook, with a different sheet displayed in each window. The individual windows are smaller than the single view in Figure 5.2, but you can see at a glance how the Summary worksheet consolidates the data from the individual worksheets. The *New Window command* (in the Window menu) is used to open each additional window. Once the windows have been opened, the *Arrange command* (in the Window menu) is used to tile or cascade the open windows.

Only one window can be active at a time, and all commands apply to just the active window. In Figure 5.3, for example, the window in the upper left is active, as can be seen by the highlighted title bar. (To activate a different window, just click in that window.)

Copying Worksheets

The workbook in Figure 5.3 summarizes the data in the individual worksheets, but how was the data placed in the workbook? You could, of course, manually type in the entries, but there is an easier way, given that each branch manager sends you a workbook with the data for his or her office. All you have to do is copy the data from the individual workbooks into the appropriate worksheets in a new corporate workbook. (The specifics for how this is done are explained in detail in a hands-on exercise.)

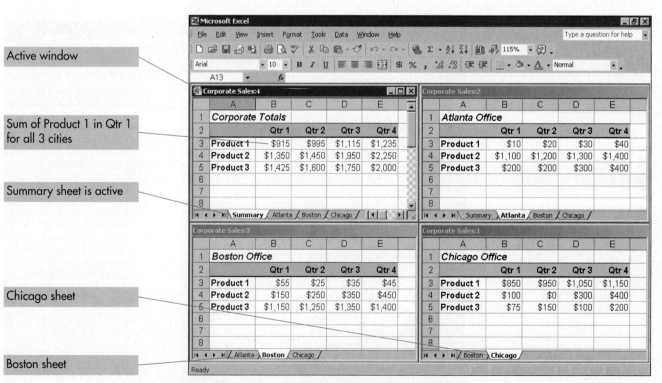

FIGURE 5.3   *Multiple Worksheets*

Consider now Figure 5.4, which at first glance appears almost identical to Figure 5.3. The two figures are very different, however. Figure 5.3 displayed four different worksheets from the same workbook. Figure 5.4, on the other hand, displays four different workbooks. There is one workbook for each city (Atlanta, Boston, and Chicago) and each of these workbooks contains only a single worksheet. The fourth workbook, Corporate Sales, contains four worksheets (Atlanta, Boston, Chicago, and Summary) and is the workbook displayed in Figure 5.3.

There are advantages and disadvantages to each technique. The single workbook in Figure 5.3 is easier for the manager in that he or she has all of the data in one file. The disadvantage is that the worksheets have to be maintained by multiple people (the manager in each city), and this can lead to confusion in that several individuals require access to the same workbook. The multiple workbooks of Figure 5.4 facilitate the maintenance of the data, but four separate files are required to produce the summary information. The choice is up to you.

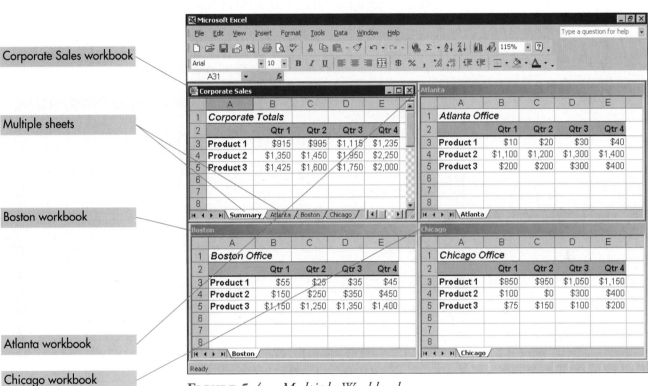

FIGURE 5.4 *Multiple Workbooks*

THE HORIZONTAL SCROLL BAR

The horizontal scroll bar contains four scrolling buttons to scroll through the worksheet tabs in a workbook. (The default workbook has three worksheets.) Click ◄ or ► to scroll one tab to the left or right. Click I◄ or ►I to scroll to the first or last tab in the workbook. Once the desired tab is visible, click the tab to select it. The number of tabs that are visible simultaneously depends on the setting of the horizontal scroll bar; that is, you can drag the *tab split bar* to change the number of tabs that can be seen at one time.

COPYING WORKSHEETS

Objective   To open multiple workbooks; to use the Windows Arrange command to tile the open workbooks; to copy a worksheet from one workbook to another. Use Figure 5.5 as a guide in the exercise.

Step 1:   **Open a New Workbook**

➤ Start Excel. Close the task pane if it is open. If necessary, click the **New button** on the Standard toolbar to open a new workbook as shown in Figure 5.5a.

➤ Delete all worksheets except for Sheet1:
  • Click the tab for **Sheet2**. Press the **Shift key** as you click the tab for **Sheet3**.
  • Point to the tab for **Sheet3** and click the **right mouse button** to display a shortcut menu. Click **Delete**.

➤ The workbook should contain only Sheet1 as shown in Figure 5.5a. Save the workbook as **Corporate Sales** in the **Exploring Excel folder**.

New button

Click Delete

Click tab for Sheet2; press
Shift and click tab for
Sheet3 to select both
sheets

Point to Sheet3 and click
right mouse button

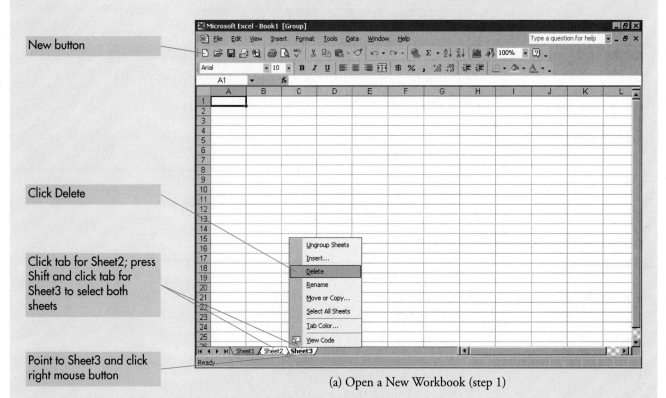

(a) Open a New Workbook (step 1)

FIGURE 5.5   *Hands-on Exercise 1*

THE RIGHT MOUSE BUTTON

Point to any object, then click the right mouse button to display a context-sensitive menu with commands appropriate to the item you are pointing to. Right clicking a cell, for example, displays a menu with selected commands from the Edit, Insert, and Format menus. Right clicking a toolbar displays a menu that lets you display (hide) additional toolbars. Right clicking a worksheet tab enables you to rename, move, copy, or delete a worksheet.

Step 2: **Open the Individual Workbooks**

➤ Pull down the **File menu**. Click **Open** to display the Open dialog box. (If necessary, open the Exploring Excel folder.)
➤ Click the **Atlanta workbook**, then press and hold the **Ctrl key** as you click the **Boston** and **Chicago workbooks** to select all three workbooks at the same time.
➤ Click **Open** to open the selected workbooks. The workbooks will be opened one after another with a brief message appearing on the status bar as each workbook is opened.
➤ Pull down the **Window menu**, which should indicate the four open workbooks at the bottom of the menu. Only the Chicago workbook is visible at this time.
➤ Click **Arrange** to display the Arrange Windows dialog box. If necessary, select the **Tiled option**, then click **OK**. You should see four open workbooks as shown in Figure 5.5b. (Do not be concerned if your workbooks are arranged differently from ours.)

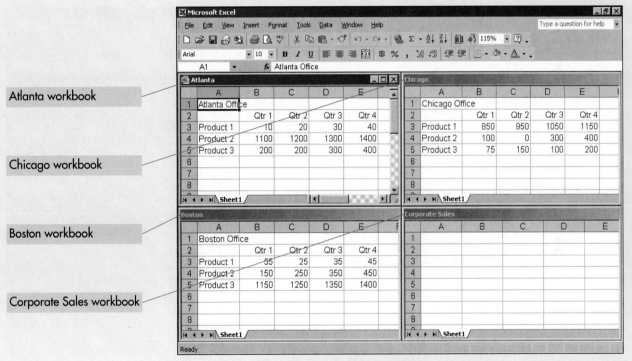

(b) Open the Individual Workbooks (step 2)

FIGURE 5.5 *Hands-on Exercise 1 (continued)*

THE DEFAULT WORKBOOK

A new workbook contains three worksheets, but you can change the default value to any number. Pull down the Tools menu, click Options, then click the General tab. Click the up (down) arrow in the Sheets in New Workbook text box to enter a new default value, then click OK to exit the Options dialog box and continue working. The next time you open a new workbook, it will contain the new number of worksheets.

Step 3: **Copy the Atlanta Data**

➤ Click in the **Atlanta workbook** to make it the active workbook. Reduce the column widths (if necessary) so that you can see the entire worksheet.

➤ Click and drag to select **cells A1** through **E5** as shown in Figure 5.5c. Pull down the **Edit menu** and click **Copy** (or click the **Copy button**).

➤ Click in cell A1 of the **Corporate Sales** workbook.

➤ Click the **Paste button** on the Standard toolbar to copy the Atlanta data into this workbook. Press **Esc** to remove the moving border from the copy range.

➤ Point to the **Sheet1 tab** at the bottom of the Corporate Sales worksheet window, then click the **right mouse button** to produce a shortcut menu. Click **Rename**, which selects the worksheet name.

➤ Type **Atlanta** to replace the existing name and press **enter**. The worksheet tab has been changed from Sheet1 to Atlanta.

➤ Click the **Save button** to save the active workbook (Corporate Sales).

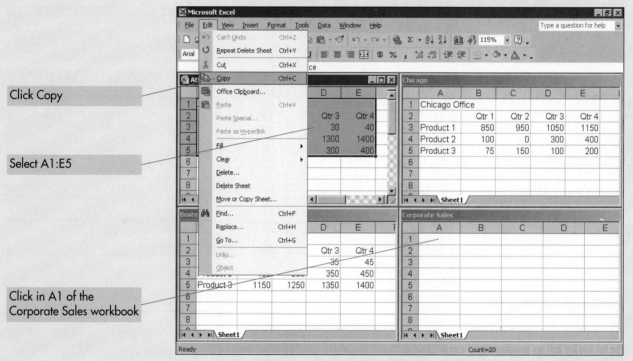

(c) Copy the Atlanta Data (step 3)

FIGURE 5.5 *Hands-on Exercise 1 (continued)*

CHANGE THE ZOOM SETTING

You can increase or decrease the size of a worksheet as it appears on the monitor by clicking the down arrow on the zoom box and selecting an appropriate percentage. If you are working with a large spreadsheet and cannot see it at one time on the screen, choose a number less than 100%. Conversely, if you find yourself squinting because the numbers are too small, select a percentage larger than 100%. Changing the magnification on the screen does not affect printing; that is, worksheets are printed at 100% unless you change the scaling within the Page Setup command.

Step 4: **Copy the Boston and Chicago Data**

➤ Click in the **Boston workbook** to make it the active workbook as shown in Figure 5.5d.

➤ Click the **Sheet1 tab**, then press and hold the **Ctrl key** as you drag the tab to the right of the Atlanta tab in the Corporate Sales workbook. You will see a tiny spreadsheet with a plus sign as you drag the tab. The plus sign indicates that the worksheet is being copied; the ▼ symbol indicates where the worksheet will be placed.

➤ Release the mouse, then release the Ctrl key. The worksheet from the Boston workbook should have been copied to the Corporate Sales workbook and appears as Sheet1 in that workbook.

➤ The Boston workbook should still be open; if it isn't, it means that you did not press the Ctrl key as you were dragging the tab to copy the worksheet. If this is the case, pull down the **File menu**, reopen the Boston workbook, and if necessary, tile the open windows.

➤ Double click the **Sheet1 tab** in the Corporate Sales workbook to rename the tab. Type **Boston** as the new name, then press the **enter key**.

➤ The Boston worksheet should appear to the right of the Atlanta worksheet; if the worksheet appears to the left of Atlanta, click and drag the tab to its desired position. (The ▼ symbol indicates where the worksheet will be placed.)

➤ Repeat the previous steps to copy the Chicago data to the Corporate Sales workbook, placing the new sheet to the right of the Boston sheet. Rename the copied worksheet **Chicago**. Remember, you must click in the window containing the Chicago workbook to activate the window before you can copy the worksheet.

➤ Save the Corporate Sales workbook. (The Summary worksheet will be built in the next exercise.)

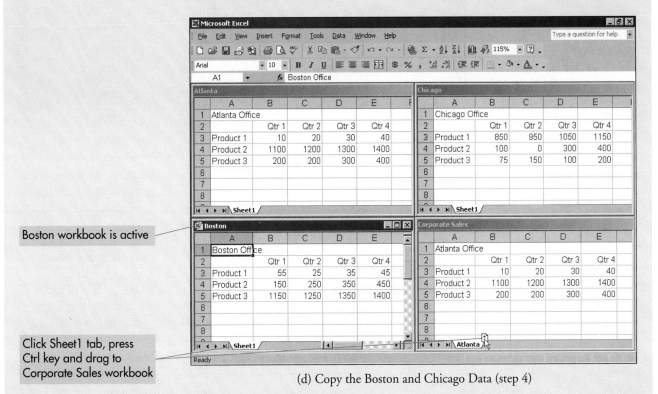

(d) Copy the Boston and Chicago Data (step 4)

FIGURE 5.5 *Hands-on Exercise 1 (continued)*

➤ Check that the Corporate Sales workbook is the active workbook. Click the **Maximize button** so that this workbook takes the entire screen.

➤ The Corporate Sales workbook contains three worksheets, one for each city, as can be seen in Figure 5.5e.

➤ Click the **Atlanta tab** to display the worksheet for Atlanta.

➤ Click the **Boston tab** to display the worksheet for Boston.

➤ Click the **Chicago tab** to display the worksheet for Chicago.

➤ Close all of the open workbooks, saving changes if requested to do so.

➤ Exit Excel if you do not want to continue with the next hands-on exercise at this time.

Click tab to display Boston worksheet

Click tab to display Chicago worksheet

(e) The Corporate Sales Workbook (step 5)

FIGURE 5.5   *Hands-on Exercise 1 (continued)*

MOVING AND COPYING WORKSHEETS

You can move or copy a worksheet within a workbook by dragging its tab. To move a worksheet, click its tab, then drag the tab to the new location (a black triangle shows where the new sheet will go). To copy a worksheet, click its tab, then press and hold the Ctrl key as you drag the tab to its new location. The copied worksheet will have the same name as the original worksheet, followed by a number in parentheses indicating the copy number. Add color to your workbook by changing the color of a worksheet tab. Right click the worksheet tab, click the View color command, select a new color, and click OK.

The presence of multiple worksheets in a workbook creates an additional requirement for cell references. You continue to use the same row and column convention when you reference a cell on the current worksheet; that is, cell A1 is still A1. What if, however, you want to reference a cell on another worksheet within the same workbook? It is no longer sufficient to refer to cell A1 because every worksheet has its own cell A1.

To reference a cell (or cell range) in a worksheet other than the current (active) worksheet, you need to preface the cell address with a ***worksheet reference***; for example, Atlanta!A1 references cell A1 in the Atlanta worksheet. A worksheet reference may also be used in conjunction with a cell range—for example, Summary!B2:E5 to reference cells B2 through E5 on the Summary worksheet. Omission of the worksheet reference in either example defaults to the cell reference in the active worksheet.

An exclamation point separates the worksheet reference from the cell reference. The worksheet reference is always an absolute reference. The cell reference can be either relative (e.g., Atlanta!A1 or Summary!B2:E5) or absolute (e.g., Atlanta!$A$1 or Summary!$B$2:$E$5).

Consider how worksheet references are used in the Summary worksheet in Figure 5.6. Each entry in the Summary worksheet computes the sum of the corresponding cells in the Atlanta, Boston, and Chicago worksheets. The cell formula in cell B3, for example, would be entered as follows:

=Atlanta!B3+Boston!B3+Chicago!B3

       └── Chicago is the worksheet reference

     └── Boston is the worksheet reference

  └── Atlanta is the worksheet reference

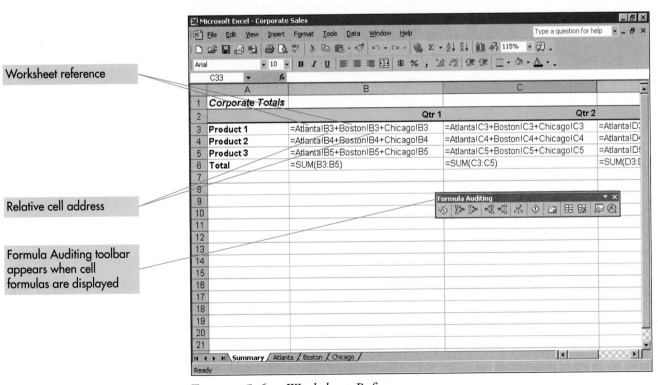

FIGURE 5.6 *Worksheet References*

The combination of relative cell references and constant worksheet references enables you to enter the formula once (in cell B3), then copy it to the remaining cells in the worksheet. In other words, you enter the formula in cell B3 to compute the total sales for Product 1 in Quarter 1, then you copy that formula to the other cells in row 3 (C3 through E3) to obtain the totals for Product 1 in Quarters 2, 3, and 4. You then copy the entire row (B3 through E3) to rows 4 and 5 (cells B4 through E5) to obtain the totals for Products 2 and 3 in all four quarters.

The proper use of relative and absolute references in the original formula in cell B3 is what makes it possible to copy the cell formulas. Consider, for example, the formula in cell C3 (which was copied from cell B3):

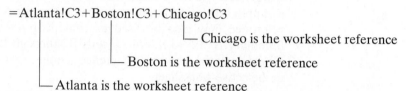

=Atlanta!C3+Boston!C3+Chicago!C3

└── Chicago is the worksheet reference

└── Boston is the worksheet reference

└── Atlanta is the worksheet reference

The worksheet references remain absolute (e.g., Atlanta!) while the cell references adjust for the new location of the formula (cell C3). Similar adjustments are made in all of the other copied formulas.

3-D Reference

A *3-D reference* is a range that spans two or more worksheets in a workbook—for example, =SUM(Atlanta:Chicago!B3) to sum cell B3 in the Atlanta, Boston, and Chicago worksheets. The sheet range is specified with a colon between the beginning and ending sheets. An exclamation point follows the ending sheet, followed by the cell reference. The worksheet references are constant and will not change if the formula is copied. The cell reference may be relative or absolute.

Three-dimensional references can be used in the Summary worksheet as an alternative way to compute the corporate total for each product–quarter combination. To compute the corporate sales for Product 1 in Quarter 1 (which appears in cell B3 of the Summary worksheet), you would use the following function:

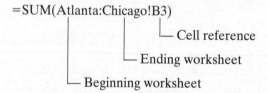

=SUM(Atlanta:Chicago!B3)

└── Cell reference

└── Ending worksheet

└── Beginning worksheet

The 3-D reference includes all worksheets between the Atlanta and Chicago worksheets. (Only one additional worksheet, Boston, is present in the example, but the reference would automatically include any additional worksheets that were inserted between Atlanta and Chicago. In similar fashion, it would also adjust for the deletion of worksheets between Atlanta and Chicago.) Note, too, that the cell reference is relative and thus the formula can be copied from cell B3 in the Summary worksheet to the remaining cells in row 3 (C3 through E3). Those formulas can then be copied to the appropriate cells in rows 4 and 5.

A 3-D reference can be typed directly into a cell formula, but it is easier to enter the reference by pointing. Click in the cell that is to contain the 3-D reference, then enter an equal sign to begin the formula. To reference a cell in another worksheet, click the tab for the worksheet you want to reference, then click the cell or cell range you want to include in the formula. To reference a range from multiple worksheets, click in the cell in the first worksheet, press the Shift key as you click the tab for the last worksheet in the range, then click in the cell in the last worksheet.

Grouping Worksheets

The worksheets in a workbook are often similar to one another in terms of content and/or formatting. In Figure 5.3, for example, the formatting is identical in all four worksheets of the workbook. You can format the worksheets individually or more easily through grouping.

Excel provides the capability for *grouping worksheets* to enter or format data in multiple worksheets at the same time. Once the worksheets are grouped, anything you do in one of the worksheets is automatically done to the other sheets in the group. You could, for example, group all of the worksheets together when you enter row and column labels, when you format data, or when you enter formulas to compute row and column totals. You must, however, ungroup the worksheets when you enter data in a specific worksheet. Grouping and ungrouping is illustrated in the following hands-on exercise.

The AutoFormat Command

The formatting commands within Excel can be applied individually (as you have done throughout the text), or automatically and collectively by choosing a predefined set of formatting specifications. Excel provides several such designs as shown in Figure 5.7. You can apply any of these designs to your worksheet by selecting the range to be formatted, then executing the *AutoFormat command* from within the Format menu. The AutoFormat command does not do anything that could not be done through the individual commands, but it does provide inspiration by suggesting several attractive designs. You can enter additional formatting commands after the AutoFormat has been executed, as you will see in our next exercise.

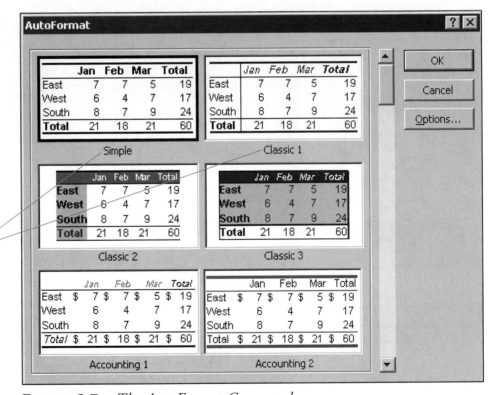

Design names

FIGURE 5.7   *The AutoFormat Command*

Objective   To use 3-D references to summarize data from multiple worksheets within a workbook; to group worksheets to enter common formatting and formulas; to open multiple windows to view several worksheets at the same time. Use Figure 5.8 as a guide in the exercise.

Step 1:   **Insert a Worksheet**

> ➤ Start Excel. Open the **Corporate Sales workbook** created in the previous exercise. The workbook contains three worksheets.
> ➤ Click the **Atlanta tab** to select this worksheet. Pull down the **Insert menu**, and click the **Worksheet command**. You should see a new worksheet, Sheet1.
> ➤ Double click the **tab** of the newly inserted worksheet to select the name. Type **Summary** and press **enter**. The name of the new worksheet has been changed.
> ➤ Click in **cell A1** of the Summary worksheet. Type **Corporate Totals** as shown in Figure 5.8a.
> ➤ Click in **cell B2**. Enter **Qtr 1**. Click in **cell B2**, then point to the fill handle in cell B2. The mouse pointer changes to a thin crosshair.
> ➤ Click and drag the fill handle over **cells C2, D2,** and **E2**. A border appears to indicate the destination range. Release the mouse. Cells C2 through E2 contain the labels Qtr 2, Qtr 3, and Qtr 4, respectively. Right align the column labels.
> ➤ Click in **cell A3**. Enter **Product 1**. Use the AutoFill capability to enter the labels **Product 2** and **Product 3** in cells A4 and A5.

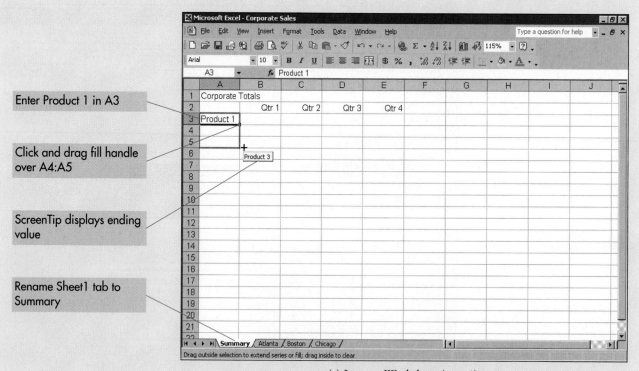

Enter Product 1 in A3

Click and drag fill handle over A4:A5

ScreenTip displays ending value

Rename Sheet1 tab to Summary

(a) Insert a Worksheet (step 1)

FIGURE 5.8   *Hands-on Exercise 2*

Step 2: **Sum the Worksheets**

➤ Click in **cell B3** of the Summary worksheet as shown in Figure 5.8b. Enter **=SUM(Atlanta:Chicago!B3)**, then press the **enter key**. You should see 915 as the sum of the sales for Product 1 in Quarter 1 for the three cities (Atlanta, Boston, and Chicago).

➤ Click the **Undo button** on the Standard toolbar to erase the function so that you can re-enter the function by using pointing.

➤ Check that you are in cell B3 of the Summary worksheet. Enter **=SUM(**.
- Click the **Atlanta tab** to begin the pointing operation.
- Press and hold the **Shift key**, click the **Chicago tab** (scrolling if necessary), then release the Shift key and click **cell B3**. The formula bar should now contain =SUM(Atlanta:Chicago!B3.
- Press the **enter key** to complete the function (which automatically enters the closing right parenthesis) and return to the Summary worksheet.

➤ You should see once again the displayed value of 915 in cell B3 of the Summary worksheet.

➤ If necessary, click in **cell B3**, then drag the fill handle over **cells C3** through **E3** to copy this formula and obtain the total sales for Product 1 in quarters.

➤ Be sure that cells B3 through E3 are still selected, then drag the fill handle to **cell E5**. You should see the total sales for all products in all quarters.

➤ Click **cell E5** to examine the formula in this cell and note that the worksheet references are constant (i.e., they remained the same), whereas the cell references are relative (they were adjusted). Click in other cells to review their formulas in similar fashion. Save the workbook.

Undo button

Sum function is entered in B3

Drag fill handle over C3:E3

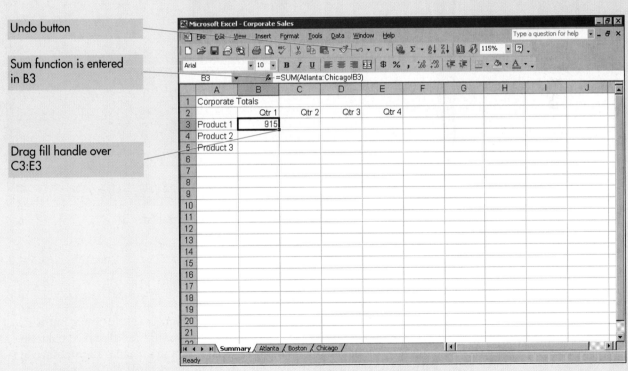

(b) Sum the Worksheets (step 2)

FIGURE 5.8 *Hands-on Exercise 2 (continued)*

Step 3: **The Arrange Windows Command**

➤ Pull down the **Window menu**, which displays the names of the open windows.
➤ The Corporate Sales workbook should be the only open workbook. Close any other open workbooks, including Book1.
➤ Click **New Window** to open a second window. Note, however, that your display will not change at this time.
➤ Pull down the **Window menu** a second time. Click **New Window** to open a third window. Open a fourth window in similar fashion.
➤ Pull down the **Window menu** once again. You should see the names of the four open windows as shown in Figure 5.8c.
➤ Click **Arrange** to display the Arrange Windows dialog box. If necessary, select the **Tile option**, then click **OK**. You should see four tiled windows.
➤ If necessary, change the column widths in the Summary worksheet so that they are approximately the same as in the other windows.

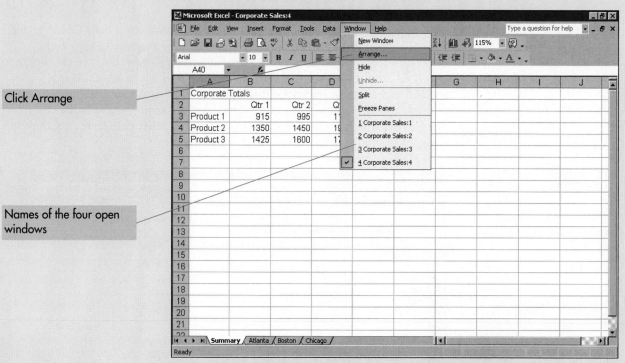

Click Arrange

Names of the four open windows

(c) The Arrange Windows Command (step 3)

FIGURE 5.8 *Hands-on Exercise 2 (continued)*

POINTING TO CELLS IN OTHER WORKSHEETS

A worksheet reference can be typed directly into a cell formula, but it is easier to enter the reference by pointing. Click in the cell that is to contain the reference, then enter an equal sign to begin the formula. To reference a cell in another worksheet, click the tab for the worksheet you want to reference, then click the cell or cell range you want to include in the formula. Complete the formula as usual, continuing to first click the tab whenever you want to reference a cell in another worksheet.

Step 4: **Changing Data**

➤ Click in the **upper-right window** in Figure 5.8d. Click the **Atlanta tab** to display the Atlanta worksheet in this window.

➤ Click the **lower-left window**. Click the **Boston tab** to display the Boston worksheet in this window.

➤ Click in the **lower-right window**. Click the **Tab scrolling button** until you can see the Chicago tab, then click the **Chicago tab**.

➤ Note that cell B3 in the Summary worksheet displays the value 915, which reflects the total sales for Product 1 in Quarter 1 for Atlanta, Boston, and Chicago (10, 55, and 850, respectively).

➤ Click in **cell B3** of the Chicago worksheet. Enter **250**. Press **enter**. The value of cell B3 in the Summary worksheet changes to 315 to reflect the decreased sales in Chicago.

➤ Click the **Undo button** on the Standard toolbar. The sales for Chicago revert to 850 and the Corporate total is again 915.

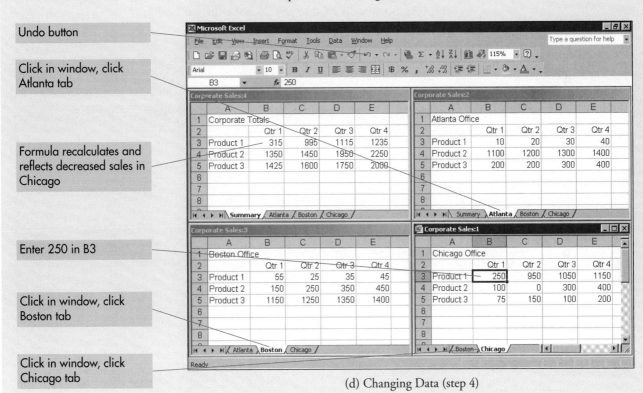

(d) Changing Data (step 4)

FIGURE 5.8   *Hands-on Exercise 2 (continued)*

CONTEXT-SENSITIVE MENUS

A context-sensitive menu provides an alternate (and generally faster) way to execute common commands. Point to a tab, then click the right mouse button to display a menu with commands to insert, delete, rename, move, copy, change color, or select all worksheets. Point to the desired command, then click the left mouse button to execute the command from the shortcut menu. Press the Esc key or click outside the menu to close the menu.

Step 5: **Group Editing**

➤ Click in the window where the Summary worksheet is active. Point to the split box separating the tab scrolling buttons from the horizontal scroll bar. (The pointer becomes a two-headed arrow.) Click and drag to the right until you can see all four tabs at the same time.

➤ If necessary, click the **Summary tab**. Press and hold the **Shift key** as you click the tab for the **Chicago worksheet**. All four tabs should be selected (and thus displayed in white) as shown in Figure 5.8e. You should also see [Group] in the title bar.

➤ Enter **Total** in **cell A6**. The text is centered in cell A6 of all four worksheets.

➤ Click in cell **B6** and enter the function **=SUM(B3:B5)**. Note that the formula is entered in all four sheets simultaneously because of group editing. Copy this formula to **cells C6** through **E6**.

➤ Stay in the Summary worksheet and scroll until you can see column F. Enter **Total** in **cell F2**. Click in **cell F3** and enter the function **=SUM(B3:E3)**. Copy this formula to **cells F4** through **F6**. Save the workbook.

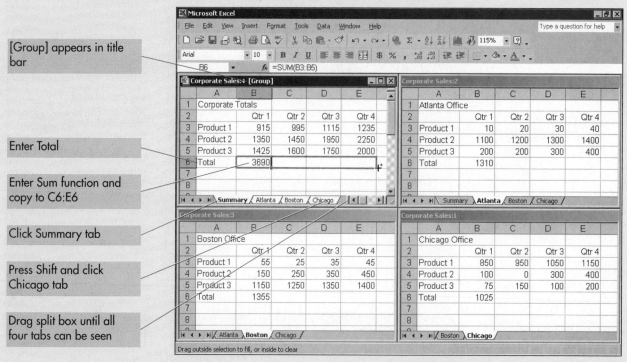

[Group] appears in title bar

Enter Total

Enter Sum function and copy to C6:E6

Click Summary tab

Press Shift and click Chicago tab

Drag split box until all four tabs can be seen

(e) Group Editing (step 5)

FIGURE 5.8 *Hands-on Exercise 2 (continued)*

THE AUTOSUM BUTTON

The AutoSum button on the Standard toolbar invokes the Sum function over a range of cells. To sum a single row or column, click in the blank cell at the end of the row or column, click the AutoSum button to see the suggested function, then click the button a second time to enter the function into the worksheet. To enter a sum function for multiple rows or columns, select the cell range prior to clicking the AutoSum button.

Step 6: **The AutoFormat Command**

➤ Be sure that all four tabs are still selected so that group editing is still in effect. Click and drag to select **cells A1** through **F6** as shown in Figure 5.8f. (You may need to scroll in the worksheet to select all of the cells.)

➤ Pull down the **Format menu** and click the **AutoFormat command** to display the AutoFormat dialog box. Choose a format that appeals to you, then click the **Options button** to determine which parts of the format you want to apply.

➤ Experiment freely by selecting different designs and/or checking and unchecking the various check boxes within a design. Set a time limit, then make a decision. We chose the **Colorful 2** format and left all of the boxes checked. Click **OK**.

➤ The format is applied to all four selected sheets. You cannot see the effects in the summary worksheet, however, until you click elsewhere in the worksheet to deselect the cells. Save the workbook.

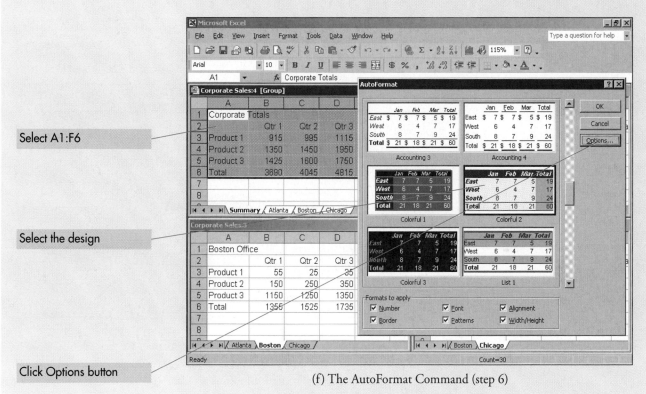

Select A1:F6

Select the design

Click Options button

(f) The AutoFormat Command (step 6)

FIGURE 5.8 *Hands-on Exercise 2 (continued)*

SELECT MULTIPLE SHEETS

You can group multiple worksheets simultaneously, then perform the same operation on the selected sheets at one time. To select adjacent worksheets, click the first sheet in the group, then press and hold the Shift key as you click the last sheet in the group. If the worksheets are not adjacent to one another, click the first tab, then press and hold the Ctrl key as you click the tab of each additional sheet. Excel indicates that grouping is in effect by appending [Group] to the workbook name in the title bar. Click any tab (other than the active sheet) to deselect the group.

Step 7:   **The Finishing Touches**

➤ Click and drag to select **cells B3** through **F6**, then pull down the **Format menu** and click the **Cells command** to display the Format Cells dialog box in Figure 5.8g. (You can also right click the selected cells, then select the **Format Cells command** from the context-sensitive menu.)
➤ Click the **Number tab**, click **Currency**, and set the number of decimal places to **zero**. Click **OK**.
➤ Change the width of columns B through F as necessary to accommodate the additional formatting. It's easiest to select all of the columns at the same time, then click and drag the border of the right-most column to change the width of all selected columns.
➤ Save the workbook. Close all four windows. Exit Excel if you do not want to continue with the next exercise at this time.

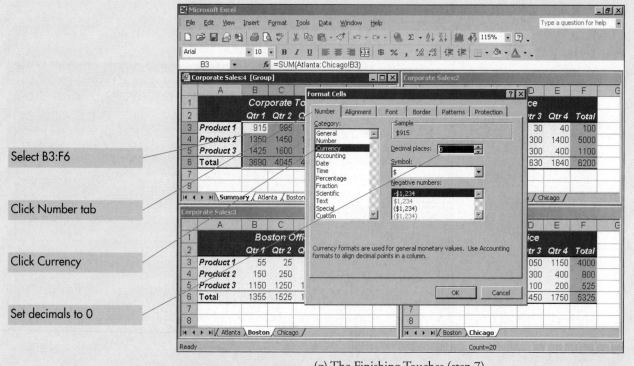

(g) The Finishing Touches (step 7)

FIGURE 5.8 *Hands-on Exercise 2 (continued)*

THE OPTIMAL (AUTOFIT) COLUMN WIDTH

The appearance of pound signs within a cell indicates that the cell width (column width) is insufficient to display the computed results in the selected format. Double click the right border of the column heading to change the column width to accommodate the widest entry in that column. For example, to increase the width of column B, double click the border between the column headings for columns B and C.

Throughout the text we have emphasized the importance of properly designing a worksheet and of isolating the assumptions and initial conditions on which the worksheet is based. A workbook can contain up to 255 worksheets, and it, too, should be well designed so that the purpose of every worksheet is evident. Documenting a workbook, and the various worksheets within it, is important because spreadsheets are frequently used by individuals other than the author. You are familiar with every aspect of your workbook because you created it. Your colleague down the hall (or across the country) is not, however, and that person needs to know at a glance the purpose of the workbook and its underlying structure. Even if you don't share your worksheet with others, you will appreciate the documentation six months from now, when you have forgotten some of the nuances you once knew so well.

One way of documenting a workbook is through the creation of a ***documentation worksheet*** that describes the contents of each worksheet within the workbook as shown in Figure 5.9. The worksheet in Figure 5.9 has been added to the Corporate Sales workbook that was created in the first two exercises. (The Insert menu contains the command to add a worksheet.)

The documentation worksheet shows the author and date the spreadsheet was last modified. It contains a description of the overall workbook, a list of all the sheets within the workbook, and the contents of each. The information in the documentation worksheet may seem obvious to you, but it will be greatly appreciated by someone seeing the workbook for the first time.

The documentation worksheet is attractively formatted and takes advantage of the ability to wrap text within a cell. The description in cell B6, for example, wraps over several lines (just as in a word processor). The worksheet also takes advantage of color and larger fonts to call attention to the title of the worksheet. The grid lines have been suppressed through the View tab in the Options command of the Tools menu. The documentation worksheet is an important addition to any workbook.

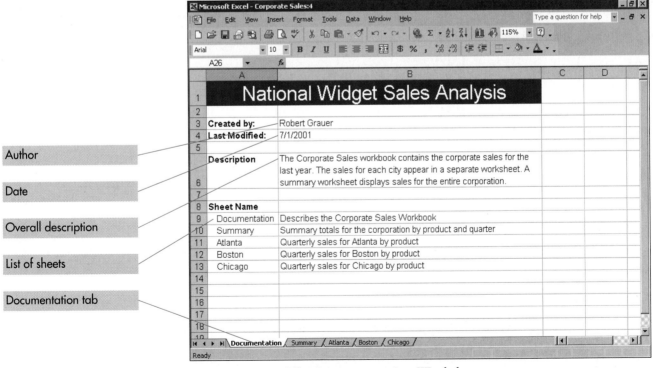

FIGURE 5.9   *The Documentation Worksheet*

THE DOCUMENTATION WORKSHEET

Objective   To improve the design of a workbook through the inclusion of a documentation worksheet; to illustrate sophisticated formatting. Use Figure 5.10 as a guide in the exercise.

Step 1:   **Add the Documentation Worksheet**

➤ Open the **Corporate Sales workbook** that was created in the previous exercise. Maximize the window. If necessary, click the **Atlanta** tab to turn off the group-editing feature. Click the **Summary tab** to select this worksheet.

➤ Pull down the **Insert menu** and click the **Worksheet command** to insert a new worksheet to the left of the Summary worksheet. Double click the **tab** of the newly inserted worksheet. Enter **Documentation** as the new name and press **enter**.

➤ Enter the descriptive entries in column A as shown in Figure 5.10a. Use boldface and indentation as appropriate. Double click the column border between columns A and B to increase the width of column A to accommodate the widest entry in the column.

➤ Enter your name in **cell B3**. Enter **=Today( )** in cell B4. Press **enter**. Click the **Left Align button** to align the date as shown in the figure.

➤ Save the workbook.

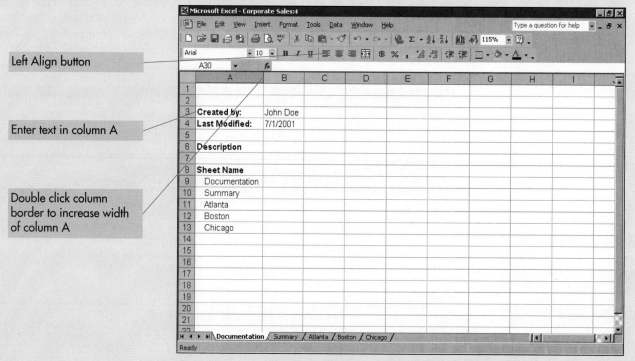

(a) Add the Documentation Worksheet (step 1)

FIGURE 5.10   *Hands-on Exercise 3*

Step 2:   **The Wrap Text Command**

➤ Increase the width of column B as shown in Figure 5.10b, then click in **cell B6** and enter the descriptive entry shown in the formula bar.

➤ Do not press the enter key until you have completed the entire entry. Do not be concerned if the text in cell B6 appears to spill into the other cells in row six. Press the **enter key** when you have completed the entry.

➤ Click in **cell B6**, then pull down the **Format menu** and click **Cells** (or right click **cell B6** and click the **Format Cells command**) to display the dialog box in Figure 5.10b.

➤ Click the **Alignment tab**, click the box to **Wrap Text** as shown in the figure, then click **OK**. The text in cell B6 wraps to the width of column B.

➤ Point to **cell A6**, then click the **right mouse button** to display a shortcut menu. Click **Format Cells** to display the Format Cells dialog box. If necessary, click the **Alignment tab**, click the **drop-down arrow** in the Vertical list box, and select **Top**. Click **OK**. Save the workbook.

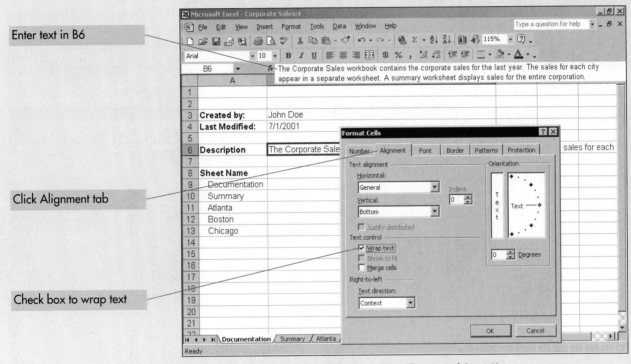

(b) The Wrap Text Command (step 2)

FIGURE 5.10   *Hands-on Exercise 3 (continued)*

EDIT WITHIN A CELL

Double click in the cell whose contents you want to change, then make the changes directly in the cell itself rather than on the formula bar. Use the mouse or arrow keys to position the insertion point at the point of correction. Press the Ins key to toggle between the insertion and overtype modes and/or use the Del key to delete a character. Press the Home and End keys to move to the first and last characters, respectively.

Step 3:   **Add the Worksheet Title**

➤ Click in **cell A1**. Enter **National Widgets Sales Analysis**. Change the font size to **22**.

➤ Click and drag to select **cells A1** and **B1**. Click the **Merge and Center button** to center the title across cells A1 and B1.

➤ Check that cells A1 and B1 are still selected. Pull down the **Format menu**. Click **Cells** to display the Format Cells dialog box as shown in Figure 5.10c.

  • Click the **Patterns tab**. Click the **Burgundy** color (to match the color used in the Colorful 2 AutoFormat that was applied in the previous exercise).

  • Click the **Font tab**. Click the drop-down arrow in the **Color list box**. Click the **White** color.

  • Click **OK** to accept the settings and close the Format Cells dialog box.

➤ Click outside the selected cells to see the effects of the formatting change. You should see white letters on a burgundy background.

➤ Complete the text entries in **cells B9** through **B13**. Add any additional documentation and formatting that you think is appropriate.

➤ Click in **cell A1**. Click the **Spelling button** to check the worksheet for spelling.

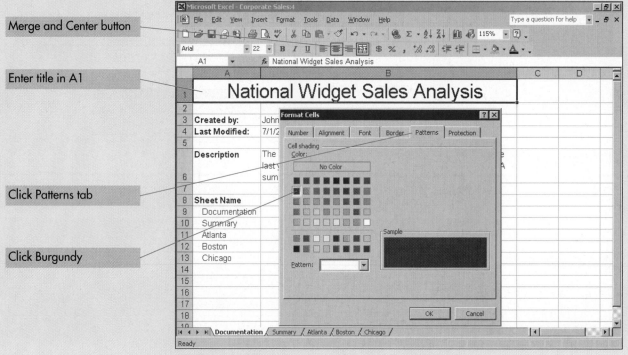

(c) Add the Worksheet Title (step 3)

FIGURE 5.10   *Hands-on Exercise 3 (continued)*

THE SPELL CHECK

Anyone familiar with a word processor takes the spell check for granted, but did you know the same capability exists within Excel? Click the Spelling button on the Standard toolbar to initiate the spell check, then implement corrections just as you do in Microsoft Word.

Step 4: **The Page Setup Command**

➤ If necessary, click the **Documentation tab** at the bottom of the window, then press and hold the **Shift key** as you click the tab for the **Chicago worksheet**. All five worksheet tabs should be selected, as shown in Figure 5.10d.

➤ Pull down the **File menu** and click the **Page Setup command** to display the Page Setup dialog box.

• Click the **Header/Footer tab**. Click the **down arrow** on the Header list box and choose **Documentation** (the name of the worksheet). Click the **down arrow** on the Footer list box and choose **Corporate Sales** (the name of the workbook).

• Click the **Margins tab**, then click the check box to center the worksheet horizontally. Change the top margin to **2 inches**.

• Click the **Sheet tab**. Check the boxes to include row and column headings and gridlines. Click **OK** to exit the Page Setup dialog box.

➤ Save the workbook. Pull down the **File menu**. Click **Print** to display the Print dialog box. Click the option button to print the **Entire Workbook**. Click **OK**.

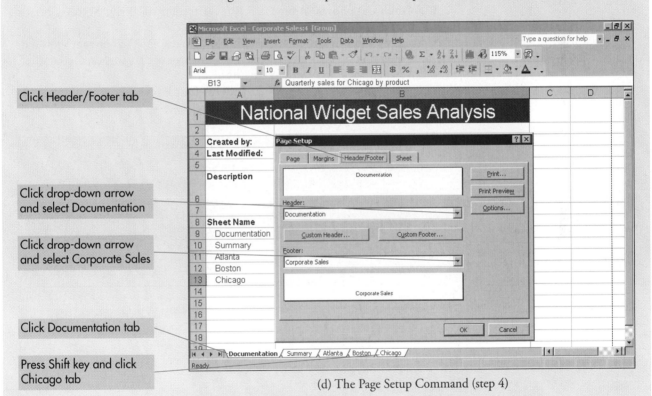

Click Header/Footer tab

Click drop-down arrow and select Documentation

Click drop-down arrow and select Corporate Sales

Click Documentation tab

Press Shift key and click Chicago tab

(d) The Page Setup Command (step 4)

FIGURE 5.10   *Hands-on Exercise 3 (continued)*

THE PRINT PREVIEW COMMAND

Use the Print Preview command to check the appearance of a worksheet to save time as well as paper. You can execute the command by clicking the Print Preview button on the Standard toolbar or from the Print Preview command button within the Page Setup or Print dialog box.

Step 5: **Print the Cell Formulas**

➤ Right click the **Summary tab** to display a context-sensitive menu, then click the **Ungroup Sheets command** to remove the group editing.

➤ Pull down the **View menu**, click **Custom Views** to display the Custom Views dialog box. Click the **Add button** to display the Add View dialog box.

➤ Enter **Displayed Values** as the name of the view (this is different from Figure 5.10e). Be sure that the Print Settings box is checked, and click **OK**.

➤ Press **Ctrl+`** to display the cell formulas. Double click the column borders between adjacent columns to increase the width of each column so that the cell formulas are completely visible.

➤ Pull down the **File menu** and click the **Page Setup command**. Click the **Page tab** and change to **Landscape orientation**. Click the option button to **Fit to 1 page**. Click **OK** to accept these settings and close the Page Setup dialog box. Click the **Print button** to print the summary worksheet.

➤ Pull down the **View menu**, click **Custom Views** to display the Custom View dialog box, then click the **Add button** to display the Add View dialog box. Enter **Cell Formulas** as shown in Figure 5.10f, verify that the Print Settings box is checked, and click **OK**.

➤ Pull down the **View menu**, click **Custom Views** to display the Custom View dialog box, then double click the **Displayed Values** view that was created earlier. You can switch back and forth at any time.

➤ Save the workbook. Close all open windows. Exit Excel if you do not want to continue with the next exercise at this time.

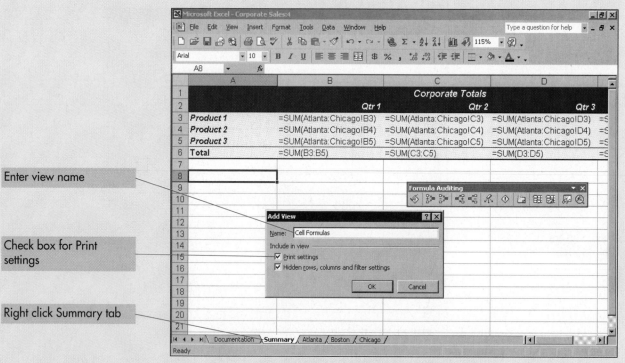

Enter view name

Check box for Print settings

Right click Summary tab

(e) Print the Cell Formulas (step 5)

FIGURE 5.10   *Hands-on Exercise 3 (continued)*

There are two approaches to combining data from multiple sources. You can store all of the data on separate sheets in a single workbook, then create a summary worksheet within that workbook that references values in the other worksheets. Alternatively, you can retain the source data in separate workbooks, and create a summary workbook that references (links to) those workbooks.

Linking is established through the creation of *external references* that specify a cell (or range of cells) in another workbook. The *dependent workbook* (the Corporate Links workbook in our next example) contains the external references and thus reflects (is dependent on) data in the source workbook(s). The *source workbooks* (the Atlanta, Boston, and Chicago workbooks in our example) contain the data referenced by the dependent workbook.

Figure 5.11 illustrates the use of linking within the context of the example we have been using. Four different workbooks are open, each with one worksheet. The Corporate Links workbook is the dependent workbook and contains external references to obtain the summary totals. The Atlanta, Boston, and Chicago workbooks are the source workbooks.

Cell B3 is the active cell, and its contents are displayed in the formula bar. The corporate sales for Product 1 in the first quarter are calculated by summing the corresponding values in the source workbooks. Note how the workbook names are enclosed in square brackets to indicate the external references to the Atlanta, Boston, and Chicago workbooks.

The formulas to compute the corporate totals for Product 1 in the second, third, and fourth quarters contain external references similar to those shown in the formula bar. The *workbook references* and sheet references are absolute, whereas the cell reference may be relative (as in this example) or absolute. Once the formula has been entered into cell B3, it may be copied to the remaining cells in this row to compute the totals for Product 1 in the remaining quarters.

Sheet reference

Workbook reference

Atlanta workbook

Chicago workbook

Boston workbook

Corporate Sales workbook (dependent workbook)

B3 is the active cell

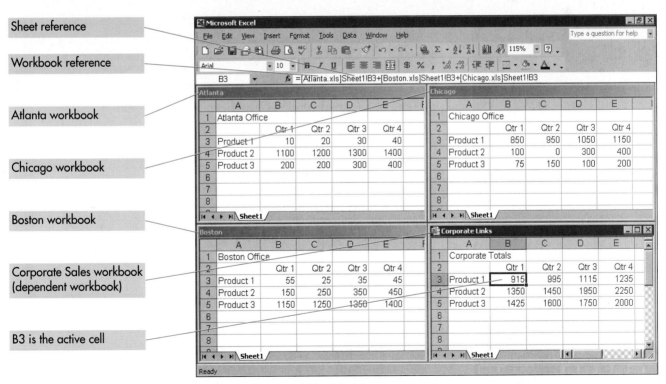

FIGURE 5.11   *File Linking*

LINKING WORKBOOKS

Objective To create a dependent workbook with external references to multiple source workbooks; to use pointing to create the external reference rather than entering the formula explicitly. Use Figure 5.12 as a guide in doing the exercise.

Step 1: **Open the Workbooks**

➤ Start Excel. If necessary, click the **New Workbook button** on the Standard toolbar to open a new workbook.

➤ Delete all worksheets except for Sheet1. Save the workbook as **Corporate Links** in the **Exploring Excel folder**.

➤ Pull down the **File menu**. Click **Open** to display the Open dialog box. Click the **Atlanta workbook**. Press and hold the **Ctrl key** as you click the **Boston** and **Chicago workbooks** to select all three workbooks at the same time as shown in Figure 5.12a.

➤ Click **Open** to open the selected workbooks. The workbooks will be opened one after another, with a brief message appearing on the status bar as each workbook is opened.

➤ Pull down the **Window menu**, which should indicate four open workbooks at the bottom of the menu. Click **Arrange** to display the Arrange Windows dialog box. If necessary, select the **Tiled option**, then click **OK**.

New Workbook button

Click Atlanta

Press Ctrl key and click Boston

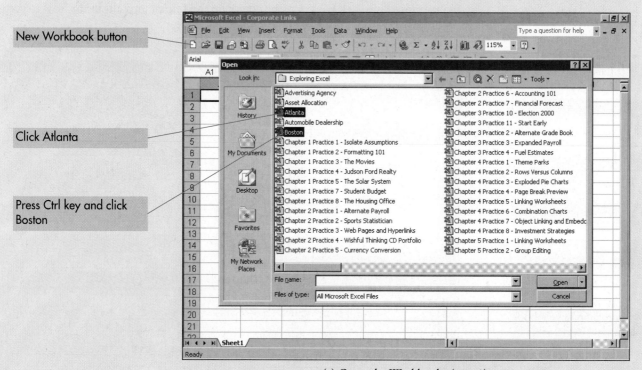

(a) Open the Workbooks (step 1)

FIGURE 5.12 *Hands-on Exercise 4*

Step 2: **The AutoFill Command**

> ➤ You should see four open workbooks as shown in Figure 5.12b, although the row and column labels have not yet been entered in the Corporate Links workbook. (Do not be concerned if your workbooks are arranged differently.)
>
> ➤ Click in **cell A1** in the **Corporate Links workbook** to make this the active cell in the active workbook. Enter **Corporate Totals**.
>
> ➤ Click **cell B2**. Enter **Qtr 1**. Click in **cell B2**, then point to the fill handle in the lower-right corner. The mouse pointer changes to a thin crosshair.
>
> ➤ Drag the fill handle over **cells C2**, **D2**, and **E2**. A border appears, to indicate the destination range. Release the mouse. Cells C2 through E2 contain the labels Qtr 2, Qtr 3, and Qtr 4, respectively.
>
> ➤ Right-align the entries in **cells B2** through **E2**, then reduce the column widths so that you can see the entire worksheet in the window.
>
> ➤ Click **cell A3**. Enter **Product 1**. Use the AutoFill capability to enter the labels **Product 2** and **Product 3** in cells A4 and A5.

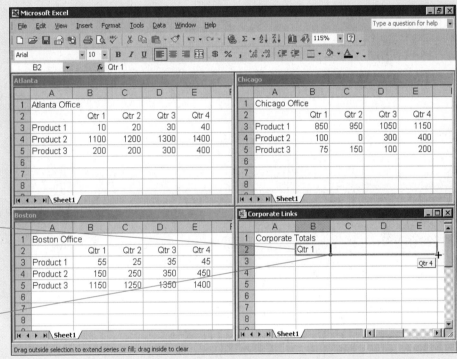

(b) The AutoFill Command (step 2)

FIGURE 5.12   *Hands-on Exercise 4 (continued)*

CREATE A CUSTOM SERIES

The AutoFill command is the fastest way to enter a series into adjacent cells. Type the first entry in the series (such as January, Monday, or Quarter 1), then click and drag the fill handle to adjacent cells to complete the series. You can also create your own series. Pull down the Tools menu, click Options, click the Custom Lists tab, and select New List. Enter the items in your series separated by commas (e.g., Tom, Dick, and Harry), click Add, and click OK. The next time you type Tom, Dick, or Harry in a cell you can use the fill handle to complete the series.

Step 3: **File Linking**

➤ Click **cell B3** of the **Corporate Links workbook**. Enter an **equal sign** so that you can create the formula by pointing:

- Click in the window for the **Atlanta workbook**. Click **cell B3**. The formula bar should display =[ATLANTA.XLS]Sheet1!$B$3. Press the **F4 key** continually until the cell reference changes to B3.
- Enter a **plus sign**. Click in the window for the **Boston workbook**. Click **cell B3**. The formula expands to include +[BOSTON.XLS]Sheet1!$B$3. Press the **F4 key** continually until the cell reference changes to B3.
- Enter a **plus sign**. Click in the window for the **Chicago workbook**. Click **cell B3**. The formula expands to include +[CHICAGO.XLS]Sheet1!$B$3. Press the **F4 key** continually until the cell reference changes to B3.
- Press **enter**. The formula is complete, and you should see 915 in cell B3 of the Corporate Links workbook. Click in **cell B3**. The entry on the formula bar should match the entry in Figure 5.12c. Save the workbook.

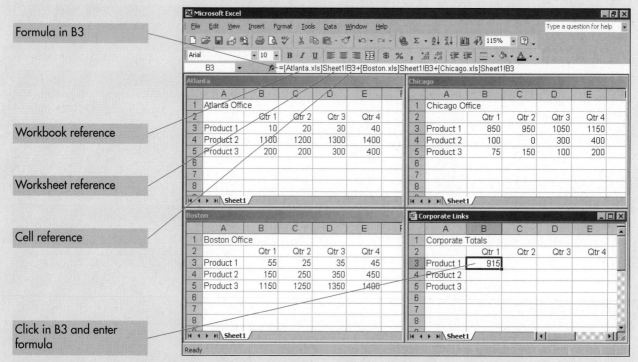

Formula in B3

Workbook reference

Worksheet reference

Cell reference

Click in B3 and enter formula

(c) File Linking (step 3)

FIGURE 5.12 *Hands-on Exercise 4 (continued)*

THE F4 KEY

The F4 key cycles through relative, absolute, and mixed addresses. Click on any reference within the formula bar; for example, click on A1 in the formula =A1+A2. Press the F4 key once, and it changes to an absolute reference, $A$1. Press the F4 key a second time, and it becomes a mixed reference, A$1; press it again, and it is a different mixed reference, $A1. Press the F4 key a fourth time, and it returns to the original relative address, A1.

Step 4: **Copy the Cell Formulas**

➤ If necessary, click **cell B3** in the **Corporate Links workbook**, then drag the fill handle over **cells C3** through **E3** to copy this formula to the remaining cells in row 3.
➤ Be sure that cells B3 through E3 are still selected, then drag the fill handle to **cell E5**. You should see the total sales for all products in all quarters as shown in Figure 5.12d.
➤ Click **cell E5** to view the copied formula as shown in the figure. Note that the workbook and sheet references are the same but that the cell references have adjusted.
➤ Save the workbook.

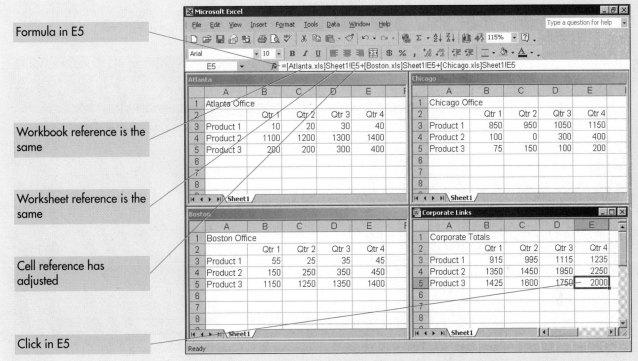

(d) Copy the Cell Formulas (step 4)

FIGURE 5.12 *Hands-on Exercise 4 (continued)*

DRIVE AND FOLDER REFERENCE

An external reference is updated regardless of whether or not the source workbook is open. The reference is displayed differently, depending on whether or not the source workbook is open. The references include the path (the drive and folder) if the source workbook is closed; the path is not shown if the source workbook is open. The external workbooks must be available to update the summary workbook. If the location of the workbooks changes (as may happen if you copy the workbooks to a different folder), pull down the Edit menu and click the Links command, then change the source of the external data.

Step 5: **Create a Workspace**

➤ Pull down the **File menu** and click the **Save Workspace command** to display the Save Workspace dialog box in Figure 5.12e.

➤ If necessary, click the **down arrow** in the Save in list box to select the **Exploring Excel folder**. Enter **Linked workbooks** as the file name. Click the **Save button** in the dialog box to save the workspace. Click **Yes** if asked whether to save the changes to the Corporate Links workbook.

➤ The workspace is saved and you can continue to work as usual. The advantage of the workspace is that you can open all four workbooks with a single command.

➤ Click the **Close button** in each window to close all four workbooks. Pull down the **File menu**, click the **Open command**, then open the **Linked workbooks** workspace that you just created.

➤ Click **Update** when asked whether you want to update the links within the Corporate Links workbook. All four workbooks are open as before.

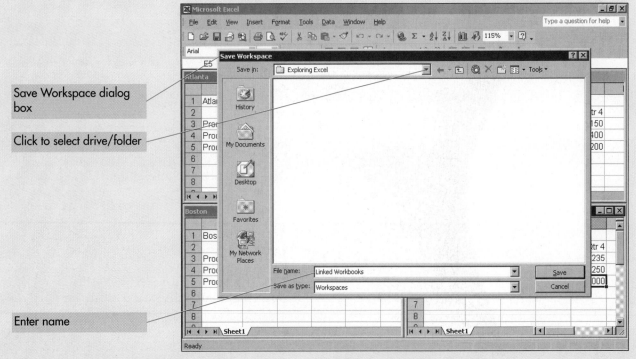

(e) Create a Workspace (step 5)

FIGURE 5.12 *Hands-on Exercise 4 (continued)*

THE WORKSPACE

A workspace enables you to open multiple workbooks in a single step, and further, will retain the arrangement of those workbooks within the Excel window. The workspace file does not contain the workbooks themselves, however, and thus you must continue to save changes you make to the individual workbooks.

Step 6: **Change the Data**

> ➤ Click **cell B3** to make it the active cell. Note that the value displayed in the cell is 915.
> ➤ Pull down the **File menu**. Click **Close**. Answer **Yes** if asked whether to save the changes.
> ➤ Click in the window containing the **Chicago workbook**, click **cell B3**, enter **250**, and press **enter**. Pull down the **File menu**. Click **Close**. Answer **Yes** if asked whether to save the changes. Only two workbooks, Atlanta and Boston, are now open.
> ➤ Pull down the **File menu** and open the **Corporate Links workbook**. You should see the dialog box in Figure 5.12f, asking whether to update the links. (Note that cell B3 still displays 915). Click **Update** to update the links.
> ➤ The value in cell B3 of the Corporate Links workbook changes to 315 to reflect the change in the Chicago workbook, even though the latter is closed.
> ➤ If necessary, click in **cell B3**. The formula bar displays the contents of this cell, which include the drive and folder reference for the Chicago workbook, because the workbook is closed.

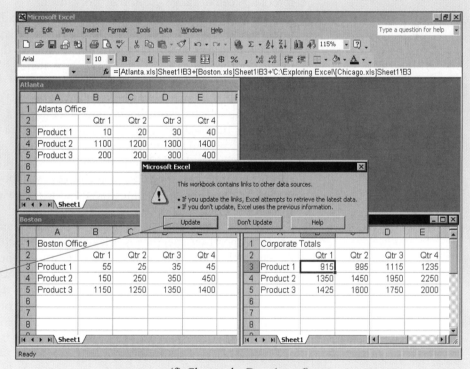

(f) Change the Data (step 6)

FIGURE 5.12 *Hands-on Exercise 4 (continued)*

Step 7: **Close the Workbooks**

> ➤ Close the Atlanta and Boston workbooks. Close the Corporate Links workbook. Click **Yes** if asked whether to save the changes.
> ➤ Saving the source workbook(s) before the dependent workbook ensures that the formulas in the source workbooks are calculated, and that all external references in the dependent workbook reflect current values.
> ➤ Exit Excel.

The chapter showed how to combine data from different sources into a summary report. The example is quite common and applicable to any business scenario requiring both detail and summary reports. One approach is to store all of the data in separate sheets of a single workbook, then summarize the data in a summary worksheet within that workbook. Alternatively, the source data can be kept in separate workbooks and consolidated through linking to a summary workbook. Both approaches are equally valid, and the choice depends on where you want to keep the source data.

An Excel workbook may contain up to 255 worksheets, each of which is identified by a tab at the bottom of the window. Worksheets may be added, deleted, moved, copied, or renamed through a shortcut menu. The highlighted tab indicates the active worksheet.

A worksheet reference is required to indicate a cell in another worksheet of the same workbook. An exclamation point separates the worksheet reference from the cell reference. The worksheet reference is absolute and remains the same when the formula is copied. The cell reference may be relative or absolute. A 3-D reference refers to a cell or range in another worksheet.

The best way to enter a reference to a cell in a different worksheet (or in a different workbook) is by pointing. Click in the cell that is to contain the formula, type an equal sign, click the worksheet tab that contains the external reference, then click in the appropriate cell. Use the F4 key to switch between relative, absolute, and mixed cell references.

Multiple worksheets may be selected (grouped) to execute the same commands on all of the selected worksheets simultaneously. An AutoFormat is a predefined set of formats that includes font size, color, boldface, alignment, and other attributes that can be applied automatically to a selected range.

A workbook should be clearly organized so that the purpose of every worksheet is evident. One way of documenting a workbook is through the creation of a documentation worksheet that describes the purpose of each worksheet within the workbook.

A workbook may also be linked to cells in other workbooks through an external reference that specifies a cell (or range of cells) in a source workbook. The dependent workbook contains the external references and uses (is dependent on) the data in the source workbook(s). The external workbooks must be available to update the summary workbook. If the location of the workbooks changes (as may happen if you copy the workbooks to a different folder), pull down the Edit menu and click the Links command, then change the source of the external data.

3-D reference (p. 228)
Arrange command (p. 220)
AutoFormat command (p. 229)
AutoSum (p. 234)
Custom view (p. 242)
Dependent workbook (p. 243)

Documentation worksheet (p. 237)
External reference (p. 243)
Grouping worksheets (p. 229)
Linking (p. 243)
New Window command (p. 220)
Source workbook (p. 243)

Tab split bar (p. 221)
Workbook reference (p. 243)
Worksheet reference (p. 227)
Workspace (p. 248)

1. Which of the following is true regarding workbooks and worksheets?
   (a) A workbook contains one or more worksheets
   (b) Only one worksheet can be selected at a time within a workbook
   (c) Every workbook contains the same number of worksheets
   (d) All of the above

2. Assume that a workbook contains three worksheets. How many cells are included in the function =SUM(Sheet1:Sheet3!A1)?
   (a) Three
   (b) Four
   (c) Twelve
   (d) Twenty-four

3. Assume that a workbook contains three worksheets. How many cells are included in the function =SUM(Sheet1:Sheet3!A1:B4)?
   (a) Three
   (b) Four
   (c) Twelve
   (d) Twenty-four

4. Which of the following is the preferred way to sum the value of cell A1 from three different worksheets?
   (a) =Sheet1!A1+Sheet2!A1+Sheet3!A1
   (b) =SUM(Sheet1:Sheet3!A1)
   (c) Both (a) and (b) are equally good
   (d) Neither (a) nor (b)

5. The reference CIS120!$A$2:
   (a) Is an absolute reference to cell A2 in the CIS120 workbook
   (b) Is a relative reference to cell A2 in the CIS120 workbook
   (c) Is an absolute reference to cell A2 in the CIS120 worksheet
   (d) Is a relative reference to cell A2 in the CIS120 worksheet

6. Assume that Sheet1 is the active worksheet and that cells A2 through A4 are currently selected. What happens if you press and hold the Shift key as you click the tab for Sheet3, then press the Del key?
   (a) Only Sheet1 will be deleted from the workbook
   (b) Only Sheet3 will be deleted from the workbook
   (c) Sheet1, Sheet2, and Sheet3 will be deleted from the workbook
   (d) The contents of cells A2 through A4 will be erased from Sheet1, Sheet2, and Sheet3

7. Which of the following is true about the reference Sheet1:Sheet3!A1:B2?
   (a) The worksheet reference is relative, the cell reference is absolute
   (b) The worksheet reference is absolute, the cell reference is relative
   (c) The worksheet and cell references are both absolute
   (d) The worksheet and cell references are both relative

8. You are in the Ready mode and are positioned in cell B2 of Sheet1. You enter an equal sign, click the worksheet tab for Sheet2, click cell B1, and press enter.
   (a) The content of cell B2 in Sheet1 is =Sheet2!B1
   (b) The content of cell B1 in Sheet2 is = Sheet1!B2
   (c) Both (a) and (b)
   (d) Neither (a) nor (b)

9. You are in the Ready mode and are positioned in cell A10 of Sheet1. You enter an equal sign, click the worksheet tab for the worksheet called This Year, and click cell C10. You then enter a minus sign, click the worksheet tab for the worksheet called Last Year, click cell C10, and press enter. What are the contents of cell A10?
    (a) =ThisYear:LastYear!C10
    (b) =(ThisYear−LastYear)!C10
    (c) =ThisYear!C10-LastYear!C10
    (d) =ThisYear:C10-LastYear:C10

10. Which of the following can be accessed from a shortcut menu?
    (a) Inserting or deleting a worksheet
    (b) Moving or copying a worksheet
    (c) Renaming a worksheet
    (d) All of the above

11. You are in the Ready mode and are positioned in cell A1 of Sheet1 of Book1. You enter an equal sign, click in the open window for Book2, click the tab for Sheet1, click cell A1, then press the F4 key continually until you have a relative cell reference. What reference appears in the formula bar?
    (a) =[BOOK1.XLS]Sheet1!$A$1
    (b) =[BOOK1.XLS]Sheet1!A1
    (c) =[BOOK2.XLS]Sheet1!$A$1
    (d) =[BOOK2.XLS]Sheet1!A1

12. The Arrange Windows command can display:
    (a) Multiple worksheets from one workbook
    (b) One worksheet from multiple workbooks
    (c) Both (a) and (b)
    (d) Neither (a) nor (b)

13. Pointing can be used to reference a cell in:
    (a) A different worksheet
    (b) A different workbook
    (c) Both (a) and (b)
    (d) Neither (a) nor (b)

14. The appearance of [Group] within the title bar indicates that:
    (a) Multiple workbooks are open and are all active
    (b) Multiple worksheets are selected within the same workbook
    (c) Both (a) and (b)
    (d) Neither (a) nor (b)

15. Which of the following is true regarding the example on file linking that was developed in the chapter?
    (a) The Atlanta, Boston, and Chicago workbooks were dependent workbooks
    (b) The Linked workbook was a source workbook
    (c) Both (a) and (b)
    (d) Neither (a) nor (b)

ANSWERS

1. a	**6.** d	**11.** d
2. a	**7.** b	**12.** c
3. d	**8.** a	**13.** c
4. b	**9.** c	**14.** b
5. c	**10.** d	**15.** d

1. Linking Worksheets: A partially completed version of the workbook in Figure 5.13 can be found on the data disk as *Chapter 5 Practice 1*. This workbook contains worksheets for the individual sections but does not contain the summary worksheet.
   a. Retrieve the *Chapter 5 Practice 1* workbook from the data disk.
   b. Group the worksheets, then add the appropriate formulas (functions) to compute the class average on each test.
   c. Ungroup the worksheets, then add a summary worksheet that includes the test averages from each of the sections as shown in the figure.
   d. Add a documentation worksheet that includes your name as the grading assistant, the date of modification, and lists of all the worksheets in the workbook.
   e. Print the entire workbook and submit it to your instructor.

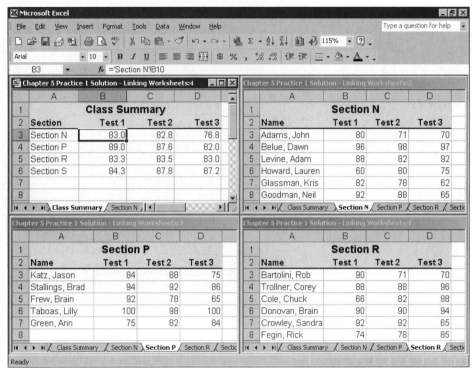

FIGURE 5.13   *Linking Worksheets (Exercise 1)*

2. A partially completed version of the workbook in Figure 5.14 can be found on the data disk as *Chapter 5 Practice 2*. The workbook contains a separate worksheet for each month of the year as well as a summary worksheet for the entire year. Thus far, only the months of January, February, and March are complete. Each monthly worksheet tallies the expenses for five divisions in each of four categories to compute a monthly total for each division. The summary worksheet displays the total expense for each division.
   a. Retrieve the *Chapter 5 Practice 2* workbook from the data disk, then open multiple windows so that the display on your monitor matches Figure 5.14.
   b. Use the Group Editing feature to select the worksheets for January, February, and March simultaneously. Enter the formula to compute the monthly total for each division and each expense category in each month.
   c. Use the Group Editing feature to format the worksheets.

d. Enter the appropriate formulas in the summary worksheet to compute the year-to-date totals for each division.

e. Add an additional worksheet for the month of April. Assume that Division 1 spends $100 in each category, Division 2 spends $200 in each category, and so on. Update the summary worksheet to include the expenses for April.

f. Add a documentation worksheet that includes your name, the date of modification, plus a description of each worksheet within the workbook.

g. Print the entire workbook (all six worksheets), then print the cell formulas for the summary worksheet only. Use an appropriate header or footer for each printout. Add a title page, then submit the assignment to your instructor.

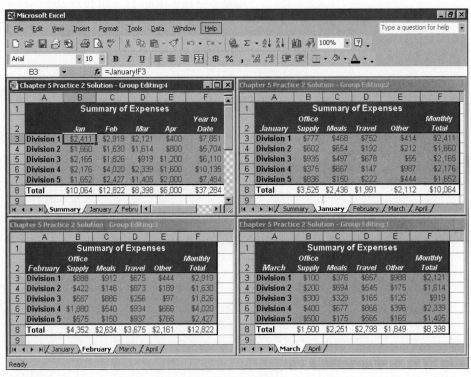

FIGURE 5.14 *Group Editing (Exercise 2)*

BUILDS ON

HANDS-ON
EXERCISE 3
PAGES 238–242

3. Object Linking and Embedding: Create the compound document in Figure 5.15, which consists of a memo, summary worksheet, and three-dimensional chart. The chart is to be created in its own chart sheet within the Corporate Sales workbook and then incorporated into the memo. Address the memo to your instructor, sign your name, then print the memo as it appears in Figure 5.15.

Prove to yourself that Object Linking and Embedding really works by returning to the Atlanta worksheet *after* you have created the document in Figure 5.15. Change the sales for Product 1 in Quarter 4 to $3,000. Switch back to the Word memo, and the chart should reflect the dramatic increase in the sales for Product 1. Add a postscript to the memo indicating that the corrected chart reflects the last-minute sale of Product 1 in Atlanta, and that you no longer want to discontinue the product. Print the revised memo and submit it to your instructor with the earlier version.

National Widgets, Inc.

Atlanta   ◆   Boston   ◆   Chicago

To: John Graves, President
           National Widgets, Inc.

From: Susan Powers
           Vice President, Marketing

Subject: Sales Analysis Data

Our overall fourth quarter sales have improved considerably over those in the first quarter. Please note, however, that Product 1, despite a growth in sales, is still trailing the other products, and discontinuing its production should be considered. I will await your reply on this matter.

Corporate Totals					
	Qtr 1	Qtr 2	Qtr 3	Qtr 4	Total
Product 1	$915	$995	$1,115	$1,235	$4,260
Product 2	$1,350	$1,450	$1,950	$2,250	$7,000
Product 3	$1,425	$1,600	$1,750	$2,000	$6,775
Total	$3,690	$4,045	$4,815	$5,485	$18,035

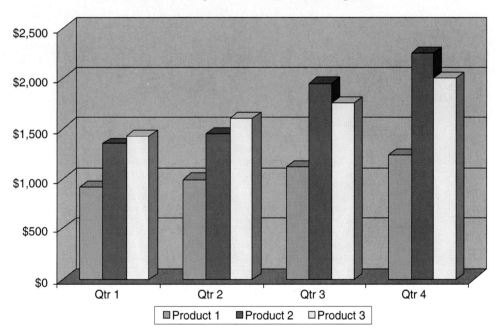

I look forward to hearing from you.

Susan

FIGURE 5.15   *Object Linking and Embedding (Exercise 3)*

4. National Computers: You will find a partially completed version of the workbook in Figure 5.16 in the *Chapter 5 Practice 4* workbook in the Exploring Excel folder. That workbook has four partially completed worksheets, one for each city. Your assignment is to complete the workbook so that it parallels the Corporate Sales workbook that was used in the first three hands-on exercises in this chapter. Proceed as follows:

a. Complete the individual worksheets by adding the appropriate formulas to compute the necessary row and column totals, then format these worksheets in attractive fashion. You can apply your own formatting, or you can use the AutoFormat command. You will find it easier, however, to use the Group editing feature as you add the totals and apply the formatting, since all of the worksheets contain parallel data. Be sure to ungroup the worksheets after you have applied the formatting.

b. Add a summary worksheet that provides corporate totals by product line and quarter. Apply the formatting from the individual worksheets to the summary worksheet.

c. Create two side-by-side column charts, each in its own chart sheet, which display the summary information in graphical fashion. One chart should compare the sales revenue for each office by product, the other should compare the revenue for each office by quarter.

d. Add a documentation worksheet similar to the sheet in Figure 5.16, then print the entire workbook for your instructor.

e. Print the cell formulas for the corporate worksheet. Add a cover sheet and submit the entire assignment to your instructor.

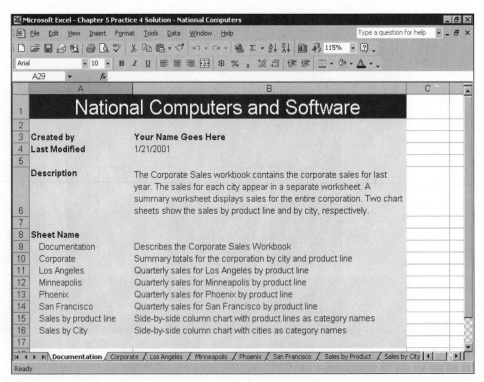

FIGURE 5.16 *National Computers (Exercise 4)*

BUILDS ON

CHAPTER 2
EXERCISE 3
PAGES 89–93

5. The Stock Portfolio: The workbook in Figure 5.17 uses Web queries (discussed in Chapter 2) to obtain current stock quotations from the Web, then uses those prices within an Excel workbook. The workbook contains five worksheets in all—a worksheet for each of three clients, Tom, Dick, and Harry; a worksheet containing stock prices as retrieved by the Web query; and a summary worksheet that shows the gain or loss for each client. Your assignment is to open the partially completed workbook in *Chapter 5 Practice 5*, and complete the workbook as follows.

a. Complete the individual worksheets for Tom, Dick, and Harry by entering the appropriate formulas to obtain the current price of each company in the client's portfolio, then determining the value of that investment by multiplying the price times the number of shares. Tom, for example, has AOL in his portfolio, the current price of which is found in cell D11 of the Stock Prices worksheet. Compute the gain or loss for each investment based on the difference between today's price and the purchase price.

b. Update the current price of each client's portfolio by right clicking anywhere within the table of prices in the Stock Prices worksheet, then clicking the Refresh Data command. (The stock symbols that appear at the top of the Stock Prices worksheet were entered manually from the investments in the individual worksheets and are the basis of the Web query.)

c. Enter the summary data for each client in the Summary worksheet using appropriate worksheet references. The total cost of Tom's portfolio, for example, is $33,000 and is found in cell D7 of Tom's worksheet. Thus the corresponding entry in the summary worksheet would be =Tom!E7, indicating that the number is to come from this cell in Tom's worksheet.

d. Add your name in row 9 of the summary worksheet as the investment adviser. Print the entire workbook for your instructor.

e. Print the cell formulas for the summary worksheet. Add a cover sheet and submit the entire assignment to your instructor.

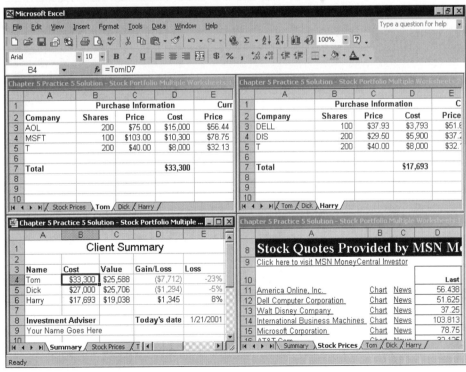

FIGURE 5.17 *The Stock Portfolio (Exercise 5)*

BUILDS ON

HANDS-ON
EXERCISE 3
PAGES 238–242

6. Creating a Web Page: Complete the first three hands-on exercises in the chapter, then pull down the File menu and click the Save as Web Page command to convert the completed workbook to its HTML equivalent. Save the file to a separate folder or desktop, then close Excel. Be sure you remember where you save the Web page.

   a. Start Windows Explorer, go the folder that contains the Web page, then double click the HTML document that you just created, to start your Web browser and display the document. You should see the corporate sales workbook displayed as a Web page within your browser, either Internet Explorer or Netscape Navigator, as shown in Figure 5.18. The address bar indicates that you are viewing the page locally (from a folder on drive C), as opposed to a Web server.

   b. Look carefully at the bottom of the page to note the various tabs corresponding to the different worksheets within the workbook. Click any tab to view the associated page. If you have trouble viewing the tabs, it is because you have an older version of the browser that does not support this feature. Pull down the Help menu within the browser, then click the About command to display the version of the browser you are currently using.

   c. Summarize the procedure to convert an Excel workbook to its HTML equivalent in a short note to your instructor. Describe how you would upload the Web page(s) to a server so that the workbook can be viewed by anyone with an Internet connection.

   d. Are you able to view the Web page in both Internet Explorer and Netscape Navigator? What differences, if any, do you see? Summarize these findings in a brief note to your instructor.

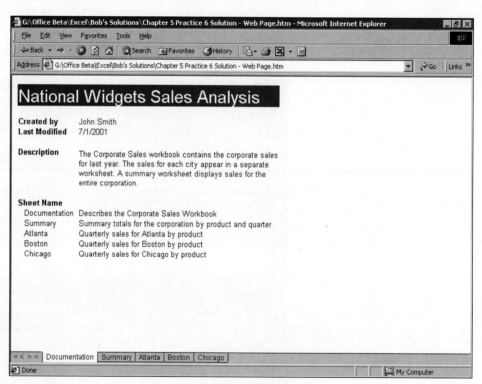

FIGURE 5.18   *Creating a Web Page (Exercise 6)*

BUILDS ON

HANDS-ON
EXERCISE 3
PAGES 238–242

7. Pivot Tables: A pivot table is an extremely flexible tool that enables you to manipulate the data in multiple worksheets to produce new reports as shown in Figure 5.19. (Pivot tables are covered in more detail in Chapter 7.) Complete the first three hands-on exercises, then follow the instructions below:

a. Open the Corporate Sales workbook that was completed at the end of the third hands-on exercise. Pull down the Data menu and click the Pivot Table and PivotChart Report command. Click the option buttons to select Multiple Consolidation Ranges and to specify Pivot Table. Click Next.

b. Click the option button that says I will create the page fields. Click Next.

c. Specify the range in step 2b of the PivotTable Wizard through pointing. Click the Sheet tab for Atlanta, select cells A2 through E5, then click the Add command button. You should see Atlanta!A$2:$E$5 in the All Ranges list box. Repeat this step for the other two cities.

d. Remain in step 2b of the PivotTable Wizard. Click the option button for 1 page field. Select (click) the Atlanta range within the All Ranges list box, then click in the Field One list box and type Atlanta. Do not press the enter key. Select (click) the Boston range within the All ranges list box, then click in the Field One list box and type Boston. Repeat this step for Chicago.

e. Click Next. Click the option button to create the pivot table on a New Worksheet. Click Finish.

f. You have a pivot table, but it does not match our figure. Click in cell B3 (the entry in the cell is Column), then click the formula bar and type Quarter (which replaces the previous Column entry). Change the entry in cell A4 from Row to Product. Change the entry in cell A1 from Page1 to City.

g. Pivot the table to match the figure. Drag Quarter to the row position (cell A4), Product to the column position (cell C3), and City to the row position below Quarter (cell A5). Release the mouse, and the Quarter and City labels will move to the positions shown in the figure.

h. Format the pivot table so that it matches Figure 5.19. Modify the description on the Documentation worksheet to include the pivot table, then print the pivot table (or the entire workbook if you haven't done so previously).

FIGURE 5.19 *Pivot Tables (Exercise 7)*

Designs by Jessica

The *Designs by Jessica* workbook on the data disk is only partially complete as it contains worksheets for individual stores, but does not yet have a summary worksheet. Your job is to retrieve the workbook and create a summary worksheet, then use the summary worksheet as the basis of a three-dimensional column chart reflecting the sales for the past year. Add a documentation worksheet containing your name as financial analyst, then print the entire workbook and submit it to your instructor.

External References

As marketing manager you are responsible for consolidating the sales information for all of the branch offices within the corporation. Each branch manager creates an identically formatted workbook with the sales information for his or her branch office. Your job is to consolidate the information into a single table, then graph the results appropriately. The branch data is to remain in the individual workbooks; that is, the formulas in your workbook are to contain external references to the *Eastern, Western,* and *Foreign workbooks* on the data disk. Your workbook is to be developed in such a way that any change in the individual workbooks should be automatically reflected in the consolidated workbook.

Pivot Tables

What advantages, if any, does a pivot table have over a conventional worksheet with respect to analyzing and consolidating data from multiple sources? What are the disadvantages? Does the underlying data have to be entered in the form of a list, or can it be taken directly from a worksheet? Use what you learn to extend the analysis of the Atlanta, Boston, and Chicago data that appeared throughout the chapter. (See practice exercise 7 for one example of a pivot table.)

Babyland

Create a new workbook based on data from the *Maplewood, Oakwood,* and *Ramblewood workbooks* in the Exploring Excel folder. The completed workbook should contain a worksheet for each store, a summary worksheet, an appropriate chart reflecting the summary data, and a documentation worksheet with your name, date, and a list of all worksheets in the workbook. Print the completed workbook, along with the cell formulas from the summary worksheet, then submit the printout to your instructor as proof you did this exercise.

CHAPTER 6

A Financial Forecast: Workgroups, Auditing, and Templates

OBJECTIVES

AFTER READING THIS CHAPTER YOU WILL BE ABLE TO:

1. Develop a spreadsheet model for a financial forecast; explain the importance of isolating the assumptions and initial conditions within a worksheet.
2. Explain how the Scenario Manager facilitates the decision-making process; create individual scenarios and a scenario summary.
3. Differentiate between precedent and dependent cells; use the Formula Auditing toolbar to detect errors that may exist within a spreadsheet.
4. Track the editing changes that are made to a spreadsheet; display, create, and edit cell comments.
5. Explain how workgroup functions enable several individuals to work on the same spreadsheet; resolve conflicts among different users.
6. Describe the use of data validation within a spreadsheet; use conditional formatting to display the value of a cell in different formats according to its value.
7. Explain how a template facilitates the creation of a new spreadsheet; create a template based on an existing worksheet.

OVERVIEW

Financial planning and budgeting are two of the most common business applications of a spreadsheet. We thought it appropriate, therefore, to use a financial forecast as the vehicle with which to illustrate several additional capabilities in Excel. We begin by developing the forecast itself, with emphasis on the importance of isolating the assumptions on which the spreadsheet is based. We introduce the Scenario Manager, which enables you to specify multiple sets of assumptions and input conditions (scenarios), then see the results at a glance.

It's important to remember, however, that a spreadsheet is first and foremost a tool for decision-making, and thus its accuracy is critical. Accordingly, we introduce the Formula Auditing toolbar and explain how its various tools can help ensure the accuracy of a spreadsheet. We describe how to share a workbook among multiple users, how to trace the editing changes that are made, and how to resolve conflicts if they occur. The last section in the chapter describes how to create a template on which to base future spreadsheets that use the same financial model. As always, the hands-on exercises help you to apply the conceptual material at the computer.

A FINANCIAL FORECAST

Figure 6.1 displays a financial forecast for Get Rich Quick Enterprises, which contains the projected income and expenses for the company over a five-year period. The spreadsheet enables management to vary any of the *assumptions* at the bottom of the spreadsheet to see the effects on the projected earnings. You don't have to be a business major to follow our forecast. All you have to realize is that the profit for any given year is determined by subtracting expenses from income.

The income is equal to the number of units sold times the unit price. The projected revenue in 2001, for example, is $300,000 based on selling 100,000 units at a price of $3.00 per unit. The variable costs for the same year are estimated at $150,000 (100,000 units times $1.50 per unit). The production facility costs $50,000 and administrative expenses add another $25,000. Subtracting the total expenses from the estimated income yields a net income before taxes of $75,000.

The income and expenses for each succeeding year are based on estimated percentage increases over the previous year, as shown at the bottom of the worksheet. It is absolutely critical to isolate the initial values and assumed rates of increase in this manner, and further, that all entries in the body of the spreadsheet are developed as formulas that reference these cells. The entry in cell C4, for example, is *not* the constant 100,000, but rather a reference to cell C18, which contains the value 100,000.

The distinction may seem trivial, but most assuredly it is not, as two important objectives are achieved. The user sees at a glance which factors affect the results of the spreadsheet (i.e., the cost and earnings projections) and, further, the user can easily change any of those values to see their effect on the overall forecast. Assume, for example, that the first-year forecast changes to 80,000 units sold and that this number will increase at 8 percent a year (rather than 10). The only changes in the worksheet are to the entries in cells C18 and E18, because the projected gross revenue is calculated using the values in these cells.

Once you appreciate the necessity of isolating the assumptions and *initial conditions,* you can design the actual spreadsheet. Ask yourself why you are building the spreadsheet in the first place and what you hope to accomplish. (The financial forecast in this example is intended to answer questions regarding projected rates of growth, and more importantly, how changes in the assumptions and initial conditions will affect the income, expenses, and earnings in later years.) By clarifying what you hope to accomplish, you facilitate the creation of the spreadsheet, which is done in five general stages:

1. Enter the row and column headings, and the values for the initial conditions and the assumed rates of change.
2. Develop the formulas for the first year of the forecast based on the initial conditions at the bottom of the spreadsheet.
3. Develop the formulas for the second year based on the values in year one and the assumed rates of change.
4. Copy the formulas for year two to the remaining years of the forecast.
5. Format the spreadsheet, then print the completed forecast.

Projected revenues

Conditional formatting

Net income

Initial values

Projected percent
increases

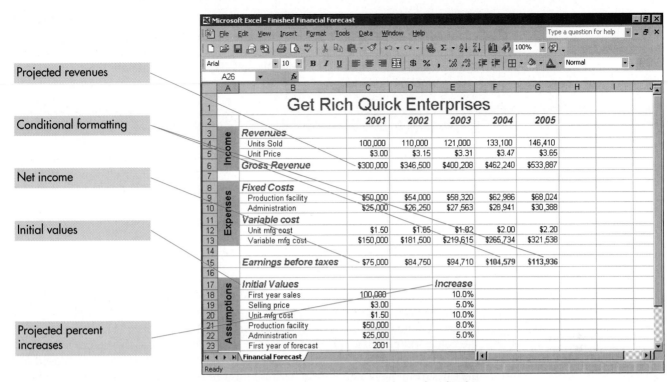

(a) Displayed Values

Rotated text

Indented text

Relative reference

Absolute reference

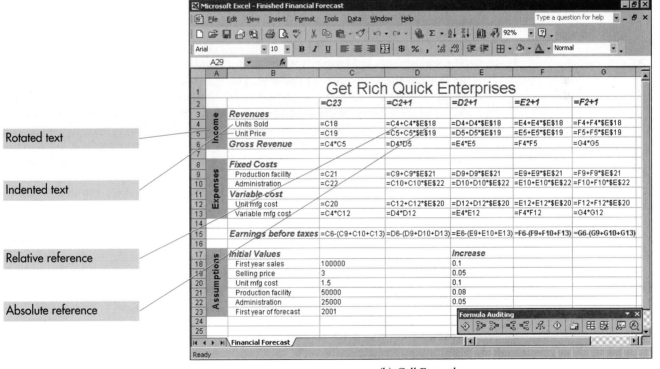

(b) Cell Formulas

FIGURE 6.1   *A Financial Forecast*

Perhaps the most critical step is the development of the formulas for the second year (2002 in Figure 6.1), which are based on the results for 2001 and the assumption about how these results will change for the next year. The units sold in 2002, for example, are equal to the sales in 2001 (cell C4) plus the estimated increase in unit sales (C4*$E$18); that is,

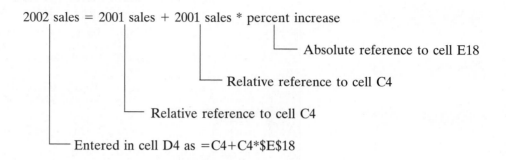

2002 sales = 2001 sales + 2001 sales * percent increase

Absolute reference to cell E18

Relative reference to cell C4

Relative reference to cell C4

Entered in cell D4 as =C4+C4*$E$18

The formula to compute the sales for the year 2002 uses both absolute and relative references, which ensures that it will be copied properly to the other columns for the remaining years in the forecast. An absolute reference ($E$18) is used for the cell containing the percent increase in unit sales, because this reference should remain the same when the formula is copied. A relative reference (C4) is used for the sales from the previous year, because this reference should change when the formula is copied. Many of the other formulas in column D are also based on percentage increases from column C, and are developed in similar fashion, as shown in Figure 6.1b.

Advanced Formatting

The spreadsheet in Figure 6.1 incorporates many of the formatting commands that have been used throughout the text. The spreadsheet also illustrates additional capabilities that will be implemented in the hands-on exercise that follows shortly. Some of these features are obvious, such as the ability to ***rotate text*** as seen in column A or the ability to ***indent text*** as was done in column B.

Other capabilities, such as ***conditional formatting***, are more subtle. Look at the projected earnings, for example, and note that amounts over $100,000 are displayed in blue, whereas values under $100,000 are not. One could simply select the two cells and change the font color to blue, but as the earnings change, the cells would have to be reformatted. Accordingly, we implemented the color by selecting the entire row of projected earnings and specifying a conditional format to display the value in blue if it exceeds $100,000, display it in red if it is negative, and default to black otherwise. The use of conditional formatting lets you vary any of the assumptions or initial conditions, which in turn change the projected earnings, yet automatically display the projected earnings in the appropriate color.

The last formatting feature in Figure 6.1 is the imposition of a user-defined style (Main Heading) for various cells in the spreadsheet. A ***style*** (or ***custom format***) is a set of formatting characteristics that is stored under a specific name. You've already used styles throughout the text that were predefined by Excel. Clicking the Comma, Currency, or Percent button on the Formatting toolbar, for example, automatically applies these styles to the selected cells. You can also define your own styles (e.g., Main Heading), as will be done in the hands-on exercise. The advantage of storing the formatting characteristics within a style, as opposed to applying the commands individually, is that you can change the definition of the style, which automatically changes the appearance of all cells defined by that style.

The ***Scenario Manager*** enables you to specify multiple sets of assumptions (***scenarios***), then see at a glance the results of any given scenario. Each scenario represents a different set of what-if conditions that you want to consider in assessing the outcome of a spreadsheet model. You could, for example, look at optimistic, pessimistic, and most likely (consensus) assumptions, as shown in Figure 6.2.

Figure 6.2a displays the Scenario Manager dialog box that contains the various scenarios that have been created. Each scenario is stored under its own name and is comprised of a set of cells whose values vary from scenario to scenario. Figure 6.2b, for example, shows the value of the ***changing cells*** for the consensus scenario. Figure 6.2c shows the values for the optimistic scenario. (The cells in the dialog box are identified by name, rather than cell reference through the ***Define Name command*** as will be shown in the next hands-on exercise. First_Year_Sales, for example, refers to cell C18 in the financial forecast. The use of a mnemonic name, as opposed to a cell reference, makes it much easier to understand precisely which values change from one scenario to the next.)

The ***scenario summary*** in Figure 6.2d compares the effects of the different scenarios to one another by showing the value of one or more ***result cells***. We see, for example, that the consensus scenario yields earnings of $113,936 in the fifth year (the same value shown earlier) compared to significantly higher or lower values for the other two scenarios.

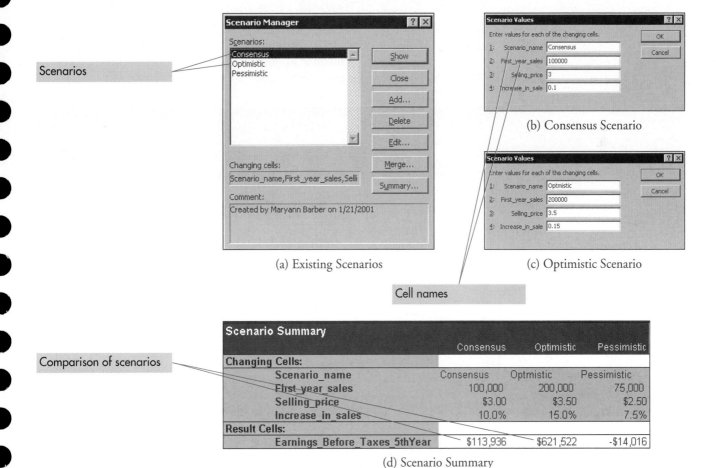

Scenarios

(a) Existing Scenarios

(b) Consensus Scenario

(c) Optimistic Scenario

Cell names

Comparison of scenarios

(d) Scenario Summary

FIGURE 6.2 *Scenario Manager*

A FINANCIAL FORECAST

Objective To develop a spreadsheet for a financial forecast that isolates the assumptions and initial values; to use conditional formatting, styles, indentation, and rotated text to format the spreadsheet. Use Figure 6.3 as a guide in the exercise.

Step 1: **Enter the Formulas for Year One**

➤ Start Excel. Open the **Financial Forecast** workbook in the **Exploring Excel folder** to display the worksheet in Figure 6.3a. (Cells C4 through C15 are currently empty.)

➤ Click in **cell C2**. Type **=C23** and press **enter**. Note that you are not entering the year explicitly, but rather a reference to the cell that contains the year, which is located in the assumptions area of the worksheet.

➤ Enter the remaining formulas for year one of the forecast:
  • Click in **cell C4**. Type **=C18**. Click in **cell C5**. Type **=C19**.
  • Click in **cell C6**. Type **=C4*C5**. Click in **cell C9**. Type **=C21**.
  • Click in **cell C10**. Type **=C22**. Click in **cell C12**. Type **=C20**.
  • Click in **cell C13**. Type **=C4*C12**.
  • Click in **cell C15**. Type **=C6-(C9+C10+C13)**.

➤ The cell contents for year one (2001 in this example) are complete. The displayed values in this column should match the numbers shown in Figure 6.3a.

➤ Save the workbook as **Finished Financial Forecast** in the **Exploring Excel Folder** you have used throughout the text.

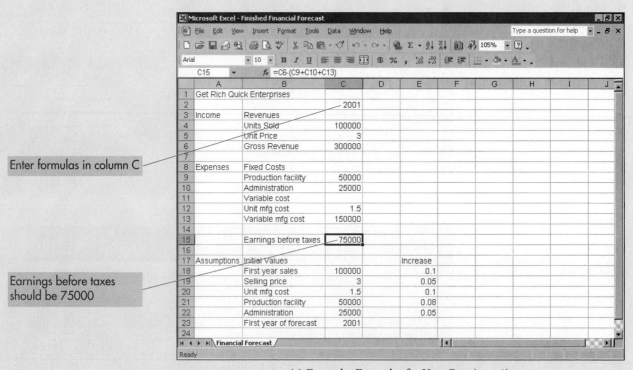

(a) Enter the Formulas for Year One (step 1)

FIGURE 6.3 *Hands-on Exercise 1*

Step 2: **Enter the Formulas for Year Two**

➤ Click in **cell D2**. Type **=C2+1** to determine the second year of the forecast.
➤ Click in **cell D4**. Type **=C4+C4*$E$18**. This formula computes the sales for year two as a function of the sales in year one and the rate of increase.
➤ Enter the remaining formulas for year two:
 • Click in **cell D5**. Type **=C5+C5*$E$19**. Copy the formula in cell C6 to D6.
 • Click in **cell D9**. Type **=C9+C9*$E$21**.
 • Click in **cell D10**. Type **=C10+C10*$E$22**.
 • Click in **cell D12**. Type **=C12+C12*$E$20**.
 • Copy the formulas in cells C13 and C15 to cells D13 and D15.
➤ The cell contents for the second year (2002) are complete. The displayed values should match the numbers shown in Figure 6.3b.
➤ Save the workbook.

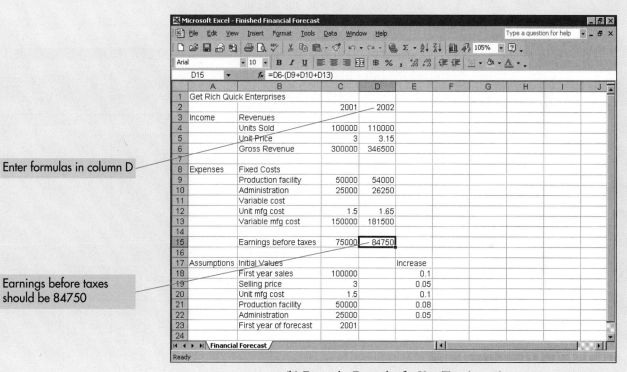

(b) Enter the Formulas for Year Two (step 2)

FIGURE 6.3 *Hands-on Exercise 1 (continued)*

USE POINTING TO ENTER CELL FORMULAS

A cell reference can be typed directly into a formula, or it can be entered more easily through pointing. The latter is also more accurate as you use the mouse or arrow keys to reference cells directly. To use pointing, select (click) the cell to contain the formula, type an equal sign to begin entering the formula, click (or move to) the cell containing the reference, then press the F4 key as necessary to change from relative to absolute references. Type any arithmetic operator to place the cell reference in the formula, then continue pointing to additional cells. Press the enter key to complete the formula.

Step 3: **Copy the Formulas to the Remaining Years**

> ➤ Click and drag to select **cells D2** through **D15** (the cells containing the formulas for year two). Click the **Copy button** on the Standard toolbar (or use the **Ctrl+C** keyboard shortcut).

> ➤ A moving border will surround these cells to indicate that their contents have been copied to the clipboard.

> ➤ Click and drag to select **cells E2** through **G15** (the cells that will contain the formulas for years three to five). Point to the selection and click the **right mouse button** to display the context-sensitive menu in Figure 6.3c.

> ➤ Click **Paste** to paste the contents of the clipboard into the selected cells. The displayed values for the last three years of the forecast should be visible in the worksheet.

> ➤ You should see earnings before taxes of 113936 for the last year in the forecast. Press **Esc** to remove the moving border.

> ➤ Save the workbook.

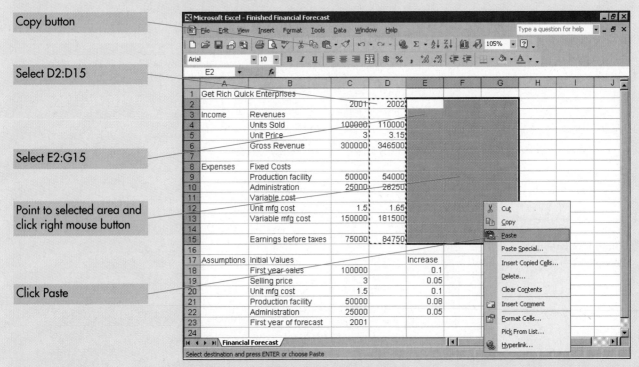

(c) Copy the Formulas to the Remaining Years (step 3)

FIGURE 6.3   *Hands-on Exercise 1 (continued)*

THE FILL HANDLE

Use the fill handle (the tiny black square) that appears in the lower-right corner of the selected cells to copy a cell (or range of cells) to an adjacent range. Select the cell (cells) to be copied, then click and drag the fill handle over the destination range. Release the mouse to complete the operation.

Step 4:   **Create a Style**

> Point to any toolbar, click the **right mouse button** to display a context-sensitive menu, then click the **Customize command** to display the Customize dialog box. Click the **Commands tab**, then select (click) the **Format category**.
> Click and drag the **Style List box** from within the command section to the right of the font color button on the Formatting toolbar. (You must drag the tool inside the toolbar and will see a large I-beam as you do so.)
> Release the mouse when you position the tool where you want. Click **Close** to close the Custom dialog box.
> The Style list box now appears on the Formatting toolbar as shown in Figure 6.3d. (The Style dialog box is not yet visible.) Click in **cell C2** and note that the Style list box indicates the Normal style (the default style for all cells in a worksheet).
> Change the font in cell C2 to **12 point Arial bold italic**. Click the **down arrow** on the Font Color tool and click **blue**. Pull down the **Format menu** and click the **Style command** to display the Style dialog box.
> The Normal style is already selected. Type **Main Heading** to define a new style according to the characteristics of the selected cell. Click **OK** to create the style and close the dialog box.
> Click and drag to select **cells D2** through **G2**. Click the down arrow on the Style list box and select the **Main Heading style** you just created to apply this style to the selected cells.
> Select **cell B3**. Press and hold the **Ctrl key** as you select **cells B6**, **B8**, **B11**, **B15**, **B17**, and **E17**, then apply the **Main Heading style** to these cells as well.
> Increase the width of column B so that you can see the text in cell B15.
> Save the workbook.

Style list box

Font Color button

Click in C2

Enter style name

Check all boxes to turn them on

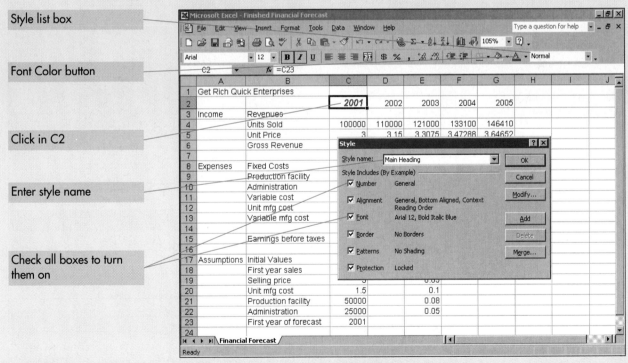

(d) Create a Style (step 4)

FIGURE 6.3   *Hands-on Exercise 1 (continued)*

Step 5: **Rotate and Indent Text**

➤ Click and drag to select **cells A3** through **A6**, as shown in Figure 6.3e. Pull down the **Format menu** and click the **Cells command** to display the Format Cells dialog box shown in the figure.
- Click the **Alignment tab** and specify **center alignment** in both the horizontal and vertical list boxes. Check the box to **Merge cells**. Click in the **Degrees text box** and enter **90**.
- Click the **Font tab**, then change the font to **12 point Arial bold**. Change the font color to **blue**.
- Click the **Patterns tab** and choose **gray shading**.
- Click **OK** to accept these changes and close the Format Cells dialog box.

➤ Apply the same formatting to **cells A8** through **A13** and **A17** through **A23**. Select **cells A8** through **A13** and click the **Merge and Center button** on the Formatting toolbar. Select **cells A17** through **A23** and merge these cells as well.

➤ Click and drag to select the labels in **cells B4** and **B5**. Click the **Increase Indent button** on the Formatting toolbar to indent these labels.

➤ Press and hold the **Ctrl key** as you select **cells B9** and **B10**, **B12** and **B13**, and **B18** through **B23**. Click the **Increase Indent button** to indent these labels.

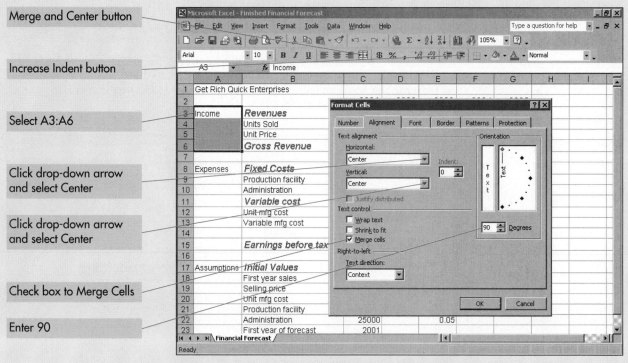

(e) Rotate and Indent Text (step 5)

FIGURE 6.3 *Hands-on Exercise 1 (continued)*

TOGGLE MERGE CELLS ON AND OFF

Click and drag to select multiple cells, then click the Merge and Center button on the Formatting toolbar to merge the cells into a single cell. Click in the merged cell, then click the Merge and Center button a second time and the cell is split. (This is different from Office 2000, where the only way to split cells was to clear the Merge cells check box within the Format Cells dialog box.)

Step 6: Conditional Formatting

➤ Click and drag to select **cells C15** through **G15**. Pull down the **Format menu** and click the **Conditional Formatting** command to display the Conditional Formatting dialog box in Figure 6.3f.

➤ Set the relationships for condition 1. Click the **Format button** to display the Format Cells dialog box and click the **Font tab**. Change the font style to **bold** and the font color to **blue**. Click **OK**.

➤ Click the **Add button** and enter the parameters for condition 2. Click the **Format button**. Change the Font style to **bold** and the color to **red**. Click **OK**.

➤ Click **OK** to close the Conditional Formatting dialog box. Click any cell to deselect cells C15 to G15. The earnings before taxes for the last two years of the forecast are displayed in bold and in blue, since they exceed $100,000.

➤ Click in **cell C19**, change the selling price to **2.00**, and press the **enter key**. The earnings before taxes are displayed in red since they are negative for every year. Click the **Undo button** to return the initial sales price to 3.00.

➤ Save the workbook.

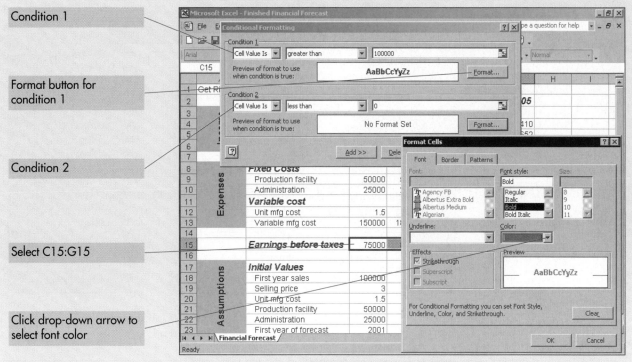

(f) Conditional Formatting (step 6)

FIGURE 6.3   *Hands-on Exercise 1 (continued)*

THE RIGHT MOUSE BUTTON

Point to a cell (or cell range), a worksheet tab, or a toolbar, then click the right mouse button to display a context-sensitive menu. Right clicking a cell, for example, displays a menu with selected commands from the Edit, Insert, and Format menus. Right clicking a toolbar displays a menu that lets you display or hide additional toolbars. Right clicking a worksheet tab enables you to rename, move, copy, or delete the worksheet.

Step 7: **Complete the Formatting**

➤ Click in **cell A1**. Change the font color to **blue**, and the font size to **22 points**. Click and drag to select **cells A1** through **G1** as shown in Figure 6.3g, then click the **Merge and Center button** to center the entry.

➤ Use Figure 6.3g as a guide to implement the appropriate formatting for the remaining entries in the worksheet. Remember to press and hold the **Ctrl key** if you want to select noncontiguous cells prior to executing a command.

➤ Add your name in **cell A2**. Save the workbook.

➤ Print the spreadsheet twice, once to show the displayed values and once to show the cell formulas. Press **Ctrl+~** to toggle between cell formulas and displayed values.

➤ Submit both printouts to your instructor.

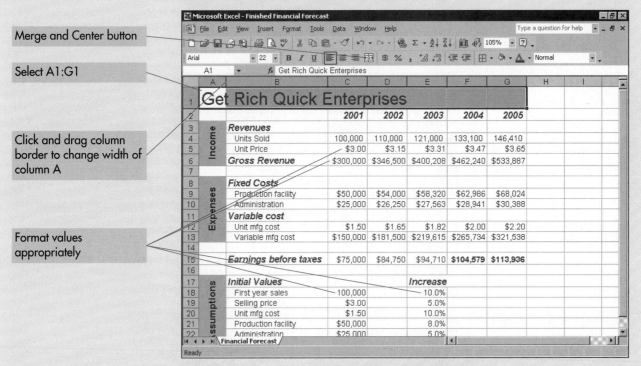

Merge and Center button

Select A1:G1

Click and drag column border to change width of column A

Format values appropriately

(g) Complete the Formatting (step 7)

FIGURE 6.3 *Hands-on Exercise 1 (continued)*

CREATE A CUSTOM VIEW

Format the spreadsheet to print the displayed values, then pull down the View menu and click Custom Views to display the Custom Views dialog box. Click the button to Add a view, enter the name (e.g., Displayed Values), and click OK. Press Ctrl+` to display the cell formulas, adjust the column widths as necessary, then pull down the View menu a second time to create a second custom view (e.g., Cell Formulas). You can switch to either view at any time by selecting the Custom Views command and selecting the appropriate view.

Step 8:   **The Insert Name Command**

➤ Click in **cell C18**, pull down the **Insert menu**, select the **Name command**, then click **Define** to display the Define Name dialog box in Figure 6.3h.

➤ **First_year_sales** is already entered as the default name (because this text appears as a label in the cell immediately to the left of the active cell. Underscores were added between the words, however, because blanks are not permitted in a cell name.) Click **OK** to accept this name.

➤ Name the other cells that will be used in the various scenarios in similar fashion. Use **Selling_price** as the name for **cell C19**, **Increase_in_sales** for **cell E18**, and **Scenario_name** for **cell E23**. (Do not be concerned that cell E23 is currently empty.)

➤ Save the workbook.

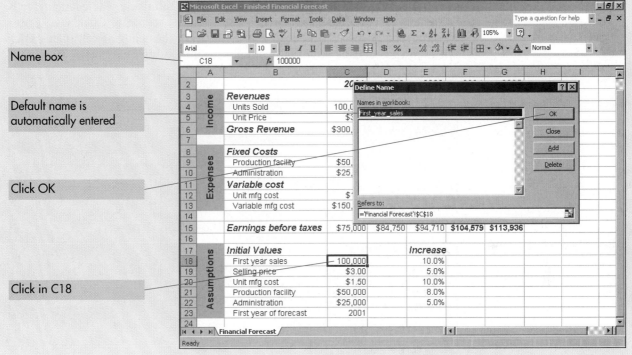

(h) The Insert Name Command (step 8)

FIGURE 6.3   *Hands-on Exercise 1 (continued)*

THE NAME BOX

Use the Name box on the formula bar to define a named range, by first selecting the cell in the worksheet to which the name is to apply, clicking in the Name box to enter the range name, and then pressing the enter key. Once the name has been defined, you can use the Name box to select a named range by clicking in the box and then typing the appropriate cell reference or name or simply by clicking the drop-down arrow next to the Name box to select the cell from a drop-down list.

Step 9: **Create the Scenarios**

➤ Click in **cell E23** and type the word **Consensus**. Click in **cell E17**, click the **Format Painter button** on the Formatting toolbar, then click in **cell E23** to copy the format from cell E17.

➤ Pull down the **Tools menu**. Click **Scenarios** to display the Scenario Manager dialog box. Click the **Add command button** to display the Add Scenario dialog box in Figure 6.3i. Type **Consensus** in the Scenario Name text box.

➤ Click in the **Changing Cells text box**. Cell E23 (the active cell) is already entered as the first cell in the scenario. Type a comma, then enter **C18**, **C19**, and **E18** as the remaining cells in the scenario. Click **OK**.

➤ You should see the Scenario Values dialog box with the values of this scenario already entered from the corresponding cells in the worksheet. Click **OK**.

➤ The Scenario Manager dialog box should still be open. Click the **Add command button** to add a second scenario called **Optimistic**. The changing cells are already entered and match the Consensus scenario. Click **OK**. Enter **Optimistic**, **200000**, **3.5**, and **.15**, as the values for the changing cells. Click **OK**.

➤ Enter a **Pessimistic scenario** in similar fashion, using **Pessimistic**, **75000**, **2.5**, and **.075**, for the changing cells. Click **OK**.

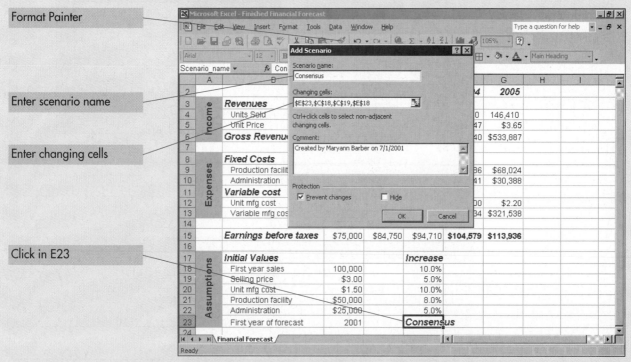

(i) Create the Scenarios (step 9)

FIGURE 6.3 *Hands-on Exercise 1 (continued)*

ISOLATE THE ASSUMPTIONS

The formulas in a worksheet should always be based on cell references that are clearly labeled, set apart from the rest of the worksheet. You can then vary the inputs (or assumptions) on which the worksheet is based to see the effect within the worksheet. You can change the values manually, or store sets of values within a specific scenario,

Step 10:   **View the Scenarios**

> ➤ The Scenario Manager dialog box should still be open as shown in Figure 6.3j. If necessary, pull down the **Tools menu** and click the **Scenarios command** to reopen the Scenario Manager.
> ➤ There should be three scenarios listed—Consensus, Optimistic, and Pessimistic—corresponding to the scenarios that were just created.
> ➤ Select the **Optimistic scenario**, then click the **Show button** (or simply double click the scenario name) to display the financial forecast under the assumptions of this scenario.
> ➤ Double click the **Pessimistic scenario**, which changes the worksheet to show the forecast under these assumptions.
> ➤ Double click the **Consensus scenario** to return to this scenario. Do you see how easy it is to change multiple assumptions at one time by storing the values in a scenario?

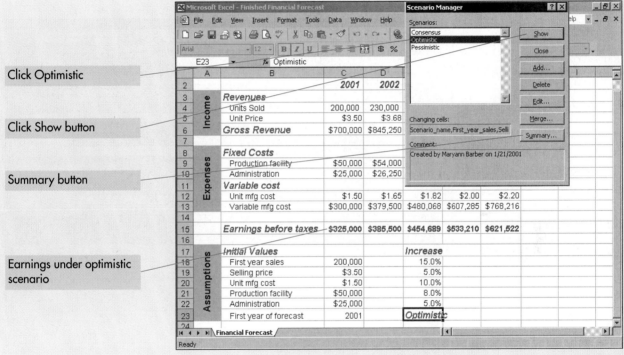

(j) View the Scenarios (step 10)

FIGURE 6.3   *Hands-on Exercise 1 (continued)*

THE SCENARIO MANAGER LIST BOX

The Scenario Manager List Box lets you select a scenario directly from a toolbar. Point to any toolbar, click the right mouse button to display a shortcut menu, then click Customize to display the Customize dialog box. Click the Commands tab, select Tools in the Categories list box, then click and drag the Scenario list box to an empty space on the toolbar. Click Close to close the dialog box and return to the workbook. Click the down arrow on the Scenario list box, which now appears on the toolbar, to choose from the scenarios that have been defined within the current workbook. See exercise 6 at the end of the chapter.

Step 11: **The Scenario Summary**

> ➤ The Scenario Manager dialog box should still be open. Click the **Summary button** to display the Scenario Summary dialog box.
> ➤ If necessary, click the **Scenario Summary option button**. Click in the **Result Cells text box**, then click in **cell G15** (the cell that contains the earnings before taxes in the fifth year of the forecast). Click **OK**.
> ➤ You should see a Scenario Summary worksheet as shown in Figure 6.3k. Each scenario has its own column in the worksheet. The changing cells, identified by name rather than cell reference, are listed in column C.
> ➤ The Scenario Summary worksheet is an ordinary worksheet to the extent that it can be modified like any other worksheet. Right click the header for **row 6**, then press and hold the **Ctrl key** as you click and drag **rows 12** to **14**. Right click the selected cells, then click the **Delete command** from the context-sensitive menu.
> ➤ Delete Column D in similar fashion. Add your name to the worksheet. Save the workbook, then print the summary worksheet for your instructor.

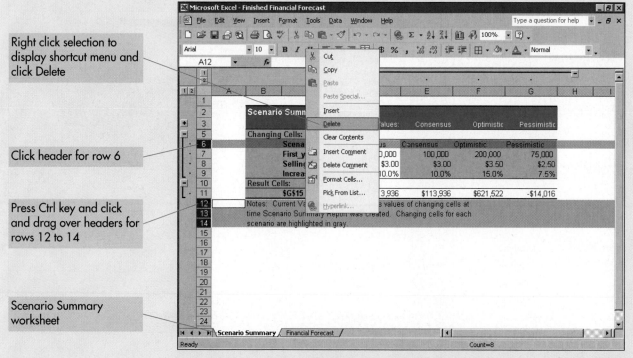

Right click selection to display shortcut menu and click Delete

Click header for row 6

Press Ctrl key and click and drag over headers for rows 12 to 14

Scenario Summary worksheet

(k) The Scenario Summary (step 11)

FIGURE 6.3 *Hands-on Exercise 1 (continued)*

THE SCENARIO SUMMARY WORKSHEET

You can return to the Scenario Manager to add or modify an individual scenario, after which you can create a new scenario summary. You must, however, modify the scenario from the original worksheet and not from the summary worksheet. Note, too, that each time you click the Summary button within the Scenario Manager, you will create another summary worksheet called Scenario Summary 2, Scenario Summary 3, and so on. You can delete the extraneous worksheets by right clicking the worksheet tab, then clicking the Delete command.

The spreadsheet containing the financial forecast is a tool that will be used by management as the basis for decision making. Executives in the company will vary the assumptions on which the spreadsheet is based to see the effects on profitability, then implement changes in policy based on the results of the spreadsheet. But what if the spreadsheet is in error? Think, for a moment, how business has become totally dependent on the spreadsheet, and what the consequences might be of basing corporate policy on an erroneous spreadsheet.

It's one thing if the assumptions about the expected increases turn out to be wrong, but the very nature of a forecast requires us to deal with uncertainty. It's inexcusable, however, if the formulas that use those numbers are invalid. Thus, it's common for several people to collaborate on the same spreadsheet to minimize the chance for error. One person creates the initial version, then distributes copies to the *workgroup* (the persons working on a project). Each person enters his or her changes, then the various workbooks can be merged into a single workbook. It's easier, however, to create a *shared workbook* and place it on a network drive to give all reviewers access to a common file.

Consider, for example, Figure 6.4, which displays an *invalid* version of the financial forecast. One of the first things you notice about Figure 6.4 is the comments by different people, Marion and Ben, who have reviewed the spreadsheet and suggested changes. Anyone with access to the shared workbook can change it using the tools on the *Reviewing toolbar* or through the *Track Changes command*. The changes made by different people to cell formulas are even displayed in different colors. You, as the developer, can then review the collective changes and resolve any conflicts that might occur.

How can you, or any of the reviewers, know when a spreadsheet displays invalid results? One way is to "eyeball" the spreadsheet and try to approximate its results.

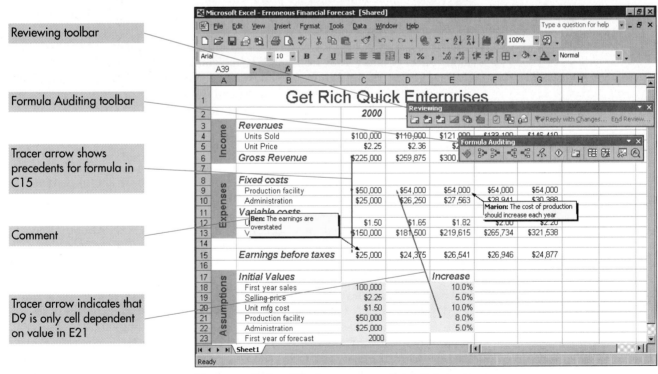

FIGURE 6.4   *Workgroups and Auditing*

Look for any calculations that are obviously incorrect. Look at the financial forecast, for example, and see whether all the values are growing at the projected rates of change. The number of units sold and the unit price increase every year as expected, but the cost of the production facility remains constant after 2001 (Marion's comment). This is an obvious error, because the production facility is supposed to increase at 8 percent annually, according to the assumptions at the bottom of the spreadsheet. The consequence of this error is that the production costs are too low and hence the projected earnings are too high. The error was easy to find, even without the use of a calculator.

A more subtle error occurs in the computation of the earnings before taxes. Look at the numbers for 2000. The gross revenue is $225,000. The total cost is also $225,000 ($50,000 for the production facility, $25,000 for administration, and $150,000 for the manufacturing cost). The projected earnings should be zero, but are shown incorrectly as $25,000 (Ben's comment), because the administration cost was not subtracted from the gross revenue in determining the profit.

You may be good enough to spot either of these errors just by looking at the spreadsheet. You can also use the *Formula Auditing toolbar* to display the relationships between the various cells in a worksheet. It enables you to trace the *precedents* for a formula and identify the cells in the worksheet that are referenced by that formula. It also enables you to trace the *dependents* of a cell and identify the formulas in the worksheet that reference that cell.

The identification of precedent and/or dependent cells is done graphically by displaying *tracers* on the worksheet. You simply click in the cell for which you want the information, then you click the appropriate button on the Formula Auditing toolbar. The blue lines (tracers) appear on the worksheet, and will remain on the worksheet until you click the appropriate removal button. The tracers always point forward, from the precedent cells to the dependent formula.

Look again at Figure 6.4 to see how the tracers are used. Cell C15 contains the formula to compute the earnings for the first year. There is a tracer (blue line) pointing to this cell and it indicates the precedents for the cell. In other words, we can see that cells C6, C9, and C13 are used to compute the value of cell C15. Cell C10 is not a precedent, however, and therein lies the error.

The analysis of the cost of the production facility is equally telling. There is a single tracer pointing away from cell E21, indicating that there is only one other cell (cell D9) in the worksheet that depends on the value of cell E21. In actuality, however, cells E9, F9, and G9 should also depend on the value of cell E21. Hence the cost of the production facility does not increase as it is supposed to.

Data Validation

The results of the financial forecast depend on the accuracy of the spreadsheet as well as the underlying assumptions. One way to stop such errors from occurring is through the *Data Validation command*, which enables the developer to restrict the values that can be entered into a cell. If the cell is to contain a text entry, you can limit the values to those that appear in a list such as Atlanta, Boston, or Chicago. In similar fashion, you can specify a quantitative relationship for numeric values such as > 0 or < 100.

Figure 6.5a displays the Settings tab in the Data Validation dialog box in which the developer requires the value in cell E18 (the annual sales increase) to be less than 15%. Figure 6.5b shows the type of error alert (a Warning) and the associated message that is to appear if the user does not enter a valid value. Figure 6.5c displays the dialog box the user sees if the criteria are violated, together with the indicated choice of actions. "Yes" accepts the invalid data into the cell despite the warning, "No" returns the user to the cell for further editing, and "Cancel" restores the previous value to the cell.

Value in E18 must be less than 15%

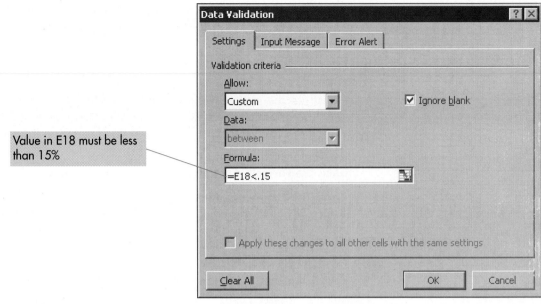

(a) Settings Tab

Title for the message box

Warning error

Warning icon

Message to be displayed if user enters a value greater than 15%

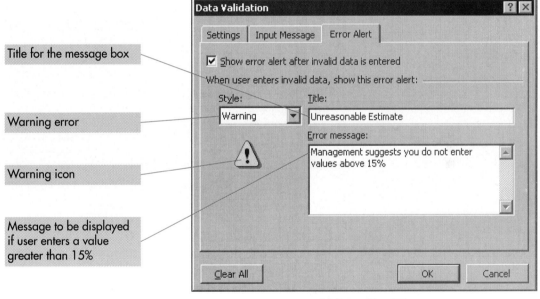

(b) Error Alert Tab

Title bar

Error message

Warning icon

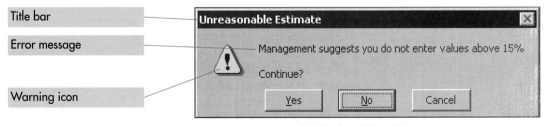

(c) Displayed Error Message

FIGURE 6.5   *The Data Validation Command*

AUDITING AND WORKGROUPS

Objective To illustrate the tools on the Formula Auditing toolbar; to trace errors in spreadsheet formulas; to identify precedent and dependent cells; to insert and delete comments. Use Figure 6.6 as a guide in the exercise.

Step 1: **Display the Formula Auditing and Reviewing Toolbars**

➤ Open the **Erroneous Financial Forecast workbook** in the **Exploring Excel folder**. Save the workbook as **Finished Erroneous Financial Forecast**.

➤ Point to any toolbar, click the **right mouse button** to display a context-sensitive menu, then click **Customize** to display the Customize dialog box.

➤ Click the **Toolbars tab**, check the boxes for the **Reviewing** and **Formula Auditing toolbars**, then close the dialog box to display the toolbars, in Figure 6.6a.

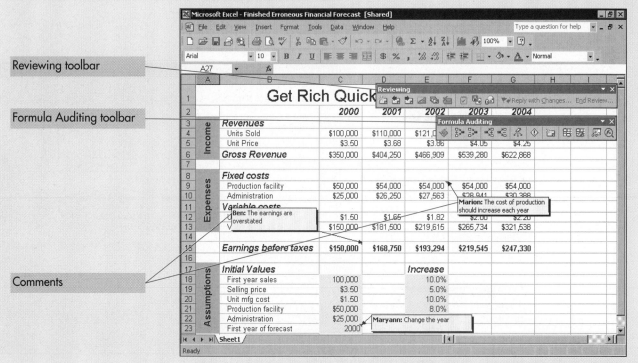

Reviewing toolbar

Formula Auditing toolbar

Comments

(a) Display the Formula Auditing and Reviewing Toolbars (step 1)

FIGURE 6.6 *Hands-on Exercise 2*

COMPARE AND MERGE WORKBOOKS

Send a copy of your workbook to one or more reviewers for comments, then merge the comments into the original workbook with a single command. Pull down the Tools menu and click the Share Workbook command, then check the box to allow changes by more than one user at a time. Send a copy of this shared workbook (with a unique file name) to each reviewer. Use the Merge and Compare workbooks command to combine the comments when they return the workbooks to you. See exercise 9 at the end of the chapter.

Step 2: **Highlight Changes**

➤ Pull down the **Tools menu**, click (or point to) the **Track Changes command**, then click **Highlight Changes** to display the Highlight Changes dialog box. Set the various options to match our selections in Figure 6.6b. Click **OK**.

➤ You should see a border around cell C19 to indicate that a change has been made to the contents of that cell. Point to the cell and you will see a ScreenTip indicating that Bob changed the contents from $2.25 to $3.50.

➤ Click in **cell C23**. Type **2001** to modify the year (as suggested by Maryann) and press **enter**. The years change automatically at the top of the forecast.

➤ Maryann's comment is now obsolete. Thus, right click in **cell C23** to display the context-sensitive menu, then click the **Delete Comment command**.

➤ The comment is removed from the cell and the red triangle disappears. The cell is still enclosed in a blue border to indicate that its value has changed.

➤ Click the **Hide All Comments button** on the Reviewing toolbar. The comments are still in the worksheet, but are no longer visible.

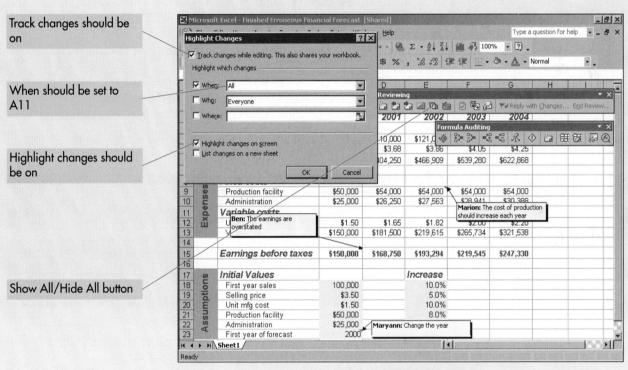

(b) Highlight Changes (step 2)

FIGURE 6.6 *Hands-on Exercise 2 (continued)*

CHANGE THE YEAR

A well-designed spreadsheet facilitates change by isolating the assumptions and initial conditions. 2000 has come and gone, but all you have to do to update the forecast is to click in cell C23, and enter 2001 as the initial year. The entries in cells C2 through G2 (containing years of the forecast) are changed automatically as they contain formulas (rather than specific values) that reference the value in cell C23.

Step 3: **Trace Dependents**

➤ Point to **cell E9** to display the comment, which indicates that the production costs do not increase after the second year. Click in **cell E21** (the cell containing the projected increase in the cost of the production facility).

➤ Click the **Trace Dependents button** on the Formula Auditing toolbar to display the dependent cells as shown in Figure 6.6c. Only one dependent cell (cell D9) is shown. This is clearly an error because cells E9 through G9 should also depend on cell E21.

➤ Click in **cell D9** to examine its formula. The production costs for the second year are based on the first-year costs (cell C9) and the rate of increase (cell E21). The latter, however, was entered as a relative rather than an absolute address.

➤ Change the formula in **cell D9** to include an absolute reference to cell E21 (i.e., the correct formula is =C9+C9*$E$21). The tracer arrow disappears due to the correction.

➤ Drag the fill handle in **cell D9** to copy the corrected formula to cells E9, F9, and G9. The displayed value for cell G9 should be $68,024. Delete Marion's comment in cell E9, which is no longer applicable.

➤ Cells D9 through G9 have a blue border to indicate that changes were made to these cells.

➤ Click in **cell E21**. Click the **Trace Dependents button**, and this time it points to the production costs for years two through five in the forecast.

➤ Click the **Remove Dependent Arrows button** on the Formula Auditing toolbar to remove the arrows.

➤ Save the workbook.

Remove Dependent Arrows button

Trace Dependents button

D9 is only dependent cell

Click in E21

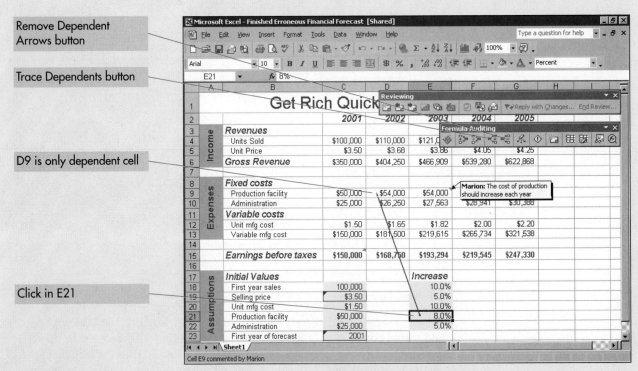

(c) Trace Dependents (step 3)

FIGURE 6.6 *Hands-on Exercise 2 (continued)*

Step 4: **Trace Precedents**

➤ Point to **cell C15** to display Ben's comment that questions the earnings before taxes. Now click the **Trace Precedents button** to display the precedent cells as shown in Figure 6.6d.

➤ There is an error in the formula because the earnings do not account for the administration expense (cell C10).

➤ Change the formula in cell C15 to **=C6-(C9+C10+C13)**. The earnings change to $125,000 after the correction.

➤ Drag the fill handle in **cell C15** to copy the corrected formula to cells D15 through G15. (The latter displays a value of $202,918 after the correction.)

➤ Delete Ben's comment in cell C15, which is no longer applicable.

➤ Save the workbook.

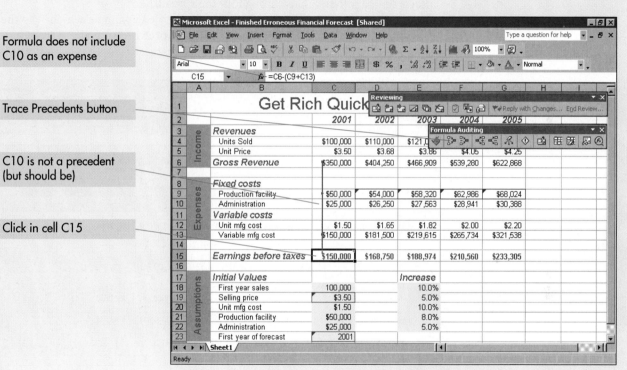

Formula does not include C10 as an expense

Trace Precedents button

C10 is not a precedent (but should be)

Click in cell C15

(d) Trace Precedents (step 4)

FIGURE 6.6 *Hands-on Exercise 2 (continued)*

THE FORMULAS ARE COLOR-CODED

The fastest way to change the contents of a cell is to double click in the cell, then make the changes directly in the cell rather than to change the entries on the formula bar. Note, too, that if the cell contains a formula (as opposed to a literal entry), Excel will display each cell reference in the formula in a different color, which corresponds to the border color of the referenced cells elsewhere in the worksheet. This makes it easy to see which cell or cell range is referenced by the formula. You can also click and drag the colored border to a different cell to change the cell formula.

Step 5: **Accept or Reject Changes (Resolve Conflicts)**

➤ Pull down the **Tools menu**, click the **Share Workbook command** to display the Share Workbook dialog box, then click the **Advanced tab**.

➤ Look for the Conflicting Changes Between Users section (toward the bottom of the dialog box), then if necessary, click the option button that says "Ask me which changes win". Click **OK**.

➤ Pull down the **Tools menu**, click (or point to) the **Track Changes command**, then click **Accept or Reject Changes**. You can accept the default selections in the Selection Changes dialog box. Click **OK**.

➤ You should see the Accept or Reject Changes dialog box in Figure 6.6e. Select (click) **$2.25**, the value that was entered by Caroline, then click the **Accept button**. (The contents of cell C19 change in the worksheet to $2.25, which in turn affects several other values throughout the spreadsheet.)

➤ Click **Accept** (or press **Ctrl+A**) to accept the next change, which was the change you made earlier in the first year of the forecast. Press the **Accept button** as you are presented with each additional change.

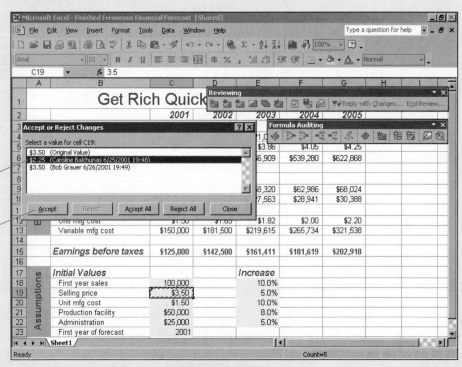

Click suggested change

Click Accept

(e) Accept or Reject Changes (Resolve Conflicts) (step 5)

FIGURE 6.6 *Hands-on Exercise 2 (continued)*

EDITING OR DELETING COMMENTS

The easiest way to edit or delete an existing comment is to point to the cell containing the comment, then click the right mouse button to display a context-sensitive menu, in which you select the appropriate command. You can use the right mouse button to insert a comment by right clicking in the cell, then choosing the Insert Comment command.

Step 6: **Insert a Comment**

➤ Click in **cell C19** (the cell containing the selling price for the first year). Pull down the **Insert menu** and click the **Comment command** (or click the **New Comment button** on the Reviewing toolbar).

➤ A comment box opens, as shown in Figure 6.6f. Enter the text of your comment as shown in the figure, then click outside the comment when you are finished.

➤ The comment box closes, but a tiny red triangle appears in the upper-right corner of cell C19. (If you do not see the triangle, pull down the **Tools menu**, click **Options**, click the **View tab**, then click the option button in the Comments area to show **Comment Indicator only**.)

➤ Point to **cell C19** and the text of your comment appears as part of the ScreenTip. Point to a different cell and the comment disappears.

New Comment button

Click in C19

Enter comment

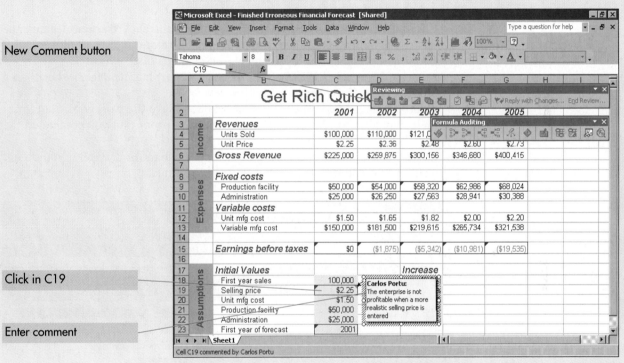

(f) Insert a Comment (step 6)

FIGURE 6.6 *Hands-on Exercise 2 (continued)*

LIMITATIONS OF SHARED WORKBOOKS

A shared workbook enables multiple people to view and/or modify a workbook simultaneously, but many of the more sophisticated features are disabled. You cannot, for example, delete worksheets, merge cells, apply conditional formats, or insert a hyperlink. Nor can you use subtotals, group or outline data, create a pivot table, or implement data validation. To use these features, you must remove the workbook from shared status as described in the next step.

Step 7:   **Data Validation**

➤ Click in cell **E18**. Type **.18**. Excel displays the error message shown in Figure 6.6g. Press **Esc** to cancel and try another entry. No matter how many times you try, you will not be able to enter a value above .15 in cell E18 because the error type was specified as "Stop" rather than a warning.

➤ Pull down the **Data menu**. The Validation command is dim and not currently accessible because the workbook is currently a shared workbook.

➤ Pull down the **Tools menu**, click (or point to) the **Track Changes command**, then click **Highlight Changes** to display the Highlight Changes dialog box. Clear the box to track changes while editing. Click **OK**. Click **Yes** when prompted to remove the workbook from shared use.

➤ Pull down the **Data menu**. Click the **Validation command** (which is now accessible) to display the Data Validation dialog box, and if necessary, click the **Error Alert tab**.

➤ Click the **drop-down arrow** on the Style list box and click **Warning**. Change the text of the message to **Management frowns on values of 15% or higher**. Click **OK** to accept the new settings and close the dialog box.

➤ Reenter **.18** in **cell E18**. This time you see a Warning message, rather than a Stop message. Click **Yes** to accept the new value.

➤ Add your name somewhere in the workbook. Save the workbook, then print the completed workbook for your professor as proof that you completed the exercise.

➤ Close the Reviewing and Formula Auditing toolbars. Exit Excel if you do not want to continue with the next exercise at this time.

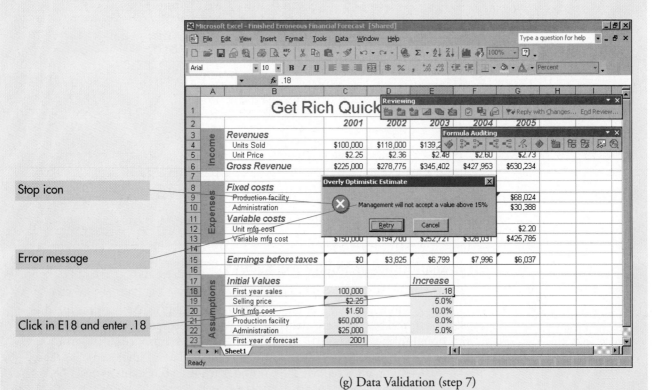

(g) Data Validation (step 7)

FIGURE 6.6   *Hands-on Exercise 2 (continued)*

The spreadsheet just completed is tailored to the needs of financial forecasting for Get Rich Quick Enterprises. It could also serve as the basis of a financial forecast for any organization, which leads in turn to the creation of a template. A *template* is a special type of workbook (it has its own file format) that is used as the basis for other workbooks. It contains text, formatting, formulas, and/or macros, but it does not contain data; the latter is entered by the end-user as he or she uses the template to create a workbook.

Figure 6.7a contains the template you will create in the next hands-on exercise. It resembles the completed forecast from earlier in the chapter, except that the assumption area has been cleared of all values except the initial year of the forecast. Even the name of the company in cell A1 has been erased. Look at the active cell (cell C15), however, and note that its contents are visible in the Formula bar. Thus, you can see that the template contains the formulas from the worksheet, but without any data. (The results of the calculations within the body of the spreadsheet are uniformly zero, but the zeros are suppressed through an option set through the Tools menu.)

The template in Figure 6.7a is used to create specific forecasts such as the one in Figure 6.7b. Look closely at the entry in the title bar for that forecast, noting that it appears as Get Rich Quick1; that is, the number 1 has been appended to the name of the template. This is done automatically by Excel, which will add the next sequential number to the name of each additional forecast during a session. To create a specific forecast, just enter the desired values in the assumption area, then as each value is entered, the formulas in the body of the spreadsheet will automatically calculate the results.

Most templates are based on *protected worksheets* that enable the user to modify only a limited number of cells within the worksheet. The template for financial forecast, for example, enables the user to change the contents of any cell in the assumption area, but precludes changes elsewhere in the worksheet. This is very important, especially when templates are used throughout an organization. The protection prevents an individual who is not familiar with Excel from accidentally (or otherwise) changing a cell formula. Any attempt to do so produces a protected-cell message on the screen.

To create a template, you start with a finished workbook and check it for accuracy. Then you clear the assumption area and protect the worksheet. The latter is a two-step process. First, you *unlock* all of the cells that are subject to change, then you protect the worksheet. Once this is done, the user will be able to change the value of any cell that was unlocked, but will be unable to change the contents of any other cell. Finally, you save the template under its own name, but as a template rather than an ordinary workbook. (Ideally, the template should be saved in a special *Templates folder* within the Microsoft Office folder so that it can be accessed automatically from the task pane. This is possible only if you have your own computer and/or if the network administrator puts the template in the folder for you.)

Once created, a template can be accessed three different ways—through the File Open command, from the task pane, or by double clicking its icon from within Windows Explorer or My Computer. The File Open command opens the actual template, enabling you to modify the template if and when that becomes necessary. The task pane provides a link to General Templates that combines the function of the File Open command with that of the Save As command. It opens a template and automatically saves it as a workbook, assigning a name to the workbook by appending a number to the name of the template (e.g., Get Rich Quick1). Double clicking a file from within My Computer or Windows Explorer has the same effect as accessing the template from the task pane.

Formula entered in C15

Name of company has
been erased

C5 is active cell

Assumption area has been
cleared

Initial year is only
assumption entered

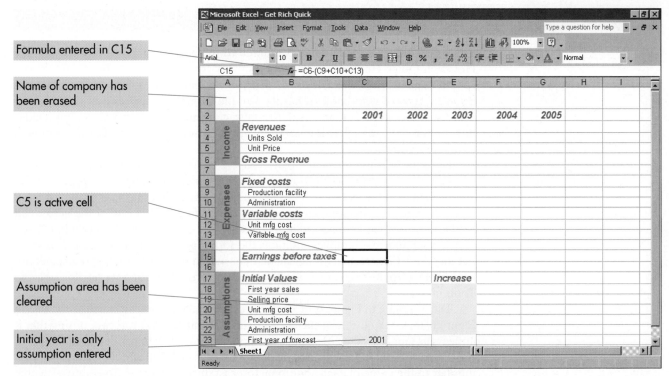

(a) Template

Get Rich Quick1 is
automatically assigned as
the name

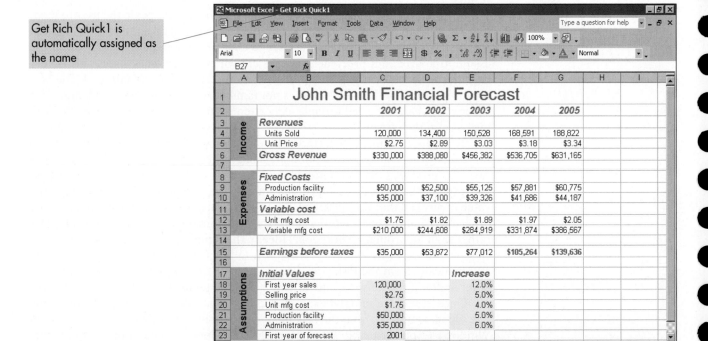

(b) Completed Worksheet

FIGURE 6.7 *The Get Rich Quick Template*

CREATING A TEMPLATE

Objective To unlock cells in a worksheet, then protect the worksheet; to create a template and then create a workbook from that template. Use Figure 6.8.

Step 1: **Clear the Assumption Area**

➤ Open the **Finished Erroneous Financial Forecast** from the previous exercise. Click in **cell A1**, then press and hold the **Ctrl key** as you click and drag to select **cells C18** through **E23**.

➤ Pull down the **Edit menu**, click (or point to) the **Clear command**, then click **Contents** to delete the contents from the selected cells as shown in Figure 6.8a. The values in the body of the spreadsheet are all zero.

➤ Pull down the **Edit menu** a second time, click the **Clear command**, then click **Comments** to delete the comments from these cells as well.

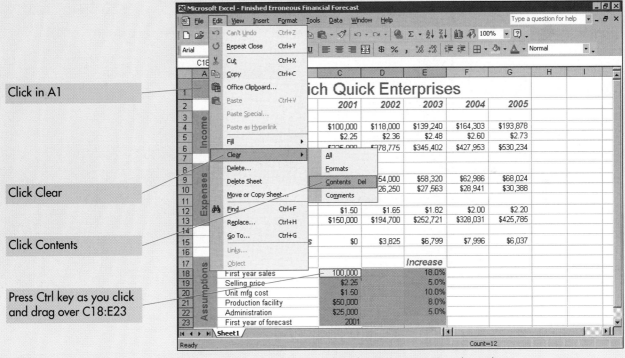

Click in A1

Click Clear

Click Contents

Press Ctrl key as you click and drag over C18:E23

(a) Clear the Assumption Area (step 1)

FIGURE 6.8 *Hands-on Exercise 3*

WORKBOOK PROPERTIES

Do you know the original author of the workbook or other Office document that is currently open? When was the file created, modified, and last accessed? This and other information are stored within the workbook and can be viewed (or changed) by pulling down the File menu and clicking the Properties command.

Step 2: Protect the Worksheet

➤ Protecting a worksheet is a two-step process. First you unlock the cells that you want to be able to change after the worksheet has been protected, then you protect the worksheet. Accordingly:

- If necessary, click in **cell A1**, then press and hold the **Ctrl key** as you click and drag to select **cells C18** through **E23**. Pull down the **Format menu**, click the **Cells command** to display the Format Cells dialog box. Click the **Protection tab**, then clear the **Locked check box**. Click **OK**.
- Pull down the **Tools menu**, click **Protection**, then click the **Protect Sheet command** to display the Protect Sheet dialog box in Figure 6.8b. Be sure that your settings match those in the figure, then click **OK**.

➤ Pull down the **Tools menu**, click the **Options command**, click the **View tab** and clear the box to show Zero values. Click **OK**. The zeros disappear.

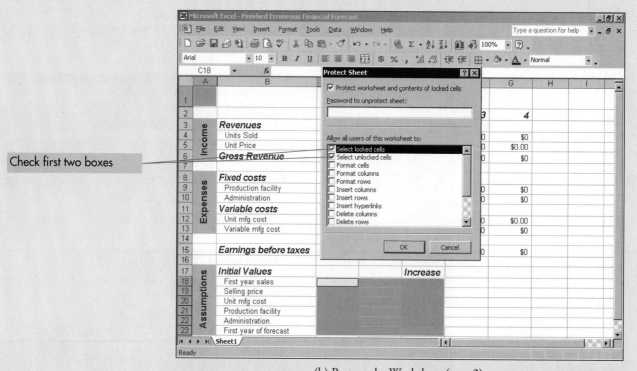

(b) Protect the Worksheet (step 2)

FIGURE 6.8   *Hands-on Exercise 3 (continued)*

THE OPTIONS MENU

Pull down the Tools menu and click the Options command to display the Options dialog box from where you can customize virtually every aspect of Excel. The General tab is especially useful as it enables you to change the default file location, the number of worksheets in a new workbook, and/or the number of recently opened files that appear on the File menu. There is no need to memorize anything, just spend a few minutes exploring the options on the various tabs, then think of the Options command the next time you want to change an Excel feature.

Step 3: **Test the Template**

➤ Test the assumption area to be sure that you can change the contents of these cells. Click in **cell A1** and enter your name followed by the words **Financial Forecast**. The text will be centered automatically across the top of the worksheet.

➤ Click in **cell C23**, type **2001**, and press the **enter key**. Excel should accept this value, and in addition, it should change the years as shown in Figure 6.8c. Enter the values **100000** and **.10** in **cells C18** and **E18**, respectively. Excel should accept these values and build the spreadsheet accordingly.

➤ If you are prevented from entering a value in the assumption area, you need to unprotect the worksheet and unlock the cells.

•   Pull down the **Tools menu**, click **Protection**, then click the **Unprotect Sheet command**.

•   Select the cells in the assumption area, pull down the **Format menu**, click the **Cells command**, click the **Protection tab**, and clear the Locked box.

•   Repeat the steps to protect the worksheet.

➤ Test the protection feature by clicking in any cell in the body of the worksheet (e.g., cell C5) and entering a value. You should see the dialog box in Figure 6.8c indicating that the cell is protected. Click **OK**. If you do not see this message, undo the entry and then repeat the commands to protect the worksheet.

➤ Clear the contents from **cells A1**, **C18**, **E18**, and **C23**. You're ready to save the template.

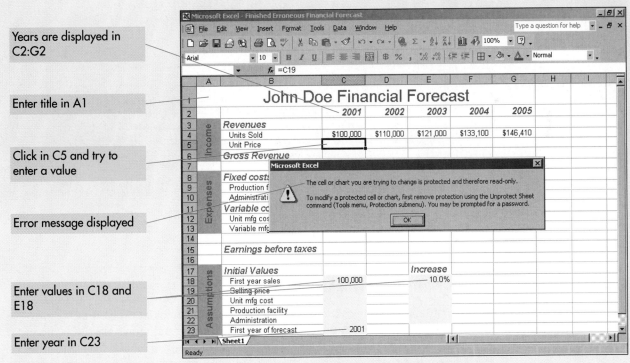

(c) Test the Template (step 3)

FIGURE 6.8   *Hands-on Exercise 3 (continued)*

Step 4: **Save the Template**

➤ Pull down the **File menu**, click the **Save As command** to display the Save As dialog box in Figure 6.8d. Enter **Get Rich Quick** as the name of the template.

➤ Click the **down arrow** in the Save as Type list box and choose **Template**. The folder where you will save the template depends on whether you have your own machine.

• If you are working on your own computer and have access to all of its folders, save the template in the **Templates folder** (the default folder that is displayed automatically).

• If you are working at school or otherwise sharing a computer, save the template in the **Exploring Excel folder** that you have used throughout the text.

➤ Click the **Save button** to save the template.

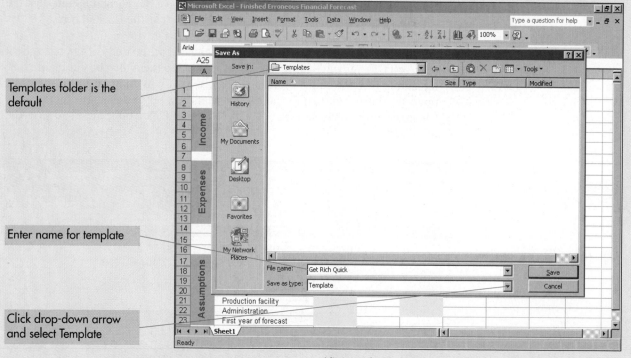

Templates folder is the default

Enter name for template

Click drop-down arrow and select Template

(d) Save the Template (step 4)

FIGURE 6.8 *Hands-on Exercise 3 (continued)*

PROTECT THE WORKBOOK

A template or workbook is not truly protected unless it is saved with a password, because a knowledgeable user can always pull down the Tools menu and access the Protect command to unprotect a worksheet. You can, however, use password protection to prevent this from happening. Pull down the File menu, click the Save As command to the Save As dialog box, then click the Tools button and click General Options to display the Save Options dialog box. You can enter one or two passwords, one to open the file, and one to modify it. Be careful, however, because once you save a workbook or template with a password, you cannot open it if you forget the password.

Step 5: **Open the Template**

➤ Close Excel, then restart the program. The way in which you open the template depends on where you saved in the previous step.
  • If you are working on your own computer, open the task pane and click the link to **General Templates** to display the dialog box in Figure 6.8e. The Get Rich Quick template appears automatically because it was saved in the Templates folder. Double click the **Get Rich Quick template** to open it.
  • If you are working at school or otherwise sharing a computer, start Windows Explorer, change to the **Exploring Excel folder**, then double click the **Get Rich Quick template** to open it.
➤ You should see a blank workbook, named Get Rich Quick1. Excel automatically saves a copy of the template as a workbook and assigns it a name consisting of the template's name followed by a number.
➤ Complete and save the financial forecast. Print the completed workbook with displayed values and with the cell formulas. Exit Excel.

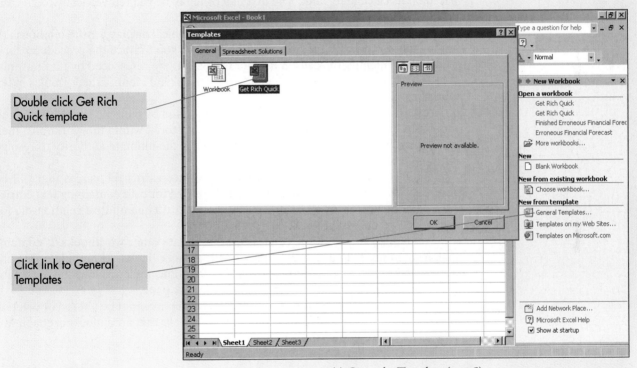

Double click Get Rich Quick template

Click link to General Templates

(e) Open the Template (step 5)

FIGURE 6.8 *Hands-on Exercise 3 (continued)*

CREATE A CHART AND ASSOCIATED TREND LINE

A chart adds impact to any type of numerical analysis. Use the template to create a financial forecast, then plot the earnings before taxes against the associated year. A simple column chart is best. Pull down the Chart menu after the chart has been drawn, then click the Add Trendline command to display the associated dialog box. Click Type tab and choose a linear (straight-line) trend. (You cannot add trendlines to data series in 3-D, stacked-column, or pie charts.) Click OK to accept the setting and close the dialog box. Print the chart for your instructor.

A spreadsheet is used frequently as a tool in decision making, and as such, is the subject of continual what-if speculation. Thus, the initial conditions and assumptions on which the spreadsheet is based should be clearly visible so that they can be easily varied. In addition, the formulas in the body of the spreadsheet should be dependent on these cells.

A style is a set of formatting instructions that has been saved under a distinct name. Styles provide a consistent appearance to similar elements throughout a workbook. Existing styles can be modified to change the formatting of all cells that are defined by that style.

The Scenario Manager lets you specify multiple sets of assumptions (scenarios), then see the results at a glance within the associated worksheet. The scenario summary compares the effects of the different scenarios to one another by showing the value of one or more result cells in a summary table.

Conditional formatting may be implemented to change the appearance of a cell based on its calculated value. The text in a cell may be rotated vertically to give the cell greater emphasis.

The Formula Auditing toolbar provides a graphical display for the relationships among the various cells in a worksheet. It enables you to trace the precedents for a formula and identify the cells in the worksheet that are referenced by that formula. It also enables you to trace the dependents of a cell and identify the formulas in the worksheet that reference that cell.

A shared workbook may be viewed and/or edited by multiple individuals simultaneously. The changes made by each user can be stored within the workbook, then subsequently reviewed by the developer, who has the ultimate authority to resolve any conflicts that might occur.

The Data Validation command enables you to restrict the values that will be accepted into a cell. You can limit the values to a list for cells containing text entries (e.g., Atlanta, Boston, or Chicago), or you can specify a quantitative relationship for cells that hold numeric values.

A template is a workbook that is used to create other workbooks. It contains text, formatting, formulas, and/or macros, but no specific data. A template that has been saved to the Templates or Spreadsheet Solutions folder is accessed automatically from the link to General Templates in the task pane.

A worksheet may be protected so that its contents cannot be altered or deleted. A protected worksheet may also contain various cells that are unlocked, enabling a user to vary the contents of these cells.

KEY TERMS

Assumptions (p. 262)
Changing cells (p. 265)
Conditional formatting (p. 264)
Custom format (p. 264)
Custom view (p. 272)
Data Validation command (p. 278)
Define Name command (p. 265)
Dependent cells (p. 278)
Formula Auditing toolbar (p. 278)
Indent text (p. 264)

Initial conditions (p. 262)
Insert Comment command (p. 285)
Insert Name command (p. 273)
Precedent cells (p. 278)
Protected worksheet (p. 287)
Result cells (p. 265)
Reviewing toolbar (p. 277)
Rotate text (p. 264)
Scenario (p. 265)
Scenario Manager (p. 265)

Scenario summary (p. 265)
Shared workbook (p. 277)
Style (p. 264)
Template (p. 287)
Templates folder (p. 287)
Tracers (p. 278)
Track Changes command (p. 277)
Unlock cells (p. 287)
Workgroup (p. 277)

1. Which of the following best describes the formula to compute the sales in the second year of the financial forecast?
   (a) It contains a relative reference to the assumed rate of increase and an absolute reference to the sales from the previous year
   (b) It contains an absolute reference to the assumed rate of increase and a relative reference to the sales from the previous year
   (c) It contains absolute references to both the assumed rate of increase and the sales from the previous year
   (d) It contains relative references to both the assumed rate of increase and the sales from the previous year

2. The estimated sales for the first year of a financial forecast are contained in cell B3. The sales for year two are assumed to be 10% higher than the first year, with the rate of increase (10%) stored in cell C23 at the bottom of the spreadsheet. Which of the following is the best way to enter the projected sales for year two, assuming that this formula is to be copied to the remaining years of the forecast?
   (a) =B3+B3*.10
   (b) =B3+B3*C23
   (c) =B3+B3*$C$23
   (d) All of the above are equivalent entries

3. Which of the following describes the placement of assumptions in a worksheet as required by Microsoft Excel?
   (a) The assumptions must appear in contiguous cells but can be placed anywhere within the worksheet
   (b) The assumptions must appear in contiguous cells and, further, must be placed below the main body of the worksheet
   (c) The assumptions are not required to appear in contiguous cells and, further, can be placed anywhere within the worksheet
   (d) None of the above

4. Given that cell D4 contains the formula =D1+D2:
   (a) Cells D1 and D2 are precedent cells for cell D4
   (b) Cell D4 is a dependent cell of cells D1 and D2
   (c) Both (a) and (b)
   (d) Neither (a) nor (b)

5. Which of the following is true, given that cell C23 is displayed with three blue tracers that point to cells E4, F4, and G4, respectively?
   (a) Cells E4, F4, and G4, and precedent cells for cell C23
   (b) Cell C23 is a precedent cell for cells E4, F4, and G4
   (c) Both (a) and (b)
   (d) Neither (a) nor (b)

6. How can you enter a comment into a cell?
   (a) Click the New Comment command on the Formula Auditing toolbar
   (b) Click the New Comment command on the Reviewing toolbar
   (c) Right click in the cell, then select the Insert Comment command
   (d) All of the above

7. Which of the following best describes how to protect a worksheet, but still enable the user to change the value of various cells within the worksheet?
   (a) Protect the entire worksheet, then unlock the cells that are to change
   (b) Protect the entire worksheet, then unprotect the cells that are to change
   (c) Unprotect the cells that are to change, then protect the entire worksheet
   (d) Unlock the cells that are to change, then protect the entire worksheet

8. Which of the following describes the protection associated with the financial forecast that was developed in the chapter?
    (a) The worksheet is protected and all cells are locked
    (b) The worksheet is protected and all cells are unlocked
    (c) The worksheet is protected and the assumption area is locked
    (d) The worksheet is protected and the assumption area is unlocked

9. Which of the following may be stored within a style?
    (a) The font, point size, and color
    (b) Borders and shading
    (c) Alignment and protection
    (d) All of the above

10. What is the easiest way to change the formatting of five cells that are scattered throughout a worksheet, each of which has the same style?
    (a) Select the cells individually, then click the appropriate buttons on the Formatting toolbar
    (b) Select the cells at the same time, then click the appropriate buttons on the Formatting toolbar
    (c) Change the format of the existing style
    (d) Reenter the data in each cell according to the new specifications

11. Each scenario in the Scenario Manager:
    (a) Is stored in a separate worksheet
    (b) Contains the value of a single assumption or input condition
    (c) Both (a) and (b)
    (d) Neither (a) nor (b)

12. The Formula Auditing and Reviewing toolbars are floating toolbars by default. Which of the following is (are) true about fixed (docked) and floating toolbars?
    (a) Floating toolbars can be changed to fixed toolbars, but the reverse is not true
    (b) Fixed toolbars can be changed into floating toolbars, but the reverse is not true
    (c) Fixed toolbars can be changed into floating toolbars and vice versa
    (d) Fixed toolbars can be displayed only at the top of the screen

13. You open a template called Expense Account but see Expense Account1 displayed on the title bar. What is the most likely explanation?
    (a) You are the first person to use this template
    (b) Some type of error must have occurred
    (c) All is in order since Excel has appended the number to differentiate the workbook from the template on which it is based
    (d) The situation is impossible

14. Two adjacent cells within the worksheet are enclosed in hairline borders of different colors. Each of these cells also contains a tiny shaded triangle in the upper-left part of the cell. Which of the following is the most likely explanation?
    (a) Conditional formatting is in effect for the cells in question
    (b) Data validation is in effect for the cells in question
    (c) A comment has been entered into each of the cells
    (d) The cells have been changed by different members of a workgroup

ANSWERS

1. b	**6.** d	**11.** d
2. c	**7.** d	**12.** c
3. c	**8.** d	**13.** c
4. c	**9.** d	**14.** d
5. a	**10.** c	

1. Erroneous Payroll: The worksheet in Figure 6.9 displays an *erroneous* version of a worksheet that computes the payroll for a fictitious company. The worksheet is nicely formatted, but several calculations are in error. You can find the worksheet shown in Figure 6.9 in the *Chapter 6 Practice 1* workbook within the Exploring Excel folder.

   Your assignment is to open the workbook, find the errors, and correct the worksheet. The *correct* specifications are shown below:

   a. The taxable income is the gross pay, minus the deduction per dependent, multiplied by the number of dependents.
   b. The withholding tax is based on the individual's taxable income. The Social Security tax is based on the individual's gross pay.
   c. The overtime bonus is entered as an assumption within the worksheet, making it possible to change the overtime rate in a single place should that become necessary.
   d. The net pay is the gross pay minus the withholding tax and the Social Security tax.
   e. You can "eyeball" the worksheet to find the mistakes and/or you can use the Formula Auditing toolbar. Figure 6.9, for example, displays the precedent cells for computing the withholding tax for the first employee and reveals the first error (i.e., that the withholding tax is incorrectly computed on the gross pay rather than on the taxable income).
   f. Print the corrected worksheet with both displayed values and cell formulas. Add a cover sheet and submit the assignment to your instructor. Do you see the importance of checking a worksheet for accuracy?

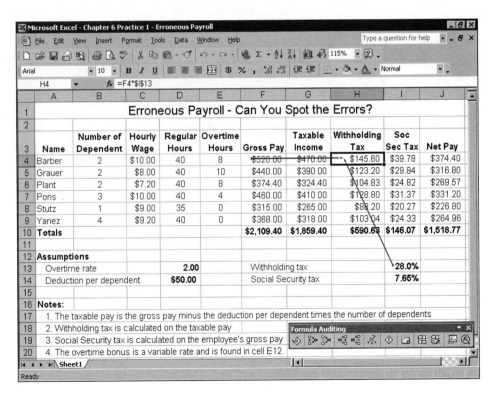

FIGURE 6.9   *Erroneous Payroll (Exercise 1)*

BUILDS ON

CHAPTER 3
PRACTICE
EXERCISE 1
PAGE 156

2. Protection and Validation: The worksheet in Figure 6.10 will calculate the value of your retirement based on a set of uniform annual contributions to a retirement account. In essence, you contribute a fixed amount of money each year ($2,000 in Figure 6.10) and the money accumulates at an estimated rate of return (9% in Figure 6.10). You indicate the age when you start to contribute, your projected retirement age, the number of years in retirement, and the rate of return you expect to earn on your money when you retire.

   a. The worksheet determines the total amount you will have contributed, the amount of money you will have accumulated, and the value of your monthly pension. The numbers are impressive, and the sooner you begin to save, the better. The calculations use the Future Value (FV) and Payment (Pmt) functions, respectively. These functions are discussed in Chapter 3.

   b. You will find the completed worksheet in the *Chapter 6 Practice 2* workbook in the Exploring Excel folder. Your assignment is to implement data validation and password protection to ensure that the user does not enter unrealistic numbers nor alter the formulas within the worksheet.

   c. Three validity checks are required as indicated in the assumption area of the worksheet. The retirement age must be 59.5 or greater (as required by current law), the rate of return during the period you are investing money cannot exceed 8%, and the rate of return during retirement cannot exceed 7%. You are to display a warning message similar to that in Figure 6.10 if the user violates any of these conditions. The warning will allow the user to override the assumptions.

   d. Unlock cells B2 through B8, where the user enters his or her name and assumptions. Protect the remainder of the worksheet. Use "password" as the password.

   e. Enter your name and your assumptions in the completed worksheet, then print the worksheet twice to show both displayed values and cell formulas for your instructor.

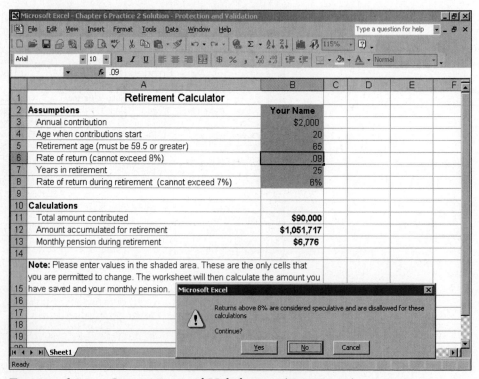

FIGURE **6.10** *Protection and Validation (Exercise 2)*

3. **Retirement Scenarios:** The worksheet in Figure 6.11 illustrates a retirement plan in which you and your employer each contribute a percentage of your salary toward your retirement. (The percentages are not necessarily equal, although Figure 6.11 shows the same percentage for both you and your employer.) The money accumulates for a specified number of years, at the specified rate of return. At that point, the "nest egg" or future value of the combined contributions will be used to fund your monthly pension in retirement.

   a. The amount of money that you will have depends on a variety of factors, as can be seen in the scenario summary of Figure 6.11. Your assignment is to open the worksheet in *Chapter 6 Practice 3,* create four different scenarios, then combine those scenarios in a scenario summary. You can match ours or you can supply your own parameters.

   b. Use the Define Name command to assign meaningful names to both the changing cells and the result cells, so that the scenario summary is easily understood.

   c. Add your name to the worksheet that performs the retirement calculations, then print that worksheet with both the displayed values and cell formulas.

   d. Print the scenario summary worksheet as well, then submit both worksheets to your instructor.

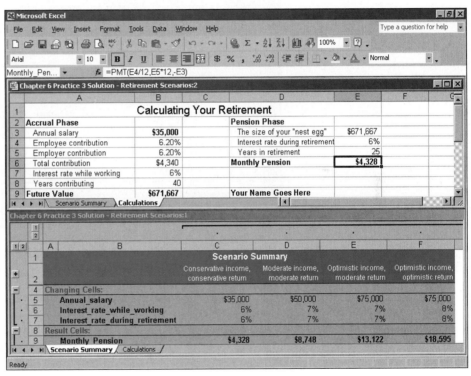

FIGURE 6.11   *Retirement Scenarios (Exercise 3)*

4. **Erroneous Grade Book:** The worksheet in Figure 6.12 is to compute class grades. The parameters (assumptions) on which the grades are based are shown in the lower portion of the worksheet. The worksheet is nicely formatted, but it contains some fundamental errors. Your assignment is to retrieve the workbook in the *Chapter 6 Practice 4* workbook and correct the errors.

   a. "Eyeball" the worksheet and/or use the Formula Auditing toolbar to determine the formulas that are in error. Figure 6.12 shows the precedent cells to determine the semester average for Charles. The cell formula is shown in the formula bar.

b. What is the meaning of the green triangle that appears in cell H5 (the cell that contains the Quiz Average for Goodman)? What command, if any, was executed to display the triangle?

c. Implement conditional formatting for the final grade after you have corrected the worksheet. All As are to be displayed in blue. All Fs are to be displayed in red.

d. Add your name as the grading assistant. Print the worksheet with both displayed values and cell formulas for your professor. Add a cover sheet to complete the assignment.

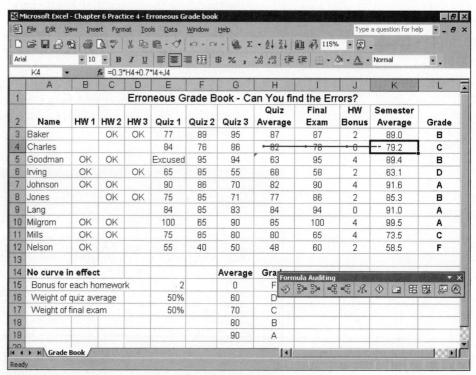

FIGURE 6.12 *Erroneous Grade Book (Exercise 4)*

BUILDS ON

PRACTICE
EXERCISE 4
PAGES 299–300

5. Grading on a Curve: Figure 6.13 displays a corrected version of the erroneous grade book from the previous problem. The formulas have been corrected, and in addition, the grading parameters have been changed to reflect a curve. The bonus for each homework assignment has been changed to three points, and the required average for each letter grade has been modified. The order of the students within the worksheet has also been changed so that students appear in descending order of the semester average.

a. Open the corrected workbook from the previous problem. Click anywhere within the semester average column, then click the Descending Sort button, so that students appear in order of descending semester average.

b. Create two scenarios, with and without a curve. The changing cells are the same for each scenario, and consist of the name of the scenario (cell A14), the homework bonus (cell E15), and the required average for each grade (cells G15 through G19). Use the parameters from the previous problem for the no curve scenario.

c. Print the displayed values for both scenarios for your professor. Add a cover sheet. Submit the completed assignment to your instructor.

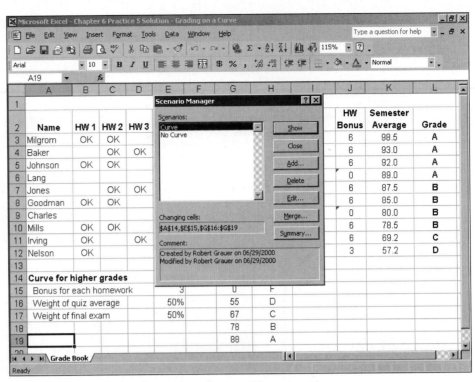

FIGURE 6.13 *Grading on a Curve (Exercise 5)*

BUILDS ON

HANDS-ON
EXERCISE 1
PAGES 266–276

6. The Scenario List Box: Look closely at Figure 6.14 and note the presence of a scenario list box on the Standard toolbar. This helpful list box lets you display a scenario (without going to the Tools menu) by clicking the down arrow and choosing the scenario from the displayed list.

   a. Choose any workbook that contains one or more scenarios (we used the Finished Financial workbook at the end of the first hands-on exercise). To display the list box, point to any toolbar, click the right mouse button to display a shortcut menu, then click Customize to display the Customize dialog box. Click the Commands tab, select Tools in the Categories list box, then click and drag the Scenario list box to an empty space on any toolbar. Click Close to close the dialog box and return to the workbook. The Scenario list box should appear on the toolbar.

   b. Prove to your instructor that you have added the list box to your toolbar by capturing the Excel screen, then pasting it into a Word document. All you have to do is press the Print Screen key within Excel (after you display the scenario list box) to copy the screen to the Windows clipboard. Start Word, then click the Paste button to add the contents of the clipboard to the Word document. Word will ask if you want to compress the picture. Click Yes.

   c. You may find it useful to modify the position of the screen within the Word document. Thus right click the figure from within Word to display a shortcut menu, click the Format Picture command to display the Format Picture dialog box, click the Layout tab, select Square wrapping, and click OK. You can now click and drag the picture anywhere within the document. You can also click and drag a sizing handle just as you can with any other Windows object.

   d. Complete the note in Figure 6.14, add your name somewhere in the document, then print the finished document for your instructor. Add a cover sheet to complete the assignment.

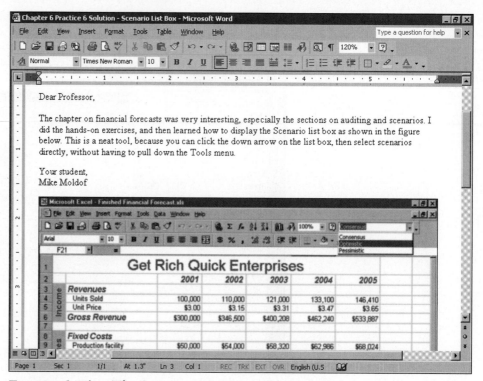

FIGURE 6.14   *The Scenario List Box (Exercise 6)*

7. The Expense Statement: Microsoft Excel includes several templates that are intended to help run a business or plan your personal finances. Pull down the View menu and open the task pane. Click the General Templates command to open the Templates dialog box, from where you can click the Spreadsheet Solutions tab to open the Expense Statement template shown in Figure 6.15. If necessary, click the command button to enable macros. Use the template to create a hypothetical business trip for yourself, then submit the completed worksheet to your instructor.

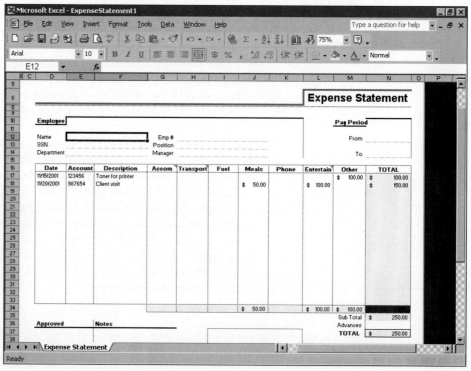

FIGURE 6.15   *The Expense Statement (Exercise 7)*

8. Excel Templates: The worksheet in Figure 6.16a was created from the loan amortization template in the Spreadsheet Solutions folder. Additional templates can be found on the Microsoft Web site. Pull down the File menu, click the New command to open the task pane, then select Templates on Microsoft.com to display the Template Gallery in Figure 6.16b. Choose at least one template, from either the Spreadsheet Solutions folder or the Template Gallery, and create a new spreadsheet based on that template.

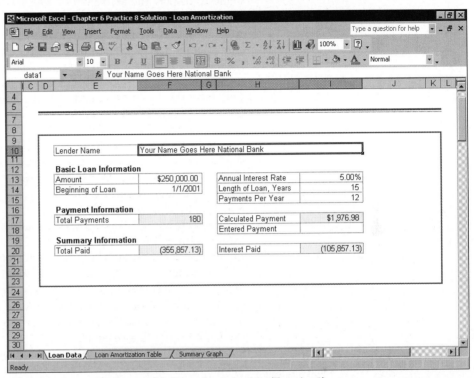

(a) Loan Amortization (Exercise 8)

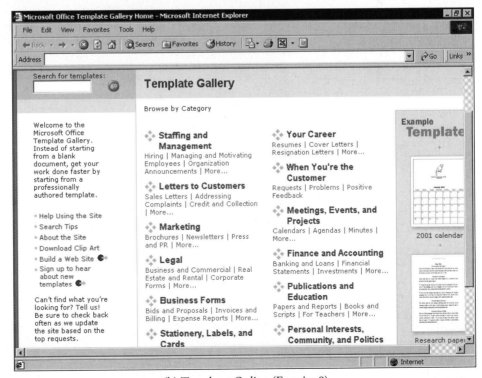

(b) Templates Online (Exercise 8)

FIGURE 6.16 *Excel Templates*

9. **Compare and Merge Workbooks:** The consensus workbook in Figure 6.17 is the result of merging three individual workbooks, provided by Tom, Dick, and Harry, each of whom added their comments to a shared workbook. Proceed as follows:

a. Open the workbook in *Chapter 6 Practice 9* that contains the original workbook sent out to each of the three reviewers.

b. Pull down the Tools menu, click the Compare and Merge Workbooks command to display the associated dialog box, select the individual workbooks for Tom's Forecast, Dick's Forecast, and Harry's Forecast, then click OK. The workbooks will be opened individually, and any changes will be automatically merged into the consensus workbook. If there are conflicting changes (e.g., two individuals make different changes to the same cell), the changes are entered in the order that the workbooks are opened.

c. Pull down the Tools menu and click the Highlight Changes command to display the Highlight Changes dialog box. Clear the Who, When, and Where check boxes so that you will see all of the changes made to the workbook. Check the box to list the changes on a new sheet. Click OK.

d. A History worksheet is created automatically that shows all of the changes made to the shared workbook. Pull down the Window menu, click New window, then pull down the Window menu a second time and tile the worksheets horizontally to match Figure 6.17.

e. Look closely at the History worksheet and note that Harry and Tom changed the value of cell E4 to $90,000 and $125,000, respectively. The value that is shown in the consensus workbook ($125,000 in our figure) depends on the order in which the workbooks were merged. Tom was last in our example, so his change dominates. You can, however, use the Track Changes command to go through all of the changes individually and accept (reject) the changes individually. If necessary, use this command to accept Tom's change ($125,000) rather than Harry's.

f. Print the completed workbook, with both worksheets, for your instructor.

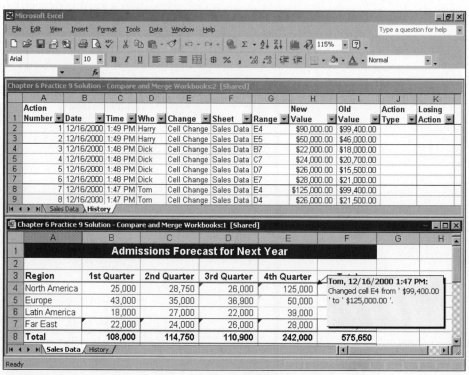

FIGURE 6.17 *Compare and Merge Workbooks (Exercise 9)*

BUILDS ON

HANDS-ON
EXERCISE 1
PAGES 266–276

10. Trend Lines: Excel 2002 extends the charting capability within Excel to include trend lines as shown in Figure 6.18. You create a chart in the usual fashion, then you use the Trend Line command in the Chart menu to add an appropriate trend line by projecting the data in a linear or exponential fashion. Your assignment is to complete the first hands-on exercise for the financial forecast, then create the chart and associated trend line. Proceed as follows:

a. Click and drag to select cells C15 through G15 (the cells that contain the projected profits) in the worksheet, then click the Chart Wizard button on the Standard toolbar.

b. Choose the two-dimensional clustered column chart in step one of the Chart Wizard. (You cannot add a trend line to a three-dimensional chart.) Click Next. The option button to display data in rows is selected.

c. Remain in step two of the Wizard and click the Series tab in the Chart Wizard dialog box. Click in the Category X labels list box, then click and drag to select cells C2 through G2 in the worksheet (the cells that contain the years of the forecast). Click Next.

d. Enter the chart title, "Our trend is up!" Remain in step three of the Wizard, and click the Legend tab in the Chart Wizard dialog box. Clear the check box to display a legend. Click Next.

e. Click the option button to create the chart as a new sheet, then click Finish.

f. Pull down the Chart menu and click the Add Trend Line command to display the Add Trend Line dialog box. Choose a linear trend, then click OK to create the line. Right click the trend line after it is created to change its color and thickness.

g. Print the completed workbook for your instructor. Add a cover sheet to complete the assignment.

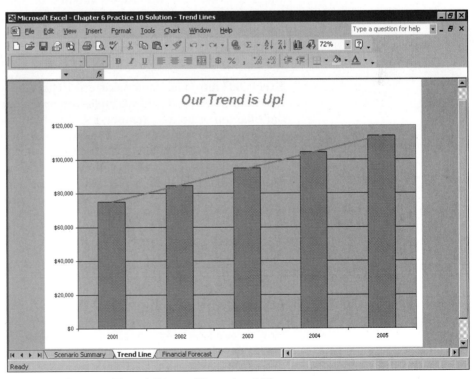

FIGURE 6.18   *Trend Lines (Exercise 10)*

The Entrepreneur

You have developed the perfect product and are seeking venture capital to go into immediate production. Your investors are asking for a projected income statement for the first four years of operation. The sales of your product are estimated at $250,000 the first year and are projected to grow at 15 percent annually. The cost of goods sold is 60 percent of the sales amount, and is expected to grow at 5% annually. You also have to pay a 10 percent sales commission, which is expected to remain constant.

Develop a financial forecast that will show the projected profits before and after taxes (assuming a tax rate of 36 percent). Your worksheet should be completely flexible and capable of accommodating a change in any of the initial conditions or projected rates of increase, *without* having to edit or recopy any of the formulas.

The worksheet should also be protected to the extent that the users can make any changes they like in the assumption area, but are prevented from making changes in the body of the worksheet. Use "password" (in lowercase) as the password.

Publishing to the Web

Use the completed financial forecast from the first hands-on exercise in the chapter as the basis for an HTML document. Complete the hands-on exercise, then use the Save as Web Page command to save the entire workbook as an HTML document. (You will see a message saying that scenarios will not be saved.) Post the document to your home page if you have one.

View the resulting page in Internet Explorer and/or Netscape Navigator. Are you able to see both worksheets in either browser? Are any Excel features lost in the conversion to HTML? Summarize this information in a brief note to your instructor.

Error Checking—Good News and Bad

Excel 2002 introduces automatic error checking, whereby a worksheet is checked for common errors. If, for example, you are adding a column of numbers and you omit the top or bottom number, Excel will flag the formula as a potential error. It will also flag an inconsistent formula within a row or column, and/or flag an unprotected cell if the cell contains a formula rather than a value. Potential errors are flagged with a green triangle, and the user is given the option to ignore or correct the error. Excel will even make the correction automatically.

This is a compelling feature, especially if you use Excel for financial calculations. Unfortunately, however, it falls short in one critical way. Your assignment is to open the workbook, *Error Checking—Good News and Bad*, and find the shortcoming. In addition, you are to use the Options command in the Tools menu to find the complete list of potential errors. Summarize your findings in a short note to your instructor.

Password Protection

How do you save a workbook with a password? Can you require one password to open a workbook and a different password to modify it? Can password protection be implemented for a shared workbook? What happens if you forget the password? Is the password case sensitive? Use the Help menu to learn about password protection in Excel, then summarize your findings in a short note to your instructor.

CHAPTER 7

List and Data Management: Converting Data to Information

OBJECTIVES

AFTER READING THIS CHAPTER YOU WILL BE ABLE TO:

1. Create a list within Excel; explain the importance of proper planning and design prior to creating the list.
2. Add, edit, and delete records in an existing list; explain the significance of data validation.
3. Use the Text Import Wizard to import data in character format.
4. Describe the TODAY( ) function and its use of date arithmetic.
5. Use the Sort command; distinguish between an ascending and a descending sort, and among primary, secondary, and tertiary keys.
6. Use DSUM, DAVERAGE, DMAX, DMIN, and DCOUNT functions.
7. Use the AutoFilter and Advanced Filter commands to display a subset of a list.
8. Use the Subtotals command to summarize data in a list; use the outline symbols to collapse and/or expand the summary information.
9. Create a pivot table and a corresponding pivot chart; save a pivot table as a Web page.

OVERVIEW

All businesses maintain data in the form of lists. Companies have lists of their employees. Magazines and newspapers keep lists of their subscribers. Political candidates monitor voter lists, and so on. This chapter presents the fundamentals of list management as it is implemented in Excel. We begin with the definition of basic terms, such as field and record, then cover the commands to create a list, to add a new record, and to modify or delete an existing record.

The second half of the chapter distinguishes between data and information and describes how one is converted to the other. We introduce the AutoFilter and Advanced Filter commands that display selected records in a list. We use the Sort command to rearrange the list. We discuss database functions and the associated criteria range. We also review date functions and date arithmetic. The chapter ends with a discussion of subtotals, pivot tables, and pivot charts—three powerful capabilities associated with lists.

Excel is the ideal application to analyze data, but other applications are better suited to collect and maintain the data. Thus, we include information on how to import data from other applications into an Excel workbook. The hands-on exercises enable you to implement the conceptual material at the computer.

LIST AND DATA MANAGEMENT

Imagine that you are the personnel director of a medium-sized company with offices in several cities, and that you manually maintain employee data for the company. Accordingly, you have recorded the specifics of every individual's employment (name, salary, location, title, and so on) in a manila folder, and you have stored the entire set of folders in a file cabinet. You have written the name of each employee on the label of his or her folder and have arranged the folders alphabetically in the filing cabinet.

The manual system just described illustrates the basics of data management terminology. The set of manila folders corresponds to a *file*. Each individual folder is known as a *record*. Each data item (fact) within a folder is called a *field*. The folders are arranged alphabetically in the file cabinet (according to the employee name on the label) to simplify the retrieval of any given folder. Likewise, the records in a computer-based system are also in sequence according to a specific field known as a *key*.

Excel maintains data in the form of a list. A *list* is an area in the worksheet that contains rows of similar data. A list can be used as a simple *database*, where the rows correspond to records and the columns correspond to fields. The first row contains the column labels or *field names*, which identify the data that will be entered in that column (field). Each additional row in the list contains a record. Each column represents a field. Each cell in the list area (other than the field names) contains a value for a specific field in a specific record. Every record (row) contains the same fields (columns) in the same order as every other record.

Figure 7.1 contains an employee list with 13 records. There are four fields in every record—name, location, title, and salary. The field names should be meaningful and must be unique. (A field name may contain up to 255 characters, but you should keep them as short as possible so that a column does not become too wide and thus difficult to work with.) The arrangement of the fields within a record is consistent from record to record. The employee name was chosen as the key, and thus the records are in alphabetical order.

Normal business operations require that you make repeated trips to the filing cabinet to maintain the accuracy of the data. You will have to add a folder whenever a new employee is hired. In similar fashion, you will have to remove the folder of any employee who leaves the company, or modify the data in the folder of any employee who receives a raise, changes location, and so on.

Changes of this nature (additions, deletions, and modifications) are known as file maintenance and constitute a critical activity within any system. Indeed, without adequate file maintenance, the data in a system quickly becomes obsolete and the information useless. Imagine the consequences of producing a payroll based on data that is six months old.

	A	B	C	D
1	Name	Location	Title	Salary
2	Adams	Atlanta	Trainee	$19,500
3	Adamson	Chicago	Manager	$52,000
4	Brown	Atlanta	Trainee	$18,500
5	Charles	Boston	Account Rep	$40,000
6	Coulter	Atlanta	Manager	$100,000
7	Frank	Miami	Manager	$75,000
8	James	Chicago	Account Rep	$42,500
9	Johnson	Chicag	Account Rep	$47,500
10	Manin	Boston	Accout Rep	$49,500
11	Marder	Chicago	Account Rep	$38,500
12	Milgrom	Boston	Manager	$57,500
13	Rubin	Boston	Account Rep	$45,000
14	Smith	Atlanta	Account Rep	$65,000

FIGURE 7.1   *The Employee List*

Nor is it sufficient simply to add (edit or delete) a record without adequate checks on the validity of the data. Look carefully at the entries in Figure 7.1 and ask yourself if a computer-generated report listing employees in the Chicago office will include Johnson. Will a report listing account reps include Manin? The answer to both questions is *no* because the data for these employees was entered incorrectly.

Chicago is misspelled in Johnson's record (the "o" was omitted). Account rep is misspelled in Manin's title. *You* know that Johnson works in Chicago, but the computer does not, because it searches for the correct spelling. It also will omit Manin from a listing of account reps because of the misspelled title. Remember, a computer does what you tell it to do, not necessarily what you want it to do. There is a difference.

GARBAGE IN, GARBAGE OUT (GIGO)

The information produced by a system is only as good as the data on which it is based. It is absolutely critical, therefore, that you validate the data that goes into a system, or else the associated information will not be correct. No system, no matter how sophisticated, can produce valid output from invalid input. In other words, garbage in—garbage out.

IMPLEMENTATION IN EXCEL

Creating a list is easy because there is little to do other than enter the data. You choose the area in the worksheet that will contain the list, then you enter the field names in the first row of the designated area. Each field name should be a unique text entry. The data for the individual records should be entered in the rows immediately below the row of field names.

Once a list has been created, you can edit any field, in any record, just as you would change the entries in an ordinary worksheet. The ***Insert Rows command*** lets you add new rows (records) to the list. The ***Insert Columns command*** lets you add additional columns (fields). The ***Delete command*** in the Edit menu enables you to delete a row or column. You can also use shortcut menus to execute commands more quickly. And finally, you can also format the entries within a list, just as you format the entries in any other worksheet.

LIST SIZE AND LOCATION

A list can appear anywhere within a worksheet and can theoretically be as large as an entire worksheet (65,536 rows by 256 columns). Practically, the list will be much smaller, giving rise to the following guideline for its placement: Leave at least one blank column and one blank row between the list and the other entries in the worksheet. Excel will then be able to find the boundaries of the list automatically whenever a cell within the list is selected. It simply searches for the first blank row above and below the selected cell, and for the first blank column to the left and right of the selected cell.

Data Form Command

A *data form* provides an easy way to add, edit, and delete records in a list. The *Form command* in the Data menu displays a dialog box based on the fields in the list and contains the command buttons shown in Figure 7.2. Every record in the list contains the same fields in the same order (e.g., Name, Location, Title, and Salary in Figure 7.2), and the fields are displayed in this order within the dialog box. You do not have to enter a value for every field; that is, you may leave a field blank if the data is unknown.

Next to each field name is a text box into which data can be entered for a new record, or edited for an existing record. The scroll bar to the right of the data is used to scroll through the records in the list. The functions of the various command buttons are explained briefly:

New — Adds a record to the end of a list, then lets you enter data in that record. The formulas for computed fields, if any, are automatically copied to the new record.

Delete — Permanently removes the currently displayed record. The remaining records move up one row.

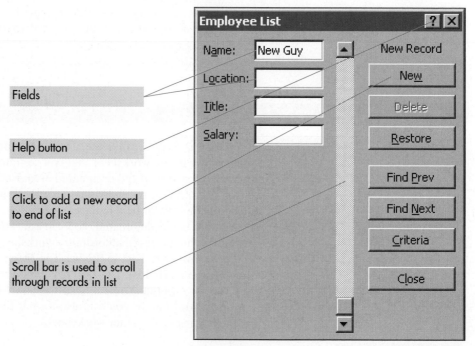

FIGURE 7.2   *The Data Form Command*

Fields

Help button

Click to add a new record to end of list

Scroll bar is used to scroll through records in list

Restore — Cancels any changes made to the current record. (You must press the Restore button before pressing the enter key or scrolling to a new record.)

Find Prev — Displays the previous record (or the previous record that matches the existing criteria when criteria are defined).

Find Next — Displays the next record (or the next record that matches the existing criteria when criteria are defined).

Criteria — Displays a dialog box in which you specify the criteria for the Find Prev and/or Find Next command buttons to limit the displayed records to those that match the criteria.

Close — Closes the data form and returns to the worksheet.

The Help button (the question mark) on the title bar of the Data Form provides access to online help. Click the Help button, then click any of the command buttons for an explanation. As indicated, the Data Form command provides an easy way to add, edit, and delete records in a list. It is not required, however, and you can use the Insert and Delete commands within the Edit menu as an alternate means of data entry.

Sort Command

The *Sort command* arranges the records in a list according to the value of one or more fields within that list. You can sort the list in *ascending* (low-to-high) or *descending* (high-to-low) *sequence.* (Putting a list in alphabetical order is considered an ascending sort.) You can also sort on more than one field at a time—for example, by location and then alphabetically by last name within each location. The field(s) on which you sort the list is (are) known as the key(s).

The records in Figure 7.3a are listed alphabetically (in ascending sequence) according to employee name. Adams comes before Adamson, who comes before Brown, and so on. Figure 7.3b displays the identical records but in descending sequence by employee salary. The employee with the highest salary is listed first, and the employee with the lowest salary is last.

Figure 7.3c sorts the employees on two keys—by location, and by descending salary within location. Location is the more important, or primary key. Salary is the less important, or secondary key. The Sort command groups employees according to like values of the primary key (location) in ascending (alphabetical) sequence, then within the like values of the primary key arranges them in descending sequence (ascending could have been chosen just as easily) according to the secondary key (salary). Excel provides a maximum of three keys—primary, secondary, and tertiary.

CHOOSE A CUSTOM SORT SEQUENCE

Alphabetic fields are normally arranged in strict alphabetical order. You can, however, choose a custom sort sequence such as the days of the week or the months of the year. Pull down the Data menu, click Sort, click the Options command button, then click the arrow on the drop-down list box to choose a sequence other than the alphabetic. You can also create your own sequence. Pull down the Tools menu, click Options, click the Custom Lists tab, select NewList, then enter the items in desired sequence in the List Entries Box. Click Add to create the sequence, then close the dialog box.

Records are listed in ascending sequence by employee name

	A	B	C	D
1	Name	Location	Title	Salary
2	Adams	Atlanta	Trainee	$19,500
3	Adamson	Chicago	Manager	$52,000
4	Brown	Atlanta	Trainee	$18,500
5	Charles	Boston	Account Rep	$40,000
6	Coulter	Atlanta	Manager	$100,000
7	Frank	Miami	Manager	$75,000
8	James	Chicago	Account Rep	$42,500
9	Johnson	Chicago	Account Rep	$47,500
10	Manin	Boston	Account Rep	$49,500
11	Marder	Chicago	Account Rep	$38,500
12	Milgrom	Boston	Manager	$57,500
13	Rubin	Boston	Account Rep	$45,000
14	Smith	Atlanta	Account Rep	$65,000
15				

(a) Ascending Sequence (by name)

Records are listed in descending sequence by salary

	A	B	C	D
1	Name	Location	Title	Salary
2	Coulter	Atlanta	Manager	$100,000
3	Frank	Miami	Manager	$75,000
4	Smith	Atlanta	Account Rep	$65,000
5	Milgrom	Boston	Manager	$57,500
6	Adamson	Chicago	Manager	$52,000
7	Manin	Boston	Account Rep	$49,500
8	Johnson	Chicago	Account Rep	$47,500
9	Rubin	Boston	Account Rep	$45,000
10	James	Chicago	Account Rep	$42,500
11	Charles	Boston	Account Rep	$40,000
12	Marder	Chicago	Account Rep	$38,500
13	Adams	Atlanta	Trainee	$19,500
14	Brown	Atlanta	Trainee	$18,500
15				

(b) Descending Sequence (by salary)

Location is the primary key (ascending sequence)

Salary is the secondary key (descending sequence)

	A	B	C	D
1	Name	Location	Title	Salary
2	Coulter	Atlanta	Manager	$100,000
3	Smith	Atlanta	Account Rep	$65,000
4	Adams	Atlanta	Trainee	$19,500
5	Brown	Atlanta	Trainee	$18,500
6	Milgrom	Boston	Manager	$57,500
7	Manin	Boston	Account Rep	$49,500
8	Rubin	Boston	Account Rep	$45,000
9	Charles	Boston	Account Rep	$40,000
10	Adamson	Chicago	Manager	$52,000
11	Johnson	Chicago	Account Rep	$47,500
12	James	Chicago	Account Rep	$42,500
13	Marder	Chicago	Account Rep	$38,500
14	Frank	Miami	Manager	$75,000
15				

(c) Multiple Keys

FIGURE 7.3 *The Sort Command*

Microsoft Excel stores a date as the integer (serial number) equivalent to the elapsed number of days since the turn of the century. Thus January 1, 1900 is stored as the number 1, January 2, 1900 as the number 2, and so on. March 16, 1981 corresponds to the number 29661 as can be seen in Figure 7.4.

The fact that dates are stored as numbers enables you to add and subtract two different dates and/or to use a date in any type of arithmetic computation. A person's age, for example, can be computed by subtracting the date of birth from today's date, and dividing the result by 365 (or more accurately by 365¼ to adjust for leap years). In similar fashion, you could add a constant (e.g., the number 30) to the date of purchase, to determine when payment is due (assuming, in this example, that payment is due 30 days after the item was purchased).

A date can be entered into a spreadsheet in various ways, most easily by typing the date in conventional fashion—for example, 1/21/97, to enter the date January 21, 1997. Any entry containing a year from 00 to 29 is assumed to be a date in the 21st century; for example, 1/21/00, will be stored as January 21, 2000. Any year between 30 and 99, however, is stored as a date in the 20th century. Thus, 3/23/48 would be stored as March 23, 1948. To avoid confusion and be sure of the date, you can enter all four digits of the year—for example, 10/31/2001 for October 31, 2001.

The **TODAY( ) function** is used in conjunction with date arithmetic and always returns the current date (i.e., the date on which the spreadsheet is opened). (The **Now( ) function** is similar in concept and includes the time of day as well as the date.) If, for example, you entered the Today() function into a spreadsheet created on March 21 and you opened the spreadsheet a month later, the value of the function would be automatically updated to April 21. The Today() function is illustrated in Figure 7.4 to calculate a person's age. Note, too, the IF function in Figure 7.4, which examines the computed age, then displays an appropriate message indicating whether the individual is of legal age or still under the age of 21.

Function displays current date

Enter 3/16/81 as a fixed date

Formula calculates person's age

	A	B	C	D
1		Cell Formulas	Date Format	Number Format
2	Today's Date	=TODAY()	7/29/01	37101
3	Birth Date	3/16/81	3/16/81	29661
4				
5	Elapsed Time (days)	=B2-B3		7440
6	Age (years)	=B5/365		20.4
7				
8		=IF(B6>=21,"You're Legal","Still a Minor")		Still a Minor

FIGURE 7.4   *Date Arithmetic*

BIRTH DATE VERSUS AGE

An individual's age and birth date provide equivalent information, as one is calculated from the other. It might seem easier, therefore, to enter the age directly into the list and avoid the calculation, but this would be a mistake. A person's age changes continually, whereas the birth date remains constant. Thus, the date, not the age, should be stored, so that the data in the list remains current. Similar reasoning applies to an employee's hire date and length of service.

It's easy to create a list in Excel and/or to modify data in that list. What if, however, the data already exists, but it is not in the form of a workbook? This is very common, especially in organizations that collect data on a mainframe, but analyze it on a PC. It can also occur when data is collected by one application, then analyzed in another. Excel provides a convenient solution in the form of the **Text Import Wizard** that converts a text (ASCII) file to an Excel workbook as shown in Figure 7.5. (Conversely, you can export an Excel workbook to another application by using the Save As command and specifying a text file.)

Figures 7.5a and 7.5b each contain the 13 records from the employee list shown, but in different formats. Both figures contain text files. The data in Figure 7.5a is in *fixed width format*, where each field requires the same number of positions in an input record. The data in Figure 7.5b is in *delimited format*, where the fields are separated from one another by a specific character.

You can access either file via the Open command in Excel, which in turn displays step 1 of the Text Import Wizard in Figure 7.5c. The Wizard prompts you for information about the external data, then it converts that data into an Excel workbook as shown in Figure 7.5d.

Name	Location	Title	Salary
Adams	Atlanta	Trainee	19500
Adamson	Chicago	Manager	52000
Brown	Atlanta	Trainee	18500
Charles	Boston	Account Rep	40000
Coulter	Atlanta	Manager	100000
Frank	Miami	Manager	75000
James	Chicago	Account Rep	42500
Johnson	Chicago	Account Rep	47500
Manin	Boston	Account Rep	49500
Marder	Chicago	Account Rep	38500
Milgrom	Boston	Manager	57500
Rubin	Boston	Account Rep	45000
Smith	Atlanta	Account Rep	65000

(a) Fixed Width

```
Name,Location,Title,Salary
Adams,Atlanta,Trainee,19500
Adamson,Chicago,Manager,52000
Brown,Atlanta,Trainee,18500
Charles,Boston,Account Rep,40000
Coulter,Atlanta,Manager,100000
Frank,Miami,Manager,75000
James,Chicago,Account Rep,42500
Johnson,Chicago,Account Rep,47500
Manin,Boston,Account Rep,49500
Marder,Chicago,Account Rep,38500
Milgrom,Boston,Manager,57500
Rubin,Boston,Account Rep,45000
Smith,Atlanta,Account Rep,65000
```

(b) Delimited

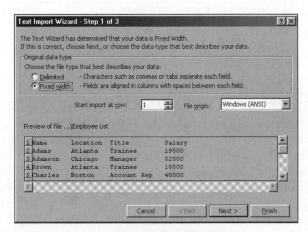

(c) Text Import Wizard

	A	B	C	D
1	Name	Location	Title	Salary
2	Adams	Atlanta	Trainee	19500
3	Adamson	Chicago	Manager	52000
4	Brown	Atlanta	Trainee	18500
5	Charles	Boston	Account Rep	40000
6	Coulter	Atlanta	Manager	100000
7	Frank	Miami	Manager	75000
8	James	Chicago	Account Rep	42500
9	Johnson	Chicago	Account Rep	47500
10	Manin	Boston	Account Rep	49500
11	Marder	Chicago	Account Rep	38500
12	Milgrom	Boston	Manager	57500
13	Rubin	Boston	Account Rep	45000
14	Smith	Atlanta	Account Rep	65000
15				

(d) Workbook

FIGURE 7.5   *Importing Data from Other Applications*

CREATING AND MAINTAINING A LIST

Objective To use the Text Import Wizard; to add, edit, and delete records in an employee list. Use Figure 7.6 as a guide in the exercise.

Step 1: **The Text Import Wizard**

> ➤ Start Excel. Pull down the **File menu** and click the **Open command** (or click the **Open button** on the Standard toolbar) to display the Open dialog box.
> ➤ Open the **Exploring Excel folder** that you have used throughout the text. Click the **drop-down arrow** on the Files of Type list box and specify **All Files**, then double click the **Employee List** text document.
> ➤ The Text Import Wizard opens automatically as shown in Figure 7.6a. The Wizard recognizes that the file is in Delimited format. Click **Next**.
> ➤ Clear the **Tab Delimiter** check box. Check the **Comma Delimiter** check box. Each field is now shown in a separate column. Click **Next**.
> ➤ There is no need to change the default format (general) of any of the fields. Click **Finish**. You see the Employee List within an Excel workbook.
> ➤ Click and drag to select **cells A1** through **D1**, then click the **Bold** and **Center buttons** to distinguish the field names from the data records. Click the **down arrow** for the **Fill Color button** and select **Pale Blue**. Adjust the column widths. Format the Salary field as Currency with zero decimals.
> ➤ Save the workbook as **Finished Employee List**. Click the **down arrow** in the Save as type list box and select **Microsoft Excel workbook**. Click **Save**.

Bold button

Center button

Fill Color button

Delimited format

Delimiter character is a comma

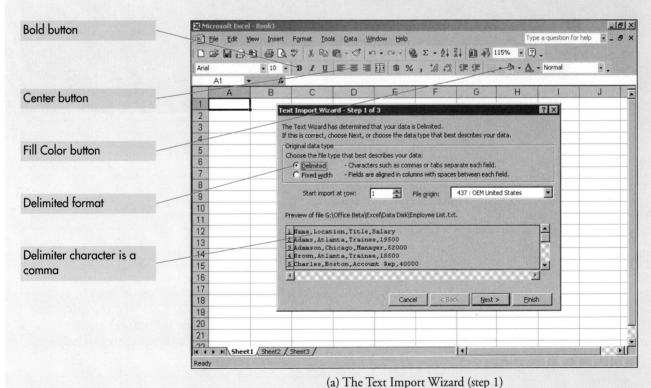

(a) The Text Import Wizard (step 1)

FIGURE 7.6   *Hands-on Exercise 1*

Step 2: **Add New Records**

➤ Click a single cell anywhere within the employee list (cells A1 through D14). Pull down the **Data menu**. Click **Form** to display a dialog box with data for the first record in the list (Adams).

➤ Click the **New command button** at the right of the dialog box to clear the text boxes and begin entering a new record.

➤ Enter the data for **Elofson** as shown in Figure 7.6b, using the **Tab key** to move from field to field within the data form.

➤ Click the **Close command button** after entering the salary. Elofson has been added to the list and appears in row 15.

➤ Add a second record for **Gillenson**, who works in **Miami** as an **Account Rep** with a salary of **$55,000**.

➤ Save the workbook.

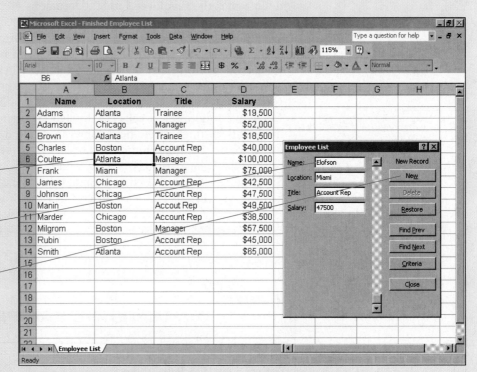

Click any cell in list

Enter data for Elofson

Click New button

(b) Add New Records (step 2)

FIGURE 7.6   *Hands-on Exercise 1 (continued)*

EMPHASIZE THE COLUMN LABELS (FIELD NAMES)

Use a different font, alignment, style (boldface and/or italics), pattern, or border to distinguish the first row containing the field names from the remaining rows (records) in a list. This ensures that Excel will recognize the first row as a header row, enabling you to sort the list simply by selecting a cell in the list, then clicking the Ascending or Descending sort buttons on the Standard toolbar.

Step 3: **The Spell Check**

➤ Select **cells B2:C16** as in Figure 7.6c. Pull down the **Tools menu** and click **Spelling** (or click the **Spelling button** on the Standard toolbar).

➤ Chicago is misspelled in cell B9 and flagged accordingly. Click the **Change command button** to accept the suggested correction and continue checking the document.

➤ Account is misspelled in cell C10 and flagged accordingly. Click **Account** in the Suggestions list box, then click the **Change command button** to correct the misspelling.

➤ Excel will indicate that it has finished checking the selected cells. Click **OK** to return to the worksheet.

➤ Save the workbook.

Spelling button

Select B2:C16

Misspelled word is detected

Suggested correction

Change button

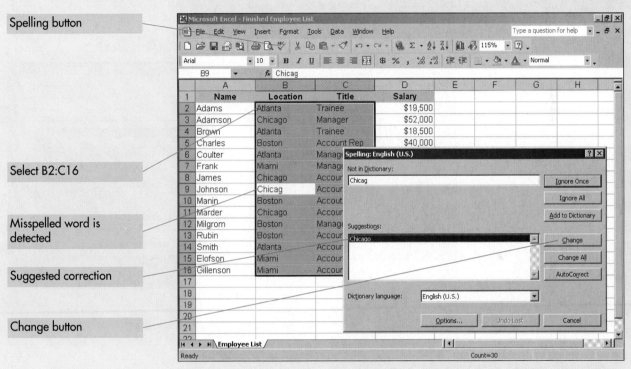

(c) The Spell Check (step 3)

FIGURE 7.6   *Hands-on Exercise 1 (continued)*

CREATE YOUR OWN SHORTHAND

Use the AutoCorrect to create your own shorthand by having it expand abbreviations such as *cis* for *Computer Information Systems.* Pull down the Tools menu, click AutoCorrect, type the abbreviation in the Replace text box and the expanded entry in the With text box. Click the Add command button, then click OK to exit the dialog box and return to the document. The next time you type *cis* in a spreadsheet, it will automatically be expanded to *Computer Information Systems.*

Step 4: **Sort the Employee List**

➤ Click a single cell anywhere in the employee list (**cells A1** through **D16**). Pull down the **Data menu**. Click **Sort** to display the dialog box in Figure 7.6d.
  • Click the **drop-down arrow** in the Sort By list box. Select **Location**.
  • Click the **drop-down arrow** in the first Then By list box. Select **Name**.
  • Be sure the **Header Row option button** is selected (so that the field names are not mixed in with the records in the list).
  • Check that the **Ascending option button** is selected for both the primary and secondary keys. Click **OK**.
➤ The employees are listed by location and alphabetically within location.
➤ Save the workbook.

Click drop-down arrow and select Location

Click drop-down arrow and select Name

Header row should be selected

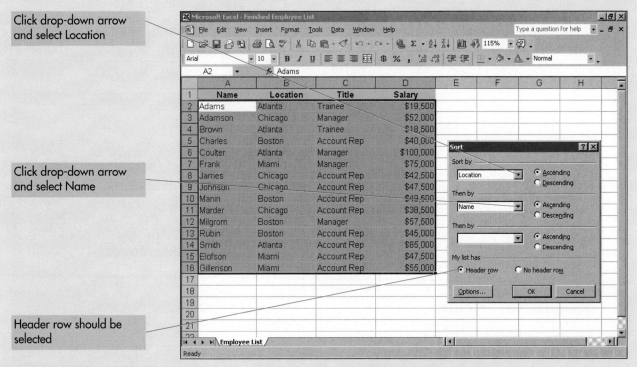

(d) Sort the Employee List (step 4)

FIGURE 7.6   *Hands-on Exercise 1 (continued)*

USE THE SORT BUTTONS

Use the Sort Ascending or Sort Descending button on the Standard toolbar to sort on one or more keys. To sort on a single key, click any cell in the column containing the key, then click the appropriate button, depending on whether you want an ascending or a descending sort. You can also sort on multiple keys, by clicking either button multiple times, but the trick is to do it in the right sequence. Sort on the least significant field first, then work your way up to the most significant. For example, to sort a list by location, and name within location, sort by name first (the secondary key), then sort by location (the primary key).

Step 5: **Delete a Record**

➤ A record may be deleted by using the Edit Delete command or the Data Form command. To delete a record by using the Edit Delete command:
  • Click the **row heading** in **row 15** (containing the record for Frank, which is slated for deletion).
  • Pull down the **Edit menu**. Click **Delete**. Frank has been deleted.
➤ Click the **Undo button** on the Standard toolbar. The record for Frank has been restored.
➤ To delete a record by using the Data Form command:
  • Click a single cell within the employee list. Pull down the **Data menu**. Click **Form** to display the data form. Click the **Criteria button**. Enter **Frank** in the Name text box, then click the **Find Next button** to locate Frank's record.
  • Click the **Delete command button**. Click **OK** in response to the warning message shown in Figure 7.6e. (The record cannot be undeleted as it could with the Edit Delete command.) Click **Close** to close the Data Form.
➤ Save the workbook.

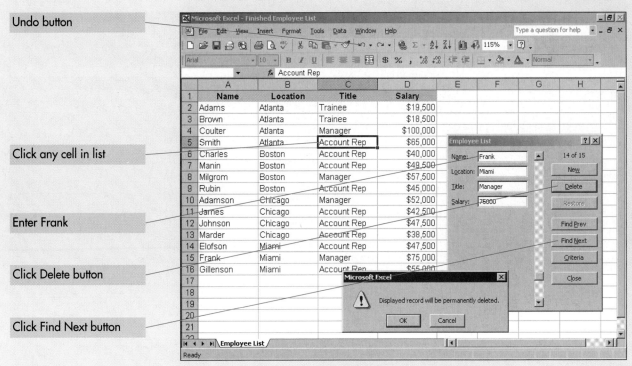

(e) Delete a Record (step 5)

FIGURE 7.6 *Hands-on Exercise 1 (continued)*

EDIT CLEAR VERSUS EDIT DELETE

The Edit Delete command deletes the selected cell, row, or column from the worksheet, and thus its execution will adjust cell references throughout the worksheet. It is very different from the Edit Clear command, which erases the contents (and/or formatting) of the selected cells, but does not delete the cells from the worksheet and hence has no effect on the cell references in other cells. Pressing the Del key erases the contents of a cell and thus corresponds to the Edit Clear command.

Step 6: **Enter the Hire Date**

➤ Click the **column heading** in column D. Point to the selection, then click the **right mouse button** to display a shortcut menu. Click **Insert**. The employee salaries have been moved to column E1, as shown in Figure 7.6f.
➤ Click **cell D1**. Type **Hire Date** and press **enter**. Adjust the column width if necessary. Dates may be entered in several different formats.
  • Type **11/24/93** in cell D2. Press the **down arrow key**.
  • Type **11/24/1993** in cell D3. Press the **down arrow key**.
  • Type **Nov 24, 1993** in cell D4. Type a **comma** after the day but do not type a period after the month. Press the **down arrow key** to move to cell D5.
  • Type **11-24-93** in cell D5. Press **enter**.
➤ For ease of data entry, assume that the next several employees were hired on the same day, 3/16/94. Click in **cell D6**. Type **3/16/94**. Press **enter**. Click in **cell D6**. Click the **Copy button** on the Standard toolbar.
➤ Drag the mouse over cells **D7** through **D10**. Click the **Paste button**. Press **Esc** to remove the moving border around cell D6.

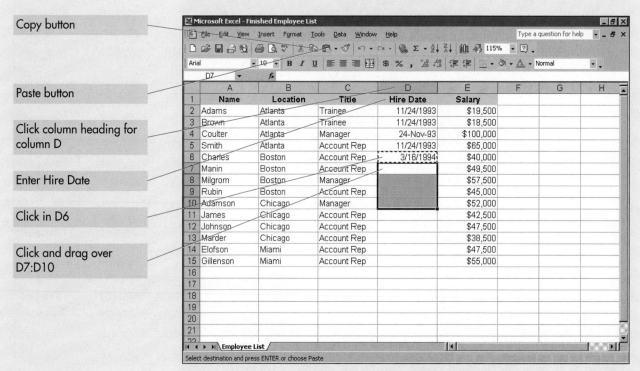

Copy button

Paste button

Click column heading for column D

Enter Hire Date

Click in D6

Click and drag over D7:D10

(f) Enter the Hire Date (step 6)

FIGURE 7.6   *Hands-on Exercise 1 (continued)*

TWO-DIGIT DATES AND THE YEAR 2000

Excel assumes that any two-digit year up to and including 29 is in the 21st century; that is, 12/31/29 will be stored as December 31, 2029. Any year after 29, however, is assumed to be in the 20th century; for example, 1/1/30 will be stored as January 1, 1930. When in doubt, however, enter a four-digit year to be sure.

Step 7:   **Format the Hire Dates**

> ➤ The five employees were hired one year apart beginning October 31, 1994.
>   • Click in cell **D11** and type **10/31/94**. Click in cell **D12** and type **10/31/95**.
>   • Select cells **D11 and D12**.
>   • Drag the **fill handle** at the bottom of cell D12 over cells **D13**, **D14**, and **D15**. Release the mouse to complete the AutoFill operation.
> ➤ Click in the column heading for **column D** to select the column of dates.
> ➤ Point to the selected cells and click the **right mouse button** to display a shortcut menu. Click **Format Cells**.
> ➤ Click the **Number tab** in the Format Cells dialog box. Click **Date** in the Category list box. Select (click) the date format shown in Figure 7.6g. Click **OK**.
> ➤ Click elsewhere in the workbook to deselect the dates. Reduce the width of column D as appropriate. Save the workbook.
> ➤ Exit Excel if you do not want to complete the next exercise at this time.

Click column heading for column D

Number tab

Click Date

Click desired format

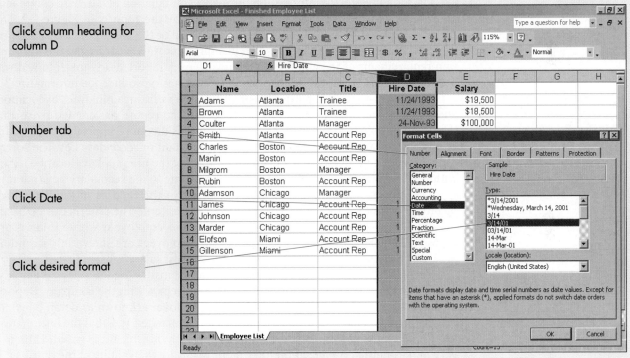

(g) Format the Hire Dates (step 7)

FIGURE 7.6   *Hands-on Exercise 1 (continued)*

DATES VERSUS FRACTIONS

A fraction is entered into a cell by preceding the fraction with an equal sign; for example, =1/4. The fraction is displayed as its decimal equivalent (.25) unless the cell is formatted to display fractions. Select the cell, pull down the Format menu, and click the Cells command. Click the Numbers tab, then choose Fraction from the Category list box. Omission of the equal sign treats the entry as a date; that is, typing 1/4 will store the entry as January 4th (of the current year).

Data and information are not synonymous. *Data* refers to a fact or facts about a specific record, such as an employee's name, title, or salary. *Information*, on the other hand, is data that has been rearranged into a form perceived as useful by the recipient. A list of employees earning more than $35,000 or a total of all employee salaries are examples of information produced from data about individual employees. Put another way, data is the raw material, and information is the finished product.

Decisions in an organization are based on information rather than raw data; for example, in assessing the effects of a proposed across-the-board salary increase, management needs to know the total payroll rather than individual salary amounts. In similar fashion, decisions about next year's hiring will be influenced, at least in part, by knowing how many individuals are currently employed in each job category.

Organizations maintain data to produce information. Data maintenance entails three basic operations—adding new records, modifying (editing or updating) existing records, and deleting existing records. The exercise just completed showed you how to maintain the data. This section focuses on using that data to create information.

Data is converted to information through a combination of database commands and functions whose capabilities are illustrated by the reports in Figure 7.7. The reports are based on the employee list as it existed at the end of the first hands-on exercise. Each report presents the data in a different way, according to the information requirements of the end-user. As you view each report, ask yourself how it was produced; that is, what was done to the data in order to produce the information?

Figure 7.7a contains a master list of all employees, listing employees by location, and alphabetically by last name within location. The report was created by sorting the list on two keys, location and name. Location is the more important field and is known as the primary key. Name is the less important or secondary key. The sorted report groups employees according to like values of the primary key (location), then within the primary key, groups the records according to the secondary key (name).

The report in Figure 7.7b displays a subset of the records in the list, which includes only those employees who meet specific criteria. The criteria can be based on any field or combination of fields—in this case, employees whose salaries are between $40,000 and $60,000 (inclusive). The employees are shown in descending order of salary so that the employee with the highest salary is listed first.

The report in Figure 7.7c displays summary statistics for the selected employees—in this example, the salaries for the account reps within the company. Reports of this nature omit the salaries of individual employees (known as detail lines), to present an aggregate view of the organization. Remember, too, that the information produced by any system is only as good as the data on which it is based. Thus, it is very important that organizations take steps to ensure the validity of the data as it is entered into a system.

CITY, STATE, AND ZIP CODE—ONE FIELD OR THREE?

The answer depends on whether the fields are referenced as a unit or individually. However, given the almost universal need to sort or select on zip code, it is almost invariably defined as a separate field. An individual's last name, first name, and middle initial are defined as individual fields for the same reason. The general rule, therefore, is to always enter data in its smallest parts.

Location Report

Name	Location	Title	Hire Date	Salary
Adams	Atlanta	Trainee	11/24/93	$19,500
Brown	Atlanta	Trainee	11/24/93	$18,500
Coulter	Atlanta	Manager	11/24/93	$100,000
Smith	Atlanta	Account Rep	11/24/93	$65,000
Charles	Boston	Account Rep	3/16/92	$40,000
Manin	Boston	Account Rep	3/16/92	$49,500
Milgrom	Boston	Manager	3/16/92	$57,500
Rubin	Boston	Account Rep	3/16/92	$45,000
Adamson	Chicago	Manager	3/16/92	$52,000
James	Chicago	Account Rep	10/31/89	$42,500
Johnson	Chicago	Account Rep	10/31/90	$47,500
Marder	Chicago	Account Rep	10/31/91	$38,500
Elofson	Miami	Account Rep	10/31/92	$47,500
Gillenson	Miami	Account Rep	10/31/93	$55,000

(a) Employees by Location and Name within Location

Employees Earning Between $40,000 and $60,000

Name	Location	Title	Hire Date	Salary
Milgrom	Boston	Manager	3/16/92	$57,500
Gillenson	Miami	Account Rep	10/31/93	$55,000
Adamson	Chicago	Manager	3/16/92	$52,000
Manin	Boston	Account Rep	3/16/92	$49,500
Johnson	Chicago	Account Rep	10/31/90	$47,500
Elofson	Miami	Account Rep	10/31/92	$47,500
Rubin	Boston	Account Rep	3/16/92	$45,000
James	Chicago	Account Rep	10/31/89	$42,500
Charles	Boston	Account Rep	3/16/92	$40,000

(b) Employees Earning between $40,000 and $60,000, inclusive

Summary Statistics
Total Salary for Account Reps:	$430,500
Average Salary for Account Reps:	$47,833
Maximum Salary for Account Reps:	$65,000
Minimum Salary for Account Reps:	$38,500
Number of Account Reps:	9

(c) Account Rep Summary Data

FIGURE 7.7   *Data versus Information*

AutoFilter Command

A *filtered list* displays a subset of records that meet a specific criterion or set of criteria. It is created by the *AutoFilter command* (or the Advanced Filter command discussed in the next section). Both commands temporarily hide those records (rows) that do not meet the criteria. The hidden records are *not* deleted; they are simply not displayed.

Figure 7.8a displays the employee list in alphabetical order. Figure 7.8b displays a filtered version of the list in which only the Atlanta employees (in rows 2, 4, 6, and 15) are visible. The remaining employees are still in the worksheet but are not shown as their rows are hidden.

Drop-down arrows appear next to each field name

Click to display only Atlanta employees

	A	B	C	D	E
1	Name	Location	Title	Hire Date	Salary
2	Adams	(All)	Trainee	11/24/93	$19,500
3	Adamson	(Top 10...)	Manager	3/16/94	$52,000
4	Brown	(Custom...)	Trainee	11/24/93	$18,500
5	Charles	Atlanta	Account Rep	3/16/94	$40,000
6	Coulter	Boston	Manager	11/24/93	$100,000
7	Elofson	Chicago	Account Rep	10/31/97	$47,500
8	Gillenson	Miami	Account Rep	10/31/98	$55,000
9	James	Chicago	Account Rep	10/31/94	$42,500
10	Johnson	Chicago	Account Rep	10/31/95	$47,500
11	Manin	Boston	Account Rep	3/16/94	$49,500
12	Marder	Chicago	Account Rep	10/31/96	$38,500
13	Milgrom	Boston	Manager	3/16/94	$57,500
14	Rubin	Boston	Account Rep	3/16/94	$45,000
15	Smith	Atlanta	Account Rep	11/24/93	$65,000

(a) Unfiltered List

Only Atlanta employees are displayed

	A	B	C	D	E
1	Name	Location	Title	Hire Date	Salary
2	Adams	Atlanta	Trainee	11/24/93	$19,500
4	Brown	Atlanta	Trainee	11/24/93	$18,500
6	Coulter	Atlanta	Manager	11/24/93	$100,000
15	Smith	Atlanta	Account Rep	11/24/93	$65,000

(b) Filtered List (Atlanta employees)

Click drop-down arrow to further filter list

	A	B	C	D	E
1	Name	Location	Title	Hire Date	Salary
2	Adams	Atlanta	(All)	11/24/93	$19,500
4	Brown	Atlanta	(Top 10...)	11/24/93	$18,500
6	Coulter	Atlanta	(Custom...)	11/24/93	$100,000
15	Smith	Atlanta	Account Rep	11/24/93	$65,000
16			Manager		
			Trainee		

(c) Imposing a Second Condition

Blue drop-down arrows indicate filter condition is in effect

	A	B	C	D	E
1	Name	Location	Title	Hire Date	Salary
6	Coulter	Atlanta	Manager	11/24/93	$100,000

(d) Filtered List (Atlanta managers)

FIGURE 7.8 *Filter Command*

Execution of the AutoFilter command places drop-down arrows next to each column label (field name). Clicking a drop-down arrow produces a list of the unique values for that field, enabling you to establish the criteria for the filtered list. Thus, to display the Atlanta employees, click the drop-down arrow for Location, then click Atlanta.

A filter condition can be imposed on multiple columns as shown in Figure 7.8c. The filtered list in Figure 7.8c contains just the Atlanta employees. Clicking the arrow next to Title, then clicking Manager, will filter the list further to display the employees who both work in Atlanta *and* have Manager as a title. Only one employee meets both conditions, as shown in Figure 7.8d. The drop-down arrows next to Location and Title are displayed in blue to indicate that a filter is in effect for these columns.

The AutoFilter command has additional options as can be seen from the drop-down list box in Figure 7.8c. (All) removes existing criteria in that column. (Custom . . .) enables you to use the relational operators (=, >, <, >=, <=, or <>) within a criterion. (Top 10 . . .) displays the records with the top (or bottom) values in the field, and makes most sense if you sort the list to see the entries in sequence.

Advanced Filter Command

The *Advanced Filter command* extends the capabilities of the AutoFilter command in two important ways. It enables you to develop more complex criteria than are possible with the AutoFilter Command. It also enables you to copy (extract) the selected records to a separate area in the worksheet. The Advanced Filter command is illustrated in detail in the hands-on exercise that follows shortly.

Criteria Range

A *criteria range* is used with both the Advanced Filter command and the database functions that are discussed in the next section. It is defined independently of the list on which it operates and exists as a separate area in the worksheet. A criteria range must be at least two rows deep and one column wide as illustrated in Figure 7.9.

The simplest criteria range consists of two rows and as many columns as there are fields in the list. The first row contains the field names as they appear in the list. The second row holds the value(s) you are looking for. The criteria range in Figure 7.9a selects the employees who work in Atlanta; that is, it selects those records where the value of the Location Field is equal to Atlanta.

Multiple values in the same row are connected by an AND and require that the selected records meet *all* of the specified criteria. The criteria range in Figure 7.9b identifies the account reps in Atlanta; that is, it selects any record in which the Location field is Atlanta *and* the Title field is Account Rep.

Values entered in multiple rows are connected by an OR in which the selected records satisfy *any* of the indicated criteria. The criteria range in Figure 7.9c will identify employees who work in Atlanta *or* whose title is Account Rep.

Relational operators may be used with date or numeric fields to return records within a designated range. The criteria range in Figure 7.9d selects the employees hired before January 1, 1993. The criteria range in Figure 7.9e returns employees whose salary is more than $40,000.

An upper and lower boundary may be established for the same field by repeating the field within the criteria range. This was done in Figure 7.9f, which returns all records in which the salary is more than $40,000 but less than $60,000.

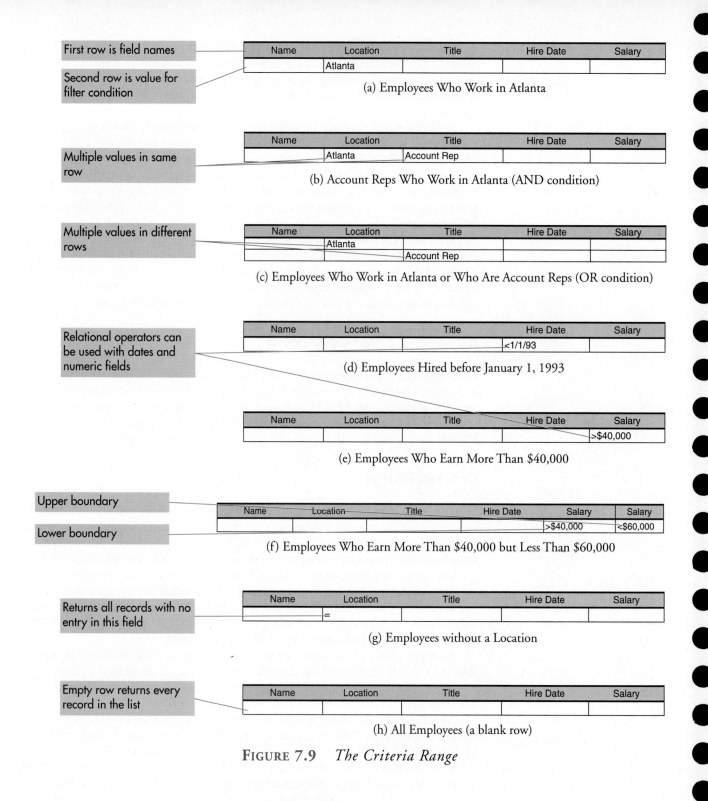

First row is field names

Second row is value for filter condition

Name	Location	Title	Hire Date	Salary
	Atlanta			

(a) Employees Who Work in Atlanta

Multiple values in same row

Name	Location	Title	Hire Date	Salary
	Atlanta	Account Rep		

(b) Account Reps Who Work in Atlanta (AND condition)

Multiple values in different rows

Name	Location	Title	Hire Date	Salary
	Atlanta			
		Account Rep		

(c) Employees Who Work in Atlanta or Who Are Account Reps (OR condition)

Relational operators can be used with dates and numeric fields

Name	Location	Title	Hire Date	Salary
			<1/1/93	

(d) Employees Hired before January 1, 1993

Name	Location	Title	Hire Date	Salary
				>$40,000

(e) Employees Who Earn More Than $40,000

Upper boundary

Lower boundary

Name	Location	Title	Hire Date	Salary	Salary
				>$40,000	<$60,000

(f) Employees Who Earn More Than $40,000 but Less Than $60,000

Returns all records with no entry in this field

Name	Location	Title	Hire Date	Salary
	=			

(g) Employees without a Location

Empty row returns every record in the list

Name	Location	Title	Hire Date	Salary

(h) All Employees (a blank row)

FIGURE 7.9   *The Criteria Range*

The equal and unequal signs select records with empty and nonempty fields, respectively. An equal sign with nothing after it will return all records without an entry in the designated field; for example, the criteria range in Figure 7.9g selects any record that is missing a value for the Location field. An unequal sign (<>) with nothing after it will select all records with an entry in the field.

An empty row in the criteria range returns *every* record in the list, as shown in Figure 7.9h. All criteria are *case-insensitive* and return records with any combination of upper- and lowercase letters that match the entry.

THE IMPLIED WILD CARD

Any text entry within a criteria range is treated as though it were followed by the asterisk **wild card**; that is, *New* is the same as *New**. Both entries will return New York and New Jersey. To match a text entry exactly, begin with an equal sign, enter a quotation mark followed by another equal sign, the entry you are looking for, and the closing quotation mark—for example, ="=New" to return only the entries that say New.

Database Functions

The **database functions** DSUM, DAVERAGE, DMAX, DMIN, and DCOUNT operate on *selected* records in a list. These functions parallel the statistical functions (SUM, AVERAGE, MAX, MIN, and COUNT) except that they affect only records that satisfy the established criteria.

The summary statistics in Figure 7.10 are based on the salaries of the managers in the list, rather than the salaries of all employees. Each database function includes the criteria range in cells A17:E18 as one of its arguments, and thus limits the employees that are included to managers. The **DAVERAGE function** returns the average salary for just the managers. The **DMAX** and **DMIN functions** display the maximum and minimum salaries for the managers. The **DSUM function** computes the total salary for all the managers. The **DCOUNT function** indicates the number of managers.

Each database function has three arguments: the range for the list on which it is to operate, the field to be processed, and the criteria range. Consider, for example, the DAVERAGE function as shown below:

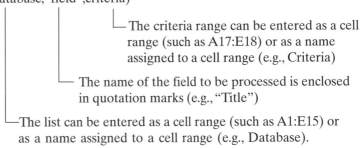

The entries in the criteria range may be changed at any time, in which case the values of the database functions are automatically recalculated. The other database functions have arguments identical to those used in the DAVERAGE function. The functions will adjust automatically if rows or columns are inserted within the specified range.

	A	B	C	D	E
1	Name	Location	Title	Hire Date	Salary
2	Adams	Atlanta	Trainee	11/24/93	$19,500
3	Adamson	Chicago	Manager	3/16/92	$52,000
4	Brown	Atlanta	Trainee	11/24/93	$18,500
5	Charles	Boston	Account Rep	3/16/92	$40,000
6	Coulter	Atlanta	Manager	11/24/93	$100,000
7	Elofson	Miami	Account Rep	10/31/92	$47,500
8	Gillenson	Miami	Account Rep	10/31/93	$55,000
9	James	Chicago	Account Rep	10/31/89	$42,500
10	Johnson	Chicago	Account Rep	10/31/90	$47,500
11	Manin	Boston	Account Rep	3/16/92	$49,500
12	Marder	Chicago	Account Rep	10/31/91	$38,500
13	Milgrom	Boston	Manager	3/16/92	$57,500
14	Rubin	Boston	Account Rep	3/16/92	$45,000
15	Smith	Atlanta	Account Rep	11/24/93	$65,000
16					
17	Name	Location	Title	Hire Date	Salary
18			Manager		
19					
20					
21			Summary Statistics		
22	Average Salary:				$69,833
23	Maximum Salary:				$100,000
24	Minimum Salary:				$52,000
25	Total Salary:				$209,500
26	Number of Employees:				3

Criteria range is A17:E18 (filters list to Managers)

Summary statistics for Managers

FIGURE 7.10   *Database Functions*

Insert Name Command

The *Name command* in the Insert menu equates a mnemonic name such as *EmployeeList* to a cell or cell range such as *A1:E15,* then enables you to use that name to reference the cell(s) in all subsequent commands. A name can be up to 255 characters in length, but must begin with a letter or an underscore. It can include upper- or lowercase letters, numbers, periods, and underscore characters but no blank spaces.

Once defined, names adjust automatically for insertions and/or deletions within the range. If, in the previous example, you were to delete row 4, the definition of *EmployeeList* would change to A1:E14. And, in similar fashion, if you were to add a new column between columns B and C, the range would change to A1:F14.

A name can be used in any formula or function instead of a cell address; for example, =SALES−EXPENSES instead of =C1−C10, where Sales and Expenses have been defined as the names for cells C1 and C10, respectively. A name can also be entered into any dialog box where a cell range is required.

THE GO TO COMMAND

Names are frequently used in conjunction with the Go To command. Pull down the Edit menu and click Go To (or click the F5 key) to display a dialog box containing the names that have been defined within the workbook. Double click a name to move directly to the first cell in the associated range and simultaneously select the entire range.

The ***Subtotals command*** uses a summary function (such as SUM, AVERAGE, or COUNT) to compute subtotals for groups of records within a list. The records are grouped according to the value in a specific field, such as location, as shown in Figure 7.11. The Subtotals command inserts a subtotal row into the list whenever the value of the designated field (location in this example) changes from one record to the next.

The subtotal for the Atlanta employees is inserted into the list as we go from the last employee in Atlanta to the first employee in Boston. In similar fashion, the subtotal for Boston is inserted into the list as we go from the last employee in Boston to the first employee in Chicago. A grand total is displayed after the last record. The list must be in sequence, according to the field on which the subtotals will be grouped, prior to executing the Subtotals command.

The summary information can be displayed with different levels of detail. Figure 7.11a displays the salary data for each employee (known as the detail lines), the subtotals for each location, and the grand total. Figure 7.11b suppresses the detail lines but shows both the subtotals and grand total. Figure 7.11c shows only the grand total. The worksheet in all three figures is said to be in outline format, as seen by the ***outline symbols*** at the extreme left of the application window.

The records within the list are grouped to compute the summary information. A plus sign indicates that the group has been collapsed, and that the detail information is suppressed. A minus sign indicates the opposite, namely that the group has been expanded and that the detail information is visible. You can click any plus or minus sign to expand or collapse that portion of the outline. You can also click the symbols (1, 2, or 3) above the plus or minus signs to collapse or expand the rows within the worksheet. Level one shows the least amount of detail and displays only the grand total. Level two includes the subtotals as well as the grand total. Level three includes the detail records, the subtotals, and the grand total.

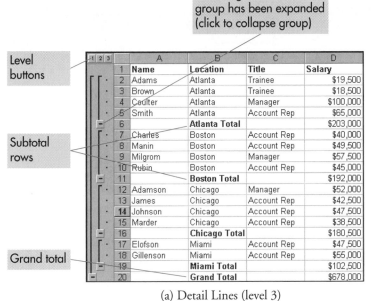

(a) Detail Lines (level 3)

(b) Location Totals (level 2)

(c) Grand Total (level 1)

FIGURE 7.11 *Subtotals and Outlining*

DATA VERSUS INFORMATION

Objective To sort a list on multiple keys; to demonstrate the AutoFilter and Advanced Filter commands; to define a named range within a worksheet; to use the DSUM, DAVERAGE, DMAX, DMIN, and DCOUNT functions. Use Figure 7.12 as a guide in the exercise.

Step 1: **Calculate the Years of Service**

> ➤ Start Excel. Open the **Finished Employee List workbook** created in the previous exercise.
> ➤ Click the **column heading** in **column D**. Point to the selection and click the **right mouse button** to display a shortcut menu. Click **Insert**. The column of hire dates has been moved to column E. Click in **cell D1**. Type **Service** and press **enter**.
> ➤ Click in **cell D2** and enter the formula to compute the years of service **=(Today( )-E2)/365** as shown in Figure 7.12a. Press **enter**; the years of service for the first employee are displayed in cell D2.
> ➤ Click in **cell D2**, then click the **Decrease Decimal button** on the Formatting toolbar several times to display the length of service with only one decimal place. Reduce the column width as appropriate.
> ➤ Drag the **fill handle** in cell D2 to the remaining cells in that column (**cells D3** through **D15**) to compute the length of service for the remaining employees.
> ➤ Save the workbook.

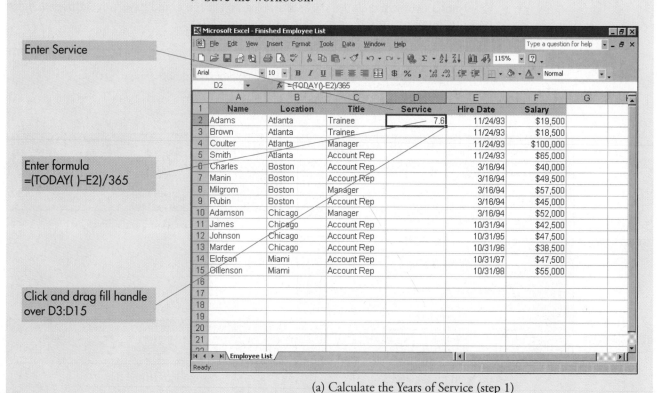

(a) Calculate the Years of Service (step 1)

FIGURE 7.12 *Hands-on Exercise 2*

Step 2: **The AutoFilter Command**

➤ Click a single cell anywhere within the list. Pull down the **Data menu**. Click the **Filter command**.
➤ Click **AutoFilter** from the resulting cascade menu to display the drop-down arrows to the right of each field name.
➤ Click the **drop-down arrow** next to **Title** to display the list of titles in Figure 7.12b. Click **Account Rep**.
➤ The display changes to show only those employees who meet the filter. The row numbers for the visible records are blue. The drop-down arrow for Title is also blue, indicating that it is part of the filter condition.
➤ Click the **drop-down arrow** next to **Location**. Click **Boston** to display only the employees in this city. The combination of the two filter conditions shows only the account reps in Boston.
➤ Click the **drop-down arrow** next to **Location** a second time. Click **(All)** to remove the filter condition on location. Only the account reps are displayed since the filter on Title is still in effect.
➤ Save the workbook.

Click drop-down arrow to right of field name

Click any cell in list

Click Account Rep

	A	B	C	D	E	F	G
1	**Name**	**Location**	**Title**	**Service**	**Hire Date**	**Salary**	
2	Adams	Atlanta	(All)	7.6	11/24/93	$19,500	
3	Brown	Atlanta	(Top 10...)	7.6	11/24/93	$18,500	
4	Coulter	Atlanta	(Custom...)	7.6	11/24/93	$100,000	
5	Smith	Atlanta	Account Rep	7.6	11/24/93	$65,000	
6	Charles	Boston	Manager	7.3	3/16/94	$40,000	
7	Manin	Boston	Trainee	7.3	3/16/94	$49,500	
8	Milgrom	Boston	Manager	7.3	3/16/94	$57,500	
9	Rubin	Boston	Account Rep	7.3	3/16/94	$45,000	
10	Adamson	Chicago	Manager	7.3	3/16/94	$52,000	
11	James	Chicago	Account Rep	6.7	10/31/94	$42,500	
12	Johnson	Chicago	Account Rep	5.7	10/31/95	$47,500	
13	Marder	Chicago	Account Rep	4.7	10/31/96	$38,500	
14	Elofson	Miami	Account Rep	3.7	10/31/97	$47,500	
15	Gillenson	Miami	Account Rep	2.7	10/31/98	$55,000	

(b) The AutoFilter Command (step 2)

FIGURE 7.12 *Hands-on Exercise 2 (continued)*

THE TOP 10 AUTOFILTER

Use the Top 10 AutoFilter option to see the top (or bottom) 10, or for that matter any number of records in a list. Just turn the AutoFilter condition on, click the down arrow in the designated field, then click Top 10 to display the associated dialog box, where you specify the records you want to view. See exercise 7 at the end of the chapter.

Step 3: **The Custom AutoFilter Command**

➤ Click the **drop-down arrow** next to **Salary** to display the list of salaries. Click **Custom** to display the dialog box in Figure 7.12c.
➤ Click the **arrow** in the leftmost drop-down list box for **Salary**, then click the **is greater than** as the relational operator.
➤ Click in the text box for the salary amount. Type **45000**. Click **OK**.
➤ The list changes to display only those employees whose title is account rep *and* who earn more than $45,000.
➤ Pull down the **Data menu**. Click **Filter**. Click **AutoFilter** to toggle the Auto-Filter command off, which removes the arrows next to the field names and cancels all filter conditions. All of the records in the list are visible.
➤ Save the workbook.

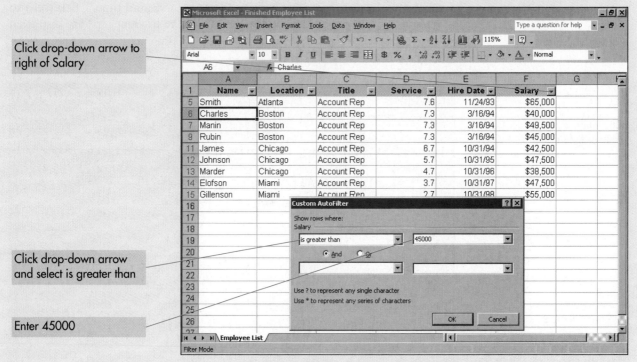

Click drop-down arrow to right of Salary

Click drop-down arrow and select is greater than

Enter 45000

(c) The Custom AutoFilter Command (step 3)

FIGURE 7.12 *Hands-on Exercise 2 (continued)*

WILD CARDS

Excel recognizes the question mark and asterisk as wild cards in the specification of criteria. A question mark stands for a single character in the exact position; for example, B?ll returns Ball, Bill, Bell, and Bull. An asterisk stands for any number of characters; for example, *son will find Samson, Johnson, and Yohanson, among others.

The Advanced Filter Command

➤ The field names in the criteria range must be spelled exactly the same way as in the associated list. The best way to ensure that the names are identical is to copy the entries from the list to the criteria range.

➤ Click and drag to select **cells A1** through **F1**. Click the **Copy button** on the Standard toolbar. A moving border appears around the selected cells. Click in **cell A17**. Click the **Paste button** on the Standard toolbar to complete the copy operation. Press **Esc** to cancel the moving border.

➤ Click in **cell C18**. Enter **Manager**. (Be sure you spell it correctly.)

➤ Click a single cell anywhere within the employee list. Pull down the **Data menu**. Click **Filter**. Click **Advanced Filter** from the resulting cascade menu to display the dialog box in Figure 7.12d. (The list range is already entered because you had selected a cell in the list prior to executing the command.)

➤ Click in the **Criteria Range** text box. Click in **cell A17** in the worksheet and drag the mouse to cell F18. Release the mouse. A moving border appears around these cells in the worksheet, and the corresponding cell reference is entered in the dialog box.

➤ Check that the **option button** to Filter the List in-place is selected. Click **OK**. The display changes to show just the managers; that is, only rows 4, 8, and 10 are visible.

➤ Click in **cell B18**. Type **Atlanta**. Press **enter**.

➤ Pull down the **Data menu**. Click **Filter**. Click **Advanced Filter**. The Advanced Filter dialog box already has the cell references for the list and criteria ranges (which were the last entries made).

➤ Click **OK**. The display changes to show just the manager in Atlanta; that is, only row 4 is visible.

➤ Pull down the **Data menu**. Click **Filter**. Click **Show All** to remove the filter condition. The entire list is visible.

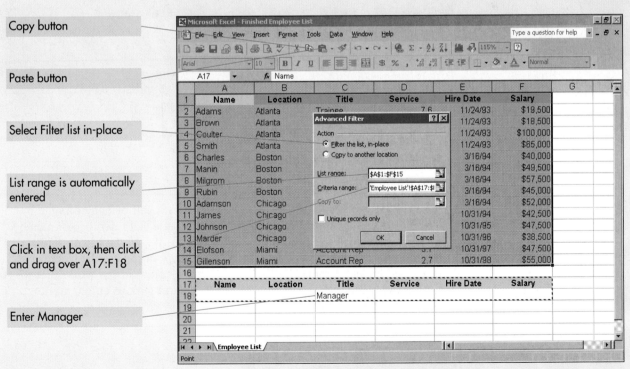

Copy button

Paste button

Select Filter list in-place

List range is automatically entered

Click in text box, then click and drag over A17:F18

Enter Manager

(d) Advanced Filter Command (step 4)

FIGURE 7.12 *Hands-on Exercise 2 (continued)*

Step 5: **The Insert Name Command**

➤ Click and drag to select **cells A1** through **F15** as shown in Figure 7.12e.
➤ Pull down the **Insert menu**. Click **Name**. Click **Define**. Type **Database** in the Define Name dialog box. Click **OK**.
➤ Pull down the **Edit menu** and click **Go To** (or press the **F5 key**) to display the Go To dialog box. There are two names in the box: Database, which you just defined, and Criteria, which was defined automatically when you specified the criteria range in step 4.
➤ Double click **Criteria** to select the criteria range (**cells A17** through **F18**). Click elsewhere in the worksheet to deselect the cells.
➤ Save the workbook.

Name box

Click and drag over A1:F15

Enter Database

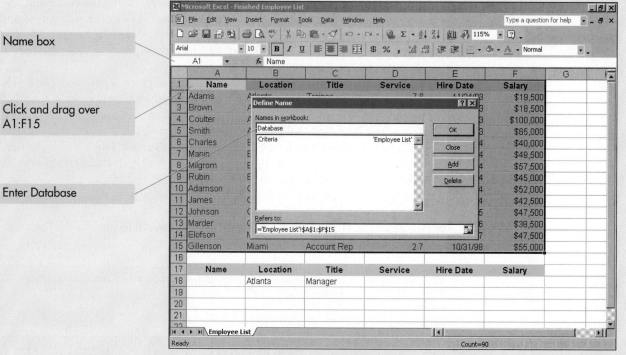

(e) The Insert Name Command (step 5)

FIGURE 7.12 *Hands-on Exercise 2 (continued)*

THE NAME BOX

Use the Name box on the formula bar to select a cell or named range by clicking in the box and then typing the appropriate cell reference or name. You can also click the drop-down arrow next to the Name box to select a named range from a drop-down list. And, finally, you can use the Name box to define a named range, by first selecting the cell(s) in the worksheet to which the name is to apply, clicking in the Name box to enter the range name, and then pressing the enter key.

Step 6: **Database Functions**

> ➤ Click in cell **A21**, type **Summary Statistics**, press the **enter key**, then click and drag to select cells **A21** through **F21**.
> ➤ Pull down the **Format menu**, click **Cells**, click the **Alignment tab**, then select **Center Across Selection** as the Horizontal alignment. Click **OK**.
> ➤ Enter the labels for **cells A22** through **A26** as shown in Figure 7.12f.
> ➤ Click in **cell B18**. Press the **Del key**. The criteria range is now set to select only managers.
> ➤ Click in **cell F22**. Click the **Insert Function button** on the formula bar to display the dialog box in Figure 7.12f.
> ➤ Select **Database** from the category list box, select **DAVERAGE** as the function name, then click **OK**.

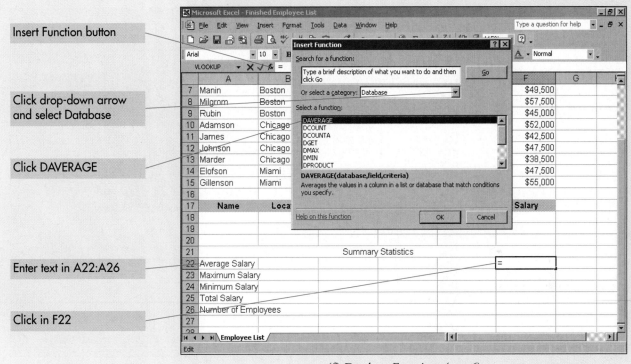

Insert Function button

Click drop-down arrow and select Database

Click DAVERAGE

Enter text in A22:A26

Click in F22

(f) Database Functions (step 6)

FIGURE 7.12 *Hands-on Exercise 2 (continued)*

HIDE A COLUMN

An individual's hire date and length of service convey essentially the same information, and thus there is no need to display both columns. Point to the column heading of the field you wish to hide, then click the right mouse button to select the column and display a shortcut menu. Click the Hide command, and the column is no longer visible (although it remains in the worksheet). To display (unhide) a column, click and drag the adjacent column headings on both sides, click the right mouse button to display a shortcut menu, then click the Unhide command.

Step 7: **The DAVERAGE Function**

> ➤ Click the **Database** text box in the dialog box as shown in Figure 7.12g. Type **Database** (the range name defined in step 5), which references the employee list.
> ➤ Click the **Field** text box. Type **"Salary"** (you must include the quotation marks), which is the name of the field (column name) within the list that you want to average.
> ➤ Click the **Criteria** text box. Type **Criteria** (the range name automatically assigned to the criteria range during the Advanced Filter operation). The dialog box displays the computed value of 69833.33333.
> ➤ Click **OK** to enter the DAVERAGE function into the worksheet.
> ➤ Save the workbook.

Enter Database

Enter "Salary"

Enter Criteria

Computed result

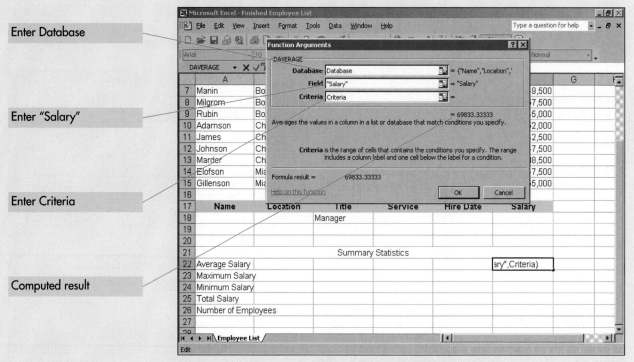

(g) The DAVERAGE Function (step 7)

FIGURE 7.12 *Hands-on Exercise 2 (continued)*

THE COLLAPSE DIALOG BUTTON

It's usually easier to enter a cell reference in the Formula Palette by clicking the underlying cell(s) within the worksheet, rather than explicitly typing the entry. The Formula Palette, however, often hides the cell(s). Should this occur, just click the Collapse Dialog button (which appears to the right of any parameter within the dialog box) to collapse (hide) the Formula Palette, enabling you to click the underlying cell(s), which is (are) now visible. Click the Collapse Dialog button a second time to display the entire dialog box.

Step 8: **The DMAX, DMIN, DSUM, and DCOUNT Functions**

➤ Enter the DMAX, DMIN, DSUM, and DCOUNT functions in cells F23 through F26, respectively. You can use the **Insert Function button** to enter each function individually, *or* you can copy the DAVERAGE function and edit appropriately:

- Click in **cell F22**. Drag the **fill handle** to **cells F23** through **F26** to copy the DAVERAGE function to these cells.
- Double click in **cell F23** to edit the contents of this cell, then click within the displayed formula to substitute **DMAX** for DAVERAGE. Press **enter**.
- Double click in the remaining cells and edit them appropriately.

➤ The computed values (except for the DCOUNT function, which has a computed value of 3) are shown in Figure 7.12h.

➤ Select **cells F22** through **F25**, then format these cells to currency with no decimals using the Formatting toolbar.

➤ Click and drag the border between columns F and G to widen column F as necessary. Save the workbook.

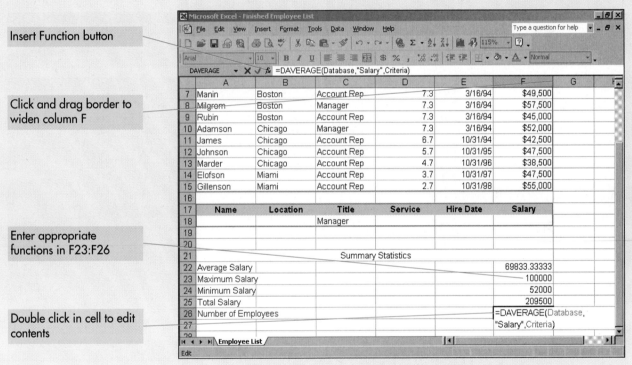

(h) The DMAX, DMIN, DSUM, DCOUNT Functions (step 8)

FIGURE 7.12   *Hands-on Exercise 2 (continued)*

IMPORT DATA FROM ACCESS

The data in a worksheet can be imported from an Access database. Pull down the Data menu, click the Import External Data command, then click Import Data to display the Select Data Source dialog box. Use the Look in list box to locate the folder containing the database and choose Access Databases as the file type. Select the database, then click the Open command to bring the Access table(s) into an Excel workbook.

Step 9: Change the Criteria

➤ Click in the **Name box**. Type **B18** and press **enter** to make cell B18 the active cell. Type **Chicago** to change the criteria to Chicago managers. Press **enter**.

➤ The values displayed by the DAVERAGE, DMIN, DMAX, and DSUM functions change to $52,000, reflecting the one employee (Adamson) who meets the current criteria (a manager in Chicago). The value displayed by the DCOUNT function changes to 1 to indicate one employee as shown in Figure 7.12i.

➤ Click in **cell C18**. Press the **Del key**.

➤ The average salary changes to $45,125, reflecting all employees in Chicago.

➤ Click in **cell B18**. Press the **Del key**.

➤ The criteria range is now empty. The DAVERAGE function displays $48,429, which is the average salary of all employees in the database.

➤ Click in **cell C18**. Type **Manager** and press the **enter key**. The average salary is $69,833, the average salary for all managers.

➤ Save the workbook.

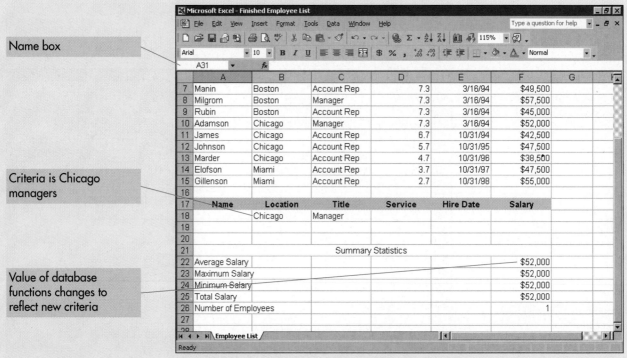

(i) Change the Criteria (step 9)

FIGURE 7.12   *Hands-on Exercise 2 (continued)*

FILTER THE LIST IN PLACE

Use the Advanced Filter command to filter the list in place and display the records that meet the current criteria. Click anywhere in the list, pull down the Data menu, click the Filter command, then choose Advanced Filter to display the Advanced Filter dialog box. Click the option button to filter the list in place, then click OK to display the selected records. You have to execute this command each time the criteria change.

Step 10: **Create the Subtotals**

➤ A list must be in sequence prior to computing the subtotals. Click any cell in the list in **Column C**, the column containing the employee titles, then click the **Sort Ascending button** on the Standard toolbar. The employees should be sequenced according to title as shown in Figure 7.12j.

➤ Pull down the **Data menu** and click the **Subtotals command**. Click the **drop-down arrow** in the **At Each Change in** list box. Click **Title** to create a subtotal whenever there is a change in title. Set the other options to match the dialog box in Figure 7.12j. Click **OK** to create the subtotals.

➤ You should see the three subtotals, one for each title, followed by the grand total for the company. The total for the Account Reps should appear first and it is equal to $430,500.

➤ The total for managers is $209,500 and matches the value obtained by the DSUM command.

➤ Save the workbook.

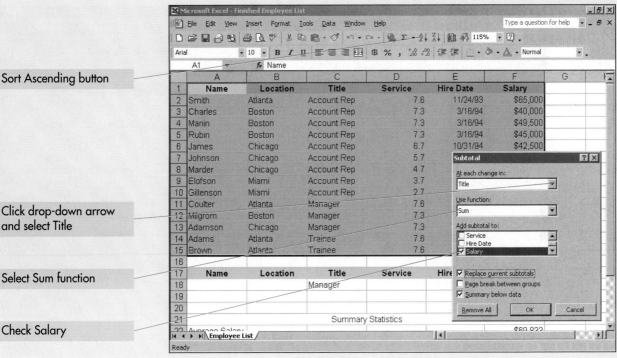

(j) Create the Subtotals (step 10)

FIGURE 7.12 *Hands-on Exercise 2 (continued)*

TWO SETS OF SUBTOTALS

You can obtain multiple sets of subtotals in the same list, provided you do the operations in the correct sequence. First sort the list according to the sequence you want, for example, by title within location. Click in the list, and compute the subtotals based on the primary key (location in this example). Click on the list a second time and compute the subtotals based on the secondary key (title in this example), but clear the check box to replace the current subtotals. You will see the subtotal for each title in the first location, followed by the subtotal for that location, and so on.

Step 11: Collapse and Expand the Subtotals

➤ The vertical lines at the left of the worksheet indicate how the data is aggregated within the list. Click the **minus sign** corresponding to the total for the Account Reps.

➤ The minus sign changes to a plus sign and the detail lines (the names of the Account Reps) disappear from the worksheet as shown in Figure 7.12k Click the **plus sign** next to the Account Rep total and you see the detailed information for each Account Rep.

➤ Click the **level 2 button** (under the Name box) to suppress the detail lines for all employees. The list collapses to display the subtotals and grand total.

➤ Click the **level 1 button** to suppress the subtotals. The list collapses further to display only the grand total. Click the **level 3 button** to restore the detail lines and subtotals.

➤ Click the **Print button** to print the list with the subtotals. Close the workbook. Exit Excel if you do not want to continue with the next exercise at this time.

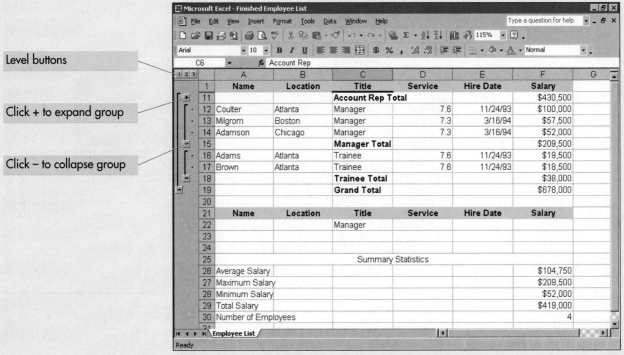

Level buttons

Click + to expand group

Click – to collapse group

(k) Collapse and Expand the Subtotals (step 11)

FIGURE 7.12   *Hands-on Exercise 2 (continued)*

DETAIL LINES VERSUS SUMMARY TOTALS

The higher you go in an organization, the more aggregated the information. The CEO, for example, requires only summary information for the company as a whole. Division managers need additional information that shows the performance of their division. Branch managers require still more detail, and so on, down the line. Excel enables you to display the information that you need by expanding or compressing the detail lines within a subtotal list.

A *pivot table* provides the ultimate flexibility in data analysis. It divides the records in a list into categories, then computes summary statistics for those categories. Pivot tables are illustrated in conjunction with the data in Figure 7.13 that displays sales information for a hypothetical advertising agency. Each record in the list in Figure 7.13a displays the name of the sales representative, the quarter in which the sale was recorded, the type of media, and the amount of the sale.

The pivot table in Figure 7.13b shows the total sales for each Media–Sales Rep combination. Look closely and you will see four shaded buttons, each of which corresponds to a different area in the table. The Media and Sales Rep buttons are in the row and column areas, respectively. Thus, each row in the pivot table displays the data for a different media type (magazine, radio, or TV), whereas each column displays data for a different sales representative. The Quarter button in the page area provides a third dimension. The value in the drop-down list box indicates that all of the records in the underlying worksheet are used to compute the totals in the body of the table. You can, however, display different pages corresponding to the totals in the first, second, third, or fourth quarters. You can also click the arrows next to the other buttons to suppress selected values for the media type or sales representative.

The best feature about a pivot table is its flexibility because you can change the orientation to provide a different analysis of the associated data. Figure 7.13c, for example, displays an alternate version of the pivot table in which the fields have been rearranged to show the total for each combination of quarter and sales representative. You go from one pivot table to another simply by clicking and dragging the buttons corresponding to the field names to different positions.

You can also change the means of computation within the data area. Both of the pivot tables in Figure 7.13 use the Sum function, but you can choose other functions such as Average, Minimum, Maximum, or Count. You can also change the formatting of any element in the table. More importantly, pivot tables are dynamic in that they reflect changes to the underlying worksheet. Thus, you can add, edit, or delete records in the associated list and see the results in the pivot table, provided you execute the *Refresh command* to update the pivot table.

The *Pivot Table Wizard* is used to create the initial pivot table in conjunction with an optional pivot chart. The *pivot chart* in Figure 7.14, for example, corresponds to the pivot table in Figure 7.13b, and at first glance, it resembles any other Excel chart. Look closely, however, and you will see shaded buttons similar to those in the pivot table, enabling you to change the chart by dragging the buttons to different areas. Reverse the position of the Media and Sales Rep buttons, for example, and you have a completely different chart. Any changes to the chart are reflected in the underlying pivot table and vice versa.

Drop-down arrows next to each button on the pivot chart let you display selected values. Click either arrow to display a drop-down list in which you select the values you want to appear in the chart. You could, for example, click the drop-down arrow next to the Sales Rep field and clear the name of any sales rep to remove his/her data from the chart.

Pivot tables may also be saved as Web pages with full interactivity as shown in Figure 7.15. The Address bar indicates that you are viewing a Web document (note the htm extension), as opposed to an Excel workbook. As with an ordinary pivot table, you can pivot the table within the Web page by repositioning the buttons for the row, column, and page fields. The plus and minus next to the various categories enable you to show or hide the detailed information. (The interactivity extends to Netscape as well as Internet Explorer, provided that you install the Office Web components.)

Pivot tables are one of the best-kept secrets in Excel, even though they have been available in the last several releases of Excel. (Pivot charts were introduced in Excel 2000.) Be sure to share this capability with your friends and colleagues.

(a) Sales Data (Excel list)

	A	B	C	D
1	**Sales Rep**	**Quarter**	**Media**	**Amount**
2	Alice	1st quarter	TV	$15,000
3	Alice	1st quarter	Radio	$4,000
4	Alice	2nd quarter	Magazine	$2,000
5	Alice	2nd quarter	Radio	$4,000
6	Alice	3rd quarter	Radio	$2,000
7	Alice	4th quarter	Radio	$4,000
8	Alice	4th quarter	Radio	$1,000
9	Bob	1st quarter	Magazine	$2,000
10	Bob	1st quarter	Radio	$1,000
11	Bob	2nd quarter	Radio	$4,000
12	Bob	3rd quarter	TV	$10,000
13	Bob	4th quarter	Magazine	$10,000
14	Bob	4th quarter	Magazine	$12,000
15	Bob	4th quarter	Radio	$1,000
16	Bob	4th quarter	Magazine	$7,000
17	Carol	1st quarter	Radio	$4,000
18	Carol	2nd quarter	Magazine	$2,000
19	Carol	2nd quarter	Magazine	$7,000
20	Carol	2nd quarter	TV	$10,000
21	Carol	3rd quarter	TV	$8,000
22	Carol	3rd quarter	TV	$18,000
23	Carol	4th quarter	TV	$13,000
24	Ted	1st quarter	Radio	$2,000
25	Ted	2nd quarter	TV	$6,000
26	Ted	2nd quarter	TV	$6,000
27	Ted	3rd quarter	TV	$20,000
28	Ted	3rd quarter	Magazine	$15,000
29	Ted	3rd quarter	Magazine	$2,000
30	Ted	4th quarter	TV	$13,000
31	Ted	4th quarter	TV	$15,000

(b) Analysis by Media Type and Sales Representative

All records are used in calculations

Quarter is in page area

Computation is Sum of Amount

Media is in row area

Sales Rep is in column area

	A	B	C	D	E	F
1	Quarter	(All) ▼				
2						
3	Sum of Amount	Sales Rep ▼				
4	Media ▼	Alice	Bob	Carol	Ted	Grand Total
5	Magazine	$2,000	$31,000	$9,000	$17,000	$59,000
6	Radio	$15,000	$6,000	$4,000	$2,000	$27,000
7	TV	$15,000	$10,000	$49,000	$60,000	$134,000
8	Grand Total	$32,000	$47,000	$62,000	$79,000	$220,000

(c) Analysis by Sales Representative and Quarter

Media is in page area

Calculation is Sum of Amount

Sales Rep is in row area

Quarter is in column area

	A	B	C	D	E	F
1	Media	(All) ▼				
2						
3	Sum of Amount	Quarter ▼				
4	Sales Rep ▼	1st quarter	2nd quarter	3rd quarter	4th quarter	Grand Total
5	Alice	$19,000	$6,000	$2,000	$5,000	$32,000
6	Bob	$3,000	$4,000	$10,000	$30,000	$47,000
7	Carol	$4,000	$19,000	$26,000	$13,000	$62,000
8	Ted	$2,000	$12,000	$37,000	$28,000	$79,000
9	Grand Total	$28,000	$41,000	$75,000	$76,000	$220,000

FIGURE 7.13   *Pivot Tables*

Quarter button

Click drop-down arrow to select value to appear in chart

Sales Rep button

Media button

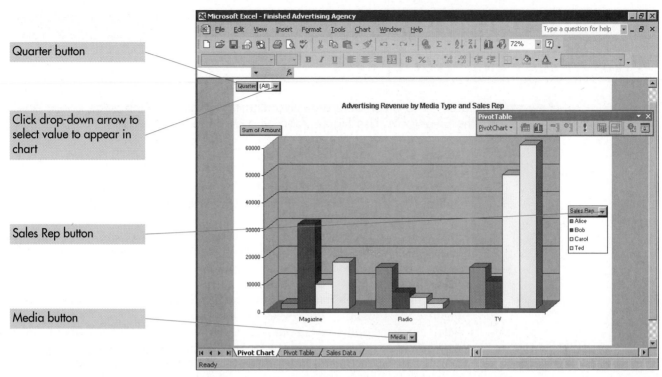

FIGURE 7.14 *A Pivot Chart*

Extension is htm

Address bar indicates a Web document

Drag button to column/row position to pivot the table

Click to show detail

Click to hide detail

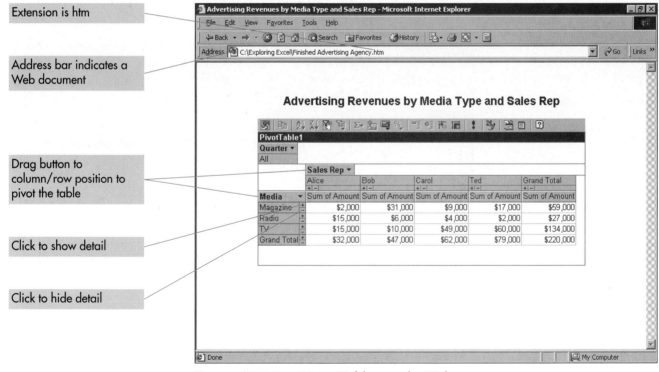

FIGURE 7.15 *Pivot Tables on the Web*

HANDS-ON EXERCISE 3

PIVOT TABLES AND PIVOT CHARTS

Objective To create a pivot table and pivot chart; to create a Web page based on the pivot table. Use Figure 7.16 as a guide in the exercise.

Step 1: **Start the Pivot Table Wizard**

> ➤ Start Excel. Open the **Advertising Agency workbook** in the **Exploring Excel folder**. Save the workbook as **Finished Advertising Agency** so that you will be able to return to the original workbook.
> ➤ The workbook contains a list of sales records for the advertising agency. Each record displays the name of the sales representative, the quarter in which the sale was recorded, the media type, and the amount of the sale.
> ➤ Click anywhere in the list of sales data. Pull down the **Data menu**. Click **PivotTable and PivotChart report** to start the Pivot Table Wizard as shown in Figure 7.16a. Close the Office Assistant, if necessary.
> ➤ Select the same options as in our figure. The pivot table will be created from data in a Microsoft Excel List or Database. In addition, you want to create a Pivot Chart report (that includes the Pivot Table). Click **Next**.
> ➤ Cells A1 through D31 have been selected automatically as the basis of the pivot table. Click **Next**.
> ➤ The option button to put the pivot table into a new worksheet is already selected. Click **Finish**. Two additional sheets have been added to the workbook, but the pivot table and chart area are not yet complete.

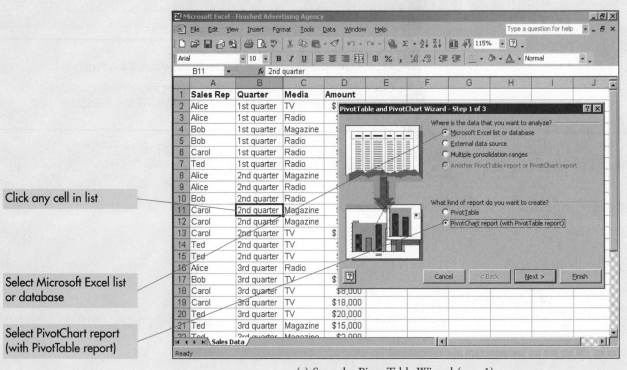

(a) Start the Pivot Table Wizard (step 1)

FIGURE 7.16 *Hands-on Exercise 3*

Step 2: **Complete the Pivot Table**

➤ Click the tab that takes you to the new worksheet (Sheet1 in our workbook). Your screen should be similar to Figure 7.16b. Complete the pivot table as follows:
- Click the **Media field button** and drag it to the row area.
- Click the **Sales Rep button** and drag it to the column area.
- Click the **Quarter field button** and drag it to the page area.
- Click the **Amount field button** and drag it to the data area.

➤ You should see the total sales for each sales representative for each type of media within a pivot table.

➤ Rename the worksheets so that they are more descriptive of their contents. Double click the **Sheet1 tab** (the worksheet that contains the pivot table) to select the name of the sheet. Type **Pivot Table** as the new name, and press **enter**.

➤ Double click the **Chart1** worksheet and change its name to **Pivot Chart** in similar fashion. Save the workbook.

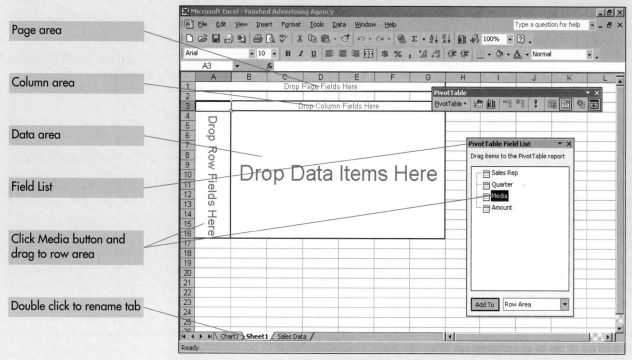

(b) Complete the Pivot Table (step 2)

FIGURE 7.16 *Hands-on Exercise 3 (continued)*

THE PAGE FIELD

A page field adds a third dimension to a pivot table. Unlike items in the row and column fields, however, the items in a page field are displayed one at a time. Creating a page field on Quarter, for example, lets you view the data for each quarter separately, by clicking the drop-down arrow on the page field list box, then clicking the appropriate quarter.

Step 3:   **Modify the Sales Data**

➤ You will replace Bob's name within the list of transactions with your own name. Click the **Sales Data tab** to return to the underlying worksheet. Pull down the **Edit menu** and click the **Replace command** to display the Find and Replace dialog box.

➤ Enter **Bob** in the Find What dialog box, type **Your Name** (first and last) in the Replace With dialog box, then click the **Replace All button**. Click **OK** after the replacements have been made. Close the Find and Replace dialog box.

➤ Click the **Pivot Table tab** to return to the pivot table as shown in Figure 7.16c. The name change is not yet reflected in the pivot table because the table must be manually refreshed whenever the underlying data changes.

➤ Click anywhere in the pivot table, then click the **Refresh Data button** on the Pivot Table toolbar to update the pivot table. (You must click the Refresh button to update the pivot table whenever the underlying data changes.) You should see your name as one of the sales representatives.

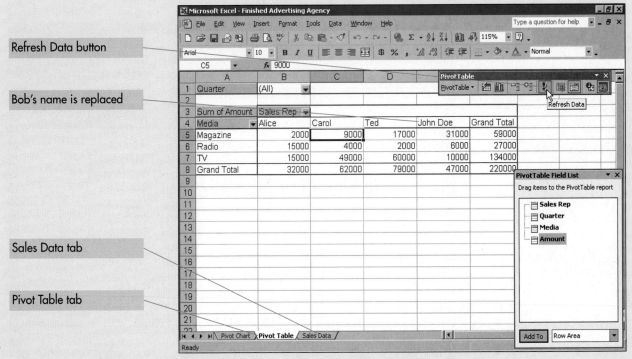

(c) Modify the Sales Data (step 3)

FIGURE 7.16   *Hands-on Exercise 3 (continued)*

THE FORMAT REPORT BUTTON

Why settle for a traditional report in black and white or shades of gray when you can choose from preformatted reports in a variety of styles and colors? Click the Format Report button on the Pivot Table toolbar to display the AutoFormat dialog box, where you select the style of your report. (To return to the default formatting, scroll to the end of the AutoFormat dialog box and select PivotTable Classic.)

Step 4: **Pivot the Table**

➤ You can change the contents of a pivot table simply by dragging fields from one area to another. Click and drag the **Quarter field** to the row area. The page field is now empty and you can see the breakdown of sales by quarter and media type.

➤ Click and drag the **Media field** to the column area, then drag the **Sales Rep field** to the page area. Your pivot table should match the one in Figure 7.16d.

➤ Click anywhere in the pivot table, then click the **Field Settings button** on the Pivot Table toolbar to display the PivotTable Field dialog box.

➤ Click the **Number button**, choose **Currency format** (with zero decimals). Click **OK** to close the Format Cells dialog box. Click **OK** a second time to close the Pivot Table Field dialog box.

➤ Save the workbook.

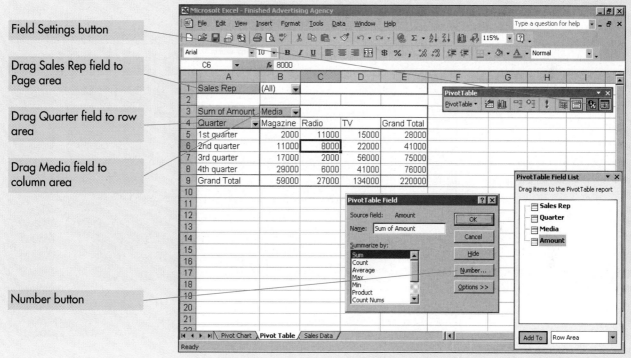

Field Settings button

Drag Sales Rep field to Page area

Drag Quarter field to row area

Drag Media field to column area

Number button

(d) Pivot the Table (step 4)

FIGURE 7.16   *Hands-on Exercise 3 (continued)*

CUSTOMIZE THE PIVOT TABLE

Right click anywhere within a pivot table to display a context-sensitive menu, then click the Table Options command to display the PivotTable Options dialog box. The default settings work well for most tables, but you can customize the table in a variety of ways. You can, for example, suppress the row or column totals or display a specific value in a blank cell. You can also change the formatting for any field within the table by right clicking the field and selecting the Format Cells button from the resulting menu.

Step 5: **Change the Chart Type**

➤ Click the **Pivot Chart tab** to view the default pivot chart as shown in Figure 7.16e. If necessary, close the field list to give yourself more room in which to work.

➤ Pull down the **Chart menu** and click the **Chart Type command** to display the dialog box in Figure 7.16e. Select the **Clustered column with a 3-D visual effect**. (Take a minute to appreciate the different types of charts that are available.)

➤ Check the box for **Default formatting**. This is a very important option, because without it, the chart is rotated in an awkward fashion. Click **OK**.

➤ The chart changes to display a three-dimensional column for each of the media in each data series.

➤ Save the workbook.

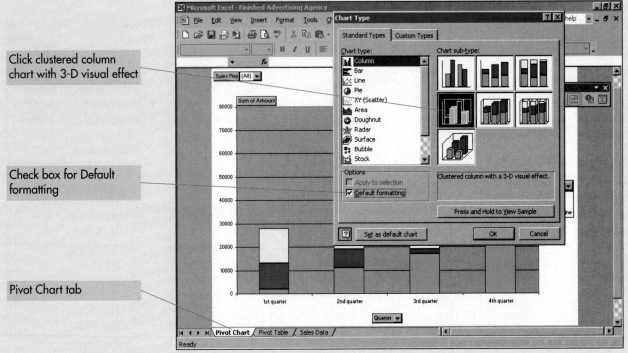

(e) Change the Chart Type (step 5)

FIGURE 7.16   *Hands-on Exercise 3 (continued)*

IT'S A PIVOT CHART

The shaded buttons for Sales Rep, Quarter, and Media that appear on the chart are similar in appearance and function to their counterparts in the underlying pivot table. Thus you can click and drag any of the buttons to a different position on the chart to change the underlying structure. You can also click and drag a field button from the PivotTable Field List to a new position on the chart. (Click the Show Field List button on the Pivot Table toolbar to show or hide the field list.)

Step 6: **Complete the Chart**

➤ Pull down the **Chart menu**, click **Chart Options** to display the Chart Options dialog box, then click the **Titles tab**. Enter **Advertising Revenue by Quarter and Media Type** as the chart title. Click **OK** to complete the chart as shown in Figure 7.16f.

➤ Click the **Sales Data tab** to select this worksheet. Press and hold the **Ctrl key** as you select the **Pivot Table tab** to select the worksheet containing the pivot table. Both worksheets are selected and hence both will be affected by the next command.

➤ Pull down the **File menu**, click the **Page Setup command**, and click the **Sheet tab**. Check the boxes to print **Gridlines** and **Row and Column headings**. Click the **Margins tab** and check the box to center the worksheet **horizontally**. Click **OK**. Save the workbook.

➤ Pull down the **File menu** and click the **Print command** to display the Print dialog box. Click the option button to print the entire workbook. Click **OK**.

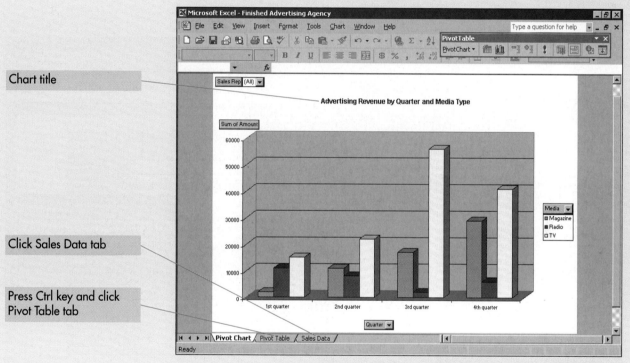

(f) Complete the Chart (step 6)

FIGURE 7.16 *Hands-on Exercise 3 (continued)*

FORMAT THE DATA SERIES

Why settle for a traditional bar chart when you can change the color, pattern, or shape of its components? Right click any column to select a data series to display a shortcut menu, then choose the Format Data Series command to display a dialog box in which you can customize the appearance of the vertical bars. We warn you that it is addictive, and that you can spend much more time than you intended initially. Set a time limit, and stop when you reach it.

Step 7: **Save the Pivot Table as a Web Page**

➤ Click the **Pivot Chart tab** to deselect the two tabs, then click the **Pivot Table tab**. Click and drag to select the entire pivot table. (If you have difficulty selecting the table, click and drag from the bottom-right cell to the top-left cell.)

➤ Pull down the **File menu**, click the **Save As Web Page command** to display the Save As dialog box, then click the **Publish button** (within the Save As dialog box) to display the Publish as Web Page dialog box in Figure 7.16g. Click **No** if the Office Assistant offers help.

➤ The default file name is **Finished Advertising Agency** and it will be saved in the **Exploring Excel folder**. There is no need to change this information.

➤ Check the box to **Add interactivity** and select **Pivot Table functionality**. Check the boxes to **AutoRepublish every time this workbook is saved** and to **Open published web page in browser**.

➤ Click the **Change button** and enter an appropriate title that includes your name. Click **OK** to close the Set Title dialog box.

➤ Check that your settings match those in Figure 7.16g. Click the **Publish button** to publish the pivot table.

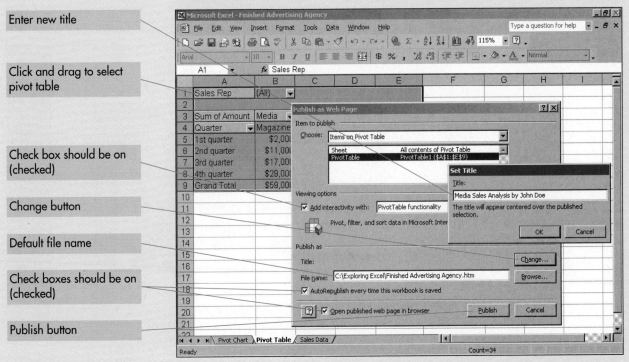

(g) Save the Pivot Table as a Web Page (step 7)

FIGURE 7.16   *Hands-on Exercise 3 (continued)*

AN EXTRA FOLDER

The Save As Web Page command creates an HTML document with the same name as the workbook on which it is based. The command also creates a folder with a similar name (the word "_files" is added to the end of the workbook name) that contains supporting Web pages to enable the interactivity. You must upload both the Web page and the folder if you intend to display the pivot table on a Web server.

Step 8: **Pivot the Web Page**

➤ The pivot table will open automatically in your browser because of the option you selected in the previous step. If Internet Explorer is your default browser, you will see the pivot table in Figure 7.16h.

➤ If Netscape Navigator is your default browser, you will be prompted to install the Microsoft Web components, after which you should see the pivot table.

➤ Pivot the table so that its appearance matches Figure 7.16h. Thus, you need to drag the **Sales Rep button** to the column area and the **Media button** to the row area. (You can click the **Fields List button** on the Pivot Table toolbar to display/hide the fields in the table, should you lose a field button.)

➤ Click the **Plus sign** next to each quarter to display the detailed information. Click the **Print button** on the Internet Explorer toolbar to print the pivot table for your instructor.

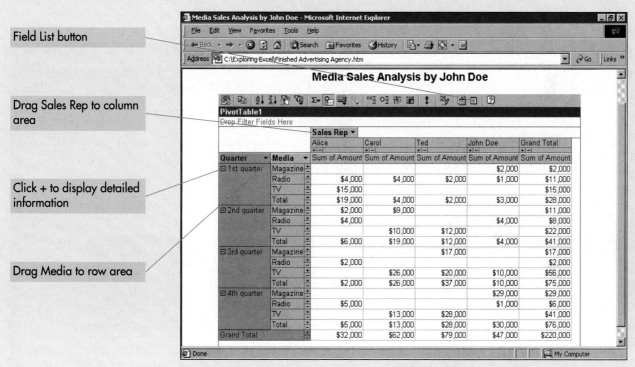

Field List button

Drag Sales Rep to column area

Click + to display detailed information

Drag Media to row area

(h) Pivot the Web Page (step 8)

FIGURE 7.16 *Hands-on Exercise 3 (continued)*

WHAT IS XML?

Extensible Markup Language (XML) takes structured data such as an Excel worksheet and converts it to a text file that can be read by a variety of applications. It enables the creator of an XML page to create his or her customized tags that enable the validation and transmission of data between applications. Formatting rules for XML are specified in style sheets. See practice exercise 10 at the end of the chapter.

Step 9: **Change the Underlying Data**

➤ Click the **Excel button** on the Windows taskbar to return to Excel. Click the **Sales Data worksheet** and change the data for John Doe's (your name) magazine sales in the first quarter from $2000 to $22000.

➤ Click the **worksheet tab** for the pivot table. Click anywhere in the pivot table and click the **refresh button** on the Pivot Table toolbar. The magazine sales in the 1st quarter increase to $22,000 and the grand total changes to $240,000.

➤ Click the **Save button** to save the changes to the worksheet. You will see the dialog box in Figure 7.16i. Click the option button to **Enable the Autopublish feature**. Click **OK**.

➤ Return to Internet Explorer. Click the **Refresh button** on the Pivot Table toolbar to update the Web page. The numbers within the Web pivot table change to reflect the change in magazine sales.

➤ Close Internet Explorer. Close Excel. Click **Yes** if prompted to save the changes.

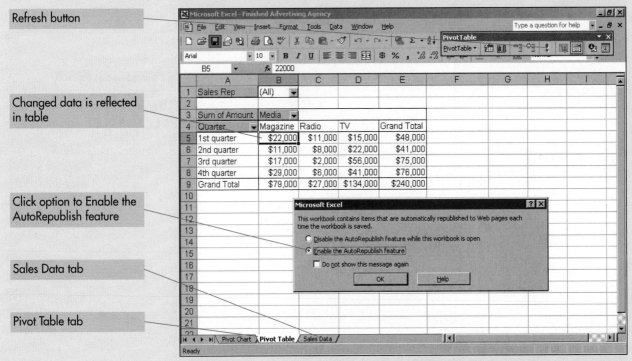

Refresh button

Changed data is reflected in table

Click option to Enable the AutoRepublish feature

Sales Data tab

Pivot Table tab

(i) Change the Underlying Data (step 9)

FIGURE 7.16 *Hands-on Exercise 3 (continued)*

THE NEED TO REFRESH

A pivot table and/or a Web page based on a pivot table do not automatically reflect changes in the underlying data. You must first refresh the pivot table as it exists within the workbook, by clicking in the pivot table, then clicking the refresh button on the Pivot Table toolbar. Next, you must save the workbook and enable the AutoPublish feature. Finally, you have to click in the Web page and click the Refresh button on the Web toolbar.

A list is an area in a worksheet that contains rows of similar data. The first row in the list contains the column labels (field names). Each additional row contains data for a specific record. A data form provides an easy way to add, edit, and delete records in a list.

A date is stored internally as an integer number corresponding to the number of days in this century. (January 1, 1900 is stored as the number 1.) The number of elapsed days between two dates can be determined by simple subtraction. The TODAY function always returns the current date (the date on which a worksheet is created or retrieved).

A filtered list displays only those records that meet specific criteria. Filtering is implemented through AutoFilter or the Advanced Filter command. The latter enables you to specify a criteria range and to copy the selected records elsewhere in the worksheet.

The Sort command arranges a list according to the value of one or more keys (known as the primary, secondary, and tertiary keys). Each key may be in ascending or descending sequence.

The database functions (DSUM, DAVERAGE, DMAX, DMIN, and DCOUNT) have three arguments: the associated list, the field name, and the criteria range. The simplest criteria range consists of two rows and as many fields as there are in the list.

The Text Import Wizard converts data in either fixed width or delimited format to an Excel workbook. The Wizard is displayed automatically if you attempt to open a text file. Data can also be imported into an Excel workbook from other applications such as Microsoft Access.

The Subtotals command uses a summary function (such as SUM, AVERAGE, or COUNT) to compute subtotals for data groups within a list. The data is displayed in outline view, where outline symbols can be used to suppress or expand the detail records.

A pivot table extends the capability of individual database functions by presenting the data in summary form. It divides the records in a list into categories, then computes summary statistics for those categories. Pivot tables provide the utmost flexibility in that you can vary the row or column categories and/or the way that the statistics are computed. A pivot chart extends the capability of a pivot table to a chart.

KEY TERMS

Advanced Filter command (p. 325)
Ascending sequence (p. 311)
AutoFilter command (p. 324)
Criteria range (p. 325)
Data (p. 322)
Data form (p. 310)
Database (p. 308)
Database functions (p. 327)
DAVERAGE function (p. 327)
DCOUNT function (p. 327)
Delete command (p. 309)
Delimited format (p. 314)
Descending sequence (p. 311)
DMAX function (p. 327)

DMIN function (p. 327)
DSUM function (p. 327)
Field (p. 308)
Field name (p. 308)
File (p. 308)
Filtered list (p. 324)
Fixed width format (p. 314)
Form command (p. 310)
Information (p. 322)
Insert Columns command (p. 309)
Insert Rows command (p. 309)
Key (p. 308)
List (p. 308)
Name command (p. 328)

Now ( ) function (p. 313)
Outline symbols (p. 329)
Pivot chart (p. 341)
Pivot table (p. 341)
Pivot Table Wizard (p. 341)
Record (p. 308)
Refresh command (p. 341)
Sort command (p. 311)
Subtotals command (p. 329)
Text Import Wizard (p. 314)
TODAY( ) function (p. 313)
Wild card (p. 327)

1. Which of the following best describes data management in Excel?
   (a) The rows in a list correspond to records in a file
   (b) The columns in a list correspond to fields in a record
   (c) Both (a) and (b)
   (d) Neither (a) nor (b)

2. How should a list be placed within a worksheet?
   (a) There should be at least one blank row between the list and the other entries in the worksheet
   (b) There should be at least one blank column between the list and the other entries in the worksheet
   (c) Both (a) and (b)
   (d) Neither (a) nor (b)

3. Which of the following is suggested for the placement of database functions within a worksheet?
   (a) Above or below the list with at least one blank row separating the database functions from the list to which they refer
   (b) To the left or right of the list with at least one blank column separating the database functions from the list to which they refer
   (c) Both (a) and (b)
   (d) Neither (a) nor (b)

4. Cells A21:B22 have been defined as the criteria range, cells A21 and B21 contain the field names City and Title, respectively, and cells A22 and B22 contain New York and Manager. The selected records will consist of:
   (a) All employees in New York, regardless of title
   (b) All managers, regardless of the city
   (c) Only the managers in New York
   (d) All employees in New York (regardless of title) or all managers

5. Cells A21:B23 have been defined as the criteria range, cells A21 and B21 contain the field names City and Title, respectively, and cells A22 and B23 contain New York and Manager, respectively. The selected records will consist of:
   (a) All employees in New York regardless of title
   (b) All managers regardless of the city
   (c) Only the managers in New York
   (d) All employees in New York or all managers

6. If employees are to be listed so that all employees in the same city appear together in alphabetical order by the employee's last name:
   (a) City and last name are both considered to be the primary key
   (b) City and last name are both considered to be the secondary key
   (c) City is the primary key and last name is the secondary key
   (d) Last name is the primary key and city is the secondary key

7. Which of the following can be used to delete a record from a database?
   (a) The Edit Delete command
   (b) The Data Form command
   (c) Both (a) and (b)
   (d) Neither (a) nor (b)

8. Which of the following is true about the DAVERAGE function?
   (a) It has a single argument
   (b) It can be entered into a worksheet using the Function Wizard
   (c) Both (a) and (b)
   (d) Neither (a) nor (b)

9. Which of the following can be converted to an Excel workbook?
   (a) A text file in delimited format
   (b) A text file in fixed width format
   (c) Both (a) and (b)
   (d) Neither (a) nor (b)

10. Which of the following is recommended to distinguish the first row in a list (the field names) from the remaining entries (the data)?
    (a) Insert a blank row between the first row and the remaining rows
    (b) Insert a row of dashes between the first row and the remaining rows
    (c) Either (a) or (b)
    (d) Neither (a) nor (b)

11. The AutoFilter command:
    (a) Permanently deletes records from the associated list
    (b) Requires the specification of a criteria range elsewhere in the worksheet
    (c) Either (a) or (b)
    (d) Neither (a) nor (b)

12. Which of the following is true of the Sort command?
    (a) The primary key must be in ascending sequence
    (b) The secondary key must be in descending sequence
    (c) Both (a) and (b)
    (d) Neither (a) nor (b)

13. What is the best way to enter January 21, 1996 into a worksheet, given that you create the worksheet on that date, and further, that you always want to display that specific date?
    (a) =TODAY()
    (b) 1/21/96
    (c) Both (b) and (b) are equally acceptable
    (d) Neither (a) nor (b)

14. Which of the following best describes the relationship between the Sort and Subtotals commands?
    (a) The Sort command should be executed before the Subtotals command
    (b) The Subtotals command should be executed before the Sort command
    (c) The commands can be executed in either sequence
    (d) There is no relationship because the commands have nothing to do with one another

15. Which of the following may be implemented in an existing pivot table?
    (a) A row field may be added or deleted
    (b) A column field may be added or deleted
    (c) Both (a) and (b)
    (d) Neither (a) nor (b)

ANSWERS

1. c	**6.** c	**11.** d
2. c	**7.** c	**12.** d
3. a	**8.** b	**13.** b
4. c	**9.** c	**14.** a
5. d	**10.** d	**15.** c

1. Election 2000: Election 2000 has been decided, but it will be remembered for its closeness and controversy. Open a partially completed version of the workbook in *Chapter 7 Practice 1*, then complete the workbook so that it matches Figure 7.17. Proceed as follows:

   a. Enter the appropriate IF function in cell C8 to determine the winner of the state's electoral votes. Use conditional formatting to display the indicated colors for Bush and Gore. Develop the formula in such a way that it can be copied to the remaining rows in this column.

   b. Enter the appropriate formulas in cells F8 and G8 to compute the difference in the number of votes and the associated percentages. (Use the absolute value function so that the difference in the number of votes is always shown as a positive number.) Copy the formulas to the remaining rows in the worksheet.

   c. Use an ordinary SUM function to determine the popular vote for each candidate as shown in cells B4 and C4. Use the DSUM function to determine the number of electoral votes for each candidate. (You will need to establish separate criteria ranges for each candidate.)

   d. Add your name somewhere in the worksheet, then print the completed worksheet to show both displayed values and cell formulas for your instructor. Be sure the worksheet fits on a single page.

   e. Print the worksheet in at least one other sequence—for example, by the smallest (or largest) vote differential.

   f. Add a cover sheet, then submit the complete assignment to your instructor.

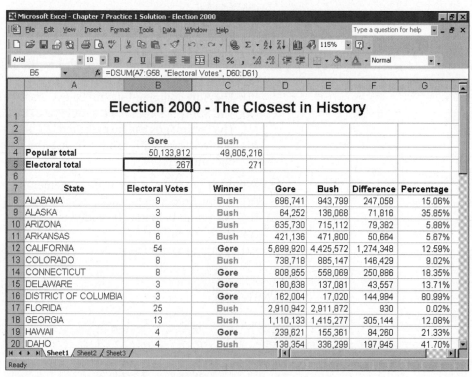

FIGURE 7.17 *Election 2000 (Exercise 1)*

2. The Dean's List: The *Chapter 7 Practice 2* workbook contains a partially completed version of the workbook in Figure 7.18. Open the workbook, then implement the following changes:

a. Add a transfer student, Jeff Borow, majoring in Engineering. Jeff has completed 14 credits and has 45 quality points. (Jeff's record can be seen in Figure 7.18, but it is not in the workbook that you will retrieve from the Exploring Excel folder.) Do not, however, enter Jeff's GPA or year in school, as both will be computed from formulas in the next two steps.

b. Enter the appropriate formula in F4 to compute the GPA for the first student (the quality points divided by the number of credits). Copy the formula to the other cells in this column.

c. Enter the appropriate formula in cell G4 to determine the year in school for the first student. (Use the HLOOKUP function based on the table in cells B24 through E25. The entries in cells A24 and A25 contain labels and are not part of the table per se.) Copy the formula to the other cells in this column.

d. Format the worksheet attractively. You can use our formatting or develop your own. Sort the list so that the students are listed alphabetically.

e. Filter the list in place so that the only visible students are those on the Dean's list (with a GPA greater than 3.2) as shown in Figure 7.18.

f. Add your name as the academic advisor in cell A28. Print the worksheet two ways, with displayed values and cell formulas, and submit both to your instructor. Use landscape printing and display gridlines and row and column headings. Be sure that each printout fits on a single sheet of paper.

g. Remove the filter condition, then print the worksheet in a different sequence—for example, by ascending or descending GPA.

h. Add a cover sheet, then submit the complete assignment to your instructor.

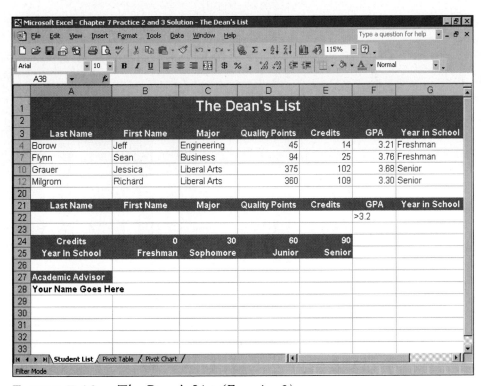

FIGURE 7.18   *The Dean's List (Exercise 2)*

3. The Pivot Chart: Complete the previous exercise, then add a pivot table and pivot chart as shown in Figure 7.19. Start by creating the pivot table in its own worksheet, but be sure to select the option to create a pivot chart with the pivot table. Rename the resulting worksheets, Sheet1 and Chart1, to Pivot Table and Pivot Chart as shown in Figure 7.19.

a. Modify the pivot table so that major and year in school are the row and column fields, respectively. Use GPA as the data field, but be sure to specify the average GPA rather than the sum. Format the GPA to two decimal places.

b. Change the format of the pivot chart to a 3-D side-by-side column chart with default formatting. Right click any column within the chart, select the Format Data Series command, then select the Series Order tab. Change the order of the columns to Freshman, Sophomore, Junior, and Senior, as opposed to the default alphabetical order.

c. Pull down the Chart menu, click the Chart Options command to display the associated dialog box, then select the Data Table tab. Check the box to display the data table below the chart. Save the workbook.

d. Print the pivot table chart as shown in Figure 7.19. You do not need to print the pivot table since the equivalent information is shown in the data table that appears below the pivot chart.

e. Pivot tables are one of the best-kept secrets in Excel, even though they have been available in the last several releases of Excel. (Pivot charts, however, were first introduced in Excel 2000.) Write a short note to a colleague that describes how this feature facilitates data analysis.

f. Add a cover sheet, then submit the complete assignment to your instructor.

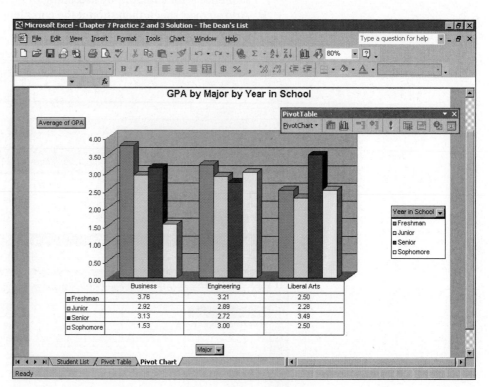

FIGURE 7.19   *The Pivot Chart (Exercise 3)*

4. **Compensation Analysis:** The workbook in Figure 7.20 is used to analyze employee compensation with respect to the dollar amount and percentage of their latest salary increase. Your assignment is to open the partially completed workbook in *Chapter 7 Practice 4* and complete the workbook to match our figure.

   a. Open the workbook, then enter the formula to compute the dollar increase for the first employee in cell G3. Note, however, that not every employee has a previous salary, and thus the formula requires an If function to work correctly. Copy this formula to the remaining rows in column G.

   b. Enter the formula to compute the percentage increase for the first employee in cell H3. The percentage increase is found by dividing the amount of the increase by the previous salary. Again, not every employee has a previous salary, and hence the formula requires an IF function to avoid dividing by zero. Copy this formula to the remaining rows in column H.

   c. Enter the indicated database functions in rows 21 and 22 to reflect only those employees who have received a raise. Thus, be sure to include the greater than zero entry in the criteria row.

   d. Format the worksheet in attractive fashion. You can copy our formatting or use your own design. Note, too, that you can suppress the display of zero values through the Options command. (If necessary, pull down the Tools menu, click the Options command, then click the View tab and clear the box to display zero values.)

   e. Add your name as a financial analyst, then print the worksheet with both displayed values and cell formulas. Use landscape printing as necessary to be sure that the worksheet fits on a single sheet of paper.

   f. Print the worksheet in at least one other sequence—for example, by the smallest (or largest) percentage increase.

   g. Add a cover sheet, then submit the complete assignment to your instructor.

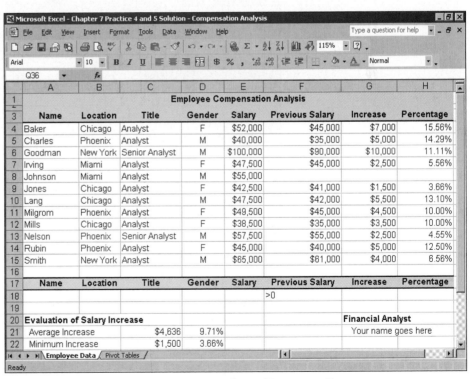

FIGURE 7.20   *Compensation Analysis (Exercise 4)*

BUILDS ON

PRACTICE
EXERCISE 4
PAGE 359

5. **Pivot Tables:** Continue the analysis from the previous exercise by creating the pivot tables shown in Figure 7.21. We have created two separate pivot tables, for the dollar and percentage increase, respectively, but you may find it more convenient to create a single table. (You can create two pivot tables on one worksheet by specifying that the second pivot table is to go on an existing worksheet, as opposed to a new worksheet.) Either solution is acceptable.

a. You will, however, have to format your pivot table to include currency and percent symbols as appropriate, as well as a reasonable number of decimal places. Note, too, we use the average (as opposed to the default sum) function for both statistics.

b. Use the same style of formatting for the text in your pivot table as in the previous exercise, so that your workbook has a uniform look. Use the Options command as described in the previous exercise to suppress the display of zero values.

c. What is the meaning of the exclamation point that appears on the Pivot Table toolbar? When do you use this tool?

d. Combine the existing pivot tables into a single table that has two data fields—the amount of the increase and the percent of the increase. Do you prefer the combined table to the individual tables?

e. Pivot tables are one of the best-kept secrets in Excel, even though they have been available in the last several releases of Excel. (Pivot charts, however, were first introduced in Excel 2000.) Write a short note to a colleague that describes how this feature facilitates data analysis.

f. Add a cover sheet, then submit the complete assignment to your instructor.

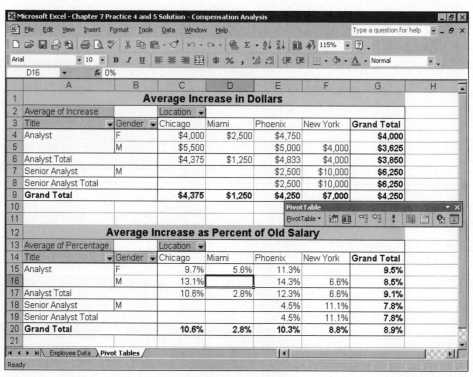

FIGURE 7.21   *Pivot Tables (Exercise 5)*

6. Consumer Loans: The worksheet in Figure 7.22 displays selected loans (those with a loan type of "A") from a comprehensive set of loan records. Your assignment is to open the partially completed *Chapter 7 Practice 6* workbook, to create the worksheet in our figure.

   a. Open the workbook, then go to cell H4, the cell containing the ending date for the first loan. Enter the formula to compute the ending date, based on the starting date and the term of the loan. For the sake of simplicity, you do not have to account for leap year. Thus, to compute the ending date, multiply the term of the loan by 365 and add that result to the starting date. Be sure to format the starting and ending dates to show a date format.

   b. Go to cell I4 and enter the PMT function to compute the monthly payment for the first loan. Copy the formulas in cells I4 and H4 to the remaining rows in the worksheet.

   c. Enter the indicated criteria in cell D31, then enter the indicated database functions toward the bottom of the worksheet.

   d. Filter the list in place to display only those loans that satisfy the indicated criteria.

   e. Format the list in attractive fashion. Add your name as the loan officer.

   f. Look closely at the bottom of Figure 7.22 and note the presence of a Pivot Table worksheet. You are to create a pivot table that has the loan type and branch location in the row and column fields, respectively. Your pivot table is to contain two data fields, the total amount of the loan type and the average interest rate.

   g. Print the entire workbook for your instructor. Print both the displayed values and cell formulas for the loans worksheet, but only the displayed values for the pivot table.

   h. Add a cover sheet, then submit the complete assignment to your instructor.

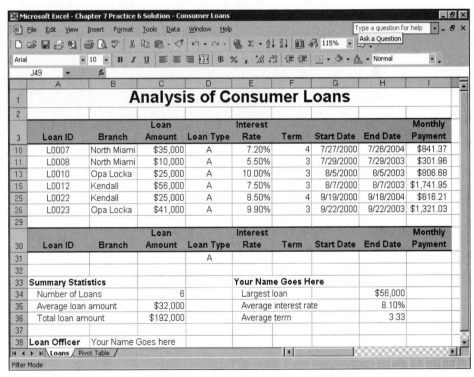

FIGURE 7.22   *Consumer Loans (Exercise 6)*

7. Top Ten Filter: Figure 7.23 displays a filtered list of the United States that displays the 10 states with the highest population density. You can duplicate the list and/or create several additional lists using the data in the *Chapter 7 Practice 7* workbook. Proceed as follows:

a. Open the workbook, and click in cell F5, the cell that contains the population density for the first state in the list, Alabama, since the states are in alphabetical order. Enter the formula to compute the density as population/area, then format the field to zero decimal places. Copy the formula to the remaining rows in the list.

b. Click anywhere in column F, the column that contains the newly created field. Pull down the Data menu, click the Filter command, and then click AutoFilter to toggle the feature on. You should see down arrows next to each of the field names in row four.

c. Click the down arrow next to the Density field, click Top 10 to display the Top 10 AutoFilter dialog box. Be sure that you have the appropriate entries in each of the three list boxes; i.e., Top rather than bottom, 10 for the number of entries, and items rather than percentages. Click OK to display the filtered list, which displays the records in the same order as in the original list. Click the Descending Sort button on the Standard toolbar to display the densities in descending sequence.

d. Format the worksheet appropriately, then add your name in cell A58 so that your instructor will know the assignment came from you.

e. Right click the worksheet tab, then select the command to Move or Copy the worksheet, check the box to create a copy, then rename the copied worksheet 13 Original States as shown in our figure.

f. Click the down arrow next to the Density field, then select the All command. Now click the down arrow next to the Year field, select the Top 10 command, then make the appropriate entries within the resulting dialog box to list the 13 original states. Sort these states in order of their admission to the Union.

g. Print the completed workbook for your instructor. Be sure to show grid lines, row and column headings, and an appropriate footer.

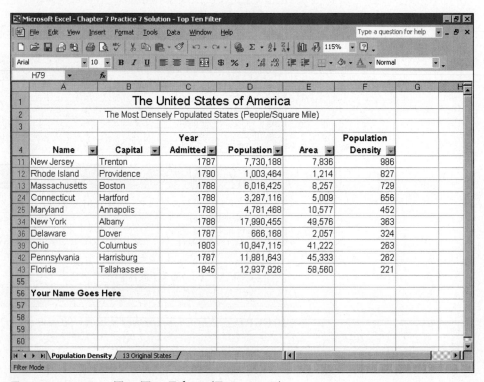

FIGURE 7.23   *Top Ten Filter (Exercise 7)*

BUILDS ON

PRACTICE
EXERCISES 4&5
PAGES 359–360

8. Compensation Report: The document in Figure 7.24 consists of a memo that was created in Microsoft Word that is linked to a pivot table from exercise 5. The document was created in such a way that any change in the pivot table within the Excel workbook will be automatically reflected in the memo.

a. Complete exercises 4 and 5 to create the pivot table that will be used in the memo. Start Word, create a simple letterhead (we used the Drop Cap command in the Format menu to create our letterhead), then enter the text of the memo in Figure 7.24. You can use our text, or modify the wording as you see fit. Be sure to include your name in the signature area.

b. Switch to Excel, copy either pivot table within the workbook to the clipboard, then use the Paste Link command within Word to bring the pivot table into the Word document.

c. Move and/or size the table as necessary. Note, too, that you may have to insert or delete hard returns within the memo to space it properly. *Print this version of the memo for your instructor.*

d. Prove to yourself that the linking really works by returning to Excel to modify the pivot table to show the total (as opposed to average) salary increase. Change the title of the pivot table as well.

e. Return to the Word memo, which should show an updated copy of the pivot table. If you did the exercise correctly, you should see $49,500 as the total amount for all salary increases. Modify the text of the memo to say "revised" salary analysis, as opposed to "preliminary," then print this version of the memo for your instructor.

f. Add a cover sheet, then submit the complete assignment to your instructor.

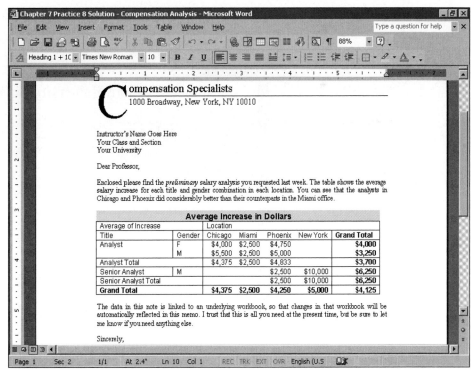

FIGURE 7.24   *Compensation Report (Exercise 8)*

BUILDS ON

PRACTICE
EXERCISE 2
PAGE 357

9. Subtotals: The document in Figure 7.25 consists of a memo that was created in Microsoft Word that is linked to an Excel worksheet from exercise 2. The document was created in such a way that any change in the worksheet will be automatically reflected in the memo.

a. Open the completed workbook from exercise 2 and, if necessary, remove the filter command that is in effect. Sort the students by major and by last name within major.

b. Click anywhere within the list, pull down the Data menu, and select the Subtotals command. Select subtotals for each change in major to display the statistics in Figure 7.25.

c. Start Word and create the text of the memo in Figure 7.25. Use the Paste Link command to link the memo to the worksheet. *Print this version of the memo for your instructor.*

d. Prove to yourself that linking really works by returning to Excel and substituting your name for Jeff Borow, but retain the other information (major, credits, and so on).

e. Use the Subtotals command in the Data menu to remove the subtotals, re-sort the list so that your name is in alphabetical order within the list of engineering students, then reexecute the Subtotals command.

f. Return to the Word memo, which should show an updated list of students with your name as an engineering student. Modify the text of the memo to say "revised" data as opposed to "preliminary," then print this version of the memo for your instructor.

g. Add a cover sheet, then submit the complete assignment to your instructor.

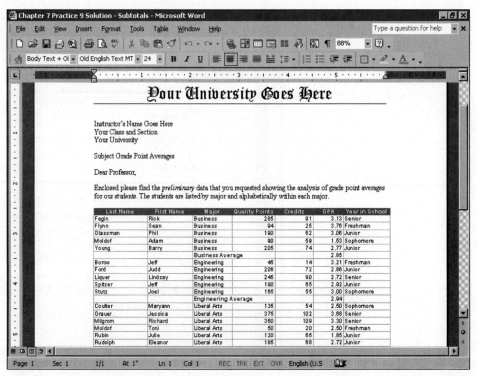

FIGURE 7.25   *Subtotals (Exercise 9)*

10. Web Pages and XML. Figure 7.26 displays the completed Election 2000 worksheet as a Web page and as an XML spreadsheet. Open the completed workbook from practice exercise 1 and proceed as follows.

   a. Pull down the File menu and click the Save As Web Page command to display the Save As dialog box. The Web Page (HTML) file format is selected by default. Click the Save button.

   b. Pull down the File menu and click the Save As Web Page command a second time to display the Save As dialog box. This time, however, select XML Spreadsheet as the file type. Click the Save button. Close the workbook. Exit Excel.

   c. Start Windows Explorer and locate the newly created Web page document. Double click the icon for the Election Web page, which in turn will display the Web page within Internet Explorer as shown in Figure 7.26.

   d. Click the Windows Explorer button a second time and locate the XML document. Double click its icon, which will display the XML page in Figure 7.26.

   e. Minimize all open applications, then click the Internet Explorer button on the taskbar for both the Web page and the XML page. Right click the taskbar to display a context-sensitive menu, then click the Tile Vertically command to display the pages side by side.

   f. Compare the appearance of the HTML page with that of XML. What is the advantage of the latter format?

   g. Add a cover sheet, then submit the complete assignment to your instructor.

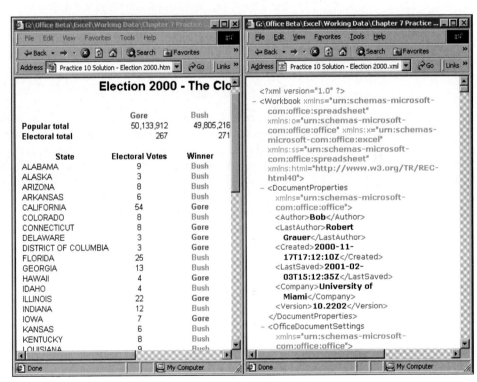

FIGURE 7.26   *Web Pages and XML (Exercise 10)*

The Super Bowl

How many times has the National Football Conference (NFC) won the Super Bowl? When was the last time the American Football Conference (AFC) won? What was the largest margin of victory? What was the closest game? What is the most points scored by two teams in one game? How many times have the Miami Dolphins appeared? How many times did they win? Use the data in the *Super Bowl workbook* to prepare a trivia sheet on the Super Bowl, then incorporate your analysis into a letter addressed to your instructor. Our workbook is almost complete, except you will have to determine the winner for each game based on the scores for the NFC and AFC teams. You can do it manually, but it's much easier if you use the IF function to determine the appropriate formula. Go to the NFL home page (www.nfl.com) to update our workbook to reflect the most recent game.

Data Validation

The best way to ensure that a workbook contains only valid data is to check the data as it is entered and reject any inappropriate values. Use the Excel Help menu to search for data validation to determine what (if any) capability is built into Excel. Is it possible, for example, to prevent a user from entering an invalid location or title in the Employee workbook that was used throughout the chapter? Summarize your findings in a brief note to your instructor. Better yet, take the final version of the Employee workbook (as it existed at the end of the last hands-on exercise) and incorporate any data validation you deem appropriate.

Asset Allocation

It's several years in the future and you find yourself happily married and financially prosperous. You and your spouse have accumulated substantial assets in a variety of accounts. Some of the money is in a regular account for use today, whereas other funds are in retirement accounts for later use. Much of the money, both regular and retirement, is invested in equities (i.e., the stock market), but a portion of your funds is also in nonequity funds such as money-market checking accounts and bank certificates of deposit. Your accounts are also in different places such as banks and brokerage houses. A summary of your accounts can be found in the *Asset Allocation workbook*. Your assignment is to open the workbook and develop a pivot table that will enable you and your spouse to keep track of your investments.

Planet Airways

Planet Airways is an independent airline offering charters and special tours. The airline has several independent agents, each of whom books trips for the airline. The data for all trips is maintained in the *Planet Airlines Access database* that is stored in the Exploring Excel folder. Your assignment is to start a new Excel workbook, then import the data from the Access database into the Excel workbook to create a pivot table for data analysis. Your pivot table should show the business by marketing representative and contract status (whether the trip is still in the proposal stage or whether it has already been signed). The data field should be the amount of the contract. The table should also have the flexibility to show which trips require passage through customs.

You may also want to explore the Access database for additional capabilities not found in Excel. In particular, look at the form and report that are contained within the database. What is the purpose of each of these objects?

CHAPTER 8

Automating Repetitive Tasks: Macros and Visual Basic for Applications

OBJECTIVES

AFTER READING THIS CHAPTER YOU WILL BE ABLE TO:

1. Define a macro; describe the relationship between macros and VBA.
2. Record and run a macro; view and edit the statements in a simple macro.
3. Use the InputBox function to obtain input for a macro as it is running; use the MsgBox statement to display a message.
4. Use a keyboard shortcut and/or a customized toolbar to run a macro; create a custom button to execute a macro.
5. Describe the function of the Personal Macro workbook.
6. Use the Step Into command to execute a macro one statement at a time.
7. Use the Copy and Paste commands to duplicate an existing macro; modify the copied macro to create an entirely new macro.
8. Use the Visual Basic If and Do statements to implement decision making and looping within an Excel macro.

OVERVIEW

Have you ever pulled down the same menus and clicked the same sequence of commands over and over? Easy as the commands may be to execute, it is still burdensome to have to continually repeat the same mouse clicks or keystrokes. If you can think of any task that you do repeatedly, whether in one workbook or in a series of workbooks, you are a perfect candidate to use macros.

A *macro* is a set of instructions that tells Excel which commands to execute. It is in essence a program, and its instructions are written in Visual Basic, a programming language. Fortunately, however, you don't have to be a programmer to write macros. Instead, you use the macro recorder within Excel to record your commands, and let Excel write the macros for you.

This chapter introduces you to the power of Excel macros. We begin by creating a simple macro to insert your name and class into a worksheet. We show you how to modify the macro once it has been created and how to execute the macro one statement at a time.

The second half of the chapter describes how to create more powerful macros that automate commands associated with list management, as presented in Chapter 7. We show you how to copy and edit a macro, and how to create customized buttons with which to execute a macro. We also show you how the power of an Excel macro can be extended through the inclusion of additional Visual Basic statements that implement loops and decision making.

INTRODUCTION TO MACROS

The *macro recorder* stores Excel commands, in the form of *Visual Basic* instructions, within a workbook. (*Visual Basic for Applications*, or *VBA*, is a subset of Visual Basic that is built into Microsoft Office.) To use the recorder, you pull down the Tools menu and click the Record New Macro command. From that point on (until you stop recording), every command you execute will be stored by the recorder. It doesn't matter whether you execute commands from pull-down menus via the mouse, or whether you use the toolbar or *keyboard shortcuts*. The macro recorder captures every action you take and stores the equivalent Visual Basic statements as a macro within the workbook.

Figure 8.1 illustrates a simple macro to enter your name and class in cells A1 and A2 of the active worksheet. The macro is displayed in the *Visual Basic Editor (VBE),* which is used to create, edit, execute, and debug Excel macros. The Visual Basic Editor is a separate application (as can be determined from its button on the taskbar in Figure 8.1), and it is accessible from any application in Microsoft Office.

The left side of the VBE window in Figure 8.1 contains the *Project Explorer,* which is similar in concept and appearance to the Windows Explorer, except that it displays only open workbooks and/or other Visual Basic projects. The Visual Basic statements for the selected module (Module1 in Figure 8.1) appear in the *Code window* in the right pane. As you shall see, a Visual Basic module consists of one or more procedures, each of which corresponds to an Excel macro. Thus, in this example, Module1 contains the NameAndCourse procedure corresponding to the Excel macro of the same name. Module1 itself is stored in the My Macros.XLS workbook.

As indicated, a macro consists of Visual Basic statements that were created through the macro recorder. We don't expect you to be able to write the Visual Basic procedure yourself, and you don't have to. You just invoke the recorder and let it capture the Excel commands for you. We do think it is important, however, to understand the macro and so we proceed to explain its statements. As you read our discussion, do not be concerned with the precise syntax of every statement, but try to get an overall appreciation for what the statements do.

A macro always begins and ends with the Sub and End Sub statements, respectively. The *Sub statement* contains the name of the macro—for example, NameAndCourse in Figure 8.1. (Spaces are not allowed in a macro name.) The *End Sub statement* is physically the last statement and indicates the end of the macro. Sub and End Sub are Visual Basic key words and appear in blue.

The next several statements begin with an apostrophe, appear in green, and are known as *comments*. They provide information about the macro, but do not affect its execution. In other words, the results of a macro are the same, whether or not the comments are included. Comments are inserted automatically by the recorder to document the macro name, its author, and *shortcut key* (if any). You can add comments (a comment line must begin with an apostrophe), or delete or modify existing comments, as you see fit.

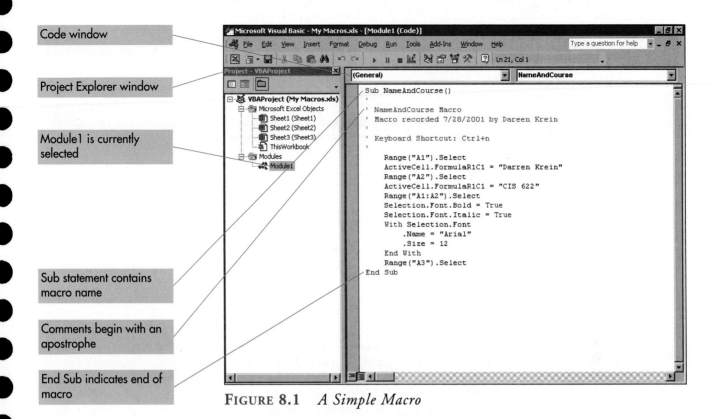

Code window

Project Explorer window

Module1 is currently selected

Sub statement contains macro name

Comments begin with an apostrophe

End Sub indicates end of macro

FIGURE 8.1 *A Simple Macro*

Every other statement is a Visual Basic instruction that was created as a result of an action taken in Excel. For example, the statements

       Range ("A1").Select

and   ActiveCell.FormulaR1C1 = "Darren Krein"

select cell A1 as the active cell, then enter the text "Darren Krein" into the active cell. These statements are equivalent to clicking in cell A1 of a worksheet, typing the indicated entry into the active cell, then pressing the enter key (or an arrow key) to complete the entry. In similar fashion, the statements

       Range ("A2").Select

and   ActiveCell.FormulaR1C1 = "CIS 622"

select cell A2 as the active cell, then enter the text entry "CIS 622" into that cell. The concept of select-then-do applies equally well to statements within a macro. Thus, the statements

     Range ("A1:A2").Select
     Selection.Font.Bold = True
     Selection.Font.Italic = True

select cells A1 through A2, then change the font for the selected cells to bold italic. The **With statement** enables you to perform multiple actions on the same object. All commands between the With and corresponding **End With statement** are executed collectively; for example, the statements

       With Selection.Font
          .Name = "Arial"
          .Size = 12
       End With

change the formatting of the selected cells (A1:A2) to 12-point Arial. The last statement in the macro, Range ("A3").Select, selects cell A3, thus deselecting all other cells, a practice we use throughout the chapter.

INTRODUCTION TO MACROS

Objective   To record, run, view, and edit a simple macro; to establish a keyboard shortcut to run a macro. Use Figure 8.2 as a guide in doing the exercise.

Step 1:   **Create a Macro**

➤ Start Excel. Open a new workbook if one is not already open. Save the workbook as **My Macros** in the **Exploring Excel folder**.

➤ Pull down the **Tools menu**, click (or point to) the **Macro command**, then click **Record New Macro** to display the Record Macro dialog box in Figure 8.2a. (If you don't see the Macro comand, click the double arrow to see more commands.)

➤ Enter **NameAndCourse** as the name of the macro. (Spaces are not allowed in the macro name.)

➤ The description is entered automatically and contains today's date and the name of the person in whose name this copy of Excel is registered. If necessary, change the description to include your name.

➤ Click in the **Shortcut Key** check box and enter a **lowercase n**. Ctrl+n should appear as the shortcut as shown in Figure 8.2a. (If you see Ctrl+Shift+N it means you typed an uppercase N rather than a lowercase letter. Correct the entry to a lowercase n.)

➤ Check that the option to Store macro in **This Workbook** is selected. Click **OK** to record the macro, which displays the Stop Recording toolbar.

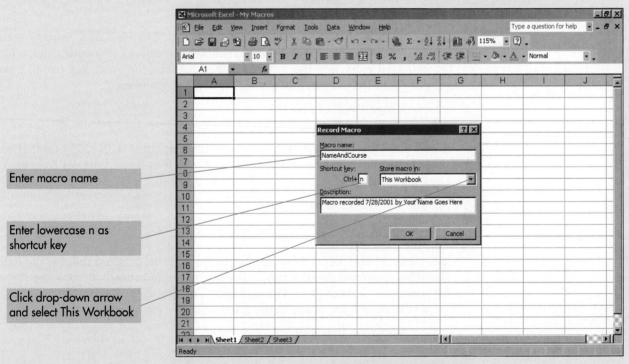

Enter macro name

Enter lowercase n as shortcut key

Click drop-down arrow and select This Workbook

(a) Create a Macro (step 1)

FIGURE 8.2   *Hands-on Exercise 1*

Step 2: **Record the Macro**

➤ Look carefully at the Relative References button on the Stop Recording button to be sure it is flush with the other buttons; that is, the button should *not* be pushed in. (See boxed tip on "Is the Button In or Out?")
➤ You should be in Sheet1, ready to record the macro, as shown in Figure 8.2b. The status bar indicates that you are in the Recording mode:
  • Click in **cell A1** even if it is already selected. Enter your name.
  • Click in **cell A2**. Enter the course you are taking.
  • Click and drag to select **cells A1** through **A2**.
  • Click the **Bold button**. Click the **Italic button**.
  • Click the arrow on the **Font Size list box**. Click **12** to change the point size.
  • Click in **cell A3** to deselect all other cells prior to ending the macro.
➤ Click the **Stop Recording button**.
➤ Save the workbook.

Click drop-down arrow on Font Size box

Click in A1 and enter your name

Click in A2 and enter your course

Stop Recording toolbar

Stop Recording button

Relative References button

Recording mode

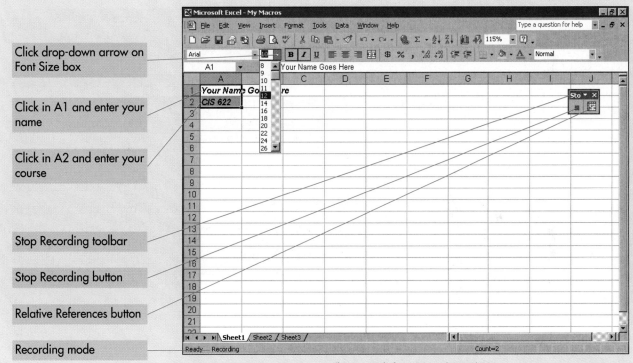

(b) Record the Macro (step 2)

FIGURE 8.2 *Hands-on Exercise 1 (continued)*

IS THE BUTTON IN OR OUT?

The distinction between relative and absolute references within a macro is critical and is described in detail at the end of this exercise. The Relative References button on the Stop Recording toolbar toggles between the two—absolute references when the button is out, relative references when the button is in. The ScreenTip, however, displays Relative References regardless of whether the button is in or out. We wish that Microsoft had made it easier to tell which type of reference you are recording, but they didn't.

Step 3: **Test the Macro**

➤ To run (test) the macro you have to remove the contents and formatting from cells A1 and A2. Click and drag to select **cells A1** through **A2**.

➤ Pull down the **Edit menu**. Click **Clear**. Click **All** from the cascaded menu to erase both the contents and formatting from the selected cells. Cells A1 through A2 are empty as shown in Figure 8.2c.

➤ Pull down the **Tools menu**. Click **Macro**, then click the **Macros ... command** to display the dialog box in Figure 8.2c.

➤ Click **NameAndCourse**, which is the macro you just recorded. Click **Run**. Your name and class are entered in cells A1 and A2, then formatted according to the instructions in the macro.

➤ Clear the contents of cells A1 and A2. Press **Ctrl+n** (the keyboard shortcut) to rerun the NameAndCourse macro. Your name and class should reappear in cells A1 and A2.

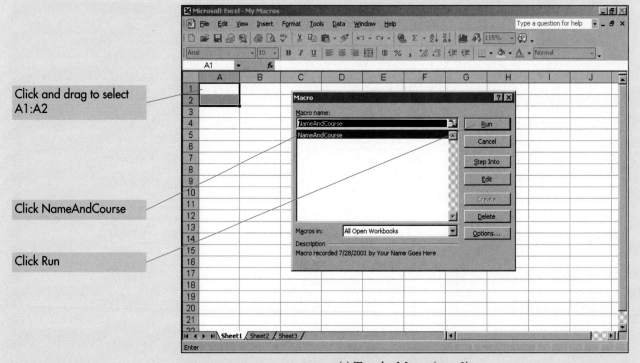

Click and drag to select
A1:A2

Click NameAndCourse

Click Run

(c) Test the Macro (step 3)

FIGURE 8.2   *Hands-on Exercise 1 (continued)*

THE EDIT CLEAR COMMAND

The Edit Clear erases the contents of a cell, its formatting, and/or its comments. Select the cell or cells to erase, pull down the Edit menu, click the Clear command, then click All, Formats, Contents, or Comments from the cascaded menu. Pressing the Del key is equivalent to executing the Edit Clear Contents command as it clears the contents of a cell, but retains the formatting and comments.

Step 4: **Start the Visual Basic Editor**

➤ Pull down the **Tools menu**, click the **Macro command**, then click **Visual Basic Editor** (or press **Alt+F11**) to open the Visual Basic Editor. Maximize the VBE window.

➤ If necessary, pull down the **View menu**. Click **Project Explorer** to open the Project Explorer window in the left pane. There is currently one open VBA project, My Macros.xls, which is the name of the open workbook in Excel.

➤ If necessary, click the **plus sign** next to the Modules folder to expand that folder, click (select) **Module1**, pull down the **View menu**, and click **Code** to open the Code window in the right pane. Click the **Maximize button** in the Code window.

➤ Your screen should match the one in Figure 8.2d. The first statement below the comments should be *Range("A1").Select,* which indicates that the macro was correctly recorded with absolute references.

➤ If you see a very different statement, *ActiveCell.FormulaR1C1,* it means that you incorrectly recorded the macro with relative references. Right click **Module1** in the Project Explorer window, select the **Remove Module1 command**, then return to step 1 and rerecord the macro.

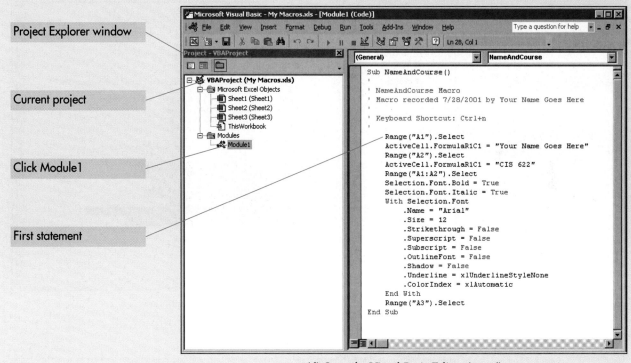

Project Explorer window

Current project

Click Module1

First statement

(d) Start the Visual Basic Editor (step 4)

FIGURE 8.2 *Hands-on Exercise 1 (continued)*

THE END RESULT

The macro recorder records only the result of the selection process, with no indication of how the selection was arrived at. It doesn't matter how you get to a particular cell. You can click in the cell directly, use the Go To command in the Edit menu, or use the mouse or arrow keys. The end result is the same and the macro indicates only the selected cell(s).

Step 5: **Edit the Macro**

➤ Edit the NameAndCourse macro by changing the font name and size to **"Times New Roman"** and **24**, respectively, as shown in Figure 8.2e.

➤ Click and drag to select the next seven statements as shown in Figure 8.2e.

➤ Press the **Del key** to delete these statements from the macro. (These statements contain default values and are unnecessary.) Delete any blank lines as well.

➤ Press **Alt+F11** to toggle back to the Excel workbook (or click the Excel button on the taskbar). Clear the entries and formatting in cells A1 and A2 as you did earlier, then rerun the NameAndCourse macro.

➤ Your name and class should once again be entered in cells A1 and A2 but in a different and larger font. (If the macro does not execute correctly, press **Alt+F11** to toggle back to the Visual Basic Editor to correct your macro.)

➤ Save the workbook.

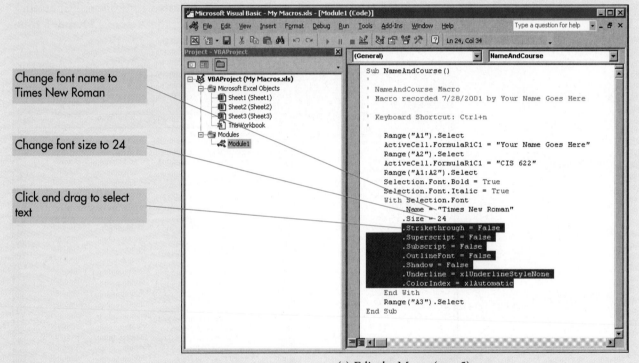

(e) Edit the Macro (step 5)

FIGURE 8.2 *Hands-on Exercise 1 (continued)*

SIMPLIFY THE MACRO

The macro recorder usually sets all possible options for an Excel command or dialog box even if you do not change those options. We suggest, therefore, that you make a macro easier to read by deleting the unnecessary statements. Take a minute, however, to review the statements prior to removing them, so that you can see the additional options. (You can click the Undo button to restore the deleted statements if you make a mistake.)

Step 6: **Create the Erase Macro**

> ➤ Pull down the **Tools menu**. Click the **Macro command**, then click **Record New Macro** from the cascaded menu. You will see the Record Macro dialog box.
> ➤ Enter **EraseNameAndCourse** as the name of the macro. Do not leave any spaces in the macro name. If necessary, change the description to include your name.
> ➤ Click in the **Shortcut Key** check box and enter a **lowercase e**. (Ctrl+e should appear as the shortcut.) Check that the option to Store macro in **This Workbook** is selected.
> ➤ Click **OK** to begin recording the macro, which displays the Stop Recording toolbar. Be sure you are recording absolute references (i.e., the Relative References button should be flush on the toolbar).
> > • Click and drag to select **cells A1** through **A2** as shown in Figure 8.2f, even if they are already selected.
> > • Pull down the **Edit menu**. Click **Clear**. Click **All** from the cascaded menu. Cells A1 through A2 should now be empty.
> > • Click in **cell A3** to deselect all other cells prior to ending the macro.
> ➤ Click the **Stop Recording button** to end the macro.

Stop Recording button

Click and drag to select A1:A2

Click All

Click Clear

Recording mode

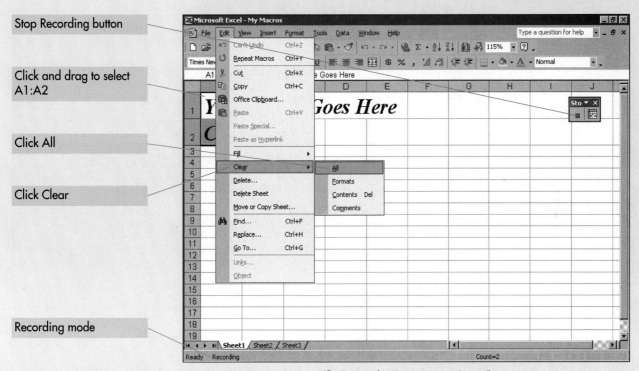

(f) Create the Erase Macro (step 6)

FIGURE 8.2 *Hands-on Exercise 1 (continued)*

TO SELECT OR NOT SELECT

If you start recording, then select a cell(s) within the macro, the selection becomes part of the macro, and the macro will always operate on the same cell. If, however, you select the cell(s) prior to recording, the macro is more general and operates on the selected cells, which may differ every time the macro is executed. Both techniques are valid, and the decision depends on what you want the macro to do.

Step 7: Shortcut Keys

➤ Press **Ctrl+n** to execute the NameAndCourse macro. (You need to reenter your name and course in order to test the newly created EraseNameAndCourse macro.)

➤ Your name and course should again appear in cells A1 and A2 as shown in Figure 8.2g.

➤ Press **Ctrl+e** to execute the EraseNameAndCourse macro. Cells A1 and A2 should again be empty.

➤ You can press **Ctrl+n** and **Ctrl+e** repeatedly, to enter and then erase your name and course. End this step after having erased the data.

➤ Save the workbook.

Press Ctrl+n to run the NameAndCourse macro

(g) Shortcut Keys (step 7)

FIGURE 8.2 *Hands-on Exercise 1 (continued)*

TROUBLESHOOTING

If the shortcut keys do not work, it is probably because they were not defined properly. Pull down the Tools menu, click Macro to display a cascaded menu, click the Macros . . . command, then select the desired macro in the Macro Name list box. Click the Options button, then check the entry in the Shortcut Key text box. A lowercase letter creates a shortcut with just the Ctrl key, whereas an uppercase letter uses Ctrl+Shift with the shortcut. Thus, "n" and "N" will establish shortcuts of Ctrl+n and Ctrl+Shift+N, respectively.

Step 8: **Step through the Macro**

➤ Press **Alt+F11** to switch back to the VBE window. Click the **Close button** to close the **Project window** within the Visual Basic Editor. The Code window expands to take the entire Visual Basic Editor window.

➤ Point to an empty area on the Windows taskbar, then click the **right mouse button** to display a shortcut menu. Click **Tile Vertically**.

➤ Your desktop should be similar to Figure 8.2h. It doesn't matter if the workbook is in the left or right window.

➤ Click in the **Visual Basic Editor window**, then click anywhere within the NameAndCourse macro. Pull down the **Debug menu** and click the **Step Into command** (or press the **F8 key**). The Sub statement is highlighted.

➤ Press the **F8 key** to move to the first executable statement (the comments are skipped). The statement is highlighted, but it has not yet been executed.

➤ Press the **F8 key** again to execute this statement (which selects cell A1 and moves to the next statement). Continue to press the **F8 key** to execute the statements one at a time. You see the effect of each statement in the Excel window.

View effects of statements as they are executed

Click anywhere within the NameAndCourse macro

Next executable statement

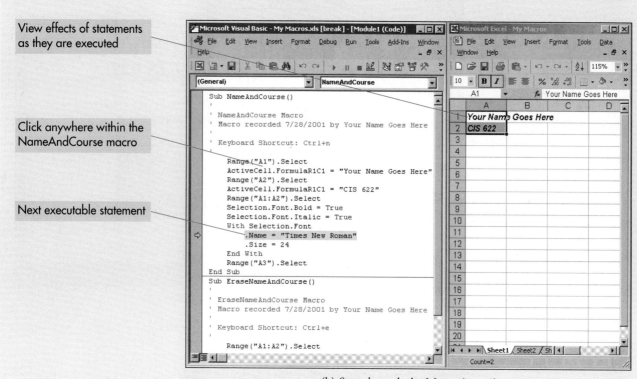

(h) Step through the Macro (step 8)

FIGURE 8.2 *Hands-on Exercise 1 (continued)*

THE STEP INTO COMMAND

The Step Into command is useful to slow down the execution of a macro in the event the macro does not perform as intended. In essence, you execute the macro one statement at a time, while viewing the results of each statement in the associated worksheet. If a statement does not do what you want it to do, just change the statement in the Visual Basic window, then continue to press the F8 key to step through the procedure.

Step 9: **Print the Module**

➤ Click in the **Visual Basic window**. Pull down the **File menu**. Click **Print** to display the Print VBA Project dialog box in Figure 8.2i.

➤ Click the option button to print the current module. Click **OK**. Submit the listing of the current module, which contains the procedures for both macros, to your instructor as proof you did this exercise.

➤ Close the My Macros workbook, which automatically closes the Visual Basic Project window (and Code window). Click **Yes** if asked to save the workbook. The macros are stored within the workbook.

➤ Exit Excel if you do not wish to continue with the next hands-on exercise at this time.

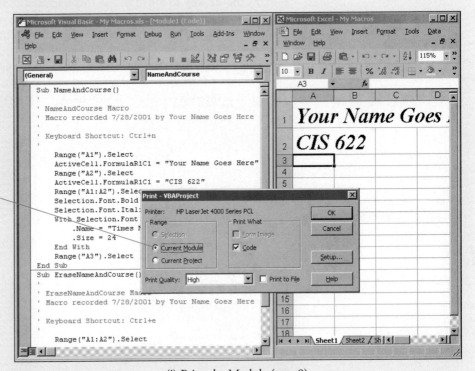

Click option button to print Current Module

(i) Print the Module (step 9)

FIGURE 8.2 *Hands-on Exercise 1 (continued)*

PROCEDURE VIEW VERSUS FULL MODULE VIEW

The procedures within a module can be displayed individually, or alternatively, multiple procedures can be viewed simultaneously. To go from one view to the other, click the Procedure View button at the bottom of the window to display just the procedure you are working on, or click the Full Module View button to display multiple procedures. You can press Ctrl+PgDn and Ctrl+PgUp to move between procedures in either view. Use the vertical scroll bar to move up and down within the VBA window.

One of the most important options to specify when recording a macro is whether the references are to be relative or absolute. A reference is a cell address. An ***absolute reference*** is a constant address that always refers to the same cell. A ***relative reference*** is variable in that the reference will change from one execution of the macro to the next, depending on the location of the active cell when the macro is executed.

To appreciate the difference, consider Figure 8.3, which displays two versions of the NameAndCourse macro from the previous exercise, one with absolute and one with relative references. Figure 8.3a uses absolute references to place your name, course, and date in cells A1, A2, and A3. The data will always be entered in these cells regardless of which cell is selected when you execute the macro.

Figure 8.3b enters the same data, but with relative references, so that the cells in which the data are entered depend on which cell is selected when the macro is executed. If cell A1 is selected, your name, course, and date will be entered in cells A1, A2, and A3. If, however, cell E4 is the active cell when you execute the macro, then your name, course, and date will be entered in cells E4, E5, and E6.

A relative reference is specified by an ***offset*** that indicates the number of rows and columns from the active cell. An offset of (1,0) indicates a cell one row below the active cell. An offset of (0,1) indicates a cell one column to the right of the active cell. In similar fashion, an offset of (1,1) indicates a cell one row below and one column to the right of the active cell. Negative offsets are used for cells above or to the left of the current selection.

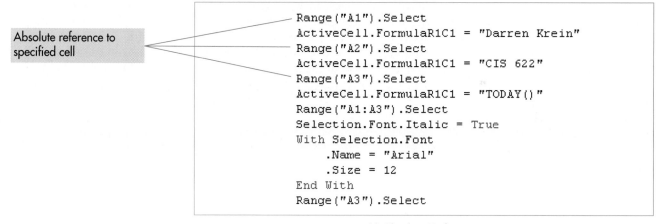

Absolute reference to specified cell

```
Range("A1").Select
ActiveCell.FormulaR1C1 = "Darren Krein"
Range("A2").Select
ActiveCell.FormulaR1C1 = "CIS 622"
Range("A3").Select
ActiveCell.FormulaR1C1 = "TODAY()"
Range("A1:A3").Select
Selection.Font.Italic = True
With Selection.Font
    .Name = "Arial"
    .Size = 12
End With
Range("A3").Select
```

(a) Absolute References

Relative reference to cell one row below active cell

Indicates a column of three cells, not cells A1 to A3

```
ActiveCell.FormulaR1C1 = "Darren Krein"
ActiveCell.Offset(1, 0).Range("A1").Select
ActiveCell.FormulaR1C1 = "CIS 622"
ActiveCell.Offset(1, 0).Range("A1").Select
ActiveCell.FormulaR1C1 = "=TODAY()"
ActiveCell.Offset(-2, 0).Range("A1:A3").Select
Selection.Font.Italic = True
With Selection.Font
    .Name = "Arial"
    .Size = 12
End With
ActiveCell.Offset(3, 0).Range("A1").Select
```

(b) Relative References

FIGURE 8.3   *Absolute versus Relative References*

Relative references may appear confusing at first, but they extend the power of a macro by making it more general. You will appreciate this capability as you learn more about macros. Let us begin by recognizing that the statement

ActiveCell.Offset (1,0).Range ("A1").Select

means select the cell one row below the active cell. It has nothing to do with cell A1, and you might wonder why the entry Range ("A1") is included. The answer is that the offset specifies the location of the new range (one row below the current cell), and the A1 indicates that the size of that range is a single cell (A1). In similar fashion, the statement

ActiveCell.Offset (−2,0).Range ("A1:A3").Select

selects a range, starting two rows above the current cell, that is one column by three rows in size. Again, it has nothing to do with cells A1 through A3. The offset specifies the location of a new range (two rows above the current cell) and the shape of that range (a column of three cells). If you are in cell D11 when the statement is executed, the selected range will be cells D9 through D11. The selection starts with the cell two rows above the active cell (cell D9), then it continues from that point to select a range consisting of one column by three rows (cells D9:D11).

RELATIVE VERSUS ABSOLUTE REFERENCES

Relative references appear confusing at first but they extend the power of a macro by making it more general. Macro statements that have been recorded with relative references include an offset to indicate the number of rows and columns the selection is to be from the active cell. An offset of (–1,0) indicates a cell one row above the active cell, whereas an offset of (0,–1) indicates a cell one column to the left of the active cell. Positive offsets are used for cells below or to the right of the current selection.

THE PERSONAL MACRO WORKBOOK

The hands-on exercise at the beginning of the chapter created the NameAndCourse macro in the My Macros workbook, where it is available to that workbook or to any other workbook that is in memory when the My Macros workbook is open. What if, however, you want the macro to be available at all times, not just when the My Macros workbook is open? This is easily accomplished by storing the macro in the Personal Macro workbook when it is first recorded.

The **Personal Macro workbook** opens automatically whenever Excel is loaded. This is because the Personal Macro workbook is stored in the XLStart folder, a folder that Excel checks each time it is loaded into memory. Once open, the macros in the Personal workbook are available to any other open workbook. The following hands-on exercise creates the NameAndCourse macro with relative references, then stores that macro in the Personal Macro workbook.

The exercise also expands the macro to enter the date of execution, and further generalizes the macro to accept the name of the course as input. The latter is accomplished through the Visual Basic **InputBox function** that prompts the user for a specific response, then stores that response within the macro. In other words, the Excel macro is enhanced through the inclusion of a VBA statement that adds functionality to the original macro. You start with the macro recorder to translate Excel commands into a VBA procedure, then you modify the procedure by adding the necessary VBA statements. (The InputBox function must be entered manually into the procedure since there is no corresponding Excel command, and hence the macro recorder would not work.)

THE PERSONAL MACRO WORKBOOK

Objective To create and store a macro in the Personal Macro workbook; to assign a toolbar button to a macro; to use the Visual Basic InputBox function. Use Figure 8.4 as a guide in the exercise.

Step 1: **The Personal Macro Workbook**

➤ Start Excel. Be sure to close the My Macros workbook from the previous exercise to avoid any conflict with an existing macro.

➤ Open a new workbook if one is not already open. Pull down the **Tools menu**, click (or point to) the **Macro command**, then click **Record New Macro** to display the Record Macro dialog box

➤ Enter **NameAndCourse** as the name of the macro. Do not leave any spaces in the macro name. Click in the **Shortcut Key** check box and enter a **lowercase n**. Ctrl+n should appear as the shortcut.

➤ Click the **drop-down arrow** in the Store macro in list box and select the Personal Macro workbook as shown in Figure 8.4a. (If you are working on a network as opposed to a standalone machine, you may not be able to access the **Personal Macro workbook**, in which case you can save the macro in this workbook.)

➤ Click **OK** to begin recording the macro, which displays the Stop Recording toolbar.

Enter macro name

Enter shortcut key

Click drop-down arrow and select Personal Macro Workbook

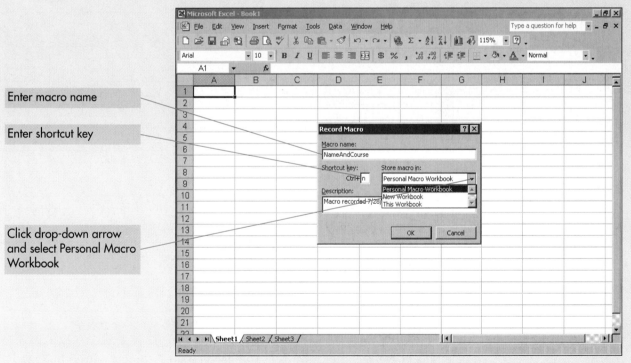

(a) The Personal Macro Workbook (step 1)

FIGURE 8.4   *Hands-on Exercise 2*

Step 2: **Record with Relative References**

➤ Click the **Relative References button** on the Stop Recording toolbar so that the button is pushed in as shown in Figure 8.4a.
➤ The Relative References button functions as a toggle switch—click it, and the button is pushed in to record relative references. Click it again, and you record absolute references. Be sure to record relative references.
➤ Enter your name in the active cell. Do *not* select the cell.
➤ Press the **down arrow key** to move to the cell immediately underneath the current cell. Enter the course you are taking.
➤ Press the **down arrow key** to move to the next cell. Enter **=TODAY()**.
➤ Click and drag to select the three cells containing the data values you just entered (cells A1 through A3 in Figure 8.4b).
  • Click the **Bold button**. Click the **Italic button**.
  • Click the arrow on the **Font Size list box**. Click **12** to change the point size.
  • If necessary, click and drag the border between the column headings for Columns A and B to increase the width of column A.
  • Click in **cell A4** to deselect all other cells prior to ending the macro.
➤ Click the **Stop Recording button** to end the macro.

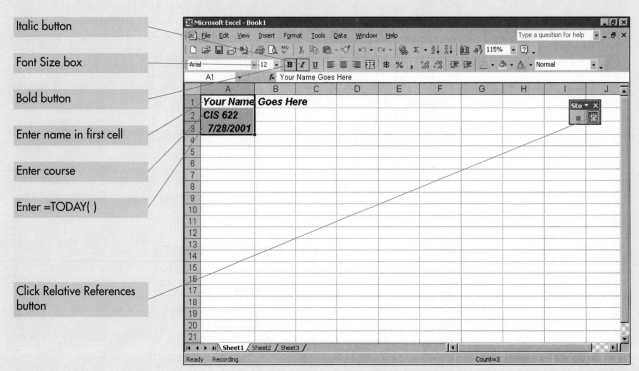

Italic button

Font Size box

Bold button

Enter name in first cell

Enter course

Enter =TODAY( )

Click Relative References button

(b) Record with Relative References (step 2)

FIGURE 8.4   *Hands-on Exercise 2 (continued)*

PLAN AHEAD

The macro recorder records everything you do, including entries that are made by mistake or commands that are executed incorrectly. Plan the macro in advance, before you begin recording. Write down what you intend to do, then try out the commands with the recorder off. Be sure you go all the way through the intended sequence of operations prior to turning the macro recorder on.

Step 3: **The Visual Basic Editor**

➤ Pull down the **Tools menu**, click the **Macro command**, then click **Visual Basic Editor** (or press **Alt+F11**) to open the Visual Basic Editor in Figure 8.4c.

➤ If necessary, pull down the **View menu**. Click **Project Explorer** to open the Project Explorer window in the left pane.

➤ There are currently two open VBA projects (Book1, the name of the open workbook, and Personal.XLS, the Personal Macro workbook).

➤ Click the **plus sign** to expand the Personal Workbook folder, then click the **plus sign** to expand the **Modules folder** within this project.

➤ Click (select) **Module1**, pull down the **View menu**, and click **Code** to open the Code window in the right pane. Maximize the Code window.

➤ Close any other open windows within the Visual Basic Editor. The first executable statement should begin with *ActiveCell.FormulaR1C1*.

➤ If you see a very different statement, *Range("A1").Select,* it means that you incorrectly recorded the macro with absolute references. Right click Module1 in the Project window, select the **Remove Module command**, then return to step 1 and rerecord the macro.

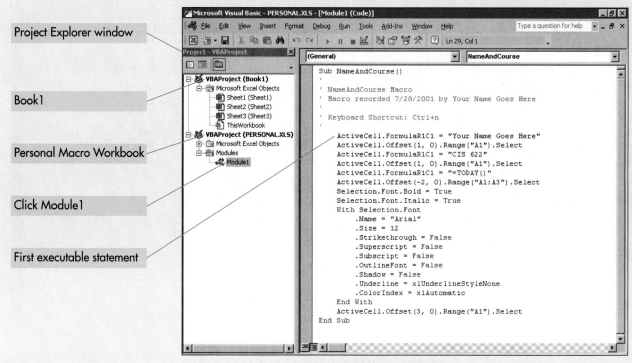

(c) The Visual Basic Editor (step 3)

FIGURE 8.4 *Hands-on Exercise 2 (continued)*

WHAT DOES RANGE ("A1:A3") REALLY MEAN?

The statement ActiveCell.Offset(−2,0).Range ("A1:A3").Select has nothing to do with cells A1 through A3, so why is the entry Range ("A1:A3") included? The effect of the statement is to select three cells (one cell under the other) starting with the cell two rows above the current cell. The offset (−2,0) specifies the starting point of the selected range (two rows above the current cell). The range ("A1:A3") indicates the size and shape of the selected range (a vertical column of three cells) from the starting cell.

Step 4: **Edit the Macro**

➤ Click and drag to select the name of the course, which is found in the third executable statement of the macro. Be sure to include the quotation marks (e.g., "CIS622" in our example) in your selection.

➤ Enter **InputBox("Enter the Course You Are Taking")** to replace the selected text. Note that as you enter the Visual Basic key word, *InputBox,* a prompt (containing the correct syntax for this statement) is displayed on the screen as shown in Figure 8.4d.

➤ Just ignore the prompt and keep typing to complete the entry. Press the **Home key** as you complete the entry to scroll back to the beginning of the line.

➤ Click immediately after the number **12**, then click and drag to select the next seven statements. Press the **Del key** to delete the highlighted statements from the macro.

➤ Delete the **Selection.Font.Bold = True** statement. Click the **Save button** to save the modified macro.

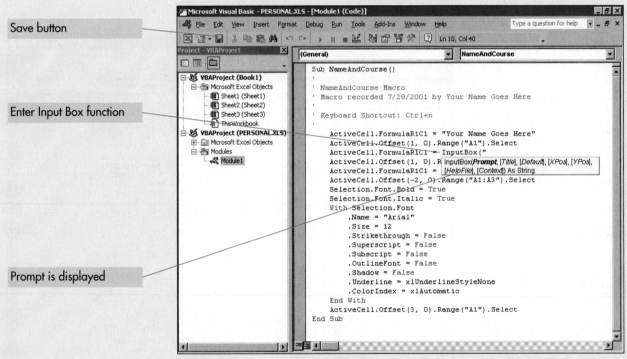

(d) Edit the Macro (step 4)

FIGURE 8.4   *Hands-on Exercise 2 (continued)*

THE INPUTBOX FUNCTION

The InputBox function adds flexibility to a macro by obtaining input from the user when the macro is executed. It is used in this example to generalize the NameAndCourse macro by asking the user for the name of the course, as opposed to storing the name within the macro. The InputBox function, coupled with storing the macro in the Personal Macro workbook, enables the user to personalize any workbook by executing the associated macro.

Step 5:   **Test the Revised Macro**

➤ Press **Alt+F11** to view the Excel workbook. Click in any cell—for example, **cell C5** as shown in Figure 8.4e.

➤ Pull down the **Tools menu**. Click **Macro**, click the **Macros ... command**, select **PERSONAL.XLS!NameAndCourse**, then click the **Run command button** to run the macro. (Alternatively you can use the **Ctrl+n** shortcut.)

➤ The macro enters your name in cell C5 (the active cell), then displays the input dialog box shown in Figure 8.4e.

➤ Enter any appropriate course and press the **enter key**. You should see the course you entered followed by the date. All three entries will be formatted according to the commands you specified in the macro.

➤ Click in a different cell, then press **Ctrl+n** to rerun the macro. The macro will enter your name, the course you specify, and the date in the selected location because it was recorded with relative references.

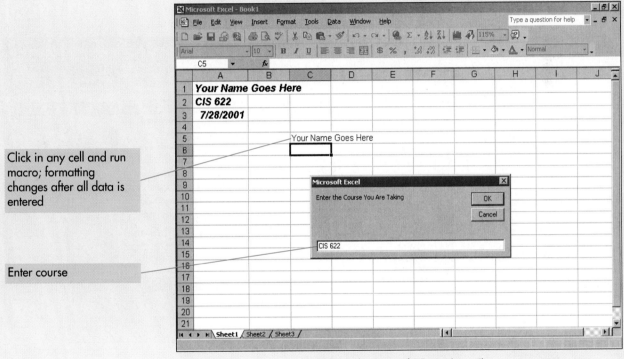

Click in any cell and run macro; formatting changes after all data is entered

Enter course

(e) Test the Revised Macro (step 5)

FIGURE 8.4   *Hands-on Exercise 2 (continued)*

RED, GREEN, AND BLUE

Visual Basic automatically assigns different colors to different types of statements (or a portion of those statements). Any statement containing a syntax error appears in red. Comments appear in green. Key words—such as Sub and End Sub, With and End With, and True and False—appear in blue.

Step 6: **Add a Custom Button**

➤ Point to any toolbar, then click the **right mouse button** to display a shortcut menu. Click **Customize** to display the Customize dialog box in Figure 8.4f.
➤ Click the **Commands tab**. Click the **down arrow** to scroll through the Categories list box until you can select the **Macros category**.
➤ Click and drag the **Custom (Happy Face) button** to an available space at the right of the Standard toolbar. Release the mouse. (You must drag the button *within* the toolbar.)
➤ Click the **Modify Selection button** within the Customize dialog box to display the cascaded menu in Figure 8.4f. Click and drag to select the name of the button (&Custom Button) and replace it with **NameAndCourse**, to create a ScreenTip for that button. Do not press the enter key.
➤ Click the **Assign Macro command** at the end of the cascaded menu to display the Assign Macro dialog box. Select **PERSONAL.XLS!NameAndCourse** and click **OK**.
➤ Click **Close** to exit the Custom dialog box.

Drag Custom button to toolbar

Enter macro name

Commands tab

Click Macro category

Click Assign Macro

Modify Selection button

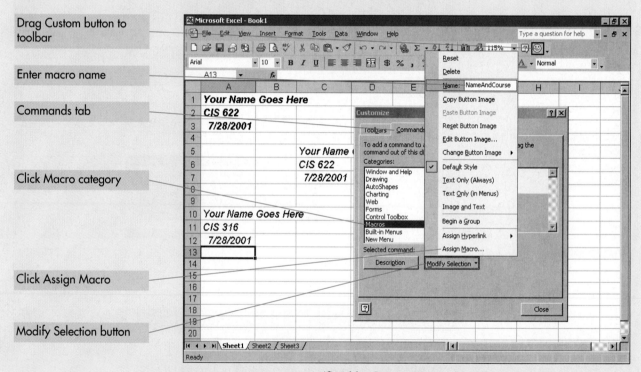

(f) Add a Custom Button (step 6)

FIGURE 8.4 *Hands-on Exercise 2 (continued)*

CUSTOMIZE THE TOOLBAR OR A MENU

You can customize any toolbar or menu to display additional buttons or commands as appropriate. Pull down the View menu, click Toolbars, click Customize to display the Customize dialog box, then click the Commands tab. Choose the category containing the button or command you want, then click and drag that object to an existing toolbar or menu.

Step 7: **Test the Custom Button**

➤ Click the **New button** on the Standard toolbar to open a new workbook (Book2 in Figure 8.4g; the book number is not important). Click **cell B2** as the active cell from which to execute the macro.

➤ Point to the **Happy Face button** to display the ScreenTip you just created. The ScreenTip will be useful in future sessions should you forget the function of this button.

➤ Click the **Happy Face button** to execute the NameAndCourse macro. Enter the name of a course you are taking. The macro inserts your name, course, and today's date in cells B2 through B4.

➤ Pull down the **File menu** and click the **Exit command** to exit the program. Click **Yes** if asked to save the changes to the Personal Workbook.

➤ Click **No** when prompted to save the changes to Book1 and/or Book2, the workbooks you created in this exercise.

Point to Custom button

New button

Click in B2

ScreenTip

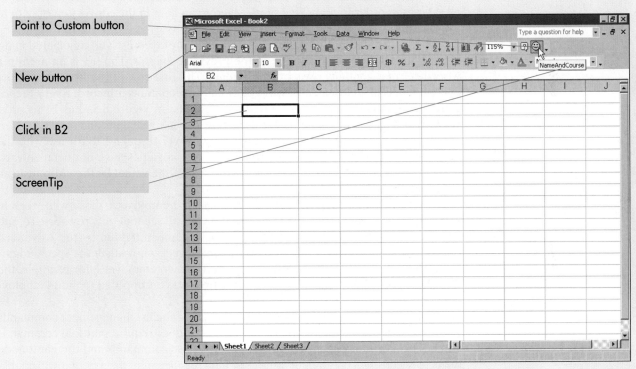

(g) Test the Custom Button (step 7)

FIGURE 8.4   *Hands-on Exercise 2 (continued)*

CHANGE THE CUSTOM BUTTON ICON

The Happy Face icon is automatically associated with the Custom Macro button. You can, however, change the image after the button has been added to a toolbar. Right click the button and click Customize to display the Customize dialog box, which must remain open to change the image. Right click the button a second time to display a different shortcut menu with commands pertaining to the specific button. Click the command to Change Button Image, select a new image, then close the Customize dialog box.

Thus far we have covered the basics of macros in the context of entering your name, course, and today's date in a worksheet. As you might expect, macros are capable of much more and can be used to automate any repetitive task. The next several pages illustrate the use of macros in conjunction with the list (data) management examples that were presented in an earlier chapter.

Data and information are not synonymous. Data is typically a fact (or facts) about a specific record (or set of records), such as an employee's name or title, or a list of all employees and their titles. Information is something more and refers to data that has been summarized, or otherwise rearranged, into a form perceived as useful by the recipient. A list of all the employees is considered raw data, whereas a subset of that list—such as the employees who worked in Chicago—could be thought of as information derived from that list. Information is also obtained by summarizing the data. Individual salaries are important to the employees who receive those salaries, whereas a manager is more interested in knowing the total of all salaries in order to make decisions. Macros can help in the conversion of data to information.

The worksheet in Figure 8.5a displays the employee list and associated summary statistics from the example in the previous chapter. The list is an area in a worksheet that contains rows of similar data. The first row in the list contains the column labels or field names. Each additional row contains a record. Every record contains the same fields in the same order. The list in Figure 8.5a has 14 records. Each record has six fields: name, location, title, service, hire date, and salary.

A criteria range has been established in cells A17 through F18 for use with the database functions in cells F22 through F26. Criteria values have not been entered in Figure 8.5a, and so the database functions reflect the values of the entire list (all 14 employees).

The worksheet in Figure 8.5b displays selected employees, those who work in Chicago. Look carefully at the worksheet and you will see that only rows 3, 9, 10, and 12 are visible. The other rows within the list have been hidden by the Advanced Filter command, which displays only those employees who satisfy the specified criteria. The summary statistics reflect only the Chicago employees; for example, the DCOUNT function in cell F26 shows four employees (as opposed to the 14 employees in Figure 8.5a).

The previous chapter described how to execute the list management commands to filter the list. The process is not difficult, but it does require multiple commands and keystrokes. Our purpose here is to review those commands and then automate the process through creation of a series of data management macros that will enable you to obtain the desired information with a single click. We begin by reviewing the commands that would be necessary to modify the worksheet in Figure 8.5b to show managers rather than the Chicago employees.

The first step is to clear the existing criterion (Chicago) in cell B18, then enter the new criterion (Manager) in cell C18. You would then execute the Advanced Filter command, which requires the specification of the list (cells A1 through F15), the location of the criteria range (cells A17 through F18), and the option to filter the list in place.

And what if you wanted to see the Chicago employees after you executed the commands to display the managers? You would have to repeat all of the previous commands to change the criterion back to what it was, then filter the list accordingly. Suffice it to say that the entire process can be simplified through creation of the appropriate macros.

The following exercise develops the macro to select the Chicago employees from the worksheet in Figure 8.5a. A subsequent exercise develops two additional macros, one to select the managers and another to select the managers who work in Chicago.

All of the macros use the concept of a ***named range*** to establish a mnemonic name (e.g., database) for a cell range (e.g., A1:F15). The advantage of using a named range in a macro over the associated cell reference is twofold. First, the macro is easier to read. Second, and perhaps more important, a named range adjusts automatically for insertions and/or deletions within the worksheet, whereas a cell reference remains constant. Thus, the use of a named range makes the macro immune to changes in the worksheet in that the macro references a flexible "database," as opposed to a fixed cell range. You can add or delete employee records within the list, and the macro will still work.

Field names

	A	B	C	D	E	F
1	**Name**	**Location**	**Title**	**Service**	**Hire Date**	**Salary**
2	Adams	Atlanta	Trainee	7.2	11/24/93	$19,500
3	Adamson	Chicago	Manager	6.9	3/16/94	$52,000
4	Brown	Atlanta	Trainee	7.2	11/24/93	$18,500
5	Charles	Boston	Account Rep	6.9	3/16/94	$40,000
6	Coulter	Atlanta	Manager	7.2	11/24/93	$100,000
7	Elofson	Miami	Account Rep	3.2	10/31/97	$47,500
8	Gillenson	Miami	Account Rep	2.2	10/31/98	$55,000
9	James	Chicago	Account Rep	6.2	10/31/94	$42,500
10	Johnson	Chicago	Account Rep	5.2	10/31/95	$47,500
11	Manin	Boston	Account Rep	6.9	3/16/94	$49,500
12	Marder	Chicago	Account Rep	4.2	10/31/96	$38,500
13	Milgrom	Boston	Manager	6.9	3/16/94	$57,500
14	Rubin	Boston	Account Rep	6.9	3/16/94	$45,000
15	Smith	Atlanta	Account Rep	7.2	11/24/93	$65,000
16						

Criteria range (A17:F18)

	A	B	C	D	E	F
17	**Name**	**Location**	**Title**	**Service**	**Hire Date**	**Salary**
18						
19						
20						
21				Summary Statistics		

Database functions (F22:F26)

	A	B	C	D	E	F
22	Average Salary					$48,429
23	Maximum Salary					$100,000
24	Minimum Salary					$18,500
25	Total Salary					$678,000
26	Number of Employees					14

(a) All Employees

Filtered list

	A	B	C	D	E	F
1	**Name**	**Location**	**Title**	**Service**	**Hire Date**	**Salary**
3	Adamson	Chicago	Manager	6.9	3/16/94	$52,000
9	James	Chicago	Account Rep	6.2	10/31/94	$42,500
10	Johnson	Chicago	Account Rep	5.2	10/31/95	$47,500
12	Marder	Chicago	Account Rep	4.2	10/31/96	$38,500
16						

Criterion

	A	B	C	D	E	F
17	**Name**	**Location**	**Title**	**Service**	**Hire Date**	**Salary**
18		Chicago				
19						
20						
21				Summary Statistics		

Database functions reflect current criteria

	A	B	C	D	E	F
22	Average Salary					$45,125
23	Maximum Salary					$52,000
24	Minimum Salary					$38,500
25	Total Salary					$180,500
26	Number of Employees					4

(b) Chicago Employees

FIGURE 8.5 *Data Management Macros*

DATA MANAGEMENT MACROS

Objective To create a data management macro in conjunction with an employee list; to create a custom button to execute a macro. Use Figure 8.6 as a guide in the exercise.

Step 1: **Data Management Functions**

➤ Start Excel. Open the **Finished Employee List workbook** that was created in the chapter on data management. Pull down the **Data Menu**, click **Subtotals**, and click the **Remove All button**.

➤ Click any cell between A2 and A15, then click the **Sort Ascending button** on the Standard toolbar. The employees should be listed in alphabetical order as shown in Figure 8.6a.

➤ Clear all entries in the range **A18** through **F18**.

➤ Click in **cell F22**, which contains the DAVERAGE function, to compute the average salary of all employees who satisfy the specified criteria. No criteria have been entered, however, so the displayed value of $48,429 represents the average salary of all 14 employees.

➤ Click **cell B18**. Enter **Chicago**. Press **enter**. The average salary changes to $45,125 to indicate the average salary of the four Chicago employees.

➤ Click **cell C18**. Enter **Manager**. Press **enter**. The average salary changes to $52,000 to indicate the average salary of the one Chicago manager.

DAVERAGE function is entered in F22

Clear entries in A18:F18

Click in F22

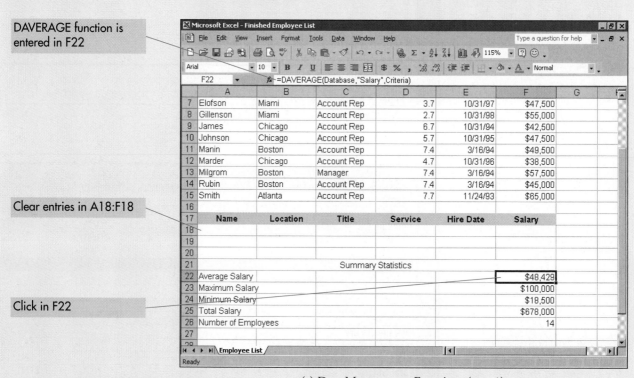

(a) Data Management Functions (step 1)

FIGURE 8.6 *Hands-on Exercise 3 (continued)*

Step 2: **The Create Name Command**

➤ Click and drag to select **cells A17** through **F18** as shown in Figure 8.6b. Pull down the **Insert menu**, click **Name**, then click **Create** to display the Create Names dialog box.

➤ The box to **Create Names in Top Row** is already checked. Click **OK**. This command assigns the text in each cell in row 17 to the corresponding cell in row 18; for example, cells B18 and C18 will be assigned the names Location and Title, respectively.

➤ Click and drag to select only **cells A18** through **F18**. (You need to assign a name to these seven cells collectively, as you will have to clear the criteria values in row 18 later in the chapter.)

➤ Pull down the **Insert menu**. Click **Name**. Click **Define**. Enter **CriteriaValues** in the Define Name dialog box. Click **OK**.

➤ Save the workbook.

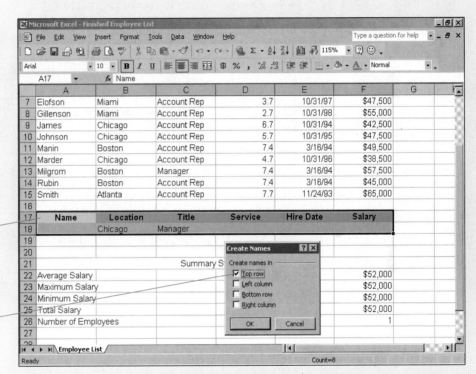

Click and drag to select A17:A18

Click Top row

(b) The Create Name Command (step 2)

FIGURE 8.6 *Hands-on Exercise 3 (continued)*

CREATE SEVERAL NAMES AT ONCE

The Insert menu contains two different commands to create named ranges. The Insert Name Define command affects only one cell or range at a time, then has you enter the name in a dialog box. The Insert Name Create command requires you to select adjacent rows or columns, then assigns multiple names from the (adjacent row or column) in one command. Both commands are very useful.

Step 3: **The Go To Command**

> ➤ Pull down the **Edit menu**. Click **Go To** to produce the Go To dialog box in Figure 8.6c. If you do not see the command, click the double arrow to display more commands.
> ➤ You should see the names you defined (CriteriaValues, Hire_Date, Location, Name, Salary, Service, and Title) as well as the two names defined previously by the authors (Criteria and Database).
> ➤ Click **Database**. Click **OK**. Cells A1 through F15 should be selected, corresponding to cells assigned to the name *Database*.
> ➤ Press the **F5 key** (a shortcut for the Edit Go To command), which again produces the Go To dialog box. Click **Criteria**. Click **OK**. Cells A17 through F18 should be selected.
> ➤ Click the **drop-down arrow** next to the Name box. Click **Location**. Cell B18 should be selected.
> ➤ You are now ready to record the macro.

Click drop-down arrow to see list of names

Click Database

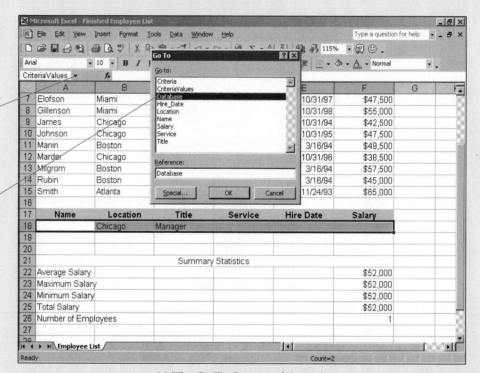

(c) The Go To Command (step 3)

FIGURE 8.6   *Hands-on Exercise 3 (continued)*

THE NAME BOX

Use the Name box (at the left of the Formula bar) to define a range by selecting the cell(s) in the worksheet to which the name is to apply, clicking the Name box, then entering the name. For example, to assign the name CriteriaValues to cells A18:F18, select the range, click in the Name box, type CriteriaValues, and press enter. The Name box can also be used to select a previously defined range by clicking the drop-down arrow next to the box and choosing the desired name from the drop-down list.

Step 4: **Record the Macro (Edit Clear Command)**

➤ Click the **Record Macro button** on the Visual Basic toolbar to display the Record Macro dialog box.

➤ Enter **Chicago** in the Macro Name text box. Verify that the macro will be stored in **This Workbook** and that the shortcut key check box is empty.

➤ Click **OK** to begin recording the macro. If necessary, click the **Relative References button** on the Stop Recording toolbar to record Absolute references (the button should be out).

➤ Pull down the **Edit menu**, click **Go To**, select **CriteriaValues** from the Go To dialog box, and click **OK**. Cells A18 through F18 should be selected as shown in Figure 8.6d. (Alternatively, you can also use the **F5 key** or the **Name box** to select CriteriaValues.)

➤ Pull down the **Edit menu**. Click **Clear**, then click **All** from the cascaded menu as shown in Figure 8.6d. Cells A18 through F18 (the criteria range) should be empty, and a new criterion can be entered into the macro.

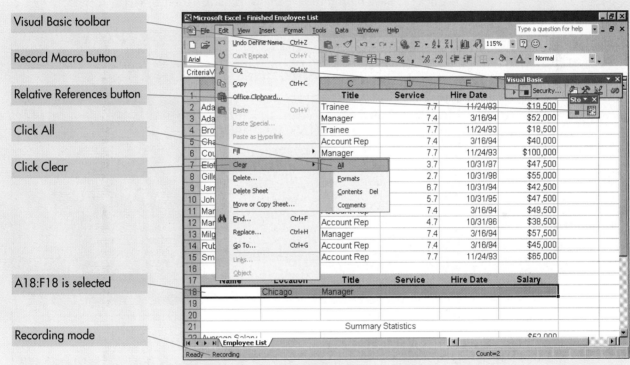

(d) Record the Macro (Edit Clear Command) (step 4)

FIGURE 8.6 *Hands-on Exercise 3 (continued)*

GOOD MACROS ARE FLEXIBLE MACROS

The macro to select Chicago employees has to be completely general and work under all circumstances, regardless of what may appear initially in the criteria row. Thus, you have to clear the entire criteria range prior to entering "Chicago" in the Location column. Note, too, the use of range names (e.g., CriteriaValues), as opposed to specific cells (e.g., A18:F18 in this example) to accommodate potential additions or deletions to the employee list.

Step 5: **Record the Macro (Advanced Filter Command)**

➤ Pull down the **Edit menu**, click **Go To**, select **Location** from the Go To dialog box, and click **OK**.

➤ Cell B18 should be selected. Enter **Chicago** to establish the criterion for both the database functions and the Advanced Filter command.

➤ Click in **cell A2** to position the active cell within the employee list. Pull down the **Data menu**. Click **Filter**, then click **Advanced Filter** from the cascaded menu to display the dialog box in Figure 8.6e.

➤ Enter **Database** as the List Range. Press the **tab key**. Enter **Criteria** as the Criteria Range.

➤ Check that the option to **Filter the List in-place** is checked.

➤ Click **OK**. You should see only those employees who satisfy the current criteria (i.e., Adamson, James, Johnson, and Marder, who are the employees who work in Chicago).

➤ Click the **Stop Recording button** to stop recording.

➤ Click the **Save button** to save the workbook with the macro.

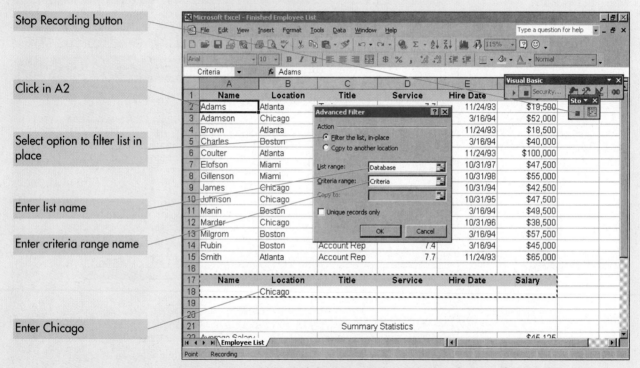

(e) Record the Macro (Advanced Filter Command) (step 5)

FIGURE 8.6 *Hands-on Exercise 3 (continued)*

THE FILTER VERSUS THE DATABASE FUNCTIONS

Change the criteria—for example, from Chicago to Chicago Managers—and the values displayed by the database functions (DAVERAGE, DSUM, and so on) change automatically. The filtered records do not change, however, until you re-execute the command to filter the records in place. The advantage of a macro becomes immediately apparent, because the macro is built to change the criteria and filter the records with a single click of the mouse.

Step 6:   **View the Macro**

➤ Click the **Visual Basic Editor button** on the Visual Basic toolbar to open the editor as shown in Figure 8.6f. If necessary, pull down the **View menu**. Click **Project Explorer** to open the Project window in the left pane.

➤ If necessary, expand the **Modules folder**, under the VBA project for Finished Employee List. Click (select) **Module1**, pull down the **View menu**, and click **Code** to open the Code window in the right pane. Maximize the Code window.

➤ Close any other open windows within the Visual Basic Editor. Your screen should match the one in Figure 8.6f. If necessary, correct your macro so that it matches ours.

➤ If the correction is minor, it is easiest to edit the macro directly; otherwise delete the macro, then return to step 4 and rerecord the macro from the beginning. (To delete a macro, pull down the Tools menu, click Macros, select the macro you wish to delete, then click the Delete button.)

➤ Click the **View Microsoft Excel button** at the left of the toolbar or press **Alt+F11** to return to the Employee worksheet.

View Microsoft Excel button

Click Module1

Code for Chicago macro

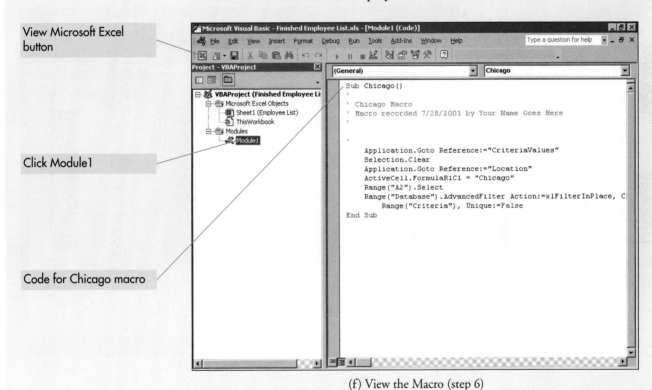

(f) View the Macro (step 6)

FIGURE 8.6   *Hands-on Exercise 3 (continued)*

THE VISUAL BASIC TOOLBAR

The Visual Basic Toolbar consists of seven buttons associated with macros and Visual Basic. You will find a button to run an existing macro, to record (or stop recording) a new macro, and to open (toggle to) the Visual Basic Editor. The toolbar can be displayed (or hidden) by right clicking any visible toolbar, then checking (or clearing) Visual Basic from the list of toolbars.

Step 7: **Assign the Macro**

➤ Pull down the **View menu**, click **Toolbars**, then click **Forms** to display the Forms toolbar as shown in Figure 8.6g.

➤ Click the **Button tool** (the mouse pointer changes to a tiny crosshair). Click and drag in the worksheet as shown in Figure 8.6g to draw a command button on the worksheet.

➤ Be sure to draw the button *below* the employee list, or the button may be hidden when a subsequent Data Filter command is executed.

➤ Release the mouse, and the Assign Macro dialog box will appear. Choose **Chicago** (the macro you just created) from the list of macro names. Click **OK**.

➤ The button should still be selected. Click and drag to select the name of the button, **Button 1**.

➤ Type **Chicago** as the new name. Do *not* press the enter key. Click outside the button to deselect it.

➤ Save the workbook.

Forms toolbar

Button tool

Click Chicago to assign macro to button

Click and drag to draw button

Click and drag to select name

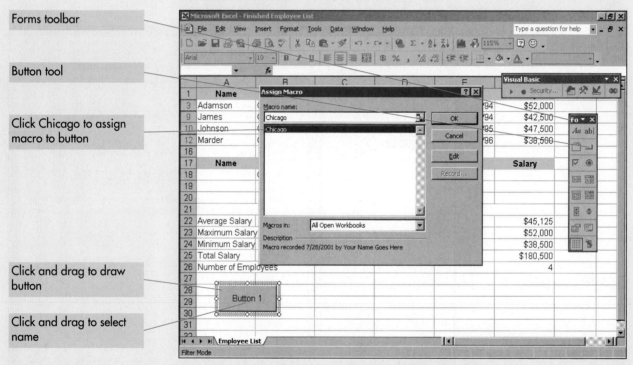

(g) Assign the Macro (step 7)

FIGURE 8.6 *Hands-on Exercise 3 (continued)*

SELECTING A BUTTON

You cannot select a Macro button by clicking it, because that executes the associated macro. Thus, to select a macro button, you must press and hold the Ctrl key as you click the mouse. (You can also select a button by clicking the right mouse button to produce a shortcut menu.) Once the button has been selected, you can edit its name, and/or move or size the button just as you can any other Windows object.

Step 8: **Test the Macro**

➤ Pull down the **Data menu**, click **Filter**, then click **Show All**.
➤ Click **cell B12**. Enter **Miami** to change the location for Marder. Press **enter**. The number of employees changes in the summary statistics area, as do the results of the other summary statistics.
➤ Click the **Chicago button** as shown in Figure 8.6h to execute the macro. Marder is *not* listed this time because she is no longer in Chicago.
➤ Pull down the **Data menu**. Click **Filter**. Click **Show All** to display the entire employee list.
➤ Click **cell B12**. Enter **Chicago** to change the location for this employee back to Chicago. Press **enter**. Click the **Chicago button** to execute the macro a second time. Marder is once again displayed with the Chicago employees.
➤ Pull down the **Data menu**. Click **Filter**. Click **Show All**.
➤ You do not have to print the workbook at this time, since we will print the entire workbook at the end of the next exercise.
➤ Save the workbook. Exit Excel if you do not want to continue with the next exercise at this time.

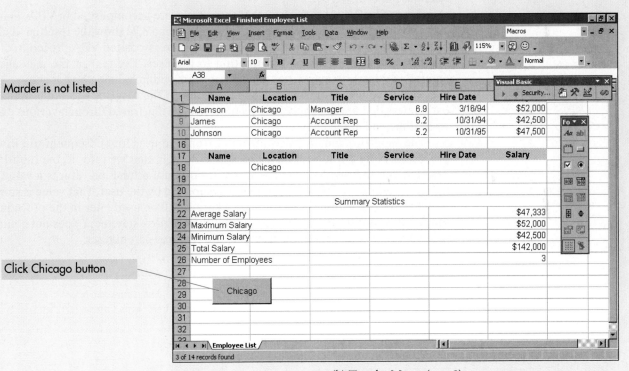

(h) Test the Macro (step 8)

FIGURE 8.6 *Hands-on Exercise 3 (continued)*

EXECUTING A MACRO

There are several different ways to execute a macro. The most basic way is to pull down the Tools menu, click Macro, click Macros to display the Macros dialog box, then double click the desired macro to run it. You can assign a macro to a button within a worksheet or to a custom button on a toolbar, then click the button to run the macro. The fastest way is to use a keyboard shortcut, provided that a shortcut has been defined.

Excel macros were originally nothing more than recorded keystrokes. Earlier versions of Excel had you turn on the macro recorder to capture the associated keystrokes, then "play back" those keystrokes when you ran the macro. Starting with Office 95, however, the recorded keystrokes were translated into Visual Basic commands, which made the macros potentially much more powerful because you could execute Visual Basic programs (known as procedures) from within Excel. (In actuality, Microsoft Office uses a subset of Visual Basic known as *Visual Basic for Applications (VBA)*, and we will use this terminology from now on.)

You can think of the macro recorder as a shortcut to generate the VBA code. Once you have that code, however, you can modify the various statements using techniques common to any programming language. You can move and/or copy statements within a procedure, search for one character string and replace it with another, and so on. And finally, you can insert additional VBA statements that are beyond the scope of ordinary Excel commands. You can, for example, display information to the user in the form of a message box any time during the execution of the macro. You can also accept information from the user into a dialog box for subsequent use in the macro.

Figure 8.7 illustrates the way that these tasks are accomplished in VBA. Figure 8.7a contains the VBA code, whereas Figures 8.7b and 8.7c show the resulting dialog boxes, as they would appear during execution of the associated VBA procedure. The **MsgBox statement** displays information to the user. The text of the message is entered in quotation marks, and the text appears within a dialog box as shown. The user clicks the OK command button to continue. (The MsgBox has other optional parameters that are not shown at this time, but are illustrated through various exercises at the end of the chapter.)

The InputBox function accepts input from the user for subsequent use in the procedure. Note the subtle change in terminology, in that we refer to the InputBox function, but the MsgBox statement. That is because a function returns a value, in this case the name of the location that was supplied by the user. That value is stored in the active cell within the worksheet, where it will be used later in the procedure. There is also a difference in syntax in that the MsgBox statement does not contain parentheses, whereas the InputBox function requires parentheses.

```
MsgBox "The MsgBox statement displays information"
ActiveCell.FormulaR1C1 = InputBox("Enter employee location")
```

(a) Visual Basic Statements

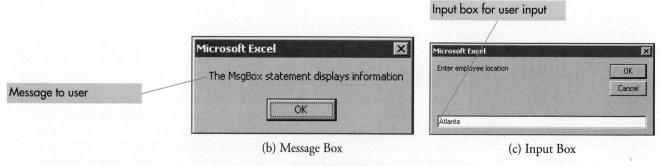

(b) Message Box   (c) Input Box

FIGURE 8.7 *VBA Statements*

CREATING ADDITIONAL MACROS

Objective To duplicate an existing macro, then modify the copied macro to create an entirely new macro. Use Figure 8.8 as a guide.

Step 1: **Enable Macros**

➤ Start Excel. Open the **Finished Employee List workbook** from the previous exercise. You should see the warning in Figure 8.8a.
➤ Click the **More Info button** to display the Help window to learn more about macro viruses. (Pull down the Tools menu, click Options, click the General tab, and check the Settings box for Micro Virus Protection if you do not see the warning message.)
➤ Click the **Close button** when you are finished reading the information.
➤ Click the **Enable Macros button** to open the Finished Employee List workbook.

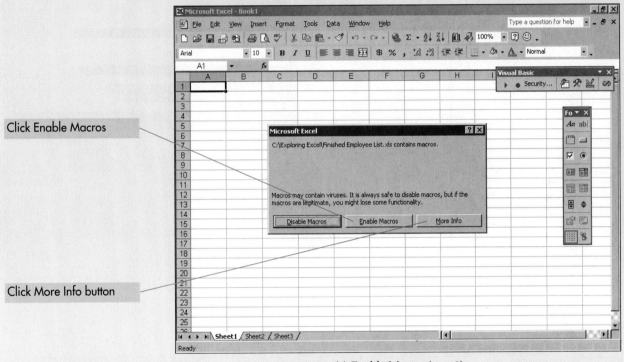

Click Enable Macros

Click More Info button

(a) Enable Macros (step 1)

FIGURE 8.8   *Hands-on Exercise 4*

MACRO VIRUSES

A computer virus is in actuality a program that can erase or delete the files on your computer. An Excel macro is also a program, and it too is capable of doing damage to your system. Thus, Excel will warn you that a workbook contains a macro, which in turn may carry a macro virus. If you are confident the workbook is safe, click the button to Enable macros; otherwise open the workbook with the macros disabled.

Step 2: **Copy the Chicago Macro**

➤ Pull down the **Tools menu**, click the **Macro command**, then click **Visual Basic Editor** (or press **Alt+F11**) to open the Visual Basic Editor.

➤ Click the **plus sign** on the Modules folder, select **Module1**, pull down the **View menu**, and click **Code**.

➤ Click and drag to select the entire Chicago macro as shown in Figure 8.8b.

➤ Pull down the **Edit menu** and click **Copy** (or click the **Copy button** on the Standard toolbar).

➤ Click below the End Sub statement to deselect the macro and simultaneously establish the position of the insertion point.

➤ Pull down the **Edit menu** and click **Paste** (or click the **Paste button** on the Standard toolbar). The Chicago macro has been copied and now appears twice in Module1.

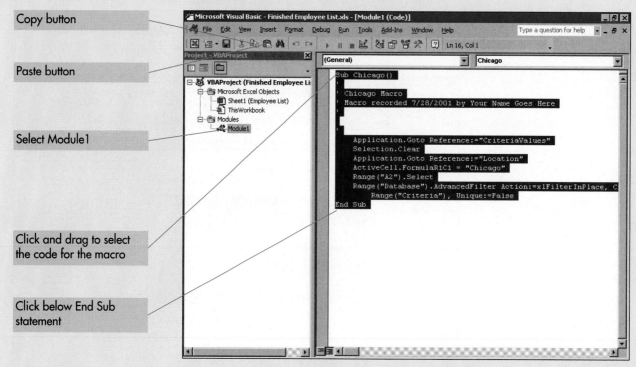

Copy button

Paste button

Select Module1

Click and drag to select
the code for the macro

Click below End Sub
statement

(b) Copy the Chicago Macro (step 2)

FIGURE 8.8   *Hands-on Exercise 4 (continued)*

THE SHIFT KEY

You can select text for editing (or replacement) with the mouse, or alternatively, you can select by using the cursor keys on the keyboard. Set the insertion point where you want the selection to begin, then press and hold the Shift key as you use the cursor keys to move the insertion point to the end of the selection.

Step 3:   **Create the Manager Macro**

- ➤ Click in front of the second (i.e., the copied) Chicago macro to set the insertion point. Pull down the **Edit menu**. Click **Replace** to display the Replace dialog box as shown in Figure 8.8c.
- ➤ Enter **Chicago** in the Find What text box. Press the **tab key**. Enter **Manager** in the Replace With text box. Select the option button to search in the *current* procedure. Click the **Find Next command button**.
- ➤ Excel searches for the first occurrence of Chicago, which should be in the Sub statement of the copied macro. (If this is not the case, click the **Find Next command button** until your screen matches Figure 8.8c.)
- ➤ Click the **Replace command button**. Excel substitutes Manager for Chicago, then looks for the next occurrence of Chicago. Click **Replace**. Click **Replace** a third time to make another substitution. Close the Replace dialog box.
- ➤ Click and drag to select **Location** within the Application.Goto.Reference statement in the Manager macro. Enter **Title**. (The criteria within the macro have been changed to employees whose title is Manager.) Save the module.

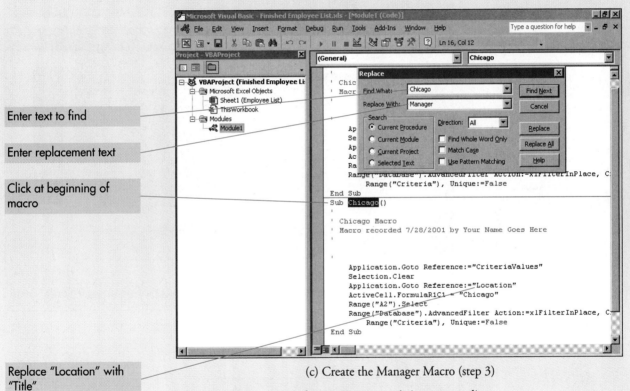

(c) Create the Manager Macro (step 3)

FIGURE 8.8   *Hands-on Exercise 4 (continued)*

THE FIND AND REPLACE COMMANDS

Anyone familiar with a word processor takes the Find and Replace commands for granted, but did you know the same capabilities exist in Excel as well as in the Visual Basic Editor? Pull down the Edit menu and choose either command. You have the same options as in the parallel command in Word, such as a case-sensitive (or insensitive) search or a limitation to a whole-word search.

Step 4: **Run the Manager Macro**

➤ Click the **Excel button** on the Windows taskbar or press **Alt+F11** to return to the Employee List worksheet.

➤ Pull down the **Tools menu**. Click **Macro**, then click the **Macros ... command** to display the Macro dialog box as shown in Figure 8.8d.

➤ You should see two macros: Chicago, which was created in the previous exercise, and Manager, which you just created. (If the Manager macro does not appear, return to the Visual Basic Editor and correct the appropriate Sub statement to include Manager() as the name of the macro.)

➤ Select the **Manager macro**, then click **Run** to run the macro, after which you should see three employees (Adamson, Coulter, and Milgrom). If the macro does not execute correctly, return to the Visual Basic Editor to make the necessary corrections, then rerun the macro.

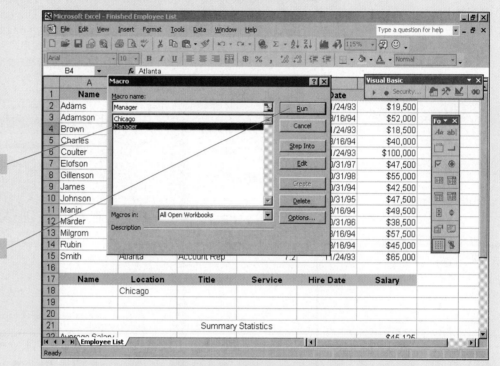

(d) Run the Manager Macro (step 4)

FIGURE 8.8   *Hands-on Exercise 4 (continued)*

THE STEP INTO COMMAND

The Step Into command helps to debug a macro, as it executes the statements one at a time. Pull down the Tools menu, click Macro, click Macros, select the macro to debug, then click the Step Into command button. Move and/or size the Visual Basic Editor window so that you can see both the worksheet and the macro. Pull down the Debug menu and click the Step Into command (or press the F8 function key) to execute the first statement in the macro and view its results. Continue to press the F8 function key to execute the statements one at a time until the macro has completed execution.

Step 5: **Assign a Button**

> ➤ Click the **Button tool** on the Forms toolbar (the mouse pointer changes to a tiny crosshair), then click and drag in the worksheet to draw a button on the worksheet. Release the mouse.
> ➤ Choose **Manager** (the macro you just created) from the list of macro names as shown in Figure 8.8e. Click **OK** to close the Assign Macro dialog box.
> ➤ The button should still be selected. Click and drag to select the name of the button, **Button 2**, then type **Manager** as the new name. Do *not* press the enter key. Click outside the button to deselect it.
> ➤ There should be two buttons on your worksheet, one each for the Chicago and Manager macros.
> ➤ Click the **Chicago button** to execute the Chicago macro. You should see four employees with an average salary of $45,125.
> ➤ Click the **Manager button** to execute the Manager macro. You should see three employees with an average salary of $69,833.

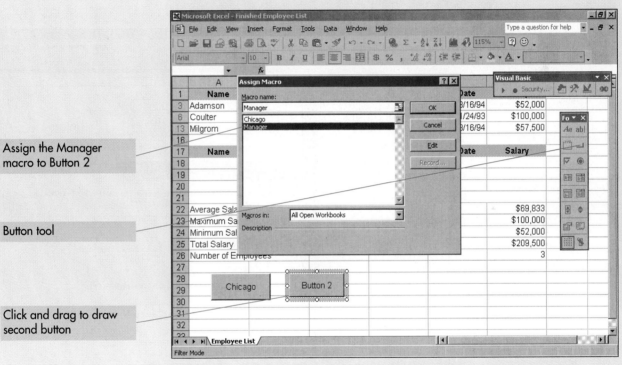

Assign the Manager macro to Button 2

Button tool

Click and drag to draw second button

(e) Assign a Button (step 5)

FIGURE 8.8 *Hands-on Exercise 4 (continued)*

CREATE UNIFORM BUTTONS

One way to create buttons of a uniform size is to create the first button, then copy that button to create the others. To copy a button, press the Ctrl key as you select (click) the button, then click the Copy button on the Standard toolbar. Click in the worksheet where you want the new button to appear, then click the Paste button. Click and drag over the name of the button and enter a new name. Right click the new button, then click Assign Macro from the shortcut menu. Select the name of the new macro, then click OK.

Step 6:   **Create the Chicago Manager Macro**

➤ Return to the Visual Basic Editor. Press **Ctrl+Home** to move to the beginning of Module1. Click and drag to select the entire Chicago macro. Be sure to include the End Sub statement in your selection.

➤ Click the **Copy button** on the Standard toolbar to copy the Chicago macro to the clipboard. Press **Ctrl+End** to move to the end of the module sheet. Click the **Paste button** on the Standard toolbar to complete the copy operation.

➤ Change **Chicago** to **ChicagoManager** in both the comment statement and the Sub statement as shown in Figure 8.8f.

➤ Click and drag to select the two statements in the **Manager macro** as shown in Figure 8.8f. Click the **Copy button**.

➤ Scroll, if necessary, until you can click in the **ChicagoManager macro** at the end of the line, ActiveCell.FormulaR1C1 = "Chicago". Press **enter** to begin a new line. Click the **Paste button** to complete the copy operation.

➤ Delete any unnecessary blank lines or spaces that may remain.

➤ Save the module.

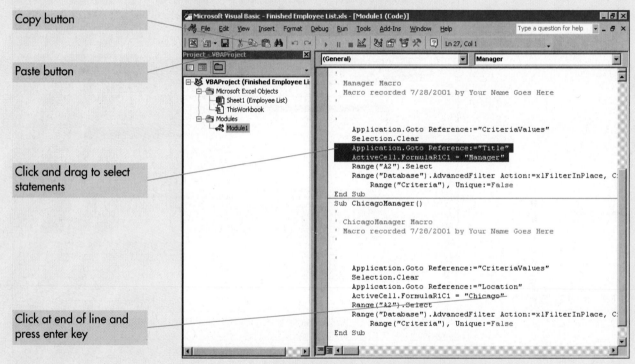

(f) Create the Chicago Manager Macro (step 6)

FIGURE 8.8   *Hands-on Exercise 4 (continued)*

ADD A SHORTCUT

You can add and/or modify the shortcut key associated with a macro at any time. Pull down the Tools menu, click the Macro command, then click Macros to display the Macro dialog box. Select the desired macro and click the Options button to display the Macro Options dialog box, where you assign a shortcut. Type a lowercase letter to create a shortcut with just the Ctrl key, such as Ctrl+m. Enter an uppercase letter to create a shortcut using the Ctrl and Shift keys, such as Ctrl+Shift+M.

Step 7: **The MsgBox Statement**

➤ Check that the statements in your ChicagoManager macro match those in Figure 8.8g. (The MsgBox statement has not yet been added.)

➤ Click immediately before the End Sub statement. Press **enter** to begin a new line, press the **up arrow** to move up one line, then press **Tab** to indent.

➤ Type the word **MsgBox** then press the **Space bar**. VBA responds with a Quick Info box that displays the complete syntax of the statement. You can ignore this information at the present time, since we are not entering any additional parameters.

➤ Enter the rest of the MsgBox statement exactly as it appears in Figure 8.8g. Be sure to include the underscore at the end of the first line, which indicates that the statement is continued to the next line.

➤ Save the module, then return to the Excel workbook.

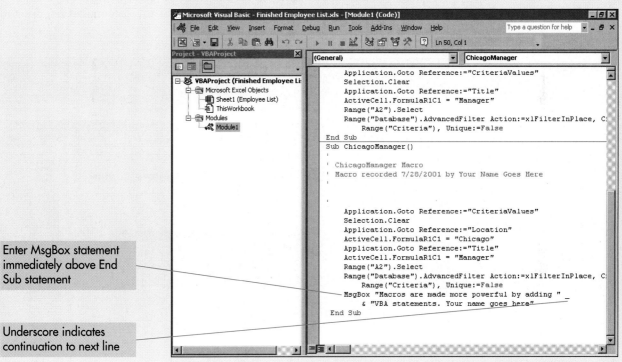

Enter MsgBox statement immediately above End Sub statement

Underscore indicates continuation to next line

(g) The MsgBox Statement (step 7)

FIGURE 8.8 *Hands-on Exercise 4 (continued)*

THE UNDERSCORE AND AMPERSAND

A VBA statement is continued from one line to the next by typing an underscore at the end of the line to be continued. You may not, however, break a line in the middle of a literal. Hence, the first line ends with a closing quotation mark, followed by a space and the underscore. The next line starts with an ampersand to indicated continuation of the previous literal, followed by the remainder of the literal in quotation marks.

Step 8: **Test the Chicago Manager Macro**

➤ You can assign a macro to a command button by copying an existing command button, then changing the name of the button and the associated macro. Right click either of the existing command buttons, click the **Copy command** from the shortcut menu, then click the **Paste button** on the Standard toolbar.

➤ Click and drag the copied button to the right of the two existing buttons. Click and drag the text of the copied button (which should still be selected) to select the text, then type **Chicago Manager** as the name of the button.

➤ Click anywhere in the worksheet to deselect the button, then **Right click** the new button, click the **Assign Macro command**, choose the newly created Chicago Manager, and click **OK**. Click anywhere in the workbook to deselect the button. Save the workbook.

➤ Click the **Chicago Manager button** to execute the macro. You should see the matching employees as shown in Figure 8.8h, followed by the message box.

➤ Click **OK**. Return to the VBA editor to correct the macro if it does not execute as intended.

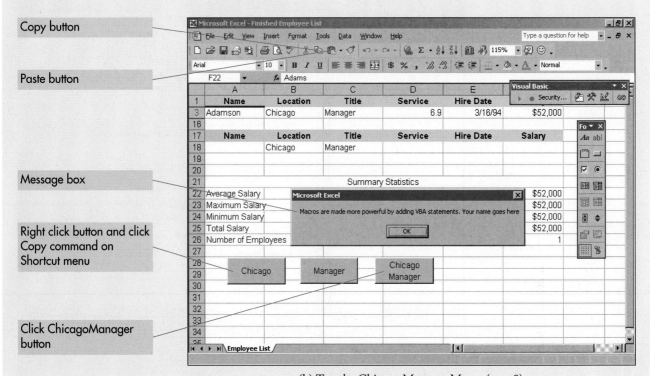

(h) Test the Chicago Manager Macro (step 8)

FIGURE 8.8 *Hands-on Exercise 4 (continued)*

CUSTOMIZE THE MESSAGE BOX

You can add a personal touch to the output of the MsgBox statement by including optional parameters to change the text of the title bar and/or include an icon within the message box. The statement, MsgBox "Hello World", vbinformation, "Your Name on Title Bar" uses both parameters. Try it.

Step 9: **Create the Any City Any Title Macro**

> ➤ Press **Alt+F11** to return to the Visual Basic editor. Click and drag to select the entire ChicagoManager macro. Click the **Copy button**, click the blank line below the End Sub statement, then click the **Paste button** to duplicate the module.
> ➤ Click and drag the name of the copied macro. Type **AnyCityAnyTitle()** to change the name of the macro. Do not leave any spaces in the macro name. Delete or modify the comments as you see fit.
> ➤ Click and drag to select **"Chicago"** as shown in Figure 8.8i. You must include the quotation marks in your selection.
> ➤ Type **InputBox("Enter the location")** to replace the specific location with the InputBox function. Be sure to use left and right parentheses and to enclose the literal in quotation marks.
> ➤ Click and drag to select **"Manager"**. Type **InputBox("Enter the title")** to replace the specific title with the InputBox function.
> ➤ Save the module and return to the Excel workbook.

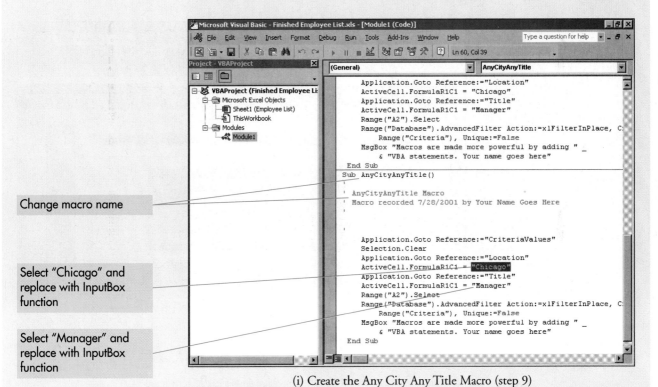

Change macro name

Select "Chicago" and replace with InputBox function

Select "Manager" and replace with InputBox function

(i) Create the Any City Any Title Macro (step 9)

FIGURE 8.8 *Hands-on Exercise 4 (continued)*

USE WHAT YOU KNOW

Use the techniques acquired from other applications such as Microsoft Word to facilitate editing within the VBA window. Press the Ins key to toggle between the insert and overtype modes as you modify the statements within a procedure. You can also cut, copy, and paste statements (or parts of statements) within a procedure and from one procedure to another. The Find and Replace commands are also useful.

Step 10: **Test the Any City Any Title Macro**

➤ Copy any of the existing command buttons to create a new button for the **Any City Any Title** macro as shown in Figure 8.8j. Be sure to assign the correct macro to this button.

➤ Click the **Any City Any Title command button** to run the macro. You will be prompted for the location. Type **Atlanta** and click **OK**. (A second input box will appear in which you will enter the title.)

➤ At this time Atlanta has been entered into the criteria area, and the summary statistics reflect the Atlanta employees. The filtered list will not change, however, until you have entered the title and completed the Advanced Filter command.

➤ Enter **Trainee** as the employee title as shown in Figure 8.8j. Click **OK**. The workbook changes to reflect the Atlanta trainees. Click **OK** in response to the message box.

➤ Return to the VBA editor if the macro does not execute as intended. Save the workbook.

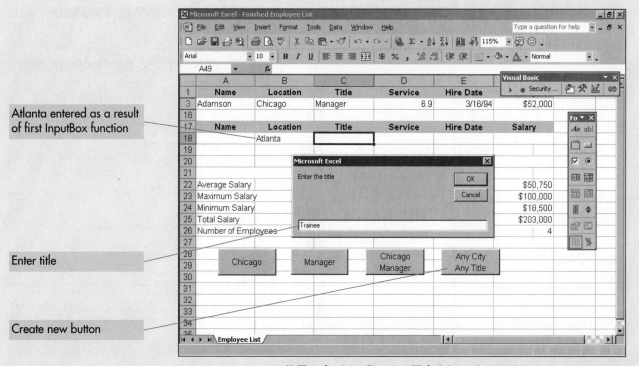

Atlanta entered as a result of first InputBox function

Enter title

Create new button

(j) Test the Any City Any Title Macro (step 10)

FIGURE 8.8   *Hands-on Exercise 4 (continued)*

ONE MACRO DOES IT ALL

The Any City Any Title macro is the equivalent of the more specific macros that were created earlier; that is, you would enter "Chicago" and "Manager" to replace the Chicago Manager macro. You can also enter "Chicago" as the city and leave the title field blank to select all Chicago employees, or alternatively, leave the city blank and enter "Manager" as the title to select all managers. And finally, you could omit both city and title to select all employees.

Step 11: **Change the Button Properties**

➤ Press and hold the **Shift** and **Ctrl keys**, then click each of the command buttons to select all four buttons as shown in Figure 8.8k.

➤ Pull down the **Format** menu and click the **Control command** to display the Format Control dialog box. Click the **Properties tab**, then check the box to **Print object** so that the command buttons will appear on the printed worksheet.

➤ Click the **Move but don't size with cells** option button. Click **OK** to exit the dialog box and return to the worksheet. Click anywhere in the worksheet to deselect the buttons.

➤ Click the **Print button** on the Standard toolbar to print the worksheet. Return to the Visual Basic Editor. Pull down the **File menu**, click the **Print command**, select **Current Module**, then click **OK**.

➤ Save the workbook a final time. Close the workbook. Exit Excel if you don't want to continue with the next exercise at this time.

Click option to Move but don't size with cells

Check box to Print object

Press and hold Shift and Ctrl keys as you click all four buttons

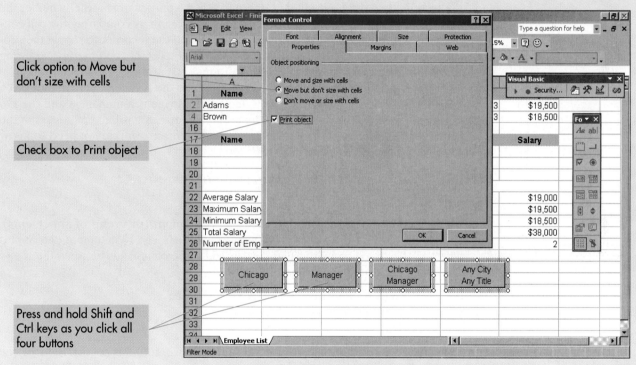

(k) Change the Button Properties (step 11)

FIGURE 8.8 *Hands-on Exercise 4 (continued)*

THE SIZE PROPERTY

Use the Size property to obtain a consistent look for your command buttons. Press and hold the Shift and Ctrl keys as you select the individual buttons. Pull down the Format menu and click the Control command to display the Format Control dialog box. Click the Size tab, enter the width and height for the selected buttons, then click OK. The buttons will be a uniform size, but they may overlap. Click anywhere in the worksheet to deselect the buttons, then right click and drag to reposition a button.

Excel macros can be made significantly more powerful by incorporating additional Visual Basic statements that enable true programming. These include the If statement for decision making, and the Do statement to implement a *loop* (one or more commands that are executed repeatedly until a condition is met).

Consider, for example, the worksheet and associated macro in Figure 8.9. The worksheet is similar to those used in the preceding exercises, except that the font color of the data for managers is red. Think for a minute how you would do this manually. You would look at the first employee in the list, examine the employee's title to determine if that employee is a manager, and if so, change the font color for that employee. You would then repeat these steps for all of the other employees on the list. It sounds tedious, but that is exactly what you would do if asked to change the font color for the managers.

Now ask yourself whether you could implement the entire process with the macro recorder. You could use the recorder to capture the commands to select a specific row within the list and change the font color. You could not, however, use the recorder to determine whether or not to select a particular row (i.e., whether the employee is a manager) because you make that decision by comparing the cell contents to a specific criterion. Nor is there a way to tell the recorder to repeat the process for every employee. In other words, you need to go beyond merely capturing Excel commands. You need to include additional Visual Basic statements.

The HighlightManager macro in Figure 8.9 uses the If statement to implement a decision (to determine whether the selected employee is a manager) and the Do statement to implement a loop (to repeat the commands until all employees in the list have been processed). To understand how the macro works, you need to know the basic syntax of each statement.

If Statement

The *If statement* conditionally executes a statement (or group of statements), depending on the value of an expression (condition). The If statement determines whether an expression is true, and if so, executes the commands between the If and the *End If statement*. For example:

```
If ActiveCell.Offset(0, 2) = "Manager" Then
    Selection.Font.ColorIndex = 3
End If
```

This If statement determines whether the cell two columns to the right of the active cell (the offset indicates a relative reference) contains the text *Manager,* and if so, changes the font color of the (previously) selected text. The number three corresponds to the color red. No action is taken if the condition is false. Either way, execution continues with the command below the End If.

IF-THEN-ELSE

The If statement includes an optional Else clause whose statements are executed if the condition is false. Consider:

If condition Then statements [Else statements] End If

The condition is evaluated as either true or false. If the condition is true, the statements following Then are executed; otherwise the statements following Else are executed. Either way, execution continues with the statement following End If. Use the Help command for additional information and examples.

Do Statement

The ***Do statement*** repeats a block of statements until a condition becomes true. For example:

```
Do Until ActiveCell = ""
    ActiveCell.Range("A1:F1").Select
    If ActiveCell.Offset(0, 2) = "Manager" Then
        Selection.Font.ColorIndex = 3
    End If
    ActiveCell.Offset(1, 0).Select
Loop
```

The statements within the loop are executed repeatedly until the active cell is empty (i.e., ActiveCell = ""). The first statement in the loop selects the cells in columns A through F of the current row. Relative references are used, and you may want to refer to the earlier discussion that indicated that A1:F1 specifies the shape of a range rather than a specific cell address.

The If statement determines whether the current employee is a manager and, if so, changes the font color for the selected cells. (The offset (0, 2) refers to the entry two columns to the right of the active cell.) The last statement selects the cell one row below the active cell to process the next employee. (Omission of this statement would process the same row indefinitely, creating what is known as an infinite loop.)

The macro in Figure 8.9 is a nontrivial example that illustrates the potential of Visual Basic to enhance a macro. Try to gain a conceptual understanding of how the macro works, but do not be concerned if you are confused initially. Do the hands-on exercise, and you'll be pleased at how much clearer it will be when you have created the macro yourself.

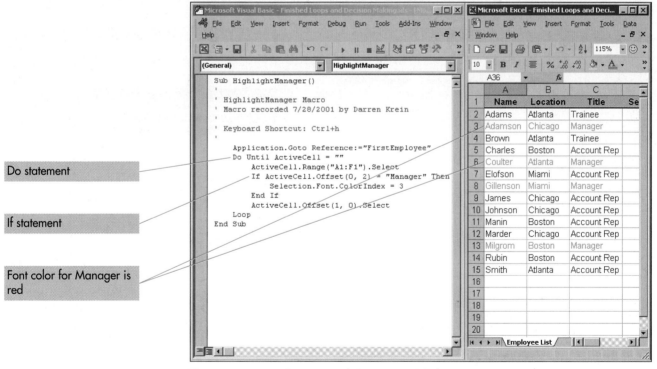

FIGURE 8.9 *Loops and Decision Making*

LOOPS AND DECISION MAKING

Objective   To implement loops and decision making in a macro through relative references and the Visual Basic Do Until and If statements. Use Figure 8.10 as a guide in doing the exercise.

Step 1:   **The ClearColor Macro**

> Open the **Loops and Decision Making workbook** in the **Exploring Excel folder**. Click the button to **Enable Macros**. Close the Forms and Visual Basic toolbars.

> Save the workbook as **Finished Loops and Decision Making workbook**. The data for the employees in rows 3, 6, 8, and 13 appears in red to indicate these employees are managers.

> Pull down the **Tools menu**. Click the **Macro command** and click **Macros** to display the dialog box in Figure 8.10a.

> Select **ClearColor**, then click **Run** to execute this macro and clear the red color from the managerial employees.

> It is important to know that the ClearColor macro works, as you will use it throughout the exercise.

> Save the workbook.

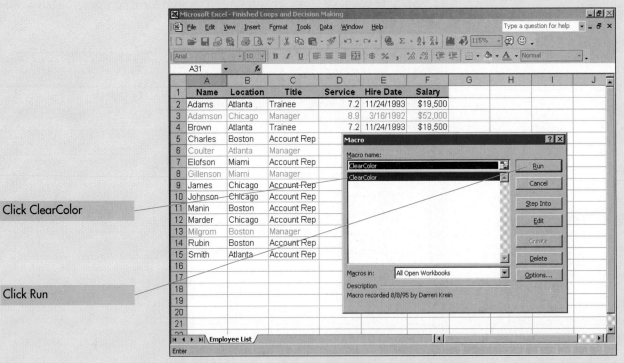

Click ClearColor

Click Run

(a) The ClearColor Macro (step 1)

FIGURE 8.10   *Hands-on Exercise 5*

Step 2:   **Record the HighlightManager Macro**

➤ You must choose the active cell before recording the macro. Click **cell A3**, the cell containing the name of the first manager.

➤ Pull down the **Tools menu**, click (or point to) the **Macro command**, then click **Record New Macro** (or click the **Record macro button** on the Visual Basic toolbar) to display the Record Macro dialog box.

➤ Enter **HighlightManager** as the name of the macro. Do not leave any spaces in the macro name. Click in the **Shortcut Key** check box and enter a **lowercase h**. Check that **This Workbook** is selected. Click **OK**.

➤ The Stop Recording toolbar appears and the status bar indicates that you are recording the macro as shown in Figure 8.10b. Click the **Relative References button** so that the button is pushed in.

➤ Click and drag to select **cells A3** through **F3** as shown in Figure 8.10b. Click the arrow in the **Font color list box**. Click **Red**. Click the **Stop Recording button**.

➤ Click anywhere in the worksheet to deselect cells A3 through F3 so you can see the effect of the macro; cells A3 through F3 should be displayed in red.

➤ Save the workbook.

Click drop-down arrow on Font Color list

Click and drag to select A3:F3

Click Red

Recording mode

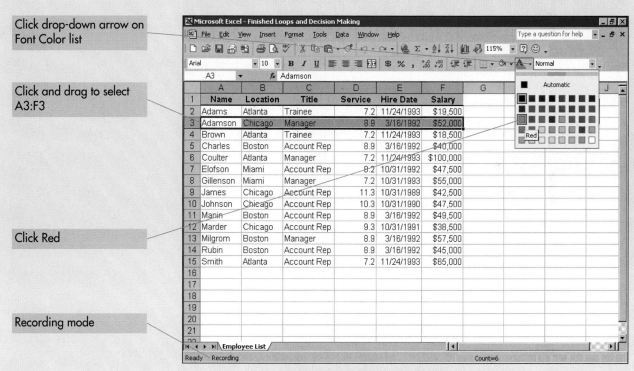

(b) Record the HighlightManager Macro (step 2)

FIGURE 8.10   *Hands-on Exercise 5 (continued)*

A SENSE OF FAMILIARITY

Visual Basic has the basic capabilities found in any other programming language. If you have programmed before, whether in Pascal, C, or even COBOL, you will find all of the familiar logic structures. These include the Do While and Do Until statements, the If-Then-Else statement for decision making, nested If statements, a Case statement, and/or calls to subprograms.

Step 3: **View the Macro**

➤ Press **Alt+F11** to open the Visual Basic Editor. If necessary, double click the **Modules folder** within the Project Explorer window to display the two modules within the workbook.

➤ Select (click) **Module2**. Pull down the **View menu** and click **Code** (or press the **F7 key**) to display the Visual Basic code for the HighlightManager macro you just created as shown in Figure 8.10c.

➤ Be sure that your code is identical to ours (except for the comments). If you see the absolute reference, Range("A3:F3"), rather than the relative reference in our figure, you need to correct your macro to match ours.

➤ Click the **close button** (the X on the Project Explorer title bar) to close the Project Explorer window. The Code window expands to occupy the entire Visual Basic Editor window.

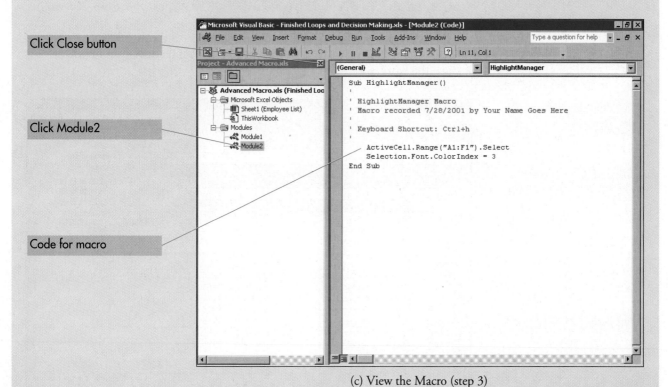

(c) View the Macro (step 3)

FIGURE 8.10 *Hands-on Exercise 5 (continued)*

WHY SO MANY MODULES?

Multiple macros that are recorded within the same Excel session are all stored in the same module. If you close the workbook, then subsequently reopen it, Excel will store subsequent macros in a new module. It really doesn't matter where (in which module) the macros are stored. You can, however, cut and paste macros from one module to another if you prefer to have all of the macros in a single module. Delete the additional (now superfluous) modules after you have copied the procedures.

Step 4:   **Test the Macro**

➤ Point to an empty area on the Windows taskbar, then click the **right mouse button** to display a shortcut menu. Click **Tile Vertically** to tile the open windows (Excel and the Visual Basic Editor).

➤ Your desktop should be similar to Figure 8.10d except that the additional employees will not yet appear in red. It doesn't matter if the workbook is in the same window as ours. (If additional windows are open on the desktop, minimize each window, then repeat the previous step to tile the open windows.)

➤ Click the **Excel window**. Click **cell A6** (the cell containing the name of the next manager). Press **Ctrl+h** to execute the HighlightManager macro. The font in cells A6 to F6 changes to red.

➤ Click **cell A7**. Press **Ctrl+h** to execute the HighlightManager macro. The font for this employee is also in red, although the employee is not a manager.

➤ Save the workbook.

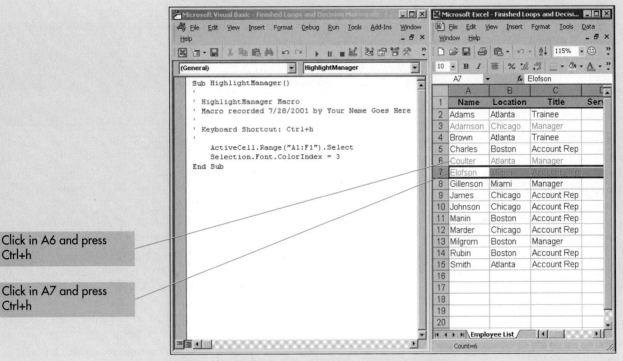

Click in A6 and press Ctrl+h

Click in A7 and press Ctrl+h

(d) Test the Macro (step 4)

FIGURE 8.10   *Hands-on Exercise 5 (continued)*

THE FIRST BUG

A bug is a mistake in a computer program; hence debugging refers to the process of correcting program errors. According to legend, the first bug was an unlucky moth crushed to death on one of the relays of the electromechanical Mark II computer, bringing the machine's operation to a halt. The cause of the failure was discovered by Grace Hopper, who promptly taped the moth to her logbook, noting, *"First actual case of bug being found."*

Step 5: **Add the If Statement**

➤ Press **Ctrl+c** to execute the ClearColor macro. The data for all employees is again displayed in black.

➤ Click in the window containing the **HighlightManager** macro. Add the **If** and **End If** statements exactly as they are shown in Figure 8.10e. Use the **Tab key** (or press the **space bar**) to indent the Selection statement within the If and End If statements.

➤ Click in the window containing the worksheet, then click **cell A3**. Press **Ctrl+h** to execute the modified HighlightManager macro. The text in cells A3 through F3 is red since this employee is a manager.

➤ Click **cell A4**. Press **Ctrl+h**. The row is selected, but the color of the font remains unchanged. The If statement prevents these cells from being highlighted because the employee is not a manager. Press **Ctrl+c** to remove all highlighting.

➤ Save the workbook.

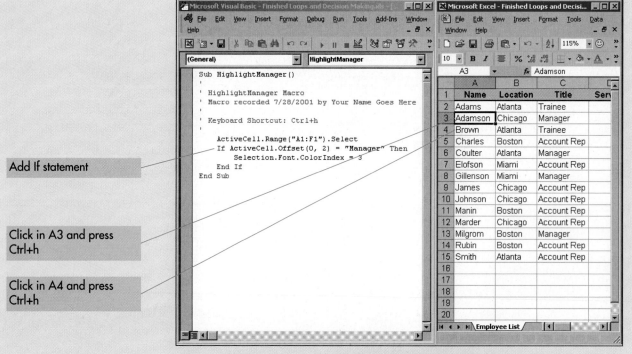

(e) Add the If Statement (step 5)

FIGURE 8.10 *Hands-on Exercise 5 (continued)*

INDENT

Indentation does not affect the execution of a macro. It, does, however, make the macro easier to read, and we suggest you follow common conventions in developing your macros. Indent the conditional statements associated with an If statement by a consistent amount. Place the End If statement on a line by itself, directly under the associated If.

Step 6: **An Endless Loop**

➤ Click in the window containing the **HighlightManager** macro. Add the **Do Until** and **Loop** statements exactly as they appear in Figure 8.10f. Indent the other statements as shown in the figure.

➤ Click **cell A3** of the worksheet. Press **Ctrl+h** to execute the macro. Cells A3 through F3 will be displayed in red, but the macro continues to execute indefinitely as it applies color to the same record over and over.

➤ Press **Ctrl+Break** to cease execution of the macro. You will see the dialog box in Figure 8.10f, indicating that an error has been encountered during the execution of the macro. Click the **End button**.

➤ Pull down the **Debug menu** and click the **Step Into command** (or press the **F8 key**) to enter the macro. The first statement is highlighted in yellow.

➤ Press the **F8 key** several times to execute the next several steps. You will see that the macro is stuck in a loop as the If statement is executed indefinitely.

➤ Click the **Reset button** in the Visual Basic window to end the debugging.

Reset button

Add Do statement and Loop

Click End button

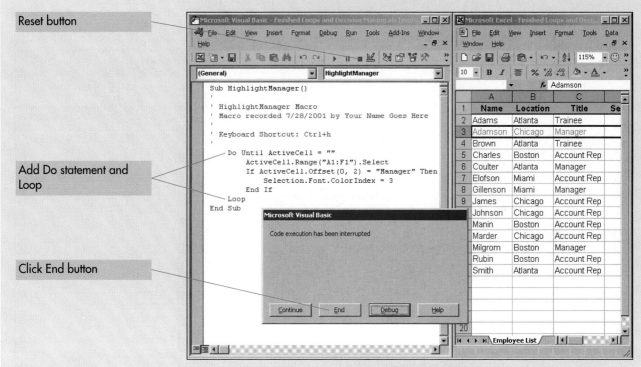

(f) An Endless Loop (step 6)

FIGURE 8.10 *Hands-on Exercise 5 (continued)*

AN ENDLESS LOOP

The glossary in the Programmer's Guide for a popular database contains the following definitions "Endless loop"—See loop, endless and "Loop, endless"—See endless loop.

We don't know whether these entries were deliberate or not, but the point is made either way. Endless loops are a common and frustrating bug. Press Ctrl+Break to halt execution, then click the Debug command button to step through the macro and locate the source of the error.

Step 7: **The Completed Macro**

➤ Click in **cell A2** of the worksheet. Click in the **Name Box**. Enter **FirstEmployee** to name this cell. Press **enter**.

➤ Click in the window containing the macro. Click after the last comment and press **enter** to insert a blank line.

➤ Add the statement to select the cell named FirstEmployee as shown in Figure 8.10g. This ensures that the macro always begins in row two by selecting the cell named FirstEmployee.

➤ Click immediately after the End If statement. Press **enter**. Add the statement containing the offset (1,0) as shown in Figure 8.10g, which selects the cell one row below the current row.

➤ Click anywhere in the worksheet except cell A2. Press **Ctrl+c** to clear the color. Press **Ctrl+h** to execute the HighlightManager macro.

➤ The macro begins by selecting cell A2, then proceeds to highlight all managers in red. Save the workbook a final time.

➤ Print the workbook and its macro for your instructor. Exit Excel.

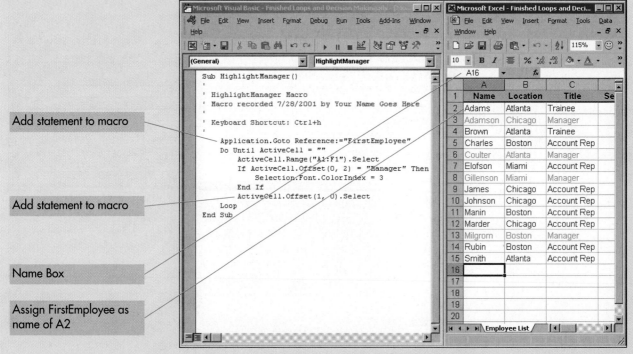

(g) The Completed Macro (step 7)

FIGURE 8.10 *Hands-on Exercise 5 (continued)*

HELP FOR VISUAL BASIC

Click within any Visual Basic key word, then press the F1 key for context-sensitive help. You will see a help screen containing a description of the statement, its syntax, key elements, and several examples. You can print the help screen by clicking the Options command button and selecting Print Topic. (If you do not see the help screens, ask your instructor to install Visual Basic Help.)

A macro is a set of instructions that automates a repetitive task. It is, in essence, a program, and its instructions are written in Visual Basic, a programming language. The macro recorder in Excel records your commands and writes the macro for you. Once a macro has been created, it can be edited by manually inserting, deleting, or changing its statements.

Macros are stored in one of two places, either in the current workbook or in a Personal Macro workbook. Macros that are specific to a particular workbook should be stored in that workbook. Generic macros that can be used with any workbook should be stored in the Personal Macro workbook.

A macro is run (executed) by pulling down the Tools menu and selecting the Run Macro command. A macro can also be executed through a keyboard shortcut, by placing a button on the worksheet, or by customizing a toolbar to include an additional button to run the macro.

A comment is a nonexecutable statement that begins with an apostrophe. Comments are inserted automatically at the beginning of a macro by the macro recorder to remind you of what the macro does. Comments may be added, deleted, or modified, just as any other statement.

A macro begins and ends with the Sub and End Sub statements, respectively. The Sub statement contains the name of the macro or VBA procedure.

The With statement enables you to perform multiple actions on the same object. All commands between the With and corresponding End With statements are executed collectively.

A macro contains either absolute or relative references. An absolute reference is constant; that is, Excel keeps track of the exact cell address and selects that specific cell. A relative reference depends on the previously selected cell, and is entered as an offset, or number of rows and columns from the current cell. The Relative Reference button on the Stop Recording toolbar toggles between the two.

An Excel macro can be made more powerful through inclusion of Visual Basic statements that enable true programming. These include the MsgBox statement to display information, the InputBox function to obtain user input, the If statement to implement decision making, and the Do statement to implement a loop. The macro recorder creates the initial macro by translating Excel commands to Visual Basic statements. The additional VBA statements are added to the resulting code using the Visual Basic Editor.

KEY TERMS

Absolute reference (p. 379)
Button tool (p. 396)
Code window (p. 368)
Comment (p. 368)
Debugging (p. 415)
Do statement (p. 411)
End If statement (p. 410)
End Sub statement (p. 368)
End With statement (p. 369)
If statement (p. 410)
InputBox function (p. 380)

Insert Name command (p. 391)
Keyboard shortcut (p. 368)
Loop (p. 410)
Macro (p. 367)
Macro recorder (p. 368)
MsgBox statement (p. 398)
Name box (p. 392)
Named range (p. 389)
Offset (p. 379)
Personal Macro workbook (p. 380)
Project Explorer (p. 368)

Relative reference (p. 379)
Shortcut key (p. 368)
Step Into command (p. 377)
Sub statement (p. 368)
Visual Basic (p. 368)
Visual Basic Editor (VBE) (p. 368)
Visual Basic for Applications (VBA) (p. 368)
With statement (p. 369)

1. Which of the following best describes recording and executing a macro?
   (a) A macro is recorded once and executed once
   (b) A macro is recorded once and executed many times
   (c) A macro is recorded many times and executed once
   (d) A macro is recorded many times and executed many times

2. Which of the following can be used to execute a macro?
   (a) A keyboard shortcut
   (b) A customized toolbar button
   (c) Both (a) and (b)
   (d) Neither (a) nor (b)

3. A macro can be stored:
   (a) In any Excel workbook
   (b) In the Personal Macro workbook
   (c) Both (a) and (b)
   (d) Neither (a) nor (b)

4. Which of the following is true regarding comments in Visual Basic?
   (a) A comment is executable; that is, its inclusion or omission affects the outcome of a macro
   (b) A comment begins with an apostrophe
   (c) Both (a) and (b)
   (d) Neither (a) nor (b)

5. Which statement must contain the name of the macro?
   (a) The Sub statement at the beginning of the macro
   (b) The first comment statement
   (c) Both (a) and (b)
   (d) Neither (a) nor (b)

6. Which of the following indicates an absolute reference within a macro?
   (a) ActiveCell.Offset(1,1).Range("A1")
   (b) $A$1
   (c) Range("A1")
   (d) All of the above

7. The statement Selection.Offset (1,0).Range ("A1").Select will select the cell:
   (a) In the same column as the active cell but one row below
   (b) In the same row as the active cell but one column to the right
   (c) In the same column as the active cell but one row above
   (d) In the same row as the active cell but one column to the left

8. The statement Selection.Offset (1,1).Range ("A1").Select will select the cell:
   (a) One cell below and one cell to the left of the active cell
   (b) One cell below and one cell to the right of the active cell
   (c) One cell above and one cell to the right of the active cell
   (d) One cell above and one cell to the left of the active cell

9. The statement Selection.Offset (1,1).Range ("A1:A2").Select will select:
   (a) Cell A1
   (b) Cell A2
   (c) Both (a) and (b)
   (d) Neither (a) nor (b)

10. Which commands are used to duplicate an existing macro so that it can become the basis of a new macro?
(a) Copy command
(b) Paste command
(c) Both (a) and (b)
(d) Neither (a) nor (b)

11. Which of the following is used to protect a macro from the subsequent insertion or deletion of rows or columns in the associated worksheet?
(a) Range names
(b) Absolute references
(c) Both (a) and (b)
(d) Neither (a) nor (b)

12. Which of the following is true regarding a customized button that has been inserted as an object onto a worksheet and assigned to an Excel macro?
(a) Point to the customized button, then click the left mouse button to execute the associated macro
(b) Point to the customized button, then click the right mouse button to select the macro button and simultaneously display a shortcut menu
(c) Point to the customized button, then press and hold the Ctrl key as you click the left mouse to select the button
(d) All of the above

13. The InputBox function:
(a) Displays a message (prompt) requesting input from the user
(b) Stores the user's response in a designated cell
(c) Both (a) and (b)
(d) Neither (a) nor (b)

14. You want to create a macro to enter your name into a specific cell. The best way to do this is to:
(a) Select the cell for your name, turn on the macro recorder with absolute references, then type your name
(b) Turn on the macro recorder with absolute references, select the cell for your name, then type your name
(c) Either (a) or (b)
(d) Neither (a) nor (b)

15. You want to create a macro to enter your name in the active cell (which will vary whenever the macro is used) and the course you are taking in the cell immediately below. The best way to do this is to:
(a) Select the cell for your name, turn on the macro recorder with absolute references, type your name, press the down arrow, and type the course
(b) Turn on the macro recorder with absolute references, select the cell for your name, type your name, press the down arrow, and type the course
(c) Select the cell for your name, turn on the macro recorder with relative references, type your name, press the down arrow, and type the course
(d) Turn on the macro recorder with relative references, select the cell for your name, type your name, press the down arrow, and type the course

ANSWERS

1. b	**6.** c	**11.** a
2. c	**7.** a	**12.** d
3. c	**8.** b	**13.** c
4. b	**9.** d	**14.** b
5. a	**10.** c	**15.** c

BUILDS ON

HANDS-ON
EXERCISE 4
PAGES 399–409

1. **Data Management Macros:** Figure 8.11 displays an alternate version of the Finished Employee List workbook that was used in the third and fourth hands-on exercises. The existing macros have been deleted and replaced by the five macros represented by the command buttons in the figure. Your assignment is to create the indicated macros and assign the macros to the command buttons. The purpose of each macro should be apparent from the name of the command button.

   a. You can "cut and paste" macros from the Finished Employee workbook as it existed at the end of the fourth hands-on exercise, or you can create the macros from scratch using the *Chapter 8 Practice 1* workbook (which contains the equivalent workbook from the beginning of hands-on exercise 3). Choose whichever technique you think is easier. You will need to use the Insert Name Create command to assign names to various cells in the worksheet for use in your macros.

   b. The All Employees macro should clear the criteria row to display all employees within the list, as well as statistics for all employees toward the bottom of the worksheet. The other four macros prompt the user for the specific criteria. Note that the user can include relational operators for service or salary, such as >60000 to display employees with salaries greater than $60,000. All of the macros should include the same MsgBox statement to display the indicated message in Figure 8.11.

   c. Run the AnySalary macro, then print the workbook as it appears in Figure 8.11. Print the worksheet with row and column headings and be sure that it fits on a single sheet of paper. Be sure to change the properties of the command buttons so that the buttons appear on the printed worksheet.

   d. Change to the Visual Basic Editor, pull down the File menu, click the Print command, then print the current project to print all of the modules (macros) within your workbook.

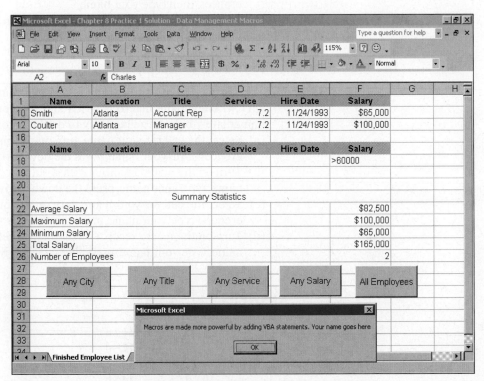

FIGURE 8.11 *Data Management Macros (Exercise 1)*

BUILDS ON

PRACTICE
EXERCISE 1
PAGE 422

2. Employee Selection: Figure 8.12 extends the previous problem to include one additional macro that prompts the user for city, title, service, and salary. The user enters all four parameters, then the macro displays the selected records within the list together with the summary statistics. Since you are specifying multiple criteria, however, it is quite possible that no employees will meet all the criteria, in which case the macro should display a message to that effect as shown in the figure. (This requires an If statement within the macro as explained in part d below.)

a. Your assignment is to complete the previous problem, then add the additional macro to prompt for the multiple criteria. The macro will always ask the user for all four parameters, but you need not enter every parameter. If, for example, you do not specify a city, the macro will return matching employees regardless of the city. Leaving all four parameters blank is equivalent to creating a blank criteria row, which in turn will display all employees.

b. You can include relational operators in the service and/or salary fields as shown in Figure 8.12. The figure is searching for Chicago Account reps, with less than eight years of service, earning more than $60,000.

c. The DAVERAGE function displays a division by zero error message, if there are no employees that meet the specified criteria. You can suppress the error message, however, by using an If statement that tests whether the number of qualified employees (the entry in cell F26) is equal to zero.

d. You need to include an If statement in your macro that tests whether the number of qualified employees is equal to zero, and if so, it should display the associated message box. It's easy to do. Use the Insert Name command within the Excel workbook to assign the name "QualifiedEmployees" to cell F26. Then insert a statement in the macro to go to this cell, which makes it the active cell. The If statement can then compare the value of the active cell to zero, and if it is zero, use the MsgBox statement to display the indicated message.

e. Print the worksheet in Figure 8.12 for your instructor. (The dialog box will not appear on your printout.) Print the module containing the macro you just developed.

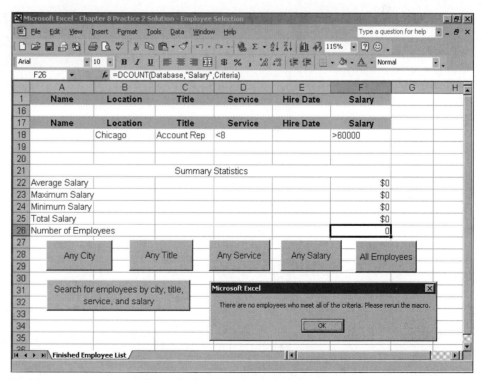

FIGURE 8.12   *Employee Selection (Exercise 2)*

3. Highlighting Employees: Figure 8.13 extends the Loops and Decision workbook from the fifth hands-on exercise to include command buttons and an additional macro. The new macro highlights the Atlanta and Chicago employees in red and blue, respectively.

a. Open the Finished Loops and Decision Making workbook from the fifth hands-on exercise. Start the Visual Basic Editor, then copy the existing HighlightManager macro so that you can use it as the basis of the new macro to highlight the employees in two locations. (You will have to change the name of the copied macro.) You will have to change the offset in the If statement to (0, 1) to reference the location column within the list, and further to compare that value to "Atlanta," as opposed to "Manager."

b. Switch to the Excel workbook, pull down the Tools menu, select the Macro command, click Macros, select the new macro, click Options, then assign a keyboard shortcut. (We used Ctrl+a). Press Ctrl+c to execute the ClearColor macro, then press Ctrl+a to test the newly created macro. The Atlanta employees should be highlighted in red.

c. Return to the VBA editor and insert the ElseIf clause immediately above the existing EndIF clause. The ElseIf should compare the value of the active cell with the appropriate offset to "Chicago," and if that condition is true, assign the selection to the appropriate color. Test the new macro.

d. Add command buttons to the worksheet as shown in Figure 8.13, then test the macros to be sure that they work properly. You should discover that the macros require one subtle adjustment; that is, if you run the Chicago and Atlanta macro, followed immediately by the Manager macro (or vice versa), employees from both macros will be highlighted. In other words, you need to run the Clear Color macro prior to running the other two. *You can make this happen automatically by including ClearColor (the name of the macro you want to run) as the first statement in the other two macros.*

e. Print the completed worksheet for your instructor. Be sure to change the properties of the command buttons so that they print with the worksheet. Print the module containing the code for all three macros.

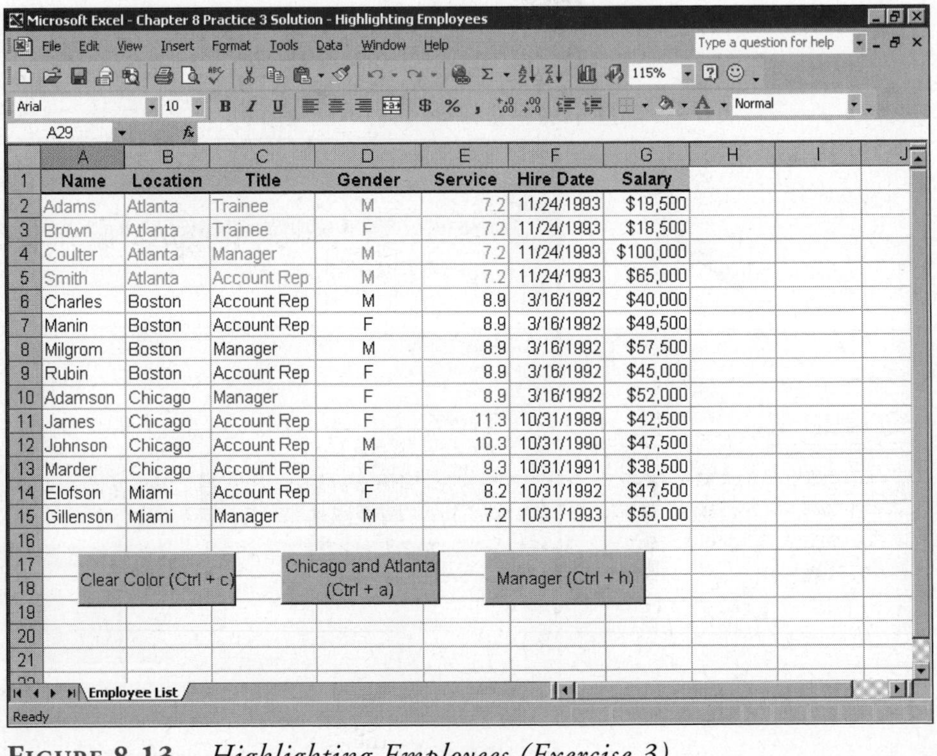

FIGURE 8.13 *Highlighting Employees (Exercise 3)*

4. Student List: The worksheet in Figure 8.14 contains multiple macros that are created for the workbook, *Chapter 8 Practice 4,* in the Exploring Excel folder. Figure 8.14 displays the worksheet after execution of the macro, Any Major – Any Year, which prompts the user for these values (Engineering and Freshman in our figure), then displays the selected students and summary statistics. The function of the remaining macros should be apparent from the associated command buttons.

a. Open the *Chapter 8 Practice 4* workbook and create the indicated macros following the techniques that were discussed in the chapter. You will find it easiest to create the first macro, then copy that macro repeatedly to create the remaining macros. Every macro should end by displaying the message box in Figure 8.14.

b. Print the completed worksheet for at least two different sets of students—for example, engineering students who are freshmen1 and business students who are seniors. Be sure to change the properties of the command buttons so that they print with the worksheet.

c. Print the module containing all of the VBA procedures. Add a cover sheet to complete the assignment.

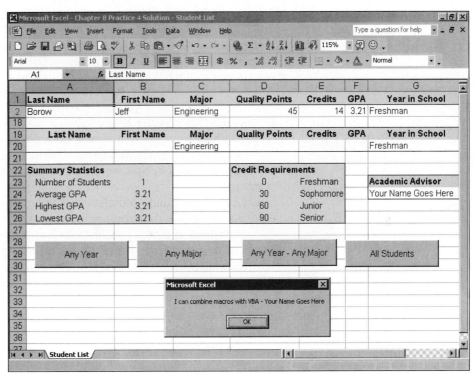

FIGURE 8.14 *Student List (Exercise 4)*

BUILDS ON

CHAPTER 7
PRACTICE
EXERCISE 1
PAGE 357

5. Election Macros: Election 2000 has come and gone, but it will be studied for years to come. Open the completed election workbook from the previous chapter (based on the workbook in *Chapter 7 Practice 1*) and add the macros shown in Figure 8.15. Each macro rearranges the states within the workbook according to the name on the corresponding button. The purpose of each macro should be evident from the name of its button.

a. Print the completed worksheet in at least two different sequences—for example, by the smallest and largest vote differential. Be sure to change the properties of the command buttons so that they print with the worksheet.

b. Print the VBA module containing all of the procedures. Add a cover sheet to complete the assignment.

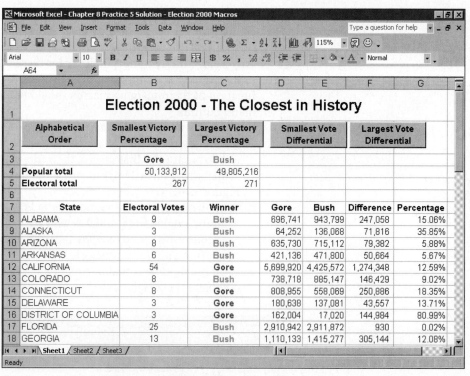

FIGURE 8.15 *Election Macros (Exercise 5)*

BUILDS ON

CHAPTER 5
PRACTICE
EXERCISE 5
PAGE 257

6. Stock Portfolio: Figure 8.16 displays a worksheet that uses macros in conjunction with Web queries to update a stock portfolio. You have seen this worksheet before, most recently in Chapter 5 when we studied worksheet references within a workbook. Now we complete the example through the introduction of macros.

a. Open the partially completed *Chapter 8 Practice 6* workbook and click the worksheet tab that contains your portfolio. The macros are already in the worksheet, and all you have to do is click the appropriate command buttons. The macro to enter your investments will prompt you for three investments for which you need to enter the company symbol, number of shares, and purchase price. This macro will also copy the stock symbols you have entered to the end of the stock symbol table in the Stock Prices worksheet.

b. Click the command button to Update Your Portfolio, which in turn will execute the Web query to retrieve the current price of your investments and automatically calculate the value of your portfolio. The worksheet is password protected to prevent you from accidentally changing any of the formulas that have been entered. (The password is "password", in lowercase letters so you can remove the protection if you like.)

c. After you have updated your portfolio, click the button to View Summary to take you to the summary worksheet. The macros for that worksheet have not been created, however, so it is up to you to create the macros and assign them to the indicated command buttons. The Update Prices macro refreshes the Web query in the Stock Prices worksheet. (It is similar to the Update Your Portfolio macro except that it returns to the Summary worksheet.) The Best Investors and Worst Investors list the portfolios in descending and ascending order according to the percentage gain or loss.

d. Print the Summary worksheet for your instructor as well as the worksheet that contains your portfolio. Print the module(s) containing all of the macros within the worksheet. Add a short note explaining the purpose of the various modules that were originally in the workbook.

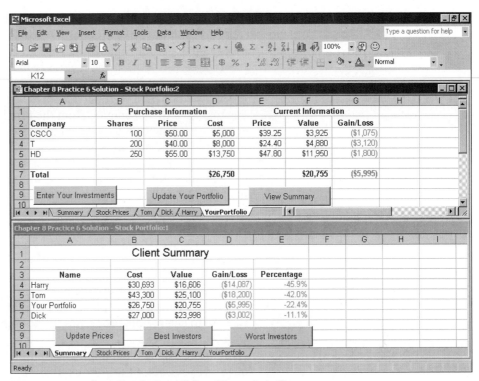

FIGURE 8.16 *Stock Portfolio (Exercise 6)*

7. Additional Practice: Figure 8.17 displays a worksheet containing hypothetical data for a series of consumer loans. The worksheet contains two macros, one to select loans by type and date, and a second macro to display all loans. The summary statistics beginning in row 31 reflect the loan records that appear in the filtered list. Your assignment is to open the workbook in *Chapter 8 Practice 7* to implement the indicated macros. You do not have to print the worksheet at this time if you continue with the next exercise.

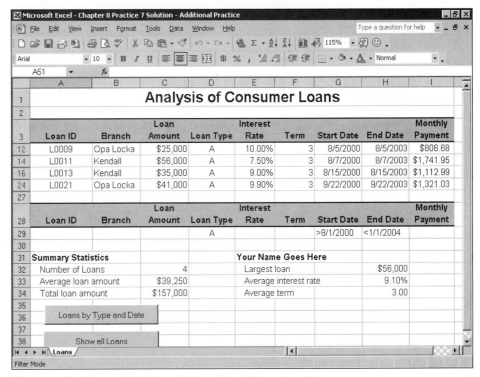

FIGURE 8.17 *Additional Practice (Exercise 7)*

BUILDS ON

PRACTICE
EXERCISE 7
PAGE 427

8. Highlight Mortgages: Figure 8.18 expands the workbook from the previous exercise to contain two additional macros, one to highlight all mortgages and the second to clear the highlighted color. Note, too, that the macro to highlight the mortgages also changes the criteria so that the summary statistics will reflect the highlighted records.

a. Open the completed workbook from the previous exercise, then add the new macros, using the techniques from the fifth hands-on exercise in the chapter. Assign each macro to its own command button. Be sure that buttons are of uniform size and appearance.

b. The assignment is not difficult, but you will need to make the macros work in conjunction with one another. You will not be able to see the highlighted mortgage records, for example, unless the macro to show all loans is run prior to highlighting the mortgages. You can execute one macro from inside another macro simply by adding a statement with the name of the macro you want to execute. In other words, add ShowAllLoans at the beginning of the HighlightMortgages, where ShowAllLoans is the name of the macro to display all of the loan records. In similar fashion, the ShowAllLoans macro should execute the ClearColor macro.

c. Print the completed worksheet with gridlines and row and column headings. Be sure to change the properties of the command buttons so that they print with the worksheet.

d. Print the module(s) containing the four macros. Add a cover sheet, then submit all of your output to your instructor.

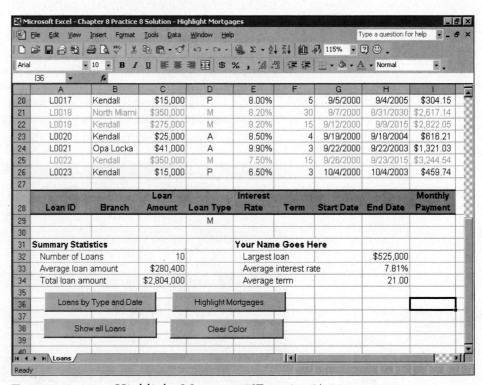

FIGURE 8.18   *Highlight Mortgages (Exercise 8)*

9. **A Look Ahead:** Figure 8.19 extends the previous exercise to include a procedure to highlight any loan, as opposed to highlighting only mortgages. The VBA code for that procedure is shown in the figure. Your job is to complete the previous hands-on exercise, delete the macro (and associated command button) for the HighlightMortgages macro, then substitute the new macro in its place. The VBA statements within the new procedure parallel those of its predecessor, but introduce some new material in Visual Basic. There are several comments within the macro to explain these statements, with additional explanation added below. Use the VBA primer that appears at the end of the Excel chapters in this text as a reference.

a. The most important concept is that of a variable to store information received from the user. The Dim statement near the beginning of the procedure assigns a name to the variable (strLoanType) and indicates that it will hold text (i.e., the variable is declared to be a character string). The subsequent Input Box statement prompts the user for the loan type, then stores that value in the strLoanType variable.

b. The If statement within the loop to highlight the selected records compares the loan type to the uppercase value of the strLoanType variable. This is important because if the user inadvertently enters a lowercase letter, the comparison would fail.

c. The MsgBox statement at the end of the procedure includes two additional parameters. The vbInformation variable indicates the type of icon that is supposed to appear within the message box. The underscore is there to show that the statement is continued to the next line, which in turn contains the text that will appear in the title bar of the message box.

d. Enter the procedure as it appears in Figure 8.19. Assign a command button to the macro within the worksheet, then test the macro.

e. Print the VBA module containing all of the procedures. Add a cover sheet to complete the assignment.

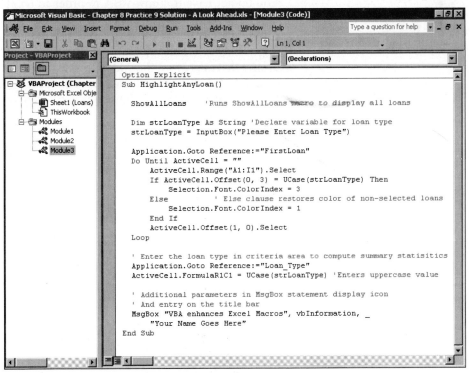

FIGURE 8.19 *A Look Ahead (Exercise 9)*

Microsoft Word

Do you use Microsoft Word on a regular basis? Are there certain tasks that you do repeatedly, whether in the same document or in a series of different documents? If so, you would do well to explore the macro capabilities within Microsoft Word. How are these capabilities similar to Excel's? How do they differ?

Starting Up

Your instructor is very impressed with the Excel workbook and associated macros that you have created. He would like you to take the automation process one step further and simplify the way in which Excel is started and the workbook is loaded. The problem is open ended, and there are many different approaches. You might, for example, create a shortcut on the desktop to open the workbook. You might also explore the use of the Startup folder in Microsoft Excel.

Antivirus Programs

What is an antivirus program and how do you get one? How do these programs supplement the macro virus protection that is built into Microsoft Excel? Use your favorite search engine to find two such programs, then summarize their capability and cost in a short note to your instructor. You can also visit the National Computer Security Association (www.ncsa.com) and the Computer Emergency Response Team (www.cert.org) to learn more about computer security.

Extending Excel Macros through VBA

You do not have to know VBA in order to create Excel macros, but knowledge of VBA will help you to create better macros. VBA is accessible from all major applications in Microsoft Office, so that anything you learn in one application is also applicable to other applications. The VBA syntax is identical. Locate the VBA primer that appears at the end of this text, study the basic statements it contains, and complete the associated hands-on exercises. Write a short note to your instructor that describes similarities and differences from one Office application to the next.

APPENDIX *A*

Toolbars

Microsoft Excel has 27 predefined toolbars that provide access to commonly used commands. The toolbars are displayed in Figure A.1 and are listed here for convenience. They are the Standard, Formatting, 3-D Settings, Borders, Chart, Circular Reference, Control Toolbox, Diagram, Drawing, Drawing Canvas, Exit Design Mode, External Data, Forms, Formula Auditing, Full Screen, Organization Chart, Picture, Pivot Table, Protection, Reviewing, Shadow Settings, Stop Recording, Text to Speech, Visual Basic, Watch Window, Web, and WordArt. The menu bar is also considered a toolbar.

The Standard and Formatting toolbars are displayed by default and appear on the same row immediately below the menu bar. The other predefined toolbars are displayed (hidden) at the discretion of the user, and in some cases are displayed automatically when their corresponding features are in use (e.g., the Chart toolbar and the Pivot Table toolbar).

The buttons on the toolbars are intended to indicate their functions. Clicking the Printer button (the fifth button from the left on the Standard toolbar), for example, executes the Print command. If you are unsure of any toolbar button, point to it, and a ScreenTip will appear that displays its name. You can display multiple toolbars, move them to new locations on the screen, customize their appearance, or suppress their display.

■ To separate the Standard and Formatting toolbars and simultaneously display all of the buttons for each toolbar, pull down the Tools menu, click the Customize command, click the Options tab, then clear the check box that has the toolbars share one row. Alternatively, the toolbars appear on the same row, so that only a limited number of buttons are visible on each toolbar and hence you may need to click the double arrow (More Buttons) tool at the end of the toolbar to view additional buttons. Additional buttons will be added to either toolbar as you use the associated feature, and conversely, buttons will be removed from the toolbar if the feature is not used.

■ To display or hide a toolbar, pull down the View menu and click the Toolbars command. Select (deselect) the toolbar(s) that you want to display (hide). The selected toolbar(s) will be displayed in the same position as when last

431

displayed. You may also point to any toolbar and click with the right mouse button to bring up a shortcut menu, after which you can select the toolbar to be displayed (hidden).

■ To change the size of the buttons or suppress the display of the ScreenTips, pull down the View menu, click Toolbars, and click Customize to display the Customize dialog box. If necessary, click the Options tab, then select (deselect) the appropriate check box. Alternatively, you can right click on any toolbar, click the Customize command from the context-sensitive menu, then select the appropriate check box from within the Options tab in the Customize dialog box.

■ Toolbars are either docked (along the edge of the window) or floating (in their own window). A toolbar moved to the edge of the window will dock along that edge. A toolbar moved anywhere else in the window will float in its own window. Docked toolbars are one tool wide (high), whereas floating toolbars can be resized by clicking and dragging a border or corner.
  • To move a docked toolbar, click anywhere in the gray background area and drag the toolbar to its new location. You can also click and drag the move handle (the vertical line) at the left of the toolbar.
  • To move a floating toolbar, drag its title bar to its new location.

■ To customize one or more toolbars, display the toolbar(s) on the screen. Then pull down the View menu, click Toolbars, and click Customize to display the Customize dialog box. Alternatively, you can click on any toolbar with the right mouse button and select Customize from the shortcut menu.
  • To move a button, drag the button to its new location on that toolbar or any other displayed toolbar.
  • To copy a button, press the Ctrl key as you drag the button to its new location on that toolbar or any other displayed toolbar.
  • To delete a button, drag the button off the toolbar and release the mouse.
  • To add a button, click the Commands tab in the Customize dialog box, select from the Categories list box the category that contains the button you want to add, then drag the button to the desired location on the toolbar. (To see a description of a tool's function prior to adding it to a toolbar, select the tool, then click the Description command button.)
  • To restore a predefined toolbar to its default appearance, click the Toolbars tab, select the desired toolbar, and click the Reset command button.

■ Buttons can also be moved, copied, or deleted without displaying the Customize dialog box.
  • To move a button, press the Alt key as you drag the button to the new location.
  • To copy a button, press the Alt and Ctrl keys as you drag the button.
  • To delete a button, press the Alt key as you drag the button off the toolbar.

■ To create your own toolbar, pull down the View menu, click Toolbars, click Customize, click the Toolbars tab, then click the New command button. Alternatively, you can click on any toolbar with the right mouse button, select Customize from the shortcut menu, click the Toolbars tab, and then click the New command button.
  • Enter a name for the toolbar in the dialog box that follows. The name can be any length and can contain spaces. Click OK.
  • The new toolbar will appear on the screen. Initially it will be big enough to hold only one button. Add, move, and delete buttons following the same procedures as outlined above. The toolbar will automatically size itself as new buttons are added and deleted.
  • To delete a custom toolbar, pull down the View menu, click Toolbars, click Customize, and click the Toolbars tab. *Verify that the custom toolbar to be deleted is the only one selected (highlighted).* Click the Delete command button. Click OK to confirm the deletion. (Note that a predefined toolbar cannot be deleted.)

MICROSOFT EXCEL 2002 TOOLBARS

Standard Toolbar

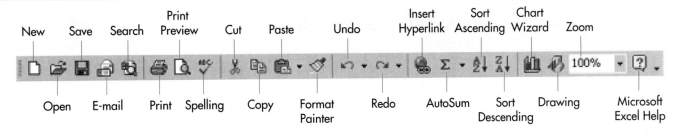

New — Open — Save — E-mail — Search — Print — Print Preview — Spelling — Cut — Copy — Paste — Format Painter — Undo — Redo — Insert Hyperlink — AutoSum — Sort Ascending — Sort Descending — Chart Wizard — Drawing — Zoom — Microsoft Excel Help

Formatting Toolbar

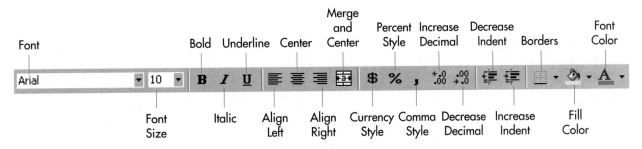

Font — Font Size — Bold — Italic — Underline — Center — Align Left — Align Right — Merge and Center — Percent Style — Currency Style — Comma Style — Increase Decimal — Decrease Decimal — Decrease Indent — Increase Indent — Borders — Fill Color — Font Color

3-D Settings Toolbar

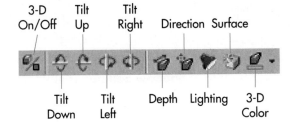

3-D On/Off — Tilt Up — Tilt Down — Tilt Right — Tilt Left — Direction — Depth — Surface — Lighting — 3-D Color

Borders Toolbar

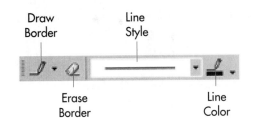

Draw Border — Erase Border — Line Style — Line Color

Chart Toolbar

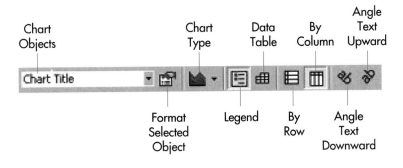

Chart Objects — Format Selected Object — Chart Type — Data Table — Legend — By Column — By Row — Angle Text Upward — Angle Text Downward

Circular Reference

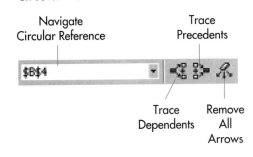

Navigate Circular Reference — Trace Precedents — Trace Dependents — Remove All Arrows

FIGURE A.1   *Toolbars*

Control Toolbox Toolbar

Design Mode • View Code • Text Box • Option Button • Combo Box • Spin Button • Label • More Controls

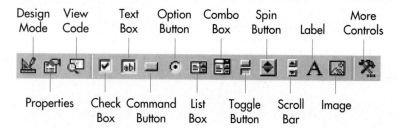

Properties • Check Box • Command Button • List Box • Toggle Button • Scroll Bar • Image

Full-Screen Toolbar

Toggle Full-Screen View

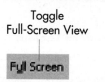

Diagram Toolbar

Insert Shape • Move Shape Forward • Layout • Change to

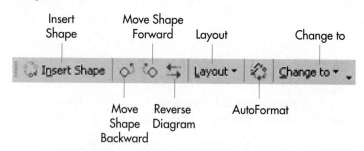

Move Shape Backward • Reverse Diagram • AutoFormat

External Data Toolbar

Edit Query • Query Parameters • Cancel Refresh • Refresh Status

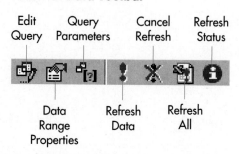

Data Range Properties • Refresh Data • Refresh All

Forms Toolbar

Label • Group Box • Check Box • List Box • Combination List-Edit • Scroll Bar • Control Properties • Toggle Grid

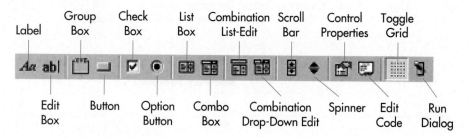

Edit Box • Button • Option Button • Combo Box • Combination Drop-Down Edit • Spinner • Edit Code • Run Dialog

Drawing Canvas Toolbar

Fit Drawing to Canvas • Scale Drawing

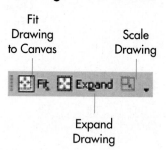

Expand Drawing

Formula Auditing Toolbar

Error Checking • Erase Precedent Arrows • Erase Dependent Arrows • Trace Error • Circle Invalid Data • Show Watch Window

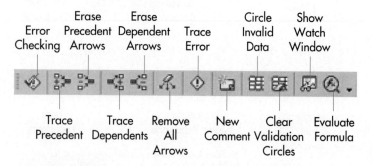

Trace Precedent • Trace Dependents • Remove All Arrows • New Comment • Clear Validation Circles • Evaluate Formula

Shadow Settings Toolbar

Shadow On/Off • Nudge Shadow Down • Nudge Shadow Right

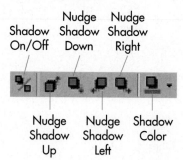

Nudge Shadow Up • Nudge Shadow Left • Shadow Color

Organization Chart Toolbar

Insert Shape • Select

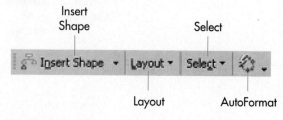

Layout • AutoFormat

Text to Speech Toolbar

Speak Cells • By Rows • Speak on Enter

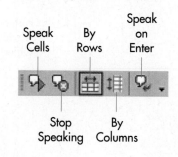

Stop Speaking • By Columns

FIGURE A.1 *Toolbars (continued)*

Drawing Toolbar

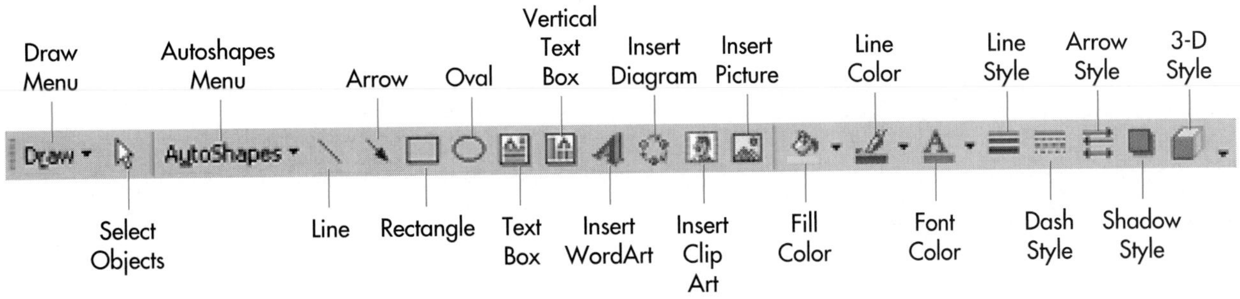
Draw Menu
Autoshapes Menu
Arrow
Oval
Vertical Text Box
Insert Diagram
Insert Picture
Line Color
Line Style
Arrow Style
3-D Style
Draw
AutoShapes
Select Objects
Line
Rectangle
Text Box
Insert WordArt
Insert Clip Art
Fill Color
Font Color
Dash Style
Shadow Style

Picture Toolbar

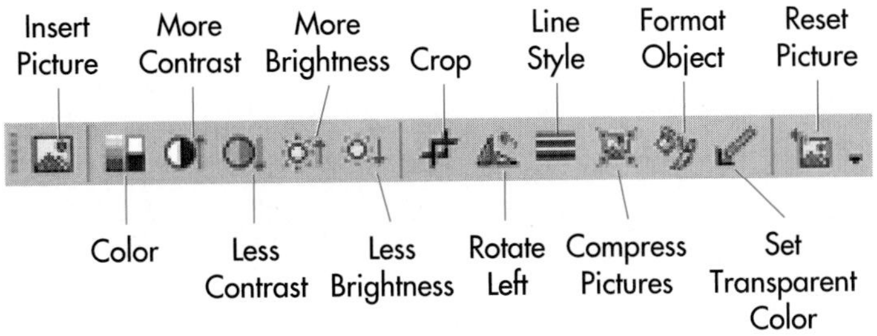
Insert Picture
More Contrast
More Brightness
Crop
Line Style
Format Object
Reset Picture
Color
Less Contrast
Less Brightness
Rotate Left
Compress Pictures
Set Transparent Color

Exit Design Mode Toolbar

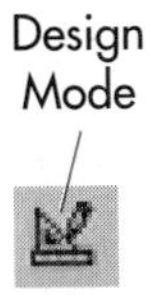
Design Mode

Pivot Table Toolbar

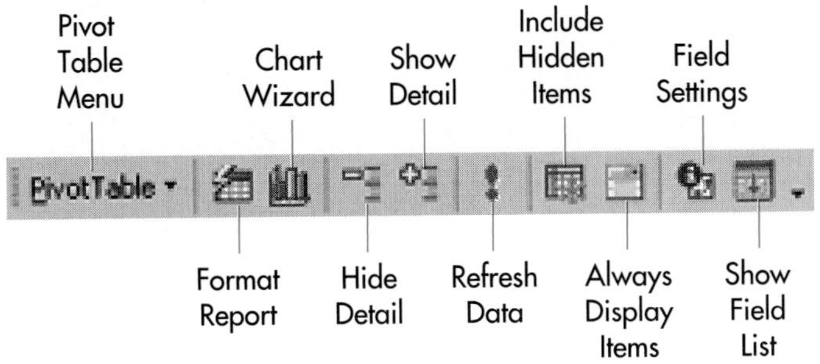
Pivot Table Menu
Chart Wizard
Show Detail
Include Hidden Items
Field Settings
PivotTable
Format Report
Hide Detail
Refresh Data
Always Display Items
Show Field List

Protection Toolbar

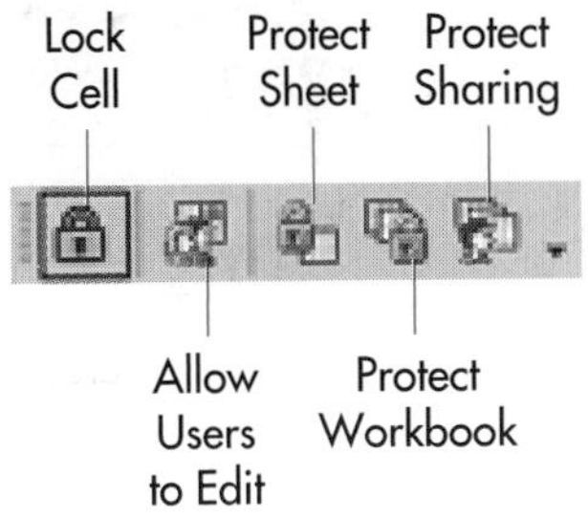
Lock Cell
Protect Sheet
Protect Sharing
Allow Users to Edit
Protect Workbook

Reviewing Toolbar

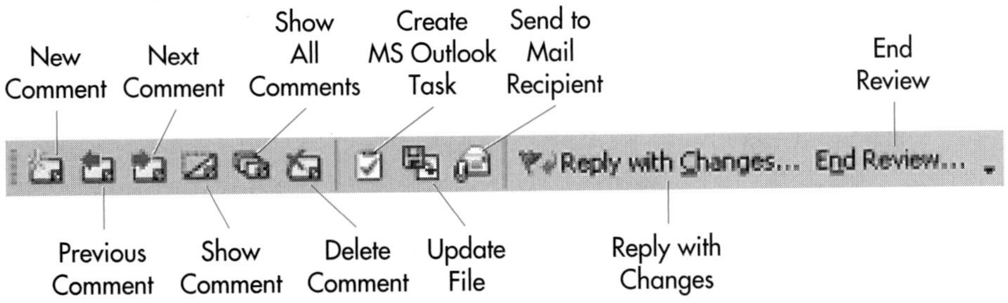
New Comment
Next Comment
Show All Comments
Create MS Outlook Task
Send to Mail Recipient
End Review
Reply with Changes...
End Review...
Previous Comment
Show Comment
Delete Comment
Update File
Reply with Changes

Stop Recording Toolbar

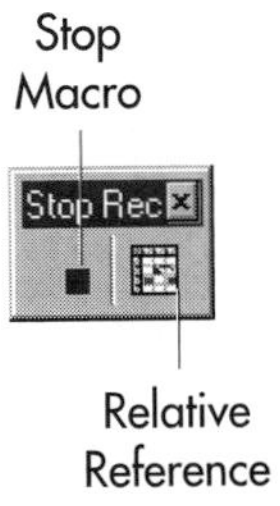
Stop Macro
Stop Rec
Relative Reference

FIGURE A.1 *(continued)*

Visual Basic Toolbar

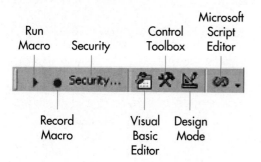

Watch Window Toolbar

Web Toolbar

WordArt Toolbar

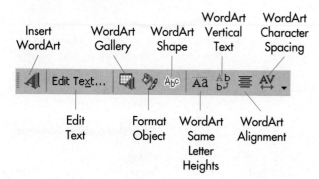

FIGURE A.1   *(continued)*

APPENDIX B

Solver: A Tool for Optimization

OVERVIEW

The use of a spreadsheet in decision making has been emphasized throughout the text. We showed you how to design a spreadsheet based on a set of initial conditions and assumptions, then see at a glance the effect of changing one or more of those values. We introduced the Scenario Manager to store sets of assumptions so that they could be easily recalled and reevaluated. We discussed the Goal Seek command, which enables you to set the value of a target cell, then determine the input needed to arrive at that target value. However, the Goal Seek command, as useful as it is, is limited to a *single* input variable. This appendix discusses **Solver**, a powerful add-in that is designed for problems involving *multiple* variables.

Solver is an optimization and resource allocation tool that helps you achieve a desired goal. You specify a goal, such as maximizing profit or minimizing cost. You indicate the constraints (conditions) that must be satisfied for the solution to be valid, and you specify the cells whose values can change to reach that goal. Solver will then determine the values for the adjustable cells (i.e., it will tell you how to allocate your resources) to reach the desired goal.

This appendix provides an introduction to Solver through two different examples. The first example shows how to maximize profit. The second example illustrates how to minimize cost. Both examples are accompanied by a hands-on exercise.

EXAMPLE 1—MAXIMIZE PROFIT

Assume that you are the production manager for a company that manufactures computers. Your company divides its product line into two basic categories—desktop computers and laptops. Each product is sold under two labels, a discount line and a premium line. As production manager you are to determine how many computers of each type, and of each product line, to make each week.

437

Your decision is subject to various constraints that must be satisfied during the production process. Each computer requires a specified number of hours for assembly. Discount and premium-brand desktops require two and three hours, respectively. Discount and premium-brand laptops use three and five hours, respectively. The factory is working at full capacity, and you have only 4,500 hours of labor to allocate among the various products.

Your production decision is also constrained by demand. The marketing department has determined that you cannot sell more than 800 desktop units, nor more than 900 laptops, per week. The total demand for the discount and premium lines is 700 and 1,000 computers, respectively, per week.

Your goal (objective) is to maximize the total profit, which is based on a different profit margin for each type of computer. A desktop and a laptop computer from the discount line have unit profits of $600 and $800, respectively. The premium desktop and laptop computers have unit profits of $1,000 and $1,300, respectively. How many computers of each type do you manufacture each week to maximize the total profit?

This is a complex problem, but one that can be easily solved provided you can design a spreadsheet that is equivalent to Figure B.1. The top half of the spreadsheet contains the information about the individual products. There are three numbers associated with each product—the quantity that will be produced, the number of hours required, and the unit profit. The bottom half of the spreadsheet contains the information about the available resources such as the total number of labor hours that are available. The spreadsheet also contains various formulas that relate the resources to the quantities that are produced. Cell E8, for example, will contain a formula that computes the total number of hours used that is based on the quantity of each computer and the associated hourly requirements.

The problem is to determine the values of cells B2 through B5, which represent the quantity of each computer to produce. You might be able to solve the problem manually through trial and error, by substituting different values and seeing the impact on profit. That is exactly what Solver will do for you, only it will do it much more quickly. (Solver uses various optimization techniques that are beyond the scope of this discussion.)

Once Solver arrives at a solution, assuming that it can find one, it creates a report such as the one shown in Figure B.2. The solution shows the value of the target cell (the profit in this example), based on the values of the adjustable cells (the quantity of each type of computer). The solution that will maximize profit is to manufacture 700 discount laptops and 800 premium desktops for a profit of $1,270,000.

The report in Figure B.2 also examines each constraint and determines whether it is binding or not binding. A **binding constraint** is one in which the resource is fully utilized (i.e., the slack is zero). The number of available hours, for example, is a binding constraint because every available hour is used, and hence the value of the target cell (profit) is limited by the amount of this resource (the number of hours). Or stated another way, any increase in the number of available hours (above 4,500) will also increase the profit.

A **nonbinding constraint** is just the opposite. It has a nonzero slack (i.e., the resource is not fully utilized), and hence it does not limit the value of the target cell. The laptop demand, for example, is not binding because a total of only 700 laptops were produced, yet the allowable demand was 900 (the value in cell E13). In other words, there is a slack value of 200 for this constraint, and increasing the allowable demand will have no effect on the profit. (The demand could actually be decreased by up to 200 units with no effect on profit.)

Need to determine values for cells B2:B5 (quantity to produce)

Will contain a formula to compute total hours

	A	B	C	D	E
1		Quantity	Hours	Unit Profit	
2	**Discount desktop**		2	$600	
3	**Discount laptop**		3	$800	
4	**Premium desktop**		3	$1,000	
5	**Premium laptop**		5	$1,300	
6					
7	Constraints				
8	Total number of hours used				
9	Labor hours available				4,500
10	Number of desktops produced				
11	Total demand for desktop computers				800
12	Number of laptops produced				
13	Total demand for laptop computers				900
14	Number of discount computers produced				
15	Total demand for discount computers				700
16	Number of premium computers produced				
17	Total demand for premium computers				1,000
18	Hourly cost of labor				$20
19	**Profit**				

FIGURE B.1 *The Initial Worksheet*

Value of target cell (E19)

Quantities to be produced (B2:B5)

Indicates whether or not constraint is binding

Target Cell (Max)

Cell	Name	Original Value	Final Value
$E$19 Profit		$0	$1,270,000

Adjustable Cells

Cell	Name	Original Value	Final Value
$B$2	Discount desktop Quantity	0	0
$B$3	Discount laptop Quantity	0	700
$B$4	Premium desktop Quantity	0	800
$B$5	Premium laptop Quantity	0	0

Constraints

Cell	Name	Cell Value	Formula	Status	Slack
$E$8	Total number of hours used	4500	$E$8<=$E$9	Binding	0
$E$10	Number of desktops produced	800	$E$10<=$E$11	Binding	0
$E$12	Number of laptops produced	700	$E$12<=$E$13	Not Binding	200
$E$14	Number of discount computers produce	700	$E$14<=$E$15	Binding	0
$E$16	Number of premium computers produce	800	$E$16<=$E$17	Not Binding	200
$B$2	Discount desktop Quantity	0	$B$2>=0	Binding	0
$B$3	Discount laptop Quantity	700	$B$3>=0	Not Binding	700
$B$4	Premium desktop Quantity	800	$B$4>=0	Not Binding	800
$B$5	Premium laptop Quantity	0	$B$5>=0	Binding	0

FIGURE B.2 *The Solution*

The information required by Solver is entered through the **Solver Parameters dialog box** as shown in Figure B.3. The dialog box is divided into three sections: the target cell, the adjustable cells, and the constraints. The dialog box in Figure B.3 corresponds to the spreadsheet shown earlier in Figure B.1.

The **target cell** identifies the goal (or objective function)—that is, the cell whose value you want to maximize, minimize, or set to a specific value. Our problem seeks to maximize profit, the formula for which is found in cell E19 (the target cell) of the underlying spreadsheet.

The **adjustable cells** (or decision variables) are the cells whose values are adjusted until the constraints are satisfied and the target cell reaches its optimum value. The changing cells in this example contain the quantity of each computer to be produced and are found in cells B2 through B5.

The **constraints** specify the restrictions. Each constraint consists of a cell or cell range on the left, a relational operator, and a numeric value or cell reference on the right. (The constraints can be entered in any order, but they always appear in alphabetical order.) The first constraint references a cell range, cells B2 through B5, and indicates that each of these cells must be greater than or equal to zero. The remaining constraints reference a single cell rather than a cell range.

The functions of the various command buttons are apparent from their names. The Add, Change, and Delete buttons are used to add, change, or delete a constraint. The Options button enables you to set various parameters that determine how Solver attempts to find a solution. The Reset All button clears all settings and resets all options to their defaults. The Solve button begins the search for a solution.

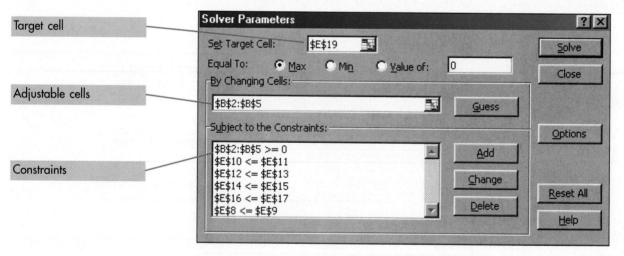

FIGURE B.3 *Solver Parameters Dialog Box*

THE GREATER-THAN-ZERO CONSTRAINT

One constraint that is often overlooked is the requirement that the value of each adjustable cell be greater than or equal to zero. Physically, it makes no sense to produce a negative number of computers in any category. Mathematically, however, a negative value in an adjustable cell may produce a higher value for the target cell. Hence the **nonnegativity** (greater than or equal to zero) **constraint** should always be included for the adjustable cells.

MAXIMIZE PROFIT

Objective To use Solver to maximize profit; to create a report containing binding and nonbinding constraints. Use Figure B.4 as a guide in the exercise.

Step 1: **Enter the Cell Formulas**

> Start Excel. Open the **Optimization workbook** in the **Exploring Excel folder**. Save the workbook as **Finished Optimization** so that you can return to the original workbook if necessary.
> If necessary, click the tab for the **Production Mix** worksheet, then click **cell E8** as shown in Figure B.4a.
> Enter the formula shown in Figure B.4a to compute the total number of hours used in production.
> Enter the remaining cell formulas as shown below:
> * Cell E10 (Number of desktops produced) **=B2+B4**
> * Cell E12 (Number of laptops produced) **=B3+B5**
> * Cell E14 (Number of discount computers produced) **=B2+B3**
> * Cell E16 (Number of premium computers produced) **=B4+B5**
> * Cell E19 (Profit) **=B2*D2+B3*D3+B4*D4+B5*D5−E18*E8**
> Save the workbook.

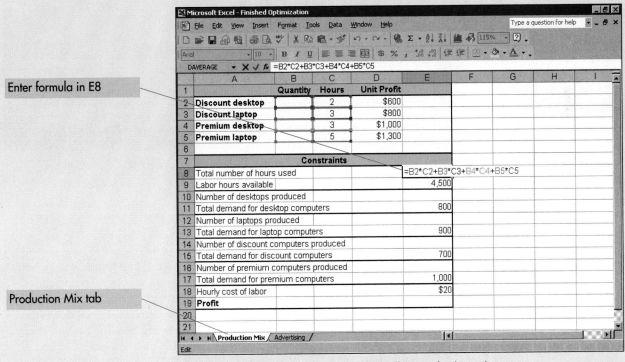

Enter formula in E8

Production Mix tab

(a) Enter the Cell Formulas (step 1)

FIGURE B.4 *Hands-on Exercise 1*

Step 2:   **Set the Target and Adjustable Cells**

➤ Check that the formula in cell E19 is entered correctly as shown in Figure B.4b. Pull down the **Tools menu**. Click **Solver** to display the Solver Parameters dialog box shown in Figure B.4b.

➤ If necessary, click in the text box for Set Target cell. Click in **cell E19** to set the target cell. The Max option button is selected by default.

➤ Click in the **By Changing Cells** text box. Click and drag **cells B2** through **B5** in the worksheet to select these cells.

➤ Click the **Add command button** to add the first constraint as described in step 3.

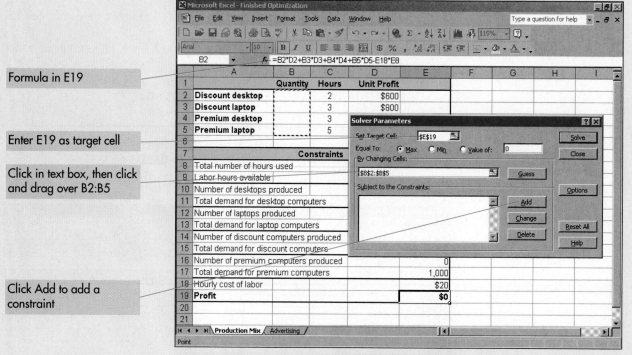

Formula in E19

Enter E19 as target cell

Click in text box, then click and drag over B2:B5

Click Add to add a constraint

(b) Set the Target and Adjustable Cells (step 2)

FIGURE B.4   *Hands-on Exercise 1 (continued)*

MISSING SOLVER

Solver is an optional component of Microsoft Excel, and hence it may not be installed on your system. If you are working on a computer at school, your instructor should be able to notify the network administrator to correct the problem. If you are working on your own machine, pull down the Tools menu, click the Add-Ins command, check the box for Solver, then click OK to close the Add-Ins dialog box. Click Yes when asked to install Solver. You will need the Microsoft Office XP CD.

Step 3: **Enter the Constraints**

➤ You should see the Add Constraint dialog box in Figure B.4c with the insertion point (a flashing vertical line) in the Cell Reference text box.
- Click in **cell E8** (the cell containing the formula to compute the total number of hours used). The <= constraint is selected by default.
- Click in the **Constraint** text box, which will contain the value of the constraint, then click **cell E9** in the worksheet to enter the cell reference.
- Click **Add** to complete this constraint and add another.

➤ You will see a new (empty) Add Constraint dialog box, which enables you to enter additional constraints. Use pointing to enter each of the constraints shown below. (Solver automatically enters each reference as an absolute reference.)
- Enter the constraint **E10<=E11**. Click **Add**.
- Enter the constraint **E12<=E13**. Click **Add**.
- Enter the constraint **E14<=E15**. Click **Add**.
- Enter the constraint **E16<=E17**. Click **Add**.

➤ Add the last constraint. Click and drag to select **cells B2** through **B5**. Click the drop-down arrow for the relational operators and click the **>=** operator. Type **0** in the text box to indicate that the production quantities for all computers must be greater than or equal to zero. Click **OK**.

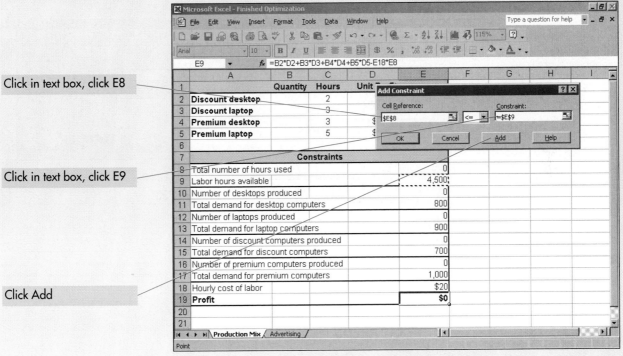

(c) Enter the Constraints (step 3)

FIGURE B.4   *Hands-on Exercise 1 (continued)*

ADD VERSUS OK

Click the Add button to complete the current constraint and display an empty dialog box to enter another constraint. Click OK only when you have completed the last constraint and want to return to the Solver Parameters dialog box to solve the problem.

Step 4: Solve the Problem

➤ Check that the contents of the Solver Parameters dialog box match those of Figure B.4d. (The constraints appear in alphabetical order rather than the order in which they were entered.)
- To change the Target cell, click the **Set Target Cell** text box, then click the appropriate target cell in the worksheet.
- To change (edit) a constraint, select the constraint, then click the **Change button**.
- To delete a constraint, select the constraint and click the **Delete button**.

➤ Click the **Solve button** to solve the problem.

➤ You should see the Solver Results dialog box, indicating that Solver has found a solution. The maximum profit is $1,270,000. The option button to Keep Solver Solution is selected by default.

➤ Click **Answer** in the Reports list box, then click **OK** to generate the report. You will see the report being generated, after which the Solver Results dialog box closes automatically.

➤ Save the workbook.

Constraints are in alphabetical order

Solve button

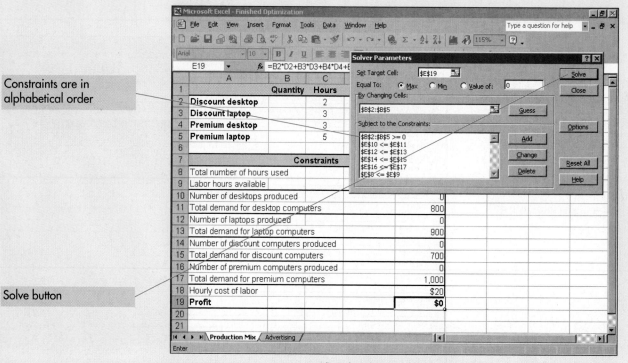

(d) Solve the Problem (step 4)

FIGURE B.4   *Hands-on Exercise 1 (continued)*

Step 5: **View the Report**

➤ Click the **Answer Report 1 worksheet tab** to view the report as shown in Figure B.4e. Click in **cell A4**, the cell immediately under the entry showing the date and time the report was created. (The gridlines and row and column headings are suppressed by default for this worksheet.)

➤ Enter your name in boldface as shown in the figure, then press **enter** to complete the entry. Print the answer sheet and submit it to your instructor as proof you did the exercise.

➤ Save the workbook. Exit Excel if you do not wish to continue with the next exercise at this time.

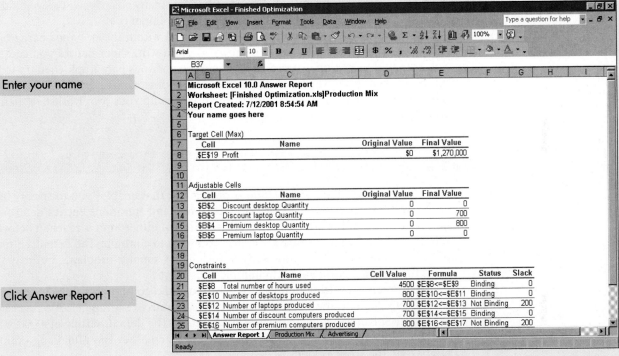

(e) View the Report (step 5)

FIGURE B.4 *Hands-on Exercise 1 (continued)*

VIEW OPTIONS

Any worksheet used to create a spreadsheet model will display gridlines and row and column headers by default. Worksheets containing reports, however, especially reports generated by Excel, often suppress these elements to make the reports easier and more appealing to read. To suppress (display) these elements, pull down the Tools menu, click Options, click the View tab, then clear (check) the appropriate check boxes under Window options.

EXAMPLE 2—MINIMIZE COST

The example just concluded introduced you to the basics of Solver. We continue now with a second hands-on exercise, to provide additional practice, and to discuss various subtleties that can occur. This time we present a minimization problem in which we seek to minimize cost subject to a series of constraints. The problem will focus on the advertising campaign that will be conducted to sell the computers you have produced.

The director of marketing has allocated a total of $125,000 in his weekly advertising budget. He wants to establish a presence in both magazines and radio, and requires a minimum of four magazine ads and ten radio ads each week. Each magazine ad costs $10,000 and is seen by one million readers. Each radio commercial costs $5,000 and is heard by 250,000 listeners. How many ads of each type should be placed to reach at least 10 million customers at minimum cost?

All of the necessary information is contained within the previous paragraph. You must, however, display that information in a worksheet before you can ask Solver to find a solution. Accordingly, reread the previous paragraph, then try to set up a worksheet from which you can call Solver. (Our worksheet appears in step 1 of the following hands-on exercise. Try, however, to set up your own worksheet before you look at ours.)

FINER POINTS OF SOLVER

Figure B.5 displays the **Solver Options dialog box** that enables you to specify how Solver will approach the solution. The Max Time and Iterations entries determine how long Solver will work on finding the solution. If either limit is reached before a solution is found, Solver will ask whether you want to continue. The default settings of 100 seconds and 100 iterations are sufficient for simpler problems, but may fall short for complex problems with multiple constraints.

The Precision setting determines how close the computed values in the constraint cells come to the specified value of the resource. The smaller the precision, the longer Solver will take in arriving at a solution. The default setting of .0000001 is adequate for most problems and should not be decreased. The remaining options are beyond the scope of our discussion.

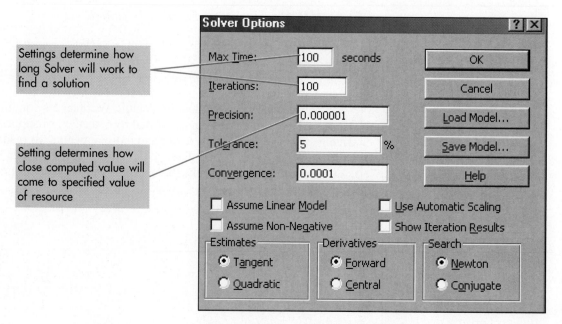

FIGURE **B.5**   *Options Dialog Box*

MINIMIZE COST

Objective To use Solver to minimize cost; to impose an integer constraint and examine its effect on the optimal solution; to relax a constraint in order to find a feasible solution. Use Figure B.6 as a guide in the exercise.

Step 1: **Enter the Cell Formulas**

➤ Open the **Finished Optimization workbook** from the previous exercise.

➤ Click the tab for the **Advertising** worksheet, then click in **cell E6**. Enter the formula **=B2*C2+B3*C3** as shown in Figure B.6a.

➤ Click in **cell E10**. Enter the formula **=B2*D2+B3*D3** to compute the size of the audience. Save the workbook.

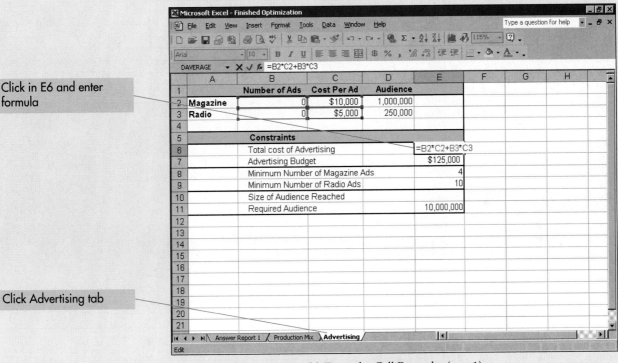

Click in E6 and enter formula

Click Advertising tab

(a) Enter the Cell Formulas (step 1)

FIGURE B.6 *Hands-on Exercise 2*

USE THE TASK PANE

The easiest way to reopen a recently used workbook is to use the task pane. Pull down the View menu and toggle the Task Pane command on so that the task pane is displayed in the right side of the application window. Click the name of the workbook in the Open a workbook area to reopen the workbook. You can also open a recently used workbook from the list that appears at the bottom of the File menu. Another way is to click the Windows Start button, click the Documents command, then click the name of the workbook when it appears in the Documents submenu.

Step 2: **Set the Target and Adjustable Cells**

➤ Pull down the **Tools menu**. Click **Solver** to display the Solver Parameters dialog box shown in Figure B.6b.

➤ Set the target cell to **cell E6**. Click the **Min (Minimize) option button**. Click in the **By Changing Cells** text box.

➤ Click and drag **cells B2** and **B3** in the worksheet to select these cells as shown in Figure B.6b.

➤ Click the **Add command button** to add the first constraint as described in step 3.

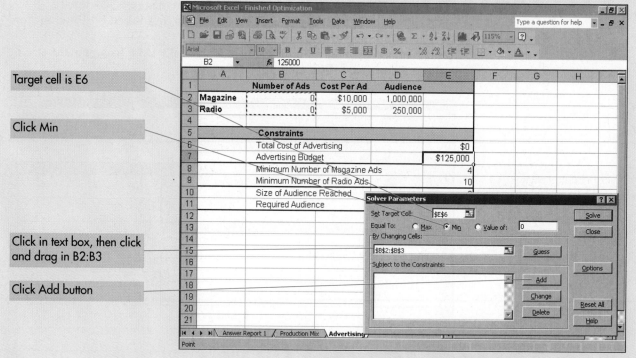

Target cell is E6

Click Min

Click in text box, then click and drag in B2:B3

Click Add button

(b) Set the Target and Adjustable Cells (step 2)

FIGURE B.6 *Hands-on Exercise 2 (continued)*

REVIEW THE TERMINOLOGY

Solver is an optimization technique that allows you to maximize or minimize the value of an objective function, such as profit or cost, respectively. The formula to compute the objective function is stored in the target cell within the worksheet. Other cells in the worksheet contain the variables or adjustable cells. Another set of cells contains the value of the available resources or constraints. This type of optimization problem is referred to as linear programming.

Step 3: **Enter the Constraints**

➤ You should see the Add Constraint dialog box in Figure B.6c with the insertion point (a flashing vertical line) in the Cell Reference text box.
  - Click in **cell E6** (the cell containing the total cost of advertising).
  - The <= constraint is selected by default.
  - Click in the text box to contain the value of the constraint, then click **cell E7** to enter the cell reference in the Add Constraint dialog box. Click **Add**.
➤ You will see a new (empty) Add Constraint dialog box, which enables you to enter additional constraints. Use pointing to enter each of the constraints shown below. (Solver converts each reference to an absolute reference.)
  - Enter the constraint **E10>=E11**. Click **Add**.
  - Enter the constraint **B2>=E8**. Click **Add**.
  - Enter the constraint **B3>=E9**. Click **OK** since this is the last constraint.

Click in text box, click in E6

Click in text box, click in E7

Click Add

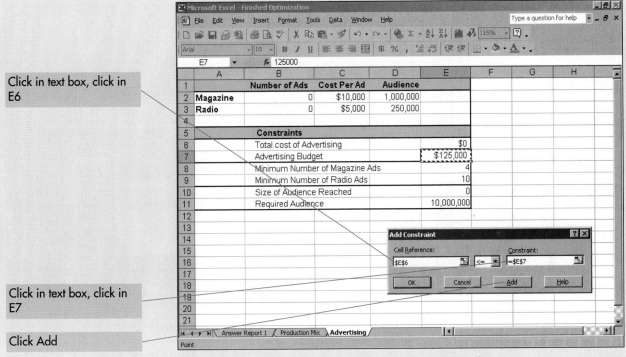

(c) Enter the Constraints (step 3)

FIGURE B.6   *Hands-on Exercise 2 (continued)*

SHOW ITERATION RESULTS

Solver uses an iterative (repetitive) approach in which each iteration (trial solution) is one step closer to the optimal solution. It may be interesting, therefore, to examine the intermediate solutions, especially if you have a knowledge of optimization techniques, such as linear programming. Click the Options command button in the Solver Parameters dialog box, check the Show Iterations Results box, click OK to close the Solver Options dialog box, then click the Solve command button in the usual fashion. A Show Trial Solutions dialog box will appear as each intermediate solution is displayed in the worksheet. Click Continue to move from one iteration to the next until the optimal solution is reached.

Step 4: **Solve the Problem**

➤ Check that the contents of the Solver Parameters dialog box match those in Figure B.6d. (The constraints appear in alphabetical order rather than the order in which they were entered.)
➤ Click the **Solve button** to solve the problem. The Solver Results dialog box appears and indicates that Solver has arrived at a solution.
➤ The option button to Keep Solver Solution is selected by default. Click **OK** to close the Solver Results dialog box and display the solution.
➤ Save the workbook.

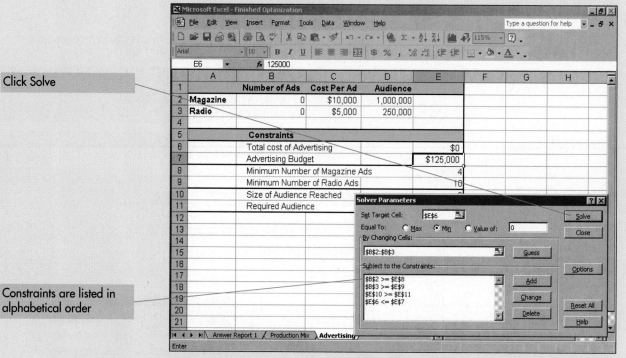

Click Solve

Constraints are listed in alphabetical order

(d) Solve the Problem (step 4)

FIGURE B.6 *Hands-on Exercise 2 (continued)*

USE POINTING TO ENTER CELL FORMULAS

A cell reference can be typed directly into a formula, or it can be entered more easily through pointing. To use pointing, select (click) the cell to contain the formula, type an equal sign to begin entering the formula, then click (or move to) the cell containing the value to be used. Type any arithmetic operator to place the cell reference into the formula, then continue pointing to additional cells. Press the enter key (instead of typing an arithmetic operator) to complete the formula.

Step 5: **Impose an Integer Constraint**

> The number of magazine ads in the solution is 7.5 as shown in Figure B.6e. This is a noninteger number, which is reasonable in the context of Solver but not in the "real world" as one cannot place half an ad.

> Pull down the **Tools menu**. Click **Solver** to once again display the Solver Parameters dialog box. Click the **Add button** to display the Add Constraint dialog box in Figure B.6e.

> The insertion point is already positioned in the Cell Reference text box. Click and drag to select **cells B2** through **B3**. Click the **drop-down arrow** in the Constraint list box and click **int** (for integer).

> Click **OK** to accept the constraint and close the Add Constraint dialog box.

> The Solver Parameters dialog box appears on your monitor with the integer constraint added. Click **Solve** to solve the problem.

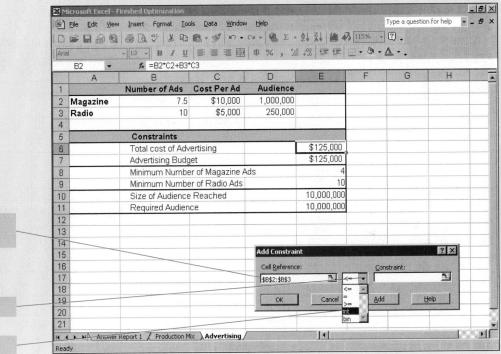

Click in box, click and drag to select B2:B3

Click drop-down arrow

Click int

(e) Impose an Integer Constraint (step 5)

FIGURE B.6 *Hands-on Exercise 2 (continued)*

DO YOU REALLY NEED AN INTEGER SOLUTION?

It seems like such a small change, but specifying an integer constraint can significantly increase the amount of time required for Solver to reach a solution. The examples in this chapter are relatively simple and did not take an inordinate amount of time to solve. Imposing an integer constraint on a more complex problem, however, especially on a slower microprocessor, may challenge your patience as Solver struggles to reach a solution.

Step 6: **The Infeasible Solution**

➤ You should see the dialog box in Figure B.6f, indicating that Solver could *not* find a solution that satisfied the existing constraints. This is because the imposition of the integer constraint would raise the number of magazine ads from 7.5 to 8, which would increase the total cost of advertising to $130,000, exceeding the budget of $125,000.

➤ The desired audience can still be reached but only by relaxing one of the binding constraints. You can, for example, retain the requisite number of magazine and radio ads by increasing the budget. Alternatively, the budget can be held at $125,000, while still reaching the audience by decreasing the required number of radio ads.

➤ Click **Cancel** to exit the dialog box and return to the worksheet.

7.5 is not an integer, and thus no solution can be reached

No solution is found

Click Cancel

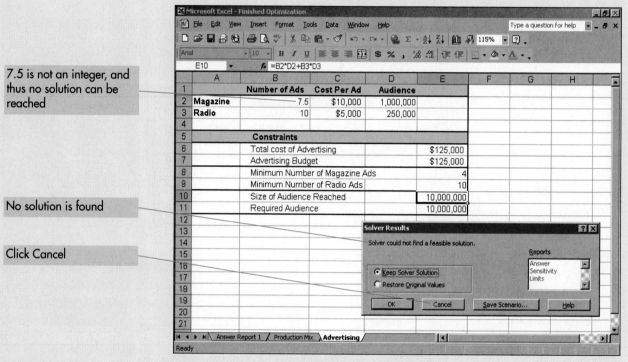

(f) The Infeasible Solution (step 6)

FIGURE B.4 *Hands-on Exercise 2 (continued)*

UNABLE TO FIND A SOLUTION

Solver is a powerful tool, but it cannot do the impossible. Some problems simply do not have a solution because the constraints may conflict with one another, and/or because the constraints exceed the available resources. Should this occur, and it will, check your constraints to make sure they were entered correctly. If Solver is still unable to reach a solution, it will be necessary to relax one or more of the constraints.

Step 7: **Relax a Constraint**

➤ Click in **cell E9** (the cell containing the minimum number of radio ads). Enter **9** and press **enter**.

➤ Pull down the **Tools menu**. Click **Solver** to display the Solver Parameters dialog box. Click **Solve**. This time Solver finds a solution as shown in Figure B.6g.

➤ Click **Answer** in the Reports list box, then click **OK** to generate the report. You will see the report being generated, after which the Solver Results dialog box closes automatically.

➤ Click the **Answer Report 2 worksheet tab** to view the report. Add your name to the report, boldface your name, print the answer report, and submit it to your instructor.

➤ Save the workbook.

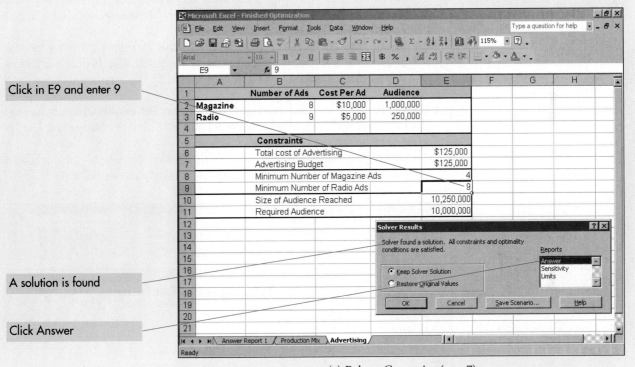

Click in E9 and enter 9

A solution is found

Click Answer

(g) Relax a Constraint (step 7)

FIGURE B.6 *Hands-on Exercise 2 (continued)*

SENSITIVITY, BINDING, AND NONBINDING CONSTRAINTS

A sensitivity report shows the effect of increasing resources associated with the binding and nonbinding constraints within the optimization problem. A binding constraint has a limiting effect on the objective value; that is, relaxing a binding constraint by increasing the associated resource will improve the value of the objective function. Conversely, a nonbinding constraint does not have a limiting effect, and increasing its resource has no effect on the value of the objective function.

Step 8: **Add the Documentation Worksheet**

➤ This step creates a documentation worksheet similar to the one in Chapter 6. Pull down the **Insert menu** and click the **Worksheet command**.

➤ Double click the **tab** of the newly inserted worksheet. Enter **Documentation** as the new name and press **enter**. If necessary, click and drag the worksheet tab to move it to the beginning of the workbook.

➤ Enter the descriptive entries in **cells A3**, **A4**, and **A6** as shown in Figure B.6h. Use boldface as shown. Increase the width of column A.

➤ Enter your name in **cell B3**. Enter **=Today( )** in **cell B4**. Press **enter**. Click the **Left Align button** to align the date as shown in the figure.

➤ Increase the width of column B, then click in **cell B6** and enter the indicated text. Do not press the enter key until you have completed the entry.

➤ Click in **cell B6**, then pull down the **Format menu** and click the **Cells command** to display the Format Cells dialog box. Click the **Alignment tab**, click the box to **Wrap Text**, then click **OK**.

➤ Point to cell **A6**, then click the **right mouse button** to display a shortcut menu. Click **Format Cells** to display the Format Cells dialog box. If necessary, click the **Alignment tab**, click the **drop-down arrow** in the Vertical list box, and select **Top**. Click **OK**.

➤ Click in **cell A1**. Enter **Solver - An Optimization Technique**. Change the font size to **18**. Click and drag to select **cells A1** and **B1**. Click the **Merge and Center button** to center the title across cells A1 and B1.

➤ Complete the entries in the remainder of the worksheet. Check the worksheet for spelling. Save the workbook. Print the documentation worksheet.

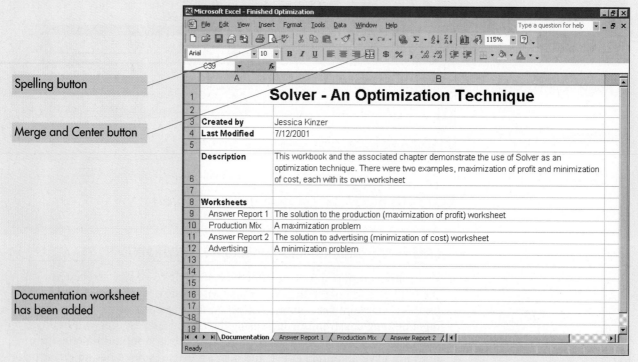

Spelling button

Merge and Center button

Documentation worksheet has been added

(h) Add the Documentation Worksheet (step 8)

FIGURE B.6 *Hands-on Exercise 2 (continued)*

Solver is an optimization and resource allocation tool that helps you achieve a desired goal, such as maximizing profit or minimizing cost. The information required by Solver is entered through the Solver Parameters dialog box, which is divided into three sections: the target cell, the adjustable cells, and the constraints.

The target cell identifies the goal (or objective function), which is the cell whose value you want to maximize, minimize, or set to a specific value. The adjustable cells are the cells whose values are changed until the constraints are satisfied and the target cell reaches its optimum value. The constraints specify the restrictions. Each constraint consists of a comparison containing a cell or cell range on the left, a relational operator, and a numeric value or cell reference on the right.

The Solver Options dialog box lets you specify how Solver will attempt to find a solution. The Max Time and Iterations entries determine how long Solver will work on finding a solution. If either limit is reached before a solution is found, Solver will ask whether you want to continue. The default settings of 100 seconds and 100 iterations are sufficient for simpler problems, but may not be enough for complex problems with multiple constraints.

KEY TERMS

Adjustable cells (p. 440)
Answer Report (p. 445)
Binding constraint (p. 438)
Constraint (p. 440)
Infeasible solution (p. 452)

Integer constraint (p. 451)
Iteration (p. 446)
Nonbinding constraint (p. 438)
Nonnegativity constraint (p. 440)
Solver (p. 437)

Solver Options dialog box (p. 446)
Solver Parameters dialog box (p. 440)
Target cell (p. 440)

CHAPTER 5

One-to-Many Relationships: Subforms and Multiple Table Queries

OBJECTIVES

AFTER READING THIS CHAPTER YOU WILL BE ABLE TO:

1. Explain how a one-to-many relationship is essential in the design of a database; differentiate between a primary key and a foreign key.
2. Use the Relationships window to implement a one-to-many relationship within an Access database.
3. Define referential integrity; explain how the enforcement of referential integrity maintains consistency within a database.
4. Distinguish between a main form and a subform; explain how a subform is used in conjunction with a one-to-many relationship.
5. Create a query based on multiple tables, then create a report based on that query.
6. Create a main form containing two subforms linked to one another

OVERVIEW

The real power of Access stems from its use as a relational database that contains multiple tables, and the objects associated with those tables. We introduced this concept at the end of Chapter 1, when we looked briefly at a database that had three tables. We revisited the concept in the previous chapter when we looked at a second relational database.

This chapter presents an entirely new case study that focuses on a relational database. The case is that of a consumer loan system within a bank. The database contains two tables, one for customers and one for loans. There is a one-to-many relationship between the tables, in that one customer can have many loans, but a loan is tied to only one customer.

The case solution includes a discussion of database concepts. It reviews the definition of a primary key and explains how the primary key of one table exists as a foreign key in a related table. It also reviews the concept of referential integrity, which ensures that the tables within the database are consistent with one another. And most important, it shows how to implement these concepts in an Access database.

The chapter builds on what you already know by expanding the earlier material on forms, queries, and reports. It describes how to create a main form and a corresponding subform that contains data from a related table. It develops a query that contains data from multiple tables, then creates a report based on that query.

Suffice it to say that this is a critically important chapter because it is built around a relational database, as opposed to a single table. Thus, when you complete the chapter, you will have a much better appreciation of what can be accomplished within Access. As always, the hands-on exercises are essential to your understanding of the material.

CASE STUDY: CONSUMER LOANS

Let us assume that you are in the Information Systems department of a commercial bank and are assigned the task of implementing a system for consumer loans. The bank needs complete data about every loan (the amount, interest rate, term, and so on). It also needs data about the customers holding those loans (name, address, telephone, etc.).

The problem is how to structure the data so that the bank will be able to obtain all of the information it needs from its database. The system must be able to supply the name and address of the person associated with a loan. The system must also be able to retrieve all of the loans for a specific individual.

The solution calls for a database with two tables, one for loans and one for customers. To appreciate the elegance of this approach, consider first a single table containing a combination of loan and customer data as shown in Figure 5.1. At first glance this solution appears to be satisfactory. You can, for example, search for a specific loan (e.g., L022) and determine that Lori Sangastiano is the customer associated with that loan. You can also search for a particular customer (e.g., Michelle Zacco) and find all of her loans (L028, L030, and L060).

There is a problem, however, in that the table duplicates customer data throughout the database. Thus, when one customer has multiple loans, the customer's name, address, and other data are stored multiple times. Maintaining the data in this form is a time-consuming and error-prone procedure, because any change to the customer's data has to be made in many places.

A second problem arises when you enter data for a new customer that occurs before a loan has been approved. The bank receives the customer's application data prior to granting a loan, and it wants to retain the customer data even if a loan is turned down. Adding a customer to the database in Figure 5.1 is awkward, however, because it requires the creation of a "dummy" loan record to hold the customer data.

The deletion (payoff) of a loan creates a third type of problem. What happens, for example, when Ted Myerson pays off loan L020? The loan record would be deleted, but so too would Ted's data as he has no other outstanding loans. The bank might want to contact Mr. Myerson about another loan in the future, but it would lose his data with the deletion of the existing loan.

The database in Figure 5.2 represents a much better design because it eliminates all three problems. It uses two different tables, a Loans table and a Customers table. Each record in the Loans table has data about a specific loan (LoanID, Date, Amount, Interest Rate, Term, Type, and CustomerID). Each record in the Customers table has data about a specific customer (CustomerID, First Name, Last Name, Address, City, State, Zip Code, and Phone Number). Each record in the

LoanID	Loan Data (Date, Amount, Interest Rate...)	Customer Data (First Name, Last Name, Address...)
L001	Loan Data for Loan L001	Customer Data for Wendy Solomon
L004	Loan Data for Loan L004	Customer Data for Wendy Solomon
L010	Loan Data for Loan L010	Customer Data for Alex Rey
L014	Loan Data for Loan L014	Customer Data for Wendy Solomon
L020	Loan Data for Loan L020	Customer Data for Tedd Myerson
L022	Loan Data for Loan L022	Customer Data for Lori Sangastiano
L026	Loan Data for Loan L026	Customer Data for Matt Hirsch
L028	Loan Data for Loan L028	Customer Data for Michelle Zacco
L030	Loan Data for Loan L030	Customer Data for Michelle Zacco
L031	Loan Data for Loan L031	Customer Data for Eileen Faulkner
L032	Loan Data for Loan L032	Customer Data for Scott Wit
L033	Loan Data for Loan L033	Customer Data for Alex Rey
L039	Loan Data for Loan L039	Customer Data for David Powell
L040	Loan Data for Loan L040	Customer Data for Matt Hirsch
L047	Loan Data for Loan L047	Customer Data for Benjamin Grauer
L049	Loan Data for Loan L049	Customer Data for Eileen Faulkner
L052	Loan Data for Loan L052	Customer Data for Eileen Faulkner
L053	Loan Data for Loan L053	Customer Data for Benjamin Grauer
L054	Loan Data for Loan L054	Customer Data for Scott Wit
L057	Loan Data for Loan L057	Customer Data for Benjamin Grauer
L060	Loan Data for Loan L060	Customer Data for Michelle Zacco
L062	Loan Data for Loan L062	Customer Data for Matt Hirsch
L100	Loan Data for Loan L100	Customer Data for Benjamin Grauer
L109	Loan Data for Loan L109	Customer Data for Wendy Solomon
L120	Loan Data for Loan L120	Customer Data for Lori Sangastiano

FIGURE 5.1   *Single Table Solution*

Loans table is associated with a matching record in the Customers table through the CustomerID field common to both tables. This solution may seem complicated, but it is really quite simple and elegant.

Consider, for example, how easy it is to change a customer's address. If Michelle Zacco were to move, you would go into the Customers table, find her record (Customer C08), and make the necessary change. You would not have to change any of the records in the Loans table, because they do not contain customer data, but only a CustomerID that indicates who the customer is. In other words, you would change Michelle's address in only one place, and the change would be automatically reflected for every associated loan.

The addition of a new customer is done directly in the Customers table. This is much easier than the approach of Figure 5.1, which required an existing loan in order to add a new customer. And finally, the deletion of an existing loan is also easier than with the single table organization. A loan can be deleted from the Loans table without losing the corresponding customer data.

The database in Figure 5.2 is composed of two tables in which there is a ***one-to-many relationship*** between customers and loans. One customer (Michelle Zacco) can have many loans (Loan numbers L028, L030, and L060), but a specific loan (L028) is associated with only one customer (Michelle Zacco). The tables are related to one another by a common field (CustomerID) that is present in both the Customers and the Loans table.

Access enables you to create the one-to-many relationship between the tables, then uses that relationship to answer questions about the database. It can retrieve information about a specific loan, such as the name and address of the customer holding that loan. It can also find all loans for a particular customer.

LoanID	Date	Amount	Interest Rate	Term	Type	CustomerID
L001	1/15/01	$475,000	6.90%	15	M	C04
L004	1/23/01	$35,000	7.20%	5	C	C04
L010	1/25/01	$10,000	5.50%	3	C	C05
L014	1/31/01	$12,000	9.50%	10	O	C04
L020	2/8/01	$525,000	6.50%	30	M	C06
L022	2/12/01	$10,500	7.50%	5	O	C07
L026	2/15/01	$35,000	6.50%	5	O	C10
L028	2/20/01	$250,000	8.80%	30	M	C08
L030	2/21/01	$5,000	10.00%	3	O	C08
L031	2/28/01	$200,000	7.00%	15	M	C01
L032	3/1/01	$25,000	10.00%	3	C	C02
L033	3/1/01	$20,000	9.50%	5	O	C05
L040	3/10/01	$129,000	8.50%	15	M	C10
L047	3/11/01	$200,000	7.25%	15	M	C03
L049	3/21/01	$150,000	7.50%	15	M	C01
L052	3/22/01	$100,000	7.00%	30	M	C01
L053	3/31/01	$15,000	6.50%	3	O	C03
L054	4/1/01	$10,000	8.00%	5	C	C02
L057	4/15/01	$25,000	8.50%	4	C	C03
L060	4/18/01	$41,000	9.90%	4	C	C08
L062	4/22/01	$350,000	7.50%	15	M	C10
L100	5/1/01	$150,000	6.00%	15	M	C03
L109	5/3/01	$350,000	8.20%	30	M	C04
L120	5/8/01	$275,000	9.20%	15	M	C07
L121	7/15/01	$20,000	8.00%	3	C	C11

(a) Loans Table

CustomerID	First Name	Last Name	Address	City	State	Zip Code	Phone Number
C01	Eileen	Faulkner	7245 NW 8 Street	Minneapolis	MN	55346	(612) 894-1511
C02	Scott	Wit	5660 NW 175 Terrace	Baltimore	MD	21224	(410) 753-0345
C03	Benjamin	Grauer	10000 Sample Road	Coral Springs	FL	33073	(305) 444-5555
C04	Wendy	Solomon	7500 Reno Road	Houston	TX	77090	(713) 427-3104
C05	Alex	Rey	3456 Main Highway	Denver	CO	80228	(303) 555-6666
C06	Ted	Myerson	6545 Stone Street	Chapel Hill	NC	27515	(919) 942-7654
C07	Lori	Sangastiano	4533 Aero Drive	Santa Rosa	CA	95403	(707) 542-3411
C08	Michelle	Zacco	488 Gold Street	Gainesville	FL	32601	(904) 374-5660
C10	Matt	Hirsch	777 NW 67 Avenue	Fort Lee	NJ	07624	(201) 664-3211

(b) Customers Table

FIGURE 5.2 *Multiple Table Solution*

Use the tables in Figure 5.2 to answer the queries below and gain an appreciation for the power of a relational database.

Query: What are the name, address, and phone number of the customer associated with loan number L010?

Answer: Alex Rey, at 3456 Main Highway is the customer associated with loan L010. His phone number is (303) 555-6666.

To determine the answer, Access searches the Loans table for loan L010 to obtain the CustomerID (C05 in this example). It then searches the Customers table for the customer with the matching CustomerID and retrieves the name, address, and phone number.

Consider a second example, that appears on the next page:

Query: Which loans are associated with Wendy Solomon?
Answer: Wendy Solomon has four loans: loan L001 for $475,000, loan L004 for $35,000, loan L014 for $12,000, and loan L109 for $350,000.

This time Access begins in the Customers table and searches for Wendy Solomon to determine the CustomerID (C04). It then searches the Loans table for all records with a matching CustomerID.

Referential Integrity

Microsoft Access automatically implements certain types of data validation during data entry to ensure that the database will produce accurate information. Access always lets you enter a record in the "one" table, the Customers table in this example, provided that all existing rules for data validation are met. You cannot, however, enter a record in the "many" table (the Loans table in this example) if that record contains an invalid (nonexistent) value for the CustomerID. This type of data validation is known as *referential integrity* and it guarantees that the tables within a database are consistent with one another. Consider:

Query: Can you add a loan to the Loans table (as it presently exists) for Customer C01? Can you add a loan for Customer C20?
Answer: Yes, you can add a loan for Customer C01 provided that the other rules for data validation are met. You cannot add a loan for Customer C20, because that customer is not in the Customers table.

Implementation in Access

Figure 5.3a displays the *Relationships window* that is used to create the one-to-many relationship between customers and loans. Each table stores data about a specific subject, such as customers or loans. Each table has a *primary key*, which is a field (or combination of fields) that uniquely identifies each record. CustomerID is the primary key in the Customers table. LoanID is the primary key in the Loans table.

The one-to-many relationship between the tables is based on the fact that the same field (CustomerID) appears in both tables. The CustomerID is the primary key in the Customers table, where its values are unique, but it is a *foreign key* in the Loans table, where its values are not unique. (A foreign key is simply the primary key of another table.) In other words, multiple records in the Loans table can have the same CustomerID to implement the one-to-many relationship between customers and loans.

To create a one-to-many relationship, you open the Relationships window in Figure 5.3a and add the necessary tables. You then drag the field on which the relationship is built from the field list of the "one" table (Customers) to the matching field in the related table (Loans). Once the relationship has been established, you will see a *relationship line* connecting the tables that indicates the one and many side of the relationship. The line extends from the primary key in the "one" table to the foreign key in the "many" table.

Figure 5.3b displays the Customers table after the one-to-many relationship has been created. A plus (or minus) sign appears to the left of the CustomerID to indicate that there are corresponding records in a related table. You can click the plus sign next to any customer record to display the related records (called a *subdatasheet*) for that customer. Conversely, you can click the minus sign (after the related records have been displayed) and the records are hidden. Look carefully at the related records for customer C04 (Wendy Solomon) and you will see the answer to one of our earlier queries.

CustomerID is the primary key in the Customers table

Relationships line

CustomerID is the foreign key in the Loans table

Referential integrity will be enforced

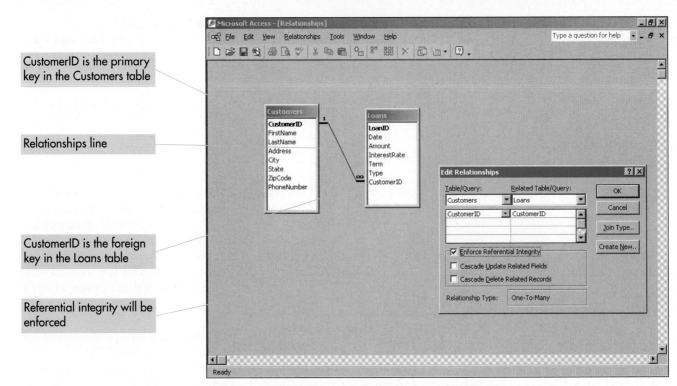

(a) The Relationships Window

+ indicates related records exist in a related table

Related records are shown for Wendy Solomon

– indicates subdatasheet is displayed

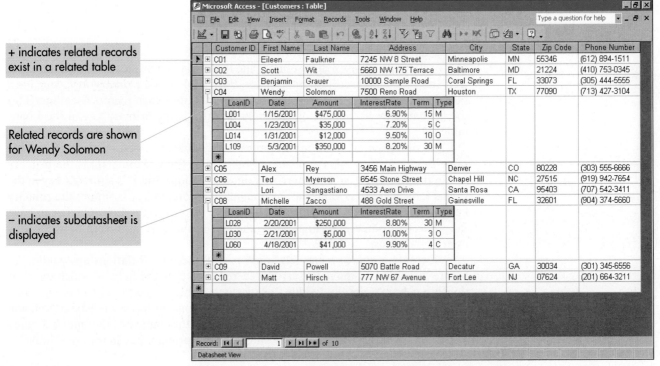

(b) The Customers Table with Related Records

FIGURE 5.3   *One-to-Many Relationship*

ONE-TO-MANY RELATIONSHIPS

Objective To create a one-to-many relationship between existing tables in a database; to demonstrate referential integrity between the tables in a one-to-many relationship. Use Figure 5.4 as a guide in the exercise.

Step 1: **The Relationships Window**

> ➤ Start Access. Open the **National Bank database** in the **Exploring Access folder**. The database contains three tables: for Customers, Loans, and Payments. (The Payments table will be used later in the chapter.)
> ➤ Pull down the **Tools menu** and click **Relationships** to open the Relationships window as shown in Figure 5.4a. (The Customers and Loans tables are not yet visible.) If you do not see the Show Table dialog box, pull down the **Relationships menu** and click the **Show Table command**.
> ➤ The **Tables tab** is selected within the Show Table dialog box. Click (select) the **Customers table**, then click the **Add Command button** to add the table to the Relationships window.
> ➤ Click the **Loans table**, then click the **Add Command button** (or simply double click the **Loans table**) to add this table to the Relationships window.
> ➤ Do *not* add the Payments table at this time. Click the **Close button** to close the Show Table dialog box.

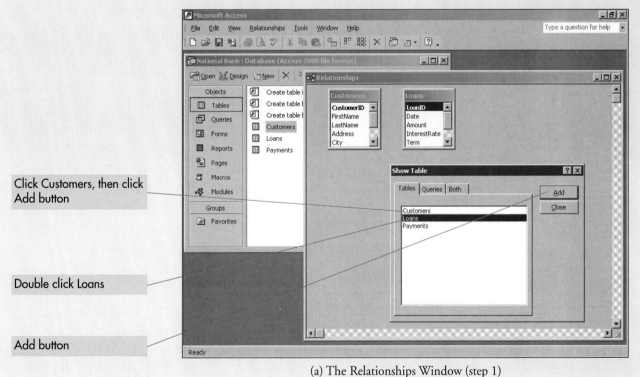

Click Customers, then click Add button

Double click Loans

Add button

(a) The Relationships Window (step 1)

FIGURE 5.4 *Hands-on Exercise 1*

Step 2: **Create the Relationship**

➤ Maximize the Relationships window. Point to the bottom border of the **Customers field list** (the mouse pointer changes to a double arrow), then click and drag the border until all of the fields are visible.

➤ Click and drag the bottom border of the **Loans field list** until all of the fields are visible. Click and drag the title bar of the **Loans field list** so that it is approximately one inch away from the Customers field list.

➤ Click and drag the **CustomerID field** in the Customers field list to the **CustomerID field** in the Loans field list. You will see the Relationships dialog box in Figure 5.4b.

➤ Check the **Enforce Referential Integrity** check box. (If necessary, clear the check boxes to Cascade Update Related Fields and Delete Related Records.)

➤ Click the **Create Command button** to establish the relationship and close the Relationships dialog box. You should see a line indicating a one-to-many relationship between the Customers and Loans tables.

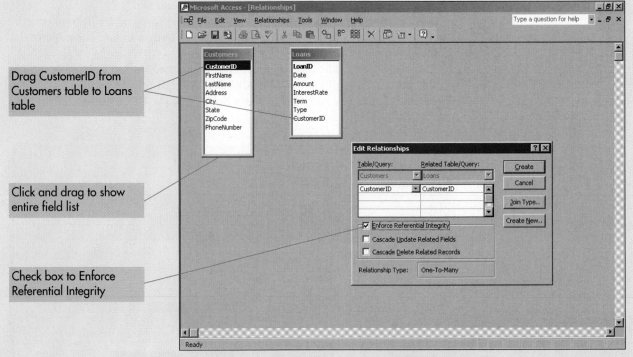

Drag CustomerID from Customers table to Loans table

Click and drag to show entire field list

Check box to Enforce Referential Integrity

(b) Create the Relationship (step 2)

FIGURE 5.4   *Hands-on Exercise 1 (continued)*

THE TABLE ANALYZER WIZARD

Duplicating data within a database results in wasted space, or worse, in erroneous information. Access, however, provides the Table Analyzer Wizard, which will examine the tables within a database to prevent such errors from occurring. The Wizard offers a brief explanation of the consequences of poor design, then it will examine your tables and make the appropriate suggestions. See exercise 10 at the end of the chapter.

Step 3: Delete a Relationship

➤ Access displays a relationship line between related tables, containing the number 1 and the infinity symbol (∞), to indicate a one-to-many relationship in which referential integrity is enforced.

➤ Point to the line indicating the relationship between the tables, then click the **right mouse button** to select the relationship and display a shortcut menu.

➤ Click the **Delete command**. You will see the dialog box in Figure 5.4c, asking whether you are sure you want to delete the relationship.

➤ Click **No** since you do *not* want to delete the relationship at this time. (Subsequently, however, it may be necessary for you to delete or edit a relationship.)

➤ Close the Relationships window. Click **Yes** if asked whether to save the layout changes.

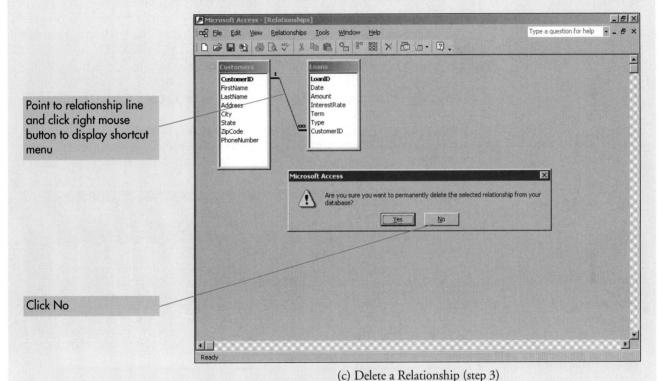

Point to relationship line and click right mouse button to display shortcut menu

Click No

(c) Delete a Relationship (step 3)

FIGURE 5.4   *Hands-on Exercise 1 (continued)*

RELATED FIELDS AND DATA TYPES

The fields on both sides of a relationship must have the same data type; for example, both fields should be text fields or both fields should be number fields. In addition, Number fields must also have the same field size. The exception is an AutoNumber (counter) field in the primary table, which is matched against a Long Integer field in the related table. AutoNumber fields are discussed in Chapter 6.

Step 4: **Add a Customer Record**

➤ The Database window is again visible with the Tables button selected. Open the **Customers table**. If necessary, click the **Maximize button** to give yourself additional room when adding a record. Widen the fields as necessary to see the data.

➤ Click the **New Record button** on the toolbar. The record selector moves to the last record (record 11).

➤ Enter **C11** as the CustomerID as shown in Figure 5.4d. The record selector changes to a pencil as soon as you enter the first character.

➤ Enter data for yourself as the new customer. Data validation has been built into the Customers table, so you must enter the data correctly, or it will not be accepted.

• The message, *Customer ID must begin with the letter C followed by a two-digit number*, indicates that the CustomerID field is invalid.

• The message, *The field 'Customers.LastName' can't contain a Null value because the Required property for this field is set to True*, indicates that you must enter a last name.

• A beep in either the ZipCode or PhoneNumber field indicates that you are entering a nonnumeric character.

• If you encounter a data validation error, press **Esc** (or Click **OK**), then re-enter the data.

➤ Press **enter** when you have completed your record. Remember your CustomerID (C11) because you will need to enter it in the corresponding loan records.

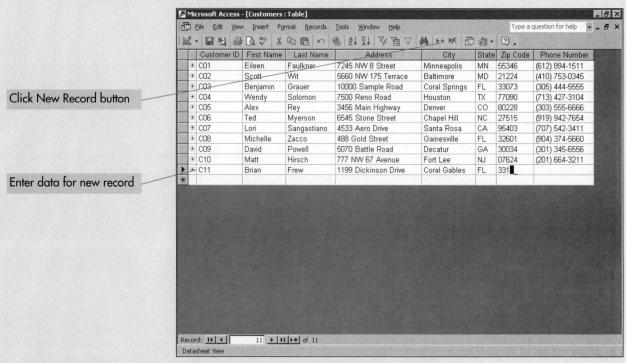

Click New Record button

Enter data for new record

(d) Add a Customer Record (step 4)

FIGURE 5.4   *Hands-on Exercise 1 (continued)*

Step 5: **Add a Loan Record**

➤ Click the **plus sign** next to the record selector for customer C03 (Benjamin Grauer). The plus sign changes to a minus sign and you see the related records as shown in Figure 5.4e. Click the **minus sign** and it changes back to a plus sign. The related records for this customer are no longer visible.

➤ Click the **plus sign** next to your customer record (record C11 in our figure). The plus sign changes to a minus sign but there are no loans as yet. Click in the **LoanID field** and enter data for a new loan record as shown in Figure 5.4e.
  • Use **L121** for the LoanID and enter the terms of the loan as you see fit.
  • Data validation has been built into the Loans table. The term of the loan, for example, cannot exceed 30 years. The interest rate must be entered as a decimal. The type of the loan must be C, M, or O for Car, Mortgage, or Other. Enter **C** for a car loan.

➤ Press **enter** when you have completed the loan record.

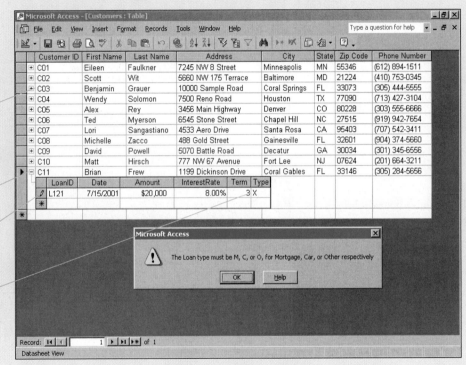

Click + sign to display related records

Click + sign, which then changes to a –

Enter Loan data

Data validation does not permit *X* to be entered

(e) Add a Loan Record (step 5)

FIGURE 5.4   *Hands-on Exercise 1 (continued)*

ADD AND DELETE RELATED RECORDS

Take advantage of the one-to-many relationship that exists between Customers and Loans to add or delete records in the Loans table from within the Customers table. Open the Customers table, then click the plus sign next to the Customer for whom you want to add or delete a loan record. To add a Loan, click in the blank row marked by the asterisk, then enter the new data. To delete a loan, select the Loan record, then click the Delete Record button on the Standard toolbar.

Step 6: **Referential Integrity**

➤ Click the **plus sign** next to the record selector for Customer C09 (David Powell). Click in the CustomerID field for this customer, then click the Delete Record button to (attempt to) delete this customer.

➤ You will see the error message in Figure 5.4f indicating that you cannot delete the customer record because there are related loan records. Click **OK**.

➤ Click in the LoanID for L039 (the loan for this customer). Click the **Delete Record button**. Click **Yes** when warned that you will not be able to undo this operation. The loan disappears.

➤ Click in the CustomerID field, click the **Delete Record button**, then click **Yes** to delete the record. The deletion was permitted because there were no longer any related records in the Loans table.

➤ Close the Customers table. Close the National Bank database. Exit Access if you do not want to continue with the next exercise at this time.

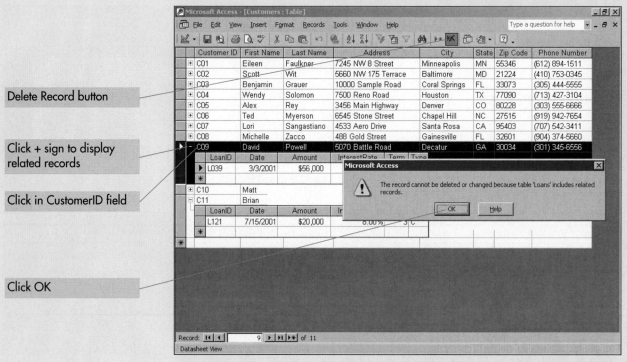

Delete Record button

Click + sign to display related records

Click in CustomerID field

Click OK

(f) Referential Integrity (step 6)

FIGURE 5.4 *Hands-on Exercise 1 (continued)*

CASCADE DELETED RECORDS

The enforcement of referential integrity will prevent the deletion of a record in the primary (Customers) table if there is a corresponding record in the related (Loans) table. (Thus, to delete a customer, you would first have to delete all loans for that customer.) This restriction is relaxed if you modify the relationship by checking the Cascade Delete Related Records option in the Relationships dialog box. The option is discussed further in the next chapter.

A *subform* is a form within a form. It appears inside a main form to display records from a related table. A main form and its associated subform, to display the loans for one customer, are shown in Figure 5.5. The *main form* (also known as the primary form) is based on the primary table (the Customers table). The subform is based on the related table (the Loans table).

The main form and the subform are linked to one another so that the subform displays only the records related to the record currently displayed in the main form. The main form shows the "one" side of the relationship (the customer). The subform shows the "many" side of the relationship (the loans). The main form displays the customer data for one record (Eileen Faulkner with Customer ID C01). The subform shows the loans for that customer. The main form is displayed in the *Form view*, whereas the subform is displayed in the *Datasheet view*. (A subform can also be displayed in the Form view, in which case it would show one loan at a time.)

Each form in Figure 5.5a has its own status bar and associated navigation buttons. The status bar for the main form indicates that the active record is record 1 of 10 records in the Customers table. The status bar for the subform indicates record 1 of 3 records. (The latter shows the number of loans for this customer rather than the number of loans in the Loans table.) Click the navigation button to move to the next customer record and you will automatically see the loans associated with that customer. If, for example, you were to move to the last customer record (C11, which contains the data you entered in the first hands-on exercise), you would see your customer and loan information.

The Loans form also contains a calculated control, the payment due, which is based on the loan parameters. Loan L031, for example (a $200,000 mortgage at 7% with a 15-year term), has a monthly payment of $1,797.66. The amount of the payment is calculated using a predefined function, as will be described in the next hands-on exercise.

Figure 5.5b displays the Design view of the Customers form in Figure 5.5a. The Loans subform control is an object on the Customers form and can be moved and sized (or deleted) just like any other object. It should also be noted that the Loans subform is a form in and of itself, and can be opened in either the Datasheet view or the Form view. It can also be opened in the Design view (to modify its appearance) as will be done in the next hands-on exercise.

Note, too, that reports can be linked to one another in exactly the same way that forms are linked to each other. Thus, you could create a main report/subreport combination to display the same information as the forms in Figure 5.5a. The choice between a form and a report depends on the information requirements of the system. Access, however, gives you the capability to create both. Everything that you learn about creating a subform also pertains to creating a subreport.

THE PMT FUNCTION

The Pmt function is one of several predefined functions built into Access. It calculates the payment due on a loan based on the principal, interest rate, and term and is similar to the PMT function in Excel. The Pmt function is reached most easily through the Expression Builder and can be entered onto any form, query, or report.

Status bar for subform

Payment Due is a calculated field

Status bar for main form

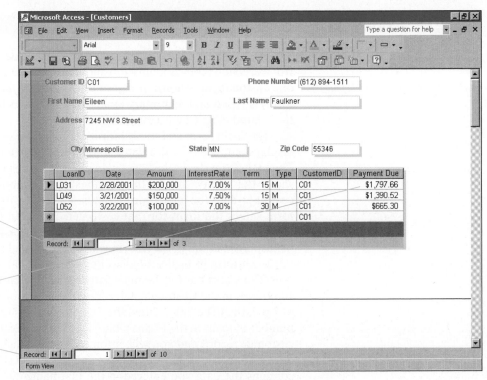

(a) Form View

Loans subform control

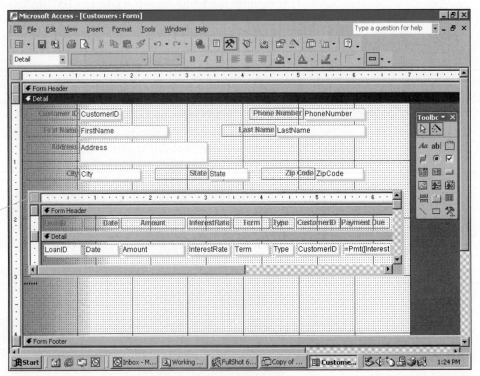

(b) Design View

FIGURE 5.5   *A Main Form and a Subform*

The Form Wizard

A subform is created in different ways depending on whether or not the main form already exists. The easiest way is to create the two forms at the same time by using the Form Wizard as depicted in Figure 5.6. The Wizard starts by asking you which fields you want to include in your form. You will need to select fields from the Customers table, as shown in Figure 5.6a, as well as from the Loans table as shown in Figure 5.6b, since these tables are the basis for the main form and subform, respectively.

The Wizard will do the rest. It gives you the opportunity to view the records by customer, as shown in Figure 5.6c. (Additional screens, not shown in Figure 5.6, let you choose the style of the forms.) Finally, you save each form as a separate object as shown in Figure 5.6d. You will find that the Wizard provides an excellent starting point, but you usually have to customize the forms after they have been created. This is done in the Form Design view using the identical techniques that were presented earlier to move and size controls and/or modify their properties.

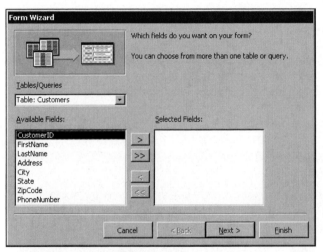

(a) The Customers Table

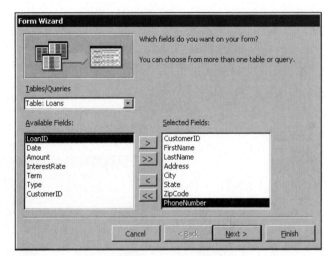

(b) The Loans Table

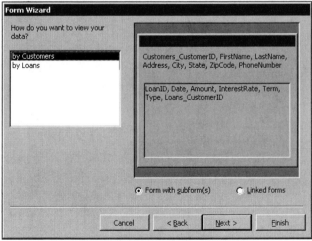

(c) View Data by Customers

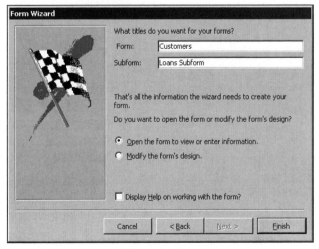

(d) Save the Forms

FIGURE 5.6   *The Form Wizard*

CREATING A SUBFORM

Objective To create a subform that displays the many records in a one-to-many relationship; to move and size controls in an existing form; to enter data in a subform. Use Figure 5.7 as a guide in doing the exercise.

Step 1: **Start the Form Wizard**

➤ Open the **National Bank database** from the previous exercise. Click the **Forms button** in the Database window, then double click the **Create form by using Wizard button** to start the Form Wizard.

➤ You should see the Form Wizard dialog box in Figure 5.7a, except that no fields have been selected.

➤ The Customers table is selected by default. Click the **>> button** to enter all of the fields in the Customers table on the form.

➤ Click the **drop-down arrow** in the Tables/Queries list box to display the tables and queries in the database.

➤ Click **Loans** to select the Loans table as shown in Figure 5.7a. Click the **>> button** to enter all of the fields in the Loans table on the form.

➤ Be sure that the Selected Fields area contains the fields from both the Loans form and the Customers form.

➤ Click **Next** to continue with the Form Wizard.

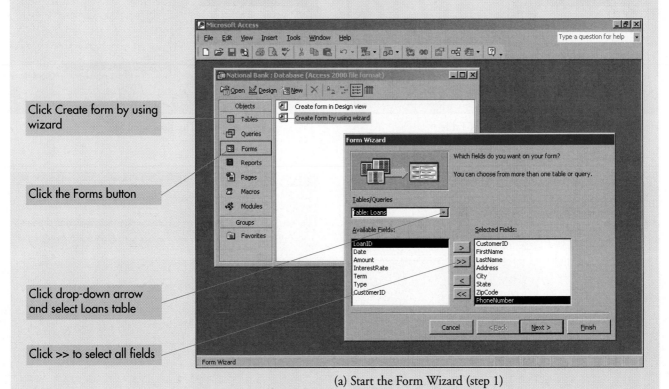

Click Create form by using wizard

Click the Forms button

Click drop-down arrow and select Loans table

Click >> to select all fields

(a) Start the Form Wizard (step 1)

FIGURE 5.7 *Hands-on Exercise 2*

Step 2: **Complete the Forms**

➤ The Wizard will prompt you for the additional information it needs to create the Customers form and the associated Loans subform:

* The next screen suggests that you view the data by customers and that you are going to create a form with subforms. Click **Next**.
* The Datasheet option button is selected as the default layout for the subform. Click **Tabular**. Click **Next**.
* Click **Blends** as the style for your form. Click **Next**.
* You should see the screen in Figure 5.7b in which the Form Wizard suggests **Customers** as the title of the form and **Loans Subform** as the title for the subform. Click the option button to **Modify the form's design**, then click the **Finish command button** to create the form and exit the Form Wizard.

➤ You should be in the Design view of the Customer form you just created. Click the **Save button** to save the form and continue working.

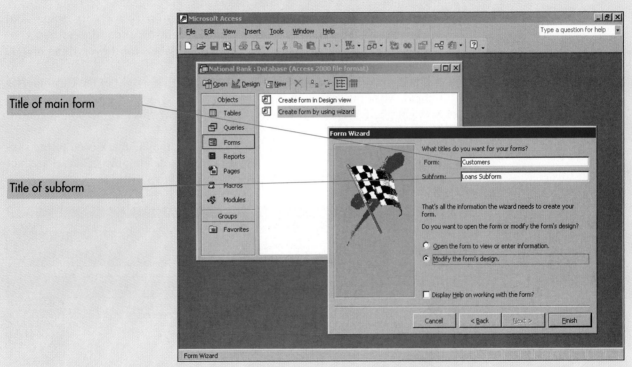

Title of main form

Title of subform

(b) Complete the Forms (step 2)

FIGURE 5.7   *Hands-on Exercise 2 (continued)*

THE NAME'S THE SAME

The Form Wizard automatically assigns the name of the underlying table (or query) to each form (subform) it creates. The Report Wizard works in similar fashion. The intent of the similar naming convention is to help you select the proper object from the Database window when you want to subsequently open the object. This becomes increasingly important in databases that contain a large number of objects.

Step 3: Modify the Customers Form

➤ You should see the Customers form in Figure 5.7c. The appearance of your form will be different from our figure, however, as you need to rearrange the position of the fields on the form. Maximize the form window.

➤ Click and drag the bottom of the Detail section down to give yourself additional room in which to work.

➤ It takes time (and a little practice) to move and size the controls within a form. Try the indicated command, then click the **Undo button** if you are not satisfied with the result.

- Move the **City**, **State**, **ZipCode**, **and PhoneNumber** to the bottom of the detail section. (This is only temporary, but we need room to work.)
- Increase the width of the form to seven inches. Click the **LastName** control to select the control and display the sizing handles, then drag the LastName control and its attached label so that it is next to the FirstName control. Align the tops of the LastName and FirstName controls.
- Move the **Address** control up. Place the controls for **City**, **State**, and **ZipCode** on the same line, then move these controls under the Address control. You may need to size some of the other labels to fit everything on one line. Align the tops of these controls as well.
- Click and drag the control for **PhoneNumber** to the right of the CustomerID field. Align the tops of the controls.
- Right align all of the labels so that they appear close to the bound control they identify.

➤ Your form should now match Figure 5.7c. Click the label attached to the subform control and press the **Del key**. Be sure you delete only the label and not the control for the subform. Save the form.

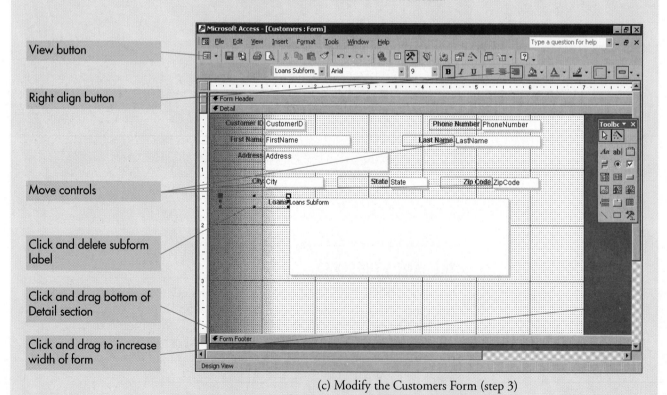

View button

Right align button

Move controls

Click and delete subform label

Click and drag bottom of Detail section

Click and drag to increase width of form

(c) Modify the Customers Form (step 3)

FIGURE 5.7 *Hands-on Exercise 2 (continued)*

➤ You should see the Customers form in the **Form View** as in Figure 5.7d. Do not be concerned about the column widths in the subform or the fact that you may not see all of the fields at this time. Our objective is simply to show the relationship between the main form and the subform.

- The customer information for the first customer (C01) is displayed in the main portion of the form. The loans for that customer are in the subform.
- The status bar at the bottom of the window (corresponding to the main form) displays record 1 of 10 records (you are looking at the first record in the Customers table).
- The status bar for the subform displays record 1 of 3 records (you are on the first of three loan records for this customer).

➤ Click the ▶ **button** on the status bar for the main form to move to the next customer record. The subform is updated automatically to display the two loans belonging to this customer.

➤ Close the Customers form. Click **Yes** if asked to save the changes.

Customer C01 is displayed

Loans displayed belong to customer C01

Status bar of subform shows record 1 of 3

Click to move to next customer record

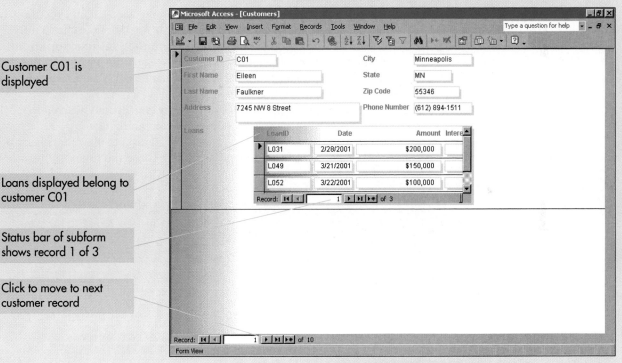

(d) View the Customers Form (step 4)

FIGURE 5.7 *Hands-on Exercise 2 (continued)*

WHY IT WORKS

The main form (Customers) and subform (Loans) work in conjunction with one another so that you always see all of the loans for a given customer. To see how the link is actually implemented, change to the Design view of the Customers form and point anywhere inside the Loans subform. Click the right mouse button to display a shortcut menu, click Properties to display the Subform/Subreport properties dialog box, and, if necessary, click the All tab within the dialog box. You should see CustomerID next to two properties (Link Child Fields and Link Master Fields).

Step 5: **Add the Payment Amount**

➤ Right click the **Form Selector button** to display a context-sensitive menu, then click **Properties** to display the Properties sheet for the form as a whole.

➤ Click the **All Tab**, click in the **Default View** text box, then select **Datasheet**. Close the Property sheet.

➤ Click the **Forms button** in the Database window. Open the **Loans subform** in Design view. Click and drag the right edge of the form to **7 inches**.

➤ Click the **Label button** on the Toolbox toolbar, then click and drag in the Form Header to create an unbound control. Enter **Payment Due** as the text for the label as shown in Figure 5.7e. Size and align the label.

➤ Click the **Text Box button**, then click and drag in the Detail section to create an unbound control that will contain the amount of the monthly payment. Click the label for the control (e.g., Text 15), then press the **Del key**.

➤ Point to the unbound control, click the **right mouse button**, then click **Properties** to open the properties dialog box. Click the **All tab**.

➤ Click the **Name property**. Enter **Payment Due** in place of the existing label.

➤ Click the **Control Source property**, then click the **Build (...) button**.
  • Double click **Functions** (if there is a plus sign in its icon), then click **Built-In Functions**. Click **Financial** in the second column, then double click **Pmt**.
  • You need to replace each of the arguments in the Pmt function with the appropriate field names from the Loans table. Select the arguments one at a time and enter the replacement for that argument exactly as shown in Figure 5.7e. Click **OK** when finished.

➤ Click the **Format property**, click the **down arrow**, and specify **Currency**. Click the **Decimal Places property**, click the **down arrow**, and select **2**.

➤ Close the Properties dialog box. Change to the Datasheet view and check the column widths, making adjustments as necessary. Close the Loans subform.

➤ Click **Yes** to save the changes.

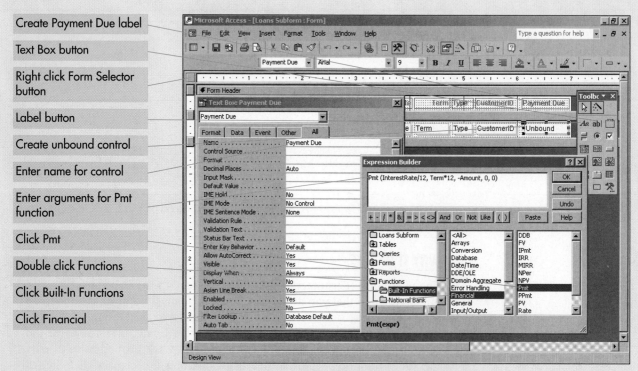

Create Payment Due label

Text Box button

Right click Form Selector button

Label button

Create unbound control

Enter name for control

Enter arguments for Pmt function

Click Pmt

Double click Functions

Click Built-In Functions

Click Financial

(e) Add the Payment Amount (step 5)

FIGURE 5.7   *Hands-on Exercise 2 (continued)*

Step 6: **Change the Column Widths**

➤ Click the **View button** to change to the Form view. You should see the first customer in the database, together with the associated loan information. You may, however, have to adjust the width of the columns within the subform and/or the size and position of the subform within the main form.

➤ To change the width of the columns within the subform:

• Click the **drop-down arrow** on the **View button** to change to the **Datasheet view**. Click the **plus sign** next to the CustomerID column for the first customer to display the associated records in the Loans table as shown in Figure 5.7f.

• Click and drag the border between the column headings until you can read all of the information. Click the **Save button** to save the new layout, then close the form. You must close the main form, then reopen the form in order for the changes in the subform to be visible.

• You should be back in the Database window. Double click the **Customers form** to reopen the form and check the width of the columns in the subform. If necessary, click the **View button** to return to the Datasheet view to further adjust the columns.

➤ It may also be necessary to change the size or position of the subform control within the main form. Click the **View button** and change to the **Design view**.

• Click the **subform control** to select it, then click and drag a sizing handle to change the size of the subform control.

• Click and drag a border of the control to change its position.

➤ You will have to switch back and forth between the Form and Design views a few times to get the correct sizing. Save the completed form.

View button

Click + to display subdatasheet

Click and drag border between column headings to size columns

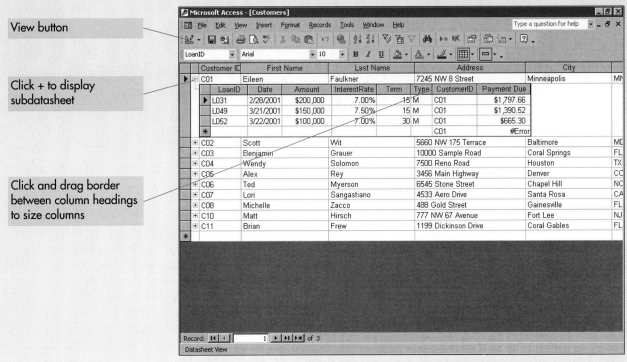

(f) Change the Column Widths (step 6)

FIGURE 5.7 *Hands-on Exercise 2 (continued)*

Step 7:   **Complete the Customers Form**

➤ Select the **Customers form**, then click the **Design button** to reopen the form as shown in Figure 5.7g.
➤ Click the **Tab Order command** to display the Tab Order dialog box. Click the **Auto Order button**, then click **OK** to accept the new tab order and close the dialog box.
➤ Click the **Page Break** tool in the toolbox, then click below the subform control. This will print one customer form per page.
➤ Save the form.

Click the Auto Order button

Click Page Break tool

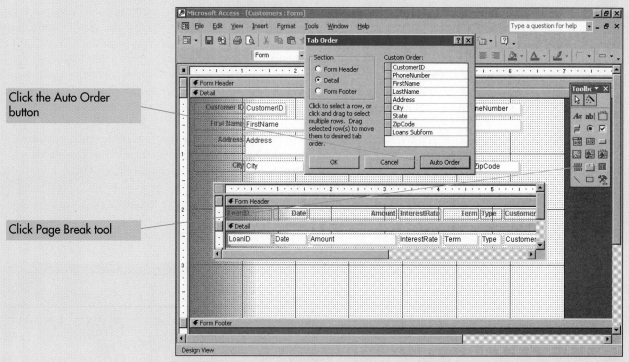

(g) Complete the Customers Form (step 7)

FIGURE 5.7   *Hands-on Exercise 2 (continued)*

#ERROR AND HOW TO AVOID IT

A #Error message will be displayed in the Form view if the Pmt function is unable to compute a payment for a new record prior to entering the term of the loan. You can, however, suppress the display of the message by using the IIf (Immediate If) function to test for a null argument. In other words, if the term of the loan has not been entered, do not display anything; otherwise compute the payment in the usual way. Use the IIf function =IIf([Term] Is Null,"",Pmt([InterestRate]/12, [Term]*12, – [Amount],)) as the control source for the payment amount. See Help for additional information.

Step 8:   **Enter a New Loan**

> ➤ Click the **View button** to switch to the Form view as shown in Figure 5.7h. (You may have to return to the Design view of the Customers form to increase the space allotted for the Loans subform. You may also have to reopen the Loans subform to adjust the column widths.)
> ➤ Click the ▶| on the status bar of the main form to move to the last record (customer C11), which is the record you entered in the previous exercise. (Click the **PgUp key** if you are on a blank record.)
> ➤ Click the **LoanID field** next to the asterisk in the subform. Enter data for the new loan as shown in Figure 5.7h:
>   • The record selector changes to a pencil as soon as you begin to enter data.
>   • The payment due will be computed automatically as soon as you complete the Term field.
>   • You do *not* have to enter the CustomerID since it appears automatically due to the relationship between the Customers and Loans tables.
> ➤ Press the **down arrow** when you have entered the last field (Type), which saves the data in the current record. (The record selector symbol changes from a pencil to a triangle.)
> ➤ Check that you are still on the record for customer 11 (the record containing your data), then click the **selection area** at the left of the form.
> ➤ Pull down the **File menu** and click **Print** (or click the **Print button**) to display the Print dialog box. Click the **Selected Record(s) option button**. Click **OK**. (It may be necessary to use the **Page Setup command** to change the margins, so that the form fits on one page.)
> ➤ Close the Customers form. Click **Yes** if asked to save the changes to the form. Close the National Bank database. Exit Access if you do not want to continue with the next hands-on exercise at this time.

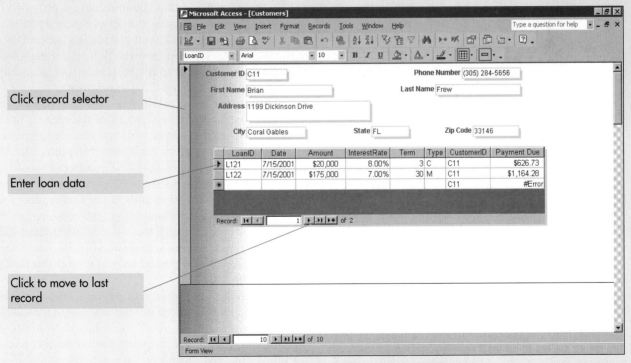

Click record selector

Enter loan data

Click to move to last record

(h) Enter a New Loan (step 8)

FIGURE 5.7   *Hands-on Exercise 2 (continued)*

The chapter began with a conceptual view of the National Bank database, in which we described the need for separate tables to store data for customers and loans. We created a database with sample data, asked several questions about various customers and their loans, then intuitively drew on both tables to derive the answers. Access simply automates the process through creation of a *multiple-table query*. This type of query was introduced in the previous chapter, but it is reviewed in this section because of its importance.

Let's assume that you wanted to know the name of every customer who held a 15-year mortgage that was issued after April 1, 2001. To answer that question, you would need data from both the Customers table and the Loans table, as shown in Figure 5.8. You would create the query using the same grid as for a simple select query, but you would have to add fields from both tables to the query. The Design view of the query is shown in Figure 5.8a. The resulting dynaset is displayed in Figure 5.8b.

The Query window contains the Field, Sort, Show, and Criteria rows that appear in simple select queries. The *Table row* is necessary only in multiple-table queries and indicates the table where the field originates. The customer's last name and first name are taken from the Customers table. All of the other fields are from the Loans table. The one-to-many relationship between the Customers table and the Loans table is shown graphically within the Query window. The tables are related through the CustomerID field, which is the primary key in the Customers table and a foreign key in the Loans table. The line between the two field lists is called a *join line*, and its properties determine how the tables will be accessed within the query.

Figure 5.8 extends the earlier discussion on multiple-table queries to include the SQL statement in Figure 5.8c and the Join Properties dialog box in Figure 5.8d. This information is intended primarily for the reader who is interested in the theoretical concepts of a relational database. *Structured Query Language* (SQL) is the universal way to access a relational database, meaning that the information provided by any database is obtained through SQL queries. Access simplifies the creation of an SQL query, however, by providing the Design grid, then converting the entries in the grid to the equivalent SQL statements. You can view the SQL statements from within Access as we did in Figure 5.8c, by changing to the SQL view, and in so doing you can gain a better appreciation for how a relational database works.

The concept of a "join" is also crucial to a relational database. In essence, Access, or any other relational database, combines (joins) all of the records in the Customers table with all of the records in the Loans table to create a temporary working table. The result is a very large table in which each record contains all of the fields from both the Customers table and the Loans table. The number of records in this table is equal to the product of the number of Customer records times the number of Loans records; for example, if there were 10 records in the Customers table, and 30 records in the Loans table, there would be 300 records in the combined table. However, Access displays only those records where the value of the joined field (CustomerID) is the same in both tables. It sounds complicated (it is), but Access does the work for you. And as we said earlier, you need only to master the Design grid in Figure 5.8a and let Access do the rest.

The power of a relational database is its ability to process multiple-table queries, such as the example in Figure 5.8. The forms and reports within a database also become more interesting when they contain information based on multiple-table queries. Our next exercise has you create a query similar to the one in Figure 5.8, then create a report based on that query.

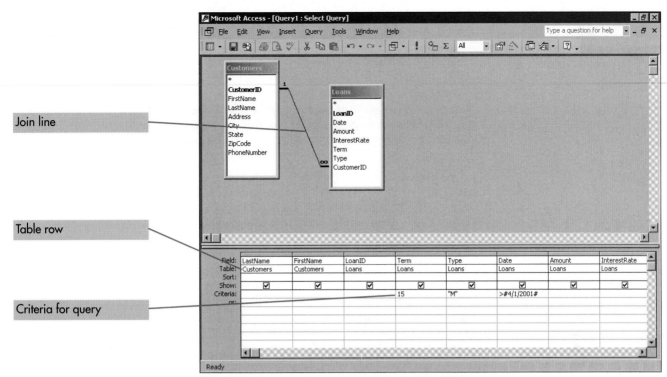

(a) Query Window

Last Name	First Name	LoanID	Term	Type	Date	Amount	InterestRate
▶ Hirsch	Matt	L062	15	M	4/22/2001	$350,000	7.50%
Grauer	Benjamin	L100	15	M	5/1/2001	$150,000	6.00%
Sangastiano	Lori	L120	15	M	5/8/2001	$275,000	9.20%
*							

(b) Dynaset

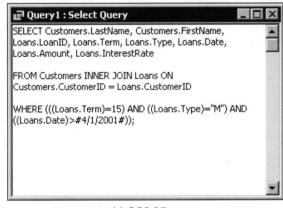

(c) SQL View

(d) Join Properties

FIGURE 5.8   *A Multiple-Table Query*

Objective To create a query that relates two tables to one another, then create a report based on that query; to use the query to update the records in the underlying tables. Use Figure 5.9 as a guide in the exercise.

Step 1: **Add the Tables**

> Open the **National Bank database** from the previous exercise.
> Click the **Queries button** in the Database window. Double click **Create query in Design view**.
> The Show Table dialog box appears as shown in Figure 5.9a, with the Tables tab already selected. Click the **Customers table,** then click the **Add button** (or double click the **Customers table**) to add the Customers table to the query.
> Double click the **Loans table** to add the Loans table to the query.
> Click **Close** to close the Show Table dialog box.

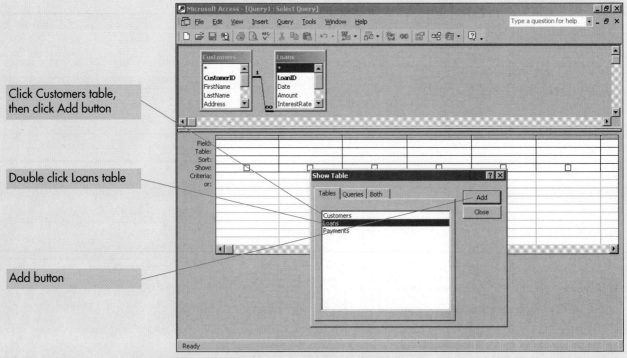

Click Customers table, then click Add button

Double click Loans table

Add button

(a) Add the Tables (step 1)

FIGURE 5.9 *Hands-on Exercise 3*

ADDING AND DELETING TABLES

To add a table to an existing query, pull down the Query menu, click Show Table, then double click the name of the table from the Table/Query list. To delete a table, click anywhere in its field list and press the Del key, or pull down the Query menu and click Remove Table.

Step 2:   **Move and Size the Field Lists**

➤ Click the **Maximize button** so that the Query Design window takes the entire desktop.
➤ Point to the line separating the field lists from the design grid (the mouse pointer changes to a cross), then click and drag in a downward direction. This gives you more space to display the field lists for the tables in the query as shown in Figure 5.9b.
➤ Click and drag the bottom of the **Customers table field list** until you can see all of the fields in the Customers table.
➤ Click and drag the bottom of the **Loans table field list** until you can see all of the fields in the Loans table.
➤ Click and drag the title bar of the **Loans table** to the right until you are satisfied with the appearance of the line connecting the tables.

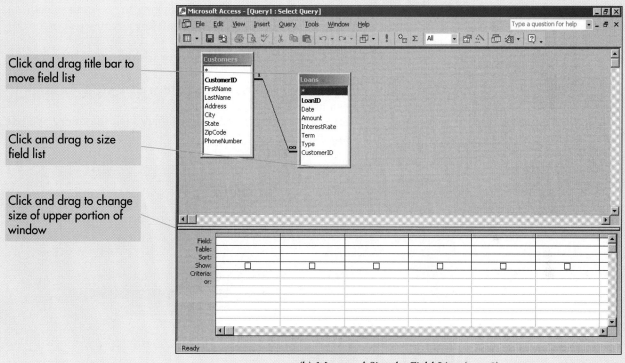

Click and drag title bar to move field list

Click and drag to size field list

Click and drag to change size of upper portion of window

(b) Move and Size the Field Lists (step 2)

FIGURE 5.9   *Hands-on Exercise 3 (continued)*

CONVERSION TO STANDARD FORMAT

Access is flexible in accepting text and date expressions in the Criteria row of a select query. A text entry can be entered with or without quotation marks (e.g., M or "M"). A date entry can be entered with or without pound signs (you can enter 1/1/96 or #1/1/96#). Access does, however, convert your entries to standard format as soon you move to the next cell in the design grid. Thus, text entries are always displayed in quotation marks, and dates are always enclosed in pound signs.

Step 3:   **Create the Query**

> ➤ The Table row should be visible within the design grid. If not, pull down the **View menu** and click **Table Names** to display the Table row in the design grid as shown in Figure 5.9c.
>
> ➤ Double click the **LastName** and **FirstName fields**, in that order, from the Customers table to add these fields to the design grid. Double click the **title bar** of the Loans table to select all of the fields, then drag the selected group of fields to the design grid.
>
> ➤ Enter the selection criteria (scrolling if necessary) as follows:
>
> • Click the **Criteria row** under the **Date field**. Type **Between 1/1/01 and 3/31/01**. (You do not have to type the pound signs.)
>
> • Click the **Criteria row** for the **Amount field**. Type **>200000**.
>
> • Type **M** in the Criteria row for the **Type field**. (You do not have to type the quotation marks.)
>
> ➤ Select all of the columns in the design grid by clicking the column selector in the first column, then pressing and holding the **Shift key** as you scroll to the last column and click its column selector.
>
> ➤ Double click the right edge of any column selector to adjust the column width of all the columns simultaneously.
>
> ➤ Click the **Sort row** under the LastName field, then click the **down arrow** to open the drop-down list box. Click **Ascending**.
>
> ➤ Click the **Save button** on the Query Design toolbar. Save the query as **First Quarter 2001 Jumbo Loans**.

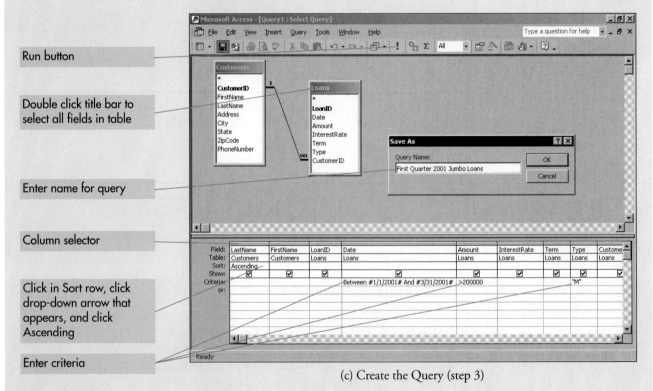

(c) Create the Query (step 3)

FIGURE 5.9   *Hands-on Exercise 3 (continued)*

Step 4: **The Dynaset**

➤ Click the **Run button** (the exclamation point) to run the query and create the dynaset in Figure 5.9d. Three jumbo loans are listed.

➤ Click the **Amount field** for loan L028. Enter **100000** as the corrected amount and press **enter**. (This will reduce the number of jumbo loans in subsequent reports to two.)

➤ Return to the Design view and rerun the query. Only two loans are listed, because loan L028 is no longer a jumbo loan. Changing a value in a dynaset automatically changes the underlying query.

➤ Click the **Close button** to close the query. Click **Yes** if asked whether to save the changes to the query.

View button

Enter 100000 as new amount

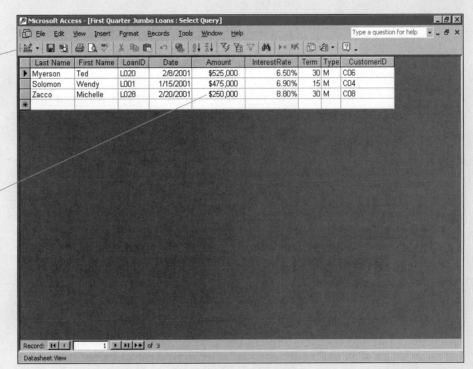

(d) The Dynaset (step 4)

FIGURE 5.9   *Hands-on Exercise 3 (continued)*

DATA TYPE MISMATCH

The data type determines the way in which criteria appear in the design grid. A text field is enclosed in quotation marks. Number, currency, and counter fields are shown as digits with or without a decimal point. Dates are enclosed in pound signs. A Yes/No field is entered as Yes or No without quotation marks. Entering criteria in the wrong format produces a Data Type Mismatch error when attempting to run the query.

Step 5: **Create a Report**

➤ The National Bank database should still be open (although the size of your window may be different from the one in the figure).
➤ Click the **Reports button** in the Database window. Double click **Create report by using Wizard**.
➤ Click the **drop-down arrow** to display the tables and queries in the database to select the one on which the report will be based.
➤ Select **First Quarter 2001 Jumbo Loans** (the query you just created) as the basis of your report as shown in Figure 5.9e.

Click Create report by using Wizard

Reports button

Click drop-down arrow to display tables and queries

Click First Quarter 2001 Jumbo loans

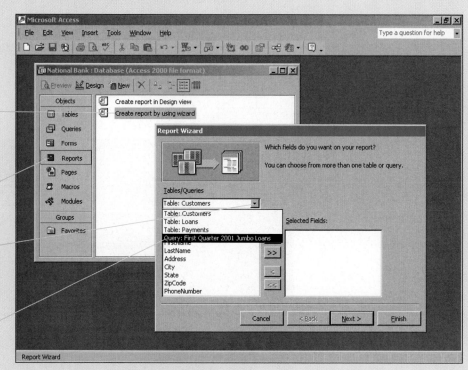

(e) Create a Report (step 5)

FIGURE 5.9 *Hands-on Exercise 3 (continued)*

CHANGE THE REPORT PROPERTIES

Do you want the page header or page footer to appear on every page of a report, or would you prefer to suppress the information on pages where there is a report header or footer? You can customize a report to accommodate this and other subtleties by changing the report properties. Open the report in Design view, right click the Report Selector button (the solid square in the upper left corner), then click the Properties command to display the property sheet for the report. Click the All tab, locate the Page Header or Page Footer property, and make the appropriate change.

Step 6: **The Report Wizard**

> ➤ Double click **LoanID** from the Available Fields list box to add this field to the report. Add the **LastName**, **FirstName**, **Date**, and **Amount** fields as shown in Figure 5.9f. Click **Next**.
> ➤ You will be asked how you want to view your data, by Customers or by Loans. Select **Customers**. Click **Next**.
> ➤ There is no need to group the records. Click **Next**.
> ➤ There is no need to sort the records. Click **Next**.
> ➤ The **Tabular layout** is selected, as is **Portrait orientation**. Be sure the box is checked to **Adjust field width so all fields fit on a page**. Click **Next**.
> ➤ Choose **Soft Gray** as the style. Click **Next**.
> ➤ Enter **First Quarter 2001 Jumbo Loans** as the title for your report. The option button to **Preview the Report** is already selected.
> ➤ Click the **Finish Command button** to exit the Report Wizard and preview the report.

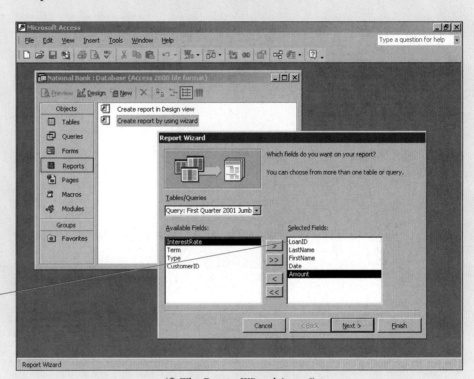

Select fields for report

(f) The Report Wizard (step 6)

FIGURE 5.9 *Hands-on Exercise 3 (continued)*

SYNCHRONIZING REPORTS

The easiest way to link two reports to one another is to create the reports simultaneously through the Report Wizard, by selecting fields from multiple tables. You can, however, add a subreport to an existing report at any time. Open the existing (main) report in Design view, click the Subform/Subreport tool on the Toolbox toolbar, then click and drag on the main report where you want the subreport to go. Supply the information requested by the Wizard and Access will do the rest. See exercise 3 at the end of the chapter.

Step 7:   **Print the Completed Report**

➤ Click the **Maximize button**. If necessary, click the **Zoom button** in the Print Preview window so that you can see the whole report as in Figure 5.9g.

➤ The report is based on the query created earlier. Michelle Zacco is *not* in the report because the amount of her loan was updated in the query's dynaset in step 4.

➤ Click the **Print button** to print the report. Close the Preview window, then close the Report window. Click **Yes** if asked to save the changes.

➤ Close the National Bank database and exit Access if you do not want to continue with the next exercise at this time.

Print button

Zoom button

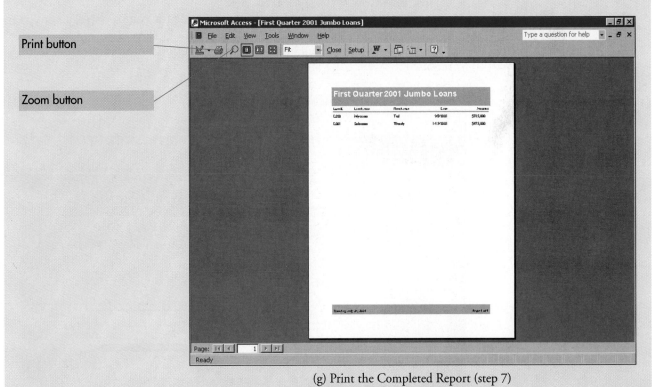

(g) Print the Completed Report (step 7)

FIGURE 5.9   *Hands-on Exercise 3 (continued)*

DATA ACCESS PAGES

The information produced by an Access database can be displayed in a query, form, or printed report. It can also be saved as a data access page that exists as a separate object within an Access database and as an HTML document. The latter can be viewed in Internet Explorer, without having Microsoft Access installed on the client computer. The data within a data access page can be grouped (e.g., by customer), and sorted within a group (e.g., by loan number).

One of the advantages of a relational database is that it can be easily expanded to include additional tables without disturbing the existing tables. The database used throughout the chapter consisted of two tables: a Customers table and a Loans table. Figure 5.10 extends the database to include a partial listing of the Payments table containing the payments received by the bank. Each record in the Payments table has three fields: LoanID, Date (the date the payment was received), and PaymentReceived (the amount sent in).

The original database had a one-to-many relationship between customers and loans. One customer may have many loans, but a given loan is associated with only one customer. The expanded database contains a second one-to-many relationship between loans and payments. One loan has many payments, but a specific payment is associated with only one loan. Thus, the primary key of the Loans table (LoanID) appears as a foreign key in the Payments table.

Look carefully at the Payments table and note that it contains multiple records with the same LoanID. Loan L001, for example, has five payments. In similar fashion, several payments were received on the same date. Payment for two loans, L001 and L002, for example, was received on 2/15/2001. The combination of LoanID and date, however, is unique (e.g., there is only one payment for L001 that was received on 2/15/2001). Thus, *the combination of the two fields*, LoanID and Date, *serves as the primary key*. (This design implies that the system will not accept two payments for the same loan on the same date.)

Query: How many payments have been received for loan L022? What was the date of the most recent payment?

Answer: Four payments have been received for loan L022. The most recent payment was received on 6/12/2001.

The query can be answered with reference to just the Payments table by finding all payments for loan L022. To determine the most recent payment, you would retrieve the records in descending order by Date and retrieve the first record.

Query: How many payments have been received from Michelle Zacco since May 1, 2001?

Answer: Three payments have been received. Two of the payments were for loan L028 on May 20th and June 20th. One payment was for loan L030 on May 21st.

To answer this query, you would look in the Customers table to determine the CustomerID for Ms. Zacco, search the Loans table for all loans for this customer, then retrieve the corresponding payments from the Payments table. (Michelle is also associated with loan L060. The Payments table, however, is truncated in Figure 5.10, and hence the payments for this loan are not visible.)

THE TRANSACTION NUMBER AND AUTONUMBER FIELD TYPE

The use of a concatenated (combined) key, such as LoanID and Date, is one way to create a unique primary key. An alternative technique is to add a new field, such as a transaction number, and assign the AutoNumber field type to that field. Each time a record is added to the Payments table, the value of the transaction number will automatically increase by one, which in turn creates a unique value for that field. This technique is illustrated in the next chapter.

CustomerID	First Name	Last Name	Address	City	State	Zip Code	Phone Number
C01	Eileen	Faulkner	7245 NW 8 Street	Minneapolis	MN	55346	(612) 894-1511
C02	Scott	Wit	5660 NW 175 Terrace	Baltimore	MD	21224	(410) 753-0345
C03	Benjamin	Grauer	10000 Sample Road	Coral Springs	FL	33073	(305) 444-5555
C04	Wendy	Solomon	7500 Reno Road	Houston	TX	77090	(713) 427-3104
C05	Alex	Rey	3456 Main Highway	Denver	CO	80228	(303) 555-6666
C06	Ted	Myerson	6545 Stone Street	Chapel Hill	NC	27515	(919) 942-7654
C07	Lori	Sangastiano	4533 Aero Drive	Santa Rosa	CA	95403	(707) 542-3411
C08	Michelle	Zacco	488 Gold Street	Gainesville	FL	32601	(904) 374-5660
C10	Matt	Hirsch	777 NW 67 Avenue	Fort Lee	NJ	07624	(201) 664-3211

(a) Customers Table

LoanID	Date	Amount	Interest Rate	Term	Type	CustomerID
L001	1/15/01	$475,000	6.90%	15	M	C04
L004	1/23/01	$35,000	7.20%	5	C	C04
L010	1/25/01	$10,000	5.50%	3	C	C05
L014	1/31/01	$12,000	9.50%	10	O	C04
L020	2/8/01	$525,000	6.50%	30	M	C06
L022	2/12/01	$10,500	7.50%	5	O	C07
L026	2/15/01	$35,000	6.50%	5	O	C10
L028	2/20/01	$250,000	8.80%	30	M	C08
L030	2/21/01	$5,000	10.00%	3	O	C08
L031	2/28/01	$200,000	7.00%	15	M	C01
L032	3/1/01	$25,000	10.00%	3	C	C02
L033	3/1/01	$20,000	9.50%	5	O	C05
L040	3/10/01	$129,000	8.50%	15	M	C10
L047	3/11/01	$200,000	7.25%	15	M	C03
L049	3/21/01	$150,000	7.50%	15	M	C01
L052	3/22/01	$100,000	7.00%	30	M	C01
L053	3/31/01	$15,000	6.50%	3	O	C03
L054	4/1/01	$10,000	8.00%	5	C	C02
L057	4/15/01	$25,000	8.50%	4	C	C03
L060	4/18/01	$41,000	9.90%	4	C	C08
L062	4/22/01	$350,000	7.50%	15	M	C10
L100	5/1/01	$150,000	6.00%	15	M	C03
L109	5/3/01	$350,000	8.20%	30	M	C04
L120	5/8/01	$275,000	9.20%	15	M	C07

(b) Loans Table

LoanID	Date	Payment Received	LoanID	Date	Payment Received	LoanID	Date	Payment Received
L001	2/15/01	$4,242.92	L010	5/25/01	$301.96	L022	5/12/01	$210.40
L001	3/15/01	$4,242.92	L010	6/25/01	$301.96	L022	6/12/01	$210.40
L001	4/15/01	$4,242.92	L014	2/28/01	$155.28	L026	3/15/01	$684.82
L001	5/15/01	$4,242.92	L014	3/31/01	$155.28	L026	4/15/01	$684.82
L001	6/15/01	$4,242.92	L014	4/30/01	$155.28	L026	5/15/01	$684.82
L004	2/15/01	$696.35	L014	5/30/01	$155.28	L026	6/15/01	$684.82
L004	3/15/01	$696.35	L014	6/30/01	$155.28	L028	3/20/01	$1,975.69
L004	4/15/01	$696.35	L020	3/8/01	$3,318.36	L028	4/20/01	$1,975.69
L004	5/15/01	$696.35	L020	4/8/01	$3,318.36	L028	5/20/01	$1,975.69
L004	6/15/01	$696.35	L020	5/8/01	$3,318.36	L028	6/20/01	$1,975.69
L010	2/25/01	$301.96	L020	6/8/01	$3,318.36	L030	3/21/01	$161.34
L010	3/25/01	$301.96	L022	3/12/01	$210.40	L030	4/21/01	$161.34
L010	4/25/01	$301.96	L022	4/12/01	$210.40	L030	5/21/01	$161.34

(c) Payments Table (partial list)

FIGURE 5.10 *Expanding the Database*

Multiple Subforms

Subforms were introduced earlier in the chapter as a means of displaying data from related tables. Figure 5.11 continues the discussion by showing a main form with two levels of subforms. The main (Customers) form has a one-to-many relationship with the first (Loans) subform. The Loans subform in turn has a one-to-many relationship with the second (Payments) subform. The Customers form and the Loans subform are the forms you created in the second hands-on exercise. (The Loans subform is displayed in the Form view, as opposed to the Datasheet view.) The Payments subform is new and will be developed in our next exercise.

The records displayed in the three forms are linked to one another according to the relationships within the database. There is a one-to-many relationship between customers and loans so that the first subform displays all of the loans for one customer. There is also a one-to-many relationship between loans and payments so that the second subform (Payments) displays all of the payments for the selected loan. Click on a different loan (for the same customer), and the Payments subform is updated automatically to show all of the payments for that loan.

The status bar for the main form indicates record 5 of 10, meaning that you are viewing the fifth of 10 Customer records. The status bar for the Loans subform indicates record 2 of 2, corresponding to the second of two loan records for the fifth customer. The status bar for the Payments subform indicates record 1 of 3, corresponding to the first of three payment records for this loan for this customer.

The three sets of navigation buttons enable you to advance to the next record(s) in any of the forms. The records move in conjunction with one another. Thus, if you advance to the next record in the Customers form, you will automatically display a different set of records in the Loans subform, as well as a different set of Payment records in the Payments subform.

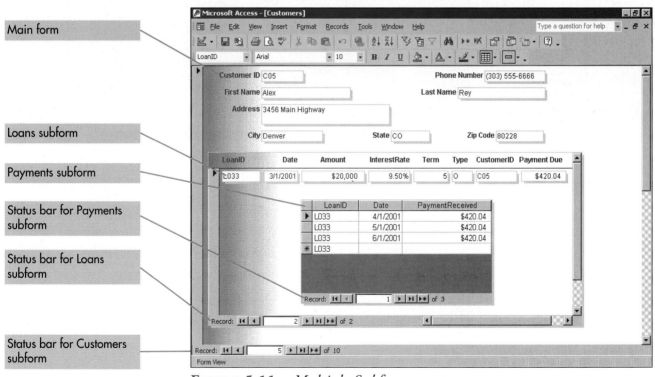

FIGURE 5.11 *Multiple Subforms*

LINKED SUBFORMS

Objective   To create a main form with two levels of subforms; to display a subform in Form view or Datasheet view. Use Figure 5.12 as a guide.

Step 1:   **Add a Relationship**

➤ Open the **National Bank database**. Pull down the **Tools menu**. Click **Relationships** to open the Relationships window as shown in Figure 5.12a.

➤ Maximize the Relationships window. Pull down the **Relationships menu**. Click **Show Table** to display the Show Table dialog box.

➤ The **Tables tab** is selected within the Show Table dialog box. Double click the **Payments table** to add the table to the Relationships window. Close the Show Table dialog box.

➤ Click and drag the title bar of the **Payments Field list** so that it is positioned approximately one inch from the Loans table.

➤ Click and drag the **LoanID field** in the Loans field list to the **LoanID field** in the Payments field list. You will see the Relationships dialog box.

➤ Check the **Enforce Referential Integrity** check box. (If necessary, clear the check boxes to Cascade Update Related Fields and Delete Related Records.)

➤ Click the **Create button** to establish the relationship. You should see a line indicating a one-to-many relationship between the Loans and Payments tables.

➤ Click the **Save button**, then close the Relationships window.

Click and drag LoanID from Loans table to Payments table

Check box to Enforce Referential Integrity

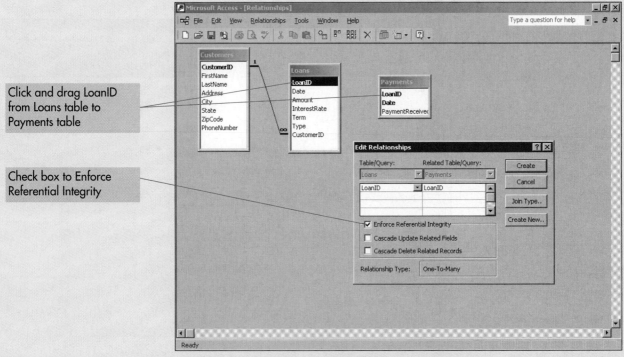

(a) Add a Relationship (step 1)

FIGURE 5.12   *Hands-on Exercise 4*

Step 2: **Create the Payments Subform**

> ➤ You should be back in the Database window. Click the **Forms button**, then open the **Loans subform** in Design view as shown in Figure 5.12b.
> ➤ Click and drag the top edge of the **Details section** so that you have approximately 2 to 2½ inches of blank space in the Detail section.
> ➤ Click the **Subform/Subreport button** on the Toolbox toolbar, then click and drag in the **Loans form** to create the Payments subform. Release the mouse.
> ➤ The **Use Existing Tables and Queries option button** is selected, indicating that we will build the subform from a table or query. Click **Next**. You should see the Subform/Subreport dialog box in Figure 5.12b.
> ➤ Click the **drop-down arrow** on the Tables and Queries list box to select the **Payments table**. Click the **>> button** to add all of the fields in the Payments table to the subform. Click **Next**.
> ➤ The Subform Wizard asks you to define the fields that link the main form to the subform. The option button to **Choose from a list** is selected, as is **Show Payments for each record in Loans using LoanID**. Click **Next**.
> ➤ **Payments subform** is entered as the name of the subform. Click **Finish**.

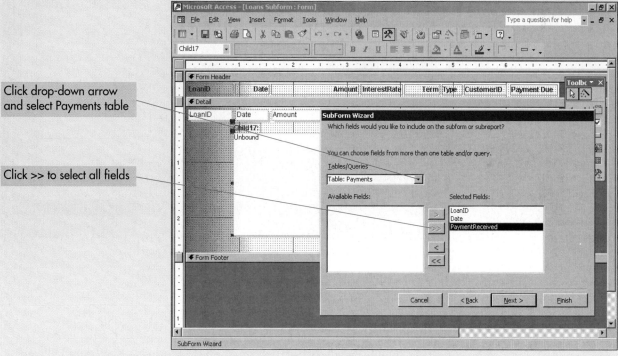

Click drop-down arrow
and select Payments table

Click >> to select all fields

(b) Create the Payments Subform (step 2)

FIGURE 5.12 *Hands-on Exercise 4 (continued)*

LINKING FIELDS, FORMS, AND SUBFORMS

Linking fields do not have to appear in the main form and subform but must be included in the underlying table or query. The LoanID, for example, links the Loans form and the Payments form and need not appear in either form. We have, however, chosen to display the LoanID in both forms to emphasize the relationship between the corresponding tables.

Step 3: **Change the Loans Subform**

➤ Maximize the window. Point to the **Form Selector box** in the upper-left corner of the Design window, click the **right mouse button** to display a shortcut menu, and click **Properties** to display the Form Properties dialog box in Figure 5.12c.
➤ The property sheet pertains to the form as a whole, as can be seen from the title bar. Click in the **Default View box**, click the **drop-down arrow** to display the views, then click **Single Form**. Close the Properties dialog box.
➤ Select the label for the Payments subform control, then press the **Del key** to delete the label.
➤ Save the form.

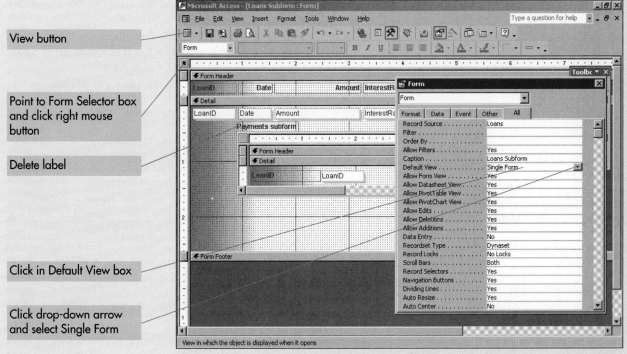

View button

Point to Form Selector box and click right mouse button

Delete label

Click in Default View box

Click drop-down arrow and select Single Form

(c) Change the Loans Subform (step 3)

FIGURE 5.12 *Hands-on Exercise 4 (continued)*

THE DEFAULT VIEW PROPERTY

The Default View property determines how a form is dislayed initially and is especially important when working with multiple forms. In general, the highest level form(s) is (are) displayed in the Single Form view and the lowest level in the Datasheet view. In this example, the Customers and Loans forms are both set to the Single Form view, whereas the Payment form is set to the Datasheet view. To change the default view, right click the Form Selector box to display the property sheet, click the All tab, then change the entry in the Default View property.

Step 4: **The Loans Subform in Form View**

➤ Click the **drop-down arrow** next to the **View button** to switch to the Form view for the Loans subform as shown in Figure 5.12d.
➤ Do not be concerned if the size and/or position of your form is different from ours as you can return to the Design view to make the necessary changes.
   • The status bar of the Loans form indicates record 1 of 26, meaning that you are positioned on the first of 26 records in the Loans table.
   • The status bar for the Payments subform indicates record 1 of 5, corresponding to the first of five payment records for this loan.
➤ Change to the **Datasheet view**, expand the first record, then expand the column widths.
➤ Change to the **Design view** to size and/or move the Payments subform control within the Loans subform. Save, then close, the Loans subform.

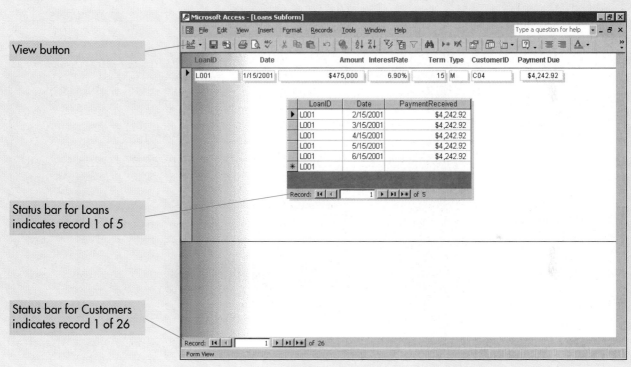

(d) The Loans Subform in Form View (step 4)

FIGURE 5.12 *Hands-on Exercise 4 (continued)*

USER-FRIENDLY FORMS

The phrase "user-friendly" appears so frequently that we tend to take it for granted. The intention is clear, however, and you should strive to make your forms as clear as possible so that the user is provided with all the information he or she may need. It may be obvious to the designer that one has to click the navigation buttons to move to a new loan, but a novice unfamiliar with Access may not know that. Adding a descriptive label to the form goes a long way toward making a system successful.

Step 5: **The Customers Form**

➤ You should be back in the Database window. Click the **Forms button** (if necessary), then open the **Customers form** as shown in Figure 5.12e.

➤ Do not be concerned if the sizes of the subforms are different from ours as you can return to the Design view to make the necessary changes.

• The status bar of the Customers form indicates record 1 of 10, meaning that you are positioned on the first of 10 records in the Customers table.

• The status bar for the Loans subform indicates record 1 of 3, corresponding to the first of three records for this customer.

• The status bar for the Payments subform indicates record 1 of 4, corresponding to the first of four payments for this loan.

➤ Change to the **Design view** to move and/or size the control for the Loans subform as described in step 6.

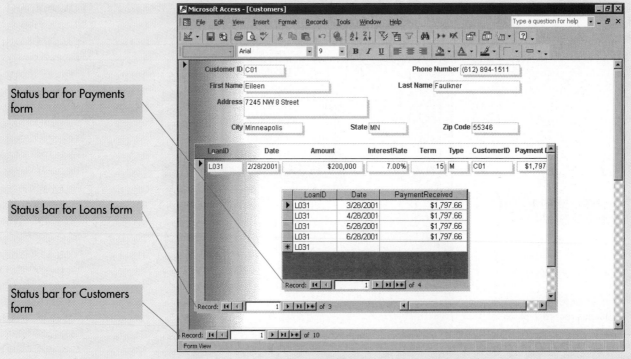

(e) The Customers Form (step 5)

FIGURE 5.12 *Hands-on Exercise 4 (continued)*

THE STARTUP PROPERTY

The Startup property determines how a database will appear when it is opened. One very common option is to open a form automatically so that the user is presented with the form without having to navigate through the Database window. Pull down the Tools menu, click Startup to display the Startup dialog box, then click the drop-down arrow in the Display Form list box. Select the desired form, such as the Customers form created in this exercise, then click OK. The next time you open the database the designated form will be opened automatically.

Step 6: **The Finishing Touches**

➤ You may need to increase the size of the Loans subform control. Click and drag the bottom edge of the **Detail Section** in Figure 5.12f to make the section larger. You may also have to click and drag the Loans subform to the left, then click and drag its right border to make it wider.

➤ We also found it necessary to decrease the size of the Amount field within the Loans subform. Click the label for the **Amount field** in the Form header. Press and hold the **Shift key** as you select the bound control for the Amount field in the detail section, then click and drag the right border to make both controls narrower.

➤ Click the **Interest Rate label**. Press and hold the **Shift key** as you select the remaining controls to the left of the amount field, then click and drag these fields to the left. Save the changes.

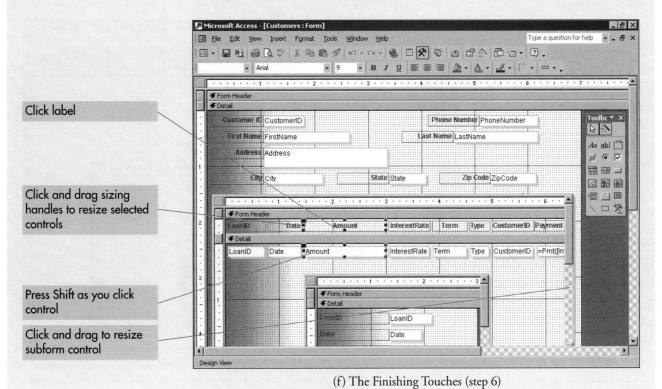

(f) The Finishing Touches (step 6)

FIGURE 5.12 *Hands-on Exercise 4 (continued)*

MULTIPLE CONTROLS AND PROPERTIES

Press and hold the Shift key as you click one control after another to select multiple controls. To view or change the properties for the selected controls, click the right mouse button to display a shortcut menu, then click Properties to display a property sheet. If the value of a property is the same for all selected controls, that value will appear in the property sheet; otherwise the box for that property will be blank. Changing a property when multiple controls are selected changes the property for all selected controls.

Step 7:   **Make Your Payments**

> ➤ Change to the **Form view.** Click the ►| on the status bar for the Customers form to move to the last record as shown in Figure 5.12g. This should be Customer C11 (your record) that you entered in the earlier exercises in this chapter. You currently have two loans, L121 and L122, the first of which is displayed.
> ➤ Click in the **Payments subform.** Enter the date of your first payment, press **Tab,** then enter the amount paid. Press **enter** to move to the next payment record and enter this payment as well. Press **enter** and enter a third payment.
> ➤ Click the **selection area** at the left of the form to select this record. Pull down the **File menu** and click **Print** to display the Print dialog box. Click the **Selected Records Option button.** Click **OK** to print the selected form.
> ➤ Close the Customers form. Click **Yes** if asked to save the changes to the form.
> ➤ Close the National Bank database. Exit Access.

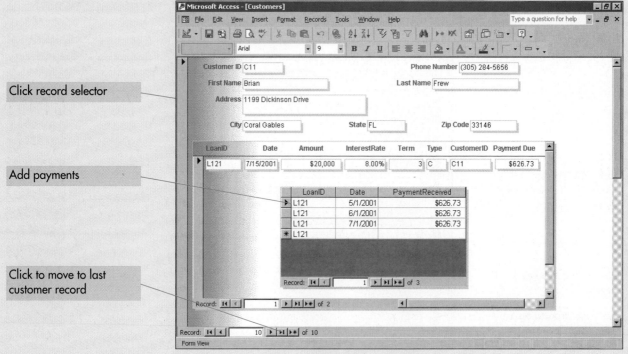

Click record selector

Add payments

Click to move to last customer record

(g) Make Your Payments (step 7)

FIGURE 5.12   *Hands-on Exercise 4 (continued)*

THREE SETS OF NAVIGATION BUTTONS

Each form or subform has its own set of navigation buttons. Thus, in this example you are looking at record 10 of 10 in the Customers form, loan 1 of 2 in the Loans form for this customer, and payment 3 of 3 in the Payments form for this loan. Click the next or previous button in the Customers form and you will be taken to the next or previous customer record, respectively. Click the next button in the Loans form, however, and you are taken to the next loan for the current customer. In similar fashion, clicking the next button in the Payments form takes you to the next payment for the current loan for the current customer.

An Access database may contain multiple tables. Each table stores data about a specific subject. Each table has a primary key, which is a field (or combination of fields) that uniquely identifies each record.

A one-to-many relationship uses the primary key of the "one" table as a foreign key in the "many" table. (A foreign key is simply the primary key of the related table.) The Relationships window enables you to graphically create a one-to-many relationship by dragging the join field from one table to the other.

Referential integrity ensures that the tables in a database are consistent with one another. When referential integrity is enforced, Access prevents you from adding a record to the "many" table if that record contains an invalid foreign key. It also prevents you from deleting a record in the "one" table if there is a corresponding record in the related table. You can, however, always add a record to the "one" table, and you can always delete a record from the "many" table.

A subform is a form within a form and is used to display data from a related table. It is created most easily with the Form Wizard, then modified in the Form Design view just as any other form. A main form can have any number of subforms. Subforms can extend to two levels, enabling a subform to be created within a subform.

The power of a select query lies in its ability to include fields from several tables. The Design view of a query shows the relationships that exist between the tables by drawing a join line that indicates how to relate the data. The Tables row displays the name of the table containing the corresponding field. Once created, a multiple table query can be the basis for a form or report.

The results of a query are displayed in a dynaset, a dynamic subset of the underlying tables that contains the records that satisfy the criteria within the query. Any changes to the dynaset are automatically reflected in the underlying table(s).

Tables can be added to a relational database without disturbing the data in existing tables. A database can have several one-to-many relationships. All relationships are created in the Relationships window.

KEY TERMS

Build button (p. 220)
Control Source property (p. 220)
Datasheet view (p. 213)
Foreign key (p. 205)
Form view (p. 213)
Join line (p. 224)
Main form (p. 213)

Multiple-table query (p. 224)
One-to-many relationship (p. 203)
PMT function (p. 213)
Primary key (p. 205)
Referential integrity (p. 205)
Relationship line (p. 205)
Relationships window (p. 205)

Startup property (p. 240)
Structured Query Language (SQL)
  (p. 224)
Subdatasheet (p. 205)
Subform (p. 213)
Table row (p. 224)

1. Which of the following will cause a problem of referential integrity when there is a one-to-many relationship between customers and loans?
   (a) The deletion of a customer record that has corresponding loan records
   (b) The deletion of a customer record that has no corresponding loan records
   (c) The deletion of a loan record with a corresponding customer record
   (d) All of the above

2. Which of the following will cause a problem of referential integrity when there is a one-to-many relationship between customers and loans?
   (a) The addition of a new customer prior to entering loans for that customer
   (b) The addition of a new loan that references an invalid customer
   (c) Both (a) and (b)
   (d) Neither (a) nor (b)

3. Which of the following is true about a database that monitors players and the teams to which those players are assigned?
   (a) The PlayerID will be defined as a primary key within the Teams table
   (b) The TeamID will be defined as a primary key within the Players table
   (c) The PlayerID will appear as a foreign key within the Teams table
   (d) The TeamID will appear as a foreign key within the Players table

4. Which of the following best expresses the relationships within the expanded National Bank database as it appeared at the end of the chapter?
   (a) There is a one-to-many relationship between customers and loans
   (b) There is a one-to-many relationship between loans and payments
   (c) Both (a) and (b)
   (d) Neither (a) nor (b)

5. A database has a one-to-many relationship between branches and employees (one branch can have many employees). Which of the following is a true statement about that database?
   (a) The EmployeeID will be defined as a primary key within the Branches table
   (b) The BranchID will be defined as a primary key within the Employees table
   (c) The EmployeeID will appear as a foreign key within the Branches table
   (d) The BranchID will appear as a foreign key within the Employees table

6. Every table in an Access database:
   (a) Must be related to every other table
   (b) Must have one or more foreign keys
   (c) Both (a) and (b)
   (d) Neither (a) nor (b)

7. Which of the following is true of a main form and subform that are created in conjunction with the one-to-many relationship between customers and loans?
   (a) The main form should be based on the Customers table
   (b) The subform should be based on the Loans table
   (c) Both (a) and (b)
   (d) Neither (a) nor (b)

8. Which of the following is true regarding the navigation buttons for a main form and its associated subform?
   (a) The navigation buttons pertain to just the main form
   (b) The navigation buttons pertain to just the subform
   (c) There are separate navigation buttons for each form
   (d) There are no navigation buttons at all

9. How do you open a subform?
   (a) Go to the Design view of the associated main form, click anywhere in the main form to deselect the subform, then double click the subform
   (b) Go to the Database window, select the subform, then click the Open or Design buttons, depending on the desired view
   (c) Either (a) and (b)
   (d) Neither (a) nor (b)

10. Which of the following is true?
   (a) A main form may contain multiple subforms
   (b) A subform may contain another subform
   (c) Both (a) and (b)
   (d) Neither (a) nor (b)

11. Which command displays the open tables in an Access database in equal-sized windows one on top of another?
   (a) The Tile command in the Window menu
   (b) The Cascade command in the Window menu
   (c) The Tile command in the Relationships menu
   (d) The Cascade command in the Relationships menu

12. Which of the following describes how to move and size a field list within the Relationships window?
   (a) Click and drag the title bar to size the field list
   (b) Click and drag a border or corner to move the field list
   (c) Both (a) and (b)
   (d) Neither (a) nor (b)

13. Which of the following is true regarding entries in a Criteria row of a select query?
   (a) A text field may be entered with or without quotation marks
   (b) A date field may be entered with or without surrounding number (pound) signs
   (c) Both (a) and (b)
   (d) Neither (a) nor (b)

14. Which of the following is true about a select query?
   (a) It may reference fields in one or more tables
   (b) It may have one or more criteria rows
   (c) It may sort on one or more fields
   (d) All of the above

15. A report may be based on:
   (a) A table
   (b) A query
   (c) Both (a) and (b)
   (d) Neither (a) nor (b)

ANSWERS

1. a	**6.** d	**11.** b
2. b	**7.** c	**12.** d
3. d	**8.** c	**13.** c
4. c	**9.** c	**14.** d
5. d	**10.** c	**15.** c

1. Widgets of America (database design): Figure 5.13 displays the relationships diagram for a database that is to be used by the Widgets of America Corporation to track the orders generated by its sales staff. Each sales representative has the exclusive rights to his or her customers; that is, each representative has many customers, but a specific customer always deals with the same sales representative. The company needs to know all of the orders placed by a specific customer as well as the total business generated by each sales representative. The data for each order includes the date the order was placed and the amount of the order.

a. We have designed the database for you. Your task is to implement our design by creating a database that contains the indicated tables and associated relationships.

b. You do not have to enter data into any of the tables, but you will need to create the tables in order to create a relationships diagram. Pay particular attention to the required field property with respect to the related fields. A customer must have an assigned sales representative to gain access to sales information. And, as you might expect, the company will not accept an order unless it (the order) is associated with a specific customer.

c. The report in Figure 5.13 is created from the Relationships window after the relationships have been specified. Pull down the Tools menu and click Relationships to open the Relationships window, then pull down the File menu and click the Print Relationships command to display the Print Preview screen of a report that displays the contents of the Relationships window. Change to the Design view and modify the report to include your name. (Our report also includes a label that describes the relationships in the system as well as a clip art image that can serve as a logo for the eventual system.) Print the completed report for your instructor as proof that you did this exercise.

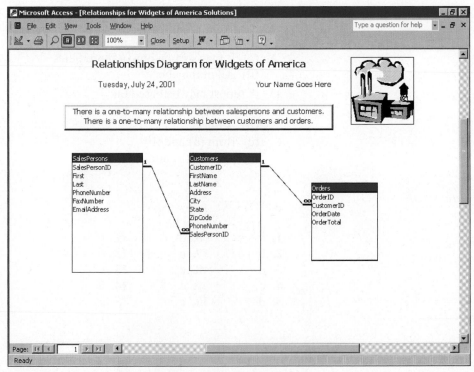

FIGURE 5.13 *Widgets of America (Exercise 1)*

BUILDS ON

HANDS-ON
EXERCISE 3
PAGES 226–232

2. Automobile Loans: Interest rates have come down and National Bank has decided to run a promotion on refinancing all of the existing automobile loans. Your assignment is to create the report in Figure 5.14, which is based on a query that contains fields from both the Customers and Loans tables, and which lists customers in alphabetical order by last name. You need not match our design exactly, but you are required to include your name as well as clip art in the report header. Print the completed report. Add a cover sheet and submit the assignment to your instructor.

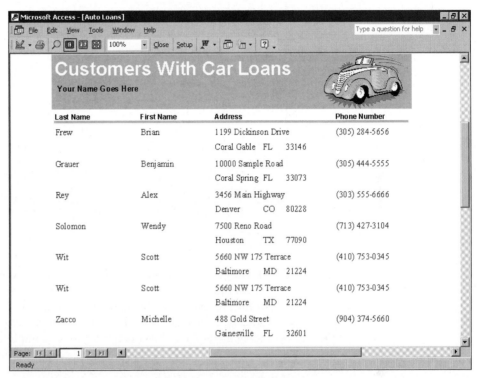

FIGURE 5.14   *Automobile Loans (Exercise 2)*

BUILDS ON

HANDS-ON
EXERCISE 3
PAGES 226–232

3. Customer List: The report in Figure 5.15 displays information about a specific customer, followed by information on all loans for that customer, followed by information about the next customer, his or her loans, and so on. It is similar in concept to the combination of a main form/subform that was created in the chapter. You can create the report in Figure 5.15 by selecting fields from both the Customers table and the Loans table when you start the Report Wizard.

Alternatively, you can create the Customers report initially, change to the Design view, then click and drag the Subform/Subreport tool to start the Subreport Wizard to create the Loan report. This approach creates two separate reports that combine to produce the equivalent information in Figure 5.15. The reports are linked automatically through the CustomerID field that appears in both the Customers and the Loans tables. Which technique do you prefer? Do the same techniques apply to the creation of a main form and a subform? Summarize your thoughts in a brief note to your instructor.

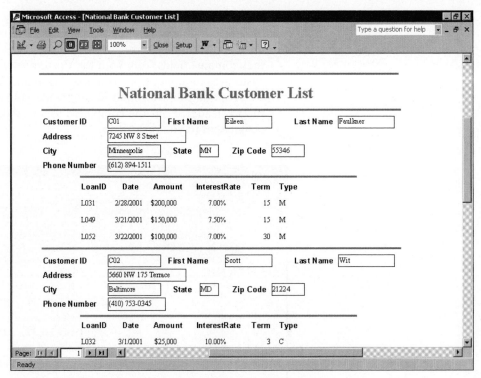

The image shows a Microsoft Access window titled "Microsoft Access - [National Bank Customer List]" with menu bar items File, Edit, View, Tools, Window, Help and a toolbar. The report displays:

National Bank Customer List

Customer ID: C01   First Name: Eileen   Last Name: Faulkner
Address: 7245 NW 8 Street
City: Minneapolis   State: MN   Zip Code: 55346
Phone Number: (612) 894-1511

LoanID	Date	Amount	InterestRate	Term	Type
L031	2/28/2001	$200,000	7.00%	15	M
L049	3/21/2001	$150,000	7.50%	15	M
L052	3/22/2001	$100,000	7.00%	30	M

Customer ID: C02   First Name: Scott   Last Name: Wit
Address: 5660 NW 175 Terrace
City: Baltimore   State: MD   Zip Code: 21224
Phone Number: (410) 753-0345

LoanID	Date	Amount	InterestRate	Term	Type
L032	3/1/2001	$25,000	10.00%	3	C

FIGURE 5.15   *Customer List (Exercise 3)*

4. Turkeys To Go Restaurants: Turkeys To Go Restaurants is a small regional chain that builds restaurants to order for individuals seeking a franchise operation. The chain encourages its franchisees to own many restaurants, but a specific restaurant is associated with only one person. A database has been partially developed, but it is up to you to complete the work. Open the *Chapter 5 Practice 4* database and create the one-to-many relationship between franchisees and restaurants. You can now create the main form/subform combination that is shown in Figure 5.16.

   a. The database already contains separate forms for both franchises and restaurants, and we want you to use those forms rather than creating the form from scratch. Accordingly, open the existing Franchisee form in Design view and size this form so that you can see the Database window at the same time. Click and drag the existing Restaurants form onto the Franchisee form. Access will automatically link the two forms together, but you will have to go back and forth between the Form view and Design view to size it properly. A restaurant will not be built unless a franchisee is already assigned to the restaurant. Thus, the form in Figure 5.16 is sufficient for all data entry in the database.

   b. Use the completed form to enter data for yourself as Franchisee number F010 as shown in Figure 5.16. Use the subform to enter data for two new restaurants, R0100, and R0101 as shown. You can enter any address and restaurant information that you deem appropriate. The annual sales of both restaurants should exceed $500,000. Click the Selector area at the left of the form, then print the record containing your personal information and associated restaurants.

   c. Add a cover sheet. Submit the completed assignment to your instructor.

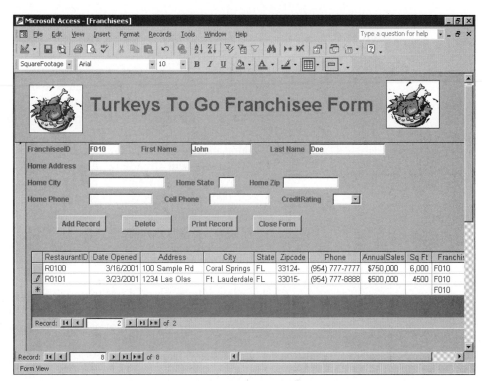

FIGURE 5.16 *Turkeys To Go Restaurants (Exercise 4)*

BUILDS ON

PRACTICE
EXERCISE 4
PAGE 248

5. Turkeys To Go Switchboard: Continue to develop the database for Turkeys To Go Restaurants by creating the switchboard in Figure 5.17. The Data Entry form is the form that you created in the previous exercise. All of the other forms and reports have been created for you, so all that you have to do is build the switchboard. Use the Startup command in the Tools menu to display the switchboard automatically whenever the database is opened. Print the switchboard form and associated table of switchboard items for your instructor.

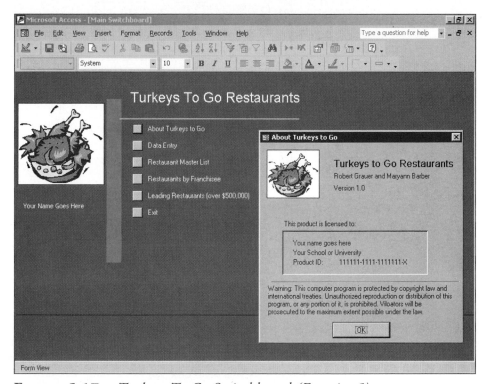

FIGURE 5.17 *Turkeys To Go Switchboard (Exercise 5)*

BUILDS ON

CHAPTER 1
PRACTICE
EXERCISE 5
PAGE 45

6. Employees by Title and Location: The form in Figure 5.18 is developed from the *Look Ahead database* that was first described in Chapter 1. That database contained three tables—Locations, Titles, and Employees. There is a one-to-many relationship between locations and employees (one location can have many employees, but a specific employee is assigned to only one location). There is also a second one-to-many relationship between titles and employees (one title can have many employees, but a specific employee is assigned only one title).

   a. Open the Look Ahead database and check to see if the necessary relationships are in place, based on the earlier work from Chapter 1.

   b. Your name will already be in the database if you have completed the earlier exercises in Chapter 1. If not, add yourself as an Account Rep earning $40,000. Your employee ID is 12345 and you are working in Los Angeles.

   c. Create a main form/subform combination that is similar to Figure 5.18. You need not follow our design exactly, but you are required to include all of the functionality. You can use our clip art or choose a different image. Print the form that displays the information for Account Reps and the associated employees for your instructor.

   d. Create a form parallel to the one in Figure 5.16 that is based on the one-to-many relationship between locations and employees. The main form should display the information for each location, and the subform should display the employees at that location. Print the form for Los Angeles (your location) for your instructor.

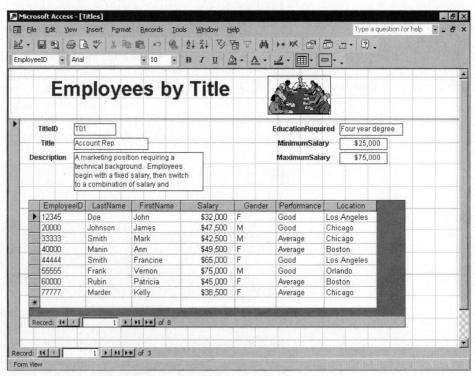

FIGURE 5.18   *Employees by Title (Exercise 6)*

BUILDS ON

PRACTICE
EXERCISE 6
PAGE 250

7. The Look Ahead Switchboard: The switchboard in Figure 5.19 completes the Look Ahead database by providing command buttons for each of the major objects within the database.

   a. Create an "About the Look Ahead database" form similar to the one shown in Figure 5.19. This form is based on similar forms that have appeared throughout the text. Use the same clip art as you did for the form in the previous problem.

b. Add command buttons corresponding to the forms you created in the previous exercise.

c. The three remaining command buttons open reports that are already in the database, and thus do not require any additional work from you. (Do not include a command button for the employee form that is in the database, since that form is now obsolete.)

d. Print the switchboard form as well as the switchboard items table for your instructor as proof that you completed this exercise.

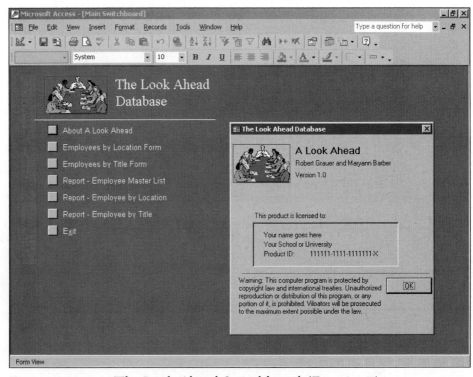

FIGURE 5.19   *The Look Ahead Switchboard (Exercise 7)*

BUILDS ON

HANDS-ON
EXERCISE 3
PAGES 226–232

8. Expanding National Bank: Expand the National Bank database to include a table for Loan Officers, the bank employees who approve each loan before it is granted. One officer will approve many loans, but a specific loan is approved by only one officer, and the loan cannot be granted until the officer approves. (The name of the loan officer will appear in the modified loans subform.) Complete the hands-on exercises in the chapter, then proceed as follows:

a. Open the National Bank database after the third hands-on exercise and create the Loan Officers table. The table contains only four fields—LoanOfficerID, LastName, FirstName, and DateHired. Add two records, Robert Grauer and Maryann Barber, as loan officers one and two, respectively.

b. Modify the Loans table to include a field for the LoanOfficerID. Switch to the Datasheet view, display the loans by LoanID (if they are not yet in this sequence), then assign each loan to an officer. Assign all loans with a LoanID of 50 or less to Bob. Assign the other loans to Maryann.

c. Change to the Design view of the Loans table and make the LoanOfficerID a required field. This ensures that all subsequent loans will be approved by a loan officer.

d. Pull down the Tools menu and expand the Relationships diagram to include the newly created table.

e. Modify the Customer form that was created at the end of the third hands-on exercise to include the Loan Officer information as shown in Figure 5.20. (This requires that you open the existing Loans subform in Design view and insert a control for the Loan Officer.) Pull down the View menu and use the Tab Order command to adjust the order in which the data is entered. In the form header add the additional information that includes your name and today's date.

f. Print the complete record for customer number 1 for your instructor.

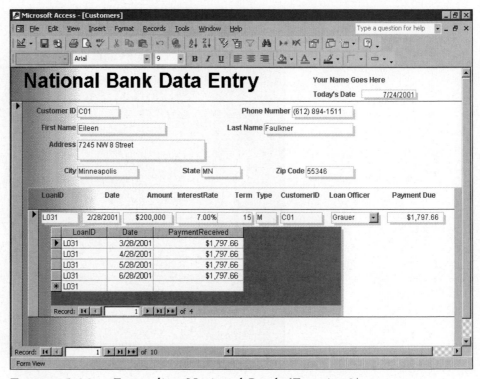

FIGURE 5.20 *Expanding National Bank (Exercise 8)*

BUILDS ON

PRACTICE
EXERCISE 8
PAGE 251

9. National Bank Switchboard: Complete the National Bank database by creating the switchboard in Figure 5.21. All of the objects (except for the "About" form) have already been created either in the hands-on exercises in the body of the chapter or in the end-of-chapter exercises. Print the switchboard form as well as the switchboard items table for your instructor.

10. The Table Analyzer Wizard: The *Chapter 5 Practice 10* database is similar to the National Bank example we have used throughout the chapter, except that its design is flawed through duplicate data. The Table Analyzer Wizard will explain how redundant data wastes space and leads to errors, and then it will suggest ways in which to improve your design.

a. Open the database, click the Tables button, and open the Loans table. Can you spot the flaw in the design that leads to redundant data?

b. Pull down the Tools menu, click the Analyze command, then choose Table to display the Table Analyzer Wizard in Figure 5.22. Let the wizard examine the Loans table for you and suggest ways in which to split the data into two or more tables. How does the wizard's design compare to the design of the National Bank database?

c. Close the Fly By Night Banking database, then open the National Bank database you have used throughout the chapter. Start the Table Analyzer Wizard and let it analyze the Customers, Loans, and Payments tables. What suggestions does the Wizard have for changing these tables?

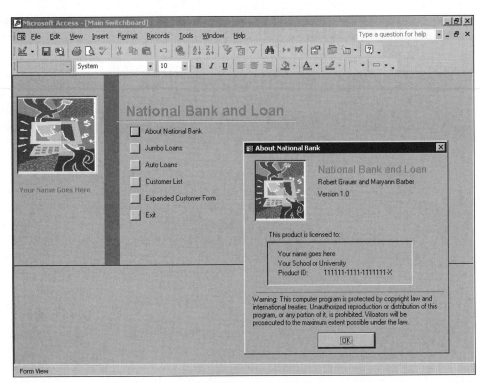

FIGURE 5.21 *National Bank Switchboard (Exercise 9)*

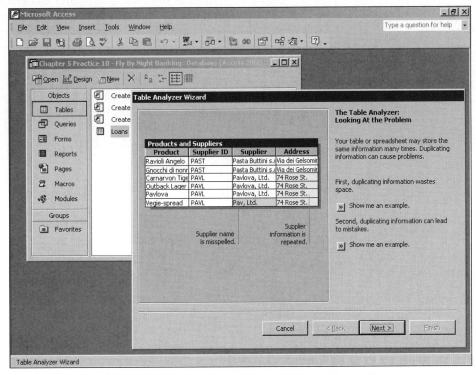

FIGURE 5.22 *The Table Analyzer Wizard (Exercise 10)*

University Apartments

You have just signed your lease for next year at University Apartments, where you have the opportunity to design a database for the complex and thereby save on your rent. The complex has 500 apartments, which are divided into various categories as determined by the number of bedrooms, and additional amenities such as a washer/dryer, patio, and so on. There are many apartments in each category, but a given apartment has only one category.

Your database is to track all apartments in the complex and the students who live in those apartments. Each apartment is leased to one or more students, who sign the identical lease with the same rent and the same starting date for the lease. The lease information is stored within the Apartment record. Each student pays his or her rent individually each month. Your database should produce a report showing the total rent received for each apartment and another report showing the total rent paid by each student.

Design a database that will satisfy the information requirements. You do not have to enter data into the tables, but you do have to create the tables in order to create the relationships diagram, which you will submit to your instructor.

The Automobile Dealership

You have been retained as a database consultant for a local automobile dealership. The dealership has been in the community for fifty years, and it places a premium on customer loyalty, as the typical customer has made repeated purchases over time. The dealership maintains the usual data about its customers—name, address, phone number, credit rating, and so on. It also maintains the usual data about its sales staff. The dealership is large and has several sales managers, each of whom is responsible for multiple salespersons.

The key to the database is the Automobiles table, which contains a record for every car that passes through the dealership. The table contains fields to indicate the date the car was received and the dealer price. It also contains fields for the sale price and sale date, information that is entered when the car is sold. The Automobiles table also contains fields that describe the vehicle such as the make, model, year, color.

Only one salesperson gets credit for each sale and that is the individual who closes the deal. The salesperson receives a commission based on the difference between the sale price and dealer cost. Managers receive an override on all sales generated by their sales staff.

Design a database that will enable the dealership to track its sales by customer, salesperson, and manager. You do not have to enter data into the tables, but you do have to create the tables in order to create the relationships diagram, which you will submit to your instructor.

CHAPTER 6

Many-to-Many Relationships: A More Complex System

OBJECTIVES

AFTER READING THIS CHAPTER YOU WILL BE ABLE TO:

1. Define a many-to-many relationship and explain how it is implemented in Access.
2. Use the Cascade Update and Cascade Delete options in the Relationships window to relax enforcement of referential integrity.
3. Explain how the AutoNumber field type simplifies the entry of a primary key for a new record.
4. Create a main and subform based on a query; discuss the advantage of using queries rather than tables as the basis for a form or report.
5. Create a parameter query; explain how a parameter query can be made to accept multiple parameters.
6. Use aggregate functions in a select query to perform calculations on groups of records.
7. Use the Get External Data command to add external tables to an existing database.

OVERVIEW

This chapter introduces a new case study to give you additional practice in database design. The system extends the concept of a relational database to include both a one-to-many and a many-to-many relationship. The case solution reviews earlier material on establishing relationships in Access and the importance of referential integrity. Another point of particular interest is the use of an AutoNumber field to facilitate the addition of new records.

The chapter extends what you already know about subforms and queries, and uses both to present information from related tables. The forms created in this chapter are based on multiple-table queries rather than tables. The queries themselves are of a more advanced nature. We show you how to create a parameter query, where the user is prompted to enter the criteria when the query is run. We also review queries that use the aggregate functions built into Access to perform calculations on groups of records.

The chapter contains four hands-on exercises to implement the case study. We think you will be pleased with what you have accomplished by the end of the chapter, working with a sophisticated system that is typical of real-world applications.

CASE STUDY: THE COMPUTER SUPER STORE

The case study in this chapter is set within the context of a computer store that requires a database for its customers, products, and orders. The store maintains the usual customer data (name, address, phone, etc.). It also keeps data about the products it sells, storing for each product a product ID, description, quantity on hand, quantity on order, and unit price. And finally, the store has to track its orders. It needs to know the date an order was received, the customer who placed it, the products that were ordered, and the quantity of each product ordered.

Think, for a moment, about the tables that are necessary and the relationships among those tables, then compare your thoughts to our solution in Figure 6.1. You probably have no trouble recognizing the need for the Customers, Products, and Orders tables. Initially, you may be puzzled by the Order Details table, but you will soon appreciate why it is there and how powerful it is.

You can use the Customers, Products, and Orders tables individually to obtain information about a specific customer, product, or order, respectively. For example:

Query: What is Jeffrey Muddell's phone number?
Answer: Jeffrey Muddell's phone is (305) 253-3909.

Query: What is the price of a Pentium III notebook? How many are in stock?
Answer: A Pentium III notebook sells for $2,599. Fifteen systems are in stock.

Query: When was order O0003 placed?
Answer: Order O0003 was placed on April 18, 2001.

Other queries require you to relate the tables to one another. There is, for example, a *one-to-many relationship* between customers and orders. One customer can place many orders, but a specific order can be associated with only one customer. The tables are related through the CustomerID, which appears as the *primary key* in the Customers table and as a foreign key in the Orders table. Consider:

Query: What is the name of the customer who placed order number O0003?
Answer: Order O0003 was placed by Jeffrey Muddell.

Query: How many orders were placed by Jeffrey Muddell?
Answer: Jeffrey Muddell placed five orders: O0003, O0014, O0016, O0024, and C0025.

These queries require you to use two tables. To answer the first query, you would search the Orders table to find order O0003 and obtain the CustomerID (C0006 in this example). You would then search the Customers table for the customer with this CustomerID and retrieve the customer's name. To answer the

(a) Customers Table

CustomerID	FirstName	LastName	Address	City	State	ZipCode	PhoneNumber
C0001	Benjamin	Lee	1000 Call Street	Tallahassee	FL	33340	(904)327-4124
C0002	Eleanor	Milgrom	7245 NW 8 Street	Margate	FL	33065	(305)974-1234
C0003	Neil	Goodman	4215 South 81 Street	Margate	FL	33065	(305)444-5555
C0004	Nicholas	Colon	9020 N.W. 75 Street	Coral Springs	FL	33065	(305)753-9887
C0005	Michael	Ware	276 Brickell Avenue	Miami	FL	33131	(305)444-3980
C0006	Jeffrey	Muddell	9522 S.W. 142 Street	Miami	FL	33176	(305)253-3909
C0007	Ashley	Geoghegan	7500 Center Lane	Coral Springs	FL	33070	(305)753-7830
C0008	Serena	Sherard	5000 Jefferson Lane	Gainesville	FL	32601	(904)375-6442
C0009	Luis	Couto	455 Bargello Avenue	Coral Gables	FL	33146	(305)666-4801
C0010	Derek	Anderson	6000 Tigertail Avenue	Coconut Grove	FL	33120	(305)446-8900
C0011	Lauren	Center	12380 S.W. 137 Avenue	Miami	FL	33186	(305)385-4432
C0012	Robert	Slane	4508 N.W. 7 Street	Miami	FL	33131	(305)635-3454

(a) Customers Table

(b) Products Table

ProductID	Product Name	Units In Stock	Units On Order	Unit Price
P0001	Pentium III/866 MHz	50	0	$1,899.00
P0002	Pentium III/1 GHz	25	5	$1,999.00
P0003	Pentium IV/1.4 GHz	125	15	$2,099.00
P0004	Pentium IV/1.5 GHz	25	50	$2,299.00
P0005	Pentium III notebook/850MHz	15	25	$2,599.00
P0006	17" CRT Monitor	50	0	$499.00
P0007	19" CRT Monitor	25	10	$899.00
P0008	21" CRT Monitor	50	20	$1,599.00
P0009	3 Years On Site Service	15	20	$399.00
P0010	36 GB SCSI Hard Drive	25	15	$799.00
P0011	73.4 GB SCSI Hard Drive	10	0	$1,245.00
P0012	2.6 GB DVD Drive	40	0	$249.00
P0013	Digital Camera	50	15	$449.95
P0014	HD Floppy Disks	500	200	$9.99
P0015	Zip Cartridges	100	50	$14.79
P0016	Digital Scanner	15	3	$179.95
P0017	Serial Mouse	150	50	$69.95
P0018	Trackball	55	0	$59.95
P0019	Joystick	250	100	$39.95
P0020	Cable Modem	35	10	$189.95
P0021	Fax/Modem 56 Kbps	20	0	$65.95
P0022	Digital Photography Package	100	15	$1,395.00
P0023	Ink Jet Printer	50	50	$249.95
P0024	Laser Printer (personal)	125	25	$569.95
P0025	Windows Me	400	200	$95.95
P0026	Windows 98	150	50	$75.95
P0027	Norton Anti-Virus	150	50	$115.95
P0028	Microsoft Scenes Screen Saver	75	25	$29.95
P0029	Microsoft Bookshelf	250	100	$129.95
P0030	Microsoft Cinemania	25	10	$59.95
P0031	Surge Protector	15	0	$45.95

(b) Products Table

(c) Orders Table

OrderID	CustomerID	OrderDate
O0001	C0004	4/15/2001
O0002	C0003	4/18/2001
O0003	C0006	4/18/2001
O0004	C0007	4/18/2001
O0005	C0001	4/20/2001
O0006	C0001	4/21/2001
O0007	C0002	4/21/2001
O0008	C0002	4/22/2001
O0009	C0001	4/22/2001
O0010	C0002	4/22/2001
O0011	C0001	4/24/2001
O0012	C0007	4/24/2001
O0013	C0004	4/24/2001
O0014	C0006	4/25/2001
O0015	C0009	4/25/2001
O0016	C0006	4/26/2001
O0017	C0011	4/26/2001
O0018	C0011	4/26/2001
O0019	C0012	4/27/2001
O0020	C0012	4/28/2001
O0021	C0010	4/29/2001
O0022	C0010	4/29/2001
O0023	C0008	4/30/2001
O0024	C0006	5/1/2001
O0025	C0006	5/1/2001

(c) Orders Table

(d) Order Details Table

OrderID	ProductID	Quantity
O0001	P0013	1
O0001	P0014	4
O0001	P0027	1
O0002	P0001	1
O0002	P0006	1
O0002	P0020	1
O0002	P0022	1
O0003	P0005	1
O0003	P0020	1
O0003	P0022	1
O0004	P0003	1
O0004	P0010	1
O0004	P0022	2
O0005	P0003	2
O0005	P0012	2
O0005	P0016	2
O0006	P0007	1
O0006	P0014	10
O0007	P0028	1
O0007	P0030	3
O0008	P0001	1
O0008	P0004	3
O0008	P0008	4
O0008	P0011	2
O0008	P0012	1
O0009	P0006	1
O0010	P0002	2
O0010	P0022	1
O0010	P0023	1
O0011	P0016	2
O0011	P0020	2
O0012	P0021	10
O0012	P0029	10
O0012	P0030	10
O0013	P0009	4
O0013	P0016	10
O0013	P0024	2
O0014	P0019	2
O0014	P0028	1
O0015	P0018	1
O0015	P0020	1
O0016	P0029	2
O0017	P0019	2
O0018	P0009	1
O0018	P0025	2
O0018	P0026	2
O0019	P0014	25
O0020	P0024	1
O0021	P0004	1
O0022	P0027	1
O0023	P0021	1
O0023	P0028	1
O0023	P0029	1
O0024	P0007	1
O0024	P0013	5
O0024	P0014	3
O0024	P0016	1
O0025	P0012	2
O0025	P0029	2

(d) Order Details Table

FIGURE 6.1 *Super Store Database*

second query, you would begin in the Customers table and search for Jeffrey Muddell to determine the CustomerID (C0006), then search the Orders table for all records with this CustomerID.

The system is more complicated than earlier examples in that there is a ***many-to-many relationship*** between orders and products. One order can include many products, and at the same time a specific product can appear in many orders. The implementation of a many-to-many relationship requires an additional table, the Order Details table, containing (at a minimum) the primary keys of the individual tables.

The Order Details table will contain many records with the same OrderID, because there is a separate record for each product in a given order. It will also contain many records with the same ProductID, because there is a separate record for every order containing that product. However, the *combination* of OrderID and ProductID is unique, and this ***combined key*** becomes the primary key in the Order Details table. The Order Details table also contains an additional field (Quantity) whose value depends on the primary key (the *combination* of OrderID and ProductID). Thus:

Query: How many units of product P0014 were included in order O0001?
Answer: Order O0001 included four units of product P0014. (The order also included one unit of Product P0013 and one unit of P0027.)

The Order Details table has four records with a ProductID of P0014. It also has three records with an OrderID of O0001. There is, however, only one record with a ProductID P0014 *and* an OrderID O0001, which is for four units.

The Order Details table makes it possible to determine all products in a given order or all orders for a given product. You can also use the Products table in conjunction with the Order Details table to determine the names of those products. Consider:

Query: Which orders include a Pentium III/866MHz computer?
Answer: A Pentium III/866MHz computer is found in orders O0002 and O0008.

Query: Which products were included in Order O0003?
Answer: Order O0003 consisted of products P0005 (a Pentium III notebook), P0020 (a cable modem), and P0022 (a digital photography package).

To answer the first query, you would begin in the Products table to find the ProductID for a Pentium III/866MHz (P0001). You would then search the Order Details table for records containing a ProductID of P0001, which in turn identifies orders O0002 and O0008. The second query is processed in similar fashion except that you would search the Order Details table for an OrderID of O0003. This time you would find three records with ProductIDs P0005, P0020, and P0022, respectively. You would then go to the Products table to look up the ProductIDs to return the name of each product.

We've emphasized that the power of a relational database comes from the inclusion of multiple tables and the relationships between those tables. As you already know, you can use data from several tables to compute the answer to more complex queries. For example:

Query: What is the total cost of order O0006? Which products are in the order and how many units of each product?
Answer: The total cost of order O0006 is $998.90. The order consists of one 19-inch monitor at $899 and ten boxes of HD floppy disks at $9.99 each.

To determine the cost of an order, you must first identify all of the products associated with that order, the quantity of each product, and the price of each product. The previous queries have shown how you would find the products in an order and the associated quantities. The price of a specific product is obtained from the Products table, which enables you to compute the invoice by multiplying the price of each product by the quantity. Thus, the total cost of order O0006 is $998.90. (One unit of P0007 at $899.00 and ten units of product P0014 at $9.99.)

The AutoNumber Field Type

Look carefully at the Customer, Order, and Product numbers in their respective tables and note that each set of numbers is consecutive. This is accomplished by specifying the *AutoNumber field* type for each of these fields in the design of the individual tables. The AutoNumber specification automatically assigns the next sequential number to the primary key of a new record. If, for example, you were to add a new customer to the existing Customers table, that customer would be assigned the number 13. In similar fashion, the next order will be order number 26, and the next product will be product number 32. (Deleting a record does not, however, renumber the remaining records in the table; that is, once a value is assigned to a primary key, the primary key will always retain that value.)

The C, O, and P that appear as the initial character of each field, as well as the high-order zeros, are *not* part of the fields themselves, but are displayed through the *Format property* associated with each field. Our Customers table, for example, uses the format \C0000, which displays a "C" in front of the field and pads it with high-order zeros. The Format property determines how a value is displayed, but does not affect how it is stored in the table. Thus, the CustomerID of the first customer is stored as the number 1, rather than C0001. The zeros provide a uniform appearance for that field throughout the table.

The Relationships Window

The *Relationships window* in Figure 6.2 shows the Computer Store database as it will be implemented in Access. The database contains the Customers, Orders, Products, and Order Details tables as per the previous discussion. The field lists display the fields within each table, with the primary key shown in bold. The OrderID and ProductID are both shown in bold in the Order Details table, to indicate that the primary key consists of the combination of these fields.

The many-to-many relationship between Orders and Products is implemented by a *pair* of one-to-many relationships. There is a one-to-many relationship between the Orders table and the Order Details table. There is a second one-to-many relationship between the Products table and the Order Details table. In other words, the Orders and Products tables are related to each other through the pair of one-to-many relationships with the Order Details table.

The *relationship lines* show the relationships among the tables. The number 1 appears next to the Products table on the relationship line connecting the Products table and the Order Details table. The infinity symbol appears at the end of the relationship line next to the Order Details table. The one-to-many relationship between these tables means that each record in the Products table can be associated with many records in the Order Details table. Each record in the Order Details table, however, is associated with only one record in the Products table.

In similar fashion, there is a second one-to-many relationship between the Orders table and the Order Details table. The number 1 appears on the relationship line next to the Orders table. The infinity symbol appears at the end of the line next to the Order Details table. Thus, each record in the Orders table can be associated with many records in the Order Details table, but each record in the Order Details table is associated with only one order.

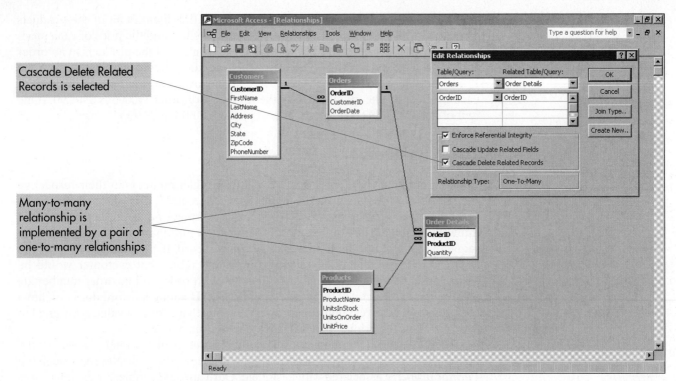

Many-to-many
relationship is
implemented by a pair of
one-to-many relationships

FIGURE 6.2   *The Relationships Window*

Referential integrity ensures that the records in related tables are consistent with one another by preventing you from adding a record to a related table with an invalid foreign key. You could not, for example, add a record to the Order Details table that referenced a nonexistent order in the Orders table. The enforcement of referential integrity will also prevent you from deleting a record in the primary (Orders) table when there are corresponding records in the related (Order Details) table.

There may be times, however, when you want to delete an order and simultaneously delete the corresponding records in the Order Details table. This is accomplished by enabling the *cascaded deletion* of related records (as shown in Figure 6.2), so that when you delete a record in the Orders table, Access automatically deletes the associated records in the Order Details table. If, for example, you were to delete order number O0006 from the Orders table, any records with this OrderID in the Order Details table would be deleted automatically.

You might also want to enable the *cascaded updating* of related fields to correct the value of an OrderID. Enforcement of referential integrity would ordinarily prevent you from changing the value of the OrderID field in the Orders table when there are corresponding records in the Order Details table. You could, however, specify the cascaded updating of related fields so that if you were to change the OrderID in the Orders table, the corresponding fields in the Order Details table would also change.

PRACTICE WITH DATABASE DESIGN

An Access database contains multiple tables, each of which stores data about a specific entity. To use Access effectively, you must be able to relate the tables to one another, which in turn requires knowledge of database design. Appendix B provides additional examples that enable you to master the principles of a relational database.

RELATIONSHIPS AND REFERENTIAL INTEGRITY

Objective To create relationships between existing tables in order to demonstrate referential integrity; to edit an existing relationship to allow the cascaded deletion of related records. Use Figure 6.3 as a guide in the exercise.

Step 1: **Add a Customer Record**

> ➤ Start Access. Open the **Computer Store database** in the **Exploring Access folder**.
> ➤ The **Tables button** is already selected in the Database window. Open the **Customers table**, then click the **Maximize button** (if necessary) so that the table takes the entire screen as shown in Figure 6.3a.
> ➤ Click the **New Record button**, then click in the **FirstName field**. Enter the first letter of your first name (e.g., "J" as shown in the figure):
>   • The record selector changes to a pencil to indicate that you are in the process of entering a record.
>   • The CustomerID is assigned automatically as soon as you begin to enter data. *Remember your customer number as you will use it throughout the chapter.* (Your CustomerID is 13, not C0013. The prefix and high-order zeros are displayed through the Format property.)
> ➤ Complete your customer record, pressing the **Tab key** to move from one field to the next. Press **Tab** after you have entered the last field (phone number) to complete the record. Close the Customers table.

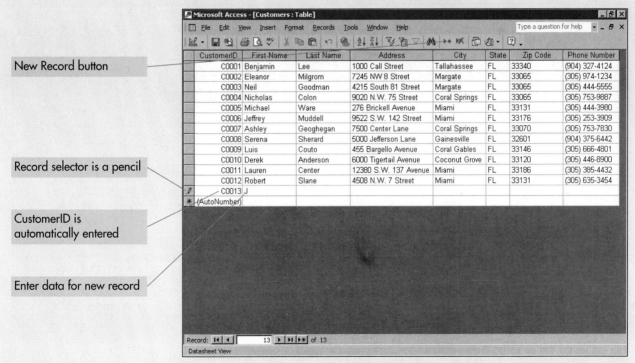

(a) Add a Customer Record (step 1)

FIGURE 6.3 *Hands-on Exercise 1*

Step 2: **Create the Relationships**

> ➤ Pull down the **Tools menu** and click **Relationships** to open the Relationships window as shown in Figure 6.3b. Maximize the Relationships window.
> ➤ Pull down the **Relationships menu** and click **Show Table** (or click the **Show Table button**) to display the Show Table dialog box.
> ➤ The **Tables tab** is selected within the Show Table dialog box, and the **Customers table** is selected. Click the **Add Command button**.
> ➤ Add the **Order Details**, **Orders**, and **Products** tables in similar fashion. Close the Show Table dialog box.
> ➤ Point to the bottom border of the **Customers field list**, then click and drag the border until all of the fields are visible.
> ➤ If necessary, click and drag the bottom border of the other tables until all of their fields are visible. Click and drag the title bars to move the field lists.
> ➤ Click and drag the **CustomerID field** in the Customers field list to the **CustomerID field** in the Orders field list. You will see the Relationships dialog box in Figure 6.3b when you release the mouse.
> ➤ Click the **Enforce Referential Integrity** check box. Click the **Create Command button** to establish the relationship.
> ➤ Click and drag the **OrderID field** in the Orders field list to the **OrderID field** in the Order Details field list. Click the **Enforce Referential Integrity** check box, then click the **Create Command button**.
> ➤ Click and drag the **ProductID field** in the Products field list to the **ProductID field** in the Order Details field list. Click the **Enforce Referential Integrity** check box, then click the **Create Command button**.
> ➤ Click the **Save button**. Close the Relationships window.

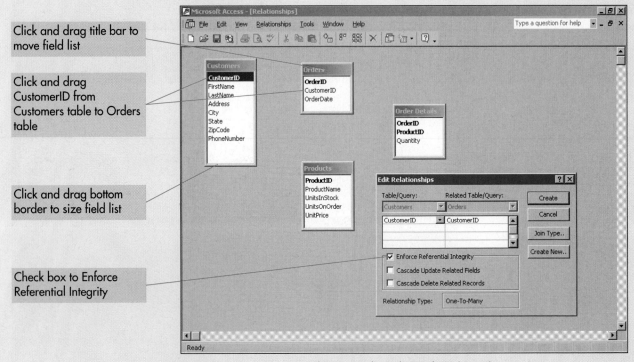

Click and drag title bar to move field list

Click and drag CustomerID from Customers table to Orders table

Click and drag bottom border to size field list

Check box to Enforce Referential Integrity

(b) Create the Relationships (step 2)

FIGURE 6.3   *Hands-on Exercise 1 (continued)*

Step 3:   **Delete an Order Details Record**

➤ You should be in the Database window. If necessary, click the **Tables button**, then open the **Orders table** as shown in Figure 6.3c.

➤ Click the **plus sign** next to order O0005. The plus sign changes to a minus sign and you see the order details for this record. Click the **row selector column** to select the Order Details record for product **P0016** in order **O0005**.

➤ Press the **Del key**. You will see a message indicating that you are about to delete one record. Click **Yes**. The Delete command works because you are deleting a "many record" in a one-to-many relationship.

➤ Click the **minus sign** next to **Order O0005**. The minus sign changes to a plus sign and you no longer see the order details. Click the **row selector column** to select the record, then press the **Del key** to (attempt to) delete the record.

➤ You will see a message indicating that you cannot delete the record. The Delete command does not work because you are attempting to delete the "one record" in a one-to-many relationship. Click **OK**.

Close button

Click + sign next to order O0005 to see related order details records

Click row selector for product P0016

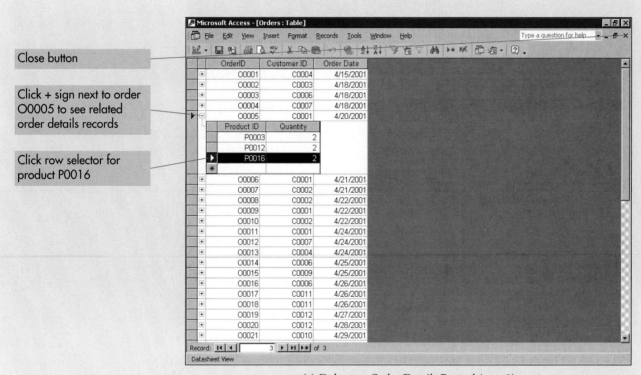

(c) Delete an Order Details Record (step 3)

FIGURE 6.3   *Hands-on Exercise 1 (continued)*

WHAT YOU CAN AND CANNOT DELETE

You can always delete a record from the "many" table, such as the Order Details table in this example. The enforcement of referential integrity, however, will prevent you from deleting a record in the "one" table (i.e., the Orders table) when there are related records in the "many" table (i.e., the Order Details table). Thus you may want to modify the relationship to permit the cascaded deletion of related records, in which case deleting a record from the "one" table will automatically delete the related records.

Step 4: **Edit a Relationship**

➤ Close the Orders table. (The tables in a relationship must be closed before the relationship can be edited.)

➤ Pull down the **Tools menu** and click **Relationships** to reopen the Relationships window (or click the **Relationships button** on the toolbar). Maximize the window.

➤ Point to the line connecting the Orders and Order Details tables, then click the **right mouse button** to display a shortcut menu. Click **Edit Relationship** to display the Relationships dialog box in Figure 6.3d.

➤ Check the box to **Cascade Delete Related Records**, then click **OK** to accept the change and close the dialog box. Click the **Save button** to save the edited relationship. Close the Relationships window.

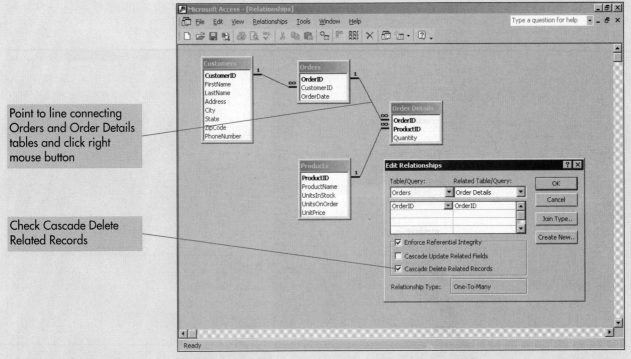

Point to line connecting Orders and Order Details tables and click right mouse button

Check Cascade Delete Related Records

(d) Edit a Relationship (step 4)

FIGURE 6.3 *Hands-on Exercise 1 (continued)*

RELATED FIELDS AND DATA TYPE

The related fields on both sides of a relationship must be the same data type—for example, both number fields or both text fields. (Number fields must also have the same field size setting.) You cannot, however, specify an AutoNumber field on both sides of a relationship. Accordingly, if the related field in the primary table is an AutoNumber field, the related field in the related table must be specified as a number field, with the Field Size property set to Long Integer.

Step 5: **Delete a Record in the Orders Table**

➤ You should be back in the Database window. Open the **Orders table**. Click the **record selector column** for **Order O0005**. Press the **Del key**.

➤ Record O0005 is deleted from the table (although you can cancel the deletion by clicking No in response to the message that is displayed on your screen). We want you to delete the record, however. Thus, click **Yes** in response to the message in Figure 6.3e.

➤ Order O0005 is permanently deleted from the Orders table as are the related records in the Order Details table. The Delete command works this time (unlike the previous attempt in step 3) because the relationship was changed to permit the deletion of related records.

➤ Close the Orders table. Close the database. Click **Yes** if prompted to save the tables or relationships.

➤ Exit Access if you do not want to continue with the next exercise at this time.

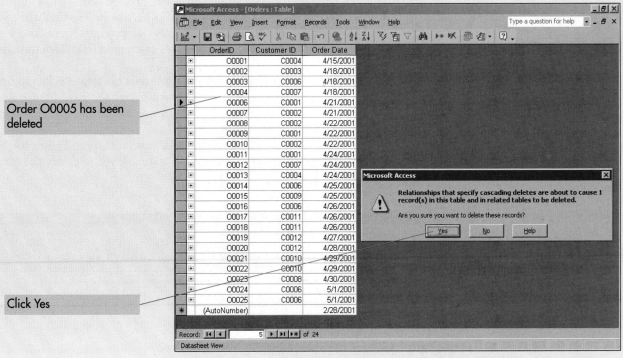

(e) Delete a Record in the Orders Table (step 5)

FIGURE 6.3 *Hands-on Exercise 1 (continued)*

USE WITH CAUTION

The cascaded deletion of related records relaxes referential integrity and eliminates errors that would otherwise occur during data entry. That does not mean, however, that the option should always be selected, and in fact, most of the time it is disabled. What would happen, for example, in an employee database with a one-to-many relationship between branch offices and employees, if cascade deleted records was in effect and a branch office was deleted?

The main and subform combination in Figure 6.4 is used by the store to enter a new order for an existing customer. The forms are based on queries (rather than tables) for several reasons. A query enables you to display data from multiple tables, to display a calculated field, and to take advantage of AutoLookup, a feature that is explained shortly. A query also lets you display records in a sequence other than by primary key.

The *main form* contains fields from both the Orders table and the Customers table. The OrderID, OrderDate, and CustomerID (the join field) are taken from the Orders table. The other fields are taken from the Customers table. The query is designed so that you do not have to enter any customer information other than the CustomerID; that is, you enter the CustomerID, and Access will automatically look up (*AutoLookup*) the corresponding customer data.

The *subform* is based on a second query containing fields from the Order Details table and the Products table. The OrderID, Quantity, and ProductID (the join field) are taken from the Order Details table. The ProductName and UnitPrice fields are from the Products table. AutoLookup works here as well so that when you enter the ProductID, Access automatically displays the Product Name and Unit Price. You then enter the quantity, and the amount (a calculated field) is determined automatically.

The queries for the main form and subform are shown in Figures 6.5a and 6.5b, respectively. The upper half of the Query window displays the field list for each table and the relationship between the tables. The lower half of the Query window contains the design grid.

The following exercise has you create the main and subform in Figure 6.4. We supply the query for the main form (Figure 6.5a), but we ask you to create the query for the subform (Figure 6.5b).

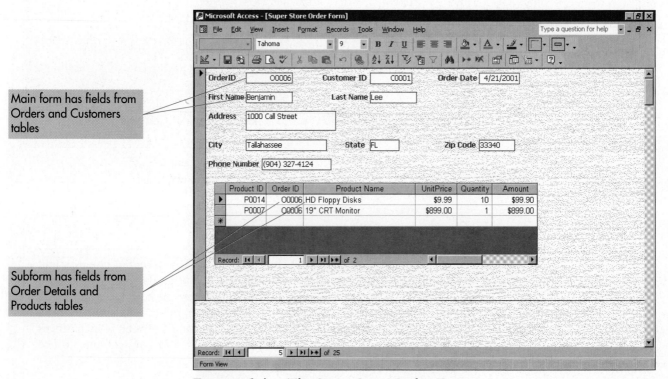

Main form has fields from Orders and Customers tables

Subform has fields from Order Details and Products tables

FIGURE 6.4 *The Super Store Order Form*

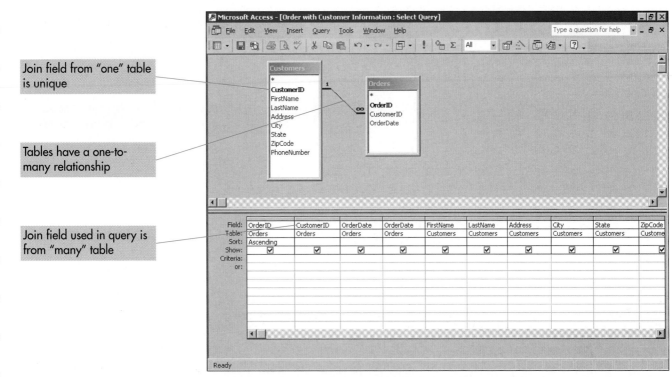

Join field from "one" table is unique

Tables have a one-to-many relationship

Join field used in query is from "many" table

(a) Order with Customer Information Query (used for the main form)

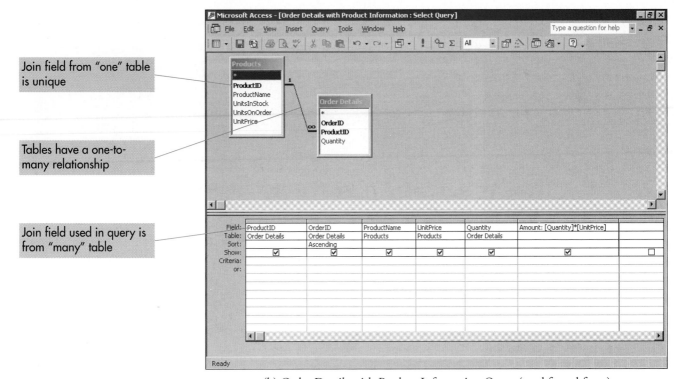

Join field from "one" table is unique

Tables have a one-to-many relationship

Join field used in query is from "many" table

(b) Order Details with Product Information Query (used for subform)

FIGURE 6.5 *Multiple-table Queries*

SUBFORMS AND MULTIPLE TABLE QUERIES

Objective   To use multiple-table queries as the basis for a main form and its associated subform; to create the link between a main form and subform manually. Use Figure 6.6 as a guide in the exercise.

Step 1:   **Create the Subform Query**

> ➤ Open the **Computer Store database** from the previous exercise. Click the **Queries button** in the Database window.
> ➤ Double click **Create query in Design view** to display the Query Design window in Figure 6.6c.
> ➤ The Show Table dialog box appears as shown in Figure 6.6a with the Tables tab already selected.
> ➤ Double click the **Products table** to add this table to the query. Double click the **Order Details table** to add this table to the query. A join line showing the one-to-many relationship between the Products and Order Details table appears automatically.
> ➤ Click **Close** to close the Show Table dialog box. If necessary, click the **Maximize button**. Resize the field lists as necessary.
> ➤ Click and drag the border separating the two parts of the query window to better display the field list. You are ready to create the query.

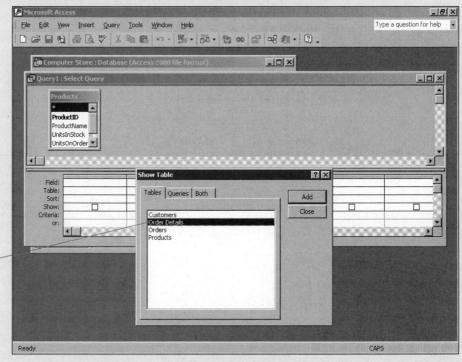

Double click Order Details table to add it to query

(a) Create the Subform Query (step 1)

FIGURE 6.6   *Hands-on Exercise 2*

Step 2:   **Create the Subform Query (continued)**

➤ Add the fields to the query as follows:
- Double click the **ProductID** and **OrderID fields** in that order from the Order Details table.
- Double click the **ProductName** and **UnitPrice fields** in that order from the Products table.
- Double click the **Quantity field** from the Order Details table.

➤ Click the **Sort row** under the **OrderID field**. Click the **drop-down arrow**, then specify an **ascending** sequence.

➤ Click the first available cell in the Field row. Type **=[Quantity]*[UnitPrice]**. Do not be concerned if you cannot see the entire expression.

➤ Press **enter**. Access has substituted Expr1: for the equal sign you typed. Drag the column boundary so that the entire expression is visible as in Figure 6.6b. (You may need to make the other columns narrower to see all of the fields in the design grid.)

➤ Click and drag to select **Expr1**. (Do not select the colon.) Type **Amount** to substitute a more meaningful field name.

➤ Point to the expression and click the **right mouse button** to display a shortcut menu. Click **Properties** to display the Field Properties dialog box in Figure 6.6b.

➤ Click the box for the **Format property**. Click the **drop-down arrow**, then scroll until you can click **Currency**. Close the Properties dialog box.

➤ Save the query as **Order Details with Product Information**. Click the **Run button** to test the query so that you know the query works prior to using it as the basis of a form.

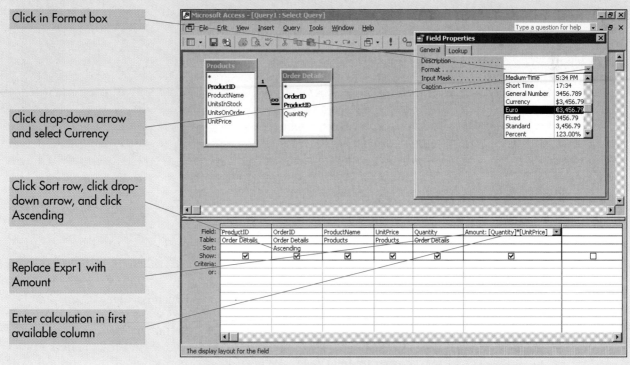

Click in Format box

Click drop-down arrow and select Currency

Click Sort row, click drop-down arrow, and click Ascending

Replace Expr1 with Amount

Enter calculation in first available column

(b) Create the Subform Query (step 2)

FIGURE 6.6   *Hands-on Exercise 2 (continued)*

Step 3: **Test the Query**

➤ You should see the dynaset shown in Figure 6.6c. (See the boxed tip if the dynaset does not appear.)

➤ Enter **1** (not P0001) to change the ProductID to 1 (from 14) in the very first record. (The Format property automatically displays the letter P and the high-order zeros.)

➤ Press **enter**. The Product Name changes to a Pentium III/866MHz system as you hit the enter key. The unit price also changes, as does the computed amount.

➤ Click the **Undo button** to cancel the change. The ProductID returns to P0014, and the Product Name changes back to HD Floppy Disks. The unit price also changes, as does the computed amount.

➤ Close the query. Save the changes to the query design if prompted to do so.

Undo button

Enter 1

Product data will change
when you press enter key

Computed amount will
also change

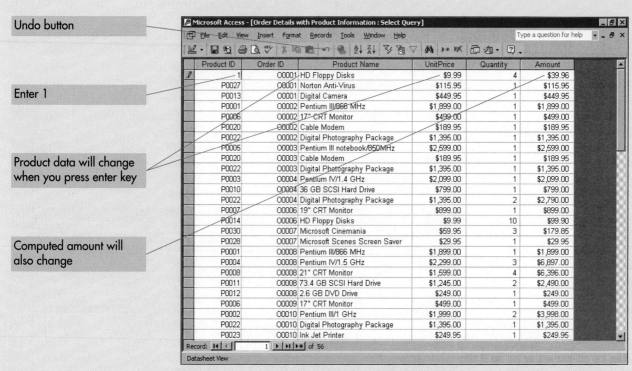

(c) Test the Query (step 3)

FIGURE 6.6 *Hands-on Exercise 2 (continued)*

A PUZZLING ERROR

If you are unable to run a query, it is most likely because you misspelled a field name in the design grid. Access interpets the misspelling as a parameter query (discussed later in the chapter) and asks you to enter a parameter value (the erroneous field name is displayed in the dialog box). Press the Esc key to exit the query and return to the Design view. Click the field row for the problem field and make the necessary correction.

Step 4: **Create the Orders Form**

➤ Click the **Forms button** in the Database window, then double click the **Create form by using wizard icon** to start the Form Wizard. You should see the dialog box in Figure 6.6d except that no tables have been selected at this time.

➤ Click the **drop-down arrow** on the Tables/Queries list box to display the tables and queries in the database. Select **Order with Customer Information** (the query we provided), then click the **>> button** to enter all of the fields from the query onto the form.

➤ Click the **drop-down arrow** to redisplay the tables and queries in the database. Click **Order Details with Product Information** to select this query as shown in Figure 6.6d. Click the **>> button**.

➤ Be sure that the Selected Fields area contains the fields from both queries. Click **Next**. The wizard will prompt you for the additional information it needs to create the form and its associated subform:

- The next screen suggests that you view the data by **Order with Customer Information** and that you create a form with subforms. Click **Next**.
- The **Datasheet option button** is selected as the default layout for the subform. Click **Next**.
- Click **Sumi Painting** as the style for your form. Click **Next**.
- Enter **Super Store Order form** as the title of the form, but accept the wizard's suggestion for the name of the subform (**Order Details with Product Information subform**).
- Click the option button to **Modify the form's design**, then click the **Finish command button** to create the form and exit the Form Wizard.

➤ You should be in the Design view of the Super Store Order form you just created. Click the **Save button** to save the form and continue working.

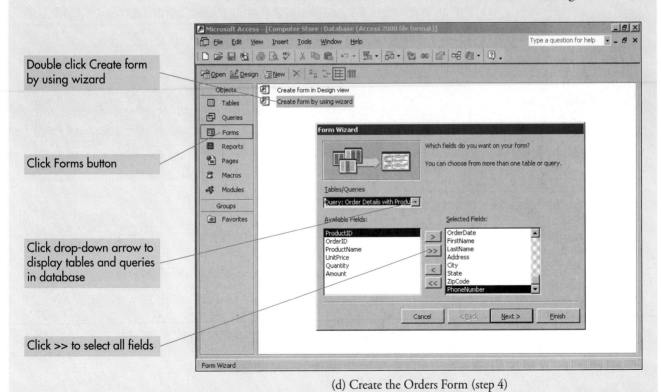

(d) Create the Orders Form (step 4)

FIGURE 6.6 *Hands-on Exercise 2 (continued)*

Step 5: **Modify the Orders Form**

➤ You are in the Design view. Maximize the window (if necessary), then **click and drag the bottom of the Details section** down to give yourself additional room in which to work.

➤ It takes time (and a little practice) to move and size the controls within a form. Try the indicated command, then click the **Undo button** if you are not satisfied with the result.

➤ Click and drag the control for the subform and its label toward the form footer. Select the label of the subform control, then press the **Del key** to delete the label as shown in Figure 6.6e. Click and drag the left border of the subform control toward the left to make the subform wider.

➤ Click the **PhoneNumber control** to select the control and display the sizing handles, then drag the control above the subform control.

➤ Click and drag the controls for **City**, **State**, and **ZipCode** (one at a time) on the line above the PhoneNumber control.

➤ Click and drag the **LastName control** so that it is next to the FirstName control. Click and drag the **Address control** under the control for FirstName.

➤ Move the **CustomerID control** to the right of the OrderID control. Click and drag the **OrderDate control** so that it is next to the CustomerID. The width of the form will change automatically if the form is not wide enough. You may, however, need to extend the width a little further when you release the mouse.

➤ Select the **Page Break tool** then click below the subform control to insert a page break on the form. The page break will print one order per page.

➤ Adjust the size, spacing, and alignment of the labels as necessary, switching back and forth between Form view and Design view. Save the form.

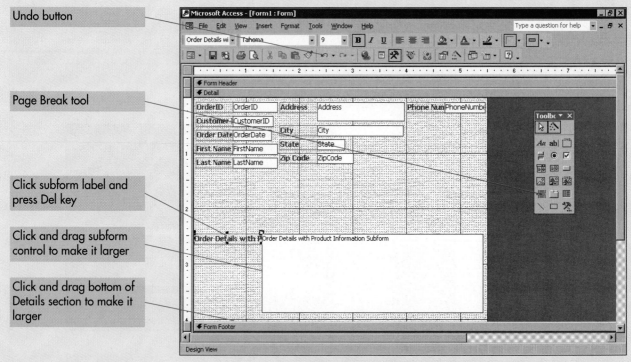

(e) Modify the Orders Form (step 5)

FIGURE 6.6 *Hands-on Exercise 2 (continued)*

Step 6:   **Change the Column Widths**

➤ Click the **View button** to change to the Form view. You should see the first order in the database together with the associated product information. You may, however, have to adjust the width of the columns within the subform and/or change the size and position of the subform within the main form.

➤ To change the width of the columns within the subform:
  • Click the **down arrow** on the **View button** and change to the **Datasheet view**. Click the **plus sign** next to the OrderID column for the first order to display the related records as shown in Figure 6.6f.
  • Click and drag the various column headings until you can read all of the information. Click the **Save button** to save the new layout, then close the form. You must close the main form, then reopen the form for the changes in the subform to be visible.
  • You should be back in the Database window. Double click the **Super Store Order form** to reopen the form and check the width of the columns in the subform. If necessary, click the **down arrow** on the **View button** to return to the Datasheet view to further adjust the columns.

➤ It may also be necessary to change the size or position of the subform within the main form. Click the **View button** and change to the **Design view**.

➤ Click and drag a sizing handle to change the size of the subform. Click and drag the subform control to change its position. If necessary, extend the width of the form.

➤ The process is one of trial and error, but it should take only a few minutes to size the subform properly. Save the completed form.

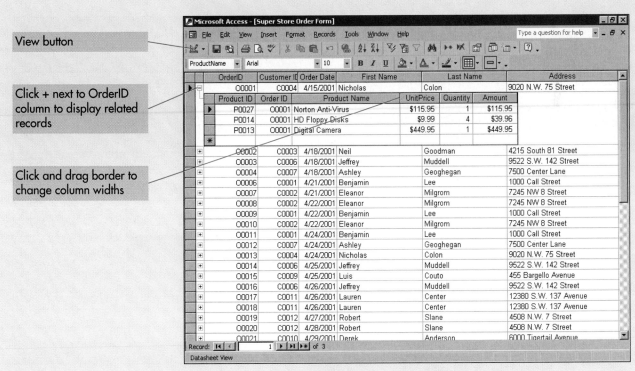

(f) Change the Column Widths (step 6)

FIGURE 6.6   *Hands-on Exercise 2 (continued)*

Step 7: **Enter a New Order**

➤ Change to the **Form view** of the Orders form as shown in Figure 6.6g. The navigation buttons on the main form let you move from one order to the next. The navigation buttons on the subform move between products in an order.

➤ Click the **New Record button** on the main form to display a blank form so that you can place an order.

➤ Click in the **Customer ID** text box. Enter **13** (your customer number from exercise 1), then press the **Tab** or **enter key** to move to the next field.

  • The OrderID is entered automatically as it is an AutoNumber field and assigned the next sequential number.

  • All of your customer information (your name, address, and phone number) is entered automatically because of the AutoLookup feature that is built into the underlying query.

  • Today's date is entered automatically because of the default value (=Date( ) that is built into the Orders table.

➤ Click the **Product ID** text box in the subform. Enter **1** (not P0001) and press the **enter key** to move to the next field. The OrderID (O0026) is entered automatically, as are the Product Name and Unit Price.

➤ Press the **Tab key** three times to move to the Quantity field, enter **1**, and press the **Tab key** twice more to move to the ProductID field for the next item. (The amount is calculated automatically.)

➤ Complete your order as shown in Figure 6.6g. The navigation buttons in the figure show that you are currently working in the third (of three) order detail records, in the 25th (of twenty-five) orders.

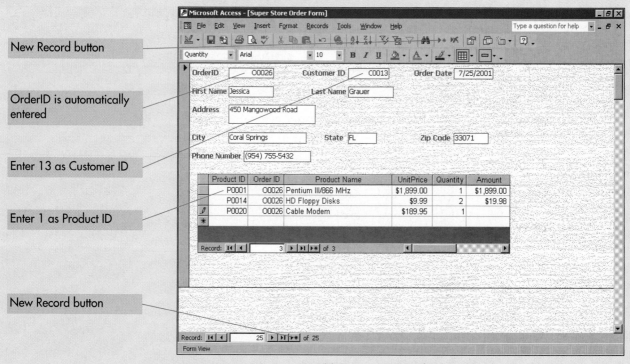

New Record button

OrderID is automatically entered

Enter 13 as Customer ID

Enter 1 as Product ID

New Record button

(g) Enter a New Order (step 7)

FIGURE 6.6 *Hands-on Exercise 2 (continued)*

Step 8: **Print the Completed Order**

➤ Click the **Selection Area** to select the current record (the order you just completed).
➤ Pull down the **File menu**. Click **Page Setup** to display the Page Setup dialog box as shown in Figure 6.6h. Click the **Page tab**, then click the **Landscape option** button so that your form will fit on the page. (Alternatively, you could click the **Margins tab** and decrease the left and right margins.) Click **OK**.
➤ Pull down the **File menu**, click **Print** to display the Print dialog box, then click the option button to specify **Selected Record(s)** as the print range. (You should not click the Print button on the toolbar, as that will print every record.)
➤ Click **OK** to print the form. Close the form, then close the database. Answer **Yes** if asked to save the changes.
➤ Exit Access if you do not want to continue with the next exercise at this time.

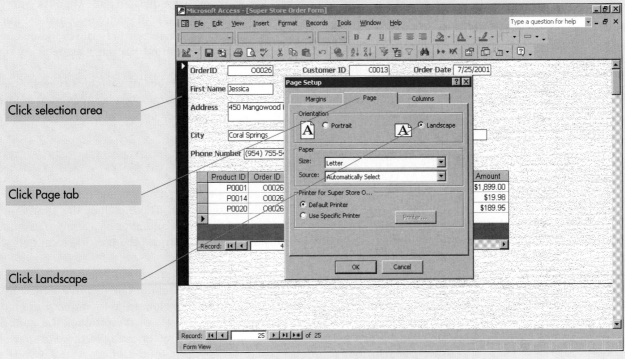

(h) Print the Completed Order (step 8)

FIGURE 6.6 *Hands-on Exercise 2 (continued)*

ADDING CUSTOMERS

The order form enables you to add an order for a new customer in the process of creating an order for that customer. Click the New Record button to add a new order, leave the CustomerID field blank, then complete the customer information (name, address, etc.) in the upper part of the form. (You need to enter at least one field, after which the CustomerID will be created automatically since it was defined as an AutoNumber field.) Press the enter key after you have entered the last field (telephone number) of customer information.

PARAMETER QUERIES

A select query, powerful as it is, has its limitations. It requires you to enter the criteria directly into the query, which means you have to change the query every time you vary the criteria. What if you wanted to use a different set of criteria (e.g., a different customer's name) every time you ran the "same" query?

A *parameter query* prompts you for the criteria each time you execute the query. It is created in similar fashion to a select query and is illustrated in Figure 6.7. The difference between a parameter query and an ordinary select query is the way in which the criteria are specified. A select query contains the actual criteria. A parameter query, however, contains a *prompt* (message) that will request the criteria when the query is executed.

The design grid in Figure 6.7a creates a parameter query that will display the orders for a particular customer. The query does not contain the customer's name, but a prompt for that name. The prompt is enclosed in square brackets and is displayed in a dialog box in which the user enters the requested data when the query is executed. Thus, the user supplies the customer's name in Figure 6.7b, and the query displays the resulting dynaset in Figure 6.7c. This enables you to run the same query with different criteria; that is, you can enter a different customer name every time you execute the query.

A parameter query may prompt for any number of variables (parameters), which are entered in successive dialog boxes. The parameters are requested in order from left to right, according to the way in which they appear in the design grid.

TOTAL QUERIES

A *total query* performs calculations on a *group* of records using one of several summary (aggregate) functions available within Access. These include the Sum, Count, Avg, Max, and Min functions to determine the total, number of, average, maximum, and minimum values, respectively. Figure 6.8 illustrates the use of a total query to compute the total amount for each order.

Figure 6.8a displays the dynaset from a select query with fields from both the Products and Order Details tables. (The dynaset contains one record for each product in each order and enables us to verify the results of the total query in Figure 6.8c.) Each record in Figure 6.8a contains the price of the product, the quantity ordered, and the amount for that product. There are, for example, three products in order O0001. The first product costs $449.95, the second product costs $39.96 (four units at $9.99 each), and the third product costs $115.95). The total for the order comes to $605.86, which is obtained by (manually) adding the amount field in each of the records for this order.

Figure 6.8b shows the Design view of the total query to calculate the cost of each order. The query contains only two fields, OrderID and Amount. The QBE grid also displays a *Total row* in which each field in the query has either a Group By or aggregate entry. The *Group By* entry under OrderID indicates that the records in the dynaset are to be grouped (aggregated) according to the like values of OrderID; that is, there will be one record in the total query for each distinct value of OrderID. The *Sum function* specifies the arithmetic operation to be performed on that field for each group of records.

The dynaset in Figure 6.8c displays the result of the total query and contains *aggregate* records, as opposed to *individual* records. There are three records for order O0001 in Figure 6.8a, but only one record in Figure 6.8c. This is because each record in a total query contains a calculated result for a group of records.

276   CHAPTER 6: MANY-TO-MANY RELATIONSHIPS

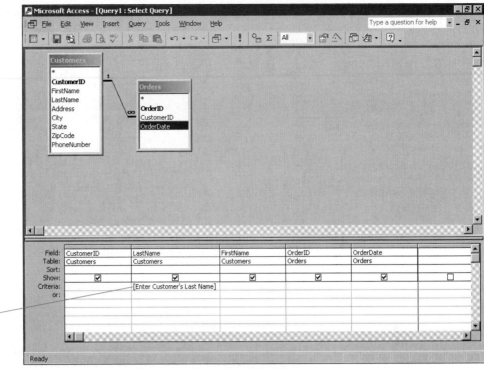

Prompt for Customer's Last Name entered in square brackets

(a) Design Grid

Prompt is displayed when query is run

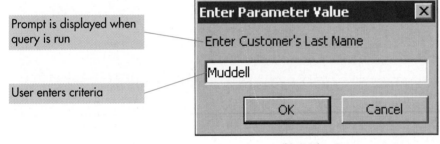

User enters criteria

(b) Dialog Box

Dynaset contains matching records

(c) Dynaset

FIGURE 6.7 Paramter Query

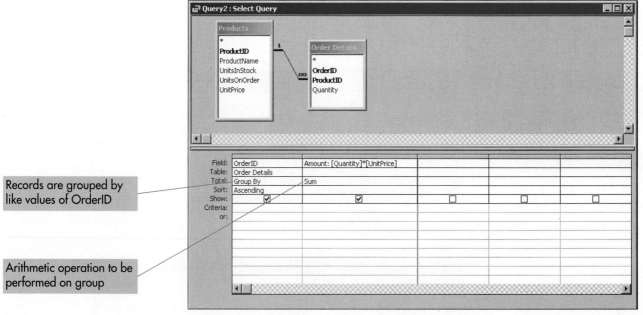

Three products are included in order O0001

Amount for each product in order O0001

(a) Order Details with Product Information Dynaset

Records are grouped by like values of OrderID

Arithmetic operation to be performed on group

(b) Design Grid

(c) Dynaset

FIGURE 6.8 *Total Query*

The exercise that follows begins by having you create the report in Figure 6.9. The report is a detailed analysis of all orders, listing every product in every order. The report is based on a query containing fields from the Orders, Customers, Products, and Order Details tables. The exercise also provides practice in creating parameter queries and total queries.

Sales Analysis by Order

Prepared by Jessica Grauer

			Product Name	Quantity	UnitPrice	Amount
O0001	Colon	4/15/2001				
			Digital Camera	1	$449.95	$449.95
			HD Floppy Disks	4	$9.99	$39.96
			Norton Anti-Virus	1	$115.95	$115.95
					Sum	$605.86
O0002	Goodman	4/18/2001				
			17" CRT Monitor	1	$499.00	$499.00
			Cable Modem	1	$189.95	$189.95
			Digital Photography	1	$1,395.00	$1,395.
			Pentium III/866 MHz	1	$1,899.00	$1,899.
					Sum	$3,982.95
O0003	Muddell	4/18/2001				
			Cable Modem	1	$189.95	$189.95
			Digital Photography	1	$1,395.00	$1,395.
			Pentium III	1	$2,599.00	$2,599.
					Sum	$4,183.95
O0004	Geoghegan	4/18/2001				
			36 GB SCSI Hard	1	$799.00	$799.00
			Digital Photography	2	$1,395.00	$2,790.
			Pentium IV/1.4 GHz	1	$2,099.00	$2,099.
					Sum	$5,688.00
O0006	Lee	4/21/2001				
			19" CRT Monitor	1	$899.00	$899.00
			HD Floppy Disks	10	$9.99	$99.90
					Sum	$998.90
O0007	Milgrom	4/21/2001				
			Microsoft Cinemania	3	$59.95	$179.85
			Microsoft Scenes	1	$29.95	$29.95

Wednesday, July 25, 2001   Page 1 of 4

FIGURE 6.9   *Sales Analysis by Order*

ADVANCED QUERIES

Objective   To copy an existing query; to create a parameter query; to create a total query using the Aggregate Sum function. Use Figure 6.10 as a guide.

Step 1:   **Create the Query**

> ➤ Open the **Computer Store database** from the previous exercise. Click the **Queries button** in the Database window. Double click **Create query in Design view** to display the Query Design window.
>
> ➤ By now you have had sufficient practice creating a query, so we will just outline the steps:
>
> - Add the **Customers**, **Orders**, **Products**, and **Order Details** tables. Move and size the field lists within the Query window to match Figure 6.10a. Maximize the window.
> - Add the indicated fields to the design grid. Be sure to take each field from the appropriate table.
> - Add the calculated field to compute the amount by multiplying the quantity by the unit price. Point to the expression, click the **right mouse button** to display a shortcut menu, then change the Format property to **Currency**.
> - Check that your query matches Figure 6.10a. Save the query as **Sales Analysis by Order**.
>
> ➤ Click the **Run button** (the exclamation point) to run the query. The dynaset contains one record for every item in every order. Close the query.

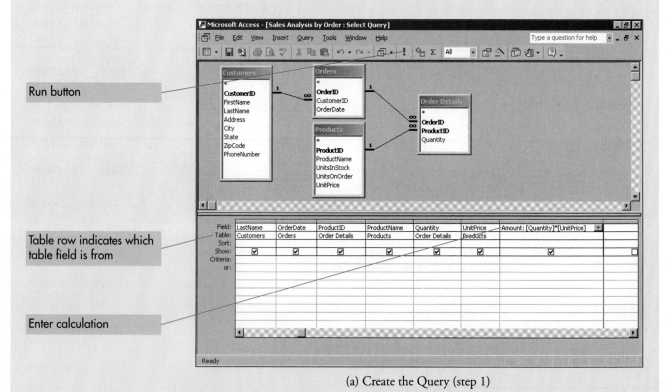

Run button

Table row indicates which table field is from

Enter calculation

(a) Create the Query (step 1)

FIGURE 6.10   *Hands-on Exercise 3*

Step 2:   **The Report Wizard**

> ➤ Click the **Reports button** in the Database window. Double click the **Create report by using Wizard** icon to start the Report Wizard.
> ➤ Click the **drop-down arrow** to display the tables and queries in the database, then select **Sales Analysis by Order** (the query you just created).
> ➤ By now you have had sufficient practice using the Report Wizard, so we will just outline the steps:
>   • Select all of the fields in the query *except* the ProductID. Click the **>> button** to move every field in the Available Fields list box to the Selected Fields list.
>   • Select the **ProductID field** in the Selected Fields list and click the **< button** to remove this field. Click **Next**.
>   • Group the report by **OrderID**. Click **Next**.
>   • Sort the report by **ProductName**. Click the **Summary Options button** to display the Summary Options dialog box in Figure 6.10b. Check **Sum** under the Amount field. The option button to **Show Detail and Summary** is selected. Click **OK** to close the Summary Options dialog box. Click **Next**.
>   • The **Stepped Layout** is selected, as is **Portrait orientation**. Be sure the box is checked to **Adjust field width so all fields fit on a page**. Click **Next**.
>   • Choose **Bold** as the style. Click **Next**.
>   • **Sales Analysis by Order** is entered as the title of the report. The option button to **Preview the Report** is selected. Click **Finish**.
> ➤ The report you see approximates the finished report, but requires several modifications to improve the formatting. The OrderDate and LastName, for example, are repeated for every product in an order, when they should appear only once in the group (OrderID) header.

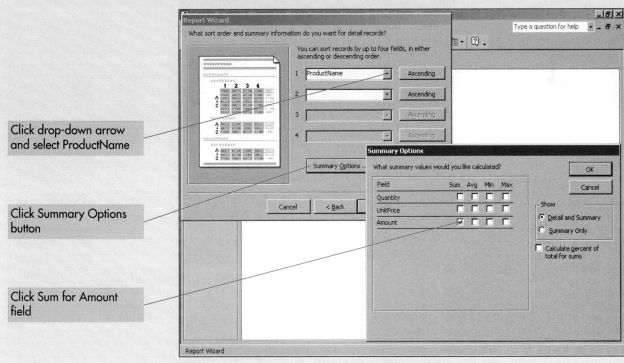

Click drop-down arrow and select ProductName

Click Summary Options button

Click Sum for Amount field

(b) The Report Wizard (step 2)

FIGURE **6.10**   *Hands-on Exercise 3 (continued)*

Step 3:   **Modify the Report Design**

➤ Click the **Close button** to change to the Design view to modify the report as shown in Figure 6.10c.

➤ Press and hold the **Shift key** as you click the **OrderDate** and **LastName** controls to select both controls, then drag the controls to the group header next to the OrderID.

➤ Click anywhere in the report to deselect the controls after they have been moved. Press and hold the **Shift key** to select the **OrderID**, **OrderDate**, and **LastName** labels in the Page Header. Press the **Del key** to delete the labels.

➤ Size the **Quantity**, **UnitPrice**, and **Amount controls** (and their **labels**). Move the **ProductName control** and its **label** closer to the other controls.

➤ Click the **OrderID control** in the OrderID header. Click the **right mouse button**, click **Properties**, and change the Border Style to **Transparent**. Close the Properties dialog box.

➤ Click the **Label** tool, then click and drag in the report header to create an unbound control under the title of the report. Type **Prepared by:** followed by your name as shown in Figure 6.10c.

➤ Select (click) the first control in the OrderID footer (which begins with "Summary for"). Press the **Del key**.

➤ Click and drag the unbound control containing the word **Sum** to the right of the group footer so that the label is next to the computed total for each order. Do the same for the Grand Total label in the Report footer.

➤ Click the **Save button** to save the report, then click the **View button** to preview the report.

Label tool

Drag OrderDate and LastName to group header

Click control and press Del key

Move Product Name label and control closer to other labels

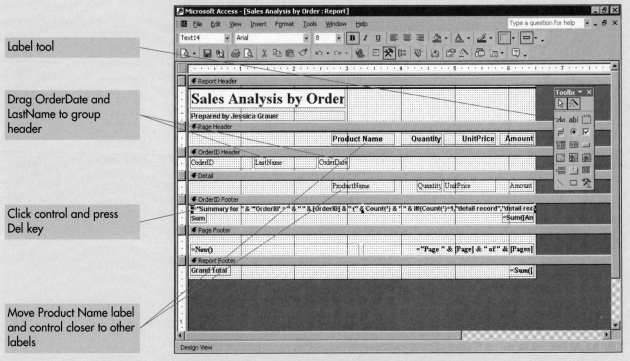

(c) Modify the Report Design (step 3)

FIGURE 6.10   *Hands-on Exercise 3 (continued)*

Step 4: **Print the Report**

> ➤ You should see the report in Figure 6.10d, which groups the reports by OrderID. The products are in alphabetical order within each order.
> ➤ Click the **Zoom button** to see the entire page. Click the **Zoom button** a second time to return to the higher magnification.
> ➤ Use the navigation buttons at the bottom of the window to see other pages in the report.
> ➤ Click the **Printer button** if you are satisfied with the appearance of the report, or return to the Design view to make any needed changes.
> ➤ Pull down the **File menu** and click **Close** to close the report. Click **Yes** if asked whether to save the changes.

Printer button

Zoom button

Report is grouped by OrderID

Products within each order are in alphabetical order

Click forward button to see next page

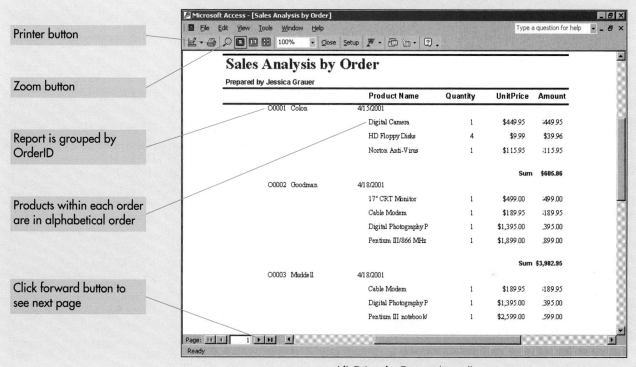

(d) Print the Report (step 4)

FIGURE 6.10 *Hands-on Exercise 3 (continued)*

Products within each order are in alphabetical order

THE UNMATCHED QUERY WIZARD

The cost of inventory is a significant expense for every business. It is one thing to maintain inventory of products that are selling well, and quite another to stock products that have never been ordered. The Unmatched Query Wizard identifies records in one table (such as the Products table) that do not have matching records in another table (such as the Order Details table). In other words, it will tell you which products (if any) have never been ordered. See exercise 2 at the end of the chapter.

Step 5: **Copy an Existing Query**

➤ If necessary, return to the Database window, then click the **Queries button** in the Database window.

➤ Click the **Sales Analysis by Order query** to select the query as shown in Figure 6.10e.

➤ Pull down the **Edit menu** and click **Copy** (or use the **Ctrl+C** shortcut) to copy the query to the clipboard.

➤ Pull down the **Edit menu** and click **Paste** (or use **Ctrl+V** shortcut) to produce the Paste As dialog box in Figure 6.10e. Type **Sales Totals**. Click **OK**.

➤ The Database window contains the original query (Sales Analysis by Order) as well as the copied version (Sales Totals) you just created.

Copy button

Paste button

Click Queries button

Click Sales Analysis by Order

Enter Sales Totals as name of new query

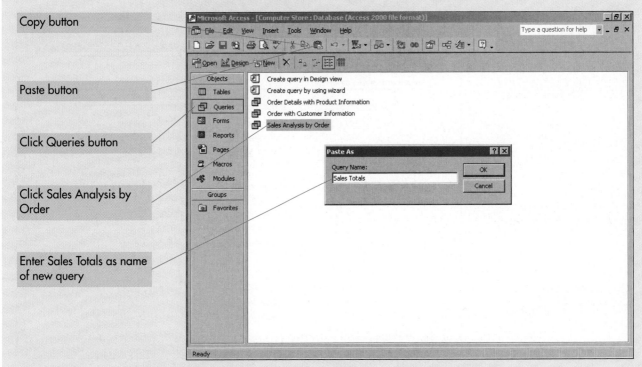

(e) Copy an Existing Query (step 5)

FIGURE 6.10 *Hands-on Exercise 3 (continued)*

COPY, DELETE, OR RENAME A REPORT

The Database window enables you to copy, delete, or rename any object (a table, form, query, or report) in an Access database. To copy an object, select the object, pull down the Edit menu, and click Copy. Pull down the Edit menu a second time, click Paste, then enter the name of the copied object. To delete or rename an object, point to the object, then click the right mouse button to display a shortcut menu, and select the desired operation.

Step 6: **Create a Total Query**

➤ Select the newly created **Sales Totals query**. Click the **Design button** to open the Query Design window in Figure 6.10f.

➤ Click the **column selector** for the **OrderDate field** to select the column. Press the **Del key** to delete the field from the query. Delete the **ProductID**, **ProductName**, **Quantity**, and **UnitPrice fields** in similar fashion.

➤ Pull down the **View menu** and click **Totals** to display the Total row (or click the **Totals button** on the toolbar).

➤ Click the **Total row** under the Amount field, then click the **drop-down arrow** to display the summary functions. Click **Sum** as shown in the figure.

➤ Save the query.

Run button

Totals button

Total row

Click drop-down arrow and select Sum

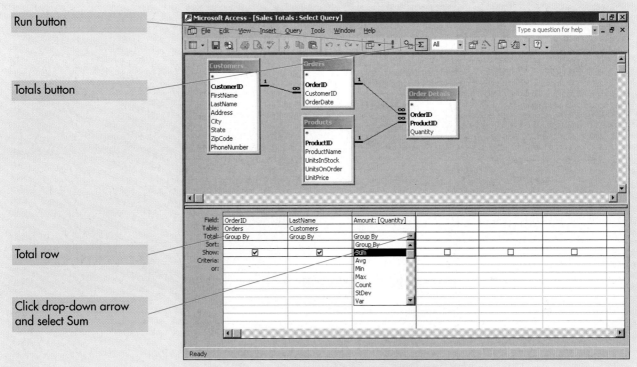

(f) Create a Total Query (step 6)

FIGURE 6.10 *Hands-on Exercise 3 (continued)*

THE DESCRIPTION PROPERTY

A working database will contain many different objects of the same type, making it all too easy to forget the purpose of the individual objects. The Description property helps you to remember. Point to any object within the Database window, click the right mouse button to display a shortcut menu, click Properties to display the Properties dialog box, enter an appropriate description, then click OK to close the Properties sheet. Once a description has been created, you can right click any object in the Database window, then click the Properties command from the shortcut menu to display the information.

Step 7: **Run the Query**

➤ Pull down the **Query menu** and click **Run** (or click the **Run button**) to run the query. You should see the datasheet in Figure 6.10g, which contains one record for each order with the total amount of that order.

➤ Click any field and attempt to change its value. You will be unable to do so as indicated by the beep and the message in the status bar, indicating that the recordset is not updatable.

➤ Click the **Design View button** to return to the Query Design view.

View button

One record for each order

Click and attempt to change any entry

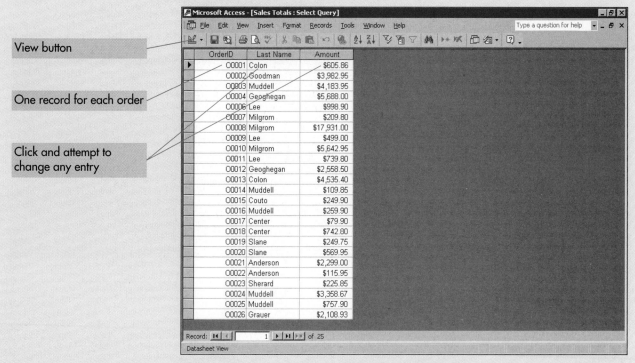

(g) Run the Query (step 7)

FIGURE 6.10   *Hands-on Exercise 3 (continued)*

UPDATING THE QUERY

The changes made to a query's dynaset are automatically made in the underlying table(s). Not every field in a query is updatable, however, and the easiest way to determine if you can change a value is to run the query, view the dynaset, and attempt to edit the field. Access will prevent you from updating a calculated field, a field based on an aggregate function (such as Sum or Count), or the join field on the "one side" of a one-to-many relationship. If you attempt to update a field you cannot change, the status bar will display a message indicating why the change is not allowed.

Step 8: **Create a Parameter Query**

> ➤ Click the **Criteria row** under **LastName**. Type **[Enter Customer's Last Name]**. Be sure to enclose the entry in square brackets.
> ➤ Pull down the **File menu**. Click **Save As**. Enter **Customer Parameter Query** in the Save Query "Sales Total" To box. Click **OK**.
> ➤ Run the query. Access will display the dialog box in Figure 6.10h, asking for the Customer's last name. Type **your name** and press **enter**. Access displays the information for your order(s). Close the query.

Run button

Enter your name in response to prompt

Enter prompt in square brackets

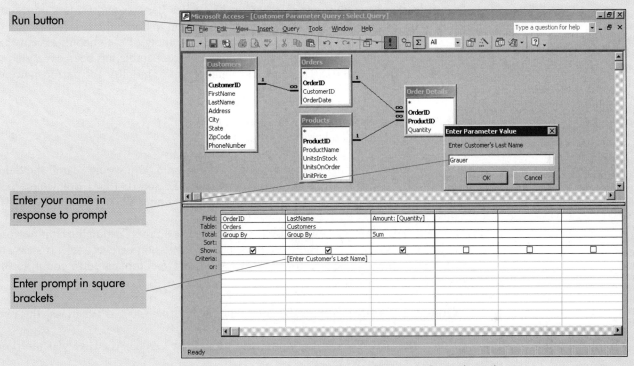

(h) Create a Parameter Query (step 8)

FIGURE 6.10   *Hands-on Exercise 3 (continued)*

THE TOPVALUES PROPERTY

The TopValues property returns a designated number of records rather than the entire dynaset. Open the query in Design view, then click the right mouse button *outside* the design grid to display a shortcut menu. Click Properties, click the box for TopValues, and enter the desired value as either a number or a percent; for example, 5 to list the top five records, or 5% to display the records that make up the top five percent. The dynaset must be in sequence according to the desired field for the TopValues property to work properly.

Step 9: **Exit Access**

> ➤ Exit Access if you do not want to continue with the next exercise. (Do not be concerned if Access indicates it will empty the clipboard.)

One of the advantages of an Access database is that it can be easily expanded to include additional data without disturbing the existing tables. The database used throughout the chapter consisted of four tables: a Customers table, a Products table, an Orders table, and an Order Details table. Figure 6.11 extends the database to include a Sales Persons table with data about each member of the sales staff.

The salesperson helps the customer as he or she comes into the store, then receives a commission based on the order. There is a one-to-many relationship between the salesperson and orders. One salesperson can generate many orders, but an order can have only one salesperson. The Sales Persons and Orders tables are joined by the SalesPersonID field, which is common to both tables.

Figure 6.11 is similar to Figure 6.1 at the beginning of the chapter except that the Sales Persons table has been added and the Orders table has been expanded to include a SalesPersonID. This enables management to monitor the performance of the sales staff. Consider:

Query: How many orders has Cori Rice taken?
Answer: Cori has taken five orders.

The query is straightforward and easily answered. You would search the Sales Persons table for Cori Rice to determine her SalesPerson ID (S03). You would then search the Orders table and count the records containing S03 in the SalesPersonID field.

The Sales Persons table is also used to generate a report listing the commissions due to each salesperson. The store pays a 5% commission on every sale. It's easy to determine the salesperson for each order. It's more complicated to compute the commission. Consider:

Query: Which salesperson is associated with order O0003? When was this person hired?
Answer: Cori Rice is the salesperson for order O0003. Ms. Rice was hired on March 15, 1993.

The determination of the salesperson is straightforward, as all you have to do is search the Orders table to locate the order and obtain the SalesPerson ID (S03). You then search the Sales Persons table for this value (S03) and find the corresponding name (Cori Rice) and hire date (3/15/93).

Query: What is the commission on order O0003?
Answer: The commission on order O0003 is $209.20.

The calculation of the commission requires a fair amount of arithmetic. First, you need to compute the total amount of the order. Thus, you would begin in the Order Details table, find each product in order O0003, and multiply the quantity of that product by its unit price. The total cost of order O0003 is $4,183.95, based on one unit of product P0005 at $2,599, one unit of product P0020 at $189.95, and one unit of product P0022 at $1,395. (You can also refer to the sales report in Figure 6.9 that was developed in the previous exercise to check these calculations.)

Now that you know the total cost of the order, you can compute the commission, which is 5% of the total order, or $209.20 (.05 × $4,183.95). The complete calculation is lengthy, but Access does it automatically, and therein lies the beauty of a relational database.

(a) Customers Table

CustomerID	FirstName	LastName	Address	City	State	ZipCode	PhoneNumber
C0001	Benjamin	Lee	1000 Call Street	Tallahassee	FL	33340	(904)327-4124
C0002	Eleanor	Milgrom	7245 NW 8 Street	Margate	FL	33065	(305)974-1234
C0003	Neil	Goodman	4215 South 81 Street	Margate	FL	33065	(305)444-5555
C0004	Nicholas	Colon	9020 N.W. 75 Street	Coral Springs	FL	33065	(305)753-9887
C0005	Michael	Ware	276 Brickell Avenue	Miami	FL	33131	(305)444-3980
C0006	Jeffrey	Muddell	9522 S.W. 142 Street	Miami	FL	33176	(305)253-3909
C0007	Ashley	Geoghegan	7500 Center Lane	Coral Springs	FL	33070	(305)753-7830
C0008	Serena	Sherard	5000 Jefferson Lane	Gainesville	FL	32601	(904)375-6442
C0009	Luis	Couto	455 Bargello Avenue	Coral Gables	FL	33146	(305)666-4801
C0010	Derek	Anderson	6000 Tigertail Avenue	Coconut Grove	FL	33120	(305)446-8900
C0011	Lauren	Center	12380 S.W. 137 Avenue	Miami	FL	33186	(305)385-4432
C0012	Robert	Slane	4508 N.W. 7 Street	Miami	FL	33131	(305)635-3454
C0013	Jessica	Grauer	450 Mangowood Road	Coral Springs	FL	33071	(305)755-5432

(a) Customers Table

(b) Products Table

ProductID	Product Name	Units In Stock	Units On Order	Unit Price
P0001	Pentium III/866 MHz	50	0	$1,899.00
P0002	Pentium III/1 GHz	25	5	$1,999.00
P0003	Pentium IV/1.4 GHz	125	15	$2,099.00
P0004	Pentium IV/1.5 GHz	25	50	$2,299.00
P0005	Pentium III notebook/850MHz	15	25	$2,599.00
P0006	17" CRT Monitor	50	0	$499.00
P0007	19" CRT Monitor	25	10	$899.00
P0008	21" CRT Monitor	50	20	$1,599.00
P0009	3 Years On Site Service	15	20	$399.00
P0010	36 GB SCSI Hard Drive	25	15	$799.00
P0011	73.4 GB SCSI Hard Drive	10	0	$1,245.00
P0012	2.6 GB DVD Drive	40	0	$249.00
P0013	Digital Camera	50	15	$449.95
P0014	HD Floppy Disks	500	200	$9.99
P0015	Zip Cartridges	100	50	$14.79
P0016	Digital Scanner	15	3	$179.95
P0017	Serial Mouse	150	50	$69.95
P0018	Trackball	55	0	$59.95
P0019	Joystick	250	100	$39.95
P0020	Cable Modem	35	10	$189.95
P0021	Fax/Modem 56 Kbps	20	0	$65.95
P0022	Digital Photography Package	100	15	$1,395.00
P0023	Ink Jet Printer	50	50	$249.95
P0024	Laser Printer (personal)	125	25	$569.95
P0025	Windows Me	400	200	$95.95
P0026	Windows 98	150	50	$75.95
P0027	Norton Anti-Virus	150	50	$115.95
P0028	Microsoft Scenes Screen Saver	75	25	$29.95
P0029	Microsoft Bookshelf	250	100	$129.95
P0030	Microsoft Cinemania	25	10	$59.95
P0031	Surge Protector	15	0	$45.95

(b) Products Table

(c) Orders Table

OrderID	CustomerID	OrderDate	SalesPersonID
O0001	C0004	4/15/2001	S01
O0002	C0003	4/18/2001	S02
O0003	C0006	4/18/2001	S03
O0004	C0007	4/18/2001	S04
O0006	C0001	4/21/2001	S05
O0007	C0002	4/21/2001	S01
O0008	C0002	4/22/2001	S02
O0009	C0001	4/22/2001	S03
O0010	C0002	4/22/2001	S04
O0011	C0001	4/24/2001	S05
O0012	C0007	4/24/2001	S01
O0013	C0004	4/24/2001	S02
O0014	C0006	4/25/2001	S03
O0015	C0009	4/25/2001	S04
O0016	C0006	4/26/2001	S05
O0017	C0011	4/26/2001	S01
O0018	C0011	4/26/2001	S02
O0019	C0012	4/27/2001	S03
O0020	C0012	4/28/2001	S04
O0021	C0010	4/29/2001	S05
O0022	C0010	4/29/2001	S01
O0023	C0008	4/30/2001	S02
O0024	C0006	5/1/2001	S03
O0025	C0006	5/1/2001	S04
O0026	C0013	7/25/2001	S05

(c) Orders Table

(d) Order Details Table

OrderID	ProductID	Quantity
O0001	P0013	1
O0001	P0014	4
O0001	P0027	1
O0002	P0001	1
O0002	P0006	1
O0002	P0020	1
O0002	P0022	1
O0003	P0005	1
O0003	P0020	1
O0003	P0022	1
O0004	P0003	1
O0004	P0010	1
O0004	P0022	2
O0005	P0003	2
O0005	P0012	2
O0005	P0016	2
O0006	P0007	1
O0006	P0014	10
O0007	P0028	1
O0007	P0030	3
O0008	P0001	1
O0008	P0004	3
O0008	P0008	4
O0008	P0011	2
O0008	P0012	1
O0009	P0006	1
O0010	P0002	2
O0010	P0022	1
O0010	P0023	1
O0011	P0016	2
O0011	P0020	2
O0012	P0021	10
O0012	P0029	10
O0012	P0030	10
O0013	P0009	4
O0013	P0016	10
O0013	P0024	2
O0014	P0019	2
O0014	P0028	1
O0015	P0018	1
O0015	P0020	1
O0016	P0029	2
O0017	P0019	2
O0018	P0009	1
O0018	P0025	2
O0018	P0026	2
O0019	P0014	25
O0020	P0024	1
O0021	P0004	1
O0022	P0027	1
O0023	P0021	1
O0023	P0028	1
O0023	P0029	1
O0024	P0007	1
O0024	P0013	5
O0024	P0014	3
O0024	P0016	1
O0025	P0012	2
O0025	P0029	2
O0026	P0001	1
O0026	P0014	2
O0026	P0020	1

(d) Order Details Table

(e) Sales Persons Table

SalesPersonID	FirstName	LastName	WorkPhone	HireDate
S01	Linda	Black	(305) 284-6105	02/03/93
S02	Michael	Vaughn	(305) 284-3993	02/10/93
S03	Cori	Rice	(305) 284-2557	03/15/93
S04	Karen	Ruenheck	(305) 284-4641	01/31/94
S05	Richard	Linger	(305) 284-4662	01/31/94

(e) Sales Persons Table

FIGURE 6.11 *Super Store Database*

The Sales Commission Query

Figure 6.12a displays the design view of a parameter query to calculate the commissions for a specific salesperson. (This query determines the commissions for Cori Rice, which you computed manually in the previous discussion.) Enter the last name of the sales associate, Rice, and the query returns the dynaset in Figure 6.12b, showing all of her commissions. Note, too, that the commission returned for order O0003 is $209.20, which corresponds to the amount we arrived at earlier.

The query in Figure 6.12a includes fields from all five tables in the database. The relationships are shown graphically in the top half of the query window and reflect the earlier discussion—for example, the one-to-many relationship between salespersons and orders. These tables are joined through the SalesPersonID field, which is the primary key in the Sales Persons table but a foreign key in the Orders table. (The Orders table has been modified to include this field.)

The following exercise has you import the Sales Persons table from another Access database. It then directs you to modify the existing Orders table to include a SalesPerson ID, which references the records in the Sales Persons table, and to modify the Super Store Order Form to include the salesperson data.

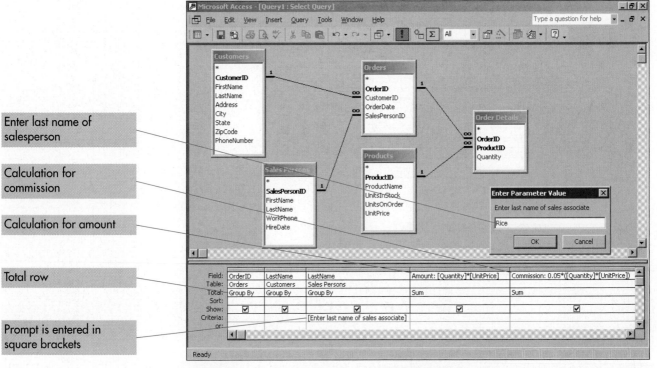

(a) Design View

(b) Dynaset

FIGURE 6.12   *Sales Commission*

EXPANDING THE DATABASE

Objective   To import a table from another database; to modify the design of an existing table. Use Figure 6.13 as a guide in the exercise.

Step 1:   **Import the Sales Persons Table**

> ➤ Open the **Computer Store database**. Click the **Tables button**. Pull down the
> **File menu**. Click **Get External Data**, then click the **Import** command.
> ➤ Click (select) the **Sales Persons database** from the **Exploring Access folder**,
> then click **Import** to display the Import Objects dialog box in Figure 6.13a.
> ➤ If necessary, click the **Tables button**, click **SalesPersons** (the only table in this
> database), then click **OK**. A dialog box will appear briefly on your screen as the
> Sales Persons table is imported into the Computer Store database.

Click Tables tab

Click Sales Persons

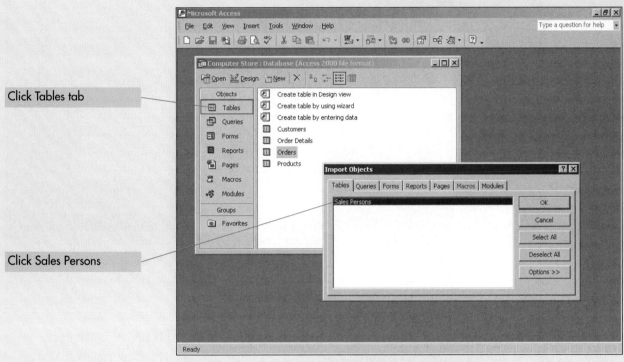

(a) Import the Sales Persons Table (step 1)

FIGURE 6.13   *Hands-on Exercise 4*

THE DOCUMENTS SUBMENU

The Documents menu contains shortcuts to the last 15 files that were
opened. Click the Start button, click (or point to) the Documents menu,
then click the document you wish to open (e.g., Computer Store), assuming
that it appears on the menu. Windows will start the application, then open
the indicated document.

Step 2: **Modify the Orders Table Design**

➤ Select the **Orders table** from the Database window as shown in Figure 6.13b. Click the **Design button**.

➤ Click in the first available row in the **Field Name** column. Enter **SalesPersonID** as shown in Figure 6.13b. Choose **Number** as the data type. The Field Size property changes to Long Integer by default.

• Click the **Format** property. Enter **\S00**.

• Click the **Default Value** property and delete the **0**.

➤ Click the **Save button** to save the modified design of the Orders table.

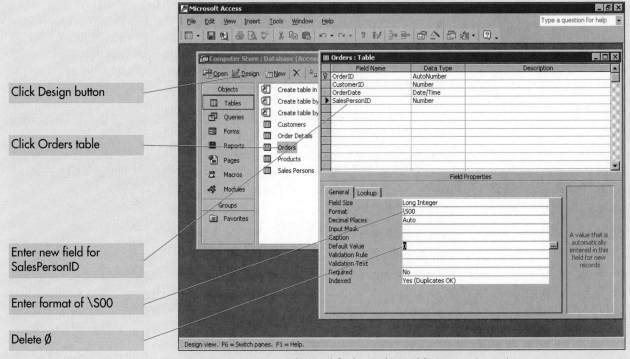

Click Design button

Click Orders table

Enter new field for SalesPersonID

Enter format of \S00

Delete Ø

(b) Modify the Orders Table Design (step 2)

FIGURE 6.13 *Hands-on Exercise 4 (continued)*

RELATIONSHIPS AND THE AUTONUMBER FIELD TYPE

The join fields on both sides of a relationship must be the same data type—for example, both number fields or both text fields. The AutoNumber field type, however, cannot be specified on both sides of a relationship. Thus, if the join field (SalesPersonID) in the primary table (Sales Persons) is an AutoNumber field, the join field in the related table (Orders) must be specified as a Number field, with the Field Size property set to Long Integer.

Step 3: **Add the Sales Person to Existing Orders**

> ➤ Click the **Datasheet View button** to change to the Datasheet view as shown in Figure 6.13c. Maximize the window.
>
> ➤ Enter the **SalesPersonID** for each existing order as shown in Figure 6.13c. (You can now modify the Required property for the SalesPersonID in the Orders table to make this a required field for new orders.)
>
> ➤ Enter only the number (e.g., 1, rather than S01) as the S and leading 0 are displayed automatically through the Format property. We are adding the data in random fashion so that we will be able to generate meaningful reports later on in the exercise.
>
> ➤ Close the Orders table.

Enter SalesPersonID for each record (enter 1, 2, 3, 4, or 5)

Type only the number

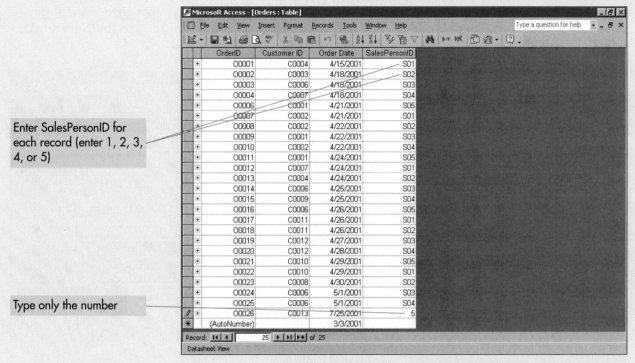

(c) Add the Sales Person to Existing Orders (step 3)

FIGURE 6.13 *Hands-on Exercise 4 (continued)*

HIDE THE WINDOWS TASKBAR

The Windows taskbar is great for novices because it makes task switching as easy as changing channels on a TV. It also takes up valuable real estate on the desktop, and hence you may want to hide the taskbar when you don't need it. Point to an empty area on the taskbar, click the right mouse button to display a shortcut menu, and click Properties to display the Taskbar Properties dialog box. Click the Taskbar Options tab (if necessary), check the box to Autohide the taskbar, and click OK. The taskbar should disappear. Now point to the bottom of the screen (or the edge where the taskbar was last displayed), and it will reappear.

Step 4: **Create the Relationship**

➤ Pull down the **Tools menu**. Click **Relationships** to open the Relationships window as shown in Figure 6.13d. (The Sales Persons table is not yet visible.) Click the **Maximize button**.

➤ If necessary, drag the bottom border of the **Orders table** until you see the SalesPersonID (the field you added in step 2).

➤ Pull down the **Relationships menu**. Click **Show Table**. Click the **Tables button** if necessary, select the **Sales Persons table**, then click the **Add button**. Close the Show Table dialog box.

➤ Drag the title bar of the **SalesPersons table** to position the table as shown in Figure 6.13d. Drag the **SalesPersonID field** from the Sales Persons table to the SalesPersonID in the Orders table.

➤ Check the box to **Enforce Referential Integrity**. Click the **Create button** to create the relationship. Click the **Save button** to save the Relationships window. Close the Relationships window.

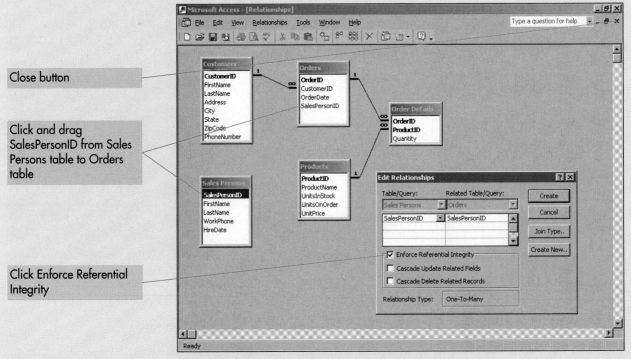

Close button

Click and drag SalesPersonID from Sales Persons table to Orders table

Click Enforce Referential Integrity

(d) Create the Relationship (step 4)

FIGURE 6.13   *Hands-on Exercise 4 (continued)*

PRINT THE RELATIONSHIPS

Pull down the Tools menu and click the Relationships command to open the Relationships window, then pull down the File menu and click the Print Relationships command. You will see the Print Preview screen of a report that displays the contents of the Relationships window. Click the Print button to print the report, or change to the Design view to modify the report, perhaps by adding your name. Save the report after printing so that it will be available at a later time.

Step 5:   **Modify the Order with Customer Information Query**

➤ You should be back in the Database window. Click the **Queries button**, select the **Order with Customer Information query**, then click the **Design button** to open the query in the Design view as shown in Figure 6.13e.

➤ If necessary, click and drag the border of the **Orders table** so that the newly added SalesPersonID field is displayed. Click the **horizontal scroll arrow** until a blank column in the design grid is visible.

➤ Click and drag the **SalesPersonID** from the Orders table to the first blank column in the design grid.

➤ Save the query. Close the query.

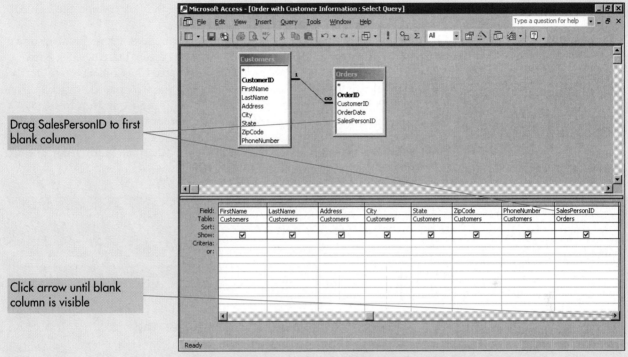

Drag SalesPersonID to first blank column

Click arrow until blank column is visible

(e) Modify the Order with Customer Information Query (step 5)

FIGURE 6.13   *Hands-on Exercise 4 (continued)*

OPTIMIZE QUERIES USING INDEXES

The performance of a database becomes important as you progress from a "student" database with a limited number of records to a real database with large tables. Thus it becomes advantageous to optimize the performance of individual queries by creating indexes in the underlying tables. Indexes should be specified for any criteria field in a query, as well as for any field that is used in a relationship to join two tables. To create an index, open the table in Design view and set the indexed property to Yes.

Step 6: **Modify the Order Form**

➤ You should be back in the Database window. Click the **Forms button**, select the **Super Store Order Form**, then click the **Design** button.

➤ Move and size the controls on the first line to make room for the SalesPersonID as shown in Figure 6.13f.

➤ Click the **Combo Box** tool, then click and drag in the form where you want the combo box to go. Release the mouse to start the Combo Box Wizard.

  • Check the option button that indicates you want the combo box to look up values in a table or query. Click **Next**.

  • Choose the **Sales Persons table** in the next screen. Click **Next**.

  • Select the **SalesPersonID** and **LastName**. Click **Next**.

  • Adjust the column width if necessary. Be sure the box to hide the key column is checked. Click **Next**.

  • Click the option button to store the value in the field. Click the **drop-down arrow** to display the fields and select the **SalesPersonID field**. Click **Next**.

  • Enter **Salesperson** as the label for the combo box. Click **Finish**.

➤ Move and/or size the combo box and its label so that it is spaced attractively on the form. Point to the combo box, click the **right mouse button** to display a shortcut menu, and click **Properties**. Click the **Other tab**.

➤ Change the name of the box to **Sales Person.** Close the dialog box.

➤ Pull down the **View menu** and click **Tab Order**. Click the **AutoOrder button**. Click **OK**. Save the form. Change to the Form view.

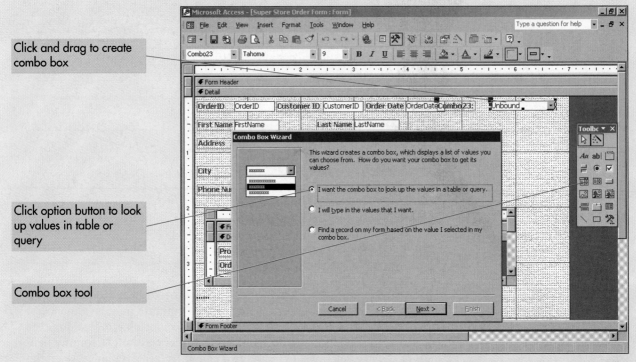

Click and drag to create combo box

Click option button to look up values in table or query

Combo box tool

(f) Modify the Order Form (step 6)

FIGURE 6.13   *Hands-on Exercise 4 (continued)*

Step 7: **The Completed Order Form**

➤ You should see the completed form as shown in Figure 6.13g. Click the **New Record button** on the Form View toolbar to display a blank form so that you can place an order.

➤ Click in the **Customer ID text box**. Enter **13** (your customer number from the first exercise), then press the **Tab key** to move to the next field.

• The OrderID is entered automatically as it is an AutoNumber field and assigned the next sequential number.

• All of your customer information (your name, address, and phone number) is entered automatically because of the AutoLookup feature that is built into the underlying query.

• Today's date is entered automatically because of the default value (=Date( )) that is built into the Orders table.

➤ Click the **drop-down arrow** on the Sales Person combo box. Select **Black** (or click in the box and type **B**), and the complete name is entered automatically.

➤ Click the **ProductID text box** in the subform. Enter **2** (not P0002) and press the **enter key** to move to the next field. The OrderID (O0027) is entered automatically, as are the Product Name and Unit Price.

➤ Press the **Tab key** three times to move to the Quantity field and enter **1**. The amount is computed automatically.

➤ Move to the ProductID field for the next item. Choose any item and enter a quantity.

➤ Close the Order form.

Click the New Record button

OrderID is automatically entered

Enter 13

Click drop-down arrow and select Black

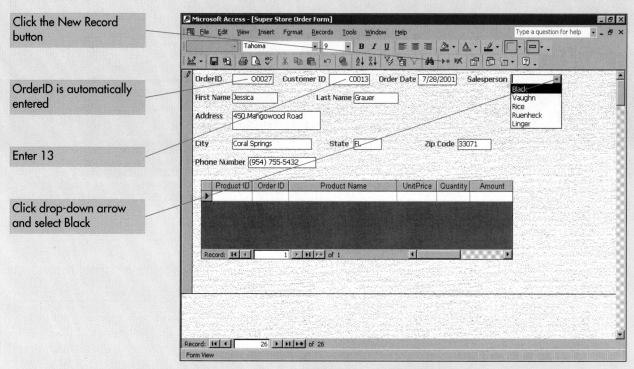

(g) The Completed Order Form (step 7)

FIGURE 6.13 *Hands-on Exercise 4 (continued)*

Step 8:   **Database Properties**

➤ You should be back in the Database window. Pull down the **File menu** and click **Database Properties** to display the dialog box in Figure 6.13h. Click the **Contents tab** to display the contents of the Computer Store database.
  • There are five tables (Customers, Order Details, Orders, Products, and Sales Persons).
  • There are five queries, which include the Total and Parameter queries you created in exercise 3.
  • There are two forms—the main form, which you have completed in this exercise, and the associated subform.
  • There is one report, the report you created in exercise 3.

➤ Click **OK** to close the dialog box. Close the Computer Store database. Exit Access.

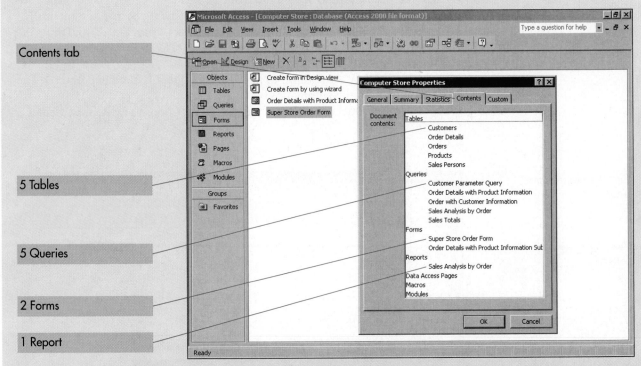

Contents tab

5 Tables

5 Queries

2 Forms

1 Report

(h) Database Properties (step 8)

FIGURE **6.13**   *Hands-on Exercise 4 (continued)*

THE STARTUP PROPERTY

The Startup property determines how a database will appear when it is opened. One very common option is to open a form automatically so that the user is presented with the form without having to navigate through the Database window. Pull down the Tools menu, click Startup to display the Startup dialog box, then click the drop-down arrow in the Display Form list box. Select the desired form (e.g., the Super Store Order form developed in this exercise), then click OK. The next time you open the database the designated form will be opened automatically.

The implementation of a many-to-many relationship requires an additional table whose primary key consists of (at least) the primary keys of the individual tables. The many-to-many table may also contain additional fields whose values are dependent on the combined key. All relationships are created in the Relationships window by dragging the join field from the primary table to the related table. A many-to-many relationship in the physical system is implemented by a pair of one-to-many relationships in an Access database.

Enforcement of referential integrity prevents you from adding a record to the related table if that record contains an invalid value of the foreign key. (You cannot, for example, add a record to the Orders table that contains an invalid value for CustomerID.) Referential integrity also prevents the deletion and/or updating of records on the "one" side of a one-to-many relationship when there are matching records in the related table. The deletion (updating) can take place, however, if the relationship is modified to allow the cascaded deletion (updating) of related records (fields).

Referential integrity does not prevent you from adding a record to the "many" table that omits a value for the field from the "one" table. You could, for example, add a record to the Orders table that omitted CustomerID. If this does not make sense in the physical situation, then you have to make the CustomerID a required field in the Orders table.

There are several reasons to base a form (or subform) on a query rather than a table. A query can contain a calculated field; a table cannot. A query can contain fields from more than one table and take advantage of AutoLookup. A query can also contain selected records from a table and/or display those records in a different sequence from that of the table on which it is based.

A parameter query prompts you for the criteria each time you execute the query. The prompt is enclosed in square brackets and is entered in the Criteria row within the Query Design view. Multiple parameters may be specified within the same query.

Aggregate functions (Avg, Min, Max, Sum, and Count) perform calculations on groups of records. Execution of the query displays an aggregate record for each group, and individual records do not appear. Updating of individual records is not possible in this type of query.

Tables may be added to an Access database without disturbing the data in existing tables. The Get External Data command enables you to import an object(s) from another database.

KEY TERMS

AutoLookup (p. 266)
AutoNumber field (p. 259)
Cascaded deletion (p. 260)
Cascaded updating (p. 260)
Combined key (p. 258)
Description property (p. 285)
Format property (p. 259)
Get External Data command (p. 291)

Group By (p. 276)
Main form (p. 266)
Many-to-many relationship (p. 258)
One-to-many relationship (p. 256)
Parameter query (p. 276)
Primary key (p. 256)
Prompt (p. 276)
Referential integrity (p. 260)
Relationship lines (p. 259)

Relationships window (p. 259)
Startup property (p. 298)
Subform (p. 266)
Sum function (p. 276)
TopValues property (p. 287)
Total query (p. 276)
Total row (p. 276)
Unmatched Query Wizard (p. 283)

1. Which table(s) is(are) necessary to implement a many-to-many relationship between students and the courses they take?
   (a) A Students table
   (b) A Courses table
   (c) A Students-Courses table
   (d) All of the above

2. Which of the following would be suitable as the primary key in a Students-Courses table, where there is a many-to-many relationship between Students and Courses, and further, when a student is allowed to repeat a course?
   (a) The combination of StudentID and CourseID
   (b) The combination of StudentID, CourseID, and semester
   (c) The combination of StudentID, CourseID, semester, and grade
   (d) All of the above are equally appropriate

3. Which of the following is necessary to add a record to the "one" side in a one-to-many relationship in which referential integrity is enforced?
   (a) A unique primary key for the new record
   (b) One or more matching records in the many table
   (c) Both (a) and (b)
   (d) Neither (a) nor (b)

4. Which of the following is necessary to add a record to the "many" side in a one-to-many relationship in which referential integrity is enforced?
   (a) A unique primary key for the new record
   (b) A matching record in the primary table
   (c) Both (a) and (b)
   (d) Neither (a) nor (b)

5. Under which circumstances can you delete a "many" record in a one-to-many relationship?
   (a) Under all circumstances
   (b) Under no circumstances
   (c) By enforcing referential integrity
   (d) By enforcing referential integrity with the cascaded deletion of related records

6. Under which circumstances can you delete the "one" record in a one-to-many relationship?
   (a) Under all circumstances
   (b) Under no circumstances
   (c) By enforcing referential integrity
   (d) By enforcing referential integrity with the cascaded deletion of related records

7. Which of the following would be suitable as the primary key in a Patients-Doctors table, where there is a many-to-many relationship between patients and doctors, and where the same patient can see the same doctor on different visits?
   (a) The combination of PatientID and DoctorID
   (b) The combination of PatientID, DoctorID, and the date of the visit
   (c) Either (a) or (b)
   (d) Neither (a) nor (b)

8. How do you implement the many-to-many relationship between patients and doctors described in the previous question?
   (a) Through a one-to-many relationship between the Patients table and the Patients-Doctors table
   (b) Through a one-to-many relationship between the Doctors table and the Patients-Doctors table
   (c) Both (a) and (b)
   (d) Neither (a) nor (b)

9. A database has a one-to-many relationship between teams and players. Which data type and field size should be assigned to the TeamID field in the Players table, if TeamID is defined as an AutoNumber field in the Teams table?
   (a) AutoNumber and Long Integer
   (b) Number and Long Integer
   (c) Text and Long Integer
   (d) Lookup Wizard and Long Integer

10. Which of the following is true about a main form and an associated subform?
    (a) The main form can be based on a query
    (b) The subform can be based on a query
    (c) Both (a) and (b)
    (d) Neither (a) nor (b)

11. A parameter query:
    (a) Displays a prompt within brackets in the Criteria row of the query
    (b) Is limited to a single parameter
    (c) Both (a) and (b)
    (d) Neither (a) nor (b)

12. Which of the following is available as an aggregate function within a select query?
    (a) Sum and Avg
    (b) Min and Max
    (c) Both (a) and (b)
    (d) Neither (a) nor (b)

13. A query designed to take advantage of AutoLookup requires:
    (a) A unique value for the join field in the "one" side of a relationship
    (b) The join field to be taken from the "many" side of a one-to-many relationship
    (c) Both (a) and (b)
    (d) Neither (a) nor (b)

14. Which of the following can be imported from another Access database?
    (a) Tables and forms
    (b) Queries and reports
    (c) Both (a) and (b)
    (d) Neither (a) nor (b)

15. Which of the following is true of the TopValues query property?
    (a) It can be used to display the top 10 records in a dynaset
    (b) It can be used to display the top 10 percent of the records in a dynaset
    (c) Both (a) and (b)
    (d) Neither (a) nor (b)

ANSWERS

1. d	**6.** d	**11.** a
2. b	**7.** b	**12.** c
3. a	**8.** c	**13.** c
4. a	**9.** b	**14.** c
5. a	**10.** c	**15.** c

BUILDS ON

HANDS-ON
EXERCISE 4
PAGES 291–298

1. Sales Commission Report: This problem continues the Computer Store database that was developed in the chapter. Complete the four hands-on exercises in the chapter, after which you will be able to develop the Sales Commission Report in Figure 6.14. The report is based on a query that is similar to the query in Figure 6.12. The Report Wizard was used to create the report after the query was completed. (The query uses fields from all five tables in the database.) You need not match our design exactly, but you have to display equivalent information. Add your name to the report header, then print the result for your instructor.

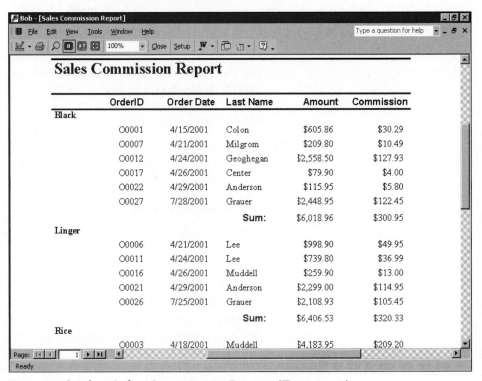

FIGURE 6.14   *Sales Commission Report (Exercise 1)*

BUILDS ON

HANDS-ON
EXERCISE 4
PAGES 291–298

2. Unmatched Query Wizard: Figure 6.15 displays a query created by the Unmatched Query Wizard to determine those products that have never been ordered. This type of information is very valuable to management, which can realize significant cost savings by eliminating these products from inventory. Proceed as follows:
   a. Complete the four hands-on exercises in this chapter.
   b. Click the Queries button in the Database window. Click the New button, select the Find Unmatched Query Wizard, and click OK. Choose Products as the table whose records you want to see in the query results. Click Next. Choose Order Details as the table that contains the related records.
   c. Product ID is selected automatically as the matching field. Click Next. Select every field from the Available Fields list. Click Next. Products without Matching Order Details is entered as the name of the query.
   d. Click Finish. You will see a list of the products (if any) that have never been ordered. Print the results of the query for your instructor. What advice would you give to management regarding the inventory of these items?
   e. Add a cover sheet to complete the assignment.

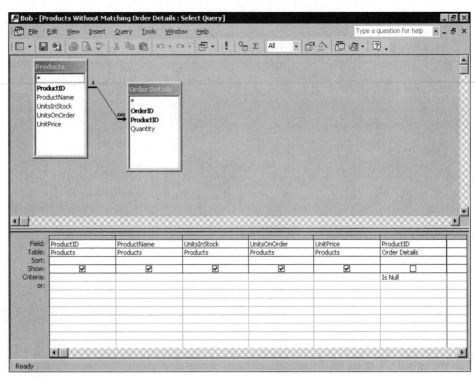

FIGURE 6.15 *Unmatched Query Wizard (Exercise 2)*

BUILDS ON

HANDS-ON
EXERCISE 4
PAGES 291–298

3. An Improved Order Form: The order form in Figure 6.16 builds on the order form that was developed in the fourth hands-on exercise in the chapter. A header has been added that includes clip art and a label for your name. Two command buttons to add a new order and close the form have also been added. The most significant change, however, is the inclusion of a Product Name combo box on the subform in place of the Product ID. Proceed as follows:

a. Open the Order Details subform in Design view. Delete the controls and associated labels for ProductID and Product Name. Click the Combo Box Wizard tool, then click and drag in the Detail area of the subform to create a combo box (where the ProductName control was previously).

b. Supply the information requested by the Wizard. Click the option button to indicate that you want the combo box to look up values in a table or query. Click Next. Specify the Products table. Click Next. Select the ProductID and ProductName fields. Click Next. Adjust the column width of the ProductName field. Click Next. Click the option button to store the value in a field and specify ProductID. Click Finish.

c. Adjust the size, position, and alignment of the newly created control. Right click the combo box, click Properties, and change the name of the combo box to Product Name.

d. Pull down the View menu, click the Tab Order command, and specify AutoOrder. Save the form.

e. Open the Super Store Order form, which should now contain a drop-down list box to facilitate data entry of new products. Adjust the column width of this field within the subform if necessary.

f. Click the add button to add a new order to demonstrate the functionality in the completed form. Click in the CustomerID and enter your CustomerID, then tab to the combo box where you can select a salesperson. Complete the order by going to the subform and selecting the individual products. Click in the Product Name list box, then click the down arrow to select the product by name, rather than by product ID. Tab to the quantity field to enter the quantity. Enter at least three products, then print the completed order.

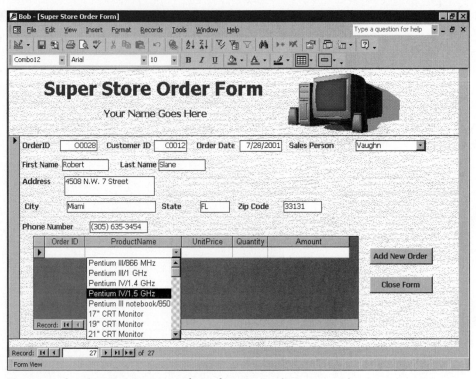

FIGURE 6.16 *An Improved Order Form (Exercise 3)*

BUILDS ON

PRACTICE
EXERCISES 1, 2, AND 3
PAGES 302–304

4. Super Store Switchboard: The switchboard in Figure 6.17 provides access to the various objects that were created for the Computer Super Store. You do not have to match our design exactly, but you should try for consistency and simplicity. The computer logo that appears in the switchboard and in the About form is the same logo as in the order form from the previous example. Print the completed switchboard as well as the table of switchboard items.

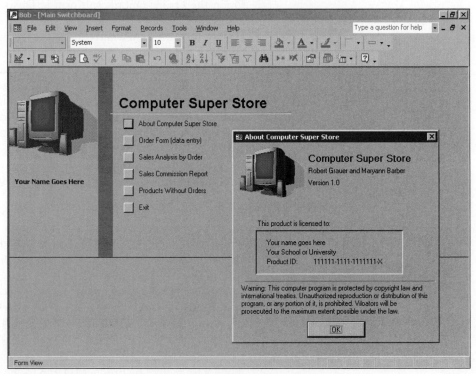

FIGURE 6.17 *Super Store Switchboard (Exercise 4)*

BUILDS ON

CHAPTER 5
PRACTICE
EXERCISE 9
PAGE 252

5. National Bank Advanced Queries: The dynaset in Figure 6.18 is the result of a total query that is associated with the National Bank database from the previous chapter. There was a one-to-many relationship between customers and loans (one customer has many loans). The amount that is displayed represents the sum of all the loans for each customer. Ted Myerson, for example, has borrowed a total of $525,000.

The query also reflects the one-to-many relationship between loan officers and loans (one loan officer is responsible for many loans) for a specific loan officer (Grauer). The name of the loan officer is entered as the query is executed since it (the officer's name) is specified as a parameter. Your assignment is to develop the query and print the dynaset shown in Figure 6.18. Add a cover sheet to complete the assignment.

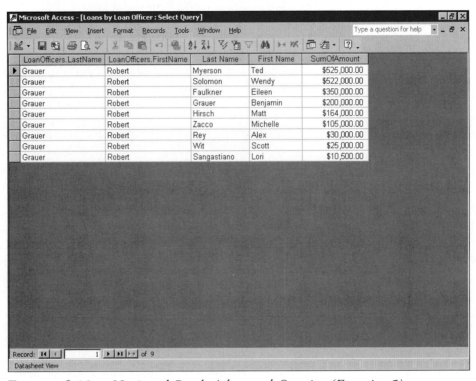

FIGURE 6.18   *National Bank Advanced Queries (Exercise 5)*

BUILDS ON

PRACTICE
EXERCISE 5
PAGE 305

6. Expanded National Bank Switchboard: The switchboard in Figure 6.19 is an expanded version of the switchboard developed in the preceding chapter. The last two items (above the Exit button) have been added to complete the switchboard. The Loans by Loan Officer button runs the query of the previous problem and displays the parameter value of the loan officer (Grauer in this example). The Loans Without Payments button uses the Unmatched Query Wizard to display all loans that have not received any payments. Only one loan should appear, and it will contain your name as the customer, provided you have followed all of the instructions in the hands-on exercises from the previous chapter. Print this loan for your instructor.

The completed switchboard ties together all of the objects that were created in the various exercises. Print the switchboard itself, together with the table of switchboard items. Add a cover sheet to complete the assignment.

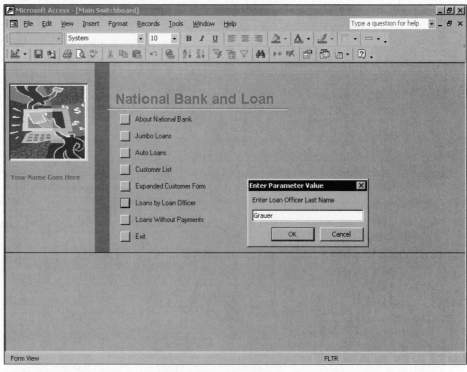

FIGURE 6.19 *Expanded National Bank Switchboard (Exercise 6)*

7. Medical Research Database Design: Figure 6.20 displays the relationships diagram for a database that is to be used by a medical research project that will track volunteers (subjects) and/or the research studies with which they are associated. A study will require several subjects, but a specific person may participate in only one study. The system should also be able to track the physicians who do the research. Many physicians can work on the same study, and a given physician may work on multiple studies.

   a. The system should be able to display all facts about a particular volunteer (subject) such as name, birth date, sex, height, weight, blood pressure, cholesterol level, and so on. It should be able to display all characteristics associated with a particular study such as the title, beginning date, ending date, as well as the names of all physicians who work on that study. It should also show whether the physician is a primary or secondary investigator in each study.

   b. Open the partially completed database in *Chapter 6 Practice 7* and implement our design. The report in Figure 6.20 is created from the Relationships window after the relationships have been specified. Print the completed report for your instructor.

BUILDS ON

PRACTICE
EXERCISE 7
PAGE 306

8. Medical Research Switchboard: The switchboard in Figure 6.21 contains several potential commands for the medical research database. Your assignment is to implement the indicated database design, then create the appropriate object for each button on the switchboard.

   Start by creating a basic switchboard that contains your name and a logo (selected clip art) for the application. The initial switchboard should contain three items—one command, to display the "About Medical Research" form that is similar to the various forms, one command to print the relationships diagram, and a command to exit the application. Print this switchboard and table of switchboard items for your instructor. Add the additional objects as directed by your instructor.

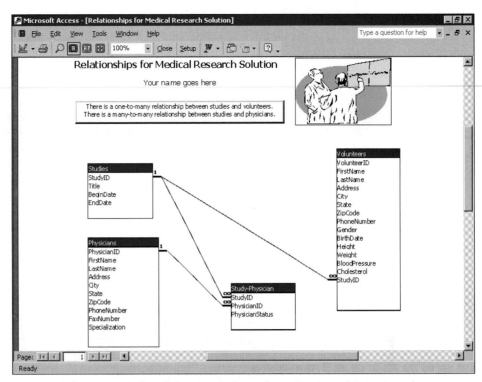

FIGURE 6.20 *Medical Research Database Design (Exercise 7)*

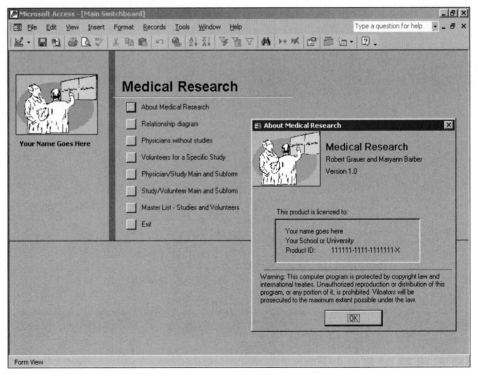

FIGURE 6.21 *Medical Research Switchboard (Exercise 8)*

9. National Conference Database Design: You have been retained as a consultant to design a database for the national conference of a professional organization. This is an annual event and the planning is extensive. Your assignment is to track the speakers and associated sessions at which they will appear in order to create a program for the conference. One speaker can participate in many sessions, and one session can have many speakers. You need to maintain the information for each speaker (name, address, telephone, e-mail, and so on). You also need to maintain information about each session (the title, a more detailed synopsis of up to 500 words, the date, starting time, duration, and the room).

a. Your database also has to track the available rooms within the hotel to facilitate the session assignments. During the course of the conference, one room will host many sessions, but a particular session will be held in only one room. The program should print the name of the session, its location, date, and starting time, as well as all of the scheduled speakers. The capacity of each room should be stored in the database so that sessions can be assigned to an appropriate room. Some rooms have large screens and/or the ability to serve refreshments, and this information should be stored as well. The database should also produce an alphabetical list of all speakers that shows all sessions at which the individual is speaking.

b. Open the partially completed database in *Chapter 6 Practice 9* and implement our design. The report in Figure 6.22 is created from the Relationships window after the relationships have been specified. Print the completed report for your instructor.

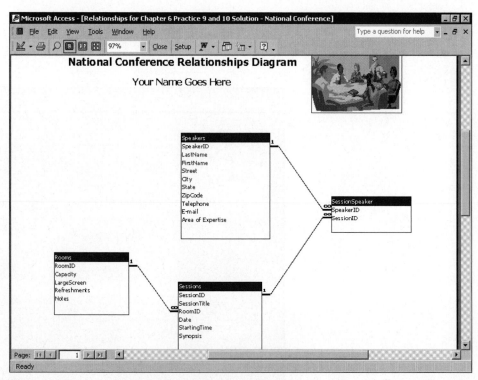

FIGURE 6.22   *National Conference Database Design (Exercise 9)*

BUILDS ON

PRACTICE
EXERCISE 9
PAGE 308

10. National Conference Switchboard: The switchboard in Figure 6.23 contains several potential commands for the national conference database. Your assignment is to implement the indicated database design, then create the appropriate object for each button on the switchboard. Print the switchboard form and table of switchboard items for your instructor.

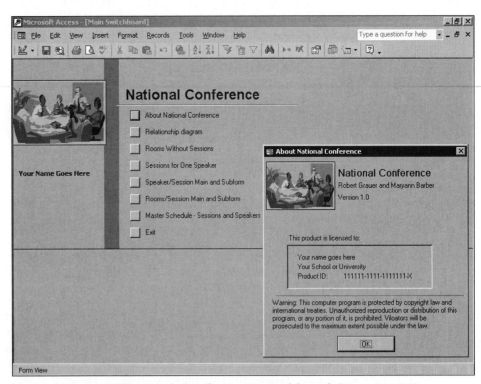

FIGURE 6.23 *National Conference Switchboard (Exercise 10)*

BUILDS ON

PRACTICE
EXERCISE 4
PAGE 304

11. A Look Ahead: Open the Computer Store database. Pull down the Tools menu, click (or point to) the Database Utilities command, then select the Database Splitter to display a screen similar to Figure 6.24. Click the button to Split the Database, then follow the onscreen instructions. Be sure to store the back end (the database containing the tables) in the same folder as the original database. You will learn the rationale for splitting a database in this fashion in Chapter 7.

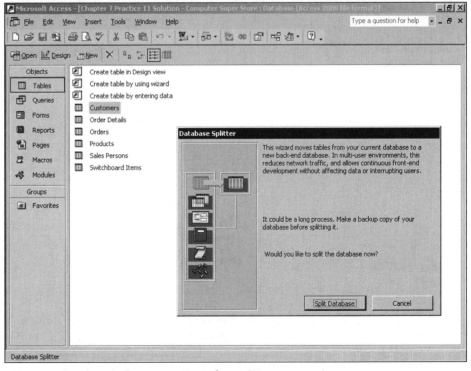

FIGURE 6.24 *Splitting a Database (Exercise 11)*

Health Clubs

Your interest in physical fitness has led to a part-time job at a local health club where you have been asked to design a database for its members and trainers. The health club runs promotions periodically, and so individuals join under different membership plans. Each plan specifies the initial fee (if any), monthly payment (if any), and duration. One plan can have many members, but a specific member has only one plan.

The health club needs to track the number of hours that each employee works, which is accomplished through time cards that record the date, time in, and time out. The health club also wants to know how often members work out, and which trainer they use—thus all members complete a simple workout form each time they are at the club. The form contains the member's identification number, date, and length of the workout (in hours). The workout form also indicates the specific facilities that were used in that session. One member can work out with different trainers, and one trainer will work out with many different members.

The database should be capable of computing the total revenue that is received by the health club. One report should show the sum of all initial fees that have been paid by all members. A second report should show the projected revenue each month, based on the monthly payment due from each member. Print the report containing the relationships diagram for your instructor as proof that you completed this exercise.

The Morning Paper

We take the delivery of our morning paper for granted, but there is a lot of planning to ensure that we receive it each day. You are to design a database for a large metropolitan newspaper that is printed at a central location within the area. Once printed, the papers are delivered to multiple warehouses. Each warehouse services multiple carriers, each of whom goes to the assigned warehouse to pick up the requisite number of papers for his or her customers. One carrier has many customers, but a particular customer has only one carrier.

The database is further complicated by the fact that the newspaper has several editions such as a Spanish edition, a daily (Monday through Saturday) edition, and a Sunday edition. One edition can go to many customers, and one customer can order many editions. There is a specific price associated with each edition. You are to design a database that will enable the paper to determine how many of each edition is to be sent to each warehouse. The database should also be capable of producing a report that shows the total amount of business that each carrier brings in. Print the report containing the relationships diagram for your instructor as proof that you completed this exercise.

The College Bookstore

The manager of a college bookstore has asked for your help in improving its database. The bookstore needs to know which books are used in which courses. One course may require several books, and the same book can be used in different courses. A book may be required in one course and merely recommended in another. The bookstore has a list of all courses taught by the university, with the faculty coordinator for each course.

The design of this database begins with the creation of a Books table that contains the ISBN for each book, its title and author, price, and publisher. Books are ordered directly from the publisher, so it is necessary to know the address and telephone for each publisher. One publisher has many books, but a specific book has only one publisher.

The bookstore places multiple orders with each publisher. One order can specify many books, and the same book can appear in multiple orders. The manager must know the date that each order was placed and the total cost of each order. The manager must also be able to create a report showing the books that are used in each course and its status for that course (i.e., whether the book is required or suggested). Your assignment is to design a database that will fulfill all of the requirements of the bookstore manager. Print the report containing the relationships diagram for your instructor as proof that you completed this exercise.

Bob's Burgers

The corporate office of Bob's Burgers has asked you to design a database to track its restaurants and managers. The database is to produce reports that show the sales of each restaurant and the performance of each manager, as measured by the total sales of all restaurants for that manager. Each restaurant has one manager, but a manager is responsible for multiple restaurants. The company stores the typical personnel data (name, salary, and so on) for each manager as well as basic data for each restaurant such as the telephone and address of each restaurant, its size in square feet, and annual sales for last year. The company would like objective ways to measure the performance of a manager such as the total revenue for which he or she is responsible, the average revenue per restaurant, the average revenue per square foot, and so on.

The database also tracks the orders that are placed by the individual restaurants to the corporate office for various food supplies. Each order is associated with a specific restaurant, and of course, one restaurant will place multiple orders during the course of the year. The company uses a standard set of product numbers, product descriptions, and associated prices that applies to every restaurant. Each order can specify multiple products, and one product may appear in several orders. The database should be capable of computing the total cost of each order. Print the report containing the relationships diagram for your instructor as proof that you completed this exercise.

The Medical Practice

Design a database for a small medical practice that has five physicians. Any patient may see any physician, and, over time, one patient will see many physicians. A patient may complain about multiple ailments, all of which can be treated in a single appointment. (The patient sees only one physician per appointment.) The practice is very efficient in its billing practices and stores all of the ailment information (description, treatment, charge, and so on) in a separate ailments table. As indicated, one appointment can deal with multiple ailments, and the same ailment (e.g., a broken arm) can be treated in different appointments.

Your solution should include separate tables for patients and physicians, with appropriate fields in each table. There is also an ailments table. Additional tables are also required to accommodate the many-to-many relationships that exist within the system. Create a database that contains all of the required tables (you do not have to enter any data) in order to print the relationships diagram for your design. Include a simple switchboard that incorporates a basic logo and color scheme.

CHAPTER 7

Building Applications: Macros and a Multilevel Switchboard

OBJECTIVES

AFTER READING THIS CHAPTER YOU WILL BE ABLE TO:

1. Use the Switchboard Manager to create and/or modify a switchboard; explain why multiple switchboards may be required within one application.
2. Use the Link Tables command to associate tables in one database with objects in a different database.
3. Describe how macros are used to automate an application; explain the special role of the AutoExec macro.
4. Describe the components of the Macro window; distinguish between a macro action and an argument.
5. Explain how prototyping facilitates the development of an application; use the MsgBox action as the basis of a prototype macro.
6. Use the Unmatched Query Wizard to identify records in one table that do not have a corresponding record in another table.
7. Create a macro group; explain how macro groups simplify the organization of macros within a database.

OVERVIEW

This chapter revisits the concept of a user interface (or switchboard) that ties the objects in a database together, so that the database is easy to use. The switchboard displays a menu, often a series of menus, which enables a nontechnical person to move easily from one Access object to another. Any database containing a switchboard is known as an application and, unlike an ordinary Access database, it does not require knowledge of Microsoft Access on the part of the user.

The development of an application may also entail the splitting of a database into two files—one containing the tables and the other containing the remaining

313

objects (the forms, reports, queries, and macros). The tables are then linked to the other objects through the Link Tables command. It sounds complicated, but this approach has several advantages, as you will see.

The chapter also covers macros and prototypes, two techniques that are used by developers in creating applications. A macro automates common command sequences and further simplifies the system for the end user. Prototypes are used in conjunction with developing the various switchboards to demonstrate the "look and feel" of an application, even before the application is complete. Three hands-on exercises are included in the chapter to progressively build the application as you develop your skills in Access.

CASE STUDY: A RECREATIONAL SPORTS LEAGUE

You have probably played in a sports league at one time or another, whether in Little League as a child or in an intramural league at school or work. Whatever the league, it had teams, players, and coaches. The typical league registers the players and coaches individually, then holds a draft among the coaches to divide the players into teams according to ability. The league may have been organized informally, with manual procedures for registering the participants and creating the teams. Now we automate the process.

Let's think for a moment about the tables and associated relationships that will be necessary to create the database. There are three tables, one each for players, coaches, and teams. There is a one-to-many relationship between teams and players (one team has many players, but a player is assigned to only one team). There is also a one-to-many relationship between teams and coaches (one team has many coaches, but a coach is assigned to only one team).

In addition to the tables, the database will contain multiple forms, queries, and reports based on these tables. A Players form is necessary in order to add a new player, or edit or delete the record of an existing player. A similar form should exist for Coaches. There might also be a sophisticated main and subform combination for the Teams table that displays the players and coaches on each team, and through which data for any table (Team, Player, or Coach) can be added, edited, or deleted. And, of course, there will be a variety of reports and queries.

Let's assume that this database has been created. It would not be difficult for a person knowledgeable in Access to open the database and select the various objects as the need arose. He or she would know how to display the Database window and how to select the various buttons to open the appropriate objects. But what if the system is to be used by someone who does not know Access, which is typically the case? You can see that the user interface becomes the most important part of the system, at least from the viewpoint of the end user. An interface that is intuitive and easy to use will be successful. Conversely, a system that is difficult to use or visually unappealing is sure to fail.

Figure 7.1a displays the *switchboard* that will be created for this application. We have added a soccer ball as a logo, but the application applies to any type of recreational sports league. The interface is intuitive and easy to use. Click the About Sports button, the first button on our menu, and the system displays the informational screen we like to include in all of our applications. Click any other button, and you display the indicated form. Click the Teams button, for example, and you see the form in Figure 7.1b, where you can add a new team, view, edit, or print the data for any existing team, then click the Close Form button to return to the main menu.

The switchboard in Figure 7.1a exists as a form within the database. Look closely, however, and you will see it is subtly different from the forms you have developed in previous chapters. The record selector and navigation buttons, for example, have been suppressed because they are not needed. In other words, this

Click About Sports button to display informational message

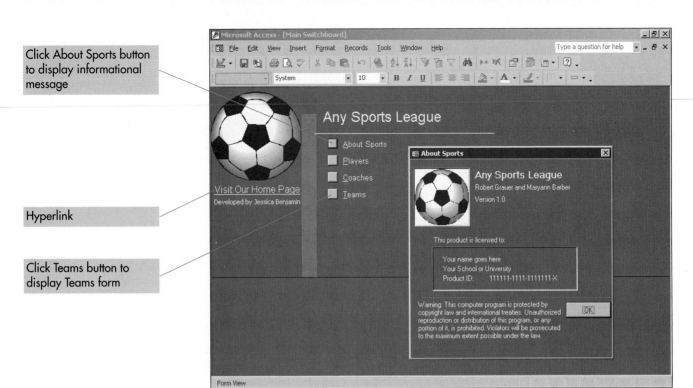

(a) The Main Menu

Hyperlink

Click Teams button to display Teams form

Add, edit, or delete a team

Add, edit, or delete a coach

Add, edit, or delete a player

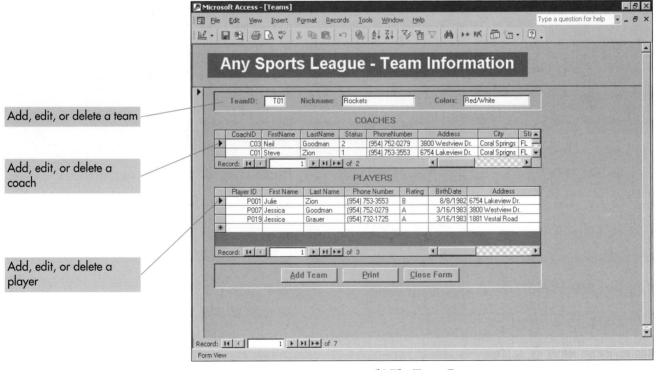

(b) The Teams Form

FIGURE 7.1 *Building a User Interface*

Switchboard can have
eight menu items

Record Source for
switchboard is
Switchboard Items table

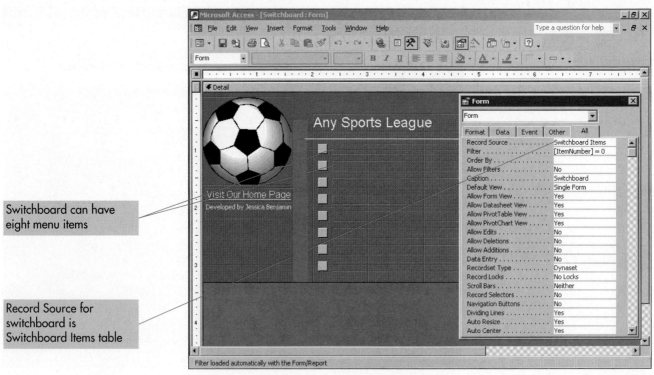

(c) Design View

SwitchboardID identifies
which switchboard item
belongs to

ItemNumber identifies
position of item on
switchboard

ItemText identifies text
displays for that item on
switchboard

Command determines
action taken when item is
selected

Argument specifies object
to be acted on (e.g., form
to be opened)

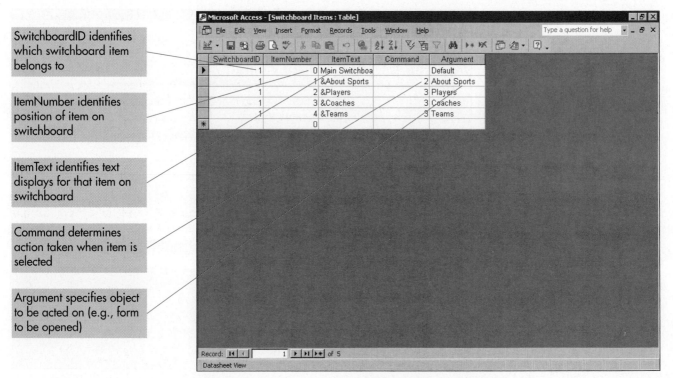

(d) Switchboard Items

FIGURE 7.1 *Building a User Interface (continued)*

form is not used for data entry, but as the basis of a menu for the user. You can even visit the league's Web site by clicking the indicated hyperlink.

The essence of the form, however, lies in the command buttons that enable the user to open the other objects in the database. Thus, when a user clicks a button, Access interprets that action as an *event* and responds with an action that has been assigned to that event. Clicking the Teams button, for example, causes Access to open the Teams form. Clicking the Players button is a different event, and causes Access to open the Players form.

The Switchboard Manager

The *Switchboard Manager* creates a switchboard automatically, by prompting you for information about each menu item. You supply the text of the item as it is to appear on the switchboard, together with the underlying command. Access does the rest. It creates a *switchboard form* that is displayed to the user and a *Switchboard Items table* that stores information about each command.

The switchboard form is shown in both the Form view and the Design view, in Figures 7.1a and 7.1c, respectively. At first, the views do not appear to correspond to one another, in that text appears next to each button in the Form view, but it is absent in the Design view. This, however, is the nature of a switchboard, because the text for each button is taken from the Switchboard Items table in Figure 7.1d, which is the record source for the form, as can be inferred from the Form property sheet. In other words, each record in the Switchboard Items table has a corresponding menu item in the switchboard form. Note, too, that you can modify the switchboard form after it has been created, perhaps by inserting a picture or a hyperlink as was done in Figure 7.1.

As indicated, the Switchboard Items table is created automatically and can be modified through the Switchboard Manager or by directly opening the table. It helps, therefore, to have an appreciation for each field in the table. The SwitchboardID field identifies the number of the switchboard, which becomes important in applications with more than one switchboard. Access limits each switchboard to eight items, but you can create as many switchboards as you like, each with a different value for the SwitchboardID. Every application has a main switchboard by default, which can in turn display other switchboards as necessary.

The ItemNumber and ItemText fields identify the position and text of the item, respectively, as it appears on the switchboard form. (The & that appears within the ItemText field will appear as an underlined letter on the switchboard to enable a keyboard shortcut; for example, &Teams is displayed as Teams and recognizes the Alt+T keyboard shortcut in lieu of clicking the button.) The Command and Argument fields determine the action that will be taken when the corresponding button is clicked. Command number 3, for example, opens a form.

The Linked Tables Manager

Every application consists of tables *and* objects (forms, queries, reports, macros, and modules) based on those tables. The tables and objects may be stored in the same database (as has been done throughout the text), or they may be stored in separate databases, as will be done for the soccer application. Look closely at the Database window in Figure 7.2a. The title bar displays "Sports Objects" and indicates the name of the database that is currently open. Note, however, the arrows that appear next to the icons for the Players, Teams, and Coaches tables to indicate that the tables are stored in a different database. The name of the second database, "Sports Tables," is seen in the Linked Table Manager dialog box in Figure 7.2b.

The tables and objects are associated with one another through the **Link Tables command** and/or through the **Linked Table Manager**. Once the linking has been established, however, it is as though the Players, Coaches, and Teams tables were in the Sports Objects database with respect to maintaining the data. In other words, you can add, edit, and delete a record in any of the three tables as if the tables were physically in the Sports Objects database.

The advantage to storing the tables and objects in separate databases is that you can enhance an application by creating a new version of the Sports Objects database, without affecting the underlying tables. The new version has the improved features, such as a new form or report, but attaches to the original data, and thus retains all of the transactions that have been processed.

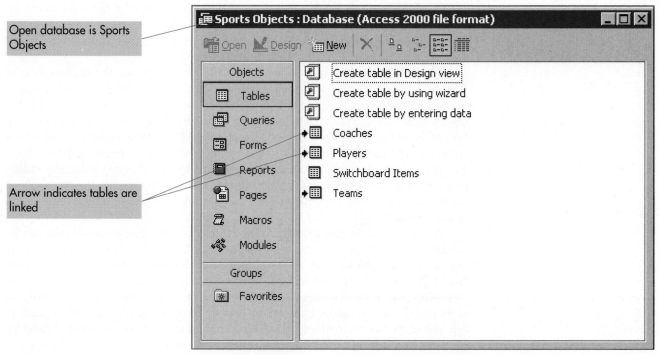

(a) The Database Window

Open database is Sports Objects

Arrow indicates tables are linked

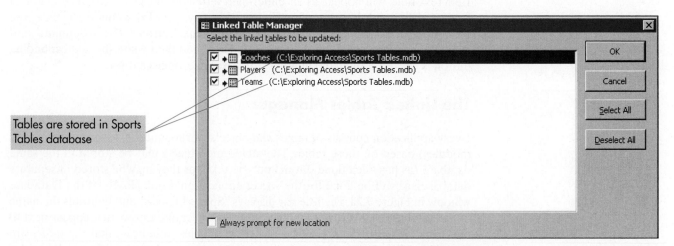

Tables are stored in Sports Tables database

(b) The Linked Table Manager

FIGURE 7.2 *Linking Tables*

THE SWITCHBOARD MANAGER

Objective To create a switchboard; to use the Link Tables command to associate tables in one database with the objects in a different database. Use Figure 7.3 as a guide in the exercise.

Step 1: **The Sports Objects Database**

> ➤ Start Access. Change to the **Exploring Access folder** as you have been doing throughout the text.
> ➤ Open the **Sports Objects database** as shown in Figure 7.3a, then click the various buttons in the Database window to view the contents of this database. This database contains the various objects (forms, queries, and reports) in the soccer application, but not the tables.
>   • Click the **Tables button**. There are currently no tables in the database.
>   • Click the **Queries button**. There is one query in the database.
>   • Click the **Forms button**. There are six forms in the database.
>   • Click the **Reports button**. There is one report in the database.
> ➤ Pull down the **File menu**, click **Database Properties**, then click the **Contents tab** to see the contents of the database as shown in Figure 7.3a. The Database Properties command enables you to see all of the objects on one screen.
> ➤ Click **OK** to close the dialog box.

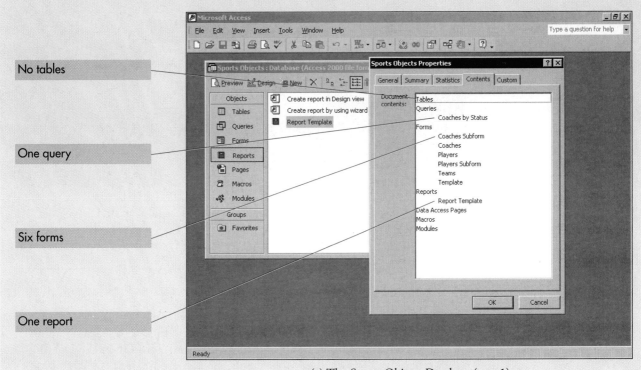

No tables

One query

Six forms

One report

(a) The Sports Objects Database (step 1)

FIGURE 7.3 *Hands-on Exercise 1*

Step 2: **The Link Tables Command**

➤ Pull down the **File menu**. Click **Get External Data**, then click **Link Tables** from the cascaded menu. You should see the Link dialog box (which is similar in appearance to the Open dialog box).

➤ Select the **Exploring Access folder**, the folder you have been using throughout the text. Scroll (if necessary) until you can select the **Sports Tables database**, then click the **Link command button**.

➤ You should see the Link Tables dialog box in Figure 7.3b. Click the **Select All command button** to select all three tables, then click **OK**.

➤ The system (briefly) displays a message indicating that it is linking the tables, after which the tables should appear in the Database window.

➤ Click the **Tables button** in the Database window. The arrow next to each table indicates that the table physically resides in another database. (You may have to relink the tables if you move the database to another computer.)

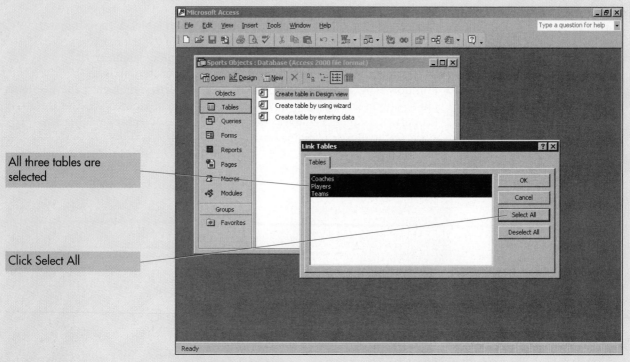

All three tables are selected

Click Select All

(b) The Link Tables Command (step 2)

FIGURE 7.3   *Hands-on Exercise 1 (continued)*

THE DATABASE SPLITTER

The tables and associated objects should always be stored in separate databases. But what if you created the application prior to learning about the ability to link tables and objects to one another? Open the existing database, pull down the Tools menu, click (or point to) the Database Utilities, select the Database Splitter command, and follow the onscreen instructions. You will wind up with two separate databases, a back end that contains the tables, and a front end that contains the other objects.

Step 3: **Import the About Sports Form**

➤ Pull down the **File menu**, click the **Get External Data command,** then click **Import** to display the Import dialog box. Select the **Exploring Access folder**, the folder you have been using throughout the text.

➤ Scroll (if necessary) until you can select the **About Sports database**, then click the **Import button** to display the Import Objects dialog box in Figure 7.3c. Click the **Forms button**, select the **About Sports** form, and click **OK**. The system pauses as the About Sports form is brought into this database.

➤ Once the importing is complete, the Database window changes to display the forms in this database, which now includes the About Sports form. Open the form in the Design view, then modify its contents to include your name and school. Save your changes, then close the form.

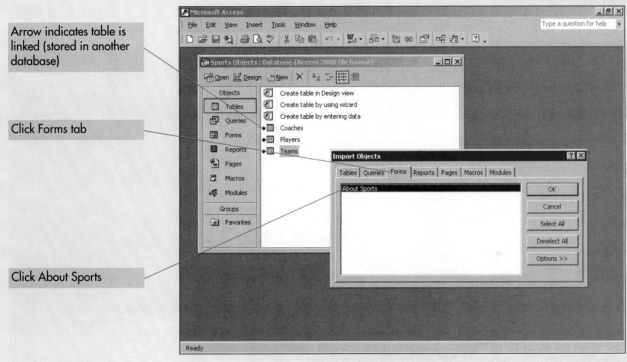

Arrow indicates table is linked (stored in another database)

Click Forms tab

Click About Sports

(c) Import the About Sports Form (step 3)

FIGURE 7.3 *Hands-on Exercise 1 (continued)*

IMPORTING VERSUS LINKING

The Get External Data command displays a cascaded menu to import or link an object from another database. Importing a table brings a copy of the table into the current database and does not maintain a tie to the original table. Linking, on the other hand, does not bring the table into the database but only a pointer to the table. All changes are stored in the original table and are reflected automatically in any database that is linked to the original table. Any type of object can be *imported* into a database. A table is the only type of object that can be *linked*.

Step 4: **Start the Switchboard Manager**

➤ Minimize the Database window. Pull down the **Tools menu**, click the **Database Utilities command**, and choose **Switchboard Manager**.

➤ Click **Yes** if you see a message indicating that there is no valid switchboard. You should see the Switchboard Manager dialog box in Figure 7.3d.

➤ Click the **Edit command button** to display the Edit Switchboard Page dialog box. Click the **New command button** to add an item to this page, which in turn displays the Edit Switchboard Item dialog box.

➤ Click in the **Text** list box and type **&About Sports**, which is the name of the command as it will appear in the switchboard.

➤ Click the **drop-down arrow** on the Command list box. Choose the command to open the form in either Add or Edit mode (it doesn't matter for this form).

➤ Click the **drop-down arrow** in the Form list box and choose **About Sports**.

➤ Click **OK** to create the switchboard item. The Edit Switchboard Item dialog box closes and the About Sports item appears in the Main Switchboard.

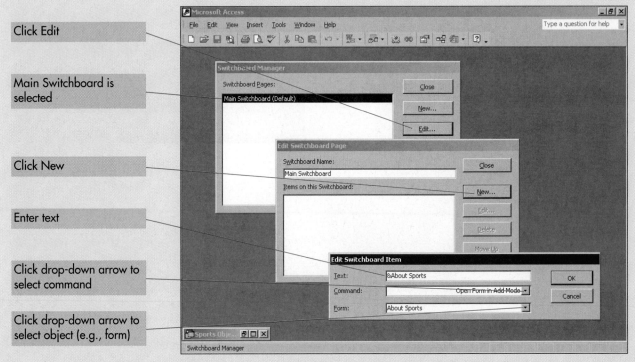

Click Edit

Main Switchboard is selected

Click New

Enter text

Click drop-down arrow to select command

Click drop-down arrow to select object (e.g., form)

(d) Start the Switchboard Manager (step 4)

FIGURE 7.3 *Hands-on Exercise 1 (continued)*

CREATE A KEYBOARD SHORTCUT

The & has special significance when used within the name of an Access object because it creates a keyboard shortcut to that object. Enter "&About Sports", for example, and the letter A (the letter immediately after the ampersand) will be underlined and appear as "<u>A</u>bout Sports" on the switchboard. From there, you can execute the item by clicking its button, or you can use the Alt+A keyboard shortcut.

Step 5: **Complete the Switchboard**

➤ Click the **New command button** in the Edit Switchboard Page dialog box to add a second item to the switchboard. Once again, you see the Edit Switchboard dialog box.

➤ Click in the **Text** list box and type **&Players**. Click the **drop-down arrow** on the Command list box and choose **Open Form in Edit Mode**. Click the **drop-down arrow** in the Form list box and choose **Players**.

➤ Click **OK** to close the Edit Switchboard Item dialog box. The &Players command appears as an item on the switchboard.

➤ Create two additional switchboard items for **&Coaches** and **&Teams** in similar fashion. Your switchboard should contain four items as shown in Figure 7.3e. Click **Close** to close the Edit Switchboard Page dialog box. Click **Close** to close the Switchboard Manager dialog box.

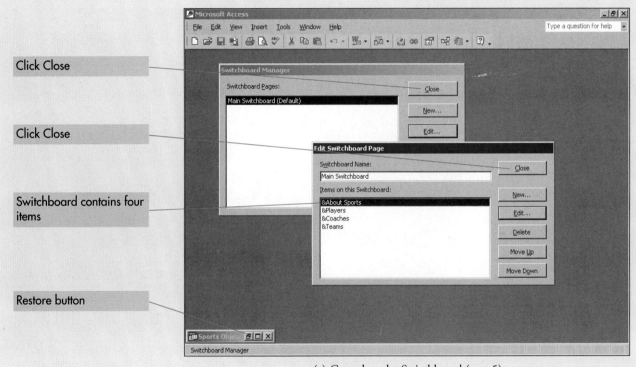

Click Close

Click Close

Switchboard contains four items

Restore button

(e) Complete the Switchboard (step 5)

FIGURE 7.3 *Hands-on Exercise 1 (continued)*

ADD MODE VERSUS EDIT MODE

It's easy to miss the difference between opening a form in the Add mode versus the Edit mode. The Add mode lets you add new records to a table, but it precludes you from viewing records that are already in the table. The Edit mode is more general and lets you add new records and/or edit existing records. Select the Add mode if you want to prevent a user from modifying existing data. Choose the Edit mode to give the user unrestricted access to the table.

Step 6: **Test the Switchboard**

➤ Click the **Restore button** in the Database window to view the objects in the database, then click the **Forms tab**. The Switchboard form has been created automatically by the Switchboard Manager.

➤ Double click the **Switchboard form** to open the Main Switchboard. Do not be concerned about the design of the switchboard at this time, as your immediate objective is to make sure that the buttons work. (We modify the design of the switchboard at the end of the exercise.) Maximize the window.

➤ Click the **About Sports button** (or use the **Alt+A** shortcut) to display the About Sports form as shown in Figure 7.3f. Click the **OK button** to close the form.

➤ Click the **Players button** (or use the **Alt+P** shortcut) to open the Players form. Click the **Maximize button** so that the Players form takes the entire window.

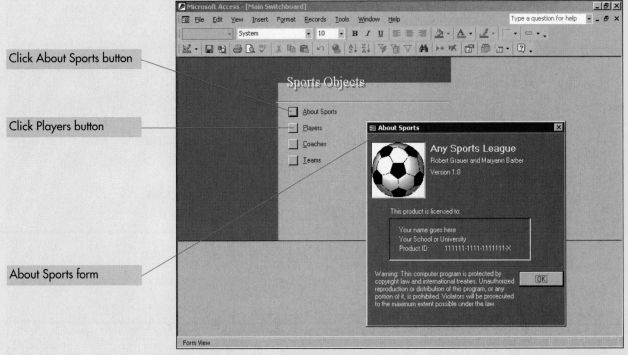

(f) Test the Switchboard (step 6)

FIGURE 7.3 *Hands-on Exercise 1 (continued)*

THE SWITCHBOARD ITEMS TABLE

You can modify an existing switchboard in one of two ways—by using the Switchboard Manager or by making changes directly in the underlying table of switchboard items. Press the F11 key to display the Database window, click the Tables button, then open the Switchboard Items table, where you can make changes to the various entries on the switchboard. We encourage you to experiment, but start by changing one entry at a time. The ItemText field is a good place to begin.

Step 7:   **Add Your Record**

> ➤ Click the **Add Player button** on the bottom of the form (or use the **Alt+A** shortcut) to display a blank record where you will enter data for yourself as shown in Figure 7.3g.
> ➤ Click the **text box** to enter your first name. (The PlayerID is an AutoNumber field that is updated automatically.) Enter your name, then press the **Tab key** to move to the next field.
> ➤ Continue to enter the appropriate data for yourself, but please assign yourself to the **Comets team**. The team is entered via a drop-down list. Type **C** (the first letter in Comets) and Comets is entered automatically from the drop-down list for teams.
> ➤ The player rating is a required field (all players are evaluated for ability in order to balance the teams) and must be A, B, C, or D.
> ➤ Click the **Close Form button** to return to the switchboard.

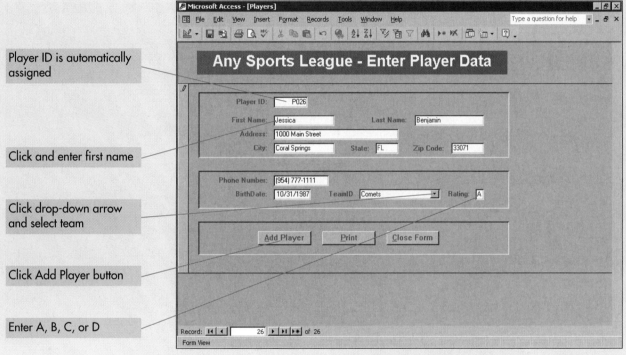

Player ID is automatically assigned

Click and enter first name

Click drop-down arrow and select team

Click Add Player button

Enter A, B, C, or D

(g) Add Your Record (step 7)

FIGURE 7.3   *Hands-on Exercise 1 (continued)*

A LOOK AHEAD

The Add Record button in the Players form was created through the Command Button Wizard. The Wizard in turn creates a VBA *event procedure* that creates a blank record at the end of the underlying table and enables you to add a new player. The procedure does not, however, position you at a specific control within the Players form; that is, you still have to click in the First Name text box to start entering the data. You can, however, add a VBA statement that automatically moves to the First Name control. See exercise 2 at the end of the chapter.

Step 8: **Complete the Data Entry**

➤ You should once again see the switchboard. Click the **Coaches button** (or use the **Alt+C** shortcut) to open the Coaches form.

➤ Click the **Add Coach button** at the bottom of the form. Click the **text box** to enter the coach's first name. (The CoachID is entered automatically.)

➤ Enter data for your instructor as the coach. Click the appropriate **option button** to make your instructor a **Head Coach**. Assign your instructor to the Comets. Click the **Close Form button** to return to switchboard.

➤ Click the **Teams command button** on the switchboard to open the Teams form and move to Team T02 (the Comets). You should see your instructor as the head coach and yourself as a player as shown in Figure 7.3h.

➤ Pull down the **Edit menu** and click **Select Record** (or click the selection area), then click the **Print button** to print the roster for your team.

➤ Click the **Close Form button** to return to the switchboard.

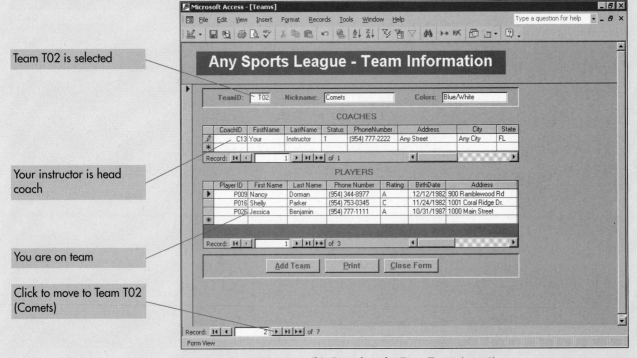

(h) Complete the Data Entry (step 8)

FIGURE 7.3   *Hands-on Exercise 1 (continued)*

THE DISPLAY WHEN PROPERTY

The Add, Print, and Close Form command buttons appear on the various forms (Team, Player, or Coach) when the forms are displayed on the screen, but not when the forms are printed. Open a form in Design view, point to an existing command button, then click the right mouse button to display a shortcut menu. Click the Properties command, click on the line for the Display When property, and choose when you want the button to appear— that is, when the form is displayed, printed, or both.

Step 9: **Insert the Clip Art**

➤ Change to the Design view. **Right click** in the Picture area of the form to display a context-sensitive menu, then click the **Properties command** to display the Property sheet. Click the **All tab**.

➤ The Picture property is currently set to "none" because the default switchboard does not contain a picture. Click in the **Picture box**, then click the **Build button** to display the Insert Picture dialog box.

➤ Click the **down arrow** in the Look In box to change to the **Exploring Access folder**, then select the **SoccerBall** as shown in Figure 7.3i. Click **OK**.

➤ Size the picture as appropriate. The dimensions of the soccer ball should be changed to a square—for example, 1.7 inches × 1.7 inches. Close the property sheet.

➤ Right click below the picture in the Detail area of the form. Point to the **Fill/Back Color command** from the context-sensitive menu to display a color palette. Choose the same shade as appears on the rest of the form. (It is the fifth square from the left in the second row.)

➤ Click the **Undo button** if the color does not match. Save the form.

Click in Picture box, then click Build button

Right click in Picture area to display shortcut menu

Click to select Exploring Access folder

Click SoccerBall

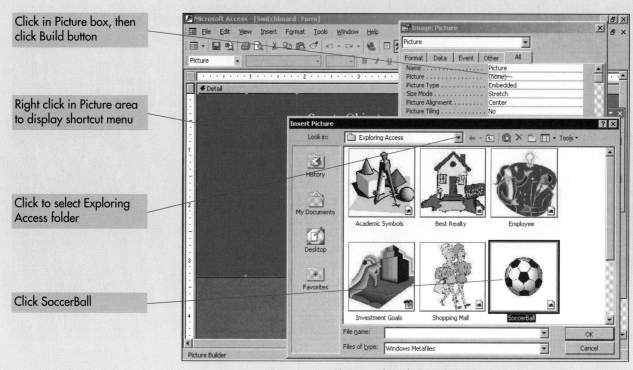

(i) Insert the Clip Art (step 9)

FIGURE 7.3   *Hands-on Exercise 1 (continued)*

THE OBJECT BOX

The easiest way to familiarize yourself with the design of the switchboard is to click the down arrow on the object box on the Formatting toolbar, scrolling as necessary to see the various objects. Select (click) any object in the Object box and it is selected automatically in the form. Right click the selected object to display its property sheet.

Step 10: **Complete the Design**

➤ Delete the label that contains the title of the switchboard, "Sports Objects". (You will have to delete two labels, because the switchboard manager automatically creates a shadow.)

➤ Click and drag the Label tool to create a new unbound control for the title of the switchboard. Enter **Any Sports League** as the title. Use 18-point Arial bold, in white for the formatting.

➤ Click the **Label** tool, then click and drag to create a text box under the picture. Enter your name in an appropriate font, point size, and color. Move and/or size the label containing your name as appropriate.

➤ Press and hold the **Shift key** as you click each text box in succession. The boxes appear to be empty, but the text will be drawn from the Switchboard Items table.

➤ Be sure that you selected all text boxes. Click the **drop-down arrow** on the Font/Fore Color button and change the color to white as shown in Figure 7.3j. Change the font and point size to **Arial** and **10pt**, respectively. Save the form.

➤ Change to the Form view to see the result of your changes. Exit Access if you do not want to continue with the next exercise at this time.

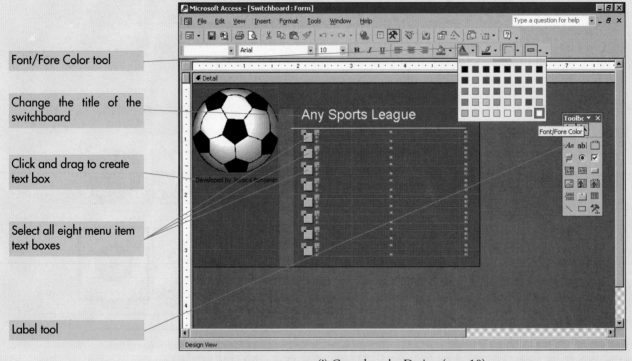

Font/Fore Color tool

Change the title of the switchboard

Click and drag to create text box

Select all eight menu item text boxes

Label tool

(j) Complete the Design (step 10)

FIGURE 7.3 *Hands-on Exercise 1 (continued)*

SET A TIME LIMIT

It's easy to spend an hour or more on the design of the switchboard, but that is counterproductive. The objective of this exercise was to develop a user interface that provides the "look and feel" of a system by selecting various menu options. That has been accomplished. Yes, it is important to fine-tune the interface, but within reason. Set a time limit for your design, then move on to the next exercise.

The exercise just completed created a switchboard that enabled a nontechnical user to access the various tables within the database. It did not, however, automate the application completely in that the user still has to open the form containing the switchboard to get started, and further may have to maximize the switchboard once it is open. You can make the application even easier to use by including macros that perform these tasks automatically.

A *macro* automates a command sequence. Thus, instead of using the mouse or keyboard to execute a series of commands, you store the commands (actions) in a macro and execute the macro. You can create a macro to open a table, query, form, or report. You can create a macro to display an informational message, then beep to call attention to that message. You can create a macro to move or size a window, or to minimize, maximize, or restore a window. In short, you can create a macro to execute any command (or combination of commands) in any Access menu and thus make an application easier to use.

The Macro Window

A macro is created in the *Macro window,* as shown in Figure 7.4. The Macro window is divided into two sections. The *actions* (commands) that comprise the macro are entered at the top. The *arguments,* or information for those actions, are entered in the lower section. Access macros are different from those in Word or Excel, in that Access lacks the macro recorder that is common to those applications. Hence, you have to enter the actions explicitly in the Macro window rather than have the recorder do it for you. In any event, macros are stored as separate objects in a database. The macro name can contain up to 64 characters (letters, numbers, and spaces), and it appears in the title bar of the Macro window (e.g., Back Up in Figure 7.4).

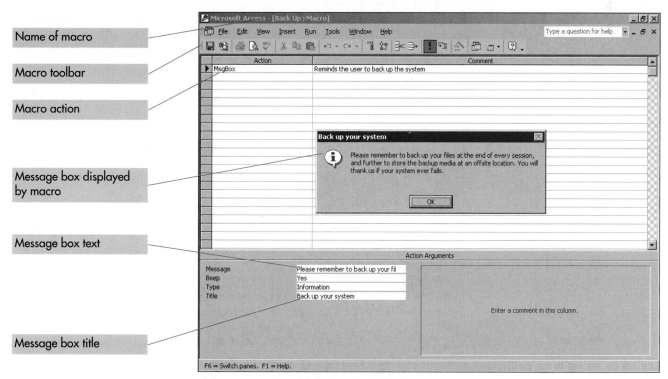

Name of macro

Macro toolbar

Macro action

Message box displayed by macro

Message box text

Message box title

FIGURE 7.4 *The Macro Window*

To create a macro, select the Macros button in the Database window, then click the New button to display the Macro window. You add actions to a macro by clicking in Action area, then choosing the action from a drop-down list, or by typing the name of the action. The arguments for an action are entered in similar fashion—that is, by choosing from a drop-down list (when available) or by typing the argument directly. The macro in Figure 7.4 consists of a single action with four arguments. As indicated, you specify the action, **MsgBox** in this example, in the top portion of the window, then you enter the values for the various arguments (Message, Beep, Type, and Title) in the bottom half of the window.

After the macro is created, you can execute it whenever the application is open. Execution of the macro in Figure 7.4, for example, will display the dialog box shown in the figure, to remind the user to back up his or her data. The contents of the dialog box are determined by the value of the arguments. The text of the dialog box is specified in the Message argument, only a portion of which is visible in the Macro window. The value of the Type argument determines the icon that is displayed within the dialog box (Information in this example). The Title argument contains the text that appears in the title bar of the dialog box.

The **macro toolbar** is displayed at the top of the Macro window and contains buttons that help create and test a macro. Many of the buttons (e.g., the Database window, Save, and Help buttons) are common to other toolbars you have used in conjunction with other objects. Other buttons are specific to the Macro window and are referenced in the hands-on exercises. As with other toolbars, you can point to a button to display its ScreenTip and determine its purpose.

The AutoExec Macro

The **AutoExec macro** is unique in that it is executed automatically whenever the database in which it is stored is opened. The macro is used to automate a system for the end user. It typically contains an OpenForm action to open the form containing the main switchboard. It may also perform other housekeeping chores, such as maximizing the current window.

Every database can have its own AutoExec macro, but there is no requirement for the AutoExec macro to be present. We recommend, however, that you include an AutoExec macro in every application to help the user get started.

Debugging

Writing a macro is similar to writing a program, in that errors occur if the actions and/or the associated arguments are specified incorrectly. Should Access encounter an error during the execution of a macro, it displays as much information as it can to help you determine the reason for the error.

Figure 7.5 contains an erroneous version of the AutoExec macro that attempts to open the Switchboard form. The macro contains two actions, Maximize and OpenForm. The Maximize action maximizes the Database window and affects all subsequent screens that will be displayed in the application. The OpenForm macro is intended to open the switchboard from the previous exercise. The name of the form is deliberately misspelled.

When the AutoExec macro is executed, Access attempts to open a form called "Switchboards", but is unable to do so, and hence it displays the informational message in the figure. Click OK, and you are presented with another dialog box, which attempts to step you through the macro and discover the cause of the error. As indicated, the error is due to the fact that the name of the form should have been "Switchboard" rather than "Switchboard*s*". The errors will not always be this easy to find, and hopefully, you will not make any. Should a bug occur, however, you will know where to begin.

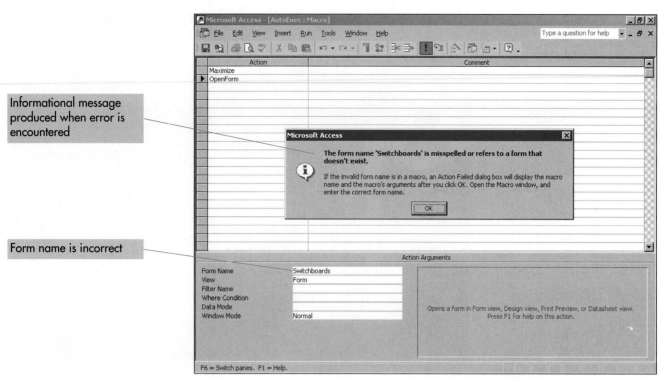

Informational message produced when error is encountered

Form name is incorrect

FIGURE 7.5 *Debugging*

APPLICATION DEVELOPMENT

Application development is an iterative process that entails continual dialog between the end user (client) and the developer. In essence, the developer presents the client with multiple versions of the application, with each successive version containing additional functionality. The user tests and evaluates each version and provides comments to the developer, who incorporates the feedback and delivers a new version (release) of the application. The process continues with each successive release containing increased functionality until the system is complete.

The user is presented with a working system (or *prototype*) at every stage of testing that captures the "look and feel" of the finished application. The switchboard in Figure 7.6a, for example, is an updated version of the main switchboard from the first hands-on exercise. Look closely and you will see a menu option to display the report switchboard in Figure 7.6b, which was created using the Switchboard Manager. The corresponding Switchboard Items table is shown in Figure 7.6c. The SwitchboardID field assumes significance in this version because there are now two different switchboards, the Main Switchboard and the Report Switchboard, with values of one and two, respectively.

The reports, however, have not yet been created, nor do they need to be, because the user can click any of the buttons on the report switchboard and see the indicated message, which was created by a simple macro. The application is "complete" in the sense that every button on the switchboard works, but it is incomplete in that the reports have not been fully developed. Nevertheless, the prototype lets the user see a working system and enables the user to provide immediate feedback.

The Report Switchboard also provides access to the report template that appears in Figure 7.6d. The purpose of the *template* is to provide additional feedback to the user with respect to the appearance of the eventual reports. It is just as easy to create an attractive report as an ugly one, and a uniform report header adds to the professional look of an application. The sooner the user communicates the requested changes to the developer, the easier (and less costly) it is for the developer to incorporate those changes.

Consistent logo throughout
the application

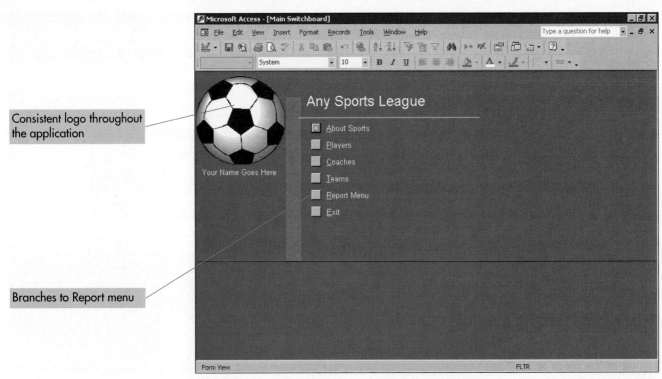

(a) Main Switchboard

Branches to Report menu

Consistent design from one
switchboard to the next

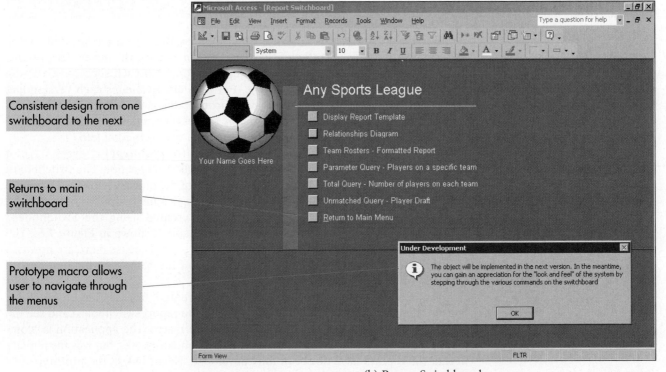

Returns to main
switchboard

Prototype macro allows
user to navigate through
the menus

(b) Report Switchboard

FIGURE 7.6 *Application Development*

Value of SwitchboardID
indicates two different
switchboards

Executes prototype macro
to indicate report is not
yet implemented

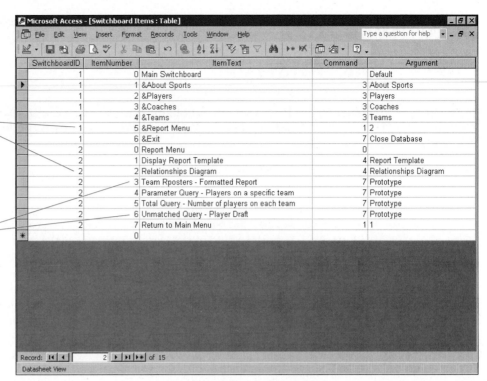

(c) Switchboard Items Table

Consistent design adds to
visual appeal

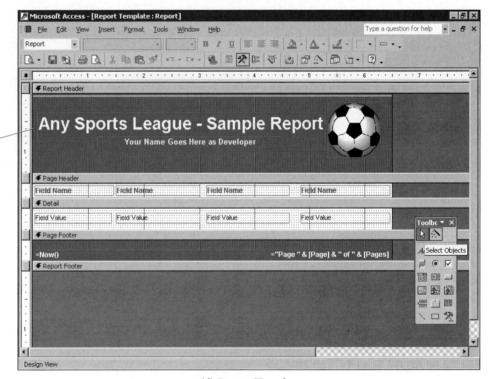

(d) Report Template

FIGURE 7.6   *Application Development (continued)*

MACROS AND PROTOTYPING

Objective To create an AutoExec and a Close Database macro; to create a subsidiary switchboard. Use Figure 7.7 as a guide in the exercise.

Step 1: **Create the AutoExec Macro**

- ➤ Start Access. Open the **Sports Objects database** from the previous exercise. Click the **Macros button** in the Database window.
- ➤ Click the **New button** to create a new macro. If necessary, click the **Maximize button** so that the Macro window takes the entire screen as in Figure 7.7a.
- ➤ Click the **drop-down arrow** to display the available macro actions. Scroll until you can select **Maximize**. (There are no arguments for this action.)
- ➤ Click the **Action box** on the second line, click the **drop-down arrow** to display the macro actions, then scroll until you can click the **OpenForm action**. Click the text box for the **Form Name** argument in the lower section of the Macro window.
- ➤ Click the **drop-down arrow** to display the list of existing forms and select **Switchboard** (the form you created in the previous exercise).
- ➤ Click the **Save button** to display the Save As dialog box in Figure 7.7a. Type **AutoExec** as the macro name and click **OK**. Click the **Run button** to run the macro and open the switchboard.
- ➤ Close the switchboard. Close the AutoExec macro.

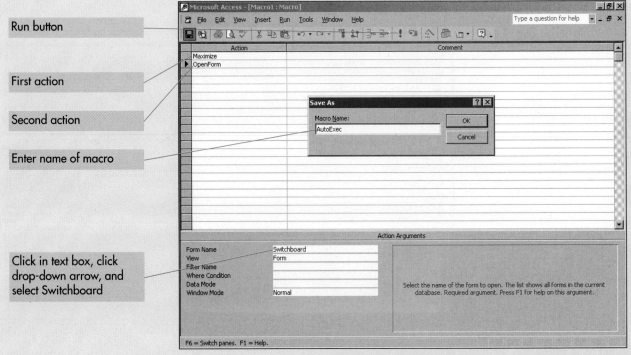

(a) Create the AutoExec Macro (step 1)

FIGURE 7.7 *Hands-on Exercise 2*

Step 2: **Create the Prototype Macro**

➤ You should be back in the Database window, which should display the name of the AutoExec macro. Click the **New button** to create a second macro.

➤ Type **Ms** (the first two letters in the MsgBox action), then press **enter** to accept this action. Enter the comment shown in Figure 7.7b.

➤ Click the text box for the **Message** argument, then press **Shift+F2** to display the zoom box so that you can see the contents of your entire message. Enter the message in Figure 7.7b. Click **OK**.

➤ Click the text box for the **Type** argument, click the **drop-down arrow** to display the list of message types, and select **Information**.

➤ Click in the text box for the **Title** argument, and enter "**Under Development**".

➤ Click the **Run button** to test the macro. You will see a message indicating that you have to save the macro. Click **Yes** to save the macro, type **Prototype** as the name of the macro, and click **OK**.

➤ You will see a dialog box containing the message you just created. Click **OK**. Close the macro.

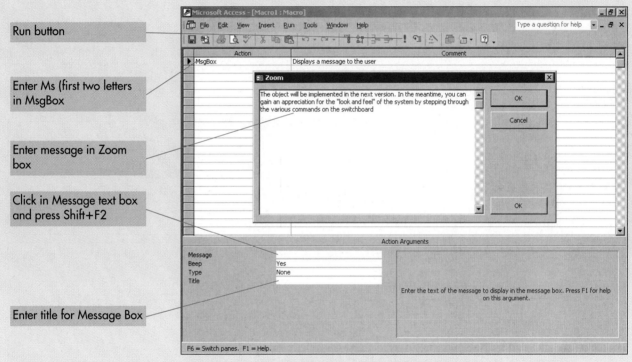

Run button

Enter Ms (first two letters in MsgBox)

Enter message in Zoom box

Click in Message text box and press Shift+F2

Enter title for Message Box

(b) Create the Prototype Macro (step 2)

FIGURE 7.7 *Hands-on Exercise 2 (continued)*

TYPE ONLY THE FIRST LETTER(S)

Click the Action box, then type the first letter of a macro action to move immediately to the first macro action beginning with that letter. Type an M, for example, and Access automatically enters the Maximize action. If necessary, type the second letter of the desired action; for example, type the letter i (after typing an M), and Access selects the Minimize action.

Step 3: **Create the Close Database Macro**

> ➤ Click the **New button** once again to create the third (and last) macro for this exercise. Specify the **MsgBox** action as the first command in the macro. Enter the comment shown in Figure 7.7c.
> ➤ Enter an appropriate message that stresses the importance of backup. Select Warning as the message type. Enter an appropriate title for the message box.
> ➤ Click the **Action box** on the second line. Type **Cl** (the first two letters in Close) and press **enter**. Enter the indicated comment as shown in Figure 7.7c.
> ➤ Click the text box for the **Object Type** argument. Click the **drop-down arrow** and choose **Form** as the Object type. Click the **Object Name** argument, click the **drop-down arrow**, and choose **Switchboard** as the Object (form) name.
> ➤ Click the **Action box** on the third line. Type **Cl** (the first two letters in Close) and press **enter**. Click the **comments line** for this macro action and enter the comment shown in the figure. No arguments are necessary.
> ➤ Save the macro as **Close Database**, then close the macro. If necessary, press the **F11 key** to return to the Database window, where you should see three macros: AutoExec, Close Database, and Prototype.

First action

Click and type Cl (first two letters in Close)

Enter macro name

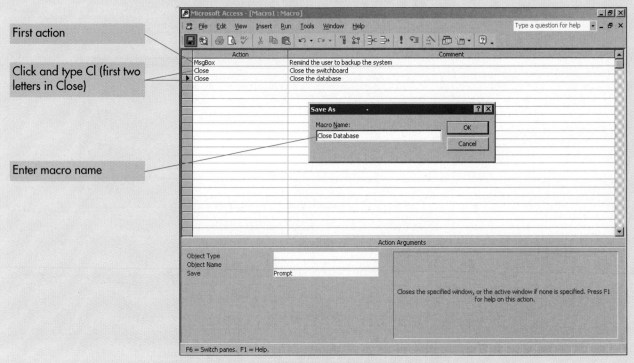

(c) Create the Close Database Macro (step 3)

FIGURE 7.7   *Hands-on Exercise 2 (continued)*

USE KEYBOARD SHORTCUTS—F6, F11, AND SHIFT+F2

Use the F6 key to move back and forth between the top and bottom halves of the Macro window. Press Shift+F2 to display a zoom box that enables you to view long arguments in their entirety. Use the F11 key at any time to display the Database window.

Step 4: **Create the Report Switchboard**

➤ Minimize the Database window to give yourself more room in which to work. Pull down the **Tools menu**, click the **Database Utilities command**, and choose **Switchboard Manager** to display the Switchboard Manager dialog box.

➤ Click **New**. Enter **Report Switchboard** as the name of the switchboard page. Click **OK**. The Create New dialog box closes and the Report Switchboard page appears in the Switchboard Manager dialog box.

➤ Select the **Report Switchboard**, click **Edit** to open the Edit Switchboard Page dialog box. Click **New** to open the Edit Switchboard Item dialog box.

➤ Add the first switchboard item. Click in the **Text** list box and type **Display Report Template** as shown in Figure 7.7d.

➤ Press the **Tab key** to move to the Command list box and type the **Open R** (the first several letters in Open Report). Press **Tab** to move to the Report list box and type **R** (the first letter in the report name, "Report Template").

➤ Click **OK** to create the switchboard item. The Edit Switchboard Item dialog box closes and Display Report Template appears on the Report Switchboard page.

➤ Add **Report 1** as the next switchboard item. Specify the **Run macro command** and choose **Prototype** as the macro. Add additional buttons for Reports 2 and 3.

➤ Add an additional item that will return the user to the main switchboard. Click **New** to open the Edit Switchboard Item dialog box. Click in the **Text** list box and type "**&Return to Main Menu . . .**"

➤ Press the **Tab key** to move to the Command list box, where the Go to Switchboard command is entered by default. Press the **Tab key** to move to the Switchboard list box, and type **M** (the first letter in the "Main Switchboard"). Click **OK** to create the switchboard item. Close the Edit Switchboard Page.

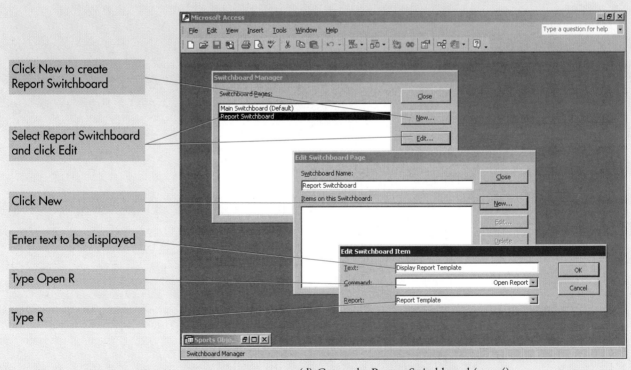

(d) Create the Report Switchboard (step 4)

FIGURE 7.7 *Hands-on Exercise 2 (continued)*

Step 5: **Modify the Main Switchboard**

➤ Select the **Main Switchboard** in the Switchboard Manager dialog box, click the **Edit button** to open the Edit Switchboard Page dialog box, then click **New** to open the Edit Switchboard Item dialog box as shown in Figure 7.7d.

➤ Add a new switchboard item to open the Report Switchboard. Click in the **Text** list box and type "**&Report Menu . . .**", the name of the command as it will appear in the switchboard.

➤ Press the **Tab key** to move to the Command list box, where "Go to Switchboard" is already entered, then press the **Tab key** a second time to move to the Switchboard list box. Type **R** (the first letter in the "Report Switchboard"). Click **OK** to create the switchboard item.

➤ The Edit Switchboard Item dialog box closes and "&Report Menu" appears on the main switchboard.

➤ The main switchboard needs one last command to close the database. Thus, click **New** to open the Edit Switchboard Item dialog box. Type **&Exit** as the name of the command.

➤ Press the **Tab key** to move to the Command list box and type **R** (the first letter in "Run Macro"). Press the **Tab key** a second time to move to the Macro list box, and type **C** (the first letter in the "Close Database" macro). Click **OK** to create the switchboard item.

➤ The main switchboard should contain six items—&About Sports, &Players, &Coaches, and &Teams from the first exercise, and &Report Menu and &Exit from this exercise.

➤ Close the Edit Switchboard Page dialog box. Close the Switchboard Manager.

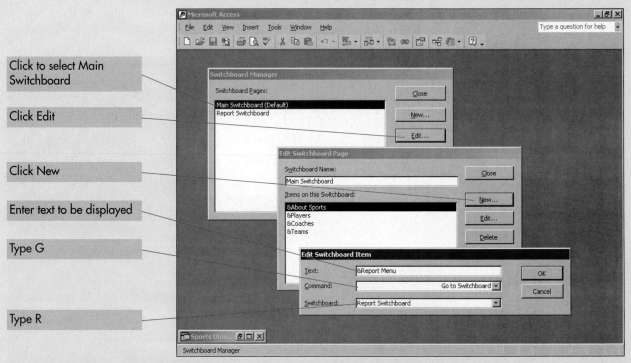

(e) Modify the Main Switchboard (step 5)

FIGURE 7.7   *Hands-on Exercise 2 (continued)*

Step 6:   **Test the Main Switchboard**

➤ Click the **Restore button** in the Database window to view the objects in the database, click the **Forms button**, then double click the **Switchboard form** to open the main switchboard.

➤ Click the **Exit button** (or use the **Alt+E** shortcut):

   • You should see an informational message similar to the one shown in the figure. (The message is displayed by the MsgBox action in the Close Database macro.)

   • Click **OK** to accept the message. The Close Database macro then closes the database.

➤ Pull down the **File menu**, then click **Sports Objects** from the list of recently opened databases. The AutoExec macro executes automatically, maximizes the current window, and displays the main switchboard.

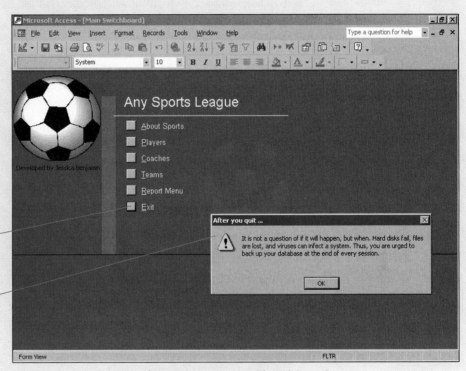

Click Exit button

Informational message is displayed

(f) Test the Main Switchboard (step 6)

FIGURE 7.7   *Hands-on Exercise 2 (continued)*

ADD A HYPERLINK

You can enhance the appeal of your switchboard through inclusion of a hyperlink. Open the switchboard form in Design view, then click the Insert Hyperlink button to display the Insert Hyperlink dialog box. Enter the text to be displayed and the Web address, then click OK to close the dialog box and return to the Design view. Right click the hyperlink to display a shortcut menu, click the Properties command to display the Properties dialog box, then change the font and/or point size as appropriate.

Step 7: **Test the Report Switchboard**

➤ Click the **Report Menu button** (or use the **Alt+R** keyboard shortcut) on the main switchboard to display the Report switchboard in Figure 7.7g.

➤ Click the button to **Display the Report Template**. Click the **Print button** to print a copy of this report for your instructor. Close the Report Preview window to return to the Report switchboard. Click the buttons for Reports 1, 2, and 3, which should display the message in Figure 7.7g.

➤ Click the **Return to Main Menu button** to exit the Report Menu and return to the main switchboard.

• To continue working, click the **Close button** on the title bar (or pull down the **File menu** and click the **Close command**) to close the form and continue working on this database. (You should not click the Exit command button as that would close the database.) You should be back in the Database window, where you can continue with the next hands-on exercise.

• To close the database, click the **Exit button** (or use the **Alt+E** shortcut).

➤ Either way, you have demonstrated the "look and feel" of the system to the extent that you can step through the various menus. Good work.

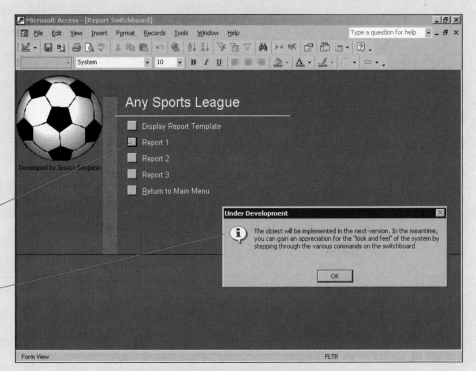

(g) Test the Report Switchboard (step 7)

FIGURE 7.7   *Hands-on Exercise 2 (continued)*

BE CONSISTENT

Consistency within an application is essential to its success. Similar functions should be done in similar ways to facilitate learning and build confidence in the application. The sports application, for example, has similar screens for the Players, Coaches, and Teams forms, each of which contains the identical buttons to add or print a record and close the form.

A player draft is essential to the operation of the league. Players sign up for the coming season at registration, after which the coaches meet to select players for their teams. All players are rated as to ability, and the league strives to maintain a competitive balance among teams. This is accomplished through a draft in which the coaches take turns selecting players from the pool of unassigned players.

The player draft is implemented through the form in Figure 7.8, which is based on a query that identifies players who have not yet been assigned to a team. The easiest way to create the underlying query is through the *Unmatched Query Wizard* that identifies records in one table (the Players table) that do not have matching records in another table (the Teams table). The Wizard prompts you for the necessary information, then it creates the required query as you will see in the next hands-on exercise. A *combo box* within the query simplifies data entry in that the user is able to click the drop-down list box to display the list of teams, rather than having to remember the TeamID.

In addition to displaying the list of unassigned players, the form in Figure 7.8 also contains three command buttons that are used during the player draft. The Find Player button moves directly to a specific player, and enables a coach to see whether a specific player has been assigned to a team, and if so, to which team. The Update List button refreshes the underlying query on which the list of unassigned players is based. It is used periodically during the draft as players are assigned to teams, to remove those players from the list of unassigned players. The End Draft button closes the form and returns to the Switchboard. Note, too, that the appearance of the form matches the other forms in the application. This type of consistency is important to give your application a professional look.

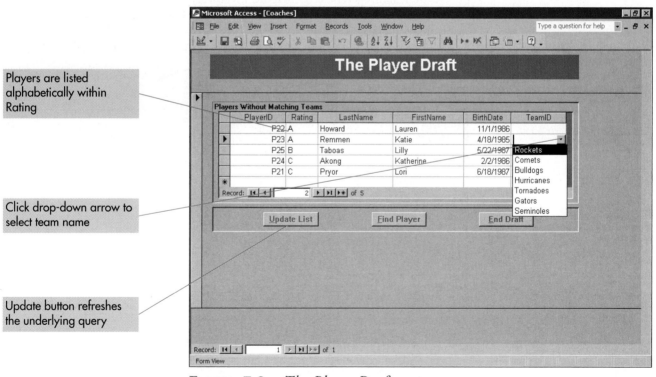

FIGURE 7.8 *The Player Draft*

Macro Groups

Implementation of the player draft requires three macros, one for each command button. Although you could create a separate macro for each button, it is convenient to create a **macro group** that contains the individual macros. The macro group has a name, as does each macro in the group. Only the name of the macro group appears in the Database window.

Figure 7.9 displays a Player Draft macro group containing three individual macros (Update List, Find Player, and End Draft), which run independently of one another. The name of each macro appears in the Macro Name column (which is displayed by clicking the Macro Names button on the Macro toolbar). The actions and comments for each macro are shown in the corresponding columns to the right of the macro name.

The advantage of storing related macros in a macro group, as opposed to storing them individually, is purely organizational. Large systems often contain many macros, which can overwhelm the developer as he or she tries to locate a specific macro. Storing related macros in macro groups limits the entries in the Database window, since only the (name of the) macro group is displayed. Thus, the Database window would contain a single entry (Player Draft, which is the name of the macro group), as opposed to three individual entries (Update List, Find Player, and End Draft, which correspond to the macros in the group).

Access must still be able to identify the individual macros so that each macro can be executed at the appropriate time. If, for example, a macro is to be executed when the user clicks a command button, the **On Click property** of that command button must specify both the individual macro and the macro group. The two names are separated by a period; for example, Player Draft.Update List to indicate the Update List macro in the Player Draft macro group.

As indicated, each macro in Figure 7.9 corresponds to a command button in the Player Draft form. The macros are created in the following hands-on exercise that implements the player draft.

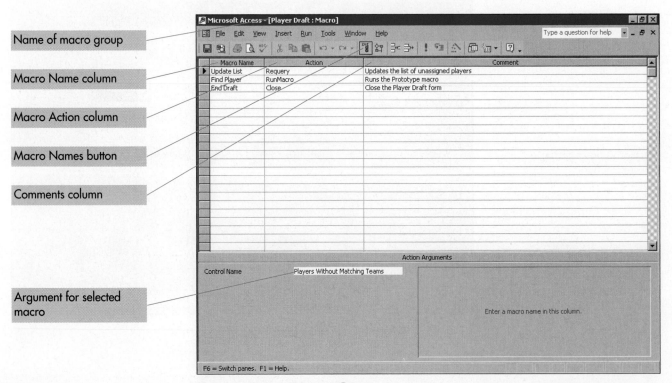

FIGURE 7.9 *Macro Group*

Objective Create a macro group containing three macros to implement a player draft. Use Figure 7.10 as a guide in the exercise.

Step 1: **The Unmatched Query Wizard**

➤ Start Access and open the **Sports Objects database**. Pull down the **File menu** and click **Close** (or click the **Close button**) to close the Main Menu form but leave the database open.

➤ Click the **Queries button** in the Database window. Click **New**, select the **Find Unmatched Query Wizard**, then click **OK** to start the wizard:

• Select **Players** as the table whose records you want to see in the query results. Click **Next**.

• Select **Teams** as the table that contains the related records. Click **Next**.

• **TeamID** is automatically selected as the matching field. Click **Next**.

• Select the following fields from the Available Fields list: **PlayerID**, **Rating**, **LastName**, **FirstName**, **BirthDate**, and **TeamID**. Click **Next**.

• **Players Without Matching Teams** is entered as the name of the query. Check that the option button to **View the results** is selected, then click **Finish** to exit the wizard and see the results of the query.

➤ You should see a dynaset containing five players (Pryor, Howard, Remmen, Akong, and Taboas) as shown in Figure 7.10a. The TeamID field for each of these players is blank, indicating that these players have not yet been assigned.

Click to switch to Design view

Dynaset shows players without a team (unassigned players)

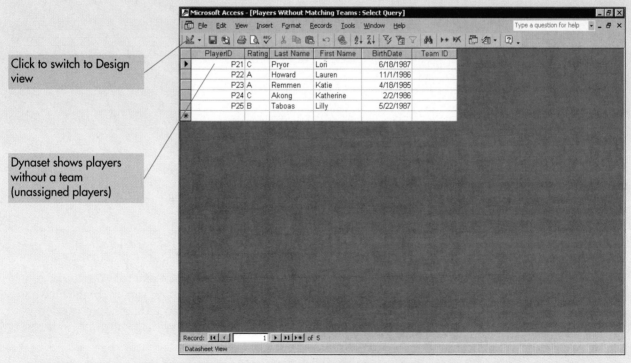

(a) The Unmatched Query Wizard (step 1)

FIGURE 7.10 *Hands-on Exercise 3*

Step 2: Modify the Query

➤ Change to Design view to see the underlying query as displayed in Figure 7.10b.

➤ Click and drag the line separating the upper and lower portions of the window. If necessary, click and drag the field lists to match the figure.

➤ Click in the **Sort row** for **Rating**, then click **Ascending** from the drop-down list. Click in the **Sort row** for **LastName**, then click **Ascending** from the drop-down list.

➤ Click the **Run button** to view the revised query, which lists players according to their player rating and alphabetically within rating.

➤ Close the query. Click **Yes** if asked whether to save the changes to the Players Without Matching Teams query.

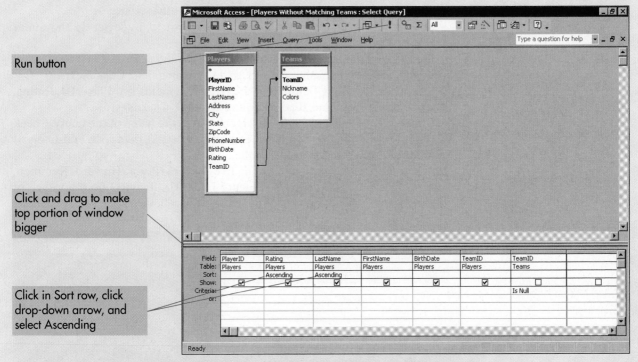

(b) Modify the Query (step 2)

FIGURE 7.10 *Hands-on Exercise 3 (continued)*

THE IS NULL CRITERION

The Is Null criterion selects those records that do not have a value in the designated field. It is the essence of the Unmatched Query Wizard, which uses the criterion to identify the records in one table that do not have a matching record in another table. The NOT operator can be combined with the Is Null criterion to produce the opposite effect; that is, the criterion Is Not Null will select records with any type of entry (including spaces) in the specified field.

Step 3: **Create the Unmatched Players Form**

➤ Click the **Forms button** in the Database window, click **New** to display the New Form dialog box and select **AutoForm:Tabular**.

➤ Click the **drop-down arrow** to choose a table or query. Select the **Players Without Matching Teams** (the query created in steps 1 and 2). Click **OK**.

➤ Maximize the window if necessary, then change to the Design view. Select the **TeamID control** in the Detail section, then press the **Del key**.

➤ Click the **Combo Box** tool. Click and drag in the Detail section, then release the mouse to start the Combo Box Wizard:

- Check the option button that indicates you want the combo box to **look up values in a table or query**. Click **Next**.
- Choose the **Teams** table in the next screen. Click **Next**.
- Select the **TeamID** and **Nickname** fields. Click **Next**.
- Adjust the column width if necessary. Be sure the box to **Hide the key column** is checked. Click **Next**.
- Click the option button to store the value in the field. Click the **drop-down arrow** to display the fields and select the **TeamID** field. Click **Next**.
- Enter **TeamID** as the label for the combo box. Click **Finish**.

➤ Click (select) the label next to the control you just created. Press the **Del key**.

➤ Point to the combo box, click the **right mouse button** to display a shortcut menu, and click **Properties**. Change the name of the control to **TeamID**.

➤ Right click the **Form Selector** box and click the **Properties command**. Click the **Default View** text box, click the **drop-down arrow**, and select **Datasheet**. Close the Properties sheet.

➤ Click the **Save button** to display the Save As dialog box in Figure 7.10c. (Players Without Matching Teams is already entered as the default name.)

➤ Click **OK** to save the form, then close the form.

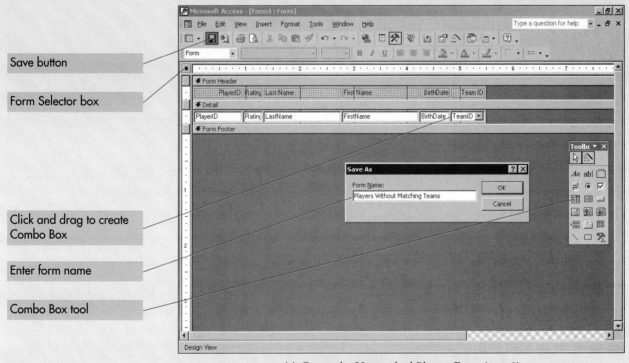

Save button

Form Selector box

Click and drag to create Combo Box

Enter form name

Combo Box tool

(c) Create the Unmatched Players Form (step 3)

FIGURE 7.10   *Hands-on Exercise 3 (continued)*

Step 4: **Create the Player Draft Macro Group**

➤ Click the **Macros button** in the Database window. Click **New** to create a new macro. Click the **Maximize button** to maximize the Macro window.

➤ If you do not see the Macro Names column, pull down the **View menu** and click **Macro Names** to display the column.

➤ Enter the macro names, comments, and actions, as shown in Figure 7.10d.

  • The Requery action (in the Update List macro) has a single argument in which you specify the control name (the name of the query). Type **Players Without Matching Teams**, which is the query you created in step 1.

  • The Find Player macro will be implemented as an assignment (see practice exercise 3), but in the interim, it will access the Prototype macro developed earlier. Choose **RunMacro** as the action and specify **Prototype**.

  • The arguments for the End Draft macro are visible in Figure 7.10d. The Player Draft form will be created in the next step. (You must enter the name manually since the form has not yet been created.)

➤ Save the Macro group as **Player Draft**. Close the Macro window.

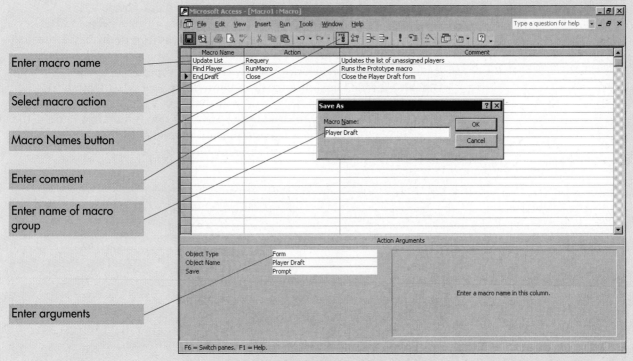

Enter macro name

Select macro action

Macro Names button

Enter comment

Enter name of macro group

Enter arguments

(d) Create the Player Draft Macro Group (step 4)

FIGURE 7.10 *Hands-on Exercise 3 (continued)*

REQUERY COMMAND NOT AVAILABLE

The macros in the Player Draft group are designed to run only when the Player Draft form is open. Do not be concerned, therefore, if you attempt to test the macros at this time and the Action Failed dialog box appears. The macros will work correctly at the end of the exercise, when the entire player draft is in place.

Step 5:   **Create the Player Draft Form**

➤ Click the **Forms button** in the Database window. Select the **Template form**, click the **Copy button** to copy the form to the clipboard, then click the **Paste button** to complete the copy operation. Type **Player Draft** as the name of the copied form. Click **OK**.

➤ Open the Player Draft form in Design view. Pull down the **Window menu** and click **Tile Horizontally** to arrange the windows as shown in Figure 7.10e. (If necessary, close any open windows besides the two in our figure, then retile the windows.)

➤ Click in the **Player Draft** form. Delete the labels and text boxes for fields 1 and 2.

➤ Click in the **Database window**. Click and drag the **Players Without Matching Teams** form into the Detail section of the Player Draft form as shown in Figure 7.10e. Maximize the Player Draft window.

Click and drag Players Without Matching Teams to Detail section of Player Draft form

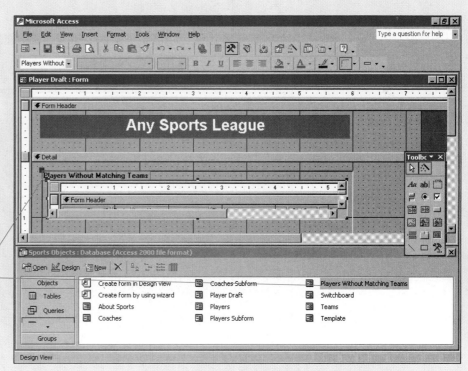

(e) Create the Player Draft Form (step 5)

FIGURE 7.10   *Hands-on Exercise 3 (continued)*

USE A TEMPLATE

Avoid the routine and repetitive work of creating a new form by basing all forms for a given application on the same template. A template is a partially completed form or report that contains graphic elements and other formatting specifications. A template does not, however, have an underlying table or query. We suggest that you create a template for your application and store it within the database, then use that template whenever you need to create a new form. It saves you time and trouble. It also promotes a consistent look that is critical to the application's overall success.

Step 6:   **Modify the Player Draft Form**

➤ Click and drag the decorative box so that it is larger than the Players Without Matching Forms control. Move the control within the decorative box.
➤ Select the control for the form, then click and drag the **sizing handles** in the Players Without Matching Team form so that its size approximates the form in Figure 7.10f.
➤ Select (click) the label, **Players Without Matching Teams**, as shown in Figure 7.10f, then press the **Del key** to remove the label. Change the text in the Form header to say **The Player Draft**.
➤ Change to the Form view. You should see the Form view of the subform, which displays the players who have not yet been assigned to a team. Change the column widths if necessary.
➤ Return to the Form Design view to change the width of the subform. Continue to switch back and forth between the Form view and the Design view until you are satisfied. Save the form.

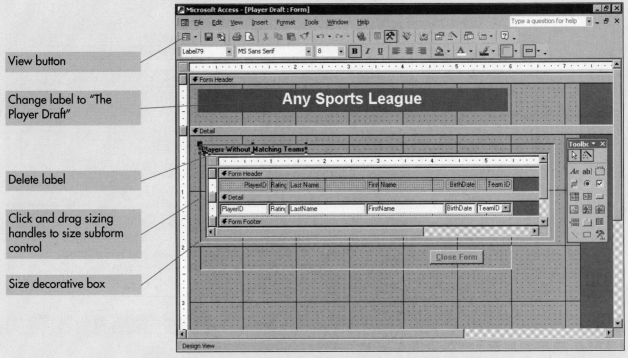

(f) Modify the Player Draft Form (step 6)

FIGURE 7.10   *Hands-on Exercise 3 (continued)*

SUPPRESS THE RECORD SELECTOR AND NAVIGATION BUTTONS

You can suppress the Record Selector and Navigation buttons on the Player Draft form, which have no active function and only confuse the user. Change to the Design view, right click the Form selector box to the left of the ruler, then click the Properties command to display the Properties dialog box. Click the Record Selectors text box and click No to disable it. Click the Navigation Buttons text box and click No to disable it. Close the Properties dialog box, then return to the Form view to see the effect of these changes, which are subtle but worthwhile.

Step 7:   **Add the Command Buttons**

➤ Click and drag the **Command Button** tool to create a command button, as shown in Figure 7.10g. Click **Miscellaneous** in the Categories list box. Select **Run Macro** from the list of actions. Click **Next**.

➤ Select **Player Draft.Update List** from the list of existing macros. Click **Next**.

➤ Click the **Text option button**. Click and drag to select the default text (Run Macro), then type **&Update List** as the text to display. Click **Next**.

➤ Enter **Update List** (in place of the button number). Click **Finish**.

➤ Create a second command button to find a player. The caption of the button should be **&Find Player** and it should run the Find Player macro.

➤ Change the caption property of the existing button on the template that closes the form to **&End Draft**.

➤ Size, align, space, and color the command buttons. Save the form.

➤ Change to the Form view. Click the **End Draft button** to close the form.

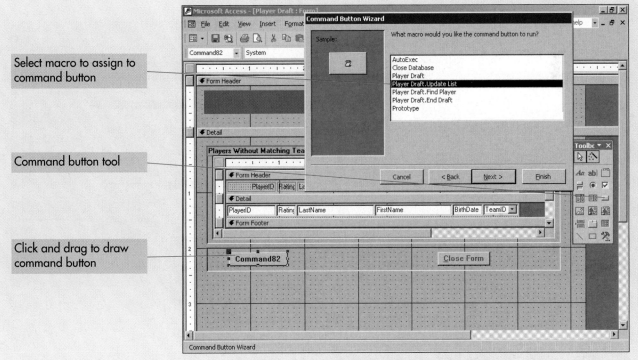

(g) Add the Command Buttons (step 7)

FIGURE 7.10   *Hands-on Exercise 3 (continued)*

ASSIGN MACROS TO CONTROLS AND COMMAND BUTTONS

Right click any command button or control to display a context-sensitive menu in which you click the Properties command, then click the Event tab in the resulting property sheet. Click in the text box of the desired event, then click the down arrow to assign an existing macro to the control or command button. Note, too, that you can click the Build button, instead of the down arrow, to select the Macro Builder and create a macro if it does not yet exist.

Step 8: **Modify the Main Switchboard**

➤ Pull down the **Tools menu**, click the **Database Utilities command**, and choose **Switchboard Manager**. Select the **Main Switchboard** in the Switchboard Manager dialog box, then click the **Edit button**.

➤ Click **New** to open the Edit Switchboard Item dialog box. Click in the **Text** list box and type **Player &Draft**. (The ampersand in front of the letter "D" establishes Alt+D as a shortcut for this button.)

➤ Press the **Tab key** to move to the Command list box. Select the command to open the form in the Edit mode. Press the **Tab key** to move to the Form list box and select the Player Draft form as shown in Figure 7.10h.

➤ Click **OK** to create the switchboard item. The Edit Switchboard Item dialog box closes and Player &Draft appears on the Main Switchboard. Select the **Player &Draft** entry, then click the **Move Up button** to move this command above the &Exit command.

➤ Close the Edit Switchboard page, then close the Switchboard Manager.

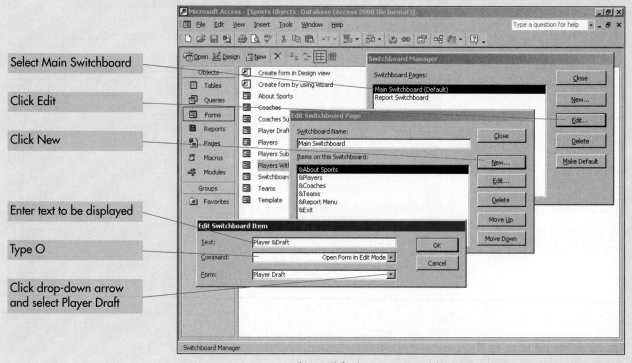

Select Main Switchboard

Click Edit

Click New

Enter text to be displayed

Type O

Click drop-down arrow and select Player Draft

(h) Modify the Main Switchboard (step 8)

FIGURE 7.10 *Hands-on Exercise 3 (continued)*

REPLICATE THE DATABASE

You can create a copy of a database, known as a replica, then take the replica with you on a laptop computer. This lets you work with the database even if you are not connected to the network, but you will eventually have to synchronize your replica with the network version. Start Windows Explorer, click and drag the Access database to the My Briefcase icon on the desktop, then follow the onscreen instructions. Use the Access Help facility for additional information. See practice exercise 12 at the end of the chapter.

Step 9: **Test the Completed System**

> ➤ Click the **Macros button** in the Database window. Double click the **AutoExec macro** to execute this macro, as though you just opened the database.
> ➤ Click the **Player Draft button** on the Main Switchboard to display the form you just created, as shown in Figure 7.10i.
> ➤ Click the **TeamID field** for Katie Remmen. Type **R** (the first letter in Rockets) and Katie is assigned automatically to this team. Click the **Update List command button**. Katie disappears from the list of unassigned players.
> ➤ Click the **Find Player button**. Click **OK** when you see the message indicating this function has not been implemented. Click the **End Draft button**.
> ➤ Click the **Teams command button** to view the team rosters. Team T01 (Rockets) is the first team you see, and Katie Remmen is on the roster. Click the **Close Form button** to return to the switchboard.
> ➤ Click the **Exit button**. Click **OK** in response to the message for backup.

Click and type R

Click Update List

Click Find Player

Click End Draft

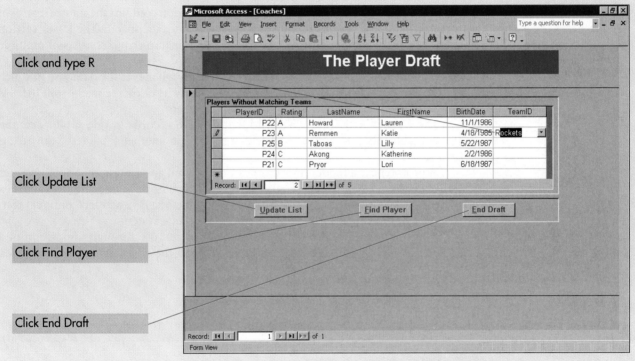

(i) Test the Completed System (step 9)

FIGURE 7.10   *Hands-on Exercise 3 (continued)*

PASSWORD PROTECT A DATABASE

Protect your database from unauthorized access through imposition of a password. It's a two-step process. First, close the database, then pull down the File menu, click the Open command to display the Open dialog box, select the database, then click the drop-down Open button and choose Open Exclusive. Next, pull down the Tools menu, click Security, click Set Database password, and follow the onscreen prompts. Be careful, however, because you cannot open the database if you forget the password. See practice exercse 5 at the end of the chapter.

An Access application is different from an ordinary database in that it contains an intuitive user interface known as a switchboard. The switchboard can be created automatically using the Switchboard Manager, a tool that prompts you for each item you want to include. You supply the text of the menu item, as it is to appear on the switchboard, together with the underlying command. Access does the rest and creates the switchboard form and associated table of switchboard items.

The tables in a database can be separated from the other objects to enable the distribution of updated versions of the application without disturbing the data. The tables are stored in one database and the objects in another. The Link Tables command associates the tables with the objects.

A template is a partially completed report or form that contains graphical elements and other formatting specifications. It is used as the basis for other objects and helps to promote a consistent look throughout an application.

A macro automates a command sequence and consists of one or more actions. The Macro window has two sections. The upper section contains the name (if any) of the macro and the actions (commands) that make up the macro. The lower section specifies the arguments for the various actions. A macro group consists of multiple macros and is used for organizational purposes.

The AutoExec macro is executed automatically whenever the database in which it is stored is opened. Each database can have its own AutoExec macro, but there is no requirement for an AutoExec macro to be present.

The Unmatched Query Wizard identifies the records in one table (e.g., the Players table) that do not have matching records in another table (e.g., the Teams table).

A prototype is a model (mockup) of a completed application that demonstrates the "look and feel" of the application. Prototypes can be developed quickly and easily through the use of simple macros containing the MsgBox action. Continual testing through prototyping is essential to the success of a system.

A database can be protected from unauthorized use through imposition of a password. Once a password has been implemented, the database cannot be opened without it.

KEY TERMS

Action (p. 329)
Argument (p. 329)
AutoExec macro (p. 330)
Combo box (p. 341)
Database properties (p. 319)
Database splitter (p. 320)
Debugging (p. 330)
Display When property (p. 326)
Event (p. 317)
Event procedure (p. 325)
Get External Data command
  (p. 320)

Is Null criterion (p. 344)
Linked Table Manager (p. 318)
Link Tables command (p. 318)
Macro (p. 329)
Macro group (p. 342)
Macro toolbar (p. 330)
Macro window (p. 329)
MsgBox action (p. 330)
On Click property (p. 342)
Password protection (p. 351)
Prototype (p. 331)

Replication (p. 350)
Requery command (p. 346)
Switchboard (p. 314)
Switchboard form (p. 317)
Switchboard Items table (p. 317)
Switchboard Manager (p. 317)
Template (p. 331)
Unmatched Query Wizard (p. 341)

1. Which of the following is created by the Switchboard Manager?
   (a) A form to hold the switchboard
   (b) A table containing the commands associated with the switchboard
   (c) Both (a) and (b)
   (d) Neither (a) nor (b)

2. Which of the following describes the storage of the tables and objects for the application developed in the chapter?
   (a) Each table is stored in its own database
   (b) Each object is stored in its own database
   (c) The tables are stored in one database and the objects in another
   (d) The tables and objects are stored in the same database

3. Which of the following is true regarding the Link Tables command as it was used in the chapter?
   (a) It was executed from the Sports Objects database
   (b) It was executed from the Sports Tables database
   (c) Both (a) and (b)
   (d) Neither (a) nor (b)

4. What happens when an Access database is opened initially?
   (a) Access executes the AutoExec macro if the macro exists
   (b) Access opens the AutoExec form if the form exists
   (c) Both (a) and (b)
   (d) Neither (a) nor (b)

5. Which statement is true regarding the AutoExec macro?
   (a) Every database must have an AutoExec macro
   (b) A database may have more than one AutoExec macro
   (c) Both (a) and (b)
   (d) Neither (a) nor (b)

6. Which of the following are examples of arguments?
   (a) MsgBox and OpenForm
   (b) Message type (e.g., critical) and Form name
   (c) Both (a) and (b)
   (d) Neither (a) nor (b)

7. Which of the following can be imported from another Access database?
   (a) Tables and forms
   (b) Queries and reports
   (c) Both (a) and (b)
   (d) Neither (a) nor (b)

8. How do you change the properties of a command button on a form?
   (a) Open the form in Form view, then click the left mouse button to display a shortcut menu
   (b) Open the form in Form view, then click the right mouse button to display a shortcut menu
   (c) Open the form in Form Design view, then click the left mouse button to display a shortcut menu
   (d) Open the form in Form Design view, then click the right mouse button to display a shortcut menu

9. Which of the following is true regarding the Unmatched Query Wizard with respect to the Sports league database?
   (a) It can be used to identify teams without players
   (b) It can be used to identify players without teams
   (c) Both (a) and (b)
   (d) Neither (a) nor (b)

10. Which of the following can be associated with the On Click property of a command button?
    (a) An event procedure created by the Command Button Wizard
    (b) A macro created by the user
    (c) Either (a) or (b)
    (d) Neither (a) nor (b)

11. Which of the following was suggested as essential to a backup strategy?
    (a) Backing up files at the end of every session
    (b) Storing the backup file(s) at another location
    (c) Both (a) and (b)
    (d) Neither (a) nor (b)

12. Which of the following is true if the On Click property of a command button contains the entry, *Player Draft.Update List*?
    (a) Update List is an event procedure
    (b) Player Draft is an event procedure
    (c) Player Draft is a macro in the Update List macro group
    (d) Update List is a macro in the Player Draft macro group

13. Which of the following is true?
    (a) An existing database may be split into two separate databases, one containing the tables, and one containing the other objects
    (b) Once the objects in a database have been linked to the tables in another database, the name and/or location of the latter database can never be changed
    (c) Both (a) and (b)
    (d) Neither (a) nor (b)

14. The F6 and F11 function keys were introduced as shortcuts. Which of the following is true about these keys?
    (a) The F6 key switches between the top and bottom sections of the Macro window
    (b) The F11 key makes the Database window the active window
    (c) Both (a) and (b)
    (d) Neither (a) nor (b)

15. Which of the following was suggested as a way to organize macros and thus limit the number of macros that are displayed in the Database window?
    (a) Avoid macro actions that have only a single argument
    (b) Avoid macros that contain only a single action
    (c) Create a macro group
    (d) All of the above

ANSWERS

1. c	**6.** b	**11.** c
2. c	**7.** c	**12.** d
3. a	**8.** d	**13.** a
4. a	**9.** c	**14.** c
5. d	**10.** c	**15.** c

BUILDS ON

HANDS-ON
EXERCISE 3
PAGES 343–351

1. Report Design: Complete the three hands-on exercises in the chapter, then create the report shown in Figure 7.11. The report prints the team rosters, which shows all the players on each team. The teams are listed alphabetically, and by last name within each team.

   a. Create a Team Rosters query that contains fields from the Teams table and the Players table. This query includes a concatenated field that contains the player's first and last name as follows, = [LastName] & ", " & [FirstName], where LastName and FirstName are field names within the Players table. The ampersands concatenate (join) the two fields together with a comma to separate the first and last names.

   b. The Report Wizard is the easiest way to create the initial report based on the query from part a. The report header can be copied directly from the Report template that appears in the database.

   c. Print the completed report for your instructor as proof that you did this exercise.

FIGURE 7.11   *Report Design (Exercise 1)*

BUILDS ON

HANDS-ON
EXERCISE 3
PAGES 343–351

2. A Look Ahead: Open the Players form, click the button to add a player, then note that to add a player you must first click the First Name text box. You can automate the process by adding a VBA statement to the event procedure that was created by the Command Button Wizard. (VBA—Visual Basic for Applications—is a powerful programming language that is covered in the next chapter.) Proceed as follows.

   a. Open the Players form in Design view. Point to the Add Player command button, then click the right mouse button to display a shortcut menu. Click Properties to display the Properties dialog box. Click the down arrow on the vertical scroll bar until you can see the On Click property, which contains the entry [Event Procedure]. Click this entry, then click the Build Button (the three dots to the right of the box) to display the associated VBA code.

b. Click under the DoCmd statement and add the line FirstName.SetFocus as shown in Figure 7.12. This tells Access to go to the control called FirstName after inserting a new record. Click the Save button, then close the VBA window.

c. Click the Form View button to switch to Form view and test the Add Player macro. Click the Add Player command button. You should be positioned in the First Name box and can start typing immediately.

d. Click the Close Form command button when you have completed the record. Click Yes if prompted to save the changes to the Players form.

e. This may seem like a lot of trouble, but the end user appreciates this type of convenience. You can modify the Coaches form in similar fashion, then submit the completed disk to your instructor as proof you completed the exercise.

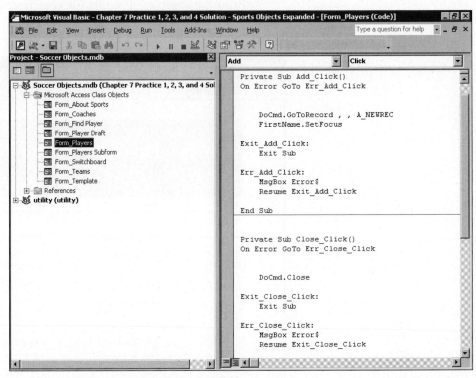

FIGURE 7.12   *A Look Ahead (Exercise 2)*

BUILDS ON

HANDS-ON
EXERCISE 3
PAGES 343–351

3. The Find Player Query: The player draft was only partially completed in the third hands-on exercise in that the Find Player button displayed the prototype macro, as opposed to locating a specific player. You can add the additional functionality in Figure 7.13 as follows:

a. Create a parameter query that requests the last name of a player, then displays all fields for that player.

b. Copy the existing Players form to a new form called Find Player. Change the Record Source property of the Find Player form to the parameter query you created in part a.

c. Change the Find Player macro in the Player Draft group so that it opens the Find Player form you just created.

d. Test the Find Player button. The player draft is now complete.

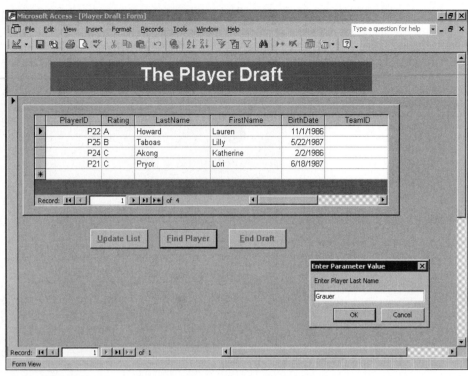

FIGURE 7.13 *The Find Player Query (Exercise 3)*

BUILDS ON

HANDS-ON
EXERCISE 3
PAGES 343–351

4. The Report Switchboard: The switchboard in Figure 7.14 is an expanded version of the switchboard from the third hands-on exercise. Your assignment is to create the indicated reports and queries, then modify the switchboard to display those objects. The Team Rosters report corresponds to the report that was created in exercise 1.

   a. The parameter query is to display the players on a specific team. Note, however, that you cannot run a query directly through the Switchboard Manager. There are two alternatives. You can create a macro to run a query, then run the macro from the Switchboard Manager. Alternatively, you can create a report based on the parameter query, and open the report from the Switchboard Manager.

   b. The Totals query is to display the team name and number of players.

   c. The Unmatched query (player draft) was implemented in the third hands-on exercise.

   d. Complete the Report Switchboard as indicated, then print each object for your instructor. Print the switchboard form itself as well as the table of switchboard items.

5. Password Protection: Close the Sports Objects database. Pull down the File menu, click the Open command to display the Open dialog box, click the Sports Objects database, then click the drop-down Open button and choose Open Exclusive. You must open the database in this way or else you will not be able to set a password. Next pull down the Tools menu, click Security, click Set Database Password, and follow the on-screen prompts as shown in Figure 7.15. Be careful, however because once you save a database with a password, you cannot open it if you forget the password.

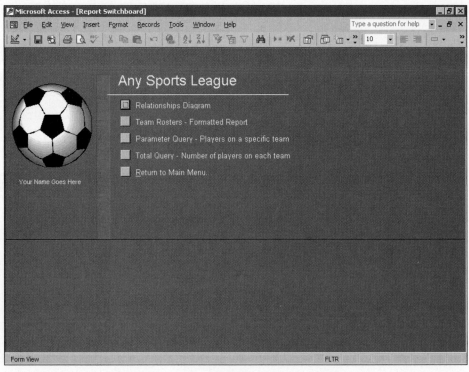

FIGURE 7.14   *The Report Switchboard (Exercise 4)*

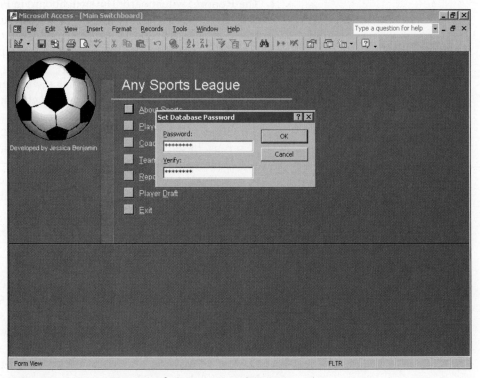

FIGURE 7.15   *Password Protection (Exercise 5)*

6. Class Scheduling: Figure 7.16 represents a database intended for class scheduling at a typical college or university. The scheduling process entails the coordination of course offerings as published in a registration schedule together with faculty assignments. The university may offer multiple sections of any given course at different times. The information about when a class meets is stored within the one-letter section designation; for example, section A meets from 9:00 to 9:50 on Mondays, Wednesdays, and Fridays.

a. The database contains separate tables for courses, sections, and faculty as can be seen in Figure 7.16. There are many-to-many relationships between courses and sections, between courses and faculty, and between faculty and sections. The key to the design is the creation of an additional Offerings table that includes the CourseID, SectionID, and FacultyID. The combination of these three fields could serve as the primary key of the Offerings table, but it is easier to add an additional field, the OfferingID with the AutoNumber field type. The additional fields, Building and Room, provide information as to where the specific course will meet.

b. We have designed the database for you. Your task is to implement our design by creating a database that contains the indicated tables and associated relationships. You do not have to enter data into any of the tables, but you will need to create the tables in order to create a relationships diagram.

c. We have embellished the report containing the relationships diagram to include a report header, with a modified font and selected clip art. These elements will be used in the next two practice exercises that develop the switchboard and a report template. The cosmetic design of a system is an important consideration that should be given careful attention. Print the completed report for your instructor.

d. Would this design be applicable to the comparable database at your school or university? Summarize your thoughts in a short note to your instructor.

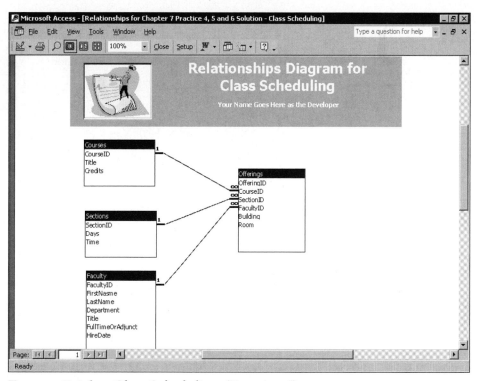

FIGURE 7.16 *Class Scheduling (Exercise 6)*

BUILDS ON

PRACTICE EXERCISE 6 PAGE 359

7. Class Scheduling Prototype: The switchboard in Figure 7.17 continues the development of the class scheduling database and represents Version 1 of the completed system. You do not have to follow our design exactly, but you are required to include the indicated functionality. It is important, however, that you use a consistent design so that all of the objects in your database have a uniform look. This attention to detail enhances the visual appeal of a database and gives it a more professional appearance. Note the following:

a. The switchboard should open automatically whenever the database is opened. This can be accomplished through the Startup property or through the creation of an AutoExec macro.

b. The About Class Scheduling form contains the same logo that appears on the switchboard and is similar to the other forms that have appeared throughout the text.

c. The second menu option should print the report containing the relationships diagram from the previous exercise.

d. Create a prototype macro to indicate items under development as shown in Figure 7.17. The associated message box will appear upon clicking either of the data entry forms, which are not yet developed.

e. The Report Switchboard button should display a secondary switchboard that contains several reports that will be available in the completed system. Clicking any of the report buttons displays the message from the prototype macro. The Report Switchboard should also contain a button to return to the main switchboard.

f. The Exit button should display a message to the user to back up the system.

g. Print each switchboard and the table of switchboard items for your instructor. Add a cover sheet to complete the assignment.

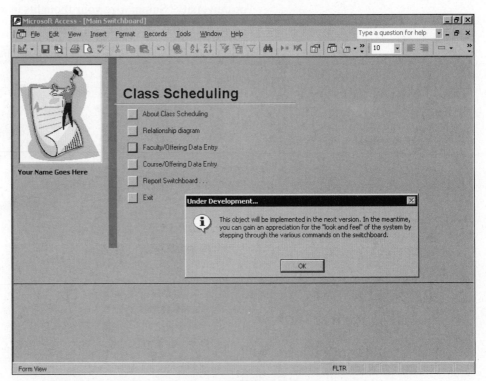

FIGURE 7.17 *Class Scheduling Prototype (Exercise 7)*

BUILDS ON

PRACTICE
EXERCISE 7
PAGE 360

8. Class Scheduling Template: Create a template for the class scheduling application that is consistent with the switchboard you developed in the previous exercise. Our template is shown in Figure 7.18. It was created in Form Design view without benefit of the Form Wizard, and it (the template) is not based on a table or query. The fields that appear in the template are labels (unbound controls) and are there to show the user the proposed color scheme that will appear on the finished form. Modify the data entry buttons on the main switchboard to display the template you just created, as opposed to the prototype macro. Print the template for your instructor.

   a. Create a simple faculty form based on the template. Start in the Database window. Select the template, press Ctrl+C to copy the template to the clipboard, press Ctrl+V to paste the contents of the clipboard into the database, then name the copied form Faculty.

   b. Go to the Design view of the newly created Faculty form as shown in Figure 7.18. Right click the Form Selector button of the form to display the Properties sheet, then change the Record Source to the Faculty table. Close the Properties sheet.

   c. The field list for the Faculty table opens automatically. Delete the dummy fields from the original template, then click and drag the fields from the field list to the form. Add the necessary command buttons and save the form.

   d. Add your instructor to the Faculty table and print the associated form.

   e. Create a report template that is based on the relationships diagram created earlier. Copy the existing report and use the duplicated object as the basis of the report template. The consistent design enhances the visual appeal of your database and gives it a professional look. Print the template for your instructor.

   f. Add a cover sheet to complete the assignment.

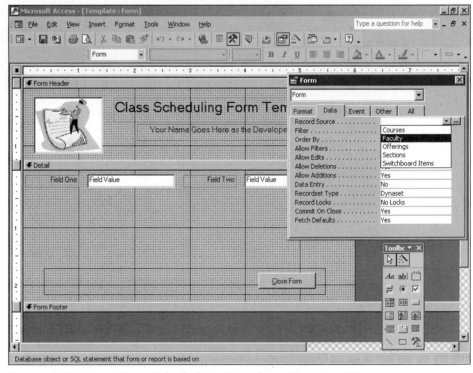

FIGURE 7.18   *Class Scheduling Template (Exercise 8)*

9. **The Video Store:** You have an internship at the local video store, which rents and/or sells tapes to customers. The store maintains the usual information about every customer (name, address, phone number, and so on). It also has detailed information about every movie such as its duration, rating, rental price, and purchase price. There is a subtlety in the design because the video store stocks multiple copies (tapes) of the same movie. Customers rent tapes (that contain movies), as opposed to renting movies.

   a. The Movies table contains the detailed information about each movie. There is a one-to-many relationship between movies and tapes; that is, one movie can have many tapes, but a specific tape is associated with only one movie.

   b. There is a many-to-many relationship between customers and tapes; that is, one customer can rent several tapes, and the same tape will (over time) be rented to many customers. This in turn gives rise to the Customer-Tape or Rentals table as shown in Figure 7.19.

   c. We have designed the database for you. Your task is to implement our design by creating a database that contains the indicated tables and associated relationships. You do not have to enter data into any of the tables, but you will need to create the tables in order to create a relationships diagram for your instructor.

   d. We have embellished the report containing the relationships diagram to include a report header, with a modified font and selected clip art. These elements will be used in the next two practice exercises that develop the switchboard and a report template. The cosmetic design of a system is an important consideration that should be given careful attention. Print the completed report for your instructor.

   e. Add a cover sheet to complete the assignment.

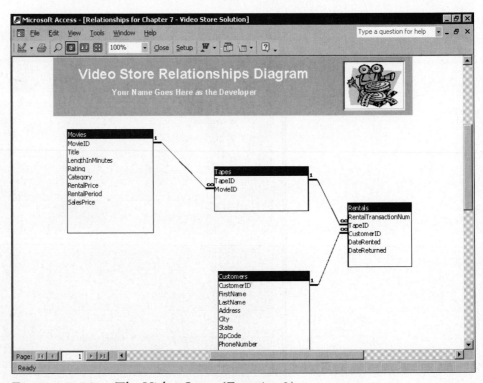

FIGURE 7.19 *The Video Store (Exercise 9)*

BUILDS ON

PRACTICE
EXERCISE 9
PAGE 362

10. Video Store Prototype: The switchboard in Figure 7.20 continues the development of the Video Store database and represents Version 1 of the completed system. You do not have to follow our design exactly, but you are required to include the indicated functionality. It is important, however, that you use a consistent design so that all of the objects in your database have a uniform look. This attention to detail enhances the visual appeal of a database and gives it a more professional appearance.

a. The switchboard should open automatically whenever the database is opened. This can be accomplished through the Startup property or through the creation of an AutoExec macro.

b. The About Video Store form contains the same logo that appears on the switchboard and is similar to the other forms that have appeared throughout the text.

c. The second menu option should print the report containing the relationships diagram from the previous exercise.

d. Create a prototype macro to indicate items under development as shown in Figure 7.20. The associated message box will appear upon clicking either of the data entry forms, which are not yet developed.

e. The Report Switchboard button should display a secondary switchboard that contains several reports that will be available in the completed system. Clicking any of the report buttons displays the message from the prototype macro. The Report Switchboard should also contain a button to return to the main switchboard.

f. The Exit button should display a message to the user to back up the system.

g. Print each switchboard and the table of switchboard items for your instructor. Add a cover sheet to complete the assignment.

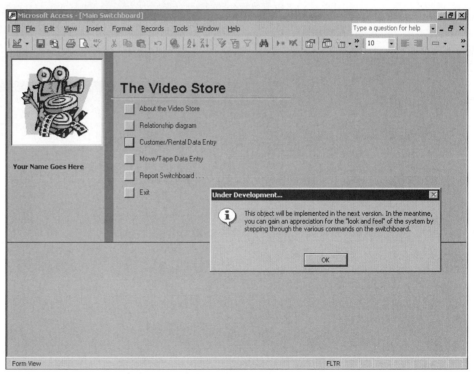

FIGURE 7.20   *Video Store Prototype (Exercise 10)*

BUILDS ON

PRACTICE
EXERCISE 10
PAGE 363

11. Video Store Templates: Continue the development of the Video Store database by creating the report and form templates shown in Figures 7.21a and 7.21b, respectively. Both templates are created in Design view, without benefit of the associated Wizard. The fields that appear are text boxes as opposed to specific controls. You do not have to follow our design exactly, but you should be consistent with the switchboard developed earlier.

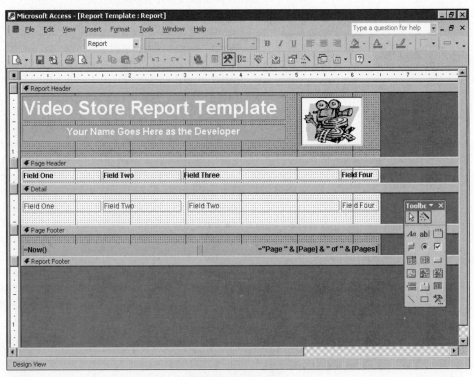

(a) Report Template

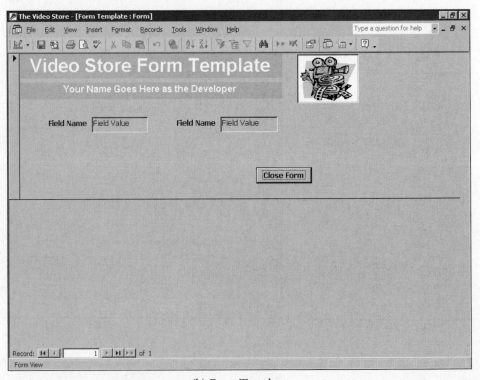

(b) Form Template

FIGURE 7.21 *Video Store Templates (Exercise 11)*

BUILDS ON

CHAPTER 5
PRACTICE EXERCISE 5
PAGE 249

12. Replicating a Database: A replica is a copy of a database that can be synchronized with other replicas to coordinate changes to the underlying data. Open the Turkeys To Go database from Chapter 5, pull down the Tools menu, click Replication, then click the Create Replica command. Click Yes when asked whether to close the database and create a replica. You will see a message suggesting that Access create a backup copy of your database. Click Yes.

a. Access creates a replica of the database and displays the Location of New Replica dialog box in which you specify the name and folder for the replica. Use the default name, but save the replica in the Exploring Access folder.

b. You will see a message similar to Figure 7.22 in which Access indicates that it converted the original database to the Design master, and further that it has created a replica. Note that the last sentence in the message indicating only the Design master can accept changes to the database structure, but that changes to the data can be made in either the Design master or the replica. Click OK. Look at the title bar of the Database window and note that "Database Master" has been appended to the name of the database.

c. Click the Data entry button on the switchboard. Add Jessica Benjamin as a new franchisee, with FranchiseeID F011. Complete the other information as you see fit. Close the data entry form. Click the Exit button on the switchboard to close this database.

d. Start Windows Explorer and open the Replica of the Turkeys To Go database in the Exploring Access folder. Pull down the Tools menu, click Replication, then click the Synchronize Now command. Click Yes when Access asks if you want to close the open objects.

e. You should see a Synchronize Database dialog box. The option button to synchronize directly with the replica is selected. Click OK. Click Yes when asked whether to close the database, after which you should get a message that the synchronization was successful. Note that the title bar indicates you are working in the replica, not the Design master.

f. Click the Data entry button on the switchboard. Locate the record for Jessica Benjamin, the franchisee you just added. Use the form to add a new restaurant (RestaurantID 8765) with any parameters you like.

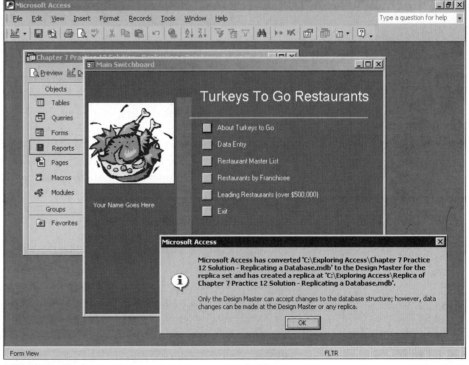

FIGURE 7.22   *Replicating a Database (Exercise 12)*

Computer Repair

The Director of the Administrative Services has come to you for assistance in implementing a system to track the repairs associated with the computers on campus. The data about each computer—such as the make and model, operating system, location on campus, and so on—is stored in a Computers table within an Access database. The faculty or staff member responsible for that computer is also indicated. The data about the faculty and staff is stored in a separate table. (One individual, such as the director of a specific computer lab, can be responsible for many computers, but a given computer is the responsibility of one person.)

Problems inevitably occur, and when they do, the faculty or staff member responsible for that computer calls the Director's office to report the problem. The nature of the problem is recorded, and a technician is assigned to fix it. (Technicians are employed as independent contractors and do not appear in the Faculty/Staff table.) One technician can work on many computers, and a specific computer may be worked on by different technicians. Your assignment is to design a database that will maintain this data and produce the associated reports. The database should be able to list all computers that are currently under repair. It should also provide a report that shows all completed repairs. Other reports might include all problems for a specific technician, or all problems reported by a particular faculty member. Your instructor has asked for a report containing the relationships diagram.

Find a Mate Dating Service

The Find a Mate Dating Service employs dating counselors to match its clients to one another. Each counselor works with many clients, but a specific client always works with the same counselor. All clients complete extensive questionnaires that describe themselves and the qualities they wish to find in a mate. The counselors evaluate this information and pair the agency's clients with one another to create a date. One client can have many dates, and a date has many (actually two) clients. Feedback is important, and each client is asked for his or her reaction to the date.

Your assignment is to design a database that will track counselors, clients, and dates. It should be able to list all dates for a specific client as well as all dates arranged by a specific counselor. Print the relationships diagram.

Security Options

Setting a password is the first step in protecting a database. You can also set different levels of password protection, by giving different permissions to different users. Pull down the Tools menu, click Security, then click User and Group Permissions to display the associated dialog box. Use help to explore the options within this dialog box. You can also encrypt a database through a different command within the Security menu. Explore the various security options, then summarize your findings in a short note to your instructor.

Compacting versus Compressing

The importance of adequate backup has been stressed throughout the text. As a student, however, your backup may be limited to what you can fit on a single floppy disk, which in turn creates a problem if the size of your database grows beyond 1.4Mb. Two potential solutions involve compacting and/or compressing the database. Compacting is done from within Access, whereas compressing requires additional software. In addition, you can split a database in two, then compact and/or compress each database. Investigate both of these techniques with respect to the Sports league database created in the chapter. Be sure to indicate to your instructor the reduction in file size that you were able to achieve.

CHAPTER *8*

Creating More Powerful Applications: Introduction to VBA

OBJECTIVES

AFTER READING THIS CHAPTER YOU WILL BE ABLE TO:

1. Describe the relationship of VBA to Microsoft Office; list several reasons to use VBA in creating an Access application.
2. Describe the components of the Module window; differentiate between the Procedure view and the Full Module view.
3. Describe two different ways to create an event procedure; explain how to navigate between existing procedures.
4. Explain how the Quick Info and Complete Word features facilitate the entry of VBA statements.
5. Create a combo box to locate a record on a form; explain why an event procedure is required for the combo box to function properly.
6. Describe the parameters associated with the MsgBox statement; explain how MsgBox can be used as a function to return a value from the user.
7. Create an event procedure to facilitate data entry through keyboard shortcuts.
8. Create an event procedure that substitutes application-specific messages for the standard Access error messages.
9. Describe several types of data validation; create an event procedure that warns the user a field has been omitted, giving the user the option to save the record without entering the data.

OVERVIEW

You can accomplish a great deal in Access without using Visual Basic. You can create an Access database consisting of tables, forms, queries, and reports, by executing commands from pull-down menus. You can use macros to create menus that tie those objects together so that the database is easier to use. Nevertheless, there comes a point where you need the power of a programming language to develop a truly useful application. Hence, this introduction to *Visual Basic for Applications* (or *VBA*), a subset of Visual Basic that is accessible from every application in Microsoft Office.

VBA is different from traditional programming languages in that it is event-driven. An *event* is any action that is recognized by Access. Opening or closing a form is an event. So is clicking a button in a form or entering data in a text box or other control on the form. The essence of VBA is the creation of *procedures* (or sets of VBA statements) that respond to specific events. Hence, the term *event procedure* will be used throughout the chapter.

To enhance an application through VBA, you decide which events are significant and what is to happen when those events occur. Then you develop the appropriate event procedures. You can, for example, create an event procedure that displays a splash (introductory) screen for the application every time a user opens the database. You can write an event procedure that creates a keyboard shortcut for data entry that executes when the user presses a particular keystroke combination. You can create an event procedure to display a specific message in place of the standard error message supplied by Access. In all instances, the execution of your procedures depends entirely on the user, because he or she triggers the underlying events through an appropriate action.

You can also use VBA to modify the event procedures that Access has created for you. If, for example, you used the Command Button Wizard to create a button to close a form, Access created the event procedure for you. The user clicks the button, and the event procedure closes the form. You can, however, use VBA to improve the procedure created by Access by adding a statement that reminds the user to back up the database after closing the form.

This chapter provides a general introduction to VBA through four hands-on exercises that enhance an application in different ways. Our approach is very different from that of other texts that run several hundred pages and cover the subject in extended detail. Our objective is to provide you with an appreciation for what can be accomplished, rather than to cover VBA in detail. We will show you how to create and modify simple procedures. We will also provide you with the conceptual framework to explore the subject in greater detail on your own.

One last point before we begin is that VBA is common to every application in Microsoft Office, and thus anything that you learn about VBA from within Access is applicable to the other applications as well. If, for example, you create a macro in Word or Excel, the macro recorder captures the keystrokes and then generates a VBA procedure that is accessible through the Word document or Excel workbook, respectively. You can modify the procedure by changing existing statements and/or by adding additional statements using the techniques in this chapter.

THE VBA PRIMER

There are two ways to learn the rudiments of VBA. You can begin your study with this chapter, which has you look at typical VBA procedures within an Access form, then proceed to the VBA primer at the end of the text to study the syntax more precisely. Alternatively, you may want to start with the primer, then return to this chapter to see the application of the various VBA statements within Access. Either way, the two chapters reinforce each other and provide a solid foundation in this important programming language.

The form in Figure 8.1 will be used throughout the chapter as the basis of our VBA examples. The form itself is unremarkable and parallels many of the forms that were developed throughout the text. It was created initially through the Form Wizard, then modified by moving and sizing controls as appropriate. What then is so special about the form, and how does it utilize VBA?

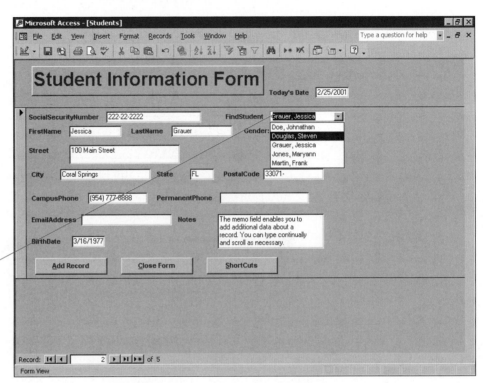

Find Student combo box

FIGURE 8.1 *User Form*

The answer lies beneath the surface and is best explained in conjunction with the dialog boxes in Figure 8.2. At first glance, the dialog boxes look like typical messages displayed by Microsoft Access. Look closely at the title bar of any message, however, and note that it has been changed to reflect the authors' introduction to Visual Basic. This is a subtle change that is easily implemented through VBA, and it gives your application a personal touch. Note, too, the different icons that are displayed in the various messages. This, too, is a subtle touch that further customizes the application and its messages.

Look closely at the content of each dialog box to learn more about the underlying VBA capability. The message in Figure 8.2a indicates that the user has omitted the e-mail address, then asks if the record should be saved anyway. This is an improvement over the built-in routines for data validation, which use the Required property to reject any record that omits the e-mail address. Should this occur, the user is notified that the field is required, but he or she cannot save the record unless a value is specified. Through VBA, however, the user has a choice and can opt to save the record even when there is no e-mail address.

The dialog box in Figure 8.2b is displayed as a result of clicking the Shortcuts command button on the form. The message implies that the user can use keyboard shortcuts to enter the city, state, and zip code for Miami or Coral Springs. True, the user could enter the data manually, but think how much time can be saved when there is extensive data entry.

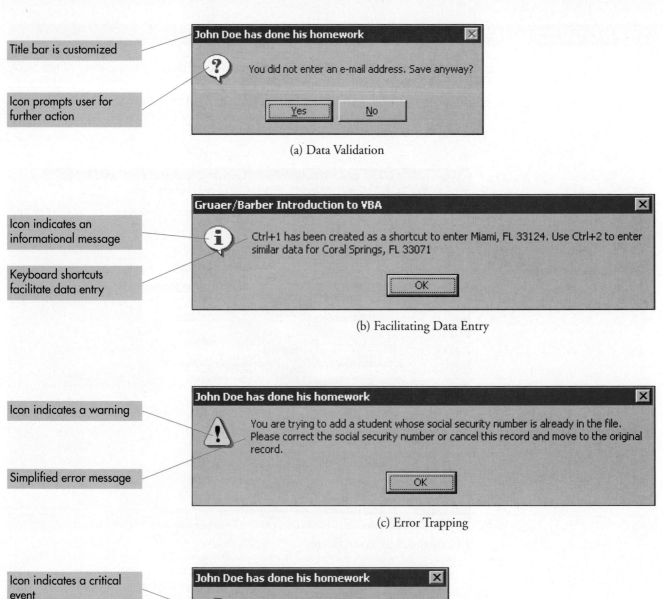

Title bar is customized

Icon prompts user for further action

(a) Data Validation

Icon indicates an informational message

Keyboard shortcuts facilitate data entry

(b) Facilitating Data Entry

Icon indicates a warning

Simplified error message

(c) Error Trapping

Icon indicates a critical event

Message alerts the user to subsequent action

(d) Enhanced Communication with User

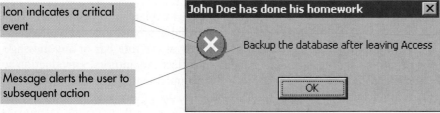

FIGURE 8.2 *Dialog Boxes*

Figure 8.2c displays a message indicating that one is attempting to add a student whose social security number is already in the file. The text is very straightforward and that is exactly the point. The default Access error message would not be as clear, and would have indicated that changes to the table were not successful because they would have created a duplicate value of the primary key. In other words, we used VBA to first detect the error, and then substituted a more explicit message. Finally, the message in Figure 8.2d simply reminds the user to back up the database upon exiting Access.

Modules and Procedures

There are, in essence, two different ways to learn VBA. The first is to immerse yourself in the theory and syntax before you attempt to develop any applications on your own. The second, and the one we follow, is to start with an overall appreciation of what it can do, then plunge right in. You need some basic vocabulary, but after that you can model your procedures on ours and create some very powerful applications in the process.

Visual Basic code is developed in units called procedures. There are two types of procedures, general procedures and event procedures. *Event procedures* are the essence of an Access application and run automatically in response to an event such as clicking a button or opening a form. *General procedures* do not run automatically, but are called explicitly from within another procedure. We focus exclusively on event procedures.

All (general and event) procedures are stored in modules; that is, one module contains one or more procedures. Every form in an Access database has its own module (known as a *class module*), which contains the procedures for that form. A procedure is either public or private. A *private procedure* is accessible only from within the module in which it is contained. A *public procedure* is accessible from anywhere.

The procedures in a module are displayed and edited through the *Module window* within the Visual Basic editor. Figure 8.3, for example, displays the Module window for the student form shown earlier in Figure 8.1. Four different procedures are visible, each of which is associated with a different event. Each procedure begins with a procedure header that names the procedure. This is followed by the executable statements within the procedure, followed by the End Sub statement to mark the end of the procedure. Do not be concerned if you do not understand the precise syntax of every statement. Try, instead, to gain an overall appreciation for what the procedures do.

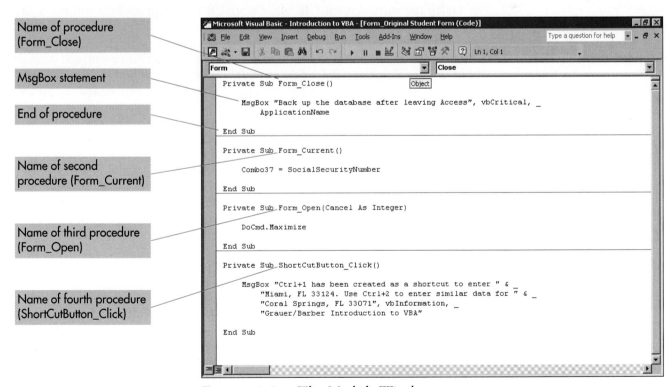

FIGURE 8.3   *The Module Window*

The first event procedure is for the **Close Form event**. The procedure header contains the key word Sub, followed by the procedure name (Form_Close). The **MsgBox statement** within the procedure displays the message box (shown earlier in Figure 8.2d) when the event occurs. Thus whenever the user closes the form, either by clicking the Close button on the form or by clicking the Close button in the document window, the event procedure is triggered and one is reminded to back up the database. (See boxed tip.)

The syntax of the MsgBox function is typical of many VBA statements and is best understood if you view the statement as it might appear in a help screen *MsgBox (prompt, buttons, title)*. The entries in parentheses are known as **arguments** (or **parameters**) and determine the contents of the message box. The first argument is contained in quotation marks, and it specifies the prompt (or message text) that appears within the message box. The second argument indicates the type of command buttons (if any) and the associated icon that appear within the dialog box. This argument is specified as an **intrinsic** (or previously defined) **constant** (vbCritical in this example), and it determines the icon that is to appear in the message box. The third argument contains the text that appears in the title bar of the message box. It, too, appears in quotation marks.

The second event procedure is associated with the **Current event** of the form and is the focus of our first hands-on exercise. The nature of this procedure is much less intuitive than the previous example, yet this event procedure is critical to the success of the form. Return to the Student Form shown in Figure 8.1 and note the presence of a combo box to find a specific student. The user clicks the drop-down arrow on the combo box and selects a student from the displayed list, after which the data for that student is displayed in the form.

The combo box was created through the Combo Box Wizard, and it works well, but it does have one limitation. If the user elects to move from one record to the next by clicking a navigation button at the bottom of the form, the combo box is out of sync in that it does not reflect the name of the new student. Hence the need to write a VBA procedure for the Current event to change the value in the combo box to match the current record. In other words, the VBA procedure will move the SocialSecurityNumber of the current record to the combo box control whenever the record changes.

The third event procedure is associated with the Open Form event, and it needs almost no explanation. The single executable statement will maximize the form when it is opened. Again, do not be concerned if you do not understand the precise syntax of every statement in our initial examples as we add further explanation in the chapter. The fourth and final procedure is associated with the Click event of the ShortCut command button, and it contains another example of the MsgBox function. Note, too, that for this procedure to make sense, other event procedures have to be created to implement the shortcuts as described.

We would be misleading you if we said that VBA is easy. It's not, but neither is it as complicated as you might think. And more importantly, VBA is extremely powerful. We think you will be pleased with what you can accomplish by the end of this chapter. Once again, it is time for a hands-on exercise.

A SIMPLE STRATEGY FOR BACKUP

We cannot overemphasize the importance of adequate backup. Backup procedures are personal and vary from individual to individual as well as from installation to installation. Our suggested strategy is very simple, namely that you back up whatever you cannot afford to lose and that you do so at the end of every session. Be sure to store the backup at a different location from the original file.

CREATE A COMBO BOX AND ASSOCIATED VBA PROCEDURE

Objective   To create a combo box to locate a record; to create a VBA procedure to synchronize the combo box with the current record. Use Figure 8.4.

Step 1:   **Open the Introduction to VBA Database**

> ➤ Start Access. Open the **Introduction to VBA database** in the **Exploring Access folder** as shown in Figure 8.4a.
> ➤ If necessary, click the **Forms button**. Select (click) the **Original Student Form**. Pull down the **Edit menu** and click the **Copy command** (or click the **Copy button** on the Database toolbar). The form is copied to the clipboard.
> ➤ Pull down the **Edit menu** a second time and click the **Paste command** (or click the **Paste button** on the Database toolbar) to display the Paste As dialog box. Type **Completed Student Form** and press **enter**.

Copy button

Paste button

Forms button

Enter name of new form

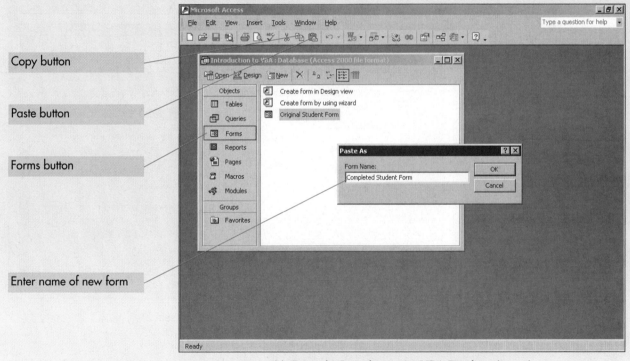

(a) Open the Introduction to VBA Database (step 1)

FIGURE 8.4   *Hands-on Exercise 1*

KEYBOARD SHORTCUTS—CUT, COPY, AND PASTE

Ctrl+X, Ctrl+C, and Ctrl+V are shortcuts to cut, copy, and paste, respectively, and apply to Windows applications in general. The shortcuts are easier to remember when you realize that the operative letters X, C, and V are next to each other at the bottom-left side of the keyboard.

Step 2: **The Combo Box Wizard**

> ➤ Open the newly created **Completed Student Form** in Design view. Maximize the window.
> ➤ Click the **Combo Box** tool on the Toolbox toolbar, then click and drag on the form next to the SSN control to create a combo box and start the Wizard.
> ➤ Select the option button to **Find a record on my form based on the value I selected in my combo box** as shown in Figure 8.4b. Click **Next**.
> ➤ Double click the **SocialSecurityNumber field** to move it from the list box of available fields (on the left of the Combo Box Wizard) to the list of selected fields. Double click the **LastName field** to move this field as well. Click **Next**.
> ➤ You should see the columns in the combo box as they will appear in the form. Be sure the Check box to Hide key column is checked. Click **Next**.
> ➤ Change the label of the combo box to **FindStudent** (do not use a space in the label). Click **Finish** to exit the Combo Box Wizard.

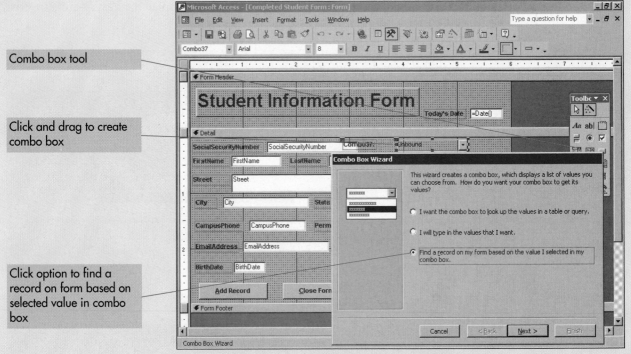

Combo box tool

Click and drag to create combo box

Click option to find a record on form based on selected value in combo box

(b) The Combo Box Wizard (step 2)

FIGURE 8.4 *Hands-on Exercise 1 (continued)*

SIZING AND MOVING A COMBO BOX AND ITS LABEL

A combo box is always created with an attached label. Select (click) the combo box, and it will have sizing handles and a move handle, but the label has only a move handle. Select the label (instead of the combo box) and the opposite occurs. To move a combo box and its label, click and drag the border of either object. To move either the combo box or its label, click and drag the move handle (a tiny square in the upper left corner) of the appropriate object.

Step 3: **Move and Size the Combo Box**

> ➤ Move and size the newly created combo box to match the layout in Figure 8.4c. The Properties sheet is not yet visible. You will most likely have to decrease the size of the combo box and/or increase the size of the label.
> ➤ To align the combo box and/or its label with the other controls on the same row of the form, press and hold the **Shift key** to select the controls you want to align. Pull down the **Format menu**, click **Align**, then click **Top** to align the top of all selected elements.
> ➤ Point to the combo box, click the **right mouse button** to display a shortcut menu, then click **Properties** to display the Properties dialog box in Figure 8.4c. If necessary, click the **All tab**.
> ➤ Write down the name of the combo box (Combo37 in our figure) as you will need it in step 7. The name of your control may be different from ours.
> ➤ Click the **Row Source property** to select it, then click the **Build button** (the button with three dots) that appears when the row is selected.

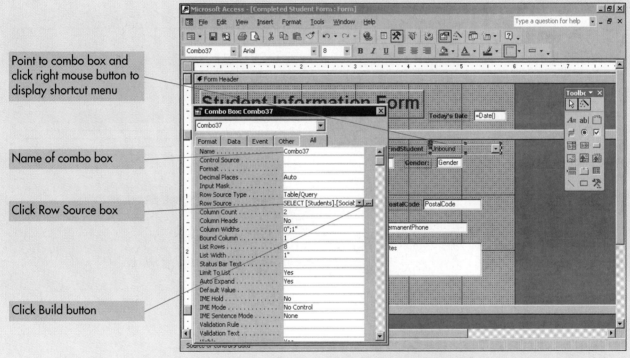

(c) Move and Size the Combo Box (step 3)

FIGURE 8.4 *Hands-on Exercise 1 (continued)*

THE PROPERTY DIALOG BOX

You can change the appearance or behavior of a control in two ways—by changing the actual control on the form itself or by changing the underlying properties. Anything you do to the control automatically changes the associated property, and conversely, any change to the property sheet is reflected in the appearance or behavior of the control. We find ourselves continually switching back and forth between the two techniques.

Step 4: **Update the Row Source**

➤ You should see the query in Figure 8.4d, except that your query has not yet been completed. Click in the second column of the Field row, immediately after the LastName control.

➤ Press the **space bar** then type **&", "& FirstName**. Leave a space after the comma within the quotation marks. Press **enter**.

➤ Double click the border between this cell and the next to increase the column width so that you can see the entire expression. Note that Expr1: has been entered automatically in front of the expression.

➤ Click in the **Sort row** of the same column, click the **down arrow** if necessary, then click **Ascending** to display the records in alphabetical order by last name.

➤ Close the query. Click **Yes** when asked whether to save the changes that were made to the SQL statement. Close the Properties sheet.

➤ Click the **View button** to return to Form view.

View button

Click in Sort row, click drop-down arrow, and select Ascending

Add &","&[FirstName]

Double click border to increase column width

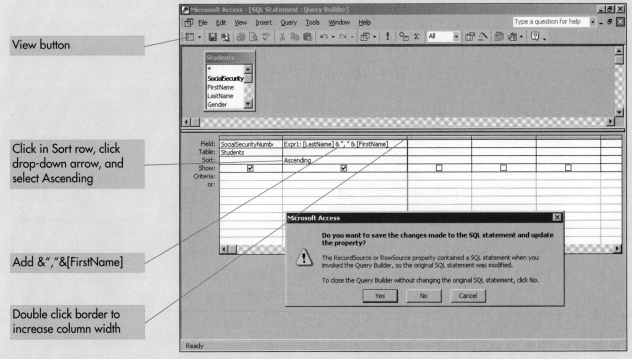

(d) Update the Row Source (step 4)

FIGURE 8.4 *Hands-on Exercise 1 (continued)*

CONCATENATING A STRING

The ampersand (&), or concatenation operator, indicates that the elements on either side of an expression are to appear adjacent to one another when the expression is displayed. You can also concatenate a literal and a field name such as "The employee's last name is" & LastName to display "The employee's last name is Smith," assuming that Smith is the current value in the LastName field.

Step 5: **Test the Find Student Combo Box**

> ➤ If necessary, click the **navigation button** above the status bar to return to the first record in the table, Maryann Jones, as shown in Figure 8.4e.
> ➤ Click the **drop-down arrow** on the combo box you just created to display a list of students in alphabetical order. (If you do not see the list of students, press **Esc** to cancel whatever operation is in effect, then return to Design view to repeat the instructions in the previous steps.)
> ➤ Select (click) **Grauer, Jessica** from the list of names in the combo box. The form is updated to display the information for this student. Click the **drop-down arrow** a second time and select **Douglas, Steven** from the combo box. Again the form is updated.
> ➤ Click the **navigation button** to return to the first student. The form displays the record for Maryann Jones, but the combo box is *not* updated; it still displays Douglas, Steven.
> ➤ Click the **View button** to return to Design view.

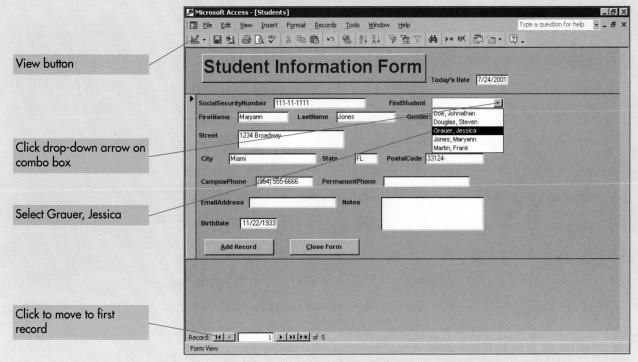

(e) Test the Find Student Combo Box (step 5)

FIGURE 8.4 *Hands-on Exercise 1 (continued)*

WHY USE VBA?

The combo box enables you to select a name from an alphabetical list, then updates the form to display the data for the corresponding record. All of this has been accomplished without the use of VBA. The problem is that the combo box is not updated automatically when records are selected via the navigation buttons. The only way to correct this problem is by writing a VBA procedure.

Step 6: **Create an Event Procedure**

> ➤ Point to the **form selector** box (the tiny square at the upper left of the form), click the **right mouse button** to display a shortcut menu, then click **Properties** to display the Form property sheet.
> ➤ Click the **Event tab**. Click the **On Current** event, then click the **Build button** to display the Choose Builder dialog box as shown in Figure 8.4f.
> ➤ Click (select) **Code Builder**, then click **OK**. A VBA window will open containing the module for the Completed Student Form.
> ➤ If necessary, maximize the VBA window and/or click the **Procedure View button** above the status bar. The insertion point is positioned automatically within a newly created event procedure.
> ➤ You should see a statement beginning Private Sub Form_Current( ) corresponding to the On Current event. You should also see the line ending End Sub, but no code appears between the Sub and End Sub statements.

Right click form selector box to display shortcut menu

Click Event tab

Click On Current box

Click Code Builder

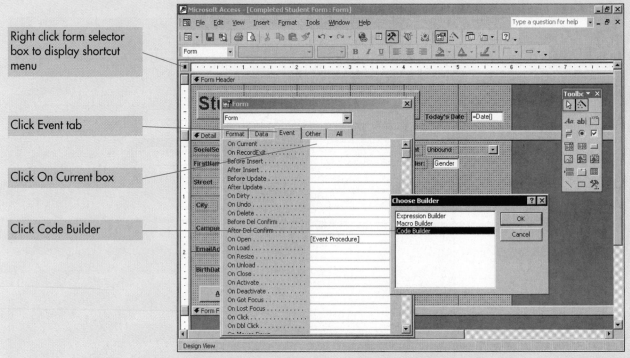

(f) Create an Event Procedure (step 6)

FIGURE 8.4 *Hands-on Exercise 1 (continued)*

CREATING AN EVENT PROCEDURE

There is only one correct way to create an event procedure, and that is the technique used in this exercise. Thus, you right click the form selector box to display the form properties, click the Event tab to select the desired event, click the Build button, and click the Code Builder. This in turn takes you to the VBA editor, where you enter the procedure. Do *not* create the event directly in the module window (without first clicking the Event tab). The latter technique appears reasonable, but it will not create the necessary association between the event and the code.

Step 7:   **Complete the On Current Event Procedure**

➤ The insertion point should be on a blank line, between the Sub and End Sub statements. If not, click on the blank line. Press the **Tab key** to indent the statements within the procedure. Indentation makes your code easier to read, but is not a syntactical requirement.

➤ Type **Combo37** (use the number of your combo box as determined in step 3).

➤ If you do not remember the name of the combo box, click the button on the taskbar to return to the Form window, click in the combo box and click the **All tab**. Look at the entry in the **Name property**.

➤ Press the **space bar** after you have entered the name of your combo box, type an **equal sign**, and press the **space bar** a second time. Type **Social** (the first several letters in the name of the SocialSecurityNumber control).

➤ Pull down the **Edit menu** and click **Complete Word** (or press **Ctrl+Space**) to display all of the objects, properties, and methods that start with these letters.

➤ SocialSecurityNumber is already selected as shown in Figure 8.4g. Press the **space bar** to copy the selected item and complete the statement.

➤ Click the **Save button** on the Visual Basic toolbar. Close the VBA window.

Save button

Procedure header

Enter name of combo box from step 3

Press space bar to copy selected item to procedure

Procedure View button

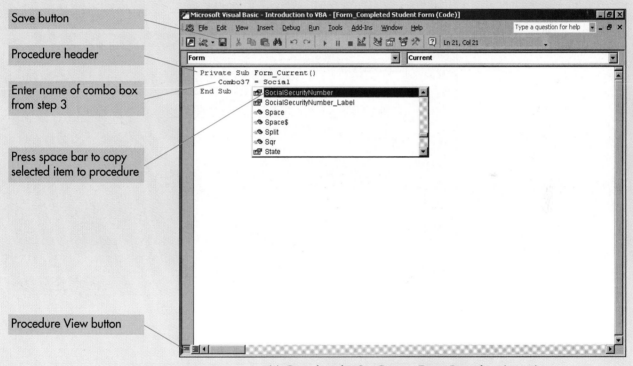

(g) Complete the On Current Event Procedure (step 7)

FIGURE 8.4   *Hands-on Exercise 1 (continued)*

USE THE RIGHT MOUSE BUTTON

The Quick Info and AutoList features are activated automatically as you create a VBA statement. The features can also be activated at any time by pulling down the Edit menu and selecting the Quick Info or List Properties/Methods commands, respectively. You can also point to any portion of a VBA statement and click the right mouse button to display a shortcut menu with options to display this information.

Step 8:   **Add Your Record**

➤ If necessary, click the button for the Access form on the task bar. Close the properties sheet. Click the **View button** to return to Form view.

➤ You should see the Student Information form. Click the **navigation button** to move to the next record. The data in the form is updated.

➤ Click the **navigation button** to return to the first record. Once again the data in the form is updated, as is the name in the combo box.

➤ Click the form's **Add Record command button**. You should see a blank form as shown in Figure 8.4h.

➤ Click in the **SocialSecurityNumber** text box and enter your Social Security number. Continue to enter your personal data.

➤ Close the form when you have finished entering data. Exit Access if you do not want to continue with the next exercise at this time.

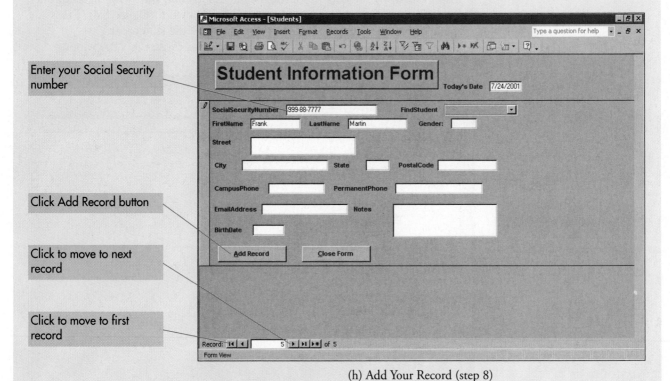

(h) Add Your Record (step 8)

FIGURE 8.4   *Hands-on Exercise 1 (continued)*

THE SET FOCUS METHOD

Ideally, clicking the Add Record button should position you in the SocialSecurityNumber field, without your having to click in the field to begin entering data. Open the Student form in Design view, right click the Add Record button and display the Properties dialog box. Click the Event tab, click the On Click property, then click the Build button. Insert the statement SocialSecurityNumber.SetFocus immediately after the DoCmd statement. Go to Form view, then click the Add button. You should be positioned in the SocialSecurityNumber field.

One of the most useful things you can accomplish through VBA is to provide the user with shortcuts for data entry. Many forms, for example, require the user to enter the city, state, and zip code for incoming records. In certain systems, such as a local store or company, this information is likely to be repeated from one record to the next. One common approach is to use the ***Default property*** in the table definition to specify default values for these fields, so that the values are automatically entered into a record.

What if, however, there are several sets of common values? Our local store, for example, may draw customers from two or three different cities, and we need to constantly switch among the different cities. The Default property is no longer effective because it is restricted to a single value. A better solution is to use VBA to provide a set of keyboard shortcuts such as Ctrl+1 for the first city, state, and zip code, Ctrl+2 for the next set of values, and so on. The user selects the appropriate shortcut, and the city, state, and zip code are entered automatically. The VBA code is shown in Figure 8.5.

Figure 8.5a displays the ***KeyDown event*** procedure to implement two shortcuts, Ctrl+1 and Ctrl+2, corresponding to Miami and Coral Springs, respectively. Figure 8.5b displays the ***Click event*** procedure for the shortcut button on the data entry form (which was shown in Figure 8.1). The user clicks the button, and a message is displayed that describes the shortcuts. The latter is very important because the system must communicate the availability of the shortcuts to the user, else how is he or she to know that they exist?

KeyCode argument

SetFocus method

```
Private Sub Form_KeyDown(KeyCode As Integer, Shift As Integer)
'The Key Preview Property of the form must be set to Yes
    If KeyCode = vbKey1 And Shift = acCtrlMask Then 'Ctrl+1 was pressed
        City = "Miami"
        State = "FL"
        PostalCode = "33124"
        CampusPhone.SetFocus
    End If
    If KeyCode = vbKey2 And Shift = acCtrlMask Then 'Ctrl+2 was pressed
        City = "Coral Springs"
        State = "FL"
        PostalCode = "33071"
        CampusPhone.SetFocus
    End If
End Sub
```

(a) Form KeyDown Event Procedure

MsgBox function

```
Private Sub ShortCutButton_Click()
    MsgBox "Ctrl+1 has been created as a shorcut to enter " & _
        "Miami, FL 33124. Use Ctrl+2 to enter similar data for " & _
        "Coral Springs, FL 33071.", vbInformation, _
        "Grauer/Barber Introduction to VBA"
End Sub
```

(b) ShortCutButton Click Event Procedure

FIGURE 8.5 *Procedure for Exercise 2*

Consider now the event procedure in Figure 8.5a and think about what it takes to implement a keyboard shortcut. In essence, the procedure must determine whether the user has used any of the existing shortcuts, and if so, enter the appropriate values in the form. There are different ways to accomplish this, the easiest being through a series of If statements, each of which checks for a specific shortcut. In other words, check to see if the user pressed Ctrl+1, and if so, enter the appropriate data. Then check to see if the user pressed Ctrl+2, etc. (If you have a previous background in programming, you may recognize alternate ways to implement this logic, either through the Else clause in the If statement, or through a Case statement. We explore these alternate structures later in the chapter, but for the time being, we want to keep our statements as simple as possible.)

Once again, we ask that you try to gain an overall appreciation for the procedure, as opposed to concerning yourself with every detail in every statement. You should recognize, for example, that the KeyDown event procedure requires two arguments, KeyCode and Shift, as can be seen from the parenthetical information in the *procedure header*. (The procedure header is created automatically as you shall see in the following hands-on exercise.)

The *KeyCode argument* tests for a specific number or letter; for example, KeyCode = vbKey1 determines whether the number 1 has been pressed by the user. (VBA defines several intrinsic constants such as vbKey1 or vbKeyA corresponding to the number 1 and letter A, respectively.) In similar fashion, the Shift argument tests for the Ctrl, Shift, or Alt key by checking for the intrinsic constants acCtrlMask, acShiftMask, and acAltMask, respectively. The And operator ensures that both keys (Ctrl and the number 1) have been pressed simultaneously.

Once a determination has been made as to whether a shortcut has been used, the corresponding values are moved to the indicated controls (City, State, and PostalCode) on the form. The *SetFocus method* then moves the insertion point to the CampusPhone control, where the user can continue to enter data into the form.

The Click event procedure in Figure 8.5b contains a single MsgBox statement which displays information about the shortcuts to the user when he or she clicks the Shortcuts button. The MsgBox statement has three parameters—a literal that is continued over two lines containing the text of the message, an intrinsic constant (vbInformation) indicating the icon that is to be displayed with the message, and a second literal indicating the text that is to appear in the title bar of the message dialog box.

The statement is straightforward, but it does illustrate the rules for continuing a VBA statement from one line to the next. To continue a statement, leave a space at the end of the line to be continued, type the underscore character, then continue the statement on the next line. You may not, however, break a line in the middle of a character string. Thus you need to complete the character string with a closing quotation mark, add an ampersand (as the concatenation operator to display this string with the character string on the next line), then leave a space followed by the underscore to indicate continuation.

BUILD CODE BY OBSERVATION AND INFERENCE

VBA is a powerful language with a subtle syntax and an almost endless variety of intrinsic constants. The expertise required to build the procedures for the keyboard shortcuts is beyond the novice, but once you are given the basic code, it is relatively easy to extend or modify the code to accommodate a specific application. Look at the code in Figure 8.5, for example, and decide how you would change the existing Ctrl+1 keyboard shortcut to reflect a different city. Can you add a third If statement to create a Ctrl+3 shortcut for a new city?

FACILITATING DATA ENTRY

Objective   Create keyboard shortcuts to facilitate data entry. Use Figure 8.6 as a guide in the exercise.

Step 1:   **Create the KeyDown Event Procedure**

> ➤ Open the **Introduction to VBA database** from the previous exercise. Click the **Forms button**, then open the **Completed Student Form** in Design view.
> ➤ Pull down the **View menu** and click **Code** (or click the **Code button** on the Database toolbar).
> ➤ If necessary, pull down the **View menu** and click **Project Explorer** to display the Project Explorer pane at the left of the window. If you are in Full Module view, click within any procedure, then click the **Procedure View button**.
> ➤ Click the **down arrow** in the Event list box and select **Form**.
> ➤ Click the **down arrow** in the Procedure list box to display the list of events for the form. Click **KeyDown** to create a procedure for this event.

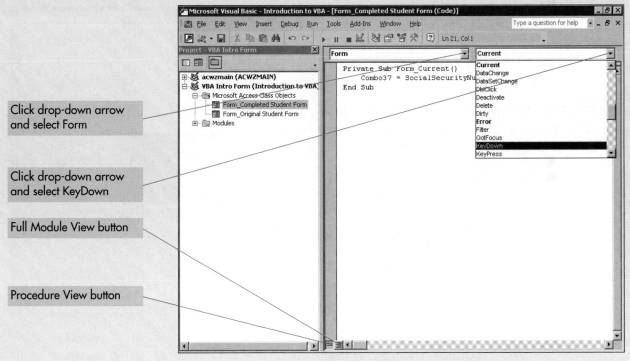

Click drop-down arrow and select Form

Click drop-down arrow and select KeyDown

Full Module View button

Procedure View button

(a) Create the KeyDown Event Procedure (step 1)

FIGURE 8.6   *Hands-on Exercise 2*

PROCEDURE VIEW VERSUS FULL MODULE VIEW

Procedures can be displayed individually, or multiple procedures can be viewed simultaneously. Click the Procedure View button to display one procedure, or click the Full Module View button to show multiple procedures. Either way, you can press Ctrl+PgDn and Ctrl+PgUp to move between procedures in the Module window.

Step 2: **Correct the Compile Error**

➤ The Procedure header and End Sub statements for the KeyDown event procedure are created automatically as shown in Figure 8.6b. The insertion point is positioned on the blank line between these two statements.

➤ Type an **apostrophe** (to indicate a comment), then enter the text of the comment as shown in the figure. Press **enter** when you have completed the comment. The line turns green to indicate it is a comment.

➤ Press the **Tab key** to indent the first line of code, then enter the statement exactly as it appears in the figure. Press **enter**. You should see the error message because we made a (deliberate) error in the If statement to illustrate what happens when you make an error.

➤ Click **OK** if you know the reason for the error, or click **Help** to display a screen describing the error, then close the Help window.

➤ Now return to the VBA statement, type a space at the end of the line, and add the key word **Then** to correct the error. Press **enter** to complete the statement. The error message should not appear.

Click to close Project Explorer window

Enter comment

Enter first line of code

Message indicating a compilation error

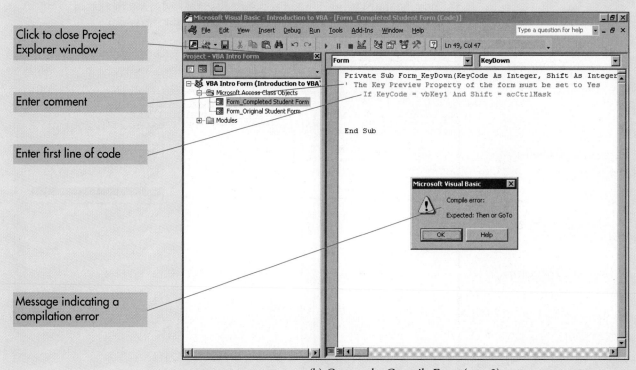

(b) Correct the Compile Error (step 2)

FIGURE 8.6 *Hands-on Exercise 2 (continued)*

RED, GREEN, AND BLUE

Visual Basic for Applications uses different colors for different types of statements (or a portion of those statements). Any statement containing a syntax error appears in red. Comments appear in green. Key words, such as Sub and End Sub, appear in blue.

Step 3: **Complete the KeyDown Event Procedure**

➤ Close the Project Explorer window and complete the KeyDown procedure as shown in Figure 8.6c. Use what you know about the Cut, Copy, and Paste commands to facilitate entering the code.

➤ You could, for example, copy the first If statement, then modify the code as appropriate, rather then typing it from scratch. Select the statements to cut or copy to the clipboard, then paste them elsewhere in the module.

➤ If the results are different from what you expected or intended, click the Undo command immediately to reverse the effects of the previous command.

➤ Be sure that your code matches the code in Figure 8.6c. The indentation is not a syntactical requirement of VBA, per se, but is used to make the statements easier to read.

➤ Click the **Save button** to save the module.

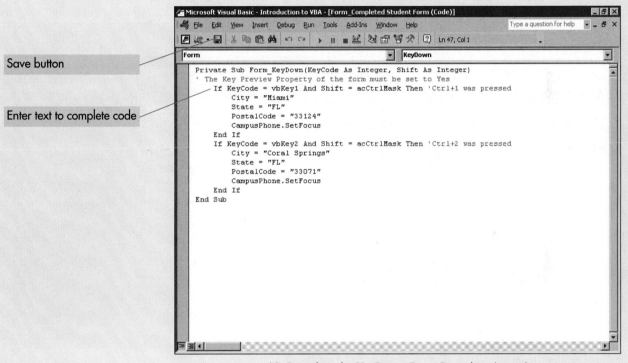

(c) Complete the KeyDown Event Procedure (step 3)

FIGURE 8.6 *Hands-on Exercise 2 (continued)*

THE COMPLETE WORD TOOL

You know that your form contains a control to reference the postal code, but you are not quite sure of the spelling. The Complete Word tool can help. Enter the first several characters, then press Ctrl+Space (or pull down the Edit menu and click Complete Word). VBA will complete the term for you if you have entered a sufficient number of letters, or it will display all of the objects, properties, and methods that begin with the letters you have entered. Use the down arrow to scroll through the list until you find the item, then press the space bar to complete the entry.

Step 4: **Set the Key Preview Property**

➤ The Key Preview property of the form must be set to Yes to complete the keyboard shortcut. Click the taskbar button to return to the **Completed Student Form**.

➤ Point to the **form selector box** (the tiny square at the upper left of the form). Click the **right mouse button** to display a context-sensitive menu with commands for the entire form.

➤ Click **Properties** to display the Form Properties dialog box. Click the **Event tab** and scroll until you can click the **Key Preview property**. Change the property to **Yes** as shown in Figure 8.6d.

➤ Close the Form Property dialog box. Save the form, which now contains the new procedure for the keyboard shortcut. The procedure should be tested as soon as it completed.

➤ Click the **View button** on the Form Design toolbar to return to Form view.

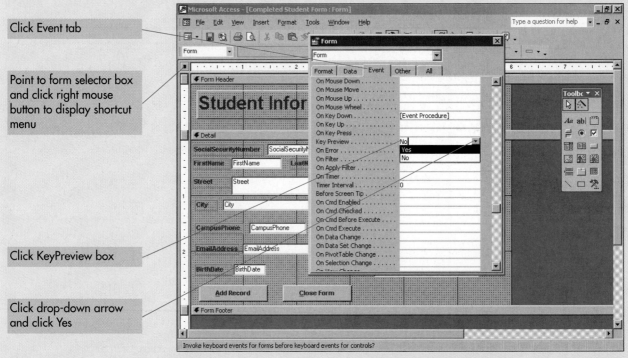

Click Event tab

Point to form selector box and click right mouse button to display shortcut menu

Click KeyPreview box

Click drop-down arrow and click Yes

(d) Set the Key Preview Property (step 4)

FIGURE 8.6 *Hands-on Exercise 2 (continued)*

USE THE PROPERTY SHEET

Every object on a form has its own property sheet. This enables you to change the appearance or behavior of a control in two ways—by changing the control through application of a menu command or toolbar button, or by changing the underlying property sheet. Anything you do to the control changes the associated property, and conversely, any change to the property sheet is reflected in the appearance or behavior of the control.

Step 5: **Test the Procedure**

➤ Click the **navigation button** to move to the first record in the table as shown in Figure 8.6e. Press **Ctrl+2** to change the City, State, and Postal Code to reflect Coral Springs, as per the shortcut you just created.

➤ The data changes automatically, and you are automatically positioned on the CampusPhone field. The record selector changes to a pencil to indicate that the data has been edited, but not yet saved.

➤ If the shortcut does not work, return to step 4 and check that the Key Preview property has been set to Yes. If the shortcut still does not work, return to the module for the form and check the VBA statements.

➤ Press **Ctrl+1** to change the city to Miami. The data should change automatically, after which you are positioned in the CampusPhone field.

➤ Click the **View button** to return to the Design view of the form.

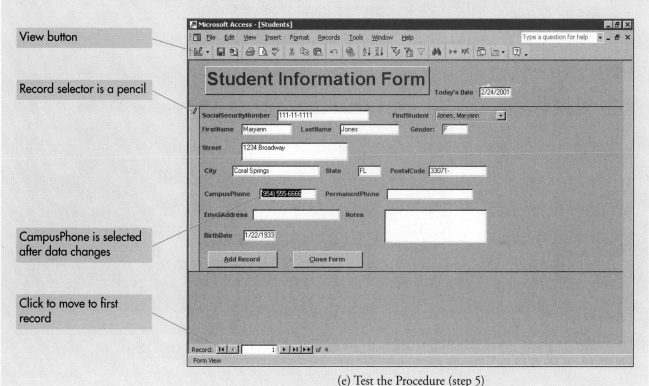

(e) Test the Procedure (step 5)

FIGURE 8.6 *Hands-on Exercise 2 (continued)*

CHANGE THE TAB ORDER

The Tab key provides a shortcut in the finished form to move from one field to the next; that is, you press Tab to move forward to the next field and Shift+Tab to return to the previous field. The order in which fields are selected corresponds to the sequence in which the controls were entered onto the form, and need not correspond to the physical appearance of the actual form. To restore a left-to-right, top-to-bottom sequence, pull down the View menu, click Tab Order, then select AutoOrder.

Step 6:   **Create the ShortCut Command Button**

➤ Click and drag the **Command Button** tool on the Toolbox toolbar to create a new command button as shown in Figure 8.6f.
➤ The Command Button Wizard starts automatically. This time, however, you want to create the Click event procedure for this button yourself.
➤ Click the **Cancel button** as soon as you see the wizard. Right click the newly created command button and display its property sheet. Click the **All tab**.
➤ Change the Name property to **ShortCutButton**. Change the Caption property to **&ShortCuts**.
➤ Click the **Event tab**. Click the **On Click property**, click the **Build button**, click **Code Builder**, then click **OK** to display the Module window.

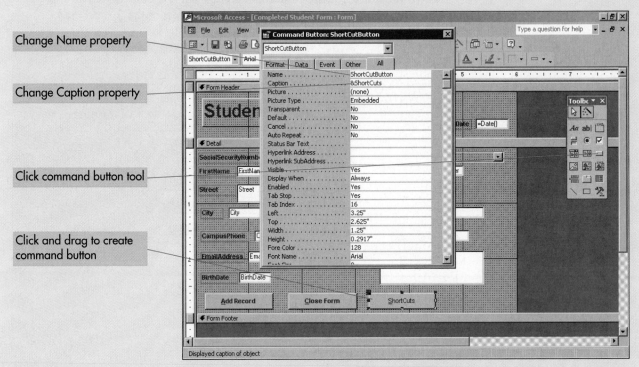

Change Name property

Change Caption property

Click command button tool

Click and drag to create command button

(f) Create the ShortCut Command Button (step 6)

FIGURE 8.6   *Hands-on Exercise 2 (continued)*

ACCELERATOR KEYS AND THE CAPTION PROPERTY

The Caption property enables you to create a keyboard shortcut for a command button. Right click the button in the Form Design view to display the Properties dialog box for the command button. Click the All tab, then modify the Caption property to include an ampersand immediately in front of the letter that will be used in the shortcut (e.g., &Help if you have a Help button). Close the dialog box, then go to Form view. The command button will contain an underlined letter (e.g., Help) that can be activated in conjunction with the Alt key (e.g., Alt+H) as a shortcut or accelerator key.

Step 7: **Create the OnClick Procedure**

➤ You should be positioned on the blank line in the ShortCutButton_Click procedure, as shown in Figure 8.6g. Press the **Tab key** to indent, then enter the VBA statement exactly as it is shown in the figure. Note the following:

- A tip (known as "Quick Info") appears as soon as you type the left parenthesis after the MsgBox function. The tip displays the syntax of the function and lists its arguments.
- Indentation is not a requirement of VBA per se, but is done to make the VBA code easier to read. Continuation is also optional and is done to make the code easier to read.

➤ Complete the statement exactly as shown in the figure, except substitute your name for Grauer/Barber. Click the **Save button**. Close the Module window.

➤ Return to the Access Design view. Close the property sheet. Size and align the new button. Save the form.

➤ Click the **View button** to change to Form view.

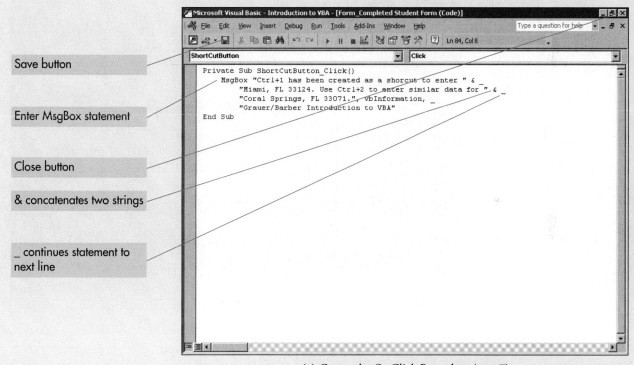

(g) Create the OnClick Procedure (step 7)

FIGURE 8.6 *Hands-on Exercise 2 (continued)*

THE MSGBOX STATEMENT

The MsgBox statement has three parameters—the text of the message to be displayed, the number of buttons and type of message, and the text that appears on the title bar. The message itself is divided into multiple character strings, which continue from one line to the next. The ampersand concatenates the two character strings to display a single message. The underscore character indicates that the statement is continued to the next line.

Step 8: **Test the ShortCuts Button**

➤ Click the **ShortCuts button.** You can also use the keyboard shortcut, **Alt+S**, as indicated by the underlined letter on the button name that was established through the Caption property for the button.

➤ You should see the message box that is displayed in Figure 8.6h. Your name should appear in the title bar of the dialog box rather than ours. Click **OK** to close the dialog box.

➤ Try the other shortcuts that have been built into the form. Press **Ctrl+1** and **Ctrl+2** to switch back and forth between Miami and Coral Springs, respectively. Press **Alt+C** to close the form. Not everyone prefers the keyboard to the mouse, but you have nonetheless created a powerful set of shortcuts.

➤ Exit Access if you do not want to continue with the next exercise at this time.

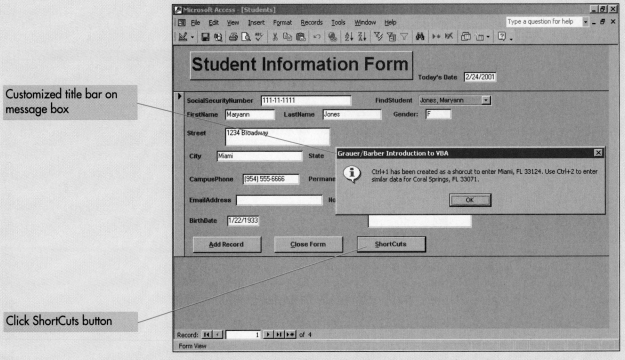

Customized title bar on message box

Click ShortCuts button

(h) Test the ShortCuts Button (step 8)

FIGURE 8.6 *Hands-on Exercise 2 (continued)*

CREATE UNIFORM COMMAND BUTTONS

A form is made more appealing if all of its command buttons have similar properties. Change to Design view, then press and hold the Shift key as you select each of the command buttons. Pull down the Format menu, click Size, then choose the desired parameters for all of the buttons such as widest and tallest. (You have to execute the command once for each parameter.) Leave the buttons selected, pull down the Format menu, select the Align command, then choose the desired alignment. Pull down the Format menu a final time, select the Horizontal Spacing command, then implement the desired (e.g., uniform) spacing for the buttons.

It is not a question of whether errors in data entry will occur, but rather how quickly a user will understand the nature of those errors in order to take the appropriate corrective action. If, for example, a user attempts to add a duplicate record for an existing customer, Access will display an error message of the form, "changes to the table were not successful because they would create duplicate values of the primary key." The issue is whether this message is clear to the nontechnical individual who is doing the data entry.

An experienced Access programmer will realize immediately that Access is preventing the addition of the duplicate record because another record with the same primary key (e.g., a Social Security or account number) is already in the file. A nontechnical user, however, may not understand the message because he or she does not know the meaning of "primary key." Wouldn't it be easier if the system displayed a message indicating that a customer with that Social Security or account number is already in the file? In other words, errors invariably occur, but it is important that the message the user sees clearly indicates the problem.

Figure 8.7 displays the event procedure that is developed in the next hands-on exercise to display application-specific error messages in place of the standard messages provided by Access. The procedure is triggered any time there is an error in data entry. Realize, however, that there are literally hundreds of errors, and it is necessary to test for each error for which we want a substitute message. Each error has a unique error number, and thus the first task is to determine the number associated for the error you want to detect. This is accomplished by forcing the error to occur, then printing the error number in the *Immediate window* (a special window within the VBA editor that enables you to display results of a procedure as it is executing). It's easier than it sounds, as you will see in the hands-on exercise.

Once you know the error numbers, you can complete the procedure by checking for the errors that you wish to trap, then displaying the appropriate error messages. One way to implement this logic is through a series of individual If statements, with one *If statement* for each error. It is more efficient, however, to use a Case statement as shown in Figure 8.7.

The *Case statement* tests the value of an incoming variable (DataErr in our example, which contains the error number), then goes to the appropriate set of statements, depending on the value of that variable. Our procedure tests for two errors, but it could be easily expanded to check for additional errors. Error 2237 occurs if the user attempts to find a record that is not in the table. Error 3022 results when the user attempts to add a duplicate record. Once an error is detected, the MsgBox statement is used to display the error message we create, after which Access will continue processing without displaying the default error message.

Note, too, the last case (Else), which is executed when Access detects an error other than 2237 or 3022. This time we do not display our own message because we do not know the nature of the error. Instead we set the Response variable to the intrinsic constant acDataErrContinue, which causes Access to display the default error message for the error that occurred.

Figure 8.7b displays the *General Declarations section,* which contains statements that apply to every procedure in the form. The section defines the constant ApplicationName as a string and sets it to the literal value "John Doe did his homework." Note, too, how the two MsgBox statements in Figure 8.7a reference this constant as the third argument, and recall that this argument contains the text that is displayed on the title bar of the message box. In other words, we can change the value of the ApplicationName constant in one place, and have that change reflected automatically in every MsgBox function.

Error numbers

MsgBox statement
displays an
improved error
message

```
Private Sub Form_Error(DataErr As Integer, Response As Integer)
' You need to determine the specific error number
'    1. Create the error in Access to determine the error number
'    2. Use the Print method of the Debug object to display the error
'    3. Press Ctrl+G to open the Immediate window

    Debug.Print "Error Number = ", DataErr

    Select Case DataErr
        Case 2237
            MsgBox "The student is not in our file. Please " & _
                "check the spelling and reenter correctly, or click the " & _
                "Add button to enter a new record.", vbExclamation, _
                ApplicationName
            Response = acDataErrContinue
        Case 3022
            MsgBox "You are trying to add a student whose " & _
                "social security number is already in the file. Please " & _
                "correct the social security number or cancel this " & _
                "record and move to the original record.", vbExclamation, _
                ApplicationName
            Response = acDataErrContinue
        Case Else
            Response = acDataErrDisplay
    End Select
End Sub
```

(a) Form Error Event Procedure

ApplicationName
constant

```
Option Compare Database
Option Explicit

Const ApplicationName As String = "John Doe has done his homework"
```

(b) General Declarations Section

FIGURE 8.7   *Procedure for Exercise 3*

THE CASE STATEMENT

The Case statement tests the value of a variable, then branches to one of several sets of statements, depending on the value of that variable. You may not be able to write a Case statement intially, but once you see the statement, you can extend the code to accommodate any application. Look at the code in Figure 8.7, for example, and decide the required modifications to reflect employees rather than students. How would you extend the existing Case statement to include an additional error message?

ERROR TRAPPING

Objective   To create an event procedure that substitutes application-specific messages for the standard Access error messages. Use Figure 8.8 as a guide.

Step 1:   **Force the Error Message**

> Open the **Introduction to VBA database**. If necessary, click the **Forms button**, then open the **Completed Student Form** in Form view.
> Click and drag to select the name in the Find Student combo box. Type **XXXX** (an obviously invalid name). Press **enter**. You should see the error message in Figure 8.8a, which may be confusing to a nontechnical user.
> Click **OK** to close the message box. Press the **Esc key** to erase the XXXX, since we are not interested in finding this student.
> Change to Design view.

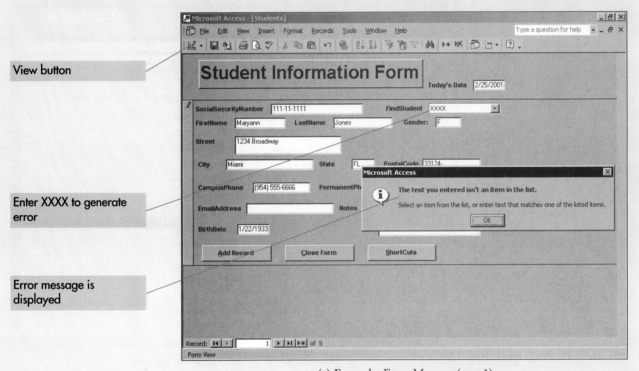

View button

Enter XXXX to generate error

Error message is displayed

(a) Force the Error Message (step 1)

FIGURE 8.8   *Hands-on Exercise 3*

EVENT-DRIVEN VERSUS TRADITIONAL PROGRAMMING

A traditional program is executed sequentially, beginning with the first line of code and continuing in order through the remainder of the program. VBA, however, is event driven, meaning that its procedures are executed when designated events occur. Thus, it is the user, and not the program, who determines which procedures are executed and when. This exercise creates a procedure that will run if specified errors occur during data entry.

Step 2: **Determine the Error Number**

➤ Pull down the **View menu** and click **Code** (or click the **Code button** on the Form Design toolbar) to display the Module window. If necessary, click the **down arrow** for the Object box and select the **Form object**.

➤ Click the **down arrow** in the Procedure box and click **Error** to display the event procedure that will execute when an error occurs in the form. Click the **Procedure View button** as shown in Figure 8.8b.

➤ We created this procedure for you. It consists of a single executable statement, to print a literal, followed by the number of the error. The comments explain how to use the procedure.

➤ Pull down the **View menu** and click **Immediate window** (or press **Ctrl+G**) to open the Immediate window. You should see number 2237.

➤ This is the error number reserved by Access to indicate that the value that was entered in the text portion of a combo box does not match any of the entries in the associated list.

➤ Close the Immediate window.

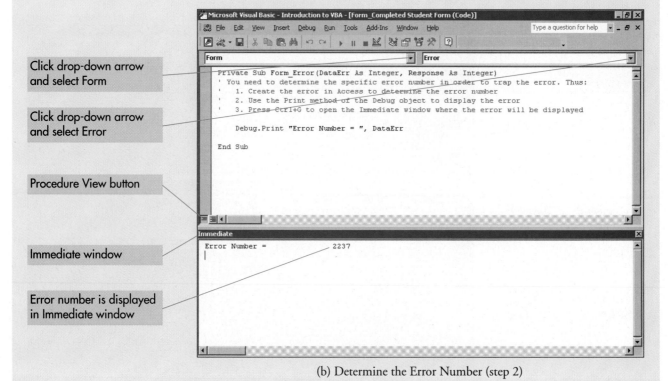

Click drop-down arrow and select Form

Click drop-down arrow and select Error

Procedure View button

Immediate window

Error number is displayed in Immediate window

(b) Determine the Error Number (step 2)

FIGURE 8.8 *Hands-on Exercise 3 (continued)*

INSTANT CALCULATOR

Use the Print method (action) in the Immediate window to use VBA as a calculator. Press Ctrl+G at any time to display the Immediate window. Type the statement Debug.Print, followed by your calculation, for example, Debug.Print 2+2, then press enter. The answer is displayed on the next line in the Immediate window.

Step 3:   **Trap the First Error**

➤ Click in the event procedure at the end of the Debug statement, press the **enter key** twice, then enter the VBA statements in Figure 8.8c. Note the following:
  • Comments appear at the beginning of the procedure.
  • The Case statement tests the value of an incoming variable (DataErr), then goes to the appropriate set of statements, depending on the value of that variable. The procedure currently tests for only one error, but it will be expanded later in the exercise to check for additional errors.
  • The indentation and blank lines within the procedure are not requirements of VBA per se, but are used to make the code easier to read.
  • A "Quick Info" tip appears as soon as you type the space after MsgBox. The tip displays the syntax of the statement.

➤ Complete the statement exactly as shown in Figure 8.8c. Save the procedure.

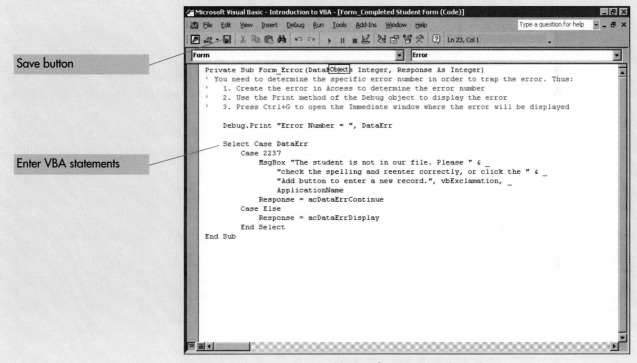

Save button

Enter VBA statements

(c) Trap the First Error (step 3)

FIGURE 8.8   *Hands-on Exercise 3 (continued)*

CONTINUING A VBA STATEMENT—THE & AND THE UNDERSCORE

A VBA statement can be continued from one line to the next by leaving a space at the end of the line to be continued, typing the underscore character, then continuing on the next line. You may not, however, break a line in the middle of a literal (character string). Thus you need to complete the character string with a closing quotation mark, add an ampersand (as the concatenation operator to display this string with the character string on the next line), then leave a space followed by the underscore to indicate continuation.

Step 4: **Test the Error Event Procedure**

➤ Click the taskbar button to return to the **Completed Student Form**. Change to the Form view. Click and drag to select the name in the Find Student combo box. Type **XXXX** (an obviously invalid name). Press **enter**.

➤ This time you should see the error message in Figure 8.8d corresponding to the text you entered in the previous step. (Note the title bar on the dialog box indicating that your name goes here. We tell you how to modify the title bar later in the exercise.)

➤ Click **OK** to close the message box. Press the **Esc key** to erase the XXXX. Return to Design view.

➤ Pull down the **View menu** and click **Code** (or click the **Code button** on the Form Design toolbar) to display the Module window.

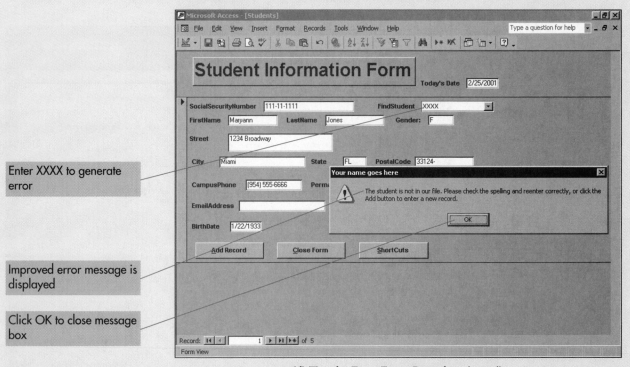

Enter XXXX to generate error

Improved error message is displayed

Click OK to close message box

(d) Test the Error Event Procedure (step 4)

FIGURE 8.8 *Hands-on Exercise 3 (continued)*

THE FIRST BUG

A bug is a mistake in a computer program; hence debugging refers to the process of correcting program errors. According to legend, the first bug was an unlucky moth crushed to death on one of the relays of the electromechanical Mark II computer, bringing the machine's operation to a halt. The cause of the failure was discovered by Grace Hopper, who promptly taped the moth to her logbook, noting, "First actual case of bug being found."

Step 5:   **Change the Application Name**

> Click the **down arrow** for the Object box and select **(General)** at the beginning of the list of objects.
> We have defined the Visual Basic constant **ApplicationName**, and initialized it to "Your name goes here." This was the text that appeared in the title bar of the dialog box in the previous step.
> Click and drag to select **Your name goes here**. Enter **John Doe has done his homework**, substituting your name for John Doe.
> Pull down the **Edit menu**, click the **Find command** to display the Find dialog box. Enter **ApplicationName** in the Find What text box. Specify the option to search the **Current module** and specify **All** as the direction.
> Click the **Find Next command button** to locate all occurrences of the ApplicationName constant. Can you appreciate the significance of this technique to customize your application? Save the procedure.

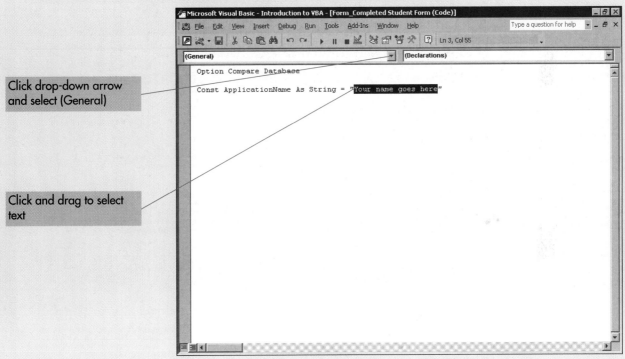

Click drop-down arrow and select (General)

Click and drag to select text

(e) Change the Application Name (step 5)

FIGURE 8.8   *Hands-on Exercise 3 (continued)*

THE MSGBOX STATEMENT—CONSTANTS VERSUS LITERALS

The third parameter in the MsgBox statement can be entered as a literal such as "John Doe's Application." It's preferable, however, to specify the argument as a constant such as ApplicationName, then define that constant in the Declarations section. That way, you can change the name of the application in one place, and have the change automatically reflected in every MsgBox statement that references the constant.

Step 6: **Complete the Error Event Procedure**

➤ Click the **down arrow** for the Object box and select the **Form object**. Click the **down arrow** for the Procedure box and click the **Error procedure**.
➤ Click immediately before the Case Else statement, then enter the additional code shown in Figure 8.8f. Use the Copy and Paste commands to enter the second Case statement. Thus:
  • Click and drag to select the first Case statement, click the **Copy button**, click above the Case Else statement, and click the **Paste button**.
  • Modify the copied statements as necessary, rather than typing the statements from scratch. Use the **Ins key** to toggle between insertion and replacement. Be sure that your code matches ours.
➤ Click the **Save button** to save the procedure. Click the taskbar button to return to the **Completed Student Form**.

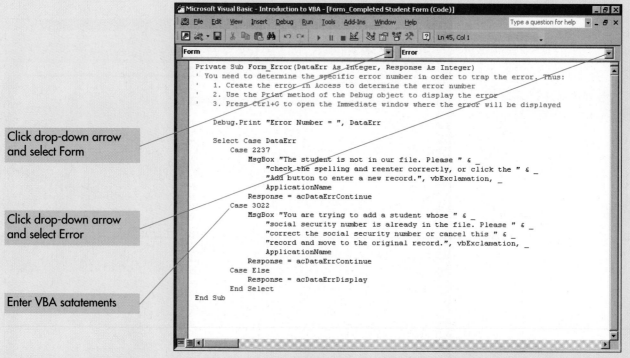

Click drop-down arrow and select Form

Click drop-down arrow and select Error

Enter VBA satatements

(f) Complete the Error Event Procedure (step 6)

FIGURE 8.8 *Hands-on Exercise 3 (continued)*

THE OBJECT AND PROCEDURE BOXES

The Object box at the top left of the Module window displays the current object, such as a form or a control on the form. The Procedure box displays the name of the current procedure for the selected object. To create or navigate between events for a form, click the down arrow on the Object box to select the Form object, then click the down arrow on the Procedure box to display the list of events. Events that already have procedures appear in bold. Clicking an event that is not bold creates the procedure header and End Sub statements for that event.

Step 7: **Complete the Testing**

➤ You should be back in Design view of the Completed Student Form. Pull down the **View menu** and change to the **Datasheet view** as shown in Figure 8.8g. (You can also click the **down arrow** next to the View button on the Form Design view and select Datasheet view.)

➤ Enter **222-22-2222** as a duplicate Social Security number for the first record. Press the **down arrow** (or click the appropriate **navigation button**) to attempt to move to the next record.

➤ You should see the error message in Figure 8.8g. The title bar displays the value of the application name entered earlier in the exercise.

➤ Click **OK** (or press **Esc**) to close the dialog box. Press **Esc** a second time to restore the original value of the Social Security number. Close the window.

➤ Exit Access if you do not want to continue with the next exercise at this time.

View button

Enter 222-22-2222
(duplicate Social Security
number)

Title bar displays
application name

Improved error message is
displayed

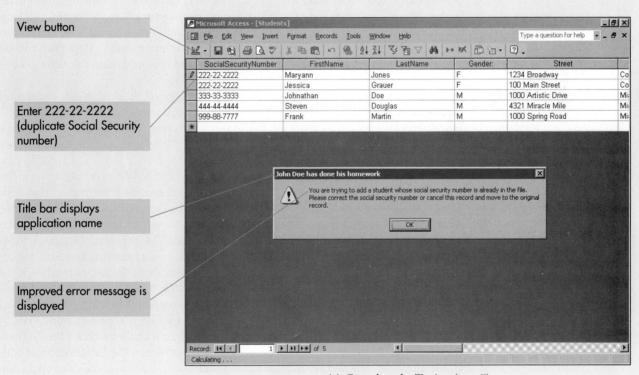

(g) Complete the Testing (step 7)

FIGURE 8.8   *Hands-on Exercise 3 (continued)*

LISTEN TO YOUR USER

One source of continual frustration to the end user is error messages steeped in technical jargon. What's obvious to you as a developer or student is often beyond the unsophisticated end user. Thus, anything that you can do to simplify a system will increase its chances for success. Listen to your users. Find out where they are having trouble and what they don't understand, then act accordingly.

Data validation is a crucial component of any system. The most basic type of validation is implemented automatically, without any additional effort on the part of the developer. A user cannot, for example, enter data that does not conform to the designated field type. The user cannot enter text into a numeric field, nor can one enter an invalid date—such as February 30—into a date field. Access also prevents you from entering a duplicate record (i.e., a record with the same primary key as another record).

Other validation checks are implemented by the developer, at either the field or record level. The former performs the validation as soon as you move from one field to the next within a table or form. The latter waits until all of the fields have been completed, then checks the entire record prior to updating the record. Both types of validation are essential to prevent invalid data from corrupting the system.

The developer can also use VBA to extend the data validation capabilities within Access. You can, for example, write an event procedure to remind the user that a field is empty and ask whether the record should be saved anyway. The field is not required and hence the Required property is not appropriate. However, you do not want to ignore the omitted field completely, and thus you need to create a VBA procedure.

The VBA code in Figure 8.9 implements this type of check through a *nested If statement* in which one If statement is contained inside another. The second (inner) If statement is executed only if the first statement is true. Thus, we first check to see whether the e-mail address has been omitted, and if it has, we ask the user whether he or she wants to save the record anyway.

The outer If statement in Figure 8.9, *If IsNull (EmailAddress),* checks to see if the e-mail address is blank, and if it is, it executes the second If statement that contains a MsgBox function, as opposed to a simple MsgBox statement. The difference between the two is that the MsgBox function displays a prompt to the user, then returns a value (such as which button a user clicked). A MsgBox statement, however, simply displays a message. MsgBox, when used as a function, requires parentheses around the arguments. MsgBox, as a statement, does not use parentheses.

Look carefully at the second argument, *vbYesNo + vbQuestion* within Figure 8.9. The intrinsic constant vbYesNo displays two command buttons (Yes and No) within the message box. The If in front of the message box function enables VBA to test the user's response and branch accordingly. Thus, if the user clicks the No button, the save operation is cancelled and the focus moves to the EmailAddress control in the form, where the user enters the address. If, however, the user clicks the Yes button, the If statement is false, and the record is saved without the e-mail address.

Nested If statement

Displays Yes and No buttons with message to user

```
Private Sub Form_BeforeUpdate(Cancel As Integer)
    If IsNull(EmailAddress) Then
        If MsgBox("You did not enter an e-mail address. Save anyway?", _
            vbYesNo + vbQuestion, ApplicationName) = vbNo Then
            Cancel = True
            EmailAddress.SetFocus
        End If
    End If
End Sub
```

FIGURE 8.9 *Procedure for Exercise 4*

DATA VALIDATION

Objective   To use Field and Table properties to implement different types of data validation. Use Figure 8.10 as a guide in the exercise.

Step 1:   **Set the Field Properties**

> ➤ Open the **Introduction to VBA database**. Click the **Tables button**, then open the **Students table** in Design view as shown in Figure 8.10a.
> ➤ Click the field selector column for the **Gender**. Click the **Validation Rule** box. Type **="M" or "F"** to accept only these values on data entry.
> ➤ Click the **Validation Text** box. Type **Please enter either M or F as the gender**.
> ➤ Click the **Required property** and change its value to **Yes**.

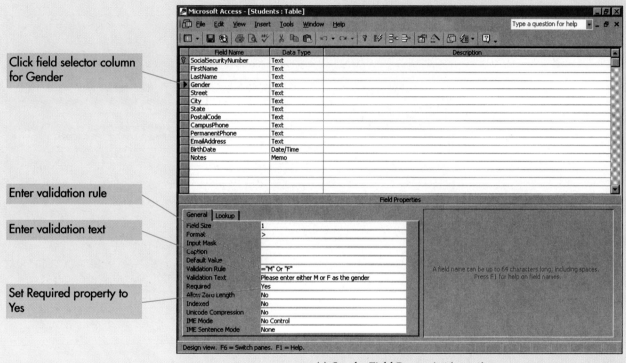

Click field selector column for Gender

Enter validation rule

Enter validation text

Set Required property to Yes

(a) Set the Field Properties (step 1)

FIGURE 8.10   *Hands-on Exercise 4*

OPTIMIZE DATA TYPES AND FIELD SIZES

The data type property determines the data that can be accepted into a field and the operations that can be performed on that data. Any field that is intended for use in a calculation should be given the numeric data type. You can, however, increase the efficiency of an Access database by specifying the appropriate value for the Field Size property of a numeric field. The Byte, Integer, and Long Integer field sizes hold values up to 256, 32,767, and 2,147,483,648, respectively.

Step 2: **Set the Table Properties**

➤ Point to the **selector** box in the upper-left corner, then click the **right mouse button** and display the Table Properties dialog box as shown in Figure 8.10b.

➤ Click in the **Validation Rule** box and enter **[CampusPhone] Is Not Null Or [PermanentPhone] Is Not Null** to ensure that the user enters one phone number or the other. (The field names should not contain any spaces and are enclosed in square brackets.)

➤ Press **enter**, then type, **You must enter either a campus or permanent phone number** (which is the validation text that will be displayed in the event of an error).

➤ Click the **Save button** to save the table. Click **No** when you see the message asking whether existing data should be tested against the new rules.

➤ Close the Table Properties dialog box. Close the Students table.

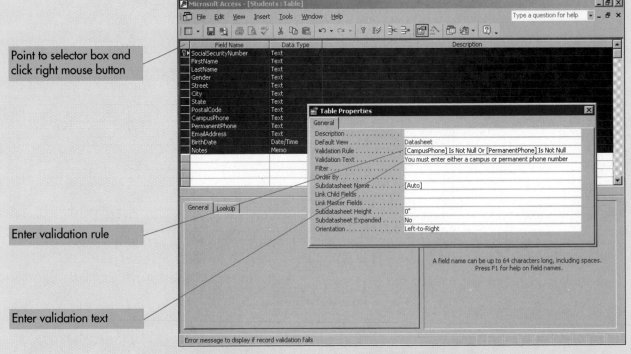

(b) Set the Table Properties (step 2)

FIGURE 8.10 *Hands-on Exercise 4 (continued)*

DAY PHONE OR PERMANENT PHONE

You can set the required property of a field to force the user to enter data for that field. But what if you wanted the user to enter one of two fields and were indifferent to which field was chosen? Setting the Required property of either or both fields would not accomplish your goal. Thus, you need to implement this type of validation at the record (rather than the field) level by setting the properties of the table as a whole, rather than the properties of the individual fields.

Step 3: **Test the Validation Rules**

➤ Open the **Completed Student Form** in Form view. If necessary, move to Maryann Jones, the first record in the table.

➤ Click and drag to select the gender field, then type **X** to replace the gender. Press **enter**. You will see an error message pertaining to the gender field.

➤ Press **Esc** (or click **OK**) to close the dialog box. Press **Esc** a second time to restore the original value.

➤ Click and drag to select the existing CampusPhone number, then press the **Del key** to erase the phone number. Press the **Tab key** to move to the PermanentPhone field. Both phone numbers should be blank.

➤ Click the ▶ **button** to move to the next record. You should see the error message in Figure 8.10c pertaining to the table properties.

➤ Press **Esc** (or click **OK**) to close the dialog box. Press **Esc** a second time to restore the original value.

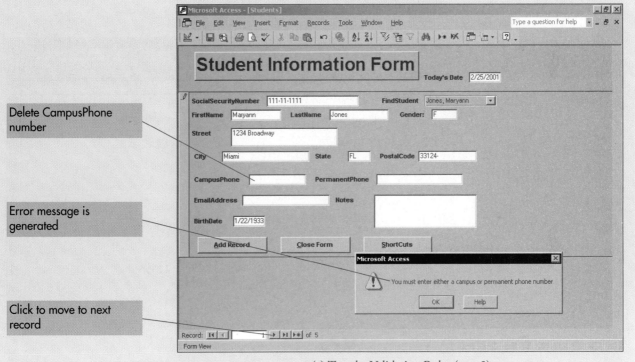

Delete CampusPhone number

Error message is generated

Click to move to next record

(c) Test the Validation Rules (step 3)

FIGURE 8.10   *Hands-on Exercise 4 (continued)*

VALIDATING AT THE FIELD VERSUS THE RECORD LEVEL

Data validation is performed at the field or record level. If it is done at the field level (e.g., by specifying the Required and Validation Rule properties for a specific field), Access checks the entry immediately as soon as you exit the field. If it is done at the record level, however (e.g., by checking that one of two fields has been entered), Access has to wait until it has processed every field in the record. Thus, it is only on attempting to move to the next record that Access informs you of the error.

Step 4: **Create the BeforeUpdate Event Procedure**

➤ Change to the Form Design view. Pull down the **View menu** and click **Code** (or click the **Code button**) on the Form Design toolbar. If necessary, click the **Procedure view button** to view one procedure at a time.

➤ Click the **down arrow** on the Objects list box and click **Form**. Click the **down arrow** on the Procedure list box to display the list of events for the form. Click **BeforeUpdate** to create a procedure for this event.

➤ Press the **Tab key** to indent, then enter the statements exactly as shown in Figure 8.10d. Note that as soon as you enter "EmailAddress," Access displays the methods and properties for the EmailAddress control.

➤ Type **set** (the first three letters in the SetFocus method), watching the screen as you enter each letter. Access moves through the displayed list automatically, until it arrives at the **SetFocus method**. Press **enter**.

➤ Add an **End If** statement to complete the If statement testing the MsgBox function. Press **enter**, then enter a second **End If** statement to complete the If statement testing the IsNull condition. Save the procedure.

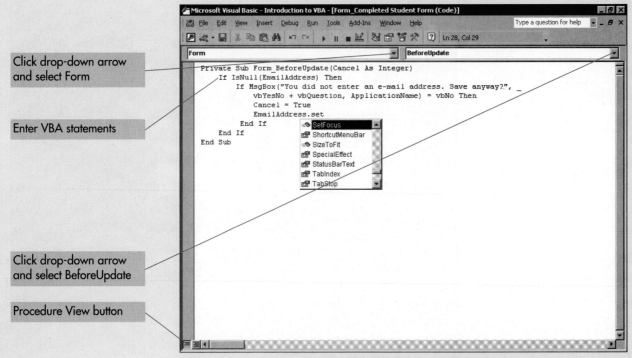

Click drop-down arrow and select Form

Enter VBA statements

Click drop-down arrow and select BeforeUpdate

Procedure View button

(d) Create the BeforeUpdate Event Procedure (step 4)

FIGURE 8.10   *Hands-on Exercise 4 (continued)*

AUTOLIST MEMBERS—HELP IN WRITING CODE

Access displays the methods and properties for a control as soon as you enter the period after the control name. Type the first several letters to select the method or property. Press the space bar to accept the selected item and remain on the same line, or press the enter key to accept the item and begin a new line.

Step 5: **Test the BeforeUpdate Event Procedure**

➤ Click the taskbar button for the Access form. Change to the **Form view**. Click in the **memo field** and enter the text shown in Figure 8.10e.
➤ Check the remaining fields, but be sure to leave the e-mail address blank. Click the navigation button to (attempt to) move to the next record.
➤ You should see the error message in Figure 8.10e. Note the entry in the title bar that corresponds to the value of the ApplicationName constant you entered earlier.
➤ Click **No** to cancel the operation, close the dialog box, and automatically position the insertion point within the text box for the e-mail address.
➤ Enter an e-mail address such as **mjones@anyschool.edu**, then move to the next record. This time Access does not display the error message and saves the record.

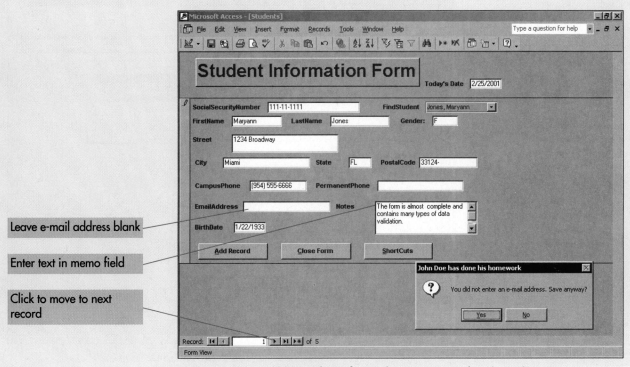

Leave e-mail address blank

Enter text in memo field

Click to move to next record

(e) Test the BeforeUpdate Event Procedure (step 5)

FIGURE 8.10 *Hands-on Exercise 4 (continued)*

MEMO FIELDS VERSUS TEXT FIELDS

A text field can store up to 255 characters. A memo field, however, can store up to 64,000 characters and is used to hold descriptive data that runs for several sentences, paragraphs, or even pages. A vertical scroll bar appears in the Form view when the memo field contains more data than is visible at one time. Note, too, that both text and memo fields store only the characters that have been entered; that is, there is no wasted space if the data does not extend to the maximum field size.

Step 6: **Create the CloseForm Event Procedure**

➤ Change to the Form Design view, then click the **Code button** on the Form Design toolbar to display the Module window. If necessary, click the **Object** box to select Form, then click the **Procedure box** to select the **Close event**.

➤ You should see the partially completed event procedure in Figure 8.10f. Press **Tab** to indent the statement, then enter **MsgBox** followed by a blank space. The Quick Info feature displays the syntax of this statement.

➤ Complete the message, ending with the closing quotation mark and comma. The AutoList feature displays the list of appropriate arguments. Type **vbc**, at which point you can select the **vbCritical** parameter by typing a **comma**.

➤ Type a **space** followed by an **underscore** to continue the statement to the next line. Enter **ApplicationName** as the last parameter. Save the module.

Click drop-down arrow and select Form

Enter MsgBox statement

QuickInfo feature displays syntax

Enter vbc, the first letters in vbCritical

Click drop-down arrow and select Close

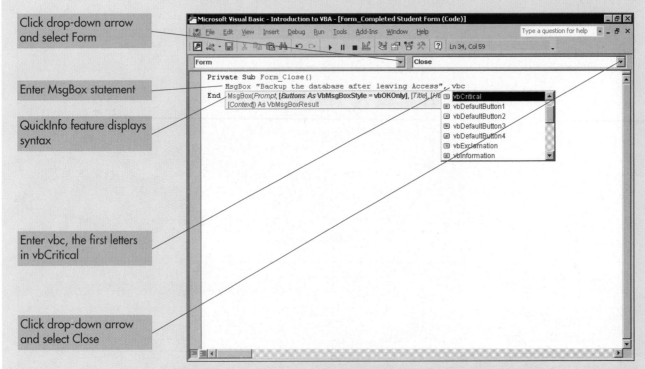

(f) Create the CloseForm Event Procedure (step 6)

FIGURE 8.10 *Hands-on Exercise 4 (continued)*

CHOOSE THE RIGHT EVENT

We associated the message prompting the user to back up the database with the Close event for the form. Would it work equally well if the message were associated with the Click event of the Close Form command button? The answer is no, because the user could bypass the command button and close the form by pulling down the File menu and choosing the Close command, and thus never see the message. Choosing the right object and associated event is one of the subtleties in VBA.

Step 7: **Close the Form**

> ➤ Click the **Access form button** on the taskbar. Return to Form view. The form looks very similar to the form with which we began, but it has been enhanced in subtle ways:
>   - The drop-down list box has been added to locate a specific student.
>   - Accelerator keys have been created for the command buttons (e.g., Alt+A to add a record).
>   - The SetFocus property was used to position the insertion point directly in the Social Security text box to add a new record.
>   - The Ctrl+1 and Ctrl+2 keyboard shortcuts have been created.
>   - The data validation has been enhanced through custom error messages.
>   - The application has been customized through the entry on the title bar.
> ➤ Click the **Close Form button** to display the dialog box in Figure 8.10g. Click **OK** to close the dialog box, which in turn closes the form.
> ➤ Close the database. Exit Access. Congratulations on a job well done.

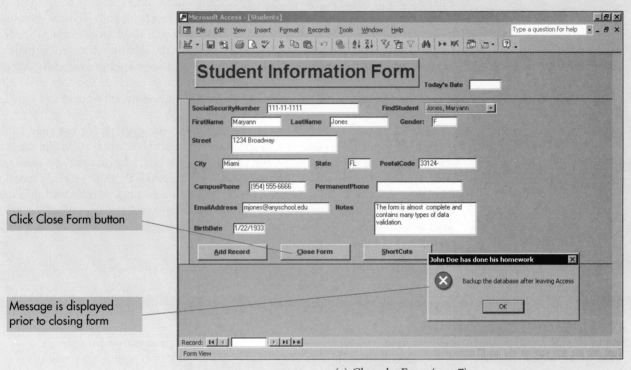

Click Close Form button

Message is displayed prior to closing form

(g) Close the Form (step 7)

FIGURE 8.10 *Hands-on Exercise 4 (continued)*

BACK UP IMPORTANT FILES

It's not a question of if it will happen, but when—hard disks die, files are lost, or viruses may infect a system. It has happened to us and it will happen to you, but you can prepare for the inevitable by creating adequate backup before the problem occurs. Decide which files to back up, how often to do the backup, and where to keep the backup. Do it!

Visual Basic for Applications (VBA) is a subset of Visual Basic that is accessible from every application in Microsoft Office. VBA is different from traditional programming languages in that it is event driven. An event is any action that is recognized by Access. Visual Basic code is developed in units called event procedures that run automatically, in response to an event such as clicking a button or opening a form.

All VBA procedures are stored in modules. Every form in an Access database has its own module that contains the event procedures for that form. All procedures are either public or private. A private procedure is accessible only from within the module in which it is contained. A public procedure is accessible from anywhere. All procedures are displayed and edited in the Module window within Access. Additional procedures can be developed by expanding the existing code through inference and observation.

Several event procedures were created in this chapter to illustrate how VBA can be used to enhance an Access application. Hands-on exercise 1 focused on the Current event to synchronize the displayed record in a form with a combo box used to locate a record by last name. Exercise 2 developed a KeyDown event procedure to facilitate data entry. Exercise 3 developed the Error event to substitute application-specific error messages for the default messages provided by Access. Exercise 4 created a BeforeUpdate event procedure to enhance the data validation for the form. Additional procedures can be developed by expanding the existing code through inference and observation.

The MsgBox statement has three arguments—the prompt (or message to the user), a VBA intrinsic constant that specifies the icon to be displayed within the box, and the text that is to appear on the title bar of the box. MsgBox may be used as a statement or a function. The difference between the two is that the MsgBox function displays a prompt to the user, then returns a value (such as which button a user clicked). A MsgBox statement, however, simply displays a message. MsgBox, when used as a function, requires parentheses around the arguments. MsgBox, as a statement, does not use parentheses.

KEY TERMS

Argument (p. 372)
BeforeUpdate event (p. 404)
Case statement (p. 391)
Class module (p. 371)
Click event (p. 381)
Close Form Event (p. 372)
Complete Word tool (p. 385)
Concalenation (p. 376)
Continuation (p. 395)
Current event (p. 372)
Data validation (p. 400)
Default property (p. 381)
Error trapping (p. 391)

Event (p. 368)
Event procedure (p. 371)
Full Module view (p. 383)
General Declarations section (p. 391)
General procedure (p. 371)
If statement (p. 391)
Immediate window (p. 391)
Intrinsic constant (p. 372)
KeyDown event (p. 381)
Key Preview property (p. 386)
KeyCode argument (p. 382)
Module window (p. 371)

MsgBox statement (p. 372)
Nested If statement (p. 400)
Object box (p. 398)
Parameter (p. 372)
Private procedure (p. 371)
Procedure (p. 368)
Procedure box (p. 398)
Procedure header (p. 382)
Procedure view (p. 383)
Public procedure (p. 371)
SetFocus method (p. 382)
Visual Basic for Applications (VBA) (p. 368)

1. Which of the following applications can be enhanced through VBA?
   (a) Word and Excel
   (b) Access and PowerPoint
   (c) Outlook
   (d) All of the above

2. Which application enhancements are accomplished using VBA event procedures?
   (a) Improved data validation
   (b) Creation of keyboard shortcuts for data entry
   (c) Substitution of customized error messages for the standard messages provided by Access
   (d) All of the above

3. Which of the following is necessary in order to establish a keyboard shortcut to facilitate data entry on a form?
   (a) Create a procedure for the KeyUp event of the form and set the Key Preview property to No
   (b) Create a procedure for the KeyUp event of the form and set the Key Preview property to Yes
   (c) Create a procedure for the KeyDown event of the form and set the Key Preview property to No
   (d) Create a procedure for the KeyDown event of the form and set the Key Preview property to Yes

4. Which of the following characters continues a VBA statement?
   (a) A hyphen
   (b) An underscore
   (c) A hyphen and an ampersand
   (d) An underscore and an ampersand

5. Which of the following types of data validation requires an event procedure?
   (a) Checking that a required field has been entered
   (b) Checking that one of two fields has been entered
   (c) Prompting the user with a message indicating that an optional field has been omitted, and asking for further instruction
   (d) All of the above

6. Which of the following is *not* used to implement a validation check that requires the user to enter a value of Atlanta or Boston for the City field?
   (a) Set the Required property for the City field to Yes
   (b) Set the Validation Rule property for the City field to either "Atlanta" or "Boston"
   (c) Set the Default property for the City field to either "Atlanta" or "Boston"
   (d) Set the Validation Text property for the City field to display an appropriate error message if the user does not enter either Atlanta or Boston

7. Which of the following techniques would you use to require the user to enter either a home phone or a business phone?
   (a) Set the Required property of each field to Yes
   (b) Set the Validation Rule property for each field to true
   (c) Set the Validation Rule for the table to [HomePhone] or [BusinessPhone]
   (d) All of the above are equally acceptable

8. Which is a true statement about the Procedure box in the Module window?
   (a) Events that have procedures appear in bold
   (b) Clicking an event that appears in boldface displays the event procedure
   (c) Clicking an event that is not in bold creates a procedure for that event
   (d) All of the above

9. Which event procedure was created in conjunction with the combo box to locate a record on the form?
   (a) An On Current event procedure for the combo box control
   (b) An On Current event procedure for the form
   (c) A KeyDown event procedure for the combo box control
   (d) A KeyDown event procedure for the form

10. Which event procedure was created to warn the user that the e-mail address was omitted and asking whether the record is to be saved anyway?
    (a) An On Error event procedure for the combo box control
    (b) An On Error event procedure for the form
    (c) A BeforeUpdate event procedure for the e-mail control
    (d) A BeforeUpdate event procedure for the form

11. Which of the following does *not* create an event procedure for a form?
    (a) Display the Properties box for the form in Design View, click the Event tab, select the event, then click the Build button
    (b) Select the form in the Object box of the Module window, then click the event (displayed in regular as opposed to boldface) in the Procedure box
    (c) Pull down the View menu in the Database window and click the code command or click the Code button on the Database toolbar
    (d) All of the above create an event procedure

12. You want to display a message in conjunction with closing a form. Which of the following is the best way to accomplish this?
    (a) Write a VBA procedure for the Close Form event
    (b) Create a Close command button for the form, then write a VBA procedure for the On Click event of the command button to display the message
    (c) Either (a) or (b)
    (d) Neither (a) nor (b)

13. Which of the following is not an Access-intrinsic constant?
    (a) ApplicationName
    (b) vbCritical
    (c) acCtrlMask
    (d) vbKey1

14. What advantage, if any, is gained by using VBA to create a keyboard shortcut to enter the city, state, and zip code in an incoming record, as opposed to using the Default Value property in the table definition?
    (a) It's easier to use VBA than to specify the Default Value property
    (b) The Default Value property cannot be applied to multiple fields for the same record, and thus VBA is the only way to accomplish this task
    (c) VBA can be used to create different shortcuts for different sets of values, whereas the Default Value property is restricted to a single value
    (d) All of the above

15. Which of the following statements was used to display the Error Number associated with an error in data entry?
    (a) Debug.Print "Error Number = "
    (b) Debug.Print "Error Number = ", DataErr
    (c) Print "Error Number = "
    (d) Print "Error Number = ", DataErr

ANSWERS

1. d	**5.** c	**9.** b	**13.** a
2. d	**6.** c	**10.** d	**14.** c
3. d	**7.** c	**11.** c	**15.** b
4. b	**8.** d	**12.** a	

1. MsgBox Examples: VBA is different from Visual Basic in that its procedures must exist within an Office document. Hence, you need to start this exercise by creating a new database to hold the procedures in Figure 8.11. Click the Modules button from within the Database window and click the New button to create a general module (called Module1 by default). This opens the VBA editor as shown in Figure 8.11.

   a. Define a public constant to hold your name. The constant is included as the third parameter in all three MsgBox statements, so that your name will appear in the title bar of the associated dialog boxes.

   b. Create the first procedure, consisting of three simple MsgBox statements, with one, two, and three parameters, respectively. Click the procedure header, then click the Run button on the VBA toolbar to test the procedure. Do you see the effect of each procedure on the associated dialog boxes?

   c. Create the second procedure that uses the MsgBox function to test the value of the user's response by comparing it to the vbYes intrinsic constant. Change the second argument to vbYesNo+vbQuestion and note the effect in the resulting dialog box.

   d. Add the third procedure and test it as well. This procedure includes a statement to exit Access, so you will have to reopen the database to print the completed module.

   e. Pull down the File menu and click the Print command to print the entire module for your instructor.

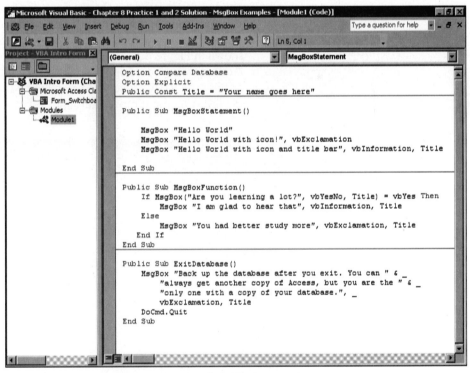

FIGURE 8.11   *MsgBox Examples (Exercise 1)*

BUILDS ON

PRACTICE
EXERCISE 1
PAGE 411

2. MsgBox Example Switchboard: Create a simple switchboard for the database in the previous exercise as shown in Figure 8.12. (The dialog box that you see in the figure appears when you click the MsgBox as a Function button.) Use the Startup property to display the switchboard automatically when the database is opened. Print the switchboard and table of switchboard items.

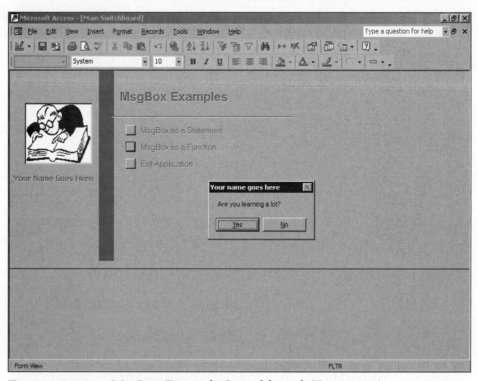

FIGURE 8.12   *MsgBox Example Switchboard (Exercise 2)*

BUILDS ON

HANDS-ON
EXERCISES
1, 2, 3, AND 4

3. Expanded Student Form: Do the four hands-on exercises in the chapter, then
   modify the completed form at the end of the fourth hands-on exercise to:
   a. Include a warning message that prompts the user if birth date is omitted as
      shown in Figure 8.13, and giving the user the option to save the record.
   b. Add a new keyboard shortcut, Ctrl+3, to enter data for New York, NY, 10010.
   c. Modify the VBA procedure associated with the Add Record button, so that
      the insertion point moves automatically to the Social Security control.

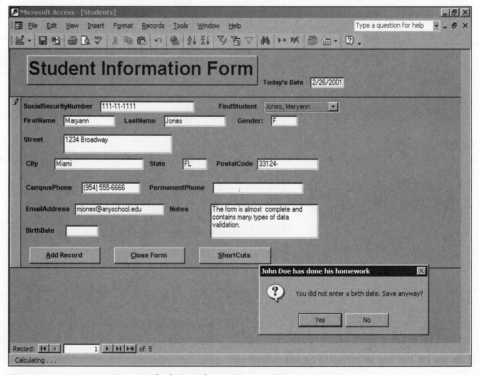

FIGURE 8.13   *Expanded Student Form (Exercise 3)*

BUILDS ON

CHAPTER 7
HANDS-ON EXERCISES
1, 2, AND 3

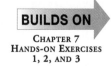

4. Return to Soccer: Figure 8.14 contains a modified version of the Players form that has been enhanced with VBA procedures. Proceed as follows:
   a. Add a combo box to the form to locate a player within the Players table. Create the necessary VBA procedure to update the contents of the combo box when the navigation buttons are used to move to a different record.
   b. Add code to the Add Player button to position the user in the First Name text box after clicking the Add button.
   c. Add a procedure to notify the user if the birth date is omitted, then ask the user if the record is to be saved anyway.
   d. Add a procedure to display a message box asking the user to try out for an all-city team if a player rating of A (upper- or lowercase) is entered.
   e. Create a Ctrl+1 keyboard shortcut to enter Miami, FL, and 33124 in the city, state, and zip code fields, respectively. Create a similar shortcut for Ctrl+2 to enter Coral Springs, FL, and 33071. Remember to set the KeyPreview property to "Yes." Add a shortcut button to display this information.
   f. Print the completed VBA module for the Players form for your instructor.

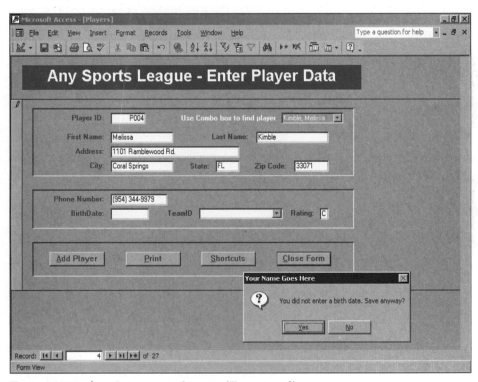

FIGURE 8.14 *Return to Soccer (Exercise 4)*

BUILDS ON

PRACTICE
EXERCISE 4
PAGE 413

5. The Coaches Form: Modify the Coaches form so that it parallels the Players form from the previous exercise. You may find it convenient to copy procedures, such as those that create and display keyboard shortcuts, from one form to another, as opposed to reentering the code. Proceed as follows:
   a. Add a combo box to the form to locate a coach within the Coaches table.
   b. Add code to the Add Coach button to position the user in the First Name text box after clicking the Add button.
   c. Add a procedure to notify the user if the phone number is omitted, then ask the user if the record is to be saved anyway.
   d. Create a Ctrl+1 keyboard shortcut to enter Miami, FL, and 33124 in the city, state, and zip code fields. Create a shortcut for Ctrl+2 to enter Coral Springs, FL, and 33071. Add a shortcut button to display this information.
   e. Print the completed VBA module for the Coaches form for your instructor.

6. Acme Computers: The database in *Chapter 8 Practice 6* contains a partially completed version of the form in Figure 8.15. Your assignment is to modify that form to accommodate all of the following:

a. Create a command button to add a new customer. The button should be created in such a way so that clicking the button takes the user directly to the FirstName field. (CustomerID is defined as an Autonumber field.)

b. Change the table properties so that the user must enter either a home phone or a business phone.

c. Create a BeforeUpdate event procedure that asks the user if the record should be saved if zip code is omitted.

d. Add a combo box to find a customer record. Be sure to change the On Current event so that the value shown in the Find Customer control matches the customer information currently displayed on the form.

e. Create a KeyDown procedure so that Ctrl+1 enters a credit rating of A and a credit limit of $10,000, Ctrl+2 enters a credit rating of B and a credit limit of $5,000, and Ctrl+3 enters a credit rating of C and a credit limit of $1,000. Create a command button to display the shortcuts for the user. Remember to set the KeyPreview property to "Yes" for the shortcuts to be operational.

f. Use the completed form to add a record for yourself as a customer, then print that form for your instructor. Print the VBA module associated with the form as well.

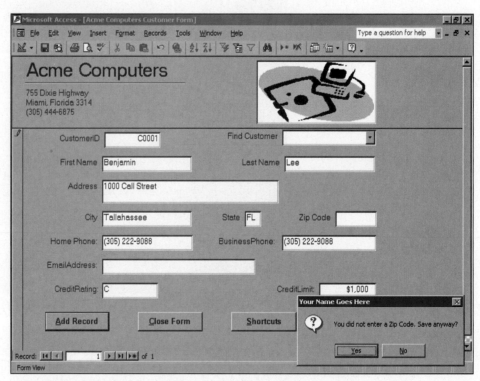

FIGURE 8.15 *Acme Computers Customer Form (Exercise 6)*

BUILDS ON

PRACTICE
EXERCISE 6
PAGE 414

7. String Processing: The procedure in Figure 8.16 consists of three simple If statements that validate the e-mail address within the Customers form of the previous problem. Use the VBA Help command to learn how the Len and InStr functions work, then create the procedure in Figure 8.16. Print the completed procedure for your instructor. Are there any other additional checks that you think should be included within this procedure?

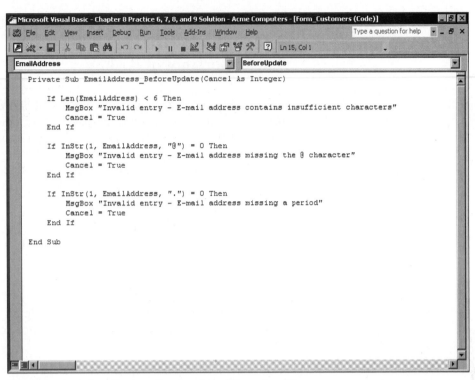

FIGURE 8.16 *String Processing (Exercise 7)*

BUILDS ON

PRACTICE
EXERCISE 7
PAGE 415

8. Acme Computers Switchboard: Create the switchboard shown in Figure 8.17 to provide access to the completed Customers form. The Exit Application button should display the message shown in the figure prior to closing the database. Use the Startup property to display the switchboard automatically when the database is opened.

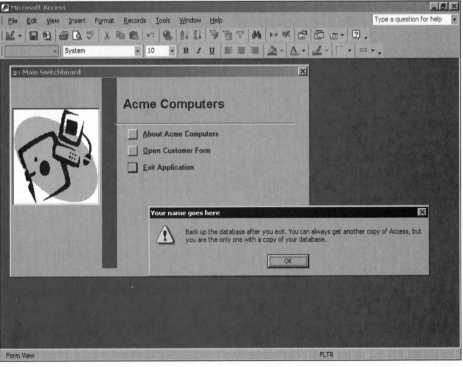

FIGURE 8.17 *Acme Computers Switchboard (Exercise 8)*

The Importance of Backup

Go to a real installation such as a doctor's or an attorney's office, the company where you work, or the computer lab at school. Determine the backup procedures that are in effect, then write a one-page report indicating whether the policy is adequate and, if necessary, offering suggestions for improvement. Your report should be addressed to the individual in charge of the business and it should cover all aspects of the backup strategy. Be sure to indicate which files are backed up, the responsible individual, how often the files are backed up, and where the backup copies are stored.

Debugging

The Debug toolbar contains several tools to help you debug a procedure if it does not work as intended. The Step Into command is especially useful as it executes the procedure one statement at a time. Choose any of the procedures you created in this chapter, then investigate the procedure in detail using the Debug toolbar. Summarize your results in a short note to your instructor.

Help for VBA

Review the hands-on exercises in the chapter to review the various ways to obtain help in VBA. In addition, you can click on any Visual Basic key word, then press the F1 key to display a context-sensitive help screen. Summarize this information in a short note to your instructor. It will be an invaluable reference as you continue to explore VBA in Access as well as other applications in Microsoft Office.

The Developer's Forum

Go to the Microsoft Developer's Forum at www.microsoft.com/office/developer to see what information is currently available. (The address of the page changes periodically, so you may have to search the site for developer resources.) In any event, locate at least one article of interest to you, then summarize your findings in a short note to your instructor.

APPENDIX A

Toolbars

OVERVIEW

Microsoft Access has 27 predefined toolbars that provide access to commonly used commands. The toolbars are displayed in Figure A.1 and are listed here for convenience: Alignment and Sizing, Database, Filter/Sort, Form Design, Form View, Formatting (Datasheet), Formatting (Form/Report), Formatting (Page), Formatting (PivotTable/PivotChart), Macro Design, Page Design, Page View, PivotChart, PivotTable, Print Preview, Query Datasheet, Query Design, Relationship, Report Design, Shortcut Menus, Source Code Control, Table Datasheet, Table Design, Toolbox, Utility 1, Utility 2, and Web.

The buttons on the toolbars are intended to indicate their functions. Clicking the Printer button (the fourth button from the left on the Database toolbar), for example, executes the Print command. If you are unsure of the purpose of any toolbar button, point to it, and a ScreenTip will appear that displays its name.

You can display multiple toolbars at one time, move them to new locations on the screen, customize their appearance, or suppress their display.

- To display or hide a toolbar, pull down the View menu and click the Toolbars command. Select (deselect) the toolbar(s) that you want to display (hide). The selected toolbar(s) will be displayed in the same position as when last displayed. You may also point to any toolbar and click with the right mouse button to bring up a shortcut menu, after which you can select the toolbar to be displayed (hidden).
- To change the size of the buttons, suppress the display of the ScreenTips, pull down the View menu, click Toolbars, and click Customize to display the Customize dialog box. If necessary, click the Options tab, then select (deselect) the appropriate check box. Alternatively, you can right click on any toolbar, click the Customize command from the context-sensitive menu, then select (deselect) the appropriate check box from within the Options tab in the Customize dialog box.
- Toolbars are either docked (along the edge of the window) or floating (in their own window). A toolbar moved to the edge of the window will dock

along that edge. A toolbar moved anywhere else in the window will float in its own window. Docked toolbars are one tool wide (high). Floating toolbars can be resized by clicking and dragging a border or corner as you would with any window.

- To move a docked toolbar, click anywhere in the gray background area and drag the toolbar to its new location. You can also click and drag the move handle (the vertical line) at the left of the toolbar.
- To move a floating toolbar, drag its title bar to its new location.

■ To customize a toolbar, display the toolbar on the screen, pull down the View menu, click Toolbars, and click Customize to display the Customize dialog box. Alternatively, you can click on any toolbar with the right mouse button and select Customize from the shortcut menu.

- To move a button, drag the button to its new location on that toolbar or any other displayed toolbar.
- To copy a button, press the Ctrl key as you drag the button to its new location on that toolbar or any other displayed toolbar.
- To delete a button, drag the button off the toolbar and release the mouse button.
- To add a button, click the Commands tab in the Customize dialog box, select the category from the Categories list box that contains the button you want to add, then drag the button to the desired location on the toolbar. (To see a description of a tool's function prior to adding it to a toolbar, select the tool, then click the Description command button.)
- To restore a predefined toolbar to its default appearance, click the Toolbars tab, select (highlight) the desired toolbar, and click the Reset command button.

■ Buttons can also be moved, copied, or deleted without displaying the Customize dialog box.

- To move a button, press the Alt key as you drag the button to the new location.
- To copy a button, press the Alt and Ctrl keys as you drag the button to the new location.
- To delete a button, press the Alt key as you drag the button off the toolbar.

■ To create your own toolbar, pull down the View menu, click Toolbars, click Customize, click the Toolbars tab, then click the New command button. Alternatively, you can click on any toolbar with the right mouse button, select Customize from the shortcut menu, click the Toolbars tab, and then click the New command button.

- Enter a name for the toolbar in the dialog box that follows. The name can be any length and can contain spaces. Click OK.
- The new toolbar will appear on the screen. Initially it will be big enough to hold only one button. Add, move, and delete buttons following the same procedures as outlined above. The toolbar will automatically size itself as new buttons are added and deleted.
- To delete a custom toolbar, pull down the View menu, click Toolbars, click Customize, and click the Toolbars tab. *Verify that the custom toolbar to be deleted is the only one selected (highlighted).* Click the Delete command button. Click OK to confirm the deletion. (Note that a predefined toolbar cannot be deleted.)

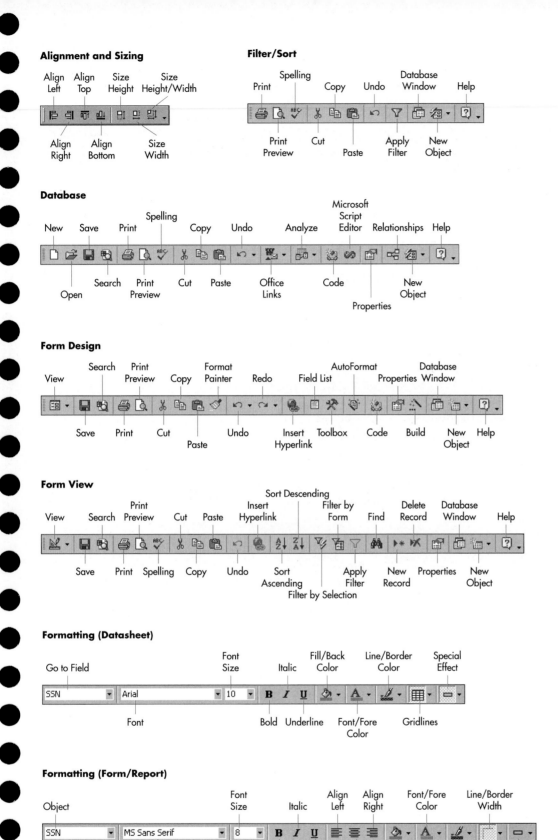

FIGURE A.1 *Access Toolbars*

Formatting (Page)

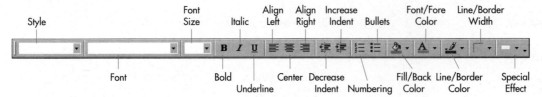

Formatting (PivotTable/Pivot Chart)

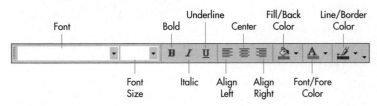

Macro Design

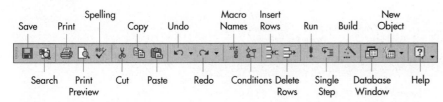

Page Design

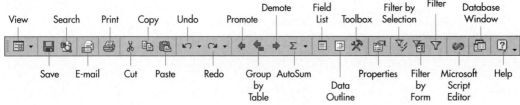

Page View

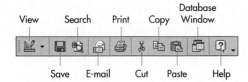

Pivot Chart

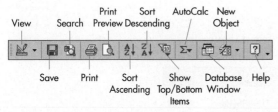

FIGURE A.1   *Access Toolbars (continued)*

Pivot Table

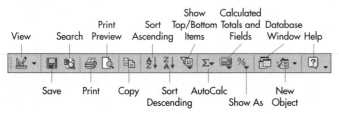

View • Search • Print Preview • Sort Ascending • Show Top/Bottom Items • Calculated Totals and Fields • Database Window • Help
Save • Print • Copy • Sort Descending • AutoCalc • Show As • New Object

Print Preview

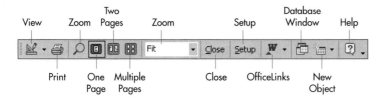

View • Zoom • Two Pages • Zoom • Setup • Database Window • Help
Print • One Page • Multiple Pages • Close • OfficeLinks • New Object

Query Datasheet

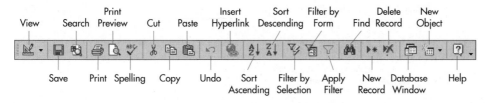

View • Search • Print Preview • Cut • Paste • Insert Hyperlink • Sort Descending • Filter by Form • Find • Delete Record • New Object
Save • Print • Spelling • Copy • Undo • Sort Ascending • Filter by Selection • Apply Filter • New Record • Database Window • Help

Query Design

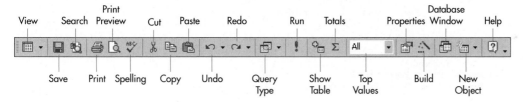

View • Search • Print Preview • Cut • Paste • Redo • Run • Totals • Properties • Database Window • Help
Save • Print • Spelling • Copy • Undo • Query Type • Show Table • Top Values • Build • New Object

Relationship

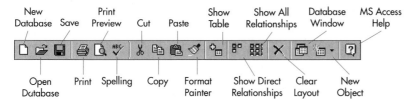

New Database • Save • Print Preview • Cut • Paste • Show Table • Show All Relationships • Database Window • MS Access Help
Open Database • Print • Spelling • Copy • Format Painter • Show Direct Relationships • Clear Layout • New Object

Report Design

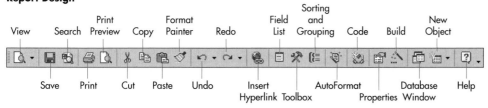

View • Search • Print Preview • Copy • Format Painter • Redo • Field List • Sorting and Grouping • Code • Build • New Object
Save • Print • Cut • Paste • Undo • Insert Hyperlink • Toolbox • AutoFormat • Properties • Database Window • Help

FIGURE A.1 *Access Toolbars (continued)*

Shortcut Menus

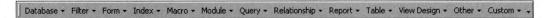

Database ▾ Filter ▾ Form ▾ Index ▾ Macro ▾ Module ▾ Query ▾ Relationship ▾ Report ▾ Table ▾ View Design ▾ Other ▾ Custom ▾

Source Code Control

Add Objects   Check   Undo   Show   Run
SourceSafe   Out   Checkout   History SourceSafe

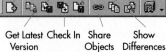

Get Latest Check In Share   Show
Version   Objects   Differences

Table Datasheet

View   Search   Print   Cut   Paste Insert   Sort   Filter by   Find   Delete   New
                   Preview   Hyperlink   Descending Form   Record   Object

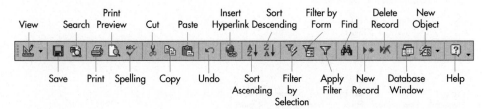

          Save   Print Spelling Copy   Undo   Sort   Filter   Apply   New   Database   Help
                                                  Ascending   by   Filter   Record   Window
                                                              Selection

Table Design

View   Search   Print   Cut   Paste   Redo   Indexes   Delete   Build   New
                   Preview   Rows   Object

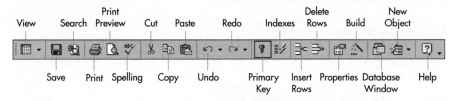

          Save   Print Spelling Copy   Undo   Primary   Insert Properties Database   Help
                                                         Key   Rows   Window

Toolbox

Select   Option Option Combo Command Unbound Page   Subform/
Objects   Label   Group   Button Box   Button   Object   Break Subreport   Rectangle
                                               Frame

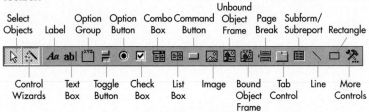

Control   Text   Toggle Check   List   Image   Bound   Tab   Line   More
Wizards   Box   Button Box   Box   Object   Control   Controls
                                                      Frame

Utility 1   **Utility 2**

Add or Remove   Add or Remove
Buttons   Buttons

Web

           Stop Current Start   Favorites   Show Only
Back   Jump   Page   Menu   Web Toolbar

Forward   Refresh   Search the   Go Menu   Address
           Current Page Web

FIGURE A.1   *Access Toolbars (continued)*

APPENDIX B

Designing a Relational Database

OVERVIEW

An Access database consists of multiple tables, each of which stores data about a specific subject. To use Access effectively, you must relate the tables to one another. This in turn requires a knowledge of database design and an understanding of the principles of a relational database under which Access operates.

Our approach to teaching database design is to present two case studies, each of which covers a common application. The first case centers on franchises for fast food restaurants and incorporates the concept of a one-to-many relationship. One person can own many restaurants, but a given restaurant is owned by only one person. The second case is based on a system for student transcripts and incorporates a many-to-many relationship. One student takes many courses, and one course is taken by many students. The intent in both cases is to design a database capable of producing the desired information.

CASE STUDY: FAST FOOD FRANCHISES

The case you are about to read is set within the context of a national corporation offering franchises for fast food restaurants. The concept of a franchise operation is a familiar one and exists within many industries. The parent organization develops a model operation, then franchises that concept to qualified individuals (franchisees) seeking to operate their own businesses. The national company teaches the franchisee to run the business, aids the person in site selection and staffing, coordinates national advertising, and so on. The franchisee pays an initial fee to open the business followed by subsequent royalties and marketing fees to the parent corporation.

The essence of the case is how to relate the data for the various entities (the restaurants, franchisees, and contracts) to one another. One approach is to develop a single restaurant table, with each restaurant record containing data about the owner and contract arrangement. As we shall see, that design leads to problems of redundancy whenever the same person owns more than one restaurant or when several restaurants have the same contract type. A better approach is to develop separate tables, one for each of the objects (restaurants, franchisees, and contracts).

The entities in the case have a definite relationship to one another, which must be reflected in the database design. The corporation encourages individuals to own multiple restaurants, creating a *one-to-many relationship* between franchisees and restaurants. One person can own many restaurants, but a given restaurant is owned by only one person. There is also a one-to-many relationship between contracts and restaurants because the corporation offers a choice of contracts to each restaurant.

The company wants a database that can retrieve all data for a given restaurant, such as the annual sales, type of contract in effect (contract types are described below), and/or detailed information about the restaurant owner. The company also needs reports that reflect the location of each restaurant, all restaurants in a given state, and all restaurants managed by a particular contract type. The various contract arrangements are described below:

Contract 1: 99-year term, requiring a one-time fee of $250,000 payable at the time the franchise is awarded. In addition, the franchisee must pay a royalty of 2 percent of the restaurant's gross sales to the parent corporation, and contribute an additional 2 percent of sales to the parent corporation for advertising.

Contract 2: 5-year term (renewable at franchisee's option), requiring an initial payment of $50,000. In addition, the franchisee must pay a royalty of 4 percent of the restaurant's gross sales to the parent corporation, and contribute an additional 3 percent of sales to the parent corporation for advertising.

Contract 3: 10-year term (renewable at franchisee's option), requiring an initial payment of $75,000. In addition, the franchisee must pay a royalty of 3 percent of the restaurant's gross sales to the parent corporation, and contribute an additional 3 percent of sales to the parent corporation for advertising.

Other contract types may be offered in the future. The company currently has 500 restaurants, of which 200 are company owned. Expansion plans call for opening an additional 200 restaurants each year for the next three years, all of which are to be franchised. There is no limit on the number of restaurants an individual may own.

Single-Table Solution

The initial concern in this, or any other, system is how best to structure the data so that the solution satisfies the information requirements of the client. We present two solutions. The first is based on a single restaurant table and will be shown to have several limitations. The second introduces the concept of a relational database and consists of three tables (for the restaurants, franchisees, and contracts).

The single-table solution is shown in Figure B.1a. Each record within the table contains data about a particular restaurant, its franchisee (owner), and contract type. There are five restaurants in our example, each with a *unique* restaurant number. At first glance, Figure B.1a appears satisfactory; yet there are three specific types of problems associated with this solution. These are:

1. Difficulties in the modification of data for an existing franchisee or contract type, in that the same change may be made in multiple places.
2. Difficulties in the addition of a new franchisee or contract type, in that these entities must first be associated with a particular restaurant.
3. Difficulties in the deletion of a restaurant, in that data for a particular franchisee or contract type may be deleted as well.

Restaurant Number	Restaurant Data (Address, annual sales . . .)	Franchisee Data (Name, telephone, address . . .)	Contract Data (Type, term, initial fee . . .)
R1	Restaurant data for Miami . . .	Franchisee data (Grauer . . .)	Contract data (Type 1 . . .)
R2	Restaurant data for Coral Gables . . .	Franchisee data (Moldof . . .)	Contract data (Type 1 . . .)
R3	Restaurant data for Fort Lauderdale. . .	Franchisee data (Grauer . . .)	Contract data (Type 2 . . .)
R4	Restaurant data for New York . . .	Franchisee data (Glassman . . .)	Contract data (Type 1 . . .)
R5	Restaurant data for Coral Springs . . .	Franchisee data (Coulter . . .)	Contract data (Type 3 . . .)

(a) Single-Table Solution

Restaurant Number	Restaurant Data	Franchisee Number	Contract Type
R1	Restaurant data for Miami . . .	F1	C1
R2	Restaurant data for Coral Gables . . .	F2	C1
R3	Restaurant data for Fort Lauderdale. . .	F1	C2
R4	Restaurant data for New York . . .	F3	C1
R5	Restaurant data for Coral Springs . . .	F4	C3

Contract Type	Contract Data
C1	Contract data. . .
C2	Contract data. . .
C3	Contract data. . .

Franchisee Number	Franchisee Data (Name, telephone, address, . . .)
F1	Grauer. . .
F2	Moldof. . .
F3	Glassman. . .
F4	Coulter. . .

(b) Multiple-Table Solution

FIGURE B.1   *Single- versus Multiple-Table Solution*

The first problem, modification of data about an existing franchisee or contract type, stems from ***redundancy***, which in turn requires that any change to duplicated data be made in several places. In other words, any modification to a duplicated entry, such as a change in data for a franchisee with multiple restaurants (e.g., Grauer, who owns restaurants in Miami and Fort Lauderdale), requires a search through the entire table to find all instances of that data so that the identical modification can be made to each of the records. A similar procedure would have to be followed should data change about a duplicated contract (e.g., a change in the royalty percentage for contract Type 1, which applies to restaurants R1, R2, and R4). This is, to say the least, a time-consuming and error-prone procedure.

The addition of a new franchisee or contract type poses a different type of problem. It is quite logical, for example, that potential franchisees must apply to the corporation and qualify for ownership before having a restaurant assigned to them. It is also likely that the corporation would develop a new contract type prior to offering that contract to an existing restaurant. Neither of these events is easily accommodated in the table structure of Figure B.1a, which would require the creation of a dummy restaurant record to accommodate the new franchisee or contract type.

The deletion of a restaurant creates yet another type of difficulty. What happens, for example, if the company decides to close restaurant R5 because of insufficient sales? The record for this restaurant would disappear as expected, but so too would the data for the franchisee (Coulter) and the contract type (C3), which is not intended. The corporation might want to award Coulter another restaurant in the future and/or offer this contract type to other restaurants. Neither situation would be possible as the relevant data has been lost with the deletion of the restaurant record.

Multiple-Table Solution

A much better solution appears in Figure B.1b, which uses a different table for each of the entities (restaurants, franchisees, and contracts) that exist in the system. Every record in the restaurant table is assigned a unique restaurant number (e.g., R1 or R2), just as every record in the franchisee table is given a unique franchisee number (e.g., F1 or F2), and every contract record a unique contract number (e.g., C1 or C2).

The tables are linked to one another through the franchisee and/or contract numbers, which also appear in the restaurant table. Every record in the restaurant table is associated with its appropriate record in the franchisee table through the franchisee number common to both tables. In similar fashion, every restaurant is tied to its appropriate contract through the contract number, which appears in the restaurant record. This solution may seem complicated, but it is really quite simple and elegant.

Assume, for example, that we want the name of the franchisee for restaurant R5, and further, that we need the details of the contract type for this restaurant. We retrieve the appropriate restaurant record, which contains franchisee and contract numbers of F4 and C3, respectively. We then search through the franchisee table for franchisee F4 (obtaining all necessary information about Coulter) and search again through the contract table for contract C3 (obtaining the data for this contract type). The process is depicted graphically in Figure B.1b.

The multiple-table solution may require slightly more effort to retrieve information, but this is more than offset by the advantages of table maintenance. Consider, for example, a change in data for contract C1, which currently governs restaurants R1, R2, and R4. All that is necessary is to go into the contract table, find record C1, and make the changes. The records in the restaurant table are *not* affected because the restaurant records do not contain contract data per se, only the number of the corresponding contract record. In other words, the change in data for contract C1 is made in one place (the contract table), yet that change would be reflected for all affected restaurants. This is in contrast to the single-table solution of Figure B.1a, which would require the identical modification in three places.

The addition of new records for franchisees or contracts is done immediately in the appropriate tables of Figure B.1b. The corporation simply adds a franchisee or contract record as these events occur, without the necessity of a corresponding restaurant record. This is much easier than the approach of Figure B.1a, which required an existing restaurant in order to add one of the other entities.

The deletion of a restaurant is also easier than with the single-table organization. You could, for example, delete restaurant R5 without losing the associated franchisee and contract data as these records exist in different tables.

Queries to the Database

By now you should be convinced of the need for multiple tables within a database and that this type of design facilitates all types of table maintenance. However, the ultimate objective of any system is to produce information, and it is in this area that the design excels. Consider now Figure B.2, which expands upon the multiple table solution to include additional data for the respective tables.

As indicated, there are three tables—for restaurants, franchisees, and contracts, respectively. The tables are linked to one another through the franchisee and/or contract numbers that also appear in the restaurant table. These fields are color-coded so that you can see the relationships more clearly.

To be absolutely sure you understand the multiple-table solution of Figure B.2, use it to answer the questions at the top of the next page. Check your answers with those provided.

Restaurant Number	Street Address	City	State	Zip Code	Annual Sales	Franchisee Number	Contract Type
R1	1001 Ponce de Leon Blvd	Miami	FL	33361	$600,000	F1	C1
R2	31 West Rivo Alto Road	Coral Gables	FL	33139	$450,000	F2	C1
R3	333 Las Olas Blvd	Fort Lauderdale	FL	33033	$250,000	F1	C2
R4	1700 Broadway	New York	NY	10293	$1,750,000	F3	C1
R5	1300 Sample Road	Coral Springs	FL	33071	$50,000	F4	C3

(a) Restaurant Table

Franchisee Number	Franchisee Name	Telephone	Street Address	City	State	Zip Code
F1	Grauer	(305) 755-1000	2133 NW 102 Terrace	Coral Springs	FL	33071
F2	Moldof	(305) 753-4614	1400 Lejeune Blvd	Miami	FL	33365
F3	Glassman	(212) 458-5054	555 Fifth Avenue	New York	NY	10024
F4	Coulter	(305) 755-0910	1000 Federal Highway	Fort Lauderdale	FL	33033

(b) Franchisee Table

Contract Type	Term (years)	Initial Fee	Royalty Pct	Advertising Pct
C1	99	$250,000	2%	2%
C2	5	$50,000	4%	3%
C3	10	$75,000	3%	3%

(c) Contract Table

FIGURE B.2 *Fast Food Franchises (database queries)*

Questions

1. Who owns restaurant R2? What contract type is in effect for this restaurant?
2. What is the address of restaurant R4?
3. Which restaurant(s) are owned by Mr. Grauer?
4. List all restaurants with a contract type of C1.
5. Which restaurants in Florida have gross sales over $300,000?
6. List all contract types.
7. Which contract type has the lowest initial fee? How much is the initial fee? Which restaurant(s) are governed by this contract?
8. How many franchisees are there? What are their names?
9. What are the royalty and advertising percentages for restaurant R3?

Answers

1. Restaurant R2 is owned by Moldof and governed by contract C1.
2. Restaurant R4 is located at 1700 Broadway, New York, NY 10293.
3. Mr. Grauer owns restaurants R1 and R3.
4. R1, R2, and R4 are governed by contract C1.
5. The restaurants in Florida with gross sales over $300,000 are R1 ($600,000) and R2 ($450,000).
6. The existing contract types are C1, C2, and C3.
7. Contract C2 has the lowest initial fee ($50,000); restaurant R3 is governed by this contract type.
8. There are four franchisees: Grauer, Moldof, Glassman, and Coulter.
9. Restaurant R3 is governed by contract C2 with royalty and advertising percentages of four and three percent, respectively.

THE RELATIONAL MODEL

The restaurant case study illustrates a ***relational database***, which requires a separate table for every entity in the physical system (restaurants, franchisees, and contracts). Each occurrence of an ***entity*** (a specific restaurant, franchisee, or contract type) appears as a row within a table. The properties of an entity (a restaurant's address, owner, or sales) appear as columns within a table.

Every row in every table of a relational database must be distinct. This is accomplished by including a column (or combination of columns) to uniquely identify the row. The unique identifier is known as the ***primary key***. The restaurant number, for example, is different for every restaurant in the restaurant table. The franchisee number is unique in the franchisee table. The contract type is unique in the contract table.

The same column can, however, appear in multiple tables. The franchisee number, for example, appears in both the franchisee table, where its values are unique, and in the restaurant table, where they are not. The franchisee number is the primary key in the franchisee table, but it is a ***foreign key*** in the restaurant table. (A foreign key is simply the primary key of a related table.)

The inclusion of a foreign key in the restaurant table enables us to implement the one-to-many relationship between franchisees and restaurants. We enter the franchisee number (the primary key in the franchisee table) as a column in the restaurant table, where it (the franchisee number) is a foreign key. In similar fashion, contract type (the primary key in the contract table) appears as a foreign key in the restaurant table to implement the one-to-many relationship between contracts and restaurants.

It is helpful perhaps to restate these observations about a relational database in general terms:

1. Every entity in a physical system requires its own table in a database.
2. Each row in a table is different from every other row because of a unique column (or combination of columns) known as a primary key.
3. The primary key of one table can appear as a foreign key in another table.
4. The order of rows in a table is immaterial.
5. The order of columns in a table is immaterial, although the primary key is generally listed first.
6. The number of columns is the same in every row of the table.

THE KEY, THE WHOLE KEY, AND NOTHING BUT THE KEY

The theory of a relational database was developed by Dr. Edgar Codd, giving rise to the phrase, "*The key, the whole key, and nothing but the key . . . so help me Codd.*" The sentence effectively summarizes the concepts behind a relational database and helps to ensure the validity of a design. Simply stated, the value of every column other than the primary key depends on the key in that row, on the entire key, and on nothing but that key.

Referential Integrity

The concept of *referential integrity* requires that the tables in a database be consistent with one another. Consider once again the first row in the restaurant table of Figure B.2a, which indicates that the restaurant is owned by franchisee F1 and governed by contract type C1. Recall also how these values are used to obtain additional information about the franchisee or contract type from the appropriate tables in Figures B.2b and B.2c, respectively.

What if, however, the restaurant table referred to franchisee number F1000 or contract C9, neither of which exists in the database of Figure B.2? There would be a problem because the tables would be inconsistent with one another; that is, the restaurant table would refer to rows in the franchisee and contract tables that do not exist. It is important, therefore, that referential integrity be strictly enforced and that such inconsistencies be prevented from occurring. Suffice it to say that data validation is critical when establishing or maintaining a database, and that no system, relational or otherwise, can compensate for inaccurate or incomplete data.

CASE STUDY: STUDENT TRANSCRIPTS

Our second case is set within the context of student transcripts and expands the concept of a relational database to implement a *many-to-many relationship*. The system is intended to track students and the courses they take. The many-to-many relationship occurs because one student takes many courses, while at the same time, one course is taken by many students. The objective of this case is to relate the student and course tables to one another to produce the desired information.

The system should be able to display information about a particular student as well as information about a particular course. It should also display information about a student-course combination, such as *when* a student took the course and *what grade* he or she received.

Solution

The (intuitive and incorrect) solution of Figure B.3 consists of two tables, one for courses and one for students, corresponding to the two entities in the physical system. The student table contains the student's name, address, major, date of entry into the school, cumulative credits, and cumulative quality points. The course table contains the unique six-character course identifier, the course title, and the number of credits.

There are no problems of redundancy. The data for a particular course (its description and number of credits) appears only once in the course table, just as the data for a particular student appears only once in the student table. New courses will be added directly to the course table, just as new students will be added to the student table.

The design of the student table makes it easy to list all courses for one student. It is more difficult, however, to list all students in one course. Even if this were not the case, the solution is complicated by the irregular shape of the student table. The rows in the table are of variable length, according to the number of courses taken by each student. Not only is this design awkward, but how do we know in advance how much space to allocate for each student?

Course Number	Course Description	Credits
ACC101	Introduction to Accounting	3
CHM100	Survey of Chemistry	3
CHM101	Chemistry Lab	1
CIS120	Microcomputer Applications	3
ENG100	Freshman English	3
MTH100	Calculus with Analytic Geometry	4
MUS110	Music Appreciation	2
SPN100	Spanish I	3

(a) Course Table

Student Number	Student Data	Courses Taken with Grade and Semester									
S1	Student data (Adams. . .)	ACC101	SP01	A	CIS120	FA00	A	MU100	FA00	B			
S2	Student data (Fox. . .)	ENG100	SP01	B	MTH100	SP01	B	SPN100	SP01	B	CIS120	FA00	A
S3	Student data (Baker. . .)	ACC101	SP01	C	ENG100	SP01	B	MTH100	FA00	C	CIS120	FA00	B
S4	Student data (Jones. . .)	ENG100	SP01	A	MTH100	SP01	A						
S5	Student data (Smith. . .)	CIS120	SP01	C	ENG100	SP01	B	CIS120	FA00	F			

(b) Student Table

FIGURE B.3 *Student Transcripts (repeating groups)*

The problems inherent in Figure B.3 stem from the many-to-many relationship that exists between students and courses. The solution is to eliminate the *repeating groups* (course number, semester, and grade), which occur in each row of the student table in Figure B.3, in favor of the additional table shown in Figure B.4. Each row in the new table is unique because the *combination* of student number, course number, and semester is unique. Semester must be included since students are allowed to repeat a course. Smith (student number S5), for example, took CIS120 a second time after failing it initially.

The implementation of a many-to-many relationship requires an additional table, with a *combined key* consisting of (at least) the keys of the individual entities. The many-to-many table may also contain additional columns, which exist as a result of the combination (intersection) of the individual keys. The combination of student S5, course CIS120, and semester SP01 is unique and results in a grade of C.

Note, too, how the design in Figure B.4 facilitates table maintenance as discussed in the previous case. A change in student data is made in only one place (the student table), regardless of how many courses the student has taken. A new student may be added to the student table prior to taking any courses. In similar fashion, a new course can be added to the course table before any students have taken the course.

Review once more the properties of a relational database, then verify that the solution in Figure B.4 adheres to these requirements. To be absolutely sure that you understand the solution, and to illustrate once again the power of the relational model, use Figure B.4 to answer the following questions about the student database.

Course Number	Course Description	Credits
ACC101	Introduction to Accounting	3
CHM100	Survey of Chemistry	3
CHM101	Chemistry Lab	1
CIS120	Microcomputer Applications	3
ENG100	Freshman English	3
MTH100	Calculus with Analytic Geometry	4
MUS110	Music Appreciation	2
SPN100	Spanish I	3

(a) Course Table

Student Number	Student Data
S1	Student data (Adams. . .)
S2	Student data (Fox. . .)
S3	Student data (Baker. . .)
S4	Student data (Jones. . .)
S5	Student data (Smith. . .)

(b) Student Table

Student Number	Course Number	Semester	Grade
S1	ACC101	SP01	A
S1	CIS120	FA00	A
S1	MU100	SP00	B
S2	ENG100	SP01	B
S2	MTH100	SP01	B
S2	SPN100	SP01	B
S2	CIS120	FA00	A
S3	ACC101	SP01	C
S3	ENG100	SP01	B
S3	MTH100	FA00	C
S3	CIS120	FA00	B
S4	ENG100	SP01	A
S4	MTH100	SP01	A
S5	CIS120	SP01	C
S5	ENG100	SP01	B
S5	CIS120	FA00	F

(c) Student-Course Table

FIGURE B.4 *Student Transcripts (improved design)*

Questions

1. How many courses are currently offered?
2. List all three-credit courses.
3. Which courses has Smith taken during his stay at the university?
4. Which students have taken MTH100?
5. Which courses did Adams take during the Fall 2000 semester?
6. Which students took Microcomputer Applications in the Fall 2000 semester?
7. Which students received an A in Freshman English during the Spring 2001 semester?

Answers

1. Eight courses are offered.
2. The three-credit courses are ACC101, CHM100, CIS120, ENG100, and SPN100.
3. Smith has taken CIS120 (twice) and ENG100.
4. Fox, Baker, and Jones have taken MTH100.
5. Adams took CIS120 during the Fall 2000 semester.
6. Adams, Fox, Baker, and Smith took Microcomputer Applications in the Fall 2000 semester.
7. Jones was the only student to receive an A in Freshman English during the Spring 2001 semester.

SUMMARY

A relational database consists of multiple two-dimensional tables. Each entity in a physical system requires its own table in the database. Every row in a table is unique due to the existence of a primary key. The order of the rows and columns in a table is immaterial. Every row in a table contains the same columns in the same order as every other row.

A one-to-many relationship is implemented by including the primary key of one table as a foreign key in the other table. Implementation of a many-to-many relationship requires an additional table whose primary key combines (at a minimum) the primary keys of the individual tables. Referential integrity ensures that the information in a database is internally consistent.

KEY TERMS

Codd, Edgar (p. 429)
Combined key (p. 431)
Entity (p. 428)
Foreign key (p. 428)

Many-to-many relationship (p. 429)
One-to-many relationship (p. 424)
Primary key (p. 428)
Redundancy (p. 425)

Referential integrity (p. 429)
Relational database (p. 428)
Repeating group (p. 431)

APPENDIX *C*

Mail Merge: An Access Database and a Word Form Letter

OVERVIEW

One of the greatest benefits of using the Microsoft Office suite is the ability to combine data from one application with another. An excellent example is a *mail merge*, in which data from an Access table or query are input into a Word document to produce a set of individualized form letters. You create the *form letter* using Microsoft Word, then you merge the letter with the *records* in the Access table or query. The merge process creates the individual letters, changing the name, address, and other information as appropriate from letter to letter. The concept is illustrated in Figure C.1, in which John Smith uses a mail merge to seek a job upon graduation. John writes the letter describing his qualifications, then merges that letter with a set of names and addresses to produce the individual letters.

The mail merge process uses two input files (a main document and a data source) and produces a third file as output (the set of form letters). The *main document* (e.g., the cover letter in Figure C.1a) contains standardized text together with one or more *merge fields* that indicate where the variable information is to be inserted in the individual letters. The *data source* (the set of names and addresses in Figure C.1b) contains the data that varies from letter to letter and is a table (or query) within an Access database. (The data source may also be taken from an Excel list, or alternatively, it can be created as a table in Microsoft Word.)

The main document and the data source work in conjunction with one another, with the merge fields in the main document referencing the corresponding fields in the data source. The first line in the address of Figure C.1a, for example, contains three merge fields, each of which is enclosed in angle brackets, *<<Title>> <<FirstName>> <<LastName>>*. (These entries are not typed explicitly but are entered through special commands as described in the hands-on exercise that follows shortly.) The merge process examines each record in the data source and substitutes the appropriate field values for the corresponding merge fields as it creates

John H. Smith

426 Jenny Lake Drive •   Coral Gables, FL 33146   • (305) 666-8888

July 25, 2001

«Title» «FirstName» «LastName»
«JobTitle»
«Company»
«Address1»
«City», «State» «PostalCode»

Dear «Title» «LastName»:

I would like to inquire about a position with «Company» as an entry-level programmer. I have just graduated from the University of Miami with a Bachelor's Degree in Computer Information Systems (May 2001) and I am very interested in working for you. I am proficient in all applications in Microsoft Office and also have experience with Visual Basic, C++, and Java. I have had the opportunity to design and implement a few Web applications, both as a part of my educational program, and during my internship with Personalized Computer Designs, Inc.

I am eager to put my skills to work and would like to talk with you at your earliest convenience. I have enclosed a copy of my résumé and will be happy to furnish the names and addresses of my references. You may reach me at the above address and phone number. I look forward to hearing from you.

Sincerely,

John H. Smith

(a) The Form Letter (a Word document)

FIGURE C.1   *The Mail Merge*

the individual form letters. For example, the first three fields in the first record will produce *Mr. Jason Frasher;* the same fields in the second record will produce, *Ms. Lauren Howard,* and so on.

The mail merge prepares the letters one at a time, with one letter created for every record in the data source until the file of names and addresses is exhausted. The individual form letters are shown in Figure C.1c. Each letter begins automatically on a new page.

A mail merge can be started from either **Microsoft Word** or **Microsoft Access**. Either way, two input files are required—the form letter (main document) and the data source. The order in which these files are created depends on how the merge is initiated. When starting in Microsoft Word, you begin with the form letter, then create the data source. The process is reversed in Access—you start with a table or query, then exit to Word to create the form letter. The merge itself, however, is always performed from within Microsoft Word.

Title	First Name	Last Name	JobTitle	Company	Address1	City	State	Postal Code
Mr.	Jason	Frasher	President	Frasher Systems	100 S. Miami Avenue	Miami	FL	33103-
Ms.	Lauren	Howard	Director of Human Resources	Unique Systems	475 LeJeune Road	Coral Gables	FL	33146-
Ms.	Elizabeth	Scherry	Director of Personnel	Custom Computing	8180 Kendall Drive	Miami	FL	33156-
*								

(b) The Data Source (an Access table or query)

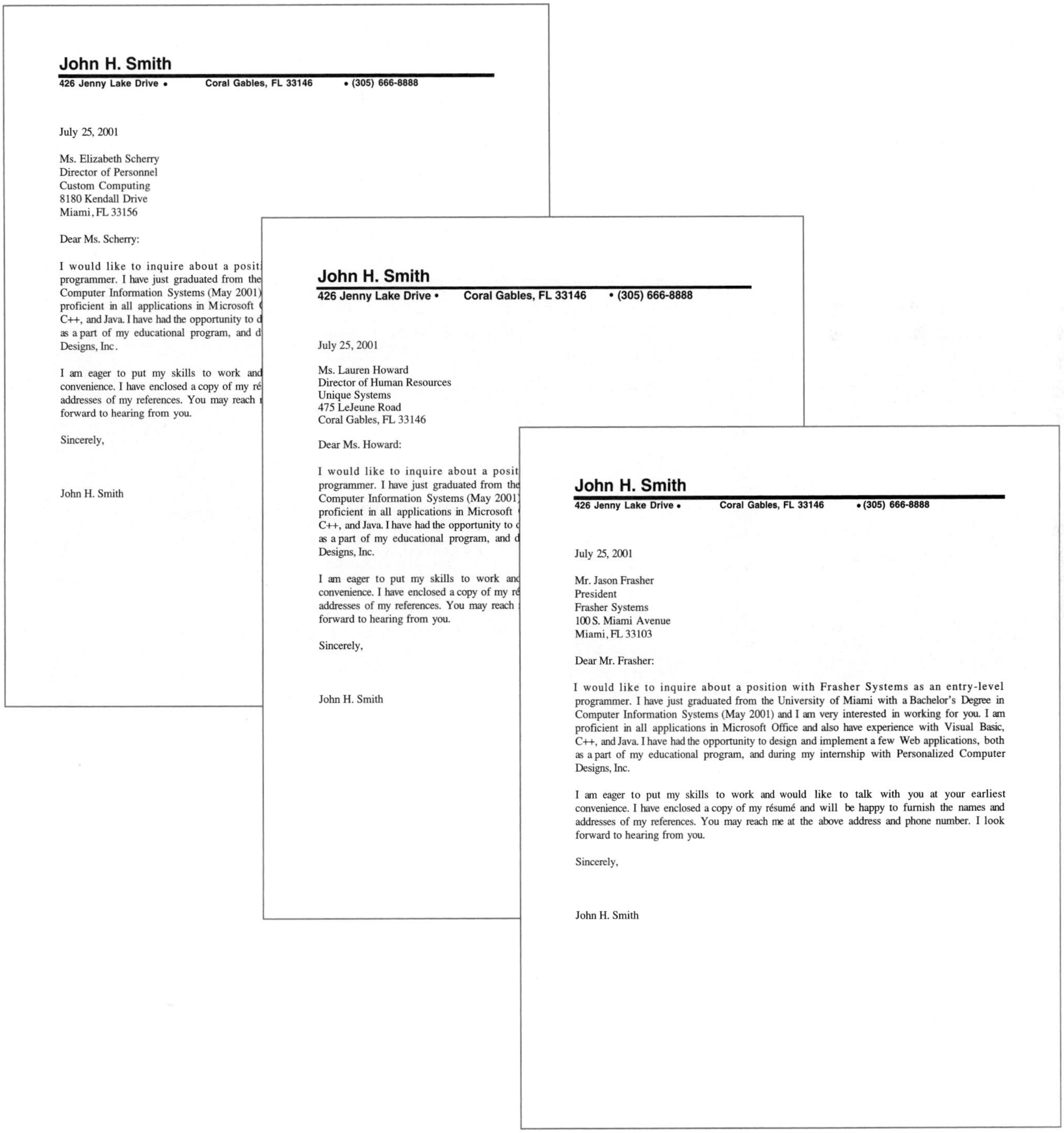

(c) The Printed Letters

FIGURE C.1   *The Mail Merge (continued)*

Objective To merge data from an Access database with a Word document to create a set of individual form letters. Use Figure C.2 as a guide.

Step 1: **Open the Names and Addresses Database**

➤ Start Access. Open the **Names and Addresses database** in the Exploring Access folder. The Tables button is selected. The Contacts table is the only table in the database.

➤ Click the **down arrow** on the **Office Links button** on the Database toolbar, then click **Merge It with Microsoft Word** to display the dialog box in Figure C.2a.

➤ The form letter has already been created for you. Thus, you can select the option to **Link your data to an existing Word document**. Click **OK**.

Click drop-down arrow on Office Links button

Click option button to link data to an existing Word document

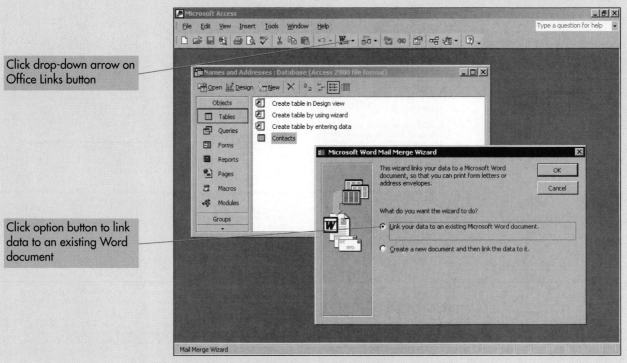

(a) Open the Names and Addresses Database (step 1)

FIGURE C.2 *Hands-on Exercise 1*

START ANYWHERE

A mail merge can be started from Microsoft Word or Microsoft Access. Either way, two input files are required, a form letter and a data source. The order in which these files are created is unimportant, and you can switch back and forth between the two. Eventually, however, the data source will be merged with the form letter to create the individual set of form letters.

Step 2: **Open the Form Letter**

> ➤ You should see the Select Microsoft Word Document dialog box as shown in Figure C.2b. Click the **down arrow** in the Look in box and select the **Exploring Access folder**.
> ➤ Select the **Form Letter** document and click the **Open button**. This starts Microsoft Word and opens the Form Letter document.
> ➤ Click anywhere within the date to select it, then press **Shift+F9** to toggle between the displayed value and the date code, which is set to always display today's date (see boxed tip below).
> ➤ The task pane also opens automatically. If necessary, maximize the application window for Word so that you have more room in which to work.
> ➤ Pull down the **File menu**, click the **Save As command** to display the Save As dialog box, and enter **Modified Form Letter** as the name of the document. Click **Save**.
> ➤ You are ready to begin the mail merge process.

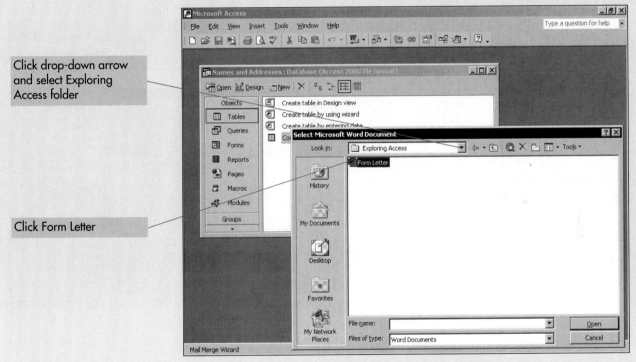

(b) Open the Form Letter (step 2)

FIGURE C.2 *Hands-on Exercise 1 (continued)*

THE INSERT DATE COMMAND

Pull down the Insert menu and click the Date and Time command to display the associated dialog box, where you choose the desired format for the date and/or time information. You can insert today's date as fixed date (by clearing the box to Update automatically). Alternatively, you can check the box, in which case the current date will appear whenever the document is opened.

Step 3:   **Edit the Recipient List**

➤ Click the link to **Edit recipient list** to display the Mail Merge Recipients dialog box, as shown in Figure C.2c. Three names appear, corresponding to the records within the Names and Addresses database that you opened to begin the exercise.

➤ Clear the check box for Elizabeth Scherry. Click **OK**. The form letter will be sent to the two remaining recipients, Jason Frasher and Lauren Howard.

➤ Modify the letterhead to reflect your name and address. Select **"Your Name Goes Here"**, then type a new entry to replace the selected text. Enter your address on the second line.

➤ Save the document. Click the link to **Next: Write your letter** at the bottom of the task pane to continue with the mail merge.

Modify letterhead to reflect your name and address

Click link to Edit Recipient list

Clear check box for Elizabeth Scherry

Click link to Next: Write your letter

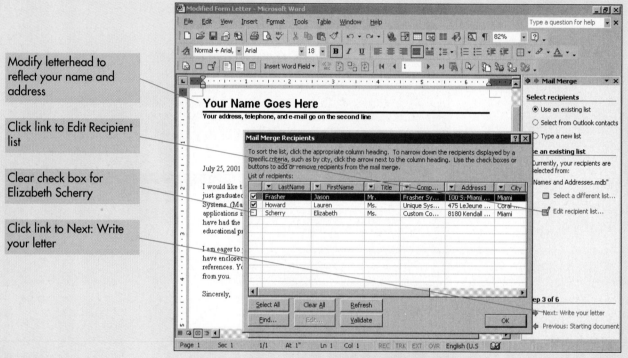

(c) Edit the Recipient List (step 3)

FIGURE C.2 *Hands-on Exercise 1 (continued)*

THE MAIL MERGE WIZARD

The Mail Merge Wizard simplifies the process of creating form letters and other types of merge documents through step-by-step directions that appear automatically in the task pane. The options for the current step appear in the top portion of the task pane and are self-explanatory. Click the link to the next step at the bottom of the pane to move forward in the process, or click the link to the previous step to return to a previous step to correct any mistakes you might have made.

Step 4: **Insert the Fields**

➤ The task pane indicates that you are in step 4 of the merge process. Click immediately after the date. Press the **enter key** twice to insert a blank line. Click the link to the **Address block** in the task pane to display the dialog box in Figure C.2d.

➤ Verify that the three check boxes have been selected as shown in Figure C.2d. Click **OK** to insert the AddressBlock field into the document.

➤ Press the **enter key** twice to leave a blank line after the address block. Click the link to the **Greeting line** to display the Greeting Line dialog box. Choose the type of greeting you want.

➤ Change the comma that appears after the greeting to a colon since this is a business letter. Click **OK**. The GreetingLine field is inserted into the document and enclosed in angled brackets.

➤ Save the document. Click **Next: Preview your letters** to continue.

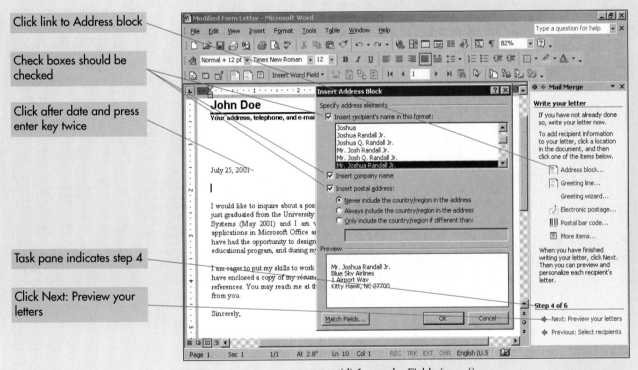

Click link to Address block

Check boxes should be checked

Click after date and press enter key twice

Task pane indicates step 4

Click Next: Preview your letters

(d) Insert the Fields (step 4)

FIGURE C.2 *Hands-on Exercise 1 (continued)*

BLOCKS VERSUS INDIVIDUAL FIELDS

The Mail Merge Wizard simplifies the process of entering field names into a form letter by supplying two predefined entries, AddressBlock and GreetingLine, which contain multiple fields that are typical of the ways in which an address and salutation appear in a conventional letter. You can still insert individual fields, by clicking in the document where you want the field to go, then clicking the Insert Merge Fields button on the Mail Merge toolbar. The blocks are easier.

Step 5: **Preview the Letters**

➤ You should be in step 5 of the mail merge, where you see the first form letter, as shown in Figure C.2e. (If you see a date code, rather than an actual date, pull down the **Tools menu** and click the **Options command** to display the Options dialog box. Click the **View tab** and clear the check box next to Field Codes.)

➤ View the records individually to be sure that the form letter is correct and that the data has been entered correctly. Use the link to the previous step(s) at the bottom of the task pane to make corrections if necessary.

➤ Save the letter. Click the link to **Next: Complete the merge** to continue.

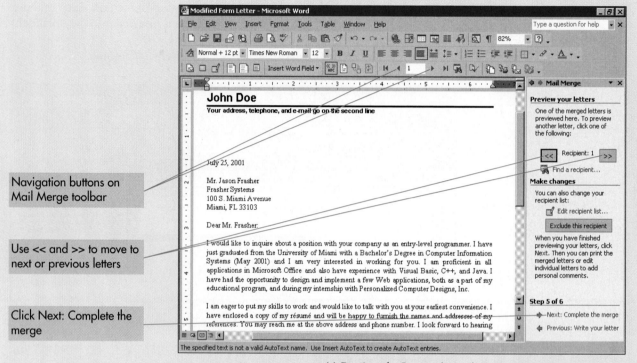

Navigation buttons on Mail Merge toolbar

Use << and >> to move to next or previous letters

Click Next: Complete the merge

(e) Preview the Letters (step 5)

FIGURE C.2   *Hands-on Exercise 1 (continued)*

THE MAIL MERGE TOOLBAR

The Mail Merge toolbar appears throughout the mail merge process and contains various buttons that apply to different steps within the process. Click the <<abc>> button to display field values rather than field codes. Click the button a second time, and you switch back to field codes from field values. Click the <<abc>> button to display the field values, then use the navigation buttons to view the different letters. Click the ▶ button, for example, and you move to the next letter. Click the ▶| button to display the form letter for the last record.

Step 6: **Edit and Print the Individual Letters**

➤ You should be in step 6 of the mail merge. Click the link to **Edit individual letters** in the task pane, which displays the Merge to New Document dialog box. The All option is selected. Click **OK** to create a third document (Letters1), consisting of the individual form letters as shown in Figure C.2f.

➤ Click the **Next (Previous) Page button** to move forward (backward) within the set of individual letters. (You have the option to personalize any of the individual letters.)

➤ Pull down the **File menu** and click the **Print command** to display the Print dialog box. Check the option to all of the letters. Click **OK**.

➤ Close the Letters1 document. Click **No** if prompted to save changes to this document because you can always re-create the individual letters from the form letter and Access database.

➤ Close the Modified Form Letter document. Click **Yes** when asked to save changes to this document.

➤ Exit Word. Exit Access.

Click to close Letters1 document

Previous Page button

Next Page button

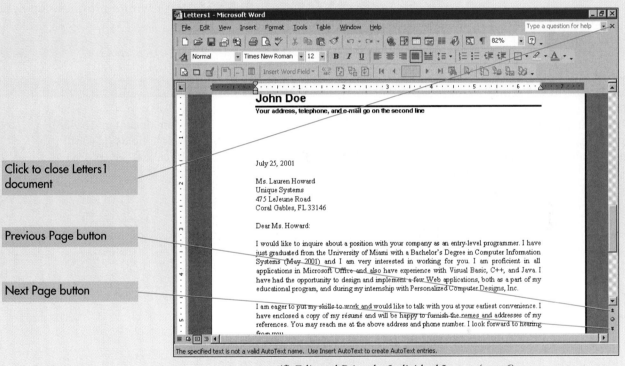

(f) Edit and Print the Individual Letters (step 6)

FIGURE C.2 *Hands-on Exercise 1 (continued)*

THREE DIFFERENT FILES

A mail merge works with a minimum of two files. The main document and data source are input to the mail merge, which creates a set of merged letters as output. The latter can be saved as a separate file, but typically that is not done. You can use the same data source (e.g., a set of names and addresses) with different main documents (a form letter and an envelope) and/or use the same main document with multiple data sources. You typically save, but do not print, the main document(s) and the data source(s). As indicated earlier, you print the set of merged letters, but typically do not save them.

One of the greatest benefits of the Microsoft Office suite is the ability to combine data from one application with that from another. A mail merge is an excellent example, as it combines data from an Access table or query with a Word document. The mail merge creates the same letter many times, changing only the variable data, such as the addressee's name and address, from letter to letter. The merge fields within the main document indicate where the variable information is to be inserted in the individual letters. The same data source can be used with different documents (e.g., to create form letters, envelopes, and/or mailing labels) for a single set of names and addresses. Conversely the same document (such as a form letter) can be used with different data sources as additional data is obtained.

A mail merge can be started from either Microsoft Word or Microsoft Access, but either way, two input files are required—the form letter and the data source. The order in which the files are created is not important. The main document and data source are saved but typically not printed. The merged file (e.g., the set of form letters) is usually printed, but not saved because you can always recreate the form letters by rerunning the mail merge. The Mail Merge Wizard provides step-by-step instructions.

KEY TERMS

Data source (p. 433)
Form letter (p. 433)
Insert Date command (p. 437)

Mail Merge toolbar (p. 440)
Mail Merge Wizard (p. 438)
Mail Merge (p. 433)

Main document (p. 433)
Merge fields (p. 433)
Recipient list (p. 438)

A Project for the Semester: Applying What You Have Learned

OVERVIEW

This appendix describes the student project we require in our course in Microsoft Access at the University of Miami. It is intended for both student and instructor, as it describes the various milestones in the administration of a class project. Our experience has been uniformly positive. Students work hard, but they are proud of the end result, and we are continually impressed at the diversity and quality of student projects. The project is what students remember most about our course, and it truly enhances the learning experience.

We begin our course with an overview of Access as it is presented in Chapter 1. We focus on the Bookstore and Employee databases, each of which contains a single table. We also touch on the concept of a relational database through the "Look Ahead" database at the end of the chapter. The initial emphasis in the course, however, is on databases with a single table, since students must develop proficiency with basic skills. This is accomplished through detailed coverage of Chapters 2 and 3, where students learn how to create tables, forms, queries, and reports.

We then move into a discussion of relational databases and database design. Students want to be proficient in Access, but it is equally important that they are comfortable with database design. Thus we present several different examples, starting in Chapter 4, followed by Appendix B, then reinforced through the opening sections in Chapters 5 and 6, and the associated case studies at the end of these chapters. It is at this point that we introduce the class project, which becomes the focal point of our course for the rest of the semester.

The Groups

The class is divided into groups of three or four students each, and students work together to submit a collective project. It is critical that the groups are balanced with respect to student abilities, and hence our groups are always formed after the first exam, when we have additional information with which to create the groups. We distribute a questionnaire in which we ask students whom they want to work with (and conversely, if there is anyone they would be uncomfortable working with). We try to honor the former requests, but will always honor the latter, so that the groups work as smoothly as possible.

Once the groups have been formed, we establish a series of milestones that are described in the remainder of the appendix. There is absolutely no requirement for you or your class to follow our milestones exactly. We have found, however, that providing detailed feedback through a series of continual assignments is the most effective way to move each group toward its final goal.

One other suggestion is to have the groups engage in a continuing presentation to the class as a whole. We allocate the beginning of each class period to group presentations of 10 to 15 minutes each on the current class assignment. The group presentations accomplish two goals—they enable students to learn from each other, and they provide valuable practice in presenting one's work to an audience.

Phase I—Preliminary Design

Describe, in a one- or two-page narrative, the relational database that your group will design and implement. You can select any of the case studies at the end of the chapters on one-to-many or many-to-many relationships, or alternatively you can choose an entirely different system. Regardless of which system you choose, the preliminary design is one of the most important aspects of the entire project since it is the foundation for the project. A good design will enable you to implement the project successfully, and hence you should give considerable thought to the document you prepare. Your project need not be unduly complex, but it must include at least three tables. The relationships between the tables can be one-to-many or many-to-many. The information can be contained in a written document to your instructor and/or a PowerPoint presentation for the class. Either way, it must do all of the following:

1. Describe the physical system for which you will create the database.
2. Develop a "wish list" describing in general terms the information the system is to produce.
3. Design a database capable of producing the required information. List the tables in the database, the fields in each table, and the relationships between the tables.
4. Describe in general terms how the database will be able to produce at least three of the reports on the wish list by describing the underlying queries, each of which references fields from multiple tables in the database.

Phase II—Detailed Design

Implement the refinements (if any) to the preliminary design from phase I, then expand that design to include all of the necessary fields in each table. You are also asked to develop the properties for each field at this time. Be sure to include adequate data validation and to use input masks as appropriate. One additional requirement is that the primary key of at least one table is an AutoNumber field.

After you have completed the design, create an Access database containing the necessary tables, with the All fields in each table, but no other objects. You do not have to enter any data at this time, but you are required to document your work. Use the Print Relationships command in the File menu to create a one-page document that gives you a visual overview of your database. Submit this document to your instructor.

You are also asked to provide detailed documentation for each table. Pull down the Tools menu, click Analyze, click Documentor. Select Tables in the Object Type drop-down list box, then select all of the tables. Click the Options button, then include for each table the Properties and Relationships but not the Permissions by User and Group. Include for each field Names, Data types, Sizes, and Properties. Do not include any information on indexes. Print the information for each table in the database and submit it to your instructor for review.

Phase III—The User Interface

Phase III focuses on the design of the switchboard and associated templates that will be replicated throughout the system. The switchboard, or user interface, is critical to the success of any system as a user spends his or her day in front of the screen. It should be functional and visually compelling. We have found that the best way to arrive at an attractive design is for each member to submit a design independently.

Thus, each member of the group creates a simple Help form for the group project, which is similar to the form that has appeared in the end-of-chapter exercises throughout the text. The form should include the names of all group members, a logo (clip art or other object), and an appropriate color scheme. All of the forms for each group are then imported into a single database (use the Get External Data command) that will be shown in class. The best design for each group can be picked by consensus, at which point the design is frozen, and development begins with the initial switchboard.

The switchboard should contain a logo for the project and establish a color scheme. The initial version need contain only two buttons—one to display the "Help About" form and one button to exit from the application. Use clip art as appropriate, but clip art for the sake of clip art is often juvenile. You may want to use different fonts and/or simple graphics (e.g., horizontal or vertical lines are often quite effective). A simple design is generally the best design.

Each group then creates a form template and a report template based on the design of the Help form and switchboard. The templates are created in Design view, without benefit of a Wizard, and neither object is based on a table or query. All subsequent forms and reports, however, are based on the templates, at which point the data source is specified. The result is a uniform look throughout the system that adds to its visual appeal. The switchboard is then expanded to include five items—the help form and exit buttons as before, new buttons to show the form and report templates, and a fifth button to print the relationships diagram from phase II. This switchboard is an essential milestone for the project because it contains the physical design (the relationships between the tables) as well as the visual design.

Phase IV—Create the Forms and Enter Test Data

Phase IV has you create the forms in which to enter test data, based on the template of Phase III. You need a form (or subform) for every table that will enable you to add, edit, and delete records in that table. You are also required to have at least one subform, and you must structure your forms to facilitate data entry in a logical way. All forms should have a consistent look (via a common template).

The forms should be user-friendly and display command buttons so that there is no requirement on the part of the end user to know Access. Each form is to include buttons to add, delete, find and print a record, and to close the form. A Help button is a nice touch. Include drop-down list boxes to facilitate data entry in at least two places. The forms should be designed so that they fit on one screen and do not require the user to scroll to access all of the fields and/or the command buttons. Decide on a common resolution, either 640 × 480 or 800 × 600, and follow that throughout.

Use the forms after they have been created to enter test data for each table. (Each table should contain 10 to 15 records.) Be sure that the data will adequately test all of the queries and reports that will be in your final system. Submit a printout of the data in each table to your instructor. (You can print the Datasheet view of each table.) In addition, submit a printed copy of each form to your instructor.

Phase V—Prototyping

Phase V has you develop a "complete" system using a switchboard and prototyping as described in Chapter 7. The main menu should be displayed automatically (via an AutoExec macro) when the database is opened, and the user should be able to step through the entire system. The final reports and queries need not be implemented at this time (a "not yet implemented" message is fine at this stage). The user should, however, be able to go from one form to the next without leaving Access or encountering an error message.

Phase VI—The Finishing Touches

The system should be "up and running" as you continue to build the various objects during the testing phase. (The reports should be based on the report template to promote a uniform look.) It is at this point that you can add the finishing touches through VBA as described in Chapter 8, if in fact you are able to cover that material during the semester. Another finishing touch to consider is the creation of a Web page for the group. The page can be simple and contain descriptive information about the project and the members in the group. Load the page onto your school server, then include a hyperlink on the main switchboard to display the page.

Phase VII—The Completed System

Submit the completed Access database that should contain all of the reports and/or queries needed to satisfy the initial wish list. To obtain a grade of A, you will need to satisfy the following requirements (many of which have been completed) in the earlier phases:

1. An approved design of sufficient complexity similar to the completed soccer database in Chapter 7.
2. Separation of the objects and tables into separate databases that are subsequently linked to one another.
3. Use of the Data Validation and Input Mask properties to validate and facilitate data entry. In addition, at least one table is to contain an AutoNumber field as its primary key.
4. Existing data in all tables with 10 to 15 records in each table.
5. An AutoExec macro to load the main menu and maximize the document window.
6. A Help button on one or more screens that displays the name of the group and an appropriate help message (e.g., a phone number). An "About" button on the opening switchboard that opens a form with introductory information about the project.

7. A working form (or subform) for each table in the database so that you can maintain each table. You must have at least one subform in your system. The forms should have a consistent look (via a common template). The system and especially the forms are to make sense; that is, just because you have all of the forms does not mean you satisfy the requirements of the project. Your forms should be designed to facilitate data entry in a logical way.

8. The forms should be user-friendly and display command buttons so that there is no requirement on the part of the end user to know Access. Each form is to include buttons to add, delete, find and print a record, and to close the form. Include drop-down list boxes to facilitate data entry in at least two places.

9. All forms should be designed for a common resolution, either 800 × 600 or 1024 × 768. The screens should be sufficiently compact so that no scrolling is required.

10. Three working reports, at least one of which is a group/total report.

11. Inclusion of a parameter query to drive a form or report.

12. At least one unmatched query. A top-value query is a nice touch, but depends on the system.

13. Various VBA modules on one or more forms that parallel the examples from Chapter 8. We suggest a combo box to locate a specific record, shortcuts for data entry (with a command button to display the shortcuts), and an error-trapping procedure for a duplicate record. Additional procedures can include a prompt to the user if a recommended field is omitted and a modified Add Record procedure to position the insertion point in the first control within the form.

14. The completed system should be as visually compelling as possible. Clip art for the sake of clip art tends to be juvenile without effect. In general, a consistent logo (one image) is much better from slide to slide than multiple images. No clip art is better than poor clip art or too much clip art.

15. You will be judged on whether your system actually works; that is, the instructor will enter and/or modify data at random. The effects of the new data should be manifest in the various reports and queries. In addition, the system cannot break; that is, the user must be able to go from one menu (form) to the next without difficulty.

The Written Document

In addition to demonstrating a working system, you are to submit a written document as described below. The submission of the written project will be an impressive (lengthy) document but easily generated, as much of the material is created directly from Access. The objective is for you to have a project of which you will be proud and something that you can demonstrate in the future. Include the following:

1. Title page plus table (list) of the contents; pages need not be numbered, but please include "loose-leaf" dividers for each section.

2. A one- or two-page description of the system taken from the earlier presentation to the class.

3. Technical documentation that includes the relationships diagram and table properties, as prepared in the detailed design phase.

4. Hard copy of each form (one per page).

5. Hard copy of each report (one per page).

6. A working disk.

Peer Evaluations

Sealed peer evaluations are to be submitted with each phase. Each member in the group is to evaluate every member in the group, including themselves, by awarding a total of 19 points; (e.g., 5, 5, 5, and 4 in a group with four people). The rationale for requesting evaluations at every milestone is to prevent problems before they occur. In assigning a final grade, I am not looking for small differences, but rather instances where one member is simply not doing his or her share. Should this occur, the instructor will meet privately with the group to correct the problem.

A Final Word

Throughout the project, you will be working with different versions of your database on different machines. You will also need to share your work with other members of your group. And, of course, you need to back up your work. The floppy disk is the medium of choice, but its capacity is only 1.4MB and an Access database can quickly exceed that. It becomes critical, therefore, that you understand the various ways of reducing the storage requirements.

In particular, you should learn how to *compact* an Access database, after which you can take advantage of a *file compression program* to reduce the size even further. You might also explore the use of *FTP* as an alternate means of transferring a file. You should also learn how to separate the data from the other objects in a database to further reduce storage requirements. And finally, you should realize that clip art and other bit map images are one of the primary reasons for a large database. Ask yourself whether you really need it.

A VBA Primer: Extending Microsoft® Office XP

OBJECTIVES

AFTER READING THIS SUPPLEMENT YOU WILL BE ABLE TO:

1. Describe the relationship of VBA to Microsoft Office XP; explain how to open the VBA editor within an Office application.
2. Distinguish between key words, statements, procedures, and modules; use the Office Assistant to obtain detailed information about any VBA statement.
3. Explain how to create, edit, and run a VBA procedure; explain how the Quick Info and Complete Word tools facilitate VBA coding.
4. Explain how to continue a VBA statement from one line to the next; add and remove comments from a procedure.
5. Distinguish between the MsgBox and InputBox statements; describe at least two arguments for each statement.
6. Explain how to debug a procedure by stepping through its statements; describe the role of the Local and Immediate windows in debugging.
7. Use the If . . . Then . . . Else statement to implement a decision; explain the advantage of the Case statement over multiple ElseIf clauses.
8. Create a custom toolbar with buttons corresponding to the VBA procedures you have developed.
9. Describe several statements used to implement a loop; explain the difference between placing a condition at the beginning or end of a loop.
10. Distinguish between event-driven and traditional programming; create event procedures associated with opening and closing an Excel workbook and with an Access database.

OVERVIEW

Visual Basic for Applications (VBA) is a powerful programming language that is accessible from all major applications in Microsoft Office XP. You do not have to

know VBA in order to use Office effectively, but even a basic understanding wi[ll] help you to create more powerful documents. Indeed, you may already have bee[n] exposed to VBA through the creation of simple macros in Word or Excel. A **mac[ro]** is a set of instructions (i.e., a program) that simplifies the execution of repetiti[ve] tasks. It is created through the **macro recorder** that captures commands as they a[re] executed, then converts those commands to a VBA program. (The macro recorder [is] present in Word, Excel, and PowerPoint, but not in Access.) You can create and ex[e]cute macros without ever looking at the underlying VBA, but you gain an appreci[a]tion for the language when you do.

The macro recorder is limited, however, in that it captures only command[s] mouse clicks, and/or keystrokes. As you will see, VBA is much more than ju[st] recorded keystrokes. It is a language unto itself, and thus, it contains all of the state[]ments you would expect to find in any programming language. This lets you enhan[ce] the functionality of any macro by adding extra statements as necessary—for exam[]ple, an InputBox function to accept data from the user, followed by an If . .[.] Then . . . Else statement to take different actions based on the information supplie[d] by the user.

This supplement presents the rudiments of VBA and is suitable for use with an[y] Office application. We begin by describing the VBA Editor and how to create, edi[t] and run simple procedures. The examples are completely general and demonstrat[e] the basic capabilities of VBA that are found in any programming language. We illu[s]trate the MsgBox statement to display output to the user and the InputBox functio[n] to accept input from the user. We describe the For . . . Next statement to impleme[nt] a loop and the If . . . Then . . . Else and Case statements for decision making. We als[o] describe several debugging techniques to help you correct the errors that invariabl[y] occur. The last two exercises introduce the concept of event-driven programming, i[n] which a procedure is executed in response to an action taken by the user. The mate[]rial here is application-specific in conjunction with Excel and Access, but it can b[e] easily extended to Word or PowerPoint.

One last point before we begin is that this supplement assumes no previou[s] knowledge on the part of the reader. It is suitable for someone who has never bee[n] exposed to a programming language or written an Office macro. If, on the oth[er] hand, you have a background in programming or macros, you will readily appreciat[e] the power inherent in VBA. VBA is an incredibly rich language that can be daunti[ng] to the novice. Stick with us, however, and we will show you that it is a flexible a[nd] powerful tool with consistent rules that can be easily understood and applied. Y[ou] will be pleased at what you will be able to accomplish.

INTRODUCTION TO VBA

VBA is a programming language, and like any other programming language its pr[o]grams (or procedures, as they are called) are made up of individual statements. Ea[ch] **statement** accomplishes a specific task such as displaying a message to the user [or] accepting input from the user. Statements are grouped into **procedures**, and pro[ce]dures, in turn, are grouped into **modules**. Every VBA procedure is classified [as] either public or private. A **private procedure** is accessible only from within the mo[d]ule in which it is contained. A **public procedure**, on the other hand, can be access[ed] from any module.

The statement, however, is the basic unit of the language. Our approa[ch] throughout this supplement will be to present individual statements, then to deve[lop] simple procedures using those statements in a hands-on exercise. As you read t[he] discussion, you will see that every statement has a precise **syntax** that describes h[ow] the statement is to be used. The syntax also determines the **arguments** (or param[e]ters) associated with that statement, and whether those arguments are required [or] optional.

The **MsgBox statement** displays information to the user. It is one of the most basic statements in VBA, but we use it to illustrate several concepts in VBA programming. Figure 1a contains a simple procedure called MsgBoxExamples, consisting of four individual MsgBox statements. All procedures begin with a **procedure header** and end with the **End Sub statement**.

The MsgBox statement has one required argument, which is the message (or prompt) that is displayed to the user. All other arguments are optional, but if they are used, they must be entered in a specified sequence. The simplest form of the MsgBox statement is shown in example 1, which specifies a single argument that contains the text (or prompt) to be displayed. The resulting message box is shown in Figure 1b. The message is displayed to the user, who responds accordingly, in this case by clicking the OK button.

Example 2 extends the MsgBox statement to include a second parameter that displays an icon within the resulting dialog box as shown in Figure 1c. The type of icon is determined by a VBA **intrinsic** (or predefined) **constant** such as vbExclamation, which displays an exclamation point in a yellow triangle. VBA has many such constants that enable you to simplify your code, while at the same time achieving some impressive results.

Example 3 uses a different intrinsic constant, vbInformation, to display a different icon. It also extends the MsgBox statement to include a third parameter that is displayed on the title bar of the resulting dialog box. Look closely, for example, at Figures 1c and 1d, whose title bars contain "Microsoft Excel" and "Grauer/Barber", respectively. The first is the default entry (given that we are executing the procedure from within Microsoft Excel). You can, however, give your procedures a customized look by displaying your own text in the title bar.

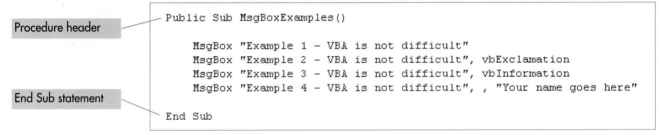

```
Public Sub MsgBoxExamples()

    MsgBox "Example 1 - VBA is not difficult"
    MsgBox "Example 2 - VBA is not difficult", vbExclamation
    MsgBox "Example 3 - VBA is not difficult", vbInformation
    MsgBox "Example 4 - VBA is not difficult", , "Your name goes here"

End Sub
```

Procedure header

End Sub statement

(a) VBA Code

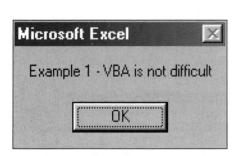

(b) Example 1—One Argument

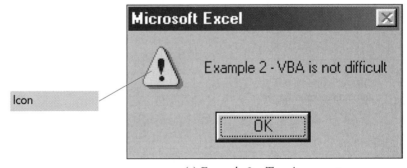

Icon

(c) Example 2—Two Arguments

FIGURE 1   *The MsgBox Statement*

Customized title bar

Icon

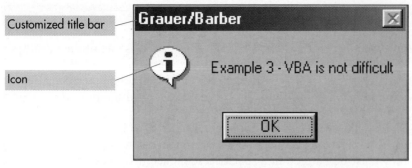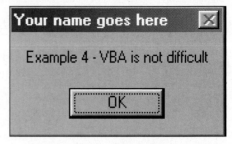

(d) Example 3—Three Arguments   (e) Example 4—Omitted Parameter

FIGURE 1   *The MsgBox Statement (continued)*

Example 4 omits the second parameter (the icon), but includes the third parameter (the entry for the title bar). The parameters are positional, however, and thus the MsgBox statement contains two commas after the message to indicate that the second parameter has been omitted.

THE INPUTBOX FUNCTION

The MsgBox statement displays a prompt to the user, but what if you want the user to respond to the prompt by entering a value such as his or her name? This is accomplished using the ***InputBox function***. Note the subtle change in terminology in that we refer to the InputBox *function*, but the MsgBox *statement*. That is because a function returns a value, in this case the user's name, which is subsequently used in the procedure. In other words, the InputBox function asks the user for information, then it stores that information (the value returned by the user) for use in the procedure.

Figure 2 displays a procedure that prompts the user for a first and last name, after which it displays the information using the MsgBox statement. (The Dim statement at the beginning of the procedure is explained shortly.) Let's look at the first InputBox function, and the associated dialog box in Figure 2b. The InputBox function displays a prompt on the screen, the user enters a value ("Bob" in this example), and that value is stored in the variable that appears to the left of the equal sign (strFirstName). The concept of a variable is critical to every programming language. Simply stated, a ***variable*** is a named storage location that contains data that can be modified during program execution.

The MsgBox statement then uses the value of strFirstName to greet the user by name as shown in Figure 2c. This statement also introduces the ampersand to ***concatenate*** (join together) two different character strings, the literal "Good morning", followed by the value within the variable strFirstName.

The second InputBox function prompts the user for his or her last name. In addition, it uses a second argument to customize the contents of the title bar (VBA Primer in this example) as can be seen in Figure 2d. Finally, the MsgBox statement in Figure 2e displays both the first and last name through concatenation of multiple strings. This statement also uses the ***underscore*** to continue a statement from one line to the next.

VBA is not difficult, and you can use the MsgBox statement and InputBox function in conjunction with one another as the basis for several meaningful procedures. You will get a chance to practice in the hands-on exercise that follows shortly.

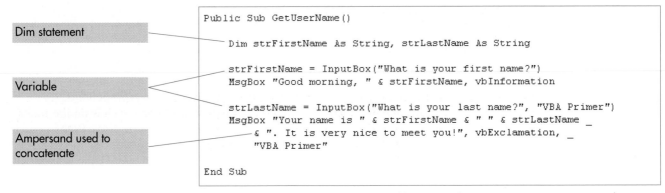

```
Public Sub GetUserName()

    Dim strFirstName As String, strLastName As String

    strFirstName = InputBox("What is your first name?")
    MsgBox "Good morning, " & strFirstName, vbInformation

    strLastName = InputBox("What is your last name?", "VBA Primer")
    MsgBox "Your name is " & strFirstName & " " & strLastName _
        & ". It is very nice to meet you!", vbExclamation, _
        "VBA Primer"

End Sub
```

Dim statement

Variable

Ampersand used to concatenate

(a) VBA Code

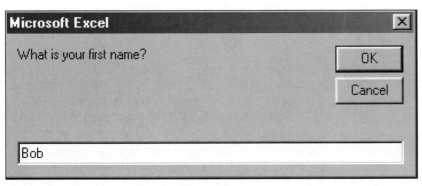

(b) InputBox

(c) Concatenation

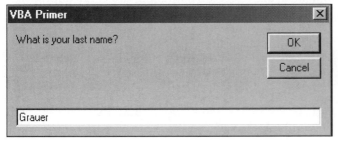

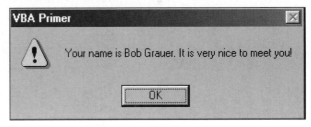

(d) InputBox includes Argument for Title Bar

(e) Concatenation and Continuation

FIGURE 2   *The InputBox Statement*

Declaring Variables

Every variable must be declared (defined) before it can be used. This is accomplished through the ***Dim*** (short for Dimension) ***statement*** that appears at the beginning of a procedure. The Dim statement indicates the name of the variable and its type (for example, whether it will hold characters or numbers), which in turn reserves the appropriate amount of memory for that variable.

A variable name must begin with a letter and cannot exceed 255 characters. It can contain letters, numbers, and various special characters such as an underscore, but it cannot contain a space or the special symbols !, @, &, $, or #. Variable names typically begin with a prefix to indicate the type of data that is stored within the variable such as "str" for a character string or "int" for integers. The use of a prefix is optional with respect to the rules of VBA, but it is followed almost universally.

All VBA procedures are created using the *Visual Basic Editor* as shown in Figure 3. You may already be familiar with the editor, perhaps in conjunction with creating and/or editing macros in Word or Excel, or event procedures in Microsoft Access. Let's take a moment, however, to review its essential components.

The left side of the editor displays the *Project Explorer*, which is similar in concept and appearance to the Windows Explorer, except that it displays the objects associated with the open document. If, for example, you are working in Excel, you will see the various sheets in a workbook, whereas in an Access database you will see forms and reports.

The VBA statements for the selected module (Module1 in Figure 3) appear in the code window in the right pane. The module, in turn, contains declarations and procedures that are separated by horizontal lines. There are two procedures, MsgBoxExamples and GetUserName, each of which was explained previously. A *comment* (nonexecutable) statement has been added to each procedure and appears in green. It is the apostrophe at the beginning of the line, rather than the color, that denotes a comment.

The *Declarations section* appears at the beginning of the module and contains a single statement, *Option Explicit*. This option requires every variable in a procedure to be explicitly defined (e.g., in a Dim statement) before it can be used elsewhere in the module. It is an important option and should appear in every module you write (see exercise 5 at the end of the chapter).

The remainder of the window should look reasonably familiar in that it is similar to any other Office application. The title bar appears at the top of the window and identifies the application (Microsoft Visual Basic) and the current document (VBA Examples.xls). The right side of the title bar contains the Minimize, Restore, and Close buttons. A menu bar appears under the title bar. Toolbars are displayed under the menu bar. Commands are executed by pulling down the appropriate menu, via buttons on the toolbar, or by keyboard shortcuts.

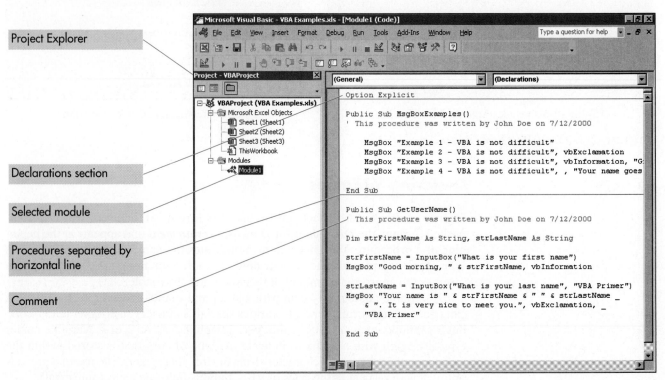

FIGURE 3   *The VBA Editor*

INTRODUCTION TO VBA

Objective   To create and test VBA procedures using the MsgBox and InputBox statements. Use Figure 4 as a guide in the exercise. You can do the exercise in any Office application.

Step 1a: **Start Microsoft Excel**

> ➤ We suggest you do the exercise in either Excel or Access (although you could use Word or PowerPoint just as easily). Go to step 1b for Access.
> ➤ Start **Microsoft Excel** and open a new workbook. Pull down the **File menu** and click the **Save command** (or click the **Save button** on the Standard toolbar) to display the Save As dialog box. Choose an appropriate drive and folder, then save the workbook as **VBA Examples**.
> ➤ Pull down the **Tools menu**, click the **Macro command**, then click the **Visual Basic Editor command** as shown in Figure 4a. Go to step 2.

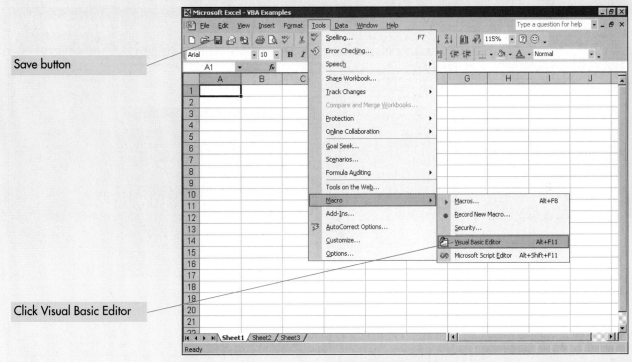

Save button

Click Visual Basic Editor

(a) Start Microsoft Excel (step 1a)

FIGURE 4   *Hands-on Exercise 1*

Step 1b: **Start Microsoft Access**

> ➤ Start **Microsoft Access** and choose the option to create a **Blank Access database**. Save the database as **VBA Examples**.
> ➤ Pull down the **Tools menu**, click the **Macro command**, then click the **Visual Basic Editor command**. (You can also use the **Alt+F11** keyboard shortcut to open the VBA editor without going through the Tools menu.)

Step 2: **Insert a Module**

➤ You should see a window similar to Figure 4b, but Module1 is not yet visible. Close the Properties window if it appears.

➤ If necessary, pull down the **View menu** and click **Project Explorer** to display the Project Explorer pane at the left of the window. Our figure shows Excel objects, but you will see the "same" window in Microsoft Access.

➤ Pull down the **Insert menu** and click **Module** to insert Module1 into the current project. The name of the module, Module1 in this example, appears in the Project Explorer pane.

➤ The Option Explicit statement may be entered automatically, but if not, click in the code window and type the statement **Option Explicit**.

➤ Pull down the **Insert menu** a second time, but this time select **Procedure** to display the Add Procedure dialog box in Figure 4b. Click in the **Name** text box and enter **MsgBoxExamples** as the name of the procedure. (Spaces are not allowed in a procedure name.)

➤ Click the option buttons for a **Sub procedure** and for **Public scope**. Click **OK**. The sub procedure should appear within the module and consist of the Sub and End Sub statements.

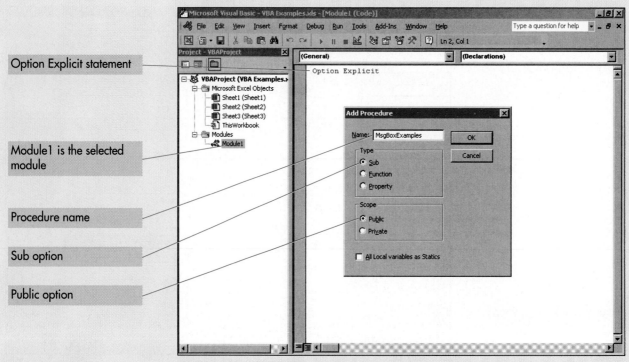

Option Explicit statement

Module1 is the selected module

Procedure name

Sub option

Public option

(b) Insert a Module (step 2)

FIGURE 4   *Hands-on Exercise 1 (continued)*

OPTION EXPLICIT

We say more about this important statement later on, but for now be sure that it appears in every module. See exercise 5 at the end of the chapter.

Step 3: **The MsgBox Statement**

> ➤ The insertion point (the flashing cursor) appears below the first statement. Press the **Tab key** to indent, type the key word **MsgBox**, then press the **space bar**. VBA responds with Quick Info that displays the syntax of the statement as shown in Figure 4c.
> ➤ Type a **quotation mark** to begin the literal, enter the text of your message, **This is my first VBA procedure**, then type the closing **quotation mark**.
> ➤ Click the **Run Sub button** on the Standard toolbar (or pull down the **Run menu** and click the **Run Sub command**) to execute the procedure. You should see a dialog box, containing the text you entered, within the Excel workbook (or other Office document) on which you are working.
> ➤ After you have read the message, click **OK** to return to the VBA Editor.

Run Sub button

Enter MsgBox statement

Quick Info displays correct syntax

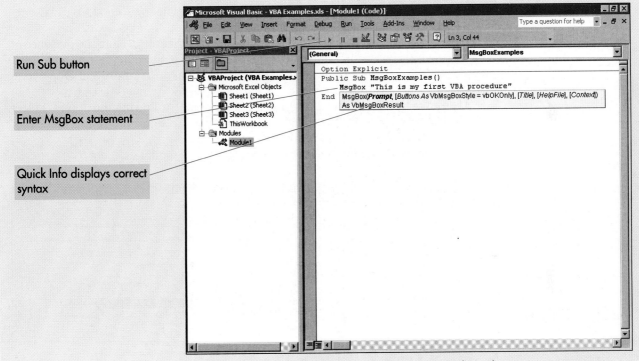

(c) The MsgBox Statement (step 3)

FIGURE 4   *Hands-on Exercise 1 (continued)*

QUICK INFO—HELP WITH VBA SYNTAX

Press the space bar after entering the name of a statement (e.g., MsgBox), and VBA responds with a Quick Info box that displays the syntax of the statement. You see the arguments in the statement and the order in which those arguments appear. Any argument in brackets is optional. If you do not see this information, pull down the Tools menu, click the Options command, then click the Editor tab. Check the box for Auto Quick Info and click OK.

Step 4:   **Complete the Procedure**

➤ You should be back within the MsgBoxExamples procedure. If necessary, click at the end of the MsgBox statement, then press **enter** to begin a new line. Type **MsgBox** and press the **space bar** to begin entering the statement.

➤ The syntax of the MsgBox statement will appear on the screen. Type a **quotation mark** to begin the message, type **Add an icon** as the text of this message, then type the closing **quotation mark**. Type a **comma**, then press the **space bar** to enter the next parameter.

➤ VBA automatically displays a list of appropriate parameters, in this case a series of intrinsic constants that define the icon or command button that is to appear in the statement.

➤ You can type the first several letters (e.g., **vbi**, for vbInformation), then press the **space bar**, or you can use the **down arrow** to select **vbInformation** and then press the **space bar**. Either way you should complete the second MsgBox statement as shown in Figure 4d. Press **enter**.

➤ Enter the third MsgBox statement as shown in Figure 4d. Note the presence of the two consecutive commas to indicate that we omitted the second parameter within the MsgBox statement. Enter your name instead of John Doe where appropriate. Press **enter**.

➤ Enter the fourth (and last) MsgBox statement following our figure. Select **vbExclamation** as the second parameter, type a **comma**, then enter the text of the title bar, as you did for the previous statement.

➤ Click the **Save button** to save the changes to the module.

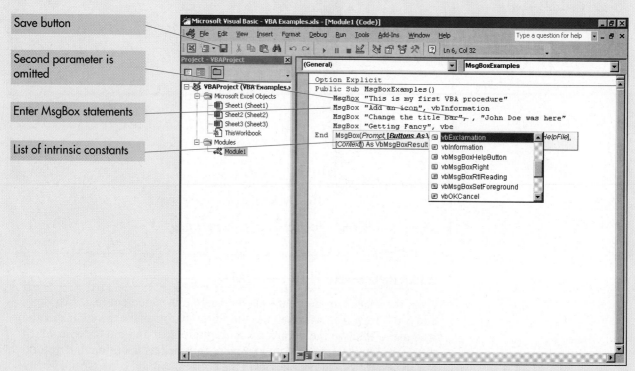

Save button

Second parameter is omitted

Enter MsgBox statements

List of intrinsic constants

(d) Complete the Procedure (step 4)

FIGURE 4   *Hands-on Exercise 1 (continued)*

Step 5:   **Test the Procedure**

➤ It's convenient if you can see the statements in the VBA procedure at the same time you see the output of those statements. Thus we suggest that you tile the VBA Editor and the associated Office application.
  • Minimize all applications except the VBA Editor and the Office application (e.g., Excel).
  • Right click the taskbar and click **Tile Windows Horizontally** to tile the windows as shown in Figure 4e. (It does not matter which window is on top. (If you see more than these two windows, minimize the other open window, then right click the taskbar and retile the windows.)
  • Click anywhere in the VBA procedure, then click the **Run Sub button** on the Standard toolbar.
  • The four messages will be displayed one after the other. Click **OK** after each message.
➤ Maximize the VBA window to continue working.

Run Sub button

Click OK

Right click empty area on taskbar

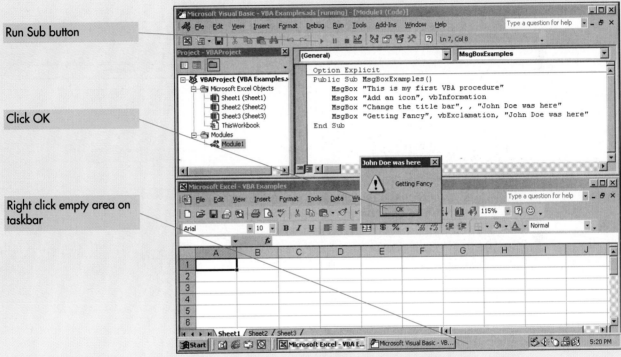

(e) Test the Procedure (step 5)

FIGURE 4   *Hands-on Exercise 1 (continued)*

HIDE THE WINDOWS TASKBAR

You can hide the Windows taskbar to gain additional space on the desktop. Right click any empty area of the taskbar to display a context-sensitive menu, click Properties to display the Taskbar properties dialog box, and if necessary click the Taskbar Options tab. Check the box to Auto Hide the taskbar, then click OK. The taskbar disappears from the screen but will reappear as you point to the bottom edge of the desktop.

Step 6: **Comments and Corrections**

➤ All VBA procedures should be documented with the author's name, date, and other comments as necessary to explain the procedure. Click after the procedure header. Press the **enter key** to leave a blank line.

➤ Press **enter** a second time. Type an **apostrophe** to begin the comment, then enter a descriptive statement similar to Figure 4f. Press **enter** when you have completed the comment. The line turns green to indicate it is a comment.

➤ The best time to experiment with debugging is when you know your procedure is correct. Go to the last MsgBox statement and delete the quotation mark in front of your name. Move to the end of the line and press **enter**.

➤ You should see the error message in Figure 4f. Unfortunately, the message is not as explicit as it could be; VBA cannot tell that you left out a quotation mark, but it does detect an error in syntax.

➤ Click **OK** in response to the error. Click the **Undo button** twice, to restore the quotation mark, which in turn corrects the statement.

➤ Click the **Save button** to save the changes to the module.

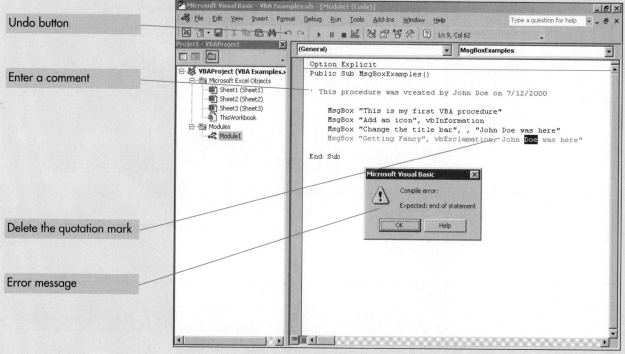

Undo button

Enter a comment

Delete the quotation mark

Error message

(f) Comments and Corrections (step 6)

FIGURE 4 *Hands-on Exercise 1 (continued)*

RED, GREEN, AND BLUE

Visual Basic for Applications uses different colors for different types of statements (or a portion of those statements). Any statement containing a syntax error appears in red. Comments appear in green. Key words, such as Sub and End Sub, appear in blue.

Step 7:   **Create a Second Procedure**

➤ Pull down the **Insert menu** and click **Procedure** to display the Add Procedure dialog box. Enter **InputBoxExamples** as the name of the procedure. (Spaces are not allowed in a procedure name.)

➤ Click the option buttons for a **Sub procedure** and for **Public scope**. Click **OK**. The new sub procedure will appear within the existing module below the existing MsgBoxExamples procedure.

➤ Enter the statements in the procedure as they appear in Figure 4g. Be sure to type a space between the ampersand and the underscore in the second MsgBox statement. Click the **Save button** to save the procedure before testing it.

➤ You can display the output of the procedure directly in the VBA window if you minimize the Excel window. Thus, **right click** the Excel button on the taskbar to display a context-sensitive menu, then click the **Minimize command**. There is no visible change on your monitor.

➤ Click the **Run Sub button** to test the procedure. This time you see the Input box displayed on top of the VBA window because the Excel window has been minimized.

➤ Enter your first name in response to the initial prompt, then click **OK**. Click **OK** when you see the message box that says "Hello".

➤ Enter your last name in response to the second prompt and click **OK**. You should see a message box similar to the one in Figure 4g. Click **OK**.

➤ Return to the VBA procedure to correct any mistakes that might occur. Save the module.

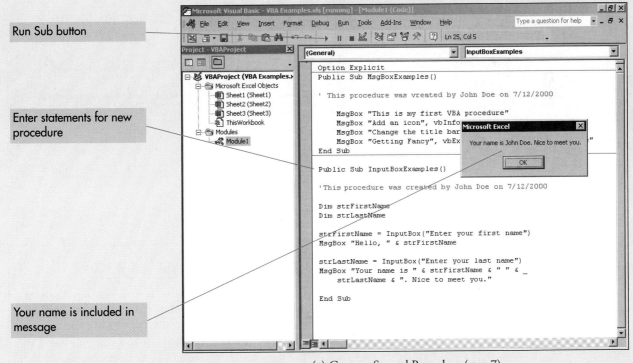

(g) Create a Second Procedure (step 7)

FIGURE 4   *Hands-on Exercise 1 (continued)*

Step 8: **Create a Public Constant**

➤ Click after the Options Explicit statement and press **enter** to move to a new line. Type the statement to define the constant, **ApplicationTitle**, as shown in Figure 4h, and press **enter**.

➤ Click anywhere in the MsgBoxExamples procedure, then change the third argument in the last MsgBox statement to ApplicationTitle. Make the four modifications in the InputBoxExamples procedure as shown in Figure 4h.

➤ Click anywhere in the InputBoxExamples procedure, then click the **Run Sub button** to test the procedure. The title bar of each dialog box will contain a descriptive title corresponding to the value of the ApplicationTitle constant.

➤ Change the value of the ApplicationTitle constant in the General Declarations section, then rerun the InputBoxExamples procedure. The title of every dialog box changes to reflect the new value. Save the procedure.

Run Sub button

Enter statement to define
Constant ApplicationTitle

Change to ApplicationTitle

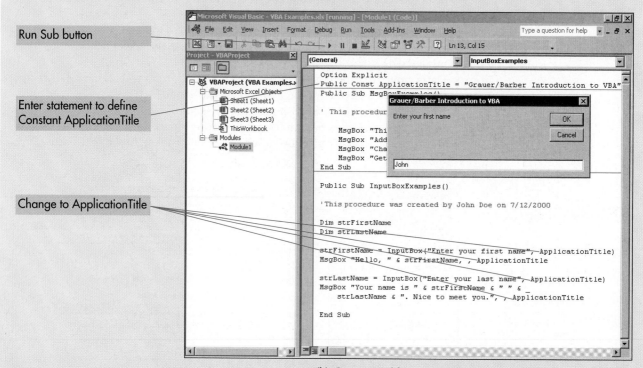

(h) Create a Public Constant (step 8)

FIGURE 4   *Hands-on Exercise 1 (continued)*

CONTINUING A VBA STATEMENT—THE & AND THE UNDERSCORE

A VBA statement can be continued from one line to the next by typing a space at the end of the line to be continued, typing the underscore character, then continuing on the next line. You may not, however, break a line in the middle of a literal (character string). Thus, you need to complete the character string with a closing quotation mark, add an ampersand (as the concatenation operator to display this string with the character string on the next line), then leave a space followed by the underscore to indicate continuation.

Step 9: **Help with VBA**

➤ You should be in the VBA editor. If necessary, pull down the **Help menu** and click **Microsoft Visual Basic Help** (or press the **F1 key**) to display the Office Assistant.

➤ Click the **Assistant**, type **InputBox**, then click the **Search button** in the Assistant's balloon for a list of topics pertaining to this entry. Click the first entry, **InputBox function**, to display the Help window.

➤ Click the **down arrow** on the Options button in the Help window, then click **Show tabs** to expand the Help window to include the Contents, Answer Wizard, and Index tabs as shown in Figure 4i.

➤ Take a minute to explore the information that is available. The Office Assistant functions identically in VBA as it does in all other Office applications. Close the Help window.

➤ Pull down the **File menu** and click the **Close command** (or click the **Close button** on the VBA title bar) to close the VBA window and return to the application. Click **Yes** if asked whether to save the changes to Module1.

➤ You should be back in the Excel (or Access) application window. Close the Office application if you do not want to continue with the next hands-on exercise at this time.

➤ Congratulations! You have just completed your first VBA procedure. Remember to use Help anytime you have a question.

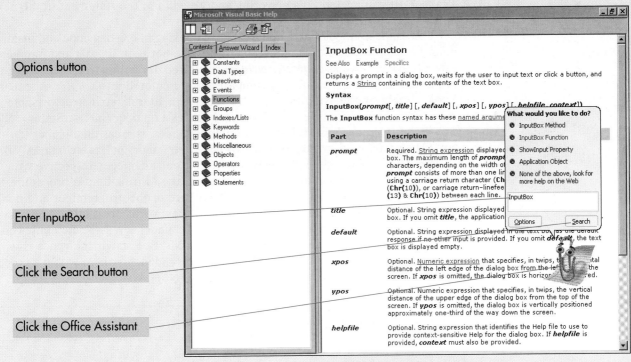

(i) Help with VBA (step 9)

FIGURE 4 *Hands-on Exercise 1 (continued)*

The ability to make decisions within a program, and then execute alternative sets of statements based on the results of those decisions, is crucial to any programming language. This is typically accomplished through an *If statement*, which evaluates a condition as either true or false, then branches accordingly. The If statement is not used in isolation, however, but is incorporated into a procedure to accomplish a specific task as shown in Figure 5a. This procedure contains two separate If statements, and the results are displayed in the message boxes shown in the remainder of the figure.

The InputBox statement associated with Figure 5b prompts the user for the name of his or her instructor, then it stores the answer in the variable strInstructorName. The subsequent If statement then compares the user's answer to the literal "Grauer". If the condition is true (i.e., Grauer was entered into the input box), then the message in Figure 5c is displayed. If, however, the user entered any other value, then the condition is evaluated as false, the MsgBox is not displayed, and processing continues with the next statement in the procedure.

The second If statement includes an optional *Else clause*. Again, the user is asked for a value, and the response is compared to the number 50. If the condition is true (i.e., the value of intUserStates equals 50), the message in Figure 5d is displayed to indicate that the response is correct. If, however, the condition is false (i.e., the user entered a number other than 50), the user sees the message in Figure 5e. Either way, true or false, processing continues with the next statement in the procedure. That's it—it's simple and it's powerful, and we will use the statement in the next hands-on exercise.

You can learn a good deal about VBA by looking at existing code and making inferences. Consider, for example, the difference between literals and numbers. *Literals* (also known as *character strings*) are stored differently from numbers, and this is manifested in the way that comparisons are entered into a VBA statement. Look closely at the condition that references a literal (strInstructorName = "Grauer") compared to the condition that includes a number (intUserStates = 50). The literal ("Grauer") is enclosed in quotation marks, whereas the number (50) is not. (The prefix used in front of each variable, "str" and "int", is a common VBA convention to indicate the variable type—a string and an integer, respectively.)

Note, too, that indentation and spacing are used throughout a procedure to make it easier to read. This is for the convenience of the programmer and not a requirement for VBA. The If, Else, and End If key words are aligned under one another, with the subsequent statements indented under the associated key word. We also indent a continued statement, such as a MsgBox statement, which is typically coded over multiple lines. Blank lines can be added anywhere within a procedure to separate blocks of statements from one another.

THE MSGBOX FUNCTION—YES OR NO

A simple MsgBox statement merely displays information to the user. MsgBox can also be used as a function, however, to accept information from the user such as clicking a Yes or No button, then combined with an If statement to take different actions based on the user's input. In essence, you enclose the arguments of the MsgBox function in parentheses (similar to what is done with the InputBox function), then test for the user response using the intrinsic constants vbYes and vbNo. See exercise 10 at the end of the chapter.

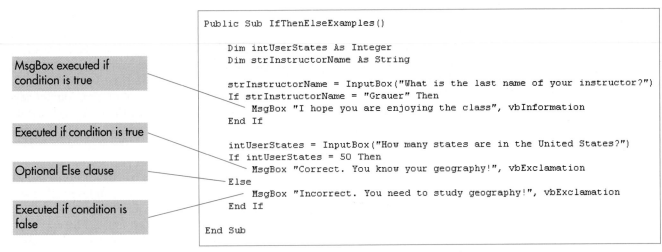

Labels pointing to the code:
- MsgBox executed if condition is true
- Executed if condition is true
- Optional Else clause
- Executed if condition is false

```
Public Sub IfThenElseExamples()

    Dim intUserStates As Integer
    Dim strInstructorName As String

    strInstructorName = InputBox("What is the last name of your instructor?")
    If strInstructorName = "Grauer" Then
        MsgBox "I hope you are enjoying the class", vbInformation
    End If

    intUserStates = InputBox("How many states are in the United States?")
    If intUserStates = 50 Then
        MsgBox "Correct. You know your geography!", vbExclamation
    Else
        MsgBox "Incorrect. You need to study geography!", vbExclamation
    End If

End Sub
```

(a) VBA Code

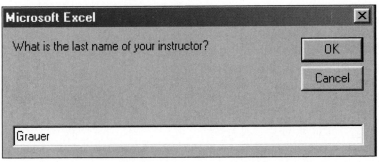

(b) Input Box Prompts for User Response

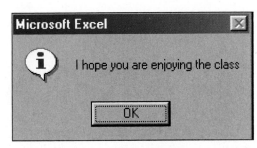

(c) Condition Is True

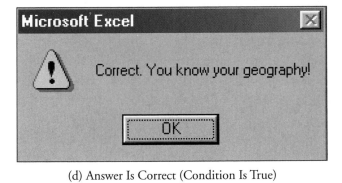

(d) Answer Is Correct (Condition Is True)

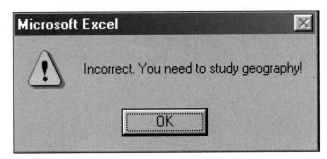

(e) Answer Is Wrong (Condition Is False)

FIGURE 5   *The If Statement*

The If statement is ideal for testing simple conditions and taking one of two actions. Although it can be extended to include additional actions by including one or more ElseIf clauses (If . . . Then . . . ElseIf . . . ElseIf . . .), this type of construction is often difficult to follow. Hence, the **Case statement** is used when multiple branches are possible.

The procedure in Figure 6a accepts a student's GPA, then displays one of several messages, depending on the value of the GPA. The individual cases are evaluated in sequence. Thus, we check first to see if the GPA is greater than or equal to 3.9, then 3.75, then 3.5, and so on. If none of the cases is true, the statement following the Else clause is executed.

Note, too, the format of the comparison in that numbers (such as 3.9 or 3.75) are not enclosed in quotation marks because the associated variable (sngUserGPA) was declared as numeric. If, however, we had been evaluating a string variable (such as, strUserMajor), quotation marks would have been required around the literal values (e.g., Case Is = "Business", Case Is = "Liberal Arts", and so on.) The distinction between numeric and character (string) variables is important.

```vba
Public Sub CaseExample()

    Dim sngUserGPA As Single

    sngUserGPA = InputBox("What is your GPA?")
    Select Case sngUserGPA
        Case Is >= 3.9
            MsgBox "Congratulations! You are graduating Summa Cum Laude!"
        Case Is >= 3.75
            MsgBox "Well Done! You are graduating Magna Cum Laude!"
        Case Is >= 3.5
            MsgBox "Congratulations! You are graduating Cum Laude!"
        Case Is >= 1.8
            MsgBox "You made it"
        Case Else
            MsgBox "Check the schedule for Summer School"
    End Select

End Sub
```

Numbers are not enclosed in quotes

Executed if none of the cases is true

(a) VBA Code

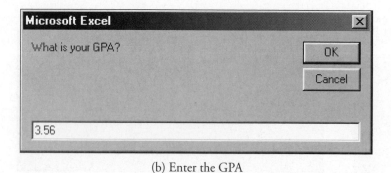

(b) Enter the GPA

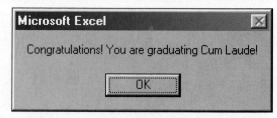

(c) Third Option Is Selected

FIGURE 6   *The Case Statement*

A VBA procedure can be executed in several different ways. It can be run from the Visual Basic Editor, by pulling down the Run menu, clicking the Run Sub button on the Standard toolbar, or using the F5 function key. It can also be run from within the Office application (Word, Excel, or PowerPoint, but not Access), by pulling down the Tools menu, clicking the Macro command, then choosing the name of the macro that corresponds to the name of the procedure.

Perhaps the best way, however, is to create a ***custom toolbar*** that is displayed within the application as shown in Figure 7. The toolbar has its own name (Bob's Toolbar), yet it functions identically to any other Office toolbar. You have your choice of displaying buttons only, text only, or both buttons and text. Our toolbar provides access to four commands, each corresponding to a procedure that was discussed earlier. Click the Case Example button, for example, and the associated procedure is executed, starting with the InputBox statement asking for the user's GPA.

A custom toolbar is created via the Toolbars command within the View menu. The new toolbar is initially big enough to hold only a single button, but you can add, move, and delete buttons following the same procedure as for any other Office toolbar. You can add any command at all to the toolbar; that is, you can add existing commands from within the Office application, or you can add commands that correspond to VBA procedures that you have created. Remember, too, that you can add more buttons to existing office toolbars.

Once the toolbar has been created, it is displayed or hidden just like any other Office toolbar. It can also be docked along any edge of the application window or left floating as shown in Figure 7. It's fun, it's easy, and as you may have guessed, it's time for the next hands-on exercise.

Custom toolbar

Buttons and text are both displayed

Input Box is displayed when procedure is executed

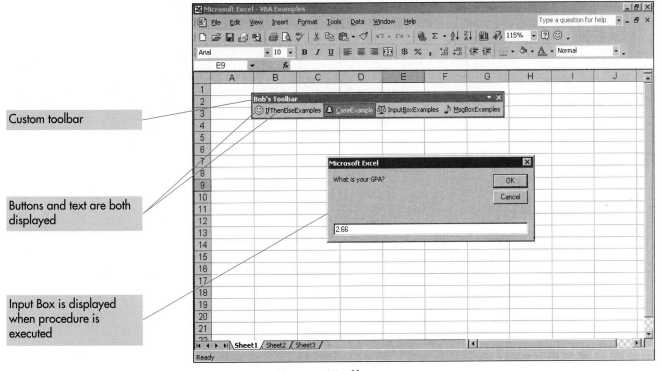

FIGURE 7   *Custom Toolbars*

DECISION MAKING

Objective   To create procedures with If . . . Then . . . Else and Case statements, then create a custom toolbar to execute those procedures. Use Figure 8 as a guide in the exercise.

Step 1:   **Open the Office Document**

> ➤ Open the **VBA Examples workbook** or Access database from the previous exercise. The procedure differs slightly, depending on whether you are using Access or Excel. In Access, you simply open the database. In Excel, however, you will be warned that the workbook contains a macro as shown in Figure 8a. Click the button to **Enable Macros**.
> ➤ Pull down the **Tools menu**, click the **Macro command**, then click the **Visual Basic Editor command**. You can also use the **Alt+F11** keyboard shortcut to open the VBA Editor without going through the Tools menu.

Click Enable Macros

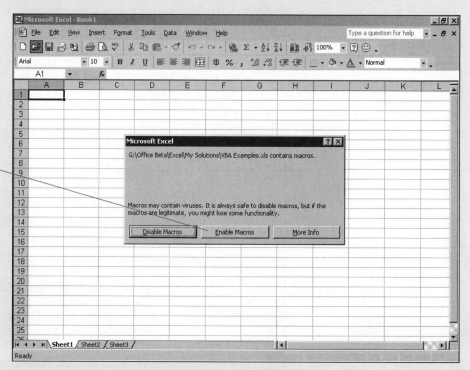

(a) Open the Office Document (step 1)

FIGURE 8   *Hands-on Exercise 2*

MACRO VIRUSES AND VBA PROCEDURES

An Excel macro is always associated with a VBA procedure. Thus, whenever Excel detects a procedure within a workbook, it warns you that the workbook contains a macro, which in turn may carry a macro virus. If you are confident the workbook is safe, click the button to Enable macros; otherwise open the workbook with the macros disabled.

Step 2: **Insert a New Procedure**

➤ You should be in the Visual Basic Editor as shown in Figure 8b. If necessary, double click **Module1** in the Explorer Window to open this module. Pull down the **Insert menu** and click the **Procedure command** to display the Add Procedure dialog box.

➤ Click in the **Name** text box and enter **IfThenElseExamples** as the name of the procedure. Click the option buttons for a **Sub procedure** and for **Public scope**. Click **OK**. The sub procedure should appear within the module and consist of the Sub and End Sub statements.

➤ Click within the newly created procedure, then click the **Procedure View button** at the bottom of the window. The display changes to show just the current procedure.

➤ Click the **Save button** to save the module with the new procedure.

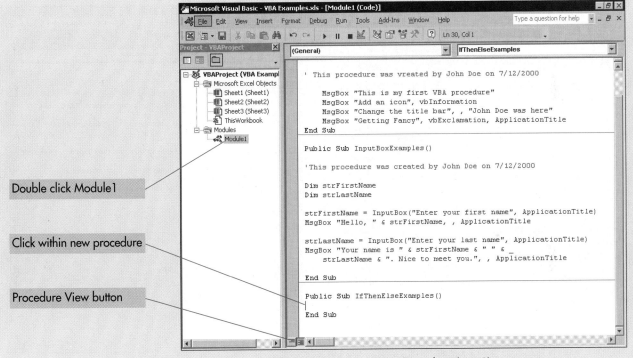

(b) Insert a New Procedure (step 2)

FIGURE 8 *Hands-on Exercise 2 (continued)*

PROCEDURE VIEW VERSUS FULL MODULE VIEW

The procedures within a module can be displayed individually, or alternatively, multiple procedures can be viewed simultaneously. To go from one view to the other, click the Procedure View button at the bottom of the window to display just the procedure you are working on, or click the Full Module View button to display multiple procedures. You can press Ctrl+PgDn and Ctrl+PgUp to move between procedures in either view.

Step 3: **Create the If ... Then ... Else Procedure**

➤ Enter the IfThenElseExamples procedure as it appears in Figure 8c, but use your instructor's name instead of Bob's. Note the following:
  • The Dim statements at the beginning of the procedure are required to define the two variables that are used elsewhere in the procedure.
  • The syntax of the comparison is different for string variables versus numeric variables. String variables require quotation marks around the comparison value (e.g., strInstructorName = "Grauer"). Numeric variables (e.g., intUserStates = 50) do not.
  • Indentation and blank lines are used within a procedure to make the code easier to read, as distinct from a VBA requirement. Press the **Tab key** to indent one level to the right.
➤ Save the procedure.

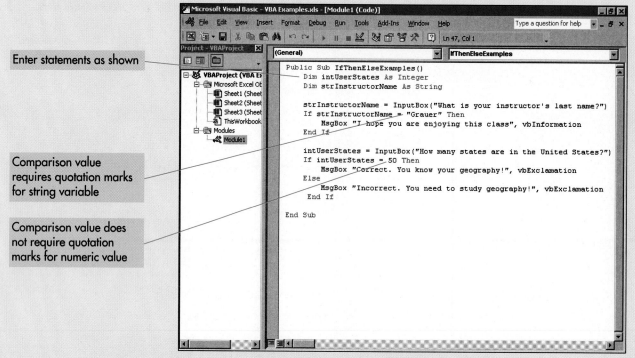

Enter statements as shown

Comparison value requires quotation marks for string variable

Comparison value does not require quotation marks for numeric value

(c) Create the If ... Then ... Else Procedure (step 3)

FIGURE 8   *Hands-on Exercise 2 (continued)*

THE COMPLETE WORD TOOL

It's easy to misspell a variable name within a procedure, which is why the Complete Word tool is so useful. Type the first several characters in a variable name (e.g., "intU" or "strI" in the current procedure), then press Ctrl+Space. VBA will complete the variable for you, if you have already entered a sufficient number of letters for a unique reference. Alternatively, it will display all of the elements that begin with the letters you have entered. Use the down arrow to scroll through the list until you find the item, then press the space bar to complete the entry.

➤ The best way to test a procedure is to display its output directly in the VBA window (without having to switch back and forth between that and the application window). Thus, right click the Excel button on the taskbar to display a context-sensitive menu, then click the **Minimize command**.

➤ There is no visible change on your monitor. Click anywhere within the procedure, then click the **Run Sub button**. You should see the dialog box in Figure 8d.

➤ Enter your instructor's name, exactly as it was spelled within the VBA procedure. Click **OK**. You should see a second message box that hopes you are enjoying the class. This box will be displayed only if you spell the instructor's name correctly. Click **OK**.

➤ You should see a second input box that asks how many states are in the United States. Enter **50** and click **OK**. You should see a message indicating that you know your geography. Click **OK** to close the dialog box.

➤ Click the **Run Sub button** a second time, but enter a different set of values in response to the prompts. Misspell your instructor's name, and you will not see the associated message box.

➤ Enter any number other than 50, and you will be told to study geography. Continue to test the procedure until you are satisfied it works under all conditions.

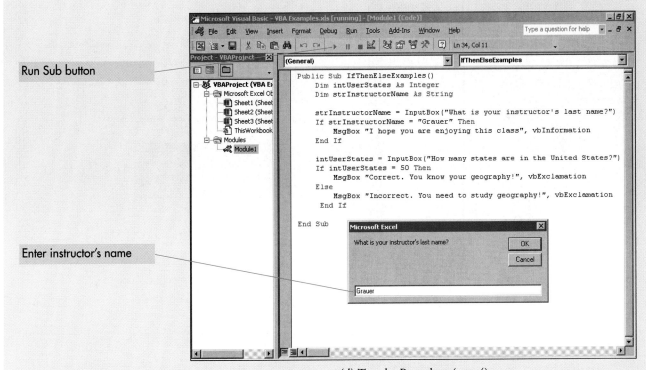

(d) Test the Procedure (step 4)

FIGURE 8   *Hands-on Exercise 2 (continued)*

Create and Test the CaseExample Procedure

➤ Pull down the **Insert menu** and create a new procedure called **CaseExample**, then enter the statements exactly as they appear in Figure 8e. Note:

• The variable sngUserGPA is declared to be a single-precision floating-point number (as distinct from the integer type that was used previously). A floating-point number is required in order to maintain a decimal point.

• You may use any editing technique with which you are comfortable. You could, for example, enter the first case, copy it four times in the procedure, then modify the copied text as necessary.

• The use of indentation and blank lines is for the convenience of the programmer and not a requirement of VBA.

➤ Click the **Run Sub button**, then test the procedure. Be sure to test it under all conditions; that is, you need to run it several times and enter a different GPA each time to be sure that all of the cases are working correctly.

➤ Save the procedure.

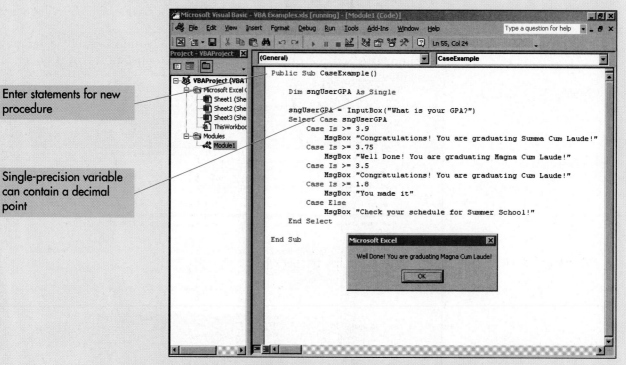

Enter statements for new procedure

Single-precision variable can contain a decimal point

(e) Create and Test the CaseExample Procedure (step 5)

FIGURE 8 *Hands-on Exercise 2 (continued)*

RELATIONAL OPERATORS

The condition portion of an If or Case statement uses one of several relational operators. These include =, <, and > for equal to, less than, or greater than, respectively. You can also use >=, <=, or <> for greater than or equal to, less than or equal to, or not equal. This is basic, but very important, information if you are to code these statements correctly.

Step 6: **Create a Custom Toolbar**

➤ Click the **Excel** (or **Access**) **button** to display the associated application window. Pull down the **View menu**, click (or point to) the **Toolbars command**, then click **Customize** to display the Customize dialog box in Figure 8f. (Bob's toolbar is not yet visible.) Click the **Toolbars tab**.

➤ Click the **New button** to display the New Toolbar dialog box. Enter the name of your toolbar—e.g., **Bob's toolbar**—then click **OK** to create the toolbar and close the dialog box.

➤ Your toolbar should appear on the screen, but it does not yet contain any buttons. If necessary, click and drag the title bar of your toolbar to move the toolbar within the application window.

➤ Toggle the check box that appears next to your toolbar within the Customize dialog box on and off to display or hide your toolbar. Leave the box checked to display the toolbar and continue with this exercise.

Custom toolbar

New button

Click to display/hide toolbar

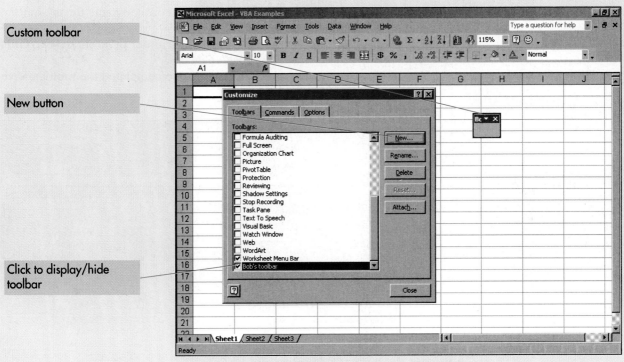

(f) Create a Custom Toolbar (step 6)

FIGURE 8 *Hands-on Exercise 2 (continued)*

FIXED VERSUS FLOATING TOOLBARS

A toolbar may be docked (fixed) along the edge of the application window, or it can be displayed as a floating toolbar anywhere within the window. You can switch back and forth by dragging the move handle of a docked toolbar to move the toolbar away from the edge. Conversely, you can drag the title bar of a floating toolbar to the edge of the window to dock the toolbar. You can also click and drag the border of a floating toolbar to change its size.

Step 7: **Add Buttons to the Toolbar**

➤ Click the **Commands tab** in the Customize dialog box, click the **down arrow** in the Categories list box, then scroll until you can select the **Macros category**. (If you are using Access and not Excel, you need to select the **File category**, then follow the steps as described in the boxed tip on the next page.)

➤ Click and drag the **Custom button** to your toolbar and release the mouse. A "happy face" button appears on the toolbar you just created. (You can remove a button from a toolbar by simply dragging the button from the toolbar.)

➤ Select the newly created button, then click the **Modify Selection command button** (or right click the button to display the context-sensitive menu) in Figure 8g. Change the button's properties as follows:

• Click the **Assign Macro command** at the bottom of the menu to display the Assign Macro dialog box, then select the **IfThenElseExamples** macro (procedure) to assign it to the button. Click **OK**.

• Click the **Modify Selection button** a second time.

• Click in the **Name Textbox** and enter an appropriate name for the button, such as **IfThenElseExamples**.

• Click the **Modify Selection button** a third time, then click **Text Only (Always)** to display text rather than an image.

➤ Close the Customize dialog box when you have completed the toolbar. Save the workbook.

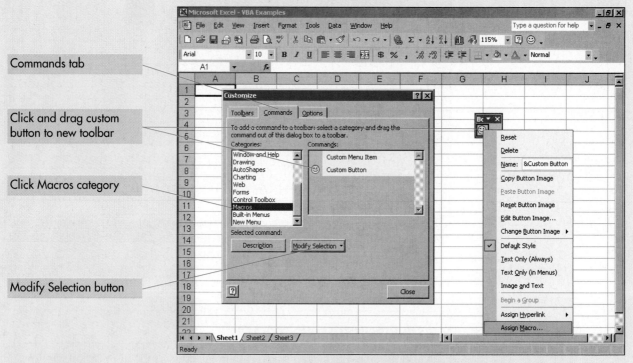

(g) Add Buttons to the Toolbar (step 7)

FIGURE 8 *Hands-on Exercise 2 (continued)*

Step 8: **Test the Custom Toolbar**

➤ Click any command on your toolbar as shown in Figure 8h. We clicked the **InputBoxExamples button**, which in turn executed the InputBoxExamples procedure that was created in the first exercise.

➤ Enter the appropriate information in any input boxes that are displayed. Click **OK**. Close your toolbar when you have completed testing it.

➤ If this is not your own machine, you should delete your toolbar as a courtesy to the next student. Pull down the **View menu**, click the **Toolbars command**, click **Customize** to display the Customize dialog box, then click the **Toolbars tab**. Select (highlight) the toolbar, then click the **Delete button** in the Customize dialog box. Click **OK** to delete the button. Close the dialog box.

➤ Exit Office if you do not want to continue with the next exercise.

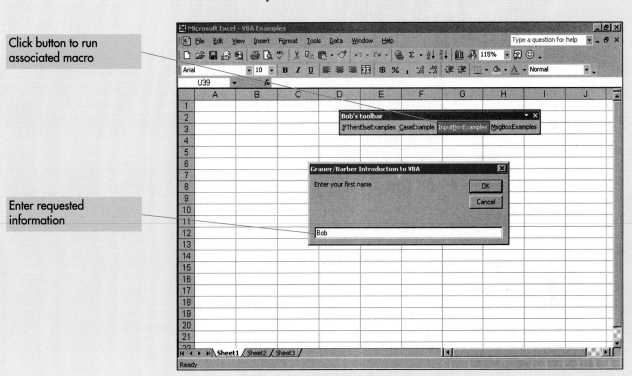

Click button to run associated macro

Enter requested information

(h) Test the Custom Toolbar (step 8)

FIGURE 8 *Hands-on Exercise 2 (continued)*

ACCESS IS DIFFERENT

The procedure to create a custom toolbar in Access is different from the procedure in Excel. Select the File category within the Customize dialog box, then click and drag the Custom command to the newly created toolbar. Select the command on the toolbar, then click the Modify Selection command button in the dialog box. Click Properties, click the On Action text box, then type the name of the procedure you want to run in the format, =procedurename(). Close the dialog boxes, then press Alt+F11 to return to the VBA Editor. Change the key word "Sub" that identifies the procedure to "Function". Return to the database window, then test the newly created toolbar.

The *For . . . Next statement* executes all statements between the words For and Next a specified number of times, using a counter to keep track of the number of times the statements are executed. The simplest form of the statement, For intCounter = 1 To N, executes the statements within the loop N times.

The procedure in Figure 9 contains two For . . . Next statements that sum the numbers from 1 to 10, counting by one and two, respectively. The Dim statements at the beginning of the procedure declare two variables, intSumofNumbers to hold the sum and intCounter to hold the value of the counter. The sum is initialized to zero immediately before the first loop. The statements in the loop are then executed 10 times, each time incrementing the sum by the value of the counter. The result (the sum of the numbers from 1 to 10) is displayed after the loop in Figure 9b.

The second For . . . Next statement increments the counter by two rather than by one. (The increment or step is assumed to be one unless a different value is specified.) The sum of the numbers is reset to zero prior to entering the second loop, the loop is entered, and the counter is initialized to the starting value of one. Each subsequent time through the loop, however, the counter is incremented by two. Each time the value of the counter is compared to the ending value, until it (the counter) exceeds the ending value, at which point the For . . . Next statement is complete. Thus the second loop will be executed for values of 1, 3, 5, 7, and 9. After the fifth time through the loop, the counter is incremented to 11, which is greater than the ending value of 10, and the loop is terminated.

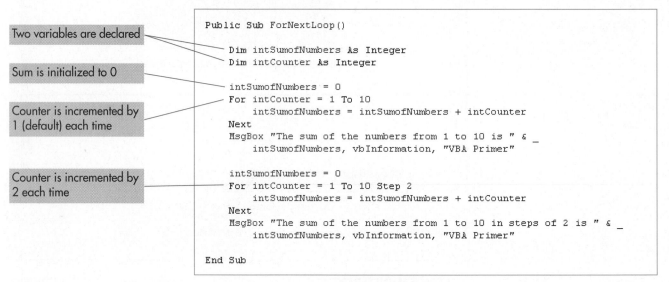

Two variables are declared

Sum is initialized to 0

Counter is incremented by 1 (default) each time

Counter is incremented by 2 each time

```
Public Sub ForNextLoop()

    Dim intSumofNumbers As Integer
    Dim intCounter As Integer

    intSumofNumbers = 0
    For intCounter = 1 To 10
        intSumofNumbers = intSumofNumbers + intCounter
    Next
    MsgBox "The sum of the numbers from 1 to 10 is " & _
        intSumofNumbers, vbInformation, "VBA Primer"

    intSumofNumbers = 0
    For intCounter = 1 To 10 Step 2
        intSumofNumbers = intSumofNumbers + intCounter
    Next
    MsgBox "The sum of the numbers from 1 to 10 in steps of 2 is " & _
        intSumofNumbers, vbInformation, "VBA Primer"

End Sub
```

(a) VBA Code

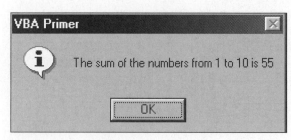

(b) In Increments of 1

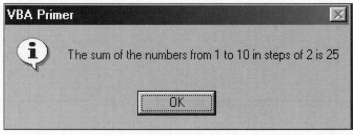

(c) In Increments of 2

FIGURE 9   *For . . . Next Loops*

The For ... Next statement is ideal when you know in advance how many times you want to go through a loop. There are many instances, however, when the number of times through the loop is indeterminate. You could, for example, give a user multiple chances to enter a password or answer a question. This type of logic is implemented through a Do loop. You can repeat the loop as long as a condition is true (Do While), or until a condition becomes true (Do Until). The choice depends on how you want to state the condition.

Regardless of which key word you choose, Do While or Do Until, two formats are available. The difference is subtle and depends on whether the key word (While or Until) appears at the beginning or end of the loop. Our discussion will use the Do Until statement, but the Do While statement works in similar fashion.

Look closely at the procedure in Figure 10a, which contains two different loops. In the first example, the Until condition appears at the end of the loop, which means the statements in the loop are executed, and then the condition is tested. This ensures that the statements in the loop will be executed at least once. The second loop, however, places the Until condition at the beginning of the loop, so that it (the condition) is tested prior to the loop being executed. Thus, if the condition is satisfied initially, the second loop will never be executed. In other words, there are two distinct statements **Do ... Loop Until** and **Do Until ... Loop**. The first statement executes the loop, then tests the condition. The second statement tests the condition, then enters the loop.

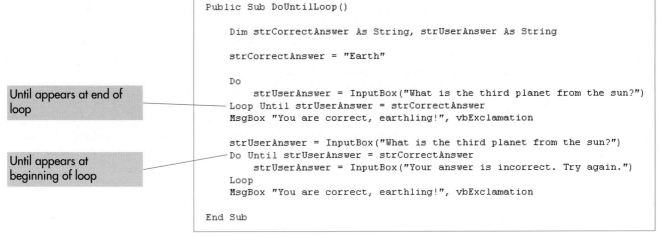

Until appears at end of loop

Until appears at beginning of loop

```
Public Sub DoUntilLoop()

    Dim strCorrectAnswer As String, strUserAnswer As String

    strCorrectAnswer = "Earth"

    Do
        strUserAnswer = InputBox("What is the third planet from the sun?")
    Loop Until strUserAnswer = strCorrectAnswer
    MsgBox "You are correct, earthling!", vbExclamation

    strUserAnswer = InputBox("What is the third planet from the sun?")
    Do Until strUserAnswer = strCorrectAnswer
        strUserAnswer = InputBox("Your answer is incorrect. Try again.")
    Loop
    MsgBox "You are correct, earthling!", vbExclamation

End Sub
```

(a) VBA Code

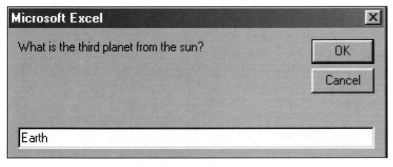

(b) Input the Answer

(c) Correct Response

FIGURE 10 *Do Until Loops*

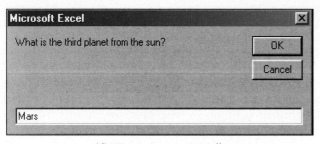
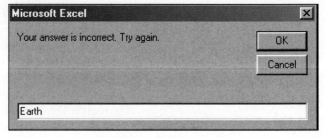

(d) Wrong Answer Initially   (e) Second Chance

FIGURE 10   *Do Until Loops (continued)*

It's tricky, but stay with us. In the first example, the user is asked the question within the loop, and the loop is executed repeatedly until the user gives the correct answer. In the second example, the user is asked the question outside of the loop, and the loop is bypassed if the user answers it correctly. The latter is the preferred logic because it enables us to phrase the question differently, before and during the loop. Look carefully at the difference between the InputBox statements and see how the question changes within the second loop.

DEBUGGING

As you learn more about VBA and develop more powerful procedures, you are more likely to make mistakes. The process of finding and correcting errors within a procedure is known as **debugging** and it is an integral part of programming. Do not be discouraged if you make mistakes. Everyone does. The important thing is how quickly you are able to find and correct the errors that invariably occur. We begin our discussion of debugging by describing two types of errors, **compilation errors** and **execution** (or **run-time**) **errors**.

A compilation error is simply an error in VBA syntax. (Compilation is the process of translating a VBA procedure to machine language, and thus a compilation error occurs when the VBA Editor is unable to convert a statement to machine language.) Compilation errors occur for many reasons, such as misspelling a key word, omitting a comma, and so on. VBA recognizes the error before the procedure is run and displays the invalid statement in red together with an associated error message. The programmer corrects the error and then reruns the procedure.

Execution errors are caused by errors in logic and are more difficult to detect because they occur without any error message. VBA, or for that matter any other programming language, does what you tell it to do, which is not necessarily what you want it to do. If, for example, you were to compute the sales tax of an item by multiplying the price by 60% rather than 6%, VBA will perform the calculation and simply display the wrong answer. It is up to you to realize that the results of the procedure are incorrect, and you will need to examine its statements and correct the mistake.

So how do you detect an execution error? In essence, you must decide what the expected output of your procedure should be, then you compare the actual results of the procedure to the intended result. If the results are different, an error has occurred, and you have to examine the logic in the procedure to find the error. You may see the mistake immediately (e.g., using 60% rather than 6% in the previous example), or you may have to examine the code more closely. And as you might expect, VBA has a variety of tools to help you in the debugging process. These tools are accessed from the **Debug toolbar** or the **Debug menu** as shown in Figure 11.

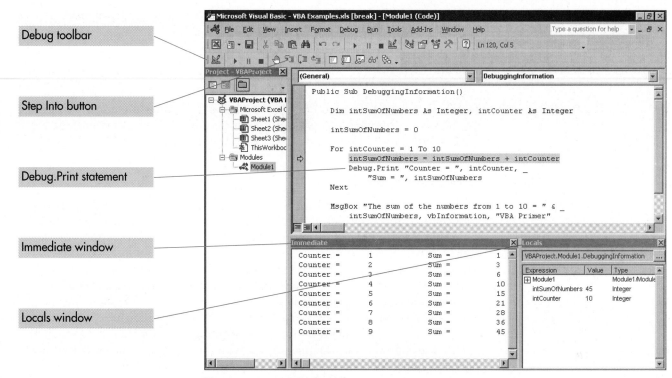

Debug toolbar

Step Into button

Debug.Print statement

Immediate window

Locals window

FIGURE 11 *Debugging*

The procedure in Figure 11 is a simple For . . . Next loop to sum the integers from 1 to 10. The procedure is correct as written, but we have introduced several debugging techniques into the figure. The most basic technique is to step through the statements in the procedure one at a time to see the sequence in which the statements are executed. Click the ***Step Into button*** on the Debug toolbar to enter (step into) the procedure, then continue to click the button to move through the procedure. Each time you click the button, the statement that is about to be executed is highlighted.

Another useful technique is to display the values of selected variables as they change during execution. This is accomplished through the ***Debug.Print statement*** that displays the values in the ***Immediate window***. The Debug.Print statement is placed within the For . . . Next loop so that you can see how the counter and the associated sum change during execution.

As the figure now stands, we have gone through the loop nine times, and the sum of the numbers from 1 to 9 is 45. The Step Into button is in effect so that the statement to be executed next is highlighted. You can see that we are back at the top of the loop, where the counter has been incremented to 10, and further, that we are about to increment the sum.

The ***Locals window*** is similar in concept except that it displays only the current values of all the variables within the procedure. Unlike the Immediate window, which requires the insertion of Debug.Print statements into a procedure to have meaning, the Locals window displays its values automatically, without any effort on the part of the programmer, other than opening the window. All three techniques can be used individually, or in conjunction with one another, as the situation demands.

We believe that the best time to practice debugging is when you know there are no errors in your procedure. As you may have guessed, it's time for the next hands-on exercise.

LOOPS AND DEBUGGING

Objective To create a loop using the For . . . Next and Do Until statements; to open the Locals and Immediate windows and illustrate different techniques for debugging. Use Figure 12 as a guide in the exercise.

Step 1: **Insert a New Procedure**

➤ Open the **VBA Examples workbook** or the Access database from the previous exercise. Either way, pull down the **Tools menu**, click the **Macro command**, then click **Visual Basic Editor** (or use the **Alt+F11** keyboard shortcut) to start the VBA editor.

➤ If necessary, double click **Module1** within the Project Explorer window to open this module. Pull down the **Insert menu** and click the **Procedure command** to display the Add Procedure dialog box.

➤ Click in the **Name** text box and enter **ForNextLoop** as the name of the procedure. Click the option buttons for a **Sub procedure** and for **Public scope**. Click **OK**. The sub procedure should appear within the module and consist of the Sub and End Sub statements.

➤ Click the **Procedure View button** at the bottom of the window as shown in Figure 12a. The display changes to show just the current procedure, giving you more room in which to work.

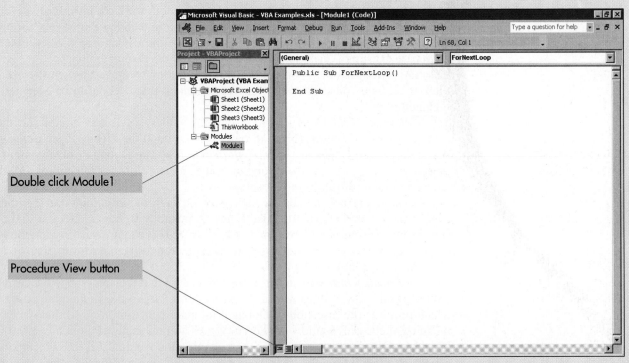

(a) Insert a New Procedure (step 1)

FIGURE 12   *Hands-on Exercise 3*

Step 2:   **Test the For . . . Next Procedure**

> Enter the procedure exactly as it appears in Figure 12b. Note the following:
>   - A comment is added at the beginning of the procedure to identify the author and the date.
>   - Two variables are declared at the beginning of the procedure, one to hold the sum of the numbers and the other to serve as a counter.
>   - The sum of the numbers is initialized to zero. The For . . . Next loop varies the counter from 1 to 10.
>   - The statement within the For . . . Next loop increments the sum of the numbers by the current value of the counter. The equal sign is really a replacement operator; that is, replace the variable on the left (the sum of the numbers) by the expression on the right (the sum of the numbers plus the value of the counter.
>   - Indentation and spacing within a procedure are for the convenience of the programmer and not a requirement of VBA. We align the For and Next statements at the beginning and end of a loop, then indent all statements within a loop.
>   - The MsgBox statement displays the result and is continued over two lines.
> Click the **Save button** to save the module. Right click the **Excel button** on the Windows taskbar to display a context-sensitive menu, then click the **Minimize command**.
> Click the **Run Sub button** to test the procedure, which should display the MsgBox statement in Figure 12b. Correct any errors that may occur.

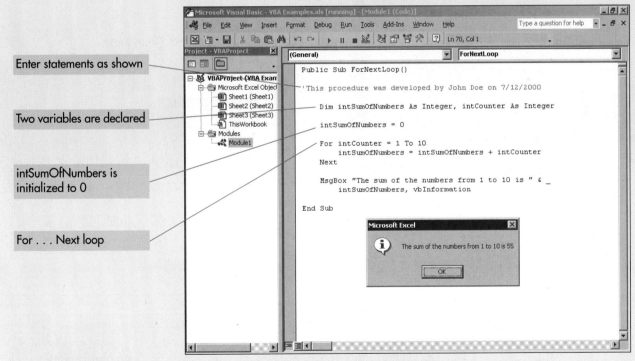

Enter statements as shown

Two variables are declared

intSumOfNumbers is initialized to 0

For . . . Next loop

(b) Test the For . . . Next Procedure (step 2)

FIGURE 12   *Hands-on Exercise 3 (continued)*

Step 3: **Compilation Errors**

➤ The best time to practice debugging is when you know that the procedure is working properly. Accordingly, we will make some deliberate errors in our procedure to illustrate different debugging techniques.

➤ Pull down the **View menu**, click the **Toolbars command**, and (if necessary) toggle the Debug toolbar on, then dock it under the Standard toolbar.

➤ Click on the statement that initializes intSumOfNumbers to zero and delete the "s" at the end of the variable name. Click the **Run Sub button**.

➤ You will see the message in Figure 12c. Click **OK** to acknowledge the error, then click the **Undo button** to correct the error.

➤ The procedure header is highlighted, indicating that execution is temporarily suspended and that additional action is required from you to continue testing. Click the **Run Sub button** to retest the procedure.

➤ This time the procedure executes correctly and you see the MsgBox statement indicating that the sum of the numbers from 1 to 10 is 55. Click **OK**.

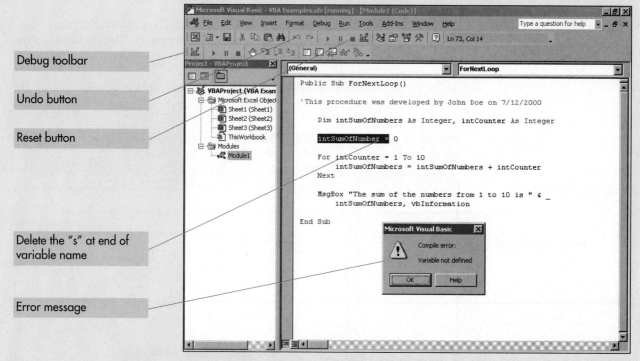

Debug toolbar

Undo button

Reset button

Delete the "s" at end of variable name

Error message

(c) Compilation Errors (step 3)

FIGURE 12   *Hands-on Exercise 3 (continued)*

USE HELP AS NECESSARY

Pull down the Help menu at any time (or press the F1 key) to access the VBA Help facility to explore at your leisure. You can also obtain context-sensitive help by clicking the Help button when it appears within a dialog box. Click the Help button in Figure 12c, for example, and you will be advised to correct the spelling of the variable.

Step 4: **Step Through a Procedure**

➤ Pull down the **View menu** a second time and click the **Locals Window command** (or click the **Locals Window button** on the Debug toolbar).

➤ If necessary, click and drag the top border of the Locals window to size the window appropriately as shown in Figure 12d.

➤ Click anywhere within the procedure. Pull down the **Debug menu** and click the **Step Into command** (or click the **Step Into button** on the Debug toolbar). The first statement (the procedure header) is highlighted, indicating that you are about to enter the procedure.

➤ Click the **Step Into button** (or use the **F8** keyboard shortcut) to step into the procedure and advance to the next executable statement. The statement that initializes intSumOfNumbers to zero is highlighted, indicating that this statement is about to be executed.

➤ Continue to press the **F8 key** to step through the procedure. Each time you execute a statement, you can see the values of intSumOfNumbers and intCounter change within the Locals window. (You can click the **Step Out button** at any time to end the procedure.)

➤ Correct errors as they occur. Click the **Reset button** on the Standard or Debug toolbars at any time to begin executing the procedure from the beginning.

➤ Eventually you exit from the loop, and the sum of the numbers (from 1 to 10) is displayed within a message box.

➤ Click **OK** to close the message box. Press the **F8 key** a final time, then close the Locals window.

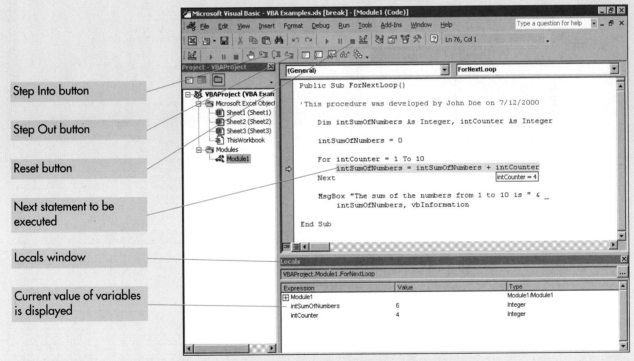

Step Into button

Step Out button

Reset button

Next statement to be executed

Locals window

Current value of variables is displayed

(d) Step Through a Procedure (step 4)

FIGURE 12 *Hands-on Exercise 3 (continued)*

Step 5: **The Immediate Window**

➤ You should be back in the VBA window. Click immediately to the left of the Next statement and press **enter** to insert a blank line. Type the **Debug.Print** statement exactly as shown in Figure 12e. (Click **OK** if you see a message indicating that the procedure will be reset.)

➤ Pull down the **View menu** and click the **Immediate Window command** (or click the **Immediate Window button** on the Debug toolbar). The Immediate window should be empty, but if not, you can click and drag to select the contents, then press the Del key to clear the window.

➤ Click anywhere within the For . . . Next procedure, then click the **Run Sub button** on the Debug toolbar to execute the procedure. You will see the familiar message box indicating that the sum of the numbers is 55. Click **OK**.

➤ You should see 10 lines within the Immediate window as shown in Figure 12e, corresponding to the values displayed by the Debug.Print statement as it was executed within the loop.

➤ Close the Immediate window.

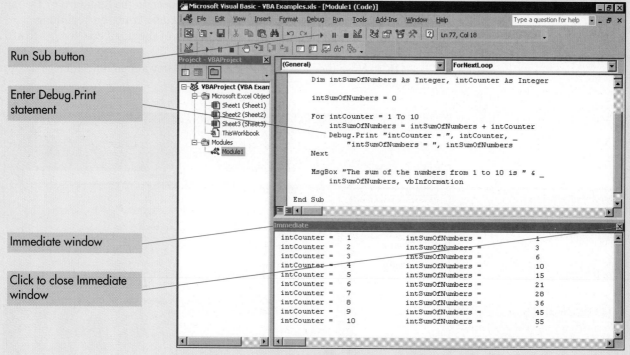

(e) The Immediate Window (step 5)

FIGURE 12 *Hands-on Exercise 3 (continued)*

INSTANT CALCULATOR

Use the Print method (action) in the Immediate window to use VBA as a calculator. Press Ctrl+G at any time to display the Immediate window. Click in the window, then type the statement Debug.Print, followed by your calculation, for example, Debug.Print 2+2, and press enter. The answer is displayed on the next line in the Immediate window.

Step 6: **A More General Procedure**

➤ Modify the existing procedure to make it more general; for example, to sum the values from any starting value to any ending value:
  • Click at the end of the existing Dim statement to position the insertion point, press **enter** to create a new line, then add the second Dim statement as shown in Figure 12f.
  • Click before the For statement, press **enter** to create a blank line, press **enter** a second time, then enter the two InputBox statements to ask the user for the beginning and ending value.
  • Modify the For statement to execute from **intStart** to **intEnd** rather than from 1 to 10.
  • Change the MsgBox statement to reflect the values of intStart and intEnd, and a customized title bar. Note the use of the ampersand and the underscore, to indicate concatenation and continuation, respectively.
➤ Click the **Save button** to save the module.

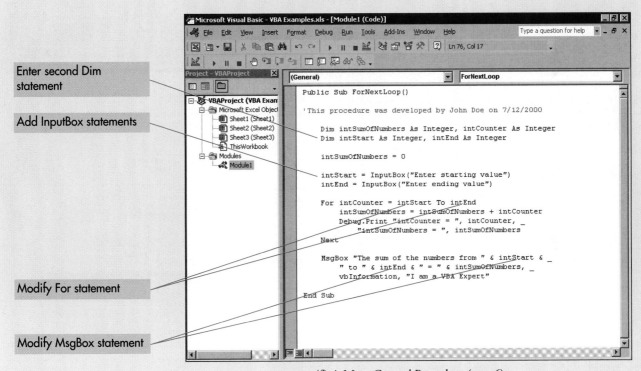

Enter second Dim statement

Add InputBox statements

Modify For statement

Modify MsgBox statement

(f) A More General Procedure (step 6)

FIGURE 12 *Hands-on Exercise 3 (continued)*

USE WHAT YOU KNOW

Use the techniques acquired from other applications such as Microsoft Word to facilitate editing within the VBA window. Press the Ins key to toggle between the insert and overtype modes as you modify the statements within a VBA procedure. You can also cut, copy, and paste statements (or parts of statements) within a procedure and from one procedure to another. The Find and Replace commands are also useful.

Step 7: **Test the Procedure**

➤ Click the **Run Sub button** to test the procedure. You should be prompted for a beginning and an ending value. Enter any numbers you like, such as 10 and 20, respectively, to match the result in Figure 12g.

➤ The value displayed in the MsgBox statement should reflect the numbers you entered. For example, you will see a sum of 165 if you entered 10 and 20 as the starting and ending values.

➤ Look carefully at the message box that is displayed in Figure 12g. Its title bar displays the literal "I am a VBA expert", corresponding to the last argument in the MsgBox statement.

➤ Note, too, the spacing that appears within the message box, which includes spaces before and after each number. Look at your results and, if necessary, modify the MsgBox statement so that you have the same output. Click **OK**.

➤ Save the procedure.

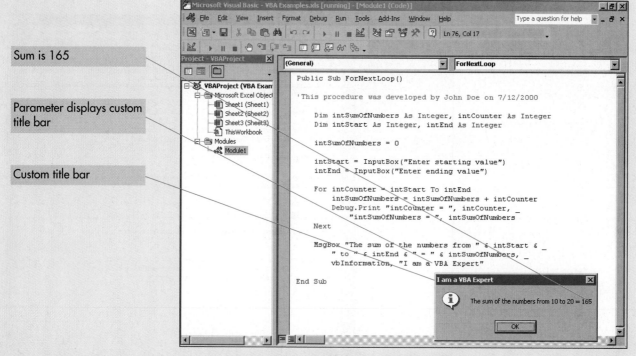

Sum is 165

Parameter displays custom title bar

Custom title bar

(g) Test the Procedure (step 7)

FIGURE 12   *Hands-on Exercise 3 (continued)*

CHANGE THE INCREMENT

The For ... Next statement can be made more general by supplying an increment within the For statement. Try For intCount = 1 To 10 Step 2, or more generally, For intCount = intStart to intEnd Step intStepValue. "Step" is a Visual Basic key word and must be entered that way. intCount, intEnd, and intStepValue are user-defined variables. The variables must be defined at the beginning of a procedure and can be initialized by requesting values from the user through the InputBox statement.

Step 8: **Create a Do Until Loop**

➤ Pull down the **Insert menu** and click the **Procedure command** to insert a new procedure called **DoUntilLoop**. Enter the procedure as it appears in Figure 12h. Note the following:

- Two string variables are declared to hold the correct answer and the user's response, respectively.
- The variable strCorrectAnswer is set to "Earth", the correct answer for our question.
- The initial InputBox function prompts the user to enter his/her response to the question. A second InputBox function appears in the loop that is executed if and only if the user enters the wrong answer.
- The Until condition appears at the beginning of the loop, so that the loop is entered only if the user answers incorrectly. The loop executes repeatedly until the correct answer is supplied.
- A message to the user is displayed at the end of the procedure after the correct answer has been entered.

➤ Click the **Run Sub button** to test the procedure. Enter the correct answer on your first attempt, and you will see that the loop is never entered.

➤ Rerun the procedure, answer incorrectly, then note that a second input box appears, telling you that your answer was incorrect.

➤ Save the procedure.

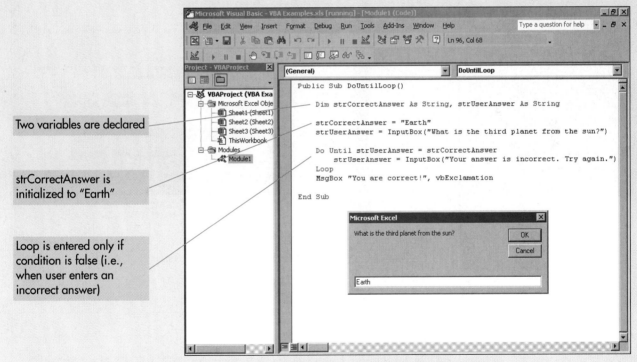

Two variables are declared

strCorrectAnswer is initialized to "Earth"

Loop is entered only if condition is false (i.e., when user enters an incorrect answer)

(h) Create a Do Until Loop (step 8)

FIGURE 12   *Hands-on Exercise 3 (continued)*

Step 9: **A More Powerful Procedure**

➤ Modify the procedure as shown in Figure 12i to include the statements to count and print the number of times the user takes to get the correct answer.
- The variable intNumberOfAttempts is declared as an integer and is initialized to 1 after the user inputs his/her initial answer.
- The Do loop is expanded to increment intNumberOfAttempts by 1 each time the loop is executed.
- The MsgBox statement after the loop is expanded prints the number of attempts the user took to answer the question.

➤ Save the module, then click the **Run Sub button** to test the module. You should see a dialog box similar to the one in Figure 12i. Click **OK**.

➤ Pull down the **File menu** and click the **Print command** to display the Print dialog box. Click the option button to print the current module. Click **OK**.

➤ Exit Office if you do not want to continue at this time.

Add Dim statement

intNumberOfAttempts is initialized to 1

Do loop keeps track of number of attempts to get the correct answer

MsgBox statement now displays number of attempts

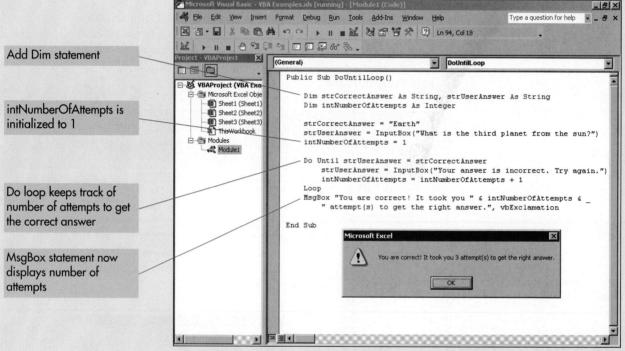

(i) A More Powerful Procedure (step 9)

FIGURE 12   *Hands-on Exercise 3 (continued)*

IT'S NOT EQUAL, BUT REPLACE

All programming languages use statements of the form N = N + 1, in which the equal sign does not mean equal in the literal sense; that is, N cannot equal N + 1. The equal sign is really a replacement operator. Thus, the expression on the right of the equal sign is evaluated, and that result replaces the value of the variable on the left. In other words, the statement N = N + 1 increments the value of N by one.

Our approach thus far has focused on VBA as an independent entity that can be run without specific reference to the applications in Microsoft Office. We have covered several individual statements, explained how to use the VBA editor to create and run procedures, and how to debug those procedures, if necessary. We hope you have found the material to be interesting, but you may be asking yourself, "What does this have to do with Microsoft Office?" In other words, how can you use your knowledge of VBA to enhance your ability in Microsoft Excel or Access? The answer is to create *event procedures* that run automatically in response to events within an Office application.

VBA is different from traditional programming languages in that it is event-driven. An *event* is defined as any action that is recognized by an application such as Excel or Access. Opening or closing an Excel workbook or an Access database is an event. Selecting a worksheet within a workbook is also an event, as is clicking on a command button on an Access form. To use VBA within Microsoft Office, you decide which events are significant, and what is to happen when those events occur. Then you develop the appropriate event procedures.

Consider, for example, Figure 13, which displays the results of two event procedures in conjunction with opening and closing an Excel workbook. (If you are using Microsoft Access instead of Excel, you can skip this discussion and the associated exercise, and move to the parallel material for Access that appears after the next hands-on exercise.) The procedure associated with Figure 13a displays a message that appears automatically after the user executes the command to close the associated workbook. The procedure is almost trivial to write, and consists of a single MsgBox statement. The effect of the procedure is quite significant, however, as it reminds the user to back up his or her work after closing the workbook. Nor does it matter how the user closes the workbook—whether by pulling down the menu or using a keyboard shortcut—because the procedure runs automatically in response to the Close Workbook event, regardless of how that event occurs.

The dialog box in Figure 13b prompts the user for a password and appears automatically when the user opens the workbook. The logic here is more sophisticated in that the underlying procedure contains an InputBox statement to request the password, a Do Until loop that is executed until the user enters the correct password or exceeds the allotted number of attempts, then additional logic to display the worksheet or terminate the application if the user fails to enter the proper password. The procedure is not difficult, however, and it builds on the VBA statements that were covered earlier.

The next hands-on exercise has you create the two event procedures that are associated with Figure 13. As you do the exercise, you will gain additional experience with VBA and an appreciation for the potential event procedures within Microsoft Office.

HIDING AND UNHIDING A WORKSHEET

Look carefully at the workbooks in Figures 13a and 13b. Both figures reference the identical workbook, Financial Consultant, as can be seen from the title bar. Look at the worksheet tabs, however, and note that two worksheets are visible in Figure 13a, whereas the Calculations worksheet is hidden in Figure 13b. This was accomplished in the Open workbook procedure and was implemented to hide the calculations from the user until the correct password was entered. See exercise 7 at the end of the chapter.

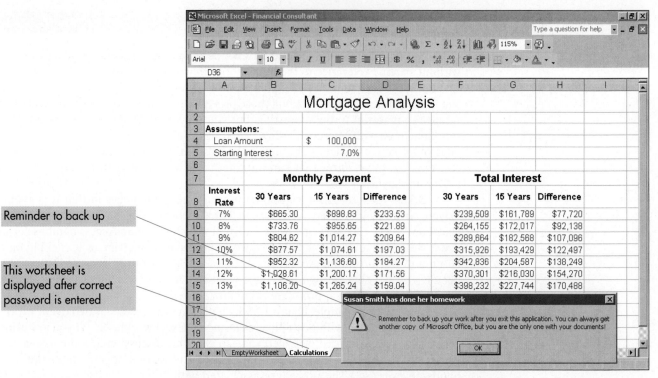

Reminder to back up

This worksheet is displayed after correct password is entered

(a) Message to the User (Close Workbook event)

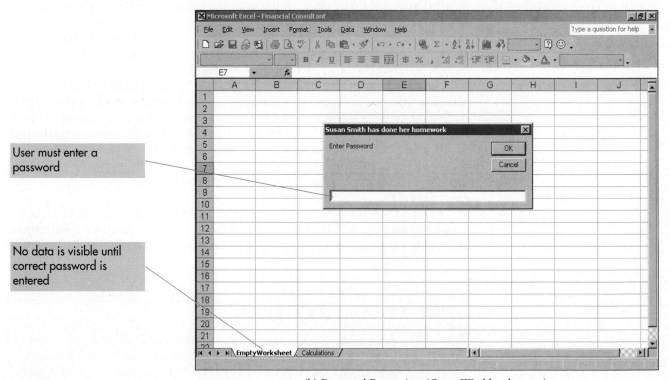

User must enter a password

No data is visible until correct password is entered

(b) Password Protection (Open Workbook event)

FIGURE 13 *Event-Driven Programming*

EVENT-DRIVEN PROGRAMMING (MICROSOFT EXCEL)

Objective To create an event procedure to implement password protection that is associated with opening an Excel workbook; to create a second event procedure that displays a message to the user upon closing the workbook. Use Figure 14 as a guide in the exercise.

Step 1: **Create the Close Workbook Procedure**

➤ Open the **VBA Examples workbook** you have used for the previous exercises and enable the macros. If you have been using Access rather than Excel, start Excel, open a new workbook, then save the workbook as **VBA Examples**.

➤ Pull down the **Tools menu**, click the **Macro command**, then click the **Visual Basic Editor command** (or use the **Alt+F11** keyboard shortcut).

➤ You should see the Project Explorer pane as shown in Figure 14a, but if not, pull down the **View menu** and click the **Project Explorer**. Double click **ThisWorkbook** to create a module for the workbook as a whole.

➤ Enter the **Option Explicit statement** if it is not there already, then press **enter** to create a new line. Type the statement to declare the variable, **Application-Title**, using your name instead of Susan Smith.

➤ Click the **down arrow** in the Object list box and select **Workbook**, then click the **down arrow** in the Procedure list box and select the **BeforeClose event** to create the associated procedure. (If you choose a different event by mistake, click and drag to select the associated statements, then press the **Del key** to delete the procedure.)

➤ Enter the MsgBox statement as it appears in Figure 14a. Save the procedure.

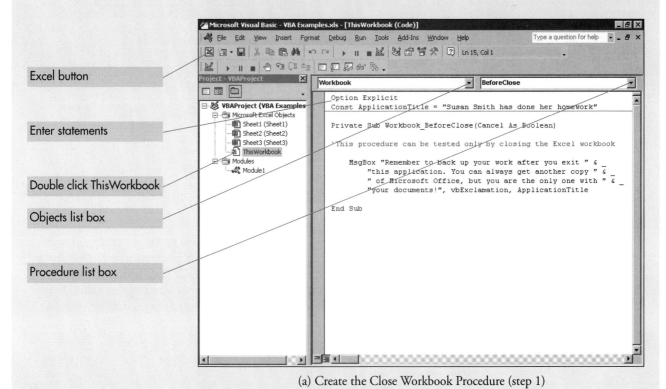

(a) Create the Close Workbook Procedure (step 1)

FIGURE 14 *Hands-on Exercise 4*

Step 2: **Test the Close Workbook Procedure**

➤ Click the **Excel button** on the Standard toolbar or on the Windows taskbar to view the Excel workbook. The workbook is not empty; that is, it does not contain any cell entries, but it does contain multiple VBA procedures.

➤ Pull down the **File menu** and click the **Close command**, which runs the procedure you just created and displays the dialog box in Figure 14b. Click **OK** after you have read the message, then click **Yes** if asked to save the workbook.

➤ Pull down the **File menu** and reopen the **VBA Examples workbook**, enabling the macros. Press **Alt+F11** to return to the VBA window to create an additional procedure.

➤ Double click **ThisWorkbook** from within the Projects Explorer pane to return to the BeforeClose procedure and make the necessary corrections, if any.

➤ Save the procedure.

Message is displayed

Click OK

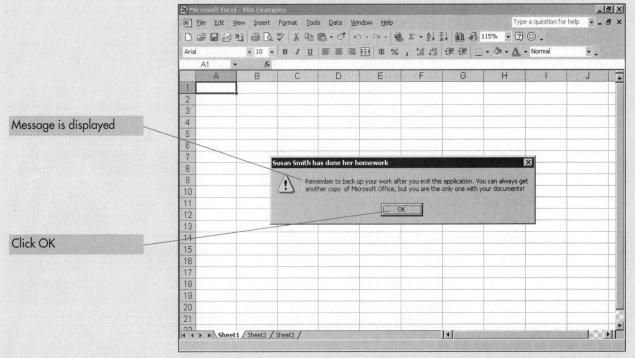

(b) Test the Close Workbook Procedure (step 2)

FIGURE 14 *Hands-on Exercise 4 (continued)*

THE MOST RECENTLY OPENED FILE LIST

One way to open a recently used workbook is to select the workbook directly from the File menu. Pull down the File menu, but instead of clicking the Open command, check to see if the workbook appears on the list of the most recently opened workbooks located at the bottom of the menu. If so, just click the workbook name, rather than having to make the appropriate selections through the Open dialog box.

Step 3:   **Start the Open Workbook Event Procedure**

➤ Click the **Procedure View button** at the bottom of the Code window. Click the **down arrow** in the Procedure list box and select the **Open event** to create an event procedure.
➤ Enter the VBA statements as shown in Figure 14c. Note the following:
  • Three variables are required for this procedure—the correct password, the password entered by the user, and the number of attempts.
  • The user is prompted for the password, and the number of attempts is set to one. The user is given two additional attempts, if necessary, to get the password correct. The loop is bypassed, however, if the user supplies the correct password on the first attempt.
➤ Minimize Excel. Save the procedure, then click the **Run Sub button** to test it. Try different combinations in your testing; that is, enter the correct password on the first, second, and third attempts. The password is **case-sensitive**.
➤ Correct errors as they occur. Click the **Reset button** at any time to begin executing the procedure from the beginning. Save the procedure.

Run Sub button

Reset button

Enter statements as shown

Procedure View button

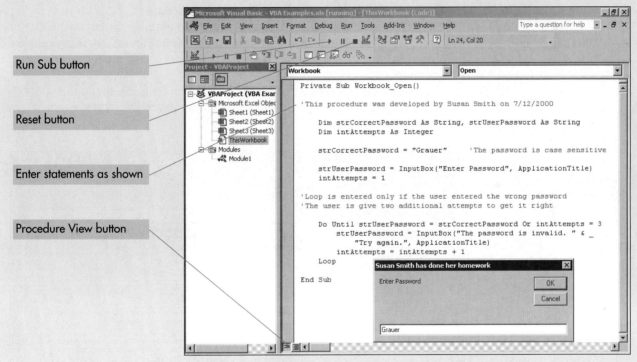

(c) Start the Open Workbook Event Procedure (step 3)

FIGURE 14   *Hands-on Exercise 4 (continued)*

THE OBJECT AND PROCEDURE BOXES

The Object box at the top of the code window displays the selected object such as an Excel workbook, whereas the Procedure box displays the name of the events appropriate to that object. Events that already have procedures appear in bold. Clicking an event that is not bold creates the procedure header and End Sub statements for that event.

Step 4: **Complete the Open Workbook Event Procedure**

➤ Enter the remaining statements in the procedure as shown in Figure 14d. Note the following:
- The If statement determines whether the user has entered the correct password and, if so, displays the appropriate message.
- If, however, the user fails to supply the correct password, a different message is displayed, and the workbook will close due to the **Workbooks.Close statement** within the procedure.
- As a precaution, put an apostrophe in front of the Workbooks.Close statement so that it is a comment, and thus it is not executed. Once you are sure that you can enter the correct password, you can remove the apostrophe and implement the password protection.

➤ Save the procedure, then click the **Run Sub button** to test it. Be sure that you can enter the correct password (**Grauer**), and that you realize the password is case-sensitive.

➤ Delete the apostrophe in front of the Workbooks.Close statement. The text of the statement changes from green to black to indicate that it is an executable statement rather than a comment. Save the procedure.

➤ Click the **Run Sub button** a second time, then enter an incorrect password three times in a row. You will see the dialog box in Figure 14d, followed by a message reminding you to back up your workbook, and then the workbook will close.

➤ The first message makes sense, the second does not make sense in this context. Thus, we need to modify the Close Workbook procedure when an incorrect password is entered.

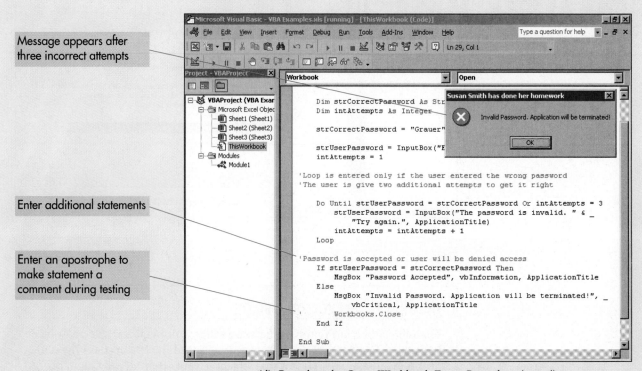

Message appears after three incorrect attempts

Enter additional statements

Enter an apostrophe to make statement a comment during testing

(d) Complete the Open Workbook Event Procedure (step 4)

FIGURE 14 *Hands-on Exercise 4 (continued)*

Step 5: **Modify the Before Close Event Procedure**

> ➤ Reopen the **VBA Examples workbook**. Click the button to **Enable Macros**.
> ➤ Enter the password, **Grauer** (the password is case-sensitive), press **enter**, then click **OK** when the password has been accepted.
> ➤ Press **Alt+F11** to reopen the VBA Editor, and (if necessary) double click **ThisWorkbook** within the list of Microsoft Excel objects.
> ➤ Click at the end of the line defining the ApplicationTitle constant, press **enter**, then enter the statement to define the **binNormalExit** variable as shown in Figure 14e. (The statement appears initially below the line ending the General Declarations section, but moves above the line when you press enter.)
> ➤ Modify the BeforeClose event procedure to include an If statement that tests the value of the binNormalExit variable as shown in Figure 14e. You must, however, set the value of this variable in the Open Workbook event procedure as described in step 6. Save the procedure.

Enter new statement

Modify procedure to include If statement

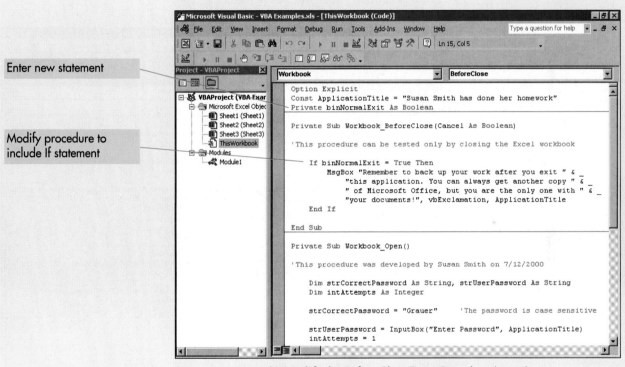

(e) Modify the Before Close Event Procedure (step 5)

FIGURE 14 *Hands-on Exercise 4 (continued)*

SETTING A SWITCH

The use of a switch (binNormalExit, in this example) to control an action within a procedure is a common programming technique. The switch is set to one of two values according to events that occur within the system, then the switch is subsequently tested and the appropriate action is taken. Here, the switch is set when the workbook is opened to indicate either a valid or invalid user. The switch is then tested prior to closing the workbook to determine whether to print the closing message.

Step 6: **Modify the Open Workbook Event Procedure**

➤ Scroll down to the Open Workbook event procedure, then modify the If statement to set the value of binNormExit as shown in Figure 14f:
  - Take advantage of the Complete Word tool to enter the variable name. Type the first few letters, "binN", then press Ctrl+Space, and VBA will complete the variable name.
  - The indentation within the statement is not a requirement of VBA per se, but is used to make the code easier to read. Blank lines are also added for this purpose.
  - Comments appear throughout the procedure to explain its logic.
  - Save the modified procedure.
➤ Click the **Run Sub button**, then enter an incorrect password three times in a row. Once again, you will see the dialog box indicating an invalid password, but this time you will not see the message reminding you to back up your workbook. The workbook closes as before.

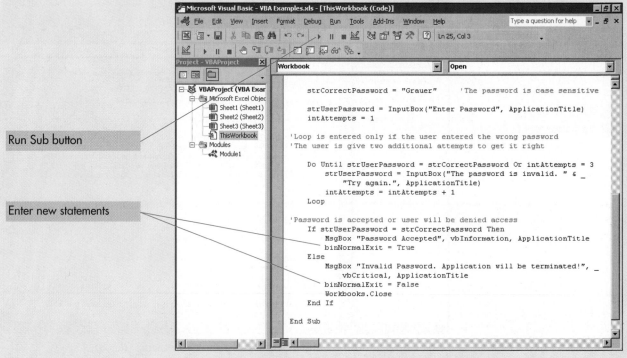

Run Sub button

Enter new statements

(f) Modify the Open Workbook Event Procedure (step 6)

FIGURE 14 *Hands-on Exercise 4 (continued)*

TEST UNDER ALL CONDITIONS

We cannot overemphasize the importance of thoroughly testing a procedure, and further, testing it under all conditions. VBA statements are powerful, but they are also complex, and a misplaced or omitted character can have dramatic consequences. Test every procedure completely at the time it is created, so that the logic of the procedure is fresh in your mind.

Step 7: **Open a Second Workbook**

➤ Reopen the **VBA Examples workbook**. Click the button to **Enable Macros**.
➤ Enter the password, **Grauer**, then press **enter**. Click **OK** when you see the second dialog box telling you that the password has been accepted.
➤ Pull down the **File menu** and click the **Open command** (or click the **Open button** on the Standard toolbar) and open a second workbook. We opened a workbook called **Financial Consultant**, but it does not matter which workbook you open.
➤ Pull down the **Window menu**, click the **Arrange command**, click the **Horizontal option button**, and click **OK** to tile the workbooks as shown in Figure 14g. The title bars show the names of the open workbooks.
➤ Pull down the **Tools menu**, click **Macro**, then click **Visual Basic Editor**.

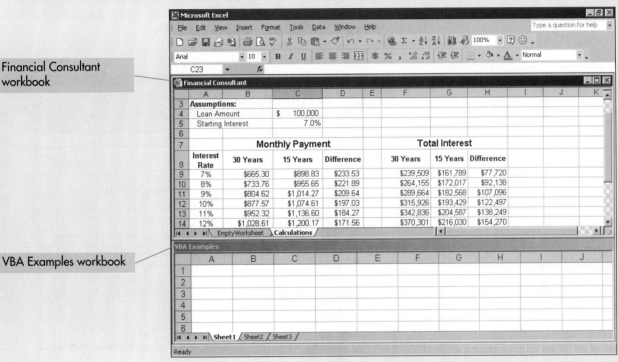

(g) Open a Second Workbook (step 7)

FIGURE 14   *Hands-on Exercise 4 (continued)*

THE COMPARISON IS CASE-SENSITIVE

Any literal comparison (e.g., strInstructorName = "Grauer") is case-sensitive, so that the user has to enter the correct name and case in order for the condition to be true. A response of "GRAUER" or "grauer", while containing the correct name, will be evaluated as false because the case does not match. You can, however, use the UCase (uppercase) function to convert the user's response to uppercase, and test accordingly. In other words, UCase(strInstructorName) = "GRAUER" will be evaluated as true if the user enters "Grauer" in any combination of upper or lowercase letters.

Step 8: **Copy the Procedure**

➤ You should be back in the Visual Basic Editor as shown in Figure 14h. Copy the procedures associated with the Open and Close Workbook events from the VBA Examples workbook to the other workbook, Financial Consultant.

- Double click **ThisWorkbook** within the list of Microsoft Excel objects under the VBA Examples workbook.
- Click and drag to select the definition of the ApplicationTitle constant in the General Declarations section plus the two procedures (to open and close the workbook) in their entirety.
- Click the **Copy button** on the Standard toolbar.
- If necessary, expand the Financial Consultant VBA Project, then double click **ThisWorkbook** with the list of Excel objects under the Financial Consultant workbook. Click underneath the **Option Explicit command**.
- Click the **Paste button** on the Standard toolbar. The VBA code should be copied into this module as shown in Figure 14h.

➤ Click the **Save button** to save the module.

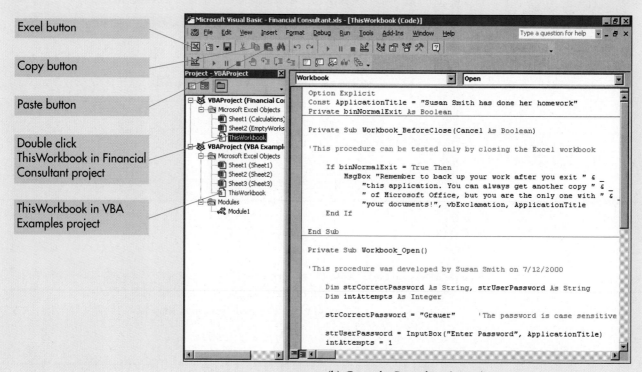

(h) Copy the Procedure (step 8)

FIGURE 14 *Hands-on Exercise 4 (continued)*

KEYBOARD SHORTCUTS—CUT, COPY, AND PASTE

Ctrl+X, Ctrl+C, and Ctrl+V are shortcuts to cut, copy, and paste, respectively, and apply to all applications in the Office suite as well as to Windows applications in general. (The shortcuts are easier to remember when you realize that the operative letters X, C, and V are next to each other at the bottom left side of the keyboard.)

Step 9: **Test the Procedure**

➤ Click the **Excel button** on the Standard toolbar within the VBA window (or click the **Excel button** on the Windows taskbar) to view the Excel workbook. Click in the window containing the Financial Consultant workbook (or whichever workbook you are using), then click the **Maximize button**.

➤ Pull down the **File menu** and click the **Close command**. (The dialog box in Figure 14i does not appear initially because the value of binNormalExit is not yet set; you have to open the workbook to set the switch.) Click **Yes** if asked whether to save the changes to the workbook.

➤ Pull down the **File menu** and reopen the workbook. Click the button to **Enable Macros**, then enter **Grauer** when prompted for the password. Click **OK** when the password has been accepted.

➤ Close this workbook, close the **VBA Examples workbook**, then pull down the **File menu** and click the **Exit command** to quit Excel.

Title bar has been customized

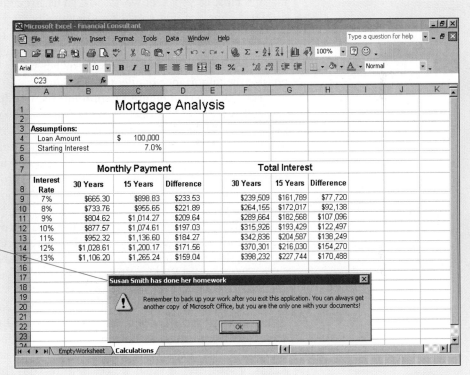

(i) Test the Procedure (step 9)

FIGURE 14 *Hands-on Exercise 4 (continued)*

SCREEN CAPTURE

Prove to your instructor that you have completed the hands-on exercise correctly by capturing a screen, then pasting the screen into a Word document. Do the exercise until you come to the screen that you want to capture, then press the PrintScreen key at the top of the keyboard. Click the Start button to start Word and open a Word document, then pull down the Edit menu and click the Paste command to bring the captured screen into the Word document. See exercise 1 at the end of the chapter.

The same VBA procedure can be run from multiple applications in Microsoft Office, despite the fact that the applications are very different. The real power of VBA, however, is its ability to detect events that are unique to a specific application and to respond accordingly. An event is defined as any action that is recognized by an application. Opening or closing an Excel workbook or an Access database is an event. Selecting a worksheet within a workbook is also an event, as is clicking on a command button on an Access form. To use VBA within Microsoft Office, you decide which events are significant, and what is to happen when those events occur. Then you develop the appropriate *event procedures* that execute automatically when the event occurs.

Consider, for example, Figure 15, which displays the results of two event procedures in conjunction with opening and closing an Access database. (These are procedures similar to those we created in the preceding pages in conjunction with opening and closing an Excel workbook.) The procedure associated with Figure 15a displays a message that appears automatically after the user clicks the Switchboard button to exit the database. The procedure is almost trivial to write, and consists of a single MsgBox statement. The effect of the procedure is quite significant, however, as it reminds the user to back up his or her work. Indeed, you can never overemphasize the importance of adequate backup.

The dialog box in Figure 15b prompts the user for a password and appears automatically when the user opens the database. The logic here is more sophisticated in that the underlying procedure contains an InputBox statement to request the password, a Do Until loop that is executed until the user enters the correct password or exceeds the allotted number of attempts, then additional logic to display the switchboard or terminate the application if the user fails to enter the proper password. The procedure is not difficult, however, and it builds on the VBA statements that were covered earlier.

The next hands-on exercise has you create the event procedures that are associated with the database in Figure 15. The exercise references a switchboard, or user interface, that is created as a form within the database. The switchboard displays a menu that enables a nontechnical person to move easily from one object in the database (e.g., a form or report) to another.

The switchboard is created through a utility called the Switchboard Manager that prompts you for each item you want to add to the switchboard, and which action you want to be taken in conjunction with that menu item. You could do the exercise with any database, but we suggest you use the database we provide to access the switchboard that we created for you. The exercise begins, therefore, by having you download a data disk from our Web site.

EVENT-DRIVEN VERSUS TRADITIONAL PROGRAMMING

A traditional program is executed sequentially, beginning with the first line of code and continuing in order through the remainder of the program. It is the program, not the user, that determines the order in which the statements are executed. VBA, on the other hand, is event-driven, meaning that the order in which the procedures are executed depends on the events that occur. It is the user, rather than the program, that determines which events occur, and consequently which procedures are executed. Each application in Microsoft Office has a different set of objects and associated events that comprise the application's object model.

Reminder to back up

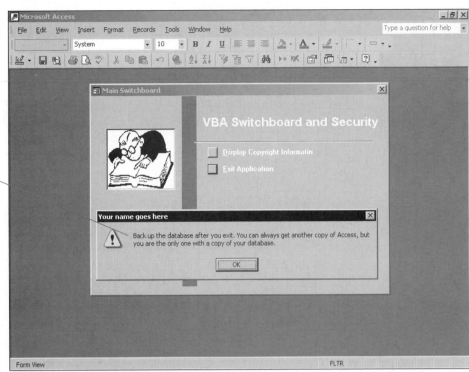

(a) Reminder to the User (Exit Application event)

User must enter a
password

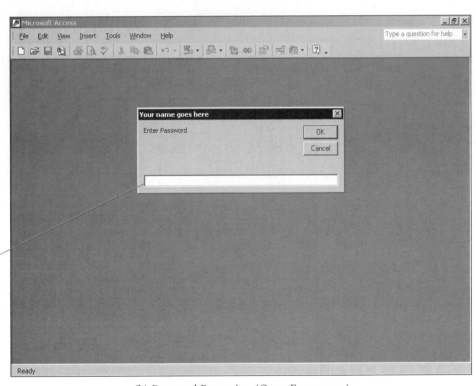

(b) Password Protection (Open Form event)

FIGURE 15   *Event-Driven Programming (Microsoft Access)*

EVENT-DRIVEN PROGRAMMING (MICROSOFT ACCESS)

Objective   To implement password protection for an Access database; to create a second event procedure that displays a message to the user upon closing the database. Use Figure 16 as a guide in the exercise.

Step 1:   **Open the Access Database**

➤ You can do this exercise with any database, but we suggest you use the database we have provided. Go to **www.prenhall.com/grauer**, click the **Office 2000 book**, click the **Student Resources tab**, then click the link to download the data disk.

➤ Scroll until you can select the disk for the **VBA Primer**. Download the file to the Windows desktop, then double click the file once it has been downloaded to your PC.

➤ Double click the file and follow the onscreen instructions to expand the self-extracting file that contains the database.

➤ Go to the newly created **Exploring VBA folder** and open the **VBA Switchboard and Security database** as shown in Figure 16a.

➤ Pull down the **Tools menu**, click the **Macro command**, then click the **Visual Basic Editor command**. Maximize the VBA Editor window.

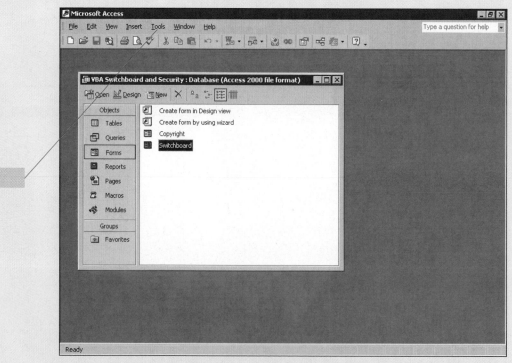

Pull down Tools menu

(a) Open the Access Database (step 1)

FIGURE 16 *Hands-on Exercise 5*

Step 2: **Create the ExitDatabase Procedure**

➤ Pull down the **Insert menu** and click **Module** to insert Module1. Complete the **General Declarations section** by adding your name to the definition of the ApplicationTitle constant as shown in Figure 16b.

➤ Pull down the **Insert menu** and click **Procedure** to insert a new procedure called **ExitDatabase**. Click the option buttons for a **Sub procedure** and for **Public scope**. Click **OK**.

➤ Complete the ExitDatabase procedure by entering the **MsgBox** and **DoCmd.Quit** statements. The DoCmd.Quit statement will close Access, but it is entered initially as a comment by beginning the line with an apostrophe.

➤ Click anywhere in the procedure, then click the **Run Sub button** to test the procedure. Correct any errors that occur, then when the MsgBox displays correctly, **delete the apostrophe** in front of the DoCmd.Quit statement.

➤ Save the module. The next time you execute the procedure, you should see the message box you just created, and then Access will be terminated.

Access button

Declarations section

Enter statements as shown

Enter apostrophe to make statement a comment for testing

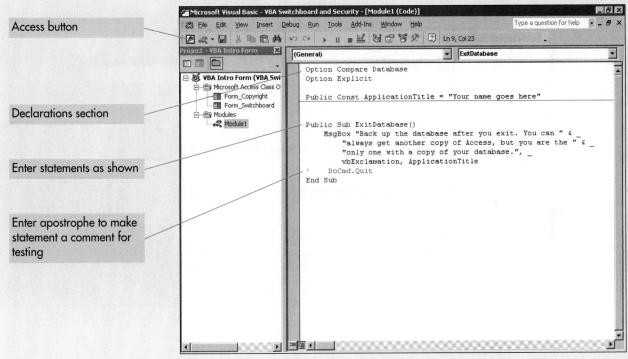

(b) Create the ExitDatabase Procedure (step 2)

FIGURE 16 *Hands-on Exercise 5 (continued)*

CREATE A PUBLIC CONSTANT

Give your application a customized look by adding your name or other identifying message to the title bar of the message and/or input boxes that you use. You can add the information individually to each statement, but it is easier to declare a public constant from within a general module. That way, you can change the value of the constant in one place and have the change reflected automatically throughout your application.

Step 3: **Modify the Switchboard**

> ➤ Click the **Access button** on the Standard toolbar within the VBA window to switch to the Database window (or use the **F11** keyboard shortcut).
>
> ➤ Pull down the **Tools menu**, click the **Database Utilities command**, then choose **Switchboard Manager** to display the Switchboard Manager dialog box in Figure 16c.
>
> ➤ Click the **Edit button** to edit the Main Switchboard and display the Edit Switchboard Page dialog box. Select the **&Exit Application command** and click its **Edit button** to display the Edit Switchboard Item dialog box.
>
> ➤ Change the command to **Run Code**. Enter **ExitDatabase** in the Function Name text box. Click **OK**, then close the two other dialog boxes. The switchboard has been modified so that clicking the Exit button will run the VBA procedure you just created.

Edit button

Edit button

Select &Exit Application

Click drop-down arrow and select Run Code

Enter ExitDatabase

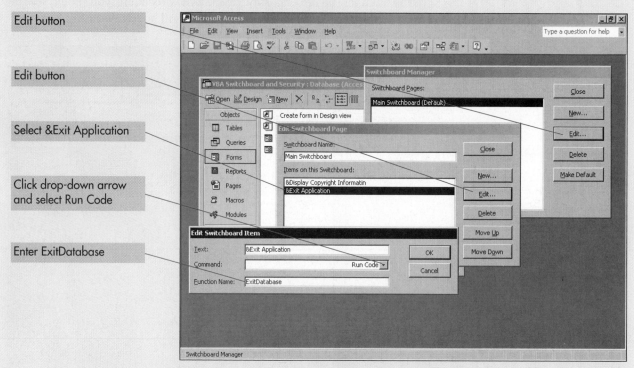

(c) Modify the Switchboard (step 3)

FIGURE 16 *Hands-on Exercise 5 (continued)*

CREATE A KEYBOARD SHORTCUT

The & has special significance when used within the name of an Access object because it creates a keyboard shortcut to that object. Enter "&Exit Application", for example, and the letter E (the letter immediately after the ampersand) will be underlined and appear as "<u>E</u>xit Application" on the switchboard. From there, you can execute the item by clicking its button, or you can use the Alt+E keyboard shortcut (where "E" is the underlined letter in the menu option).

Step 4: **Test the Switchboard**

➤ If necessary, click the **Forms tab** in the Database window. Double click the **Switchboard form** to open the switchboard as shown in Figure 16d. The switchboard contains two commands.

➤ Click the **Display Copyright Information command** to display a form that we use with all our databases. (You can open this form in Design view and modify the text to include your name, rather than ours. If you do, be sure to save the modified form, then close it.)

➤ Click the **Exit Application command** (or use the **Alt+E** keyboard shortcut). You should see the dialog box in Figure 16d, corresponding to the MsgBox statement you created earlier. Click **OK** to close the dialog box.

➤ Access itself will terminate because of the DoCmd.Quit statement within the ExitDatabase procedure. (If this does not happen, return to the VBA Editor and remove the apostrophe in front of the DoCmd statement.)

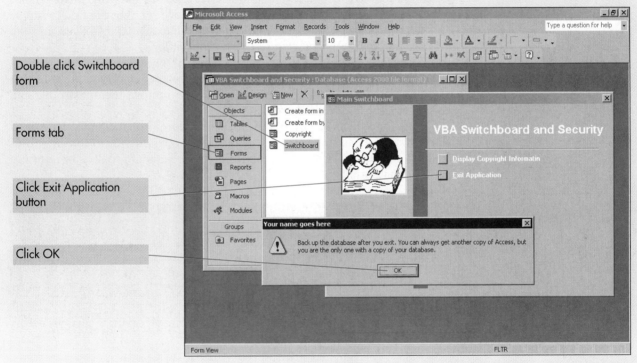

Double click Switchboard form

Forms tab

Click Exit Application button

Click OK

(d) Test the Switchboard (step 4)

FIGURE 16 *Hands-on Exercise 5 (continued)*

BACK UP IMPORTANT FILES

It's not a question of if it will happen, but when—hard disks die, files are lost, or viruses may infect a system. It has happened to us and it will happen to you, but you can prepare for the inevitable by creating adequate backup before the problem occurs. The essence of a backup strategy is to decide which files to back up, how often to do the backup, and where to keep the backup. Do it!

Step 5: **Complete the Open Form Event Procedure**

➤ Start Access and reopen the **VBA Switchboard and Security database**. Press **Alt+F11** to start the VBA Editor. Click the **plus sign** next to Microsoft Access Class objects, double click the module called **Form_Switchboard**, then look for the **Form_Open procedure** as shown in Figure 16e.

➤ The procedure was created automatically by the Switchboard Manager. You must, however, expand this procedure to include password protection. Note the following:

• Three variables are required—the correct password, the password entered by the user, and the number of attempts.

• The user is prompted for the password, and the number of attempts is set to one. The user is given two additional attempts, if necessary, to get the correct password.

• The If statement at the end of the loop determines whether the user has entered the correct password, and if so, it executes the original commands that are associated with the switchboard. If, however, the user fails to supply the correct password, an invalid password message is displayed and the **DoCmd.Quit** statement terminates the application.

• We suggest you place an **apostrophe** in front of the statement initially so that it becomes a comment, and thus it is not executed. Once you are sure that you can enter the correct password, you can remove the apostrophe and implement the password protection.

➤ Save the procedure. You cannot test this procedure from within the VBA window; you must cause the event to happen (i.e., open the form) for the procedure to execute. Click the **Access button** on the Standard toolbar to return to the Database window.

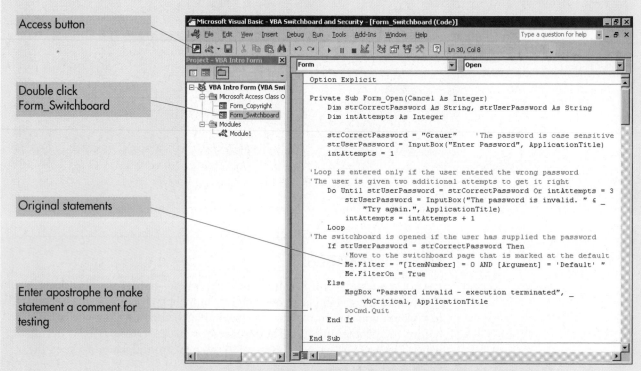

(e) Complete the Open Form Event Procedure (step 5)

FIGURE 16 *Hands-on Exercise 5 (continued)*

Step 6:   **Test the Procedure**

➤ Close all open windows within the Access database except for the Database window. Click the **Forms tab**, then double click the **Switchboard Form**.

➤ You should be prompted for the password as shown in Figure 16f. The password (in our procedure) is **Grauer**.

➤ Test the procedure repeatedly to include all possibilities. Enter the correct password on the first, second, and third attempts to be sure that the procedure works as intended. Each time you enter the correct password, you will have to close the switchboard, then reopen it.

➤ Test the procedure one final time, by failing to enter the correct password. You will see a message box indicating that the password is invalid and that execution will be terminated. Termination will not take place, however, because the DoCmd.Quit statement is currently entered as a comment.

➤ Press **Alt+F11** to reopen the VBA Editor. Delete the apostrophe in front of the DoCmd.Quit statement. The text of the statement changes from green to black to indicate that it is an executable statement. Save the procedure.

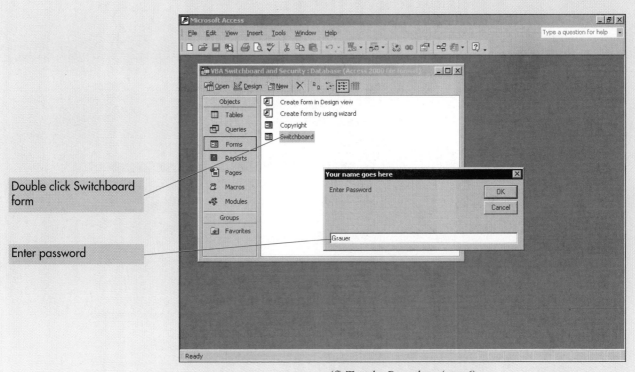

Double click Switchboard form

Enter password

(f) Test the Procedure (step 6)

FIGURE 16   *Hands-on Exercise 5 (continued)*

TOGGLE COMMENTS ON AND OFF

Comments are used primarily to explain the purpose of VBA statements, but they can also be used to "comment out" code as distinct from deleting the statement altogether. Thus you can add or remove the apostrophe in front of the statement, to toggle the comment on or off.

Change the Startup Properties

➤ Click the **Access button** on the VBA Standard toolbar to return to the Database window. Pull down the **Tools menu** and click **Startup** to display the Startup dialog box as shown in Figure 16g.

➤ Click in the **Application Title** text box and enter the title of the application, **VBA Switchboard and Security** in this example.

➤ Click the **drop-down arrow** in the Display Form/Page list box and select the **Switchboard form** as the form that will open automatically in conjunction with opening the database.

➤ Clear the check box to display the Database window. Click **OK** to accept the settings and close the dialog box. The next time you open the database, the switchboard should open automatically, which in turn triggers the Open Form event procedure that will prompt the user to enter a password.

➤ Close the Switchboard form.

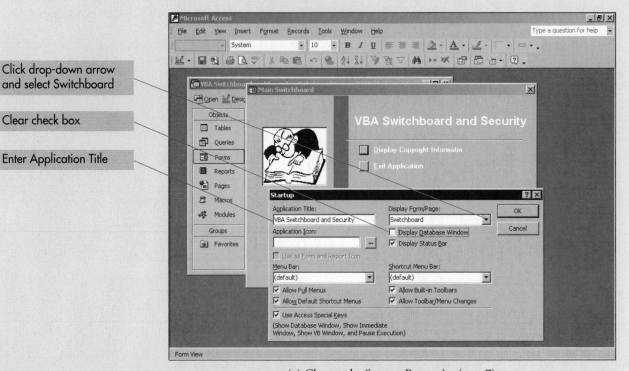

(g) Change the Startup Properties (step 7)

FIGURE 16 *Hands-on Exercise 5 (continued)*

HIDE THE DATABASE WINDOW

Use the Startup property to hide the Database window from the novice user. You avoid confusion and you may prevent the novice from accidentally deleting objects in the database. Of course, anyone with some knowledge of Access can restore the Database window by pulling down the Window menu, clicking the Unhide command, then selecting the Database window from the associated dialog box. Nevertheless, hiding the Database window is a good beginning.

Step 8: **Test the Database**

➤ Close the database, then reopen the database to test the procedures we have created in this exercise. The sequence of events is as follows:
  • The database is loaded and the switchboard is opened but is not yet visible. The Open Form procedure for the switchboard is executed, and you are prompted for the password as shown in Figure 16h.
  • The password is entered correctly and the switchboard is displayed. The Database window is hidden, however, because the Startup Properties have been modified.
➤ Click the **Exit Application command** (or use the **Alt+E** keyboard shortcut). You will see the message box reminding you to back up the system, after which the database is closed and Access is terminated.
➤ Testing is complete and you can go on to add the other objects to your Access database. Congratulations on a job well done.

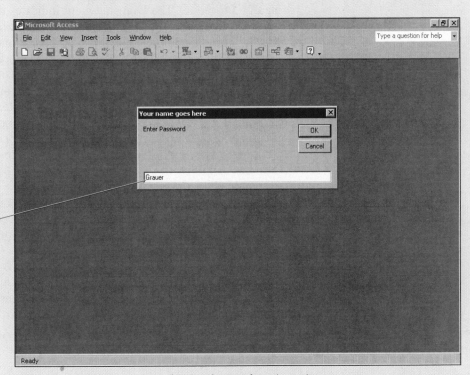

Enter password

(h) Test the Database (step 8)

FIGURE 16   *Hands-on Exercise 5 (continued)*

HIDE MENUS AND TOOLBARS

You can use the Startup property to hide menus and/or toolbars from the user by clearing the respective check boxes. A word of caution, however— once the menus are hidden, it is difficult to get them back. Start Access, pull down the File menu, and click Open to display the Open dialog box, select the database to open, then press and hold the Shift key when you click the Open button. This powerful technique is not widely known.

Visual Basic for Applications (VBA) is a powerful programming language that is accessible from all major applications in Microsoft Office XP. A VBA statement accomplishes a specific task such as displaying a message to the user or accepting input from the user. Statements are grouped into procedures, and procedures in turn are grouped into modules. Every procedure is classified as either private or public.

The MsgBox statement displays information to the user. It has one required argument, which is the message (or prompt) that is displayed to the user. The other two arguments, the icon that is to be displayed in the dialog box and the text of the title bar, are optional. The InputBox function displays a prompt to the user requesting information, then it stores that information (the value returned by the user) for use later in the procedure.

Every variable must be declared (defined) before it can be used. This is accomplished through the Dim (short for Dimension) statement that appears at the beginning of a procedure. The Dim statement indicates the name of the variable and its type (for example, whether it will hold a character string or an integer number), which in turn reserves the appropriate amount of memory for that variable.

The ability to make decisions within a procedure, then branch to alternative sets of statements is implemented through the If . . . Then . . . Else or Case statements. The Else clause is optional, but may be repeated multiple times within an If statement. The Case statement is preferable to an If statement with multiple Else clauses.

The For . . . Next statement (or For . . . Next loop as it is also called) executes all statements between the words For and Next a specified number of times, using a counter to keep track of the number of times the loop is executed. The Do . . . Loop Until and/or Do Until . . . Loop statements are used when the number of times through the loop is not known in advance.

VBA is different from traditional programming languages in that it is event-driven. An event is defined as any action that is recognized by an application, such as Excel or Access. Opening or closing an Excel workbook or an Access database is an event. Selecting a worksheet within a workbook is also an event, as is clicking on a command button on an Access form. To use VBA within Microsoft Office, you decide which events are significant, and what is to happen when those events occur. Then you develop the appropriate event procedures.

KEY TERMS

Argument (p. 2)
Case statement (p. 18)
Character string (p. 16)
Comment (p. 6)
Compilation error (p. 30)
Complete Word tool (p. 22)
Concatenate (p. 4)
Custom toolbar (p. 19)
Debug menu (p. 30)
Debug toolbar (p. 30)
Debug.Print statement (p. 31)
Debugging (p. 30)
Declarations section (p. 6)
Dim statement (p. 5)
Do Loops (p. 29)
Else clause (p. 16)
End Sub statement (p. 3)
Event (p. 41)

Event procedure (Access) (p. 52)
Event procedure (Excel) (p. 41)
Execution error (p. 30)
For . . . Next Statement (p. 28)
Full Module view (p. 21)
Help (p. 15)
If statement (p. 16)
Immediate window (p. 31)
InputBox function (p. 4)
Intrinsic constant (p. 3)
Literal (p. 16)
Locals window (p. 31)
Macro (p. 2)
Macro recorder (p. 2)
Module (p. 2)
MsgBox statement (p. 3)
Object box (p. 45)
Option Explicit (p. 6)

Private procedure (p. 2)
Procedure (p. 2)
Procedure box (p. 45)
Procedure header (p. 3)
Procedure view (p. 21)
Project Explorer (p. 6)
Public procedure (p. 2)
Quick Info (p. 9)
Run-time error (p. 30)
Statement (p. 2)
Step Into button (p. 31)
Syntax (p. 2)
Underscore (p. 4)
Variable (p. 4)
VBA (p. 1)
Visual Basic Editor (p. 6)
Visual Basic for Applications (p. 2)

1. Which of the following applications in Office XP has access to VBA?
   (a) Word
   (b) Excel
   (c) Access
   (d) All of the above

2. Which of the following is a valid name for a VBA variable?
   (a) Public
   (b) Private
   (c) strUserFirstName
   (d) int Count Of Attempts

3. Which of the following is true about an If statement?
   (a) It evaluates a condition as either true or false, then executes the statement(s) following the keyword "Then" if the condition is true
   (b) It must contain the keyword Else
   (c) It must contain one or more ElseIf statements
   (d) All of the above

4. Which of the following lists the items from smallest to largest?
   (a) Module, procedure, statement
   (b) Statement, module, procedure
   (c) Statement, procedure, module
   (d) Procedure, module, statement

5. Given the statement, MsgBox "Welcome to VBA" , , "Bob was here", which of the following is true?
   (a) "Welcome to VBA" will be displayed within the resulting message box
   (b) "Welcome to VBA" will appear on the title bar of the displayed dialog box
   (c) The two adjacent commas will cause a compilation error
   (d) An informational icon will be displayed with the message

6. Where are the VBA procedures associated with an Office document stored?
   (a) In the same folder, but in a separate file
   (b) In the Office document itself
   (c) In a special VBA folder on drive C
   (d) In a special VBA folder on the local area network

7. The Debug.Print statement is associated with the:
   (a) Locals window
   (b) Immediate window
   (c) Project Explorer
   (d) Debug toolbar

8. Which of the following is the proper sequence of arguments for the MsgBox statement?
   (a) Text for the title bar, prompt, button
   (b) Prompt, button, text for the title bar
   (c) Prompt, text for the title bar, button
   (d) Button, prompt, text for the title bar

9. Which of the following is a true statement about Do loops?
   (a) Placing the Until clause at the beginning of the loop tests the condition prior to executing any statements in the loop
   (b) Placing the Until clause at the end of the loop executes the statements in the loop, then it tests the condition
   (c) Both (a) and (b)
   (d) Neither (a) nor (b)

10. Given the statement, For intCount = 1 to 10 Step 3, how many times will the statements in the loop be executed (assuming that there are no statements in the loop to terminate the execution)?
    (a) 10
    (b) 4
    (c) 3
    (d) Impossible to determine

11. Which of the following is a *false* statement?
    (a) A dash at the end of a line indicates continuation
    (b) An ampersand indicates concatenation
    (c) An apostrophe at the beginning of a line signifies a comment
    (d) A pair of quotation marks denotes a character string

12. What is the effect of deleting the apostrophe that appears at the beginning of a VBA statement?
    (a) A compilation error will occur
    (b) The statement is converted to a comment
    (c) The color of the statement will change from black to green
    (d) The statement is made executable

13. Which of the following If statements will display the indicated message if the user enters a response other than "Grauer" (assuming that "Grauer" is the correct password)?
    (a) If strUserResponse <> "Grauer" Then MsgBox "Wrong password"
    (b) If strUserResponse = "Grauer" Then MsgBox "Wrong password"
    (c) If strUserResponse > "Grauer" Then MsgBox "Wrong password"
    (d) If strUserResponse < "Grauer" Then MsgBox "Wrong password"

14. Which of the following will execute the statements in the loop at least once?
    (a) Do . . . Loop Until
    (b) Do Until ..... Loop
    (c) Both (a) and (b)
    (d) Neither (a) nor (b)

15. The copy and paste commands can be used to:
    (a) Copy statements within a procedure
    (b) Copy statements from a procedure in one module to a procedure in another module within the same document
    (c) Copy statements from a module in an Excel workbook to a module in an Access database
    (d) All of the above

ANSWERS

1. d	**6.** b	**11.** a
2. c	**7.** b	**12.** d
3. a	**8.** b	**13.** a
4. c	**9.** c	**14.** a
5. a	**10.** b	**15.** a

BUILDS ON

HANDS-ON
EXERCISE 4
PAGES 43–51

1. Screen Capture: The ability to capture a screen, then print the captured screen as part of a document, is very useful. The Word document in Figure 17, for example, captures the Excel screen as a workbook is opened, with the dialog box in place.

    Open the completed workbook from the fourth hands-on exercise. Press the PrintScreen key when prompted for the password to copy the screen to the Windows clipboard, an area of memory that is accessible to any Windows application. Next, start (or switch to) a Word document, and then execute the Paste command in the Edit menu to paste the contents of the clipboard into the current document. That's all there is to it. The screen is now part of the Word document, where it can be moved and sized like any other Windows object. Print the Word document for your instructor.

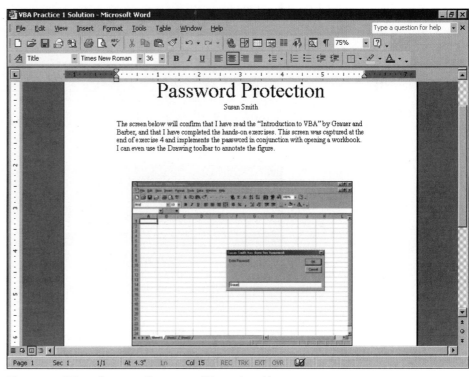

FIGURE 17   *Screen Capture (Exercise 1)*

2. VBA in a Word Document: Everything that you have learned with respect to creating VBA event procedures in Excel or Access is also applicable to Microsoft Word. Accordingly, start Microsoft Word and create the document in Figure 18. Read the document carefully, then create the Document_Close event procedure to display the indicated message box, adding your name to the title bar. Prove to your professor that you have completed this assignment by capturing the screen in Figure 18, as described in the previous exercise.

BUILDS ON

HANDS-ON
EXERCISE 4
PAGES 43–51

3. The Before Print Event: Open the Excel workbook that you used in the fourth hands-on exercise to create an event procedure associated with the Before_Print event. The procedure is to contain a MsgBox statement to remind the user to print a workbook with both displayed values and cell contents as shown in Figure 19.

    The easiest way to switch between the two views is to press Ctrl+~. (The tilde is located at the upper-left of the keyboard.) Prove to your professor that you have completed this assignment by capturing the screen in Figure 19.

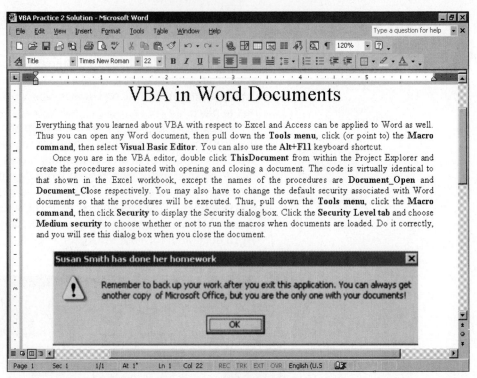

FIGURE 18   *VBA in a Word Document (Exercise 2)*

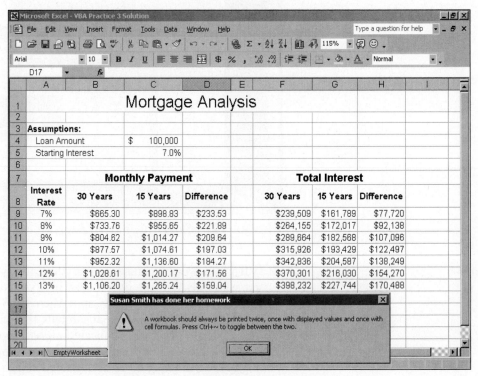

FIGURE 19   *The Before Print Event (Exercise 3)*

BUILDS ON

HANDS-ON
EXERCISE 5
PAGES 54–61

4. The On Click Event: Open the Access database that you used in the fifth hands-on exercise to create an event procedure associated with the On Click event for the indicated command button.

   a. Open the Copyright form from the switchboard, then change to the Design view. Modify the form so that it contains your name rather than ours.

   b. Right click the Technical Support button to display a context-sensitive menu, click Properties, click the Event tab, then select the On Click event. Click the Build button, select Code Builder as shown in Figure 20, and click OK.

   c. The VBA Editor will position you within the On Click event procedure for the command button. All you need to do is add a single MsgBox statement to identify yourself as "Tech Support". Be sure to include the parameter to display your name on the title bar of the message box.

   d. Save the form, then go to form view and click the button to view the message box you just created. Prove to your professor that you have completed this assignment by capturing the associated screen, as described in exercise 1.

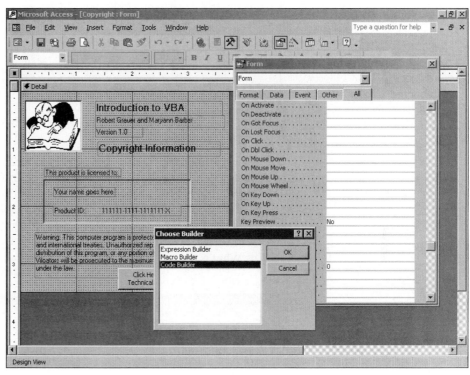

FIGURE 20   *The On Click Event (Exercise 4)*

5. The Option Explicit Statement: The Option Explicit statement should appear at the beginning of every module, but this is not a VBA requirement, only a suggestion from the authors. Omitting the statement can have serious consequences in that the results of a procedure are incorrect, a point that is illustrated in Figure 21.

   a. What is the answer that is displayed in the message box of Figure 21? What is the answer that should be displayed?

   b. Look at the statements within the For ... Next loop to see if you can detect the reason for the error. (*Hint:* Look closely at the variable names.)

   c. What does the Option Explicit statement do? How would including the statement in the procedure of Figure 21 help to ensure the correct result?

   d. Summarize your answers in a note to your instructor.

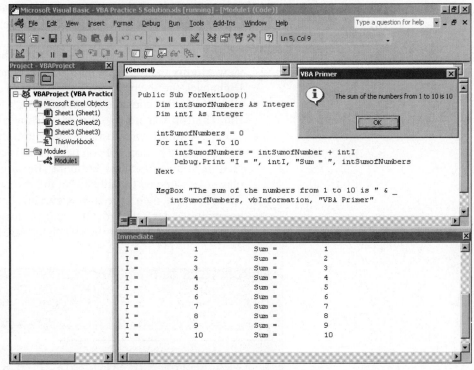

FIGURE 21 *The Option Explicit Statement (Exercise 5)*

6. String Processing: The procedure in Figure 22 illustrates various string processing functions to validate a user's e-mail address. Answer the following:
   a. What are the specific checks that are implemented to check the user's e-mail address? Are these checks reasonable?
   b. What does the VBA Len function do? What does the InStr function do? (Use the VBA Help menu to learn more about these functions.)
   c. What is the purpose of the variable binValidEmail within the procedure?

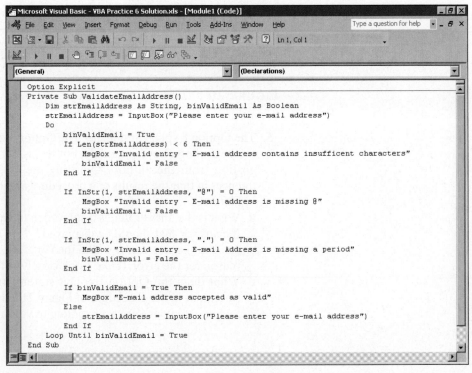

FIGURE 22 *String Processing (Exercise 6)*

BUILDS ON

HANDS-ON
EXERCISE 4
PAGES 43–51

7. Hiding a Worksheet: Figure 23 expands on the procedure to implement password protection in an Excel workbook by hiding the worksheet until the correct password has been entered.
   a. What additional statements have been added to the procedure in Figure 23 that were not present in Hands-on Exercise 4? What is the purpose of each statement?
   b. What statement could you add to the procedure to hide the empty worksheet after the correct password has been entered?
   c. Summarize your answers in a note to your instructor.

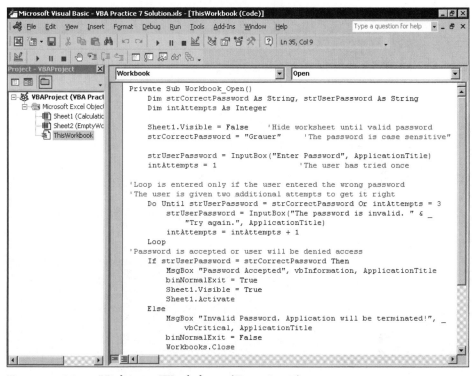

FIGURE 23 *Hiding a Worksheet (Exercise 7)*

8. Help with VBA: Help is just a mouse click away and it is invaluable. Use the Help facility to look up detailed information that expands a topic that was discussed in the chapter. The screen in Figure 24, for example, explains the integer data type and its use within a Dim statement. The information is quite detailed, but if you read carefully, you will generally find the answer. Print three different Help-screens for your instructor.

9. Invoking a Procedure: The same statement (or set of statements) is often executed from many places within a single procedure or from multiple procedures within an application. You can duplicate the code as necessary, but it is far more efficient to create a single procedure that contains the repeated statements, and then invoke that procedure. The advantage to this approach is that you have to write (or modify) the procedure only once.

   The module in Figure 25 illustrates how this is accomplished. The History-Quiz procedure asks the user multiple questions, then displays one of two messages, depending on whether the response is correct. These messages are contained in two separate procedures, then the appropriate procedure (CorrectAnswer or IncorrectAnswer) is called from within the HistoryQuiz procedure, depending on whether the user's answer is right or wrong. Create and test the module in Figure 25 to be sure you understand this technique.

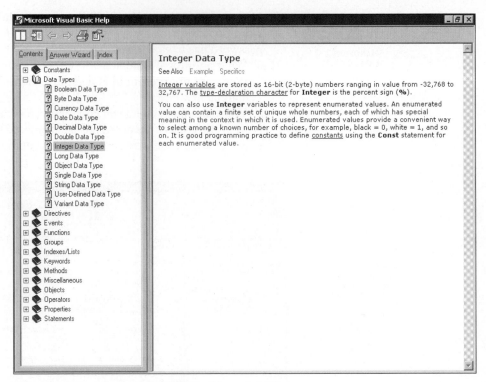

FIGURE 24 *Help with VBA (Exercise 8)*

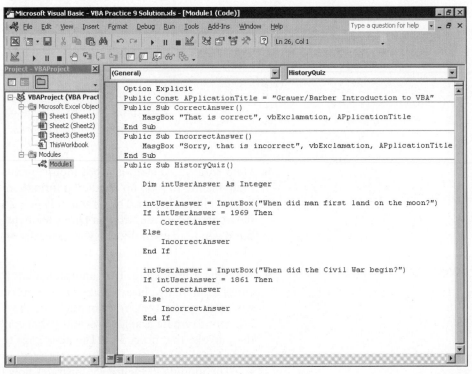

FIGURE 25 *Invoking a Procedure (Exercise 9)*

10. The MsgBox Function: The procedure in Figure 26 shows how the MsgBox statement can accept information from the user and branch accordingly. A simple MsgBox statement merely displays a message. If, however, you enclose the parameters of the MsgBox statement in parentheses, it becomes a function and returns a value (in this example, a mouse click indicating whether the user clicked yes or no). The use of parentheses requires that you include a second parameter such as vbYesNo to display the Yes and No command buttons. You then embed the MsgBox function within an If statement that tests for the intrinsic contstants, vbYes and vbNo, respectively.

You can concatenate the vbYesNo intrinsic constant with another constant such as vbQuestion to display an icon next to the buttons as shown in Figure 26. You can also use other intrinsic constants such as vbOKCancel to display different sets of command buttons.

Add the procedure in Figure 26 to the VBA Examples workbook (or Access database) that you created in the chapter. Print the procedure for your instructor.

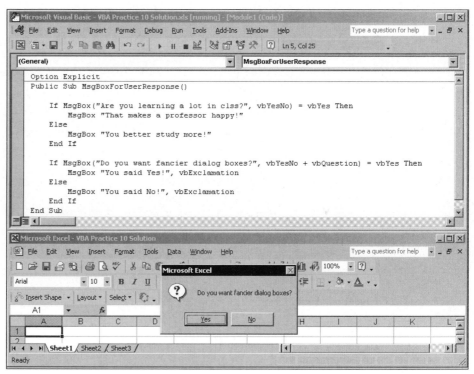

FIGURE 26   *The MsgBox Function (Exercise 10)*

GLOSSARY

Absolute Cell Reference In Excel, Absolute Cell Reference (or address) refers to cell references that will not change when copied to another cell, and is specified with a dollar sign in front of the column and row designation.

Accept and Review Changes command In Word, the Accept and Review Changes command helps users to look over documents and then make desired changes.

Access time All disks have an access time, which on average is the amount of time it takes a disk to retrieve a document.

Action Items slide In PowerPoint, Action Items slides are slides created during a presentation.

Active Cell An Active Cell in Excel is a cell where information or data will be input, indicated by a black border surrounding it.

Address book This function is a section of Outlook that acts like a personal telephone and address book, having the e-mail program retrieve numbers and addresses.

Aggregate (Summary) Functions In Access, the Aggregate (Summary) Functions are used to determine the total number, average, or maximum values of a group of records.

Alignment In all applications, Alignment defines the positioning of text within documents: flush left/flush right, left aligned, right aligned, and centered with the margin.

AND condition AND condition specifies that records selected must include ALL criteria.

Animation effects In PowerPoint, the program has Animation effects, such as stars flying from the top left-hand corner to the bottom right-hand corner.

Arguments In Excel, arguments are values as input which perform an indicated calculation, and then return another value as output.

Arrange command In Excel, once windows are open, the Arrange command under the Windows menu can be used to cascade the open windows.

Ascending sequence In Word while working on a table, the Ascending sequence button helps sort information in rows in an ascending manner.

Assumptions In Excel, Assumptions are initial conditions or scenarios that spreadsheets are based on.

Asterisks In Access, an asterisk (record selector symbol) is visible next to the end of every table, showing users the status of the record.

AutoContent Wizard In PowerPoint, the AutoContent Wizard helps users to create new presentations.

AutoCorrect The AutoCorrect function instantly changes spelling mistakes as they are typed.

AutoFill capability AutoFill capability allows users to enter data into adjacent cells by dragging the fill handle to desired new cells.

AutoFormat command In Excel, the AutoFormat command presents already formatted designs for users to choose from.

Automatic replacement In Word, Automatic replacement is pre-determined correction and replacement of words or phrases.

AutoNumber field An AutoNumber field is a data type that makes Access format consecutive numbers every time a new record is added.

AutoShapes button In PowerPoint, Access and Word, AutoShapes buttons, located on the Drawing toolbar, can allow users to add lines, rectangles, ovals, callouts, and banners to documents.

AutoSum The AutoSum button on the Standard toolbar causes various cells to add up. By clicking certain rows and columns, their addition is also invoked.

Auxiliary storage Auxiliary storage or secondary storage is a section of the computer whose function is to keep information for an extended period of time and then moved to and from the RAM.

Background command In PowerPoint, the Background command changes the coloring to all or each slide in a presentation.

Bit Stands for binary digit, and represents zero and one. Alone, bits do not have significant meaning; however, when combined they equal bytes.

Boldface Boldface is the darkening of letters or numbers in order to emphasize texture in documents.

Bookmark Within a Web browser, bookmarks mark a favorite or frequently used site.

Bound control Bound controls are fields that are used to change and input data of a table.

Bug A Bug is a mistake in a computer program in any Microsoft program.

Bullets and Numbering command In Word, the Bullets and Numbering command under the Format menu gives users a number of choices in styles for bulleting, numbering and outline numbering.

Bulleted list In Word, by clicking on the button with three vertical squares, a list can be made with various choices of bullets.

Byte Byte equals eight bits, and is the smallest significant unit of memory. Different computers are capable of holding different sizes of bytes or memory; a gigabyte (Gb) is one example.

Calculated control In Access, calculated controls deals with expressions rather than fields for its data source.

Calculated field In Access and Excel, a calculated field is where values from formulas that work with a designated field or fields are determined.

Caption property In Access, the Caption property explicitly names labels.

Case statement In Access, the Case statement tests values of a variable as they are input into the program.

Category labeling In charts, the category labeling is the written language used to describe entries.

CD-ROM An acronym for Compact Disk, Read-Only Memory. It is a disk that stores information in large quantities, but does not allow the user to write on the CD.

Cell In Excel, Access and Mircrosoft Office XP, a Cell is the intersection of a row and column.

Cell Reference In Excel, Access and Microsoft Office XP, the intersection of a row and column is designated a Column and a number equaling the Cell Reference.

Central processing unit (CPU) The CPU is the main part of a computer responsible for executing computations.

Character style In Access, Word, and PowerPoint, character style function harbors the formatting of characters.

Chart A Chart in Access and Excel is a graphical representation of data in a worksheet.

Chart Wizard The Chart Wizard is a guide in helping create tables or queries to build desired charts within Access.

Check box In Access, Check boxes are used as YES/NO fields for data entry of two choices.

Clip art Clip art in many Microsoft applications is used to create special effect with words, letters, and photographs.

Clock speed Clock speed is how much time that it takes data to be transmitted in a microprocessor.

Close command In any Microsoft Program, the Close command allows users to close a document, spreadsheet, or workbook.

Color Scheme In PowerPoint, a set of eight colors defines the programs Color Scheme.

Column Chart A Column Chart in Excel displays data in a column formation and can be converted to a bar chart.

Columnar Report A Columnar report is the easiest kind of report detailing fields for records in a column.

Columns command In Word, Columns command calls up the window to insert one to three columns in a document.

Command buttons In Access, Command buttons help users to modify tables, for example, by clicking on Add Records or New Record.

Comment statements Comment statements are symbols (non-executable statements) placed at the beginning of macros to remind users what the macro does.

Compact and Repair Database command The Compact and Repair Database command plays two roles: to eliminate fragmentation and waste on a disk and to repair databases if Access is unable to read them.

Compressed file A Compressed file allows users to download large amounts of information from the Web or Internet by reducing the time it takes to transfer the file into the desired program.

Conditional Formatting command Conditional Formatting command allows users to display values within a spreadsheet in different manners, red values versus blue values.

Constant In any spreadsheet, the entry that does not change is called the constant.

Constraints Constraints in Excel represent restrictions placed in cells or cell ranges.

Controls In Access, Control displays data in numerical or descriptive forms. There are three types of controls: bound, unbound, and calculated controls.

Convert Database command The Convert Database command changes the file format of an Access 2002 database from earlier versions.

Copy Command The Copy command is located under the Edit menu, allowing users to copy a desired text, graph, or picture.

Create New Folder command In Word, the Create New Folder command make new folders for different sets of documents.

Create Subdocument command In Word, the Create Subdocument command allows users to make subdocument files when saving or working on master documents.

Currency field In Access or Excel, the Currency field is used to store monetary figures.

Current record In Access, a current record refers to an active set of fields.

Cut Command The Cut command is located under the Edit menu, letting users cut a desired text, graph, or picture.

Data Data are facts about records or sets of records.

Database In Access, Databases are one or more tables.

Database window The Database window shows users the many tables, queries, forms, reports, pages, macros, and modules in Access.

Data points In charts for Excel or Microsoft Graph, Data points are numeric values used to describe entries.

Data series In charts for Excel or Microsoft Graph, Data series is another way of describing a group of data points on worksheets.

Datasheet In the Microsoft Graph program or Excel, Datasheets record data values (data points) in order to create graphs or data series for presentations.

Datasheet view In Access, the Datasheet view function helps users to add, edit or delete records.

Data type In Access, Data types exist in every field of a table, and they decide on the types of data limitations and function to be executed within each field.

Data Validation command In Excel and Access, the Data Validation command gives users the ability to prevent errors from happening by restricting the values accepted in cells.

Date/Time field In Access and Excel, the Date/Time field holds dates or times.

Debugging Debugging is the act of ridding any program of bugs (mistakes).

Default Value property In Access, the Default Value property self-activates a default value each time a record is input into the table.

Delete command The Delete command takes information or lists away from a document or spreadsheet.

Dependent Workbook In Excel, the Dependent Workbook holds the external and is contingent in operation on source workbooks.

Descending sequence In Word while working on a table, the Descending sequence button helps sort information in rows in an descending manner.

Design view In Access, the Design view allow users to create and choose tables, and to indicate the fields that will be put in the tables.

Desktop publishing Desktop publishing is bringing text and graphics together to make a polished document without depending on outside sources.

Dialog box Dialog boxes appear immediately after any command has been selected giving users additional options in order to complete a command.

Do Statement In Excel, the Do Statement copies a block of statements until a condition comes to fruition.

Documentation Worksheets In Excel, Documentation Worksheets contain descriptive explanations of each worksheet within a workbook.

Drawing toolbar In Word, the Drawing toolbar offers users additional choices in drawing lines, shapes, boxes with text, and many other options.

Drop-down list box In Access, Drop-down list boxes have choices or indicators to pick from for input into a table.

Dropped-capital letters In Word, a Dropped-capital letter is a larger, dominant bold letter placed at the beginning of a paragraph; used for emphasis.

DVD A DVD is equivalent to a CD-ROM disk, but can store much more data (up to 17 Gb).

Edit The Edit Button changes the contents of a cell or deletes text from a document.

Embedded Object In PowerPoint, Embedded Objects are placed and stored within a presentation.

Endnote In Word and Access documents, Endnotes are like footnotes, but are located at the end of a document.

Event Events are actions such as clicking a button or closing a file that are recognized by Access.

Event procedures In Access, Event procedures are one of the two kind found in the Visual Basic code, and are the various actions automatically recognized by Access application.

Exit command In any Windows application, the Exit command closes and leaves any application.

Exploded Pie Chart In Excel, Exploded Pie Charts display relationships between data by dividing data according to slices of a pie.

Export command The Export command allows users to copy an Access database object from an outside source.

Expression In Access, a combination of operators, field names, constants and/or functions are expressions.

Field Fields are the individual data found in folders.

Field name In Access, Field names are located in the first row of a table.

Field Size property In Access, the Field Size property restricts and amends the text size of a field.

File While working with spreadsheets, files are in correspondence with manila folders.

File Menu The File Menu is an integral part of any Windows application, allowing users to open and save documents on a disk.

File Name The File name allows users to "name" a document while saving it on a disk.

File Transfer Protocol File Transfer Protocol (FTP) in Word gives users the ability to upload files from PCs to the server through this function.

File Type The File type lets users know what application the document was saved under.

Fill Handle In Excel, a small black square appearing in the bottom-right corner of a cell allowing data to be entered in cells.

Filter by Form In Access, Filter by Form allows users to choose criteria to be input in various relationships within tables or charts, and also can use the and/or function in the criterion selection.

Filter by Selection button In Access, the Filter by Selection button on the Database toolbar allows users to choose only certain desired criterion, and excludes others.

Filtered List Filtered Lists in Excel and Access are only records that match specific criteria.

Find command The Find command shares a dialog box with the Replace and Go to Commands. This command finds various occurrences of the same word or phrase.

Floppy disk A square, plastic apparatus used to store completed documents created on a microprocessor program such as Microsoft Word.

Folder In any Microsoft Program, folders organize and store files or documents, and are key components to the Windows storage system.

Font Font (Typeface) means the entire group of upper- and lowercase letters, numbers, punctuation marks, and symbols used in documents.

Footer In Word, Footers are one or many lines placed at the bottom of a page.

Footnote In Word and Access, Footnotes are located at the bottom of document pages detailing additional information.

Format property In Access, the Format property alters the method in which a field is shown or printed.

Format Font command In many applications, Format Font command allows users to change and alter the typeface, size, and style of text in documents.

Format Picture command In Word, Format Picture command gives users the option to alter a picture in documents.

Formatting Toolbar In any Microsoft Application, it appears under the Standard toolbar, and provides access to common formatting operations such as boldface and italics.

Forms In Access, Forms are ways to input, show, and print data in a table.

Forms toolbar In Word, the Forms toolbar allows users to make three kinds of fields: text boxes, check boxes, and drop-down list boxes.

Formula In a spreadsheet, the combination of constants, cell references, arithmetic operations, and/or functions displayed in a calculation is a Formula.

Formula Bar In Excel or Access, the Formula Bar shows the contents of the spreadsheet's formula and is located at the top of the worksheet.

Form view In Access, the Form view allows user to see information on forms without the designs.

Form Wizard In Access, the Form Wizard displays and makes forms for users by asking users a sequence of questions.

Function In Access or Excel, a Function indicates a predefined computational task, such as SUM or AVERAGE.

General Procedure In Access, General procedures are one of the two kinds of procedures. This kind of procedure, however, is not automatically recognized by the Access application.

Get External Data command In Access or Excel, the Get External Data command bring data from outside sources such as Microsoft Office, a text file, Excel, or Access.

Goal Seek command In Excel, the Goal Seek command solves mathematical problems and enables the user to set up an end result in order to determine the input to produce that result.

Go To command The Go To command shares a dialog box with the Replace and Find To commands. This command finds a word or phrase that the user is looking for.

Graphics Graphics are designs, pictures, or any other feature used to enhance a document.

Grid A Grid in Word is an invisible set of horizontal and vertical lines used to place text in a document.

Group Footer A Group Footer reveals the last record and summary information about the group.

Group Header A Group Header reveals the name of the group of records and is located at a record's beginning.

Hard disk A hard disk or fixed disk is the apparatus located inside of a computer used to store and to access data.

Hard page break In Word, users can put a Hard page break in documents on purpose in order to begin a new page or paragraph

Hard Return Hard Return takes place when the Enter key is hit at the end of a paragraph.

Header In Word, Headers are one or more lines at the top of every printed page.

Header and Footer command In PowerPoint, the Header and Footer command inserts additional information at the bottom or top of slides.

Help Command The Help Command answers questions that users have about functions of any of the Microsoft Programs.

Hidden Slide In PowerPoint, experienced speakers who think certain questions may be posed during a presentation use Hidden Slides; therefore, they create hidden slides. Hidden slides can be denoted by a square with a line through it located below the slide in the bottom right-hand corner.

Hide Slide Button In PowerPoint, the Hide Slide button allows users to conceal slides during a presentation.

Homepage Each time a user logs into a Web browser, the homepage of that Web browser or site appears.

Hyperlink A Hyperlink can be defined as a reference to another document located on the Internet.

Hyperlink field This is a field that stores Web addresses or URL addresses enabling an Access database to show the Internet link.

HTML HTML or HyperText Markup Language is an address bar recognized by Internet Explorer and Netscape Navigator.

IF Function The IF Function decides on certain numerical augmentations within a worksheet.

Immediate window In Access during computations in VBA, the VBA editor allows data computations to be shown in the Immediate window.

Import External Data command In Excel, the Import External Data command allows users to bring in information or data from an outside source.

Import Spreadsheet Wizard The Import Spreadsheet Wizard aids users in creating spreadsheets in Excel and imports them into tables for Access.

Imported Data Imported Data is data that is brought to Access or Excel from an outside source.

Indents In Word, Indents is the spacing between the text and the margins.

Index In Word, after users complete long documents, an Index will can be created.

Index and Tables command In Word from the Insert menu, the Index and Tables command helps users to create tables of contents.

Indexed property In Access, the Indexed property ensures speedy and efficient searches for desired fields.

Information Information refers to summarized data or non-factual materials.

In-place Editing In the PowerPoint program, modifications to graphs in Microsoft Graph are allowed through In-place editing.

Input devices Any exterior source that takes information, changes it to electronic signals, and transfers it to the CPU. The keyboard, mouse, joystick, scanner, microphone, and auxiliary storage are input devices.

InputBox Function In Excel, the Input-Box Function accepts information (input) from users for later use in a procedure. InputBox Function information must be placed in parentheses.

Input Mask Property This property places data in a specific pattern where numeric data or symbols must be typed in a specific order or way.

Insert Bookmark command The Insert Bookmark command copies sites or web pages and stores them in folders for future quick access.

Insert Columns command The Insert Columns command puts new columns (fields) on to lists.

Insert Date command In Word, the Insert Date command puts a date on a document and can be accessed through the Insert menu.

Insert Footnote command In Word, the Insert footnote command places footnotes at the bottom of desired pages, and gives each note a number.

Insert Function command The Insert Function command in Excel allows users to insert a function into a workbook.

Insert Hyperlink command In many applications, the Insert Hyperlink command lets users bring in a Hyperlink from the Web.

Insert Menu In Word, the Insert Menu function allows users to make various sections in a document.

Insert Mode By pressing the insert key once, users can amend or add text, missing letters or symbols

Insert Page Numbers command In Word located under the Insert Menu, the Insert Page Numbers command puts page numbers in five places of alignment and three page positions, according to the user's desired location.

Insert Picture command In PowerPoint, the Insert Picture command downloads pictures into presentations.

Insert Rows command The Insert Rows command puts new rows (records) on to lists.

Insert Subdocument command In Word, the Insert Subdocument command creates a subdocument while working on a master document.

Insert Symbol command In Access, Word, and PowerPoint, the Insert Symbol command places symbols and characters in documents.

Insert Table command In PowerPoint, the Insert Table command brings a variety of table choices to users.

Insertion Point The Insertion Point is a blinking line that allows users to type text where the line appears; present at the beginning of a new document.

Intel Corporation Intel is known for the creation of the microprocessor.

Internet Explorer When searching for information on the Internet, Internet Explorer is one search tool to be used.

Key In computer-based systems, keys are the records kept in sequence in particular fields known as Keys.

KeyCode Argument In Access, a KeyCode Argument finds specific numbers or letters which may or may not have been used by the user.

Label In Access, Label is an example of an unbound control.

Landscape orientation In many Microsoft applications, Landscape orientation allows users to print documents the dimensions of $11 \times 8\frac{1}{2}''$.

Linked object In PowerPoint, a Linked object is an object that is placed and stored in its own file.

Linking In Excel, Linking allows multiple data sets to be connected through an external reference in a source workbook.

List In Excel, data is kept in Lists, rows of similar data.

List box A List box shows available choices within any Dialog box.

Macro Stored in current workbooks or Personal Macro workbooks, Macros are sets of instructions that automatically repeat a task within a program.

Macro Recorder In Excel, the Macro Recorder remembers users instructions and automatically writes the macro.

Master document In Word, Master documents have many subdocuments, filed away in separate files.

Masthead In any newsletter, the title identifying a newsletter or paper is called the Masthead, and is usually located at the top of the document.

Meeting Minder During a PowerPoint presentation, Meeting Minder keeps track of questions or problems arising during a presentation.

Megabyte (Mb) Nowadays the memory of a computer is measured in megabytes (Mb). One Kb and Mb equal about one thousand and one million characters.

Megahertz (MHz) MHz is defined as *millions of cycles*, and determines how fast a microprocessor works.

Memo field Memo field in Excel and Access are used to store sentences and paragraphs, and can store up to 640,000 characters in length.

Memory For all computers, Memory is another term used to define random-access memory or RAM. On a short-term basis, Memory keeps computer programs and information from other working programs.

Menu bar The Menu bar provides users with access to pull-down menus needed to execute tasks within any of the Microsoft programs.

Microcomputer A microcomputer or Personal Computer (PC) has only one person who can access it at a time unlike a minicomputer that has many users.

Microprocessor A microprocessor is a single silicon chip containing the PC's or microcomputer's CPU. An example is Intel's Pentium III, a well-known name of a microprocessor.

Microsoft Clip Gallery In Office 2002, Microsoft Clip Gallery offers users pictures and fancy letter for use in documents and newsletters.

Microsoft Graph A supplementary application found in Microsoft Office XP that allows users to create graphs or charts within an Access report.

Microsoft Organization Chart Microsoft Organization Chart allows users to design an organization chart and import it into PowerPoint.

Microsoft WordArt Microsoft WordArt adds special effects to text and text objects, and can be brought in to PowerPoint by clicking the WordArt tool.

Minicomputer Like mainframes or servers, minicomputers also uphold many users; however, not as many.

Multitasking Multitasking gives users the choice to work on as many programs as desired at the same time.

Musical Instrument Digital Interface (MIDI) file MIDI files create sounds equivalent to sheet music.

My Documents My Documents is a folder where users can store their working or complete documents.

Name Box In Excel, the Name Box is another name for the cell reference for the cell being used in the worksheet, and is located at the left of the formula bar.

Navigation controls On the Internet, Navigation controls give users additional choices for viewing within Internet Explorer.

New Window command Under the Window menu in Excel, the New Window command creates various windows for users.

Normal style In Word, the normal style function contains the typical paragraph settings and is used for every paragraph unless indicated as another style.

Normal view In Word and PowerPoint, The Normal view is the typical way in which a document is seen.

NOT Function The NOT Function during the selection of criteria for records in Access determines that records selected must not be included in the specified value or criteria.

Notes Page view In PowerPoint, the Notes Page view is similar to the Slide view, except it allows users to attach notes below the slide.

Number Field In Access or Excel, a Number Field has the values that are in a calculation.

Numbered List In Word, by clicking on the button with the numbers one, two and three, a list using numbers can be incorporated into a document.

Object box In Access, the Object box shows the current object being used at the top left of the Module window.

Object Linking and Embedding (OLE) In PowerPoint, OLE gives users the ability to link or embed information designed in other applications.

Office clipboard Office clipboard in Office 2002 allows users to cut, paste, copy, and move many documents, objects, or text in a sequential order.

OLE Object field An OLE Object field in Access or Excel contains pictures, sounds, or graphics.

Open command The Open command lets users retrieve documents off of the hard drive or disk.

Operating system An operating system is the programs that connect the computer's hardware contents to each other. This system is located on the hard drive, and becomes a part of the computer when switched on. After these programs enter the computer's memory, the operating system takes over and controls the system during the needed time.

Option Group In Access, Option Groups provide users with choices from lists of three.

OR condition An OR condition during the selection of criteria for records in Access determine that records selected must only include some of the specified criteria.

Outline numbered list In Word, Outline numbered lists are lists formed into outlines with numbers that are automatically updated as users add information.

Outlining toolbar In Word, the Outlining toolbar helps users to work on master documents, allowing users to collapse and expand subdocuments.

Outline view In Word and PowerPoint, the outline view gives users the option to view a document's style in an outline form.

Output devices These devices generally take electronic signals from input devices or the CPU, and translate them to the correct output configuration. Typical devices known as output devices are monitors, printers, speakers, and the auxiliary storage.

Overtype Mode By pressing the insert key twice, users can amend or add text, missing letters, or symbols

Pack and Go Wizard In PowerPoint, the Pack and Go Wizard keeps all files from your presentation on a single file, allowing presenters never to be unprepared for a presentation.

Page Footer The Page Footer is found at the bottom of each page, showing the page number and descriptive information.

Page Header The Page Header is found at the top of each page, showing the page numbers, column headings, and other descriptive information.

Page numbers In Access and Word, Page numbers can be placed in five alignment locations at the bottom, right, or left side, of a document.

Page Setup command The Page Setup command in Access, Excel, and Word allows users to alter the margins, footnotes, and headers of a working document.

Paragraph style In Word, the Paragraph style function preserves the formatting of paragraphs, such as alignment, indents, and line spacing.

Password protection In Word, Password protection is of two different kinds when saving a document: a password to open and a password to amend your document.

Paste Command After cutting or copying a text, picture, or graph, the Paste Command moves that text, picture, or graph to another location within the document or another document.

Paste Special Command The Paste Special Command can be used in place of the Paste Command to move a text without the associated formatting.

Pen In PowerPoint, during presentations Pens are used to draw or write on the slides.

Pencils In Access, Pencils (record selector symbol) shows users the record that they are working on and reveals alterations to users.

Picture toolbar In Word and Power Point, the Picture toolbar has crop options for imported pictures.

Pie Charts In Excel, Pie Charts are one way to display relations that proportions have with each other.

Placeholders In PowerPoint, the Placeholders are fragmented lines encircling shapes where text, titles, graphs, or photos can be inserted.

Places bar In PowerPoint, the Places bar allows quick access to commonly frequented folders.

PMT Function PMT Function in Excel spreadsheets requires three arguments in order to calculate the periodic payment on a loan.

Pointing In Excel, Pointing is using the mouse or arrow keys to select the cell directly in creating a formula in a spreadsheet.

Portrait orientation In many Microsoft applications, Portrait orientation can be found under the File Menu and then by clicking the PageSetup button. It is the default for printing orientation and documents print as they appear on screen.

Primary Key A Primary Key is a field that can reveal records for tables.

Print command The Print command in any Microsoft Program allows users to print documents, spreadsheets, or workbooks.

Print Layout view The Print Layout view is located under the Page Setup of the File button. This view allows users to see how the printed version of the document looks.

Program Microsoft Word, Microsoft PowerPoint, and Microsoft Excel are programs whose written guidelines help execute the desired tasks of the users.

Project Explorer In Word, the Project Explorer like Windows Explorer shows users open Word documents and/or other Visual Basic projects.

Property A property is what determines an object's role within a program.

Property sheet In Access, Property sheets present an object's property, and alterations to the property can be made here.

Pull-down menus Through the menu bar, pull-down menus allow users to complete commands within any Microsoft program. Pull-down menus are many within each program and can either be accessed by a sequence of commands or by clicking a command button.

Pull-quote In Word, Pull-quotes are phrases or sentences set in larger type in order to stand out from other sections of the page.

Query A Query allows users to pick records from tables, and put some of those records into other selected tables, and/or perform calculations on that data.

Query Window The Query Window shows users the field list and design grid in Access.

Read-only memory (ROM) In every computer, this is the memory that is available when a user starts up a computer; it is the guidelines that reveal to the computer that it must examine and start up its operating systems into its CPU.

Record When working with spreadsheets, Records are the individual files within folders.

Recycle Bin The Recycle Bin stores unwanted documents or files until emptied.

Redo command Located under the Edit button, the Redo command *repeats* the same text by copying the same text in another location within a working document.

Referential Integrity Referential Integrity in Access is having the tables in a database harmonious with one another.

Rehearse Timings Rehearse Timings is a feature in PowerPoint letting users time a presentation while practicing.

Relative Reference In Excel, Relative Reference refers to cell references in the formula that will change when copied to another cell.

Removable mass storage This is another term for Zip drive, an external or internal storage apparatus, which can keep as much as 250Mb of information. It operates like a huge floppy disk.

Repeat command Located under the Edit button, the Repeat command lets users paste the same text over again in another location within a working document.

Replace command The Replace command shares a dialog box with the Find and Go To commands. After the Find command finds the text or phrase that the user is looking for, the Replace command allows the user to "replace" the text or phrase.

Report A report in Access is a printed document for a database.

Report Footer A Report Header is a section of a report found at the end of a report, containing summary information about the report.

Report Header A Report Header is a section of a report found at the beginning of a report, containing information such as the title and date of the report.

Report Wizard The Report Wizard in Microsoft Access is the most simple way to make and construct a report.

Required property In Access, the Required property discards records not corresponding to the value in field.

Résumé Wizard In Word, the Résumé Wizard aids users in completing professional résumés by asking them a series of questions, and later presenting templated résumé.

Reverse In Word for text emphasis, Reverse is a popular text and background technique where light text is put on a dark background.

Revision mark In Word, a vertical line inside of the left margin denotes a Revision mark, showing that a change has been made at that place in the document.

Revision Toolbar In Word, the Revision Toolbar harbors editing tools for users.

Round trip HTML A function that can be found in all applications of Office 2002, which enables users to subsequently edit a Web page while in another application and vice versa.

Sans serif typeface Sans serif typeface does not have small lines extending on the bottoms and tops of letters.

Save As command The Save As command lets users change the name of the source where a document is saved or change the place where the document is saved.

Save As Web Page command The Save As Web Page command in Excel allows a worksheet to be changed into a Web page. In other Microsoft Programs, this function allows documents on the Web to be transported into programs to be used in working documents.

Save command The Save command allows users to "save" documents on disks or the hard drive.

Scenario In Excel, Scenarios are "what-if" situations put into a spreadsheet.

Scenario Manager In Excel, the Scenario Manager enables users to speculate on various situations or outcomes of working spreadsheets.

Scenario Summary In Excel, the Scenario Summary allows users to compare various results of different scenarios in a summary table.

Screen Tip In many applications, Screen Tips pop up and allow users to learn new information about the program.

Scroll bar Vertical and horizontal scroll bars are located within any window, and are used to find unseen areas within any working document.

Scrolling In many Microsoft applications in order to view different parts of any document, users scroll up and down, or from right to left by pushing the arrow buttons on the keyboard of the computer or by using the mouse and arrow button.

Section In Word, one of the three ways of formatting is a section which is different parts of a document, and each part can be formatted in various ways.

Section break In a Word document, a Section break is a disconnection of space within a document.

Select-then-do In Word, the Select-then-do methodology is choosing a text, and then moving it to the desired location and working it.

Selective replacement In Word by using Selective replacement, users can replace words by clicking the Find Next command button, and then the Replace button to change the word.

Send To command In many Windows applications, the Send To command allows users to send documents or information to email or other applications of their choice.

Serif Typeface Serif Typeface has small lines extending on the bottoms and tops of letters.

Server On the Internet, information is stored on servers, large computers.

SetFocus method In Access, the SetFocus method brings users back to the point needed to begin work again.

Shared Workbook In Excel, when working in Workgroups, Shared Workbooks are placed on networks, making it easier for groups to asses and share ideas and amendments.

Sizing handles In PowerPoint and Word, Sizing handles let users move and size pictures in documents.

Slide Layouts In PowerPoint, there are 24 pre-created slide formats that show where different objects, texts, pictures, graphs, and titles belong on the text.

Slide master In PowerPoint, Slide master reveals the formatting for individual slides.

Slide Navigator In PowerPoint, Slide Navigator gives users the opportunity to find any slide within a presentation.

Slide Show view In PowerPoint, the Slide Show view shows one slide after another as it would appear during the PowerPoint presentation.

Slide Sorter toolbar In PowerPoint, located in the bottom left-hand corner, the Slide Sorter toolbar allows users to change views for their slideshow.

Slide Sorter view In PowerPoint, the Slide Sorter view shows user each slide on a smaller scale.

Slide view In PowerPoint, after clicking the Slide view button, users can work on one slide at a time.

Soft page break In Word, the Soft page break function pushes text that no longer fits on a page on to the next page.

Soft Return Soft Return occurs when the word processor moves text from line to line while the user is in a document.

Solver Solver in Excel is an add-in that helps users solve problems with many variables.

Sort In Word, Sort lets users move rows around within tables.

Sort command The Sort command puts lists in ascending or descending order according to specified keys.

Sound Through a sound board and speakers, sound can be used in Power-Point presentations.

Source workbook In Excel, information must be derived from an original source or dependent workbooks.

Spellcheck In many Windows applications, spellcheck is used to make sure users have not made any spelling mistakes; sentence structures can also be checked.

Spreadsheet In Excel, a Spreadsheet is composed of a grid of rows and columns allowing users to organize data and to recompute formulas with any changes made.

Standard toolbar The Standard toolbar has buttons that give users choices in what to execute next.

Startup Property The Startup Property is needed in order to present users with the main switchboard.

Status Bar In Excel, the Status Bar can be found at the bottom of the worksheet and allows users to know what is going on as they work.

Style Style is defined as a series of characteristics created for diversity.

Style command In Word, in the Format menu, the Style command adds and changes style types to documents.

Switchboard In order for non-technical users to identify pertinent information or data, Switchboards let data or objects to be moved easily from one place to another within Access or Excel.

Switchboard Items table The Switchboard Items table is the base for the Switchboard.

Switchboard Manager The Switchboard Manager is an Access Utility used to create switchboards.

Tab key This key when pushed allows the tab to indent for a paragraph or for indentation purposes.

Table In Access, Tables are made up of records and fields organized in rows and columns for the purpose of storing information.

Tables and Borders toolbar Tables and Borders toolbar (Table menu) gives users an array of choices when making tables and adding borders to them.

Table feature In Word, the Table feature creates many different kinds of tables for users to choose from.

Tables menu In Word, after clicking the Table menus, users can choose to draw or to insert tables of varying sizes.

Table of Contents In Word, a Table of Contents can be created automatically after clicking on the Index and Table command key.

Table Row In Access, a Table Row is a row that is contained in the Design grid of the lower half of the Query window in order to distinguish the table from where the field was taken.

Table Wizard In Access or Excel, Table Wizard has already created tables for users to choose from.

Tabular report A Tabular report is a report detailing information in rows rather than columns.

Tape backup unit This term means to store large amounts of data, like a Zip Drive, used for backing up entire systems.

Task Manager The Task Manager helps users to complete tasks, such as shutting down or starting up the computer.

Telnet Telnet is a program used with a PC to connect to other programs like the Web or email.

Template Templates are also known as "empty" worksheets or documents in many of the applications.

Terminal session A Terminal session is when users connect to and maintain a Web page.

Text box In PowerPoint, after clicking onto the empty square in the toolbar, the Text box allows text to be inserted in presentations.

Text field A Text field keeps information such as student names, address, or numbers, and can store up to 255 characters.

Theme A Theme (template) is a set of designs and graphics or colors that could be used in a Microsoft document.

Three-Dimensional Pie Charts In Excel, Three-Dimensional Pie Charts are pie charts that are seen in a three-dimensional view.

Today ( ) Function This function in Excel when placed in an active cell always returns to the current date of when the spreadsheet was opened.

Toggle Switch A toggle switch is an apparatus that allows the computer to execute two tasks at the same time; for example, the changing of uppercase letters to lowercase letters while pressing the Caps Lock key.

Tool bar The Tool bar in any Windows application reveals the button available for the execution of various tasks while working within each application.

Total Query In Access, by using one of many summary or aggregate functions, a Total Query does calculations on groups of records.

Track Changes command Under the Tools menu in Word, the Track Changes command highlights changes, accepts or rejects changes, or compares documents during the editing process.

Transition effect In PowerPoint, Transition effects regulate the way one screen appears on the screen and how the next appears.

Triangle In Access, Triangles (record selector symbol) reveal the place where records are being stored (saved).

Typeface Typeface is another term for font, meaning the entire group of upper- and lowercase letters, numbers, punctuation marks, and symbols used in documents.

Type size Type size is a measurement used to determine the size of text in documents, and the typeface ranges from 8 points and up.

Unbound Control In Access, Unbound controls are fields that have no data for entry.

Undo Command Located under the Edit button, the Undo Command brings back the users previous work(s) that were erased. This button can only be used when an initial mistake is made.

Validation Rule property In Access, the Validation Rule property discards unknown data records.

Validation Text property In Access, the Validation Text property presents an "error message" any time the validation rule is broken.

Versions command In Word, instead of using the Save As command, users can click on the Versions command under the File menu, allowing users to save multiple versions of the same document.

View menu The View menu supplies various views of a document through different magnifications.

Visual Basic for Applications (VBA) Easily accessible from any application in Microsoft Office, VBA is an event-driven programming language.

Visual Basic Editor (VBE) In Word, the Visual Basic Editor (VBE) shows Project Explorer at the left side of the VBE window, and it is used to edit, build, and debug modules.

WAV file WAV files are digitized recording of actual sound and is less compact than MIDI files.

Web Page A Web page (HTML document) is a document located on the Internet.

Web Page Wizard By asking users many questions, Web Page Wizard helps users to create their own Web sites.

Web Query Web Queries can be executed from almost any Web page by pulling the Data menu down, click Import External Data command, click New Web Query, and enter the new Web page.

Web Site On the Web, Web sites are numerous, and sites are places where information is distributed about specific topics, companies, or issues.

Whole word replacement In Word, under the Replace command, Whole word replacement looks and finds only whole words and replaces them.

Wild Card Wild Cards allow users to search for a pattern within a text field.

Windows clipboard Windows clipboard is a transitory place in Windows application where users can move text or objects by selecting cut, copy, and paste commands located under the Edit Menu.

With Statement The With Statement in Excel allows users to perform many tasks at the same time on objects.

Wizard In many applications, Wizards ask users questions and when finished create from the questions the desired document.

Word Wrap Word wrap occurs as the word processor "wraps" text from line to line.

Workbook A Workbook in Excel is made of more than one worksheet.

Workgroup Workgroups are people who are working on projects. In Excel, the program has the capability to allow changes to the workbook from each member of the workgroup, and later merge into a single workbook.

Workplace In Excel, a Workplace allows users to open multiple workbooks in a single step.

Worksheet Worksheets in Excel refer to spreadsheets. (Workbook and Worksheet are unique to Excel).

Worksheet References In Excel, Worksheet References help label cells and remains constant.

World Wide Web The World Wide Web (www or the Web) is a smaller part of the Internet.

Write-enabled When open, the square holes located in the upper left- and right-hand corners of any disk allow users to alter files saved on disk.

Write-protected When closed, the square holes located in the upper left- and right-hand corners of any disk allow users to to protect files saved on disk.

WYSIWYG WYSIWYG means What You See Is What You Get and is pronounced "wizzywig." This interface means that the way in which a document appears on a microprocessor's screen is how it will look when it prints out.

X Axis The X Axis on a graph or chart in Excel is the horizontal axis point.

Y Axis The Y Axis on a graph or chart in Excel is the vertical axis point.

Yes/No field In Excel and Access, the Yes/No field is used to evaluate two values: Yes/No, True/False, or On/Off.

Zoom command The Zoom command shows a document on the screen at magnifications ranging from 10% to 500%.

INDEX

A = Access   E = Excel   W = Word   VB = VBA

Visual Basic for Applications (*See* VBA)
Visual Basic toolbar, E395

W

Web Layout command, W269
Web Page Wizard, W282–W286
Web site (creation of), W282–W292
Wild card, E327, E332
With Statement, E369
WordArt, W243
Workbook
  compare and merge, E280
  linking of, E243–E249
  properties of, E289
  protection of, E292
Workbook reference, E243
Workgroup, E277, W304–W305
Worksheet
  copying of, E225–E226
  grouping of, E229, E234
  inserting of, E230, E238
  linking of, W248–W249
  moving of, E226
  selecting of, E235
  summing of, E231
  ungrouping of, E242
Worksheet reference, E227–E228, E232
Workspace, E248
Wrap Text command, E239

X

XML, E351

Z

Zoom, E224
Zoom box, A336